Fundamentals of
C++

and Data Structures,
Advanced Course,
Second Edition

Dr. Kenneth A. Lambert
and
Dr. Thomas Naps

**COURSE
TECHNOLOGY**

THOMSON LEARNING

Australia • Canada • Mexico • Singapore • Spain • United Kingdom • United States

COURSE TECHNOLOGY

TM

THOMSON LEARNING

**Fundamentals of C++ and Data Structures,
Advanced Course, Second Edition**
by Dr. Kenneth Lambert and Dr. Thomas Naps

Managing Editor:
Melissa Ramondetta

Development Editor:
Betsy Newberry, Custom
Editorial Productions

Marketing Manager:
Kim Wood

Senior Product Manager:
Dave Lafferty

Editorial Assistant:
Jodi Dreissig

Production Editor:
Karen Jacot

Cover Design:
Abby Scholz

Compositor:
GEX Publishing Services

Printer:
Transcontinental

Disclaimer
Course Technology reserves the right to revise this publication and make changes from time to time in its content without notice.

ISBN 0-538-69565-X Softcover

ISBN 0-538-69564-1 Hardcover

We've got it all for
C++ Programming!

Our new C++ texts offer hands-on practice with everything needed to master the C++ programming language. These texts cover everything from beginning to advanced topics to meet your programming needs.

PREFACE

The recurring themes of abstraction, theory, and design are important in all areas of computer science. A student's first two courses in computer science are pivotal in emphasizing these themes. In the first course, students are introduced to top-down design, structured programming techniques, procedural and data abstraction, and a high-level programming language as a vehicle for solving problems. Where the programming language has object-oriented features, such as C++, students can also receive exposure to the ways in which object-oriented methods can support effective design and abstraction. In the second course, students can then encounter more rigorous strategies for developing large, effective programs that solve problems frequently encountered by computer scientists.

Fundamentals of C++ and Data Structures, Advanced Course begins with the assumption that the reader has a working knowledge of problem solving with C++. This should include familiarity with control structures, functions (used nonrecursively), parameter passing, strings, files, arrays (in their AP incarnations as vectors and matrices), and the definition and use of classes. We refer uninitiated readers to *Fundamentals of C++, Introductory Course* by Kenneth A. Lambert and Douglas W. Nance. From this starting point, the current text is organized around several objectives:

1. To demonstrate the application of software engineering principles in design, coding, and testing of large programs.

2. To introduce students to the essential data structures such as linked lists, stacks, queues, trees, and (to a lesser extent) graphs. This introduction emphasizes the specification of each structure as an abstract data type before discussing implementations and applications of that structure.

3. To make students aware of the importance of object-oriented methods in developing software, particularly in the design and implementation of abstract data types.

4. To provide a systematic approach to the study of algorithms, an approach that focuses first on understanding the action of the algorithm and then on analyzing the algorithm from a space/time perspective. In particular, searching, sorting, and recursive algorithms are covered in detail.

5. To give students an overview of what lies ahead in computer science.

Overview and Organization

Throughout the text, we have attempted to explain and develop concepts carefully and illustrate them by frequent examples and diagrams. New concepts are then used in complete programs to show how they aid in solving problems. We place an early and consistent emphasis on good writing habits and neat, readable documentation. We frequently offer communication and style tips where appropriate. The opening prologue of the text explicitly states and briefly reviews the C++ prerequisites assumed in the rest of the text. The prologue should be skimmed before starting Lesson 1. Students should feel confident of their ability to work with all of the C++ topics discussed in the prologue before proceeding in the text. The text is designed for students who are using any C++ compiler.

Lessons 1 and 2 collectively present a detailed treatment of the software engineering principles. Lesson 1 introduces big-O analysis as the essential tool used by the computer scientist in evaluating alternative strategies from a time/space perspective. Simple sorting and searching algorithms are used as examples for the application of big-O analysis.

Lesson 2 is a critical lesson in that it introduces the formalism used to present abstract data types used throughout the text. This formalism consists of specifying an ADT's attributes and operations as a set of language-independent preconditions and postconditions before moving to a C++ class declaration as an interface for the ADT. Rules for using and implementing ADTs are developed. Ordered collections, sorted collections, one-key tables, and two-key tables are presented as examples of ADTs. Because these ADTs lend themselves naturally to the use of keys and elements of different data types, the notions of generic ADTs and parameterized types can be introduced in this lesson and can be implemented with C++ class templates. Because students have studied big-O analysis in the preceding lesson, they are well equipped to compare and contrast the efficiencies of various implementations of these ADTs. These four ADTs and the use of class templates recur in the remainder of the text as we explore more advanced techniques for implementing other ADTs.

Lesson 2 also pulls together and expands on the software engineering issues introduced in earlier chapters. The lesson presents a detailed treatment of the analysis, design, implementation, testing, and maintenance stages of the software system life cycle. This treatment emphasizes a more object-oriented perspective on software engineering.

Lessons 3 through 6 cover the use of essential data structures and recursion in advanced problem-solving techniques. Each data structure is first defined as an abstract data type and then declared as a C++ class. Various implementations are discussed and compared using the big-O terminology of Lesson 1. This provides a convincing demonstration of the utility of big-O analysis. Lesson 3, devoted to dynamic memory management, pointers, and linked lists, discusses how linked lists might be used as an alternative implementation of the ADTs that were introduced in Lesson 2. Lesson 4 covers stacks and queues, discussing parsing and simulation as applications of these ADTs. Lesson 5 explores recursion in depth. A graduated series of examples is presented, culminating with the use of trial-and-error back-tracking as a problem-solving technique. Lesson 6 provides examples of the utility of recursion by using it as the primary technique for processing data in binary trees, general trees, and graphs. The importance of binary search trees as an alternative way of representing keyed tables is also discussed, with comparisons drawn to the array and linked list implementations previously covered in Lessons 2 and 3. The material on general trees, graphs, and networks in the final two sections of Lesson 6 can be omitted without affecting a student's understanding of the lessons that follow.

The background in software engineering and data structures found in Lessons 1 through 6 prepares the student for the more complex sorting and searching algorithms of Lessons 7 and 8. In Lesson 7, sorting methods that break the $O(n^2)$ barrier are investigated. These methods include the shell sort, quick sort, heap sort, and merge sort. Lesson 8 scrutinizes search techniques such as hashing, indexing, indexed sequential search, B-trees, and tries.

We have made a large effort to acknowledge the increasing importance of object-oriented methods in the computer science community. However, object-oriented methods must be seen in the larger context of the concern with abstraction, design, and theory that makes up computer science. In this text, objects are used where relevant in developing designs and abstractions that solve interesting problems.

Additional Features of This Text

As a result of extensive feedback from many reviewers and users of our college-edition text, we have covered the following in this edition:

1. The AP classes for strings, vectors, matrices, stacks, and queues are used throughout.

2. The material on ADTs and software engineering has been streamlined and consolidated into one lesson.

3. Linked lists (Lesson 3) are developed in a top-down manner, with a discussion of abstract operations preceding the implementation details of pointers.

In addition, this text has a number of noteworthy pedagogical features.

- *Objectives*: Each lesson starts with a concise list of topics and learning objectives.
- *Exercises*: Short-answer questions appear at the end of each section that is intended to build analytical skills.
- *End-of-lesson projects*: Lengthy lists of suggestions for complete programs and projects are given at the end of each lesson. These cover different problem areas in computer science, such as data processing and mathematics. Some problems and projects run from lesson to lesson, providing students with a sense of problem solving as a cumulative enterprise that often requires programming in the large. Several assignments focus explicitly on improving students' communication skills in refining designs and writing documentation.
- *Module specifications*: Specifications are given for many program modules.
- *Structure charts*: We provide charts that reflect modular development and include the use of data flow arrows to emphasize transmission of data to or from each module. These charts set the stage for understanding the use of value and reference parameters when functions are introduced.
- *Special features*: These are tidbits of information intended to create awareness of and interest in various aspects of computer science, including its historical context. Special attention is paid to issues of computer ethics and security.
- *Suggestions for test programs*: Ideas included in the exercises are intended to encourage students to use the computer to determine answers to questions and to see how to implement concepts in short programs.
- *Case studies*: A complete program is listed at the end of each lesson that illustrates utilization of the concepts developed within the lesson. This section includes the complete development of a project, from user requirements to specifications to pseudocode design to implementation and testing.
- *Run-time trace diagrams*: In addition to use of *graphic documentation* to help students visualize algorithms, run-time trace diagrams are introduced as a means of analyzing recursive algorithms.
- *Running, testing, and debugging tips*: These tips will be useful to students as they work on the programming projects at the end of each lesson.
- *Tables in lesson-end summaries*: These are frequently used to compare and evaluate various C++ features, data structures, and algorithms. Such compact, side-by-side comparisons emphasize the importance of knowing the relative advantages and disadvantages of the various techniques studied.
- *Reading references*: When appropriate, pointers are given to excellent sources for further reading on topics introduced in the text.
- *Vocabulary terms*: New terms are bold faced and italicized when introduced.

A comprehensive glossary, as well as appendices on reserved words, useful library functions, syntax diagrams, and character sets are also included.

This book covers only that portion of C++ necessary for the first two courses in computer science. It is designed to be "generic," so that learners can build code and execute programs using any C++ compiler.

Ancillaries

It is our belief that a broad-based teaching support package is essential for an introductory course using C++. Thus, the following ancillary materials are available:

1. *Instructor's manual*. Available in electronic format on the *Instructor Resource Kit*. It contains teaching suggestions, answers to section exercises, and solutions for selected end-of-lesson projects and critical-thinking activities.

2. *Activities Workbook*. This 144-page supplement contains many "pen-and-pencil" activities, as well as hands-on computer programming projects.

3. *Lesson plans*, as well as *Student study guides*, help to guide students through the lesson text and exercises.

4. *Source code files*. Files that demonstrate the successful operation of a program, or that students can use to develop their programs, have been provided for many exercises and the *Case Studies*. The programs are written in platform-independent C++, which can be run immediately on most implementations. The files are on the *Instructor Resource Kit*.

5. *Computerized test bank*. Adopters of this edition will receive a computerized test-generation system. This provides a test bank system that allows adopters to edit, add, or delete test questions.

Each program segment in the text has been compiled and run. Hence, original versions were all working. Unfortunately, the publication process does allow errors in code to occur after a program has been run. Every effort has been made to produce an error-free text, although this cannot be guaranteed with certainty. We assume full responsibility for all errors and omissions. If you detect any, please be tolerant and notify us so they can be corrected in subsequent printings and editions.

This text has been designed to mesh with the text by Kenneth A. Lambert and Douglas W. Nance mentioned earlier.

Acknowledgments

We would like to take this opportunity to thank those who in some way contributed to the completion of this text. Several reviewers contributed significant constructive comments during various phases of manuscript development. They include Dr. Ashraf Saad of the University of Cincinnati and Dave Clausen of La Cañada High School in La Cañada, CA.

We would also like to thank the following:

Dave Lafferty at Course Technology, who saw the vision for this project and assembled and managed the resources to get it completed it successfully.

Developmental editor Betsy Newberry of Custom Editorial Productions, Inc., who worked with reviewers to generate valuable analyses of the text, and who managed the development of all the supplements.

Technical editor Tom Bockerstette. He made many useful suggestions for improving not only style, but content as well. We also acknowledge his effort in preparing the *Activities Workbook*.

Lori Hunt who prepared the entire *Instructor's manual* for the book.

Kenneth A. Lambert
Thomas L. Naps

How to Use this Book

What makes a good computer programming text? Sound pedagogy and the most current, complete materials. That is what you will find in the new *Fundamentals of C++ and Data Structures, Advanced Course.* Not only will you find an inviting layout, but also many features to enhance learning.

Objectives— Objectives are listed at the beginning of each lesson, along with a suggested time for completion of the lesson. This allows you to look ahead to what you will be learning and to pace your work.

Enhanced Screen Shots— Screen shots now come to life on each page.

Program Code Examples— Many examples of program code are included in the text to illustrate concepts under discussion.

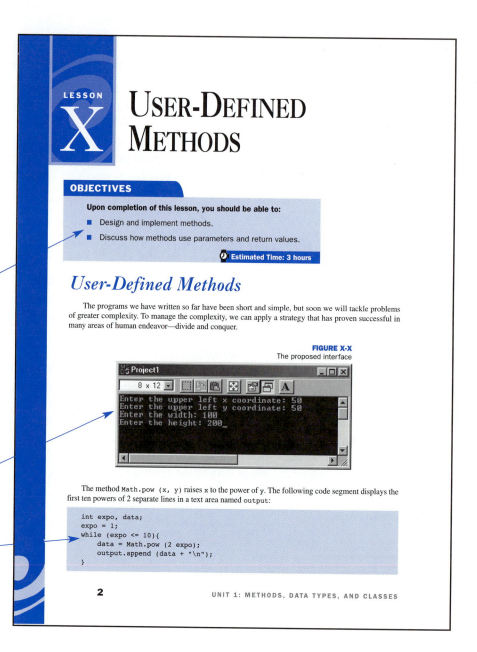

LESSON X

USER-DEFINED METHODS

OBJECTIVES

Upon completion of this lesson, you should be able to:

■ Design and implement methods.

■ Discuss how methods use parameters and return values.

🕐 **Estimated Time: 3 hours**

User-Defined Methods

The programs we have written so far have been short and simple, but soon we will tackle problems of greater complexity. To manage the complexity, we can apply a strategy that has proven successful in many areas of human endeavor—divide and conquer.

FIGURE X-X
The proposed interface

```
Project1                                    _ □ ×
 8 x 12       ▭ ▭ ▭ ▭ ▭ ▭  A
Enter the upper left x coordinate: 50
Enter the upper left y coordinate: 50
Enter the width: 100
Enter the height: 200_
```

The method `Math.pow (x, y)` raises x to the power of y. The following code segment displays the first ten powers of 2 separate lines in a text area named `output`:

```
int expo, data;
expo = 1;
while (expo <= 10){
    data = Math.pow (2 expo);
    output.append (data + "\n");
}
```

How to Use this Book

Case Studies— Case studies present Java program solutions to specific user requests and show the analysis, design, and implementation stages of the software development life cycle.

Summary— At the end of each lesson, you will find a summary to help you complete the end-of-lesson activities.

Review Questions— Review material at the end of each lesson and each unit enables you to prepare for assessment of the content presented.

Lesson Projects— End-of-lesson hands-on application of what has been learned in the lesson allows you to actually apply the techniques covered.

SCANS— (Secretary's Commision on Achieving Necessary Skills)— The U.S. Department of Labor has identified the school-to-careers competencies. The five workplace competencies (resource, interpersonal skills, information, systems, and technology) and foundation skills (basic skills, thinking skills, and personal qualities) are identi-

fied in Case Studies and Projects throughout the text. More information on SCANS can be found on the *Electronic Instructor.*

Critical Thinking— Each lesson and each unit review gives you an opportunity to apply creative analysis to situations presented.

End-of-Unit Applications— End-of-unit hands-on application of concepts learned in the unit provides opportunity for a comprehensive review.

Lesson 1 Algorithm Analysis: Space and Time Considerations

CASE STUDY: A Sales Table

Request

Write a program that allows the user to enter the names and annual sales figures for any number of salespeople. The program should display a formatted table of salespeople, their sales, and their commissions (at 10% of the sales amount).

Summary

In this lesson you learned:

■ The modern computer age began in the late 1940s with the development of ENIAC. Business computing became practical in the 1950s, and time-sharing computers advanced computing in large organizations in the 1960s.

LESSON 1 REVIEW QUESTIONS

FILL IN THE BLANK

Complete the following sentences by writing the correct word or words in the blanks provided.

1. What are the three major hardware components of a computer _____.

2. Name three input devices _____.

LESSON 1 PROJECTS

1. Java's `Integer` class defines public constants, `MIN_VALUE` and `MAX_VALUE`, that name the minimum and maximum `int` values supported by the language. Thus, the expression `Integer.MAX_VALUE` returns the maximum `int` value. The `Double` class defines similar constants. Write a program that displays the values of these four constants.

CRITICAL THINKING

SCANS

You have an idea for a program that will help the local pizza shop handle take-out orders. Your friend suggests an interview with the shop's owner to discuss her user requirements before you get started on the program. Explain why this is a good suggestion, and list the questions you would ask the owner to help determine the user requirements.

UNIT 1 APPLICATIONS

1. Light travels at 3 * 108 meters per second. A light-year is the distance a light beam would travel in 1 year. Write a program that calculates and displays the value of a light year.

3

CONTENTS

PROLOGUE—A REVIEW OF C++ ESSENTIALS

This is *not* an introductory programming text. Rather, it assumes that you have acquired basic programming skills and now want to use these skills to explore more advanced problems in computer science.

The purpose of this prologue is to review those C++ tools that are prerequisite to the lessons that follow. These tools are:

- Main program and library files
- Program comments
- Reserved words and identifiers
- Simple data types
- Literals
- Variables
- Symbolic constants
- Expressions and assignment
- Type conversion
- Interactive input and output
- Functions (not including recursion)
- Value and reference parameters
- Selection
- Iteration
- `typedef`
- Enumerated data types
- Structured data types (apstrings, apvectors, apmatrices, files, structs)
- Implementation of simple classes
- Class templates

If you are confident in your ability to use these tools, feel free to skim the rest of the prologue and begin Lesson 1 in earnest. If you feel you need a quick review of these C++ topics, read the prologue thoroughly. If you are not familiar with some of the topics, read the prologue in conjunction with a more detailed introductory text on C++ programming, such as *Fundamentals of C++, Introductory Course* by Kenneth A. Lambert and Douglas W. Nance.

Main Program and Library Files

A C++ program typically consists of one or more modules. The top-level or main program module appears in a main program file. Other modules, which may consist of data and function definitions, appear in library files. Some library files are standard and come with any C++ implementation, while others must be constructed by the programmer.

1

The form of a typical main program module is:

```
<preprocessor directives>
<global data and function declarations>

int main()
{
    <local data declarations>

    <statements>
    return 0;
}


<main program function implementations>
```

All of the items in angle brackets are optional, but are usually present in most C++ programs. Data and function declarations and function implementations are discussed in the following sections. Preprocessor directives are used at compile time to make the contents of library files available to the main program module or to other modules. The use of the most important of these, #include, is shown in the following example:

```
#include <iostream.h>
#include <math.h>
#include "mylib.h"
```

The angle brackets should be used to specify the name of a standard library file, and double quotes should enclose the name of a programmer-defined library file.

The main program function begins with the word int and ends with the } symbol. The area of code within the { and } symbols is referred to as the main program block. The last statement in a main program block should be return 0;.

Each of the other modules in a C++ program is specified as a library consisting of two files: a header file (having a **.h** extension) and an implementation file (having a **.cpp** extension). The header file contains data definitions and function declarations that are to be made available to modules wishing to use this code. The form of a typical header file is:

```
#ifndef <header name>

<preprocessor directives>

<data and function declarations>

#define <header name>

#endif
```

The preprocessor directives #ifndef, #define, and #endif are used to prevent multiple inclusions of the library file in one application. At compile time, if this library file has already been included by another module, the <header name> (which can be any C++ identifier) will be visible and control will branch to the end of this file. Otherwise, the contents of the library file will be included and the <header name> will be made visible.

The implementation file contains function implementations. The form of a typical implementation file is:

```
<preprocessor directives>

<function implementations>
```

One of the preprocessor directives should include the header file of this library.

Program Comments

C++ programmers usually document their code with end-of-line comments. The form of such a comment is:

```
// <text of comment>
```

The compiler ignores the text of the comment until the end of the current line.

Multiline comments are used primarily for debugging. For example, when you want the compiler to ignore a troublesome chunk of code, you can mark it off as follows:

```
/*
<troublesome chunk of code>
*/
```

Reserved Words and Identifiers

A table of reserved words in C++ appears in Appendix A. C++ is case sensitive. All reserved words must be spelled in lowercase. Identifiers must begin with a letter or an underscore. This initial character is followed by zero or more letters, digits, or underscores. Remember that the compiler will treat IF as an identifier, not a reserved word, and that number and Number are two different identifiers.

This text adopts a convention of using uppercase letters for constant identifiers, lowercase letters for all other identifiers, and underscores where needed to suggest multiword identifiers.

Simple Data Types

The simple data types used in this text are int, float, and char. int represents integer values, float represents real numbers, and char represents the ASCII character set. Occasionally, we use double to represent real numbers having greater precision than float, and prefix int with long or unsigned to represent large or nonnegative integers, respectively. Boolean values in most C++ implementations consist of two integers: 0, meaning false, and a nonzero value, usually 1, meaning true.

Literals

The values of simple data types are represented in program code as literals. An integer in decimal format is represented as a sequence of one or more digits. A real number is represented either in fixed point format or in floating point format. A printing character in the ASCII range from ' ' to '~' is represented by enclosing the character in single quotes. Some other characters are represented by an escape sequence, as in the following table:

Literal	Name
\n	new line
\t	tab
\"	double quote
\\	backslash
\0	null

String literals are represented by enclosing zero or more characters, including escaped characters, in double quotes.

Variables

Variables can be declared with or without default initial values. The form for declaring variables without default values is:

```
<data type> <list of identifiers>;
```

where `<data type>` is any C++ data type and `<list of identifiers>` is one or more identifiers separated by commas. The form for initializing a variable if a simple data type to a default value within a declaration is:

```
<data type> <identifier> = <initial value>;
```

where `<initial value>` is the value of any expression. Note that the second form permits only one variable per declaration.

In general, a variable can be declared anywhere it is needed in a program. The scope of a variable is either global, if it is declared in a library file or above the main program block or is restricted to the block within which it is declared.

Symbolic Constants

A symbolic constant definition looks just like a variable declaration that specifies a default value, except that the definition begins with the word `const`. For example, the following lines of code define π to two decimal places, an upper bound for integer input and a symbol for the blank space character:

```
const float PI = 3.14;
const int UPPER_BOUND = 100;
const char BLANK = ' ';
```

Expressions and Assignment

Standard operators are provided to construct expressions that perform arithmetic, comparisons, logic, and assignment. The following table lists the most important of these operators:

Operator	Meaning
+	Addition (binary or unary)
–	Subtraction or negation
*	Multiplication
/	Division
%	Modulus
==	Is equal to
<	Is less than
>	Is greater than
<=	Is less than or equal to
>=	Is greater than or equal to
!=	Is not equal to
&&	Logical and
||	Logical or
!	Logical not
( )	Parentheses
=	Assignment

The precedence of the operators governs the order in which they are executed within a compound expression. The following table lists the operators in decreasing order of precedence:

```
( )
!
*, /, %
+, –
<, <=, >, >=, ==, !=
&&
||
=
```

Most of these operators are left associative, meaning that operators of the same precedence are executed from left to right. The programmer can use parentheses to force earlier execution of operators of lower precedence in an expression. For example, the expression 2 + 3 * 5 evaluates to 17, and the expression (2 + 3) * 5 evaluates to 25.

The / operator is overloaded for integers and real numbers. Thus, when both operands of / are integers, the value returned is the integer quotient. Otherwise, the value returned is a real number. The % operator should be used only with integers. All of the other operators in the preceding table can be used in mixed-mode operations with any combination of int, float, and char data values (see the discussion of type conversion following).

Compound expressions that produce Boolean values are executed by using short-circuit evaluation. An expression containing || (logical or) returns nonzero (true) if the first operand returns nonzero; otherwise, the second operand is evaluated and its value is returned. An expression containing && (logical and) returns zero (false) if the first operand returns zero; otherwise, the second operand is evaluated and its value is returned. Thus, assuming that b = 0, the following example would return zero after evaluating just the first operand:

```
(b != 0) && (a / b)
```

An assignment expression has the side effect of storing a value in a variable, called the target of the assignment. The value returned by an assignment expression depends on the context. When the assignment expression is being used to compute a value, the value returned is the value stored during the assignment operation. This is sometimes called an r-value, to indicate that it can be used on the right side of another assignment expression. In this case, for example, the assignment expression c = 5 would have the effect of storing the value 5 in the variable c and returning the value 5. The assignment operator is right associative. This means that cascaded assignment expressions are evaluated from right to left. Assuming that a, b, and c are integer variables, the following expression would first store the value 5 in c, then store it in b, and finally store it in a:

```
a = b = c = 5
```

When the assignment operation is being used as the target of another assignment, the value returned is the address or memory location of the variable into which a value can be stored. This is sometimes called an l-value. The following cascaded assignment expression uses parentheses to override the right associativity of the assignment operators in the previous example, with very different effects:

```
((a = b) = c) = 5
```

In this example, the innermost enclosed assignment expression is evaluated first, storing the value of b in a. This expression returns the address of a as the target of the next assignment expression, which stores the value of c in a. This expression also returns the address of a as the target of the outermost parenthesized assignment expression, which stores the value 5 in a. Thus, b and c are not modified at all in this expression.

The fact that assignment expressions return values can cause subtle errors in C++ programs. Assuming that variable a contains the value 3, the following two expressions both return zero but have very different consequences for a program:

```
a == 0
a = 0
```

The first expression just compares the values of a and zero and returns zero. The second expression also has the side effect of resetting a to zero.

Most assignment expressions occur in assignment statements, which are formed by ending the expression with a semicolon. Thus, the statement:

```
a = 5;
```

has the side effect of storing 5 in variable a, and the computer discards the value returned.

Type Conversion

The computer performs implicit type conversion during mixed-mode operations. For example, any arithmetic or comparison operation on a float and an int first converts the int to a float before execution. During assignment, if the left operand is a float and the right operand is an int, the int is converted to a float. If the target is an int and the right operand is a float, then the float is truncated to an int.

The programmer can perform an explicit type conversion by using either of the following two forms:

```
<type name>(<expression>)

(<type name>) <expression>
```

Thus, int(3.14) would return the value 3, and (float) 3 would return the value 3.0.

Interactive Input and Output

Input and output for interactive users can be performed by using the standard input and output streams. The standard output stream, cout, is by default connected to the terminal screen. The standard output operator or inserter, <<, can be used to send data of numeric, character, or string types to the stream. For example, the following output statement would display the message "Hi, I'm 6 years old." followed by a carriage return on the screen:

```
cout << "Hi, I'm " << 6 << " years old" << '.' << endl;
```

The new line character is sent by specifying the endl manipulator or by specifying the new line character '/n'. Each data value is implicitly converted to characters before being sent to the stream.

The standard input stream, cin, is connected to the keyboard. The standard input operator or extractor, >>, can be used to receive data from the stream. For example, the following statements would prompt the user for an integer, a real number, and a string, and input these values into the corresponding variables:

```
cout << "Enter an int, a float, and a string, "
     << "separated by spaces: ";
cin >> intValue >> floatValue >> stringValue;
```

Whitespace characters (space, tab, or new line) are used to separate data values during input. All whitespace characters are skipped during input. In the previous example, digits are taken from the stream and converted to an integer value that is stored in the integer variable. The same process takes place for the real number and the string value, though these data types increase the range of characters accepted. Integer values input into float variables are implicitly converted to real numbers. Nondigit characters typed during input into an integer variable terminate the input operation for that variable. Thus, if the input characters typed at the keyboard in our example are 675.35 dollars, three values are actually stored and the entire statement completes execution. The integer value will be 675, the real number will be .35, and the string will be "dollars".

Functions (Not Including Recursion)

Standard library functions are made available by including the desired library header file. A function interface is specified by a function declaration. A declaration consists of the return type of the function, the function's name, and a parenthesized list of zero or more formal parameters declarations. A semicolon must terminate a function declaration. For example, the declaration of the **math** library function pow follows:

```
double pow(double base, double exponent);
```

A function can be called either as a complete statement or within an expression. For example, the pow function could be used to compute a value for output or to throw away the result:

```
cout << pow(2, 5) << endl; // Output the result.

pow(2, 5);                  // Throw the result away.
```

Function declarations of programmer-defined functions should appear either in a library header file or directly before the main program heading in the main program file. They may be listed in any order that is convenient.

For each function declaration there should exist a function implementation. It should appear either in a library implementation file or below the main program block. A function implementation consists of a function heading and a block of code enclosed in curly braces. The function heading should be an exact copy of the function declaration, with the trailing semicolon omitted. The block of code can contain data declarations and statements. Functions that return a value should do this by executing a `return` statement at the logical end of the function. For example, the following code might implement a function that returns the square of its argument:

```
double square(double x)
{
    return x * x;
}
```

Functions that return no value but are executed for their side effects are called `void` functions. The following function displays "Hello world!" on the screen:

```
void helloWorld()
{
    cout << "Hello world!" << endl;
}
```

Note that this function also declares no parameters. This is the kind of function normally called as a standalone statement:

```
helloWorld();
```

The parentheses must be included in the call, even though no arguments are expected.

Value and Reference Parameters

C++ supports two primary parameter passing modes, pass by value and pass by reference. Pass by value is safe, in that the function works on a local copy of the actual parameter. Pass by reference allows side effects, in that the address of the actual parameter is referenced within the function. For example, the following function declaration is intended to specify an operation that computes the roots of a quadratic equation:

```
void computeRoots(float a, float b, float c,
    float &root1, float &root2);
```

The first three formal parameters are declared as value parameters to specify the input arguments to the function. The last two parameters are declared as reference parameters (using the ampersand) to specify the return values of the function.

In general, the scope of the formal parameters and locally declared data names is the body of the function.

Selection

There are three kinds of selection statements in C++. The `if` statement supports one-way decisions. For example, the following code increments a counter if a number is odd:

```
if (odd(x))
    oddCount = oddCount + 1;
```

The parentheses enclosing the Boolean expression are required.

The `if...else` statement supports two-way or multiway decisions. For example, the following code divides one number by another or outputs an error message if the second number is zero:

```cpp
if (second != 0)
   cout << first / second << endl;
else
{
   cout << "ERROR: the program cannot divide << first << " by ";
   cout << second << endl;
}
```

Note the use of a compound statement in the `else` clause. In general, simple statements in C++ end with a semicolon and compound statements end with a curly brace.

The `switch` statement supports multiway decisions involving comparisons of the value of a selector expression to a series of constants. For example, the following code represents a command interpreter for a simple text editor:

```cpp
switch (command)
{
   case 'E':
   case 'e': edit();
         break;
   case 'P':
   case 'p': print();
         break;
   case 'Q':
   case 'q': quit();
         break;
   default: cout << "ERROR: commands are e, p, or q." << endl;
}
```

The parentheses enclosing the selector expression (the variable `command`) are required. The `break` statement must be included in each case if the programmer wishes control to branch to the end of the `switch` statement. Otherwise, the next case is always evaluated. The `default` clause is optional but highly recommended.

Iteration

There are three kinds of loop structures in C++. The `for` loop is normally used to count from one limit to another, either up or down. The following two loops output the numbers between 1 and 5, first in ascending order and then in descending order:

```cpp
for (int i = 1; i <= 5; ++i)
   cout << i << endl

for (int j = 5; j >= 1; --j)
   cout << j << endl;
```

The form of a `for` loop heading is:

```
for (<initialization>; <termination>; <update>)
```

The termination condition is tested at loop entry and causes the loop to exit if it returns zero (false). Otherwise, the body of the loop executes and the update is run before the termination condition is re-examined. Note that the updates for the two loops use the increment and the decrement operators, respectively.

The `while` loop is normally used as an entry controlled loop with sentinel values or Boolean flags. For example, the following code adds numbers entered by the user until the value -999 is entered:

```
cout << "Enter a number: ";
cin >> number;
while (number != -999)
{
    sum = sum + number;
    cout << "Enter a number: ";
    cin >> number;
}
```

The parentheses enclosing the Boolean expression are required.

The `do...while` loop can be used instead of a `while` loop when it is known that a process must be performed at least once. For example, the following code takes input data until it falls within a range of values specified by a lower bound and an upper bound:

```
do
{
    cout << "Enter a value: ";
    cin >> value;
} while ((value < lowerBound) || (value > upperBound));
```

The parentheses enclosing the Boolean expression are required.

Typedef

Sometimes it is convenient to create a name for a data type and use this name to declare variables, function parameters, and so forth. For example, if you are using an older compiler, it might not provide a `bool` data type. Using `typedef`, you could create a type name, `boolean`, to represent Boolean values, as follows:

```
const int TRUE = 1;
const int FALSE = 0;


typedef int boolean;
```

Then one can use these names to define a Boolean function that tests data for validity, as follows:

```
boolean isValid(int data, int lowerBound, int upperBound)
{
    if ((data >= lowerBound) && (data <= upperBound))
        return TRUE;
    else
        return FALSE;
}
```

Enumerated Data Types

Occasionally, a programmer needs to use mnemonic symbols to represent data values such as the days of the week or the primary colors. Rather than use strings, which require memory space that is a linear function of the number of characters needed in a symbol, the programmer can use enumerated values. An enumerated type in C++ specifies a set of symbolic constants that map to integers at run time. For example, the following code declares types and variables to represent the weekdays and the primary colors:

```
enum weekday {MON, TUE, WED, THUR, FRI};
enum primaryColor {RED, YELLOW, BLUE};

weekday day = MON;
primaryColor color = RED;
```

Enumerated values of the same type can be compared and assigned. Any enumerated value can be cast to its underlying integer representation, and integers within the range of an enumerated type can be cast to the corresponding enumerated value. Thus, the code:

```
cout << int(MON) << endl;
```

would display the value 0 on the screen, and the code:

```
color = primaryColor(2);
```

would assign the enumerated value BLUE to the variable color. C++ does not implicitly convert between integers and enumerated values.

Structured Data Types (apstrings, apvectors, apmatrices, files, structs)

An apvector object is constructed in C++ by specifying the base type, the name of the object, and the physical size of the vector. For example, the following code declares a vector of characters and a vector of integers, capable of storing 10 data values:

```
apvector<int> intArray(10);
```

Vectors can have any base type, including other vectors. Vector index positions are numbered from 0 to N - 1, where N is the physical size of the vector specified in its declaration. This implies that a[0] is the first possible data value in the vector a and a[n - 1] is the last possible value.

Care should be taken in three areas when programming with vectors in C++. First, loops that process entire vectors should be checked by hand carefully. A `for` loop should usually have the form:

```
for (int i = 0; i < MAX; ++ i)
    process(a[i]);
```

where MAX represents either the last physical location in the vector or the location of the last element currently used by the program in the vector. Note that the initial value of i is 0 and its last value as an index is MAX - 1.

Second, vector parameters that are intended to be modified in functions can be declared as in the following example, assuming a base type of element:

```
void changeVector(apvector<int> &theVector);
```

1 1

Note that the size of the vector is not specified. Because the vector is passed by reference, vectors of elements of any size can be passed to this function.

Third, vector parameters that are not intended to be modified can be passed as constant reference parameters, as in the following example:

```
void displayVector(const apvector<int> &theVector);
```

The actual vector is passed by reference to this function also, but the compiler will disallow assignments to the constant parameter in the function body. Passing vectors in this fashion avoids the considerable overhead involved in copying an entire vector when it is passed by value.

Strings can be conveniently represented using the `apstring` class. For example, you could define a string type, declare two variables, input data into them, and output results in the following code:

```
apstring firstName, lastName;

cout << "Enter you first name:";
cin >> firstName;
cout << "Enter you last name:";
cin >> lastName;
cout << "Hi, " << firstName << " " << lastName << "!" << endl;
```

A two-dimensional grid can be declared using an `apmatrix`. For example, the following code:

```
apmatric<int> f(10,20);
```

constructs a matrix called `f` with 10 rows and 20 columns. The rows are indexed from 0 through 9 inclusive, and the columns are indexed from 0 through 19. The following nested loop construct would call a function `process` for each of the integers in the matrix `f`.

```
for (int i = 0; i < 9; i++)
  for (int j = 0; j < 19; j++)
    process(f[i][j]);
```

Complete documentation for the `apvector, apstring, and apmatrix` classes can be found in Appendix E.

Data values of different types can be combined into one data structure by using a `struct`. This is similar to the record facility in other programming languages. For example, the following code defines a type for representing a person's name, address, phone number, salary, and age and declares two variables of this type:

```
struct person
{
    string name, address, phoneNumber;
    float salary;
    int age;
};

person manager, clerk;
```

Note the semicolon, which is required, following the right curly brace. The items enclosed in the curly braces are called the members of the `struct`. They can be of any data type (including `string`, which we assume to be defined by the programmer elsewhere). Members are referenced by using the selector or dot operator, as follows:

```
manager.name = "Sandra Speedup";
manager.address = "300 Park Avenue/nRoanoke, VA/n24018";
manager.phoneNumber = "703-775-3316";
manager.salary = 60000.00;
manager.age = 25;
```

File processing in C++ is accomplished by means of file streams. The program gains access to these by:

```
#include <fstream.h>
```

The following code opens a file stream for output to a file named "myfile", prints an integer, a real number, and a string to the file, closes the file, and then performs input on it as well:

```
int intValue;
float floatValue;
apstring stringValue[20];
ofstream outFile;
ifstream inFile;

outFile.open("myfile");
outFile << 45 endl << 3.14 << endl << "Hi!" << endl;
outFile.close();
inFile.open("myfile");
inFile >> intValue >> floatValue >> stringValue;
inFile.close();
```

File stream input and output operations work in essentially the same way as input and output operations on the standard streams (cin and cout). To control a loop for the input of an arbitrary number of data values from an input file stream, one can use a while loop with a priming input statement. The following example copies integers from one file stream to another:

```
inFile >> data;
while (! inFile.eof())
{
    outFile << data << endl;
    inFile >> data;
}
```

Note that an attempt to input data must be made before the end-of-file condition can be tested with the eof function.

Implementation of Simple Classes

The first step in developing a new class to solve a problem is to draw up a list of user requirements. These state the *attributes* and *operations* that users expect the class to have. For example, a minimal set of attributes for a bank account might be the following:

1. A password (a string)

2. A balance (a real number)

1 3

The operations that users expect to perform on bank accounts follow:

1. Create a new account with default password and balance

2. Create a new account with user-specified password and balance

3. Change the password

4. Deposit money

5. Withdraw money

6. Observe the balance

Assuming that a class called `account` has been defined in a library file, the following client program shows how to create and access a bank account object:

```
// Program file: bankdriv.cpp

#include <iostream.h>
#include <iomanip.h>

#include "account.h"

int main()
{
    // Create two accounts and a dummy target

    account judy("beelzebub", 50.00);
    account jim("gadzooks", 100.00);
    account target;

    cout << setiosflags(ios::fixed | ios::showpoint)
        << setprecision(2);

    // Look up balances

    cout << "Judy's balance = $"
        << judy.getBalance("beelzebub") << endl;

    cout << "Jim's balance = $"
        << jim.getBalance("gadzooks") << endl;

    // An invalid password

    cout << "Result of invalid password = "
        << jim.getBalance("rosebud") << endl;

    // Make a deposit

    cout << "Depositing $20.00 to Jim, new balance = $"
        << jim.deposit("gadzooks", 20.00) << endl;

    // An attempted overdraft
```

```
    cout << "Result of overdraft from Judy ($51.00) = "
        << judy.withdraw("beelzebub", 51.00) << endl;

    // Copy to dummy target

    target = judy;
    cout << "Target's balance = $"
        << target.getBalance("beelzebub") << endl;
    return 0;
}
```

The output that this program produces is:

```
Judy's balance = $50.00
Jim's balance = $100.00
Result of invalid password = -1.00
Depositing $20.00 to Jim, new balance = $120.00
Result of overdraft from Judy ($51.00) = -2.00
Target's balance = $50.00
```

The implementation of a class in C++ consists of two parts, a class *declaration section* and a class *implementation section*, which are usually placed in separate files. The first file for the account class, called account.h, contains the declaration section of the class.

```
// Class declaration file: account.h

#ifndef ACCOUNT_H
#define ACCOUNT_H

#include "apstring.h"

class account
{
    public:

    // Constructors

    account();
    account(const apstring &password, double balance);
    account(const account &a);

    // Accessor

    double getBalance(const apstring &password) const;

    // Modifiers

   int setPassword(const apstring &password,
          const apstring newPassword);
    double deposit(const apstring &password,
          double amount);
```

```
      double withdraw(const apstring &password,
              double amount);

      // Assignment

      const account& operator = (const account &a);

      private:

      // Data members

      apstring myPassword;
      double myBalance;
};

#endif
```

The general form for writing a simple class declaration section in C++ is:

```
<preprocessor directives>

<constant definitions>

class <class name>
{
          public:

          <public data declarations>
          <public function declarations>

          private:

          <private data declarations>
          <private function declarations>
};
```

The account class implementation file will have the form:

```
// Class implementation file: account.cpp

<member function implementation 1>
.
.
<member function implementation n>
```

The headings of the function implementations must have the form:

```
<return type> <class name>::<function name> (<optional parameter list>)
```

<u>Constructors</u>: The `account` class declaration specifies three class constructors. The first constructor, `account()`, is run when a program declares string variables as in the following code:

```
account first, second;
```

This kind of constructor is called a *default constructor*. The implementation of the default constructor for an account sets the password to an empty string and the balance to zero.

```
account::account()
{
  myPassword = "";
  myBalance = 0.00;
}
```

The second constructor:

```
account(const apstring &password, double balance);
```

is run when users wish to declare an account variable with specified attributes, as in the code:

```
account judy("beelzebub", 100.00);
```

The implementation of this constructor assigns the values of the parameters to the corresponding data members of the account object.

```
account::account(const apstring &password,
        double balance)
{
  myPassword = password;
  myBalance = balance;
}
```

The third constructor is called the *copy constructor* for the `account` class. This function is run whenever an account object is passed by value as a parameter to a function. To guarantee a complete copy in all situations, we define a copy constructor that takes another account object as a parameter:

```
account::account(const account &a)
{
  myPassword = a.myPassword;
  myBalance = a.myBalance;
}
```

The data members of the new account object, called the *receiver object*, are referenced by name. The data members of the account object to be copied, called the *parameter object*, are accessed by the selector notation used with C++ structs.

<u>Accessors</u>: The role of accessor functions is to allow users to observe the attributes of an object without changing them. To guarantee that no changes occur, we can declare an accessor function as a *const function*, using the form:

```
<return type> <function name>(<formal parameter declarations>) const;
```

The implementation of the accessor function for account objects, `getBalance`, follows:

```cpp
double account::getBalance(const apstring &password) const
{
  if (password == myPassword)
   return myBalance;
  else
   return -1;
}
```

Modifiers: The role of modifier functions is to set one or more of the attributes of an object to new values. Here we illustrate by providing the implementation of the modifier function `withdraw` for account objects.

```cpp
double account::withdraw(const apstring &password,
            double amount)
{
  if (password == myPassword)
   if ((amount >= 0) && (amount <= myBalance))
   {
     myBalance = myBalance - amount;
     return myBalance;
   }
   else
     return -2; // Invalid amount
  else
     return -1; // Invalid password
}
```

The Assignment Operator, Polymorphism, and Overloading: Many of the built-in operators in C++ are *polymorphic*, which means "many structures." For example, the operators +, ==, and >> are polymorphic for integers and real numbers. This means that the same operators designate the same general operations (arithmetic, comparisons, input/output), even though the actual operations performed may vary with the type or structure of the operands.

C++ allows a programmer to reuse any built-in operator (or function name, also) to designate an operation on new data types. This process is called *overloading an operation*. We begin by specifying the declaration of the member function to be overloaded:

```cpp
const account& operator = (const account &a);
```

Note that `operator` is a reserved word in C++. The receiver object will be the left operand of the assignment, and the parameter object will serve as the right operand. The general form for specifying operators is:

```
<return type> operator <standard operator symbol> (<parameter list>);
```

The implementation is written by placing a similar form in the function heading. If the target and the source objects are not the same object, the function copies the data members of the source object to the target object. The function returns a reference to the target object.

```cpp
const account& account::operator = (const account &a)
{
```

```
      if (this != &a)
      {
       myPassword = a.myPassword;
       myBalance = a.myBalance;
      }
      return *this;
}
```

Note the following points:

1. The reserved word `this` always refers to the address of the receiver object. The expression `&a` returns the address of the parameter object `a`. Thus, the expression `(this != &a)` returns `True` if the operands are addresses of different objects.

2. The assignment operator in C++ normally returns an *l-value*. An l-value is an object that can be the target of an assignment operation in C++. For this mechanism to work correctly, the return type of an assignment operator should be a reference to the class of the target object. However, in this book, we discourage the return of an l-value from an assignment. Instead, we return a constant reference, specified in this example as `const account&`. By returning a constant reference, we do not allow the programmer to assign to the same variable more than once in an assignment expression, so the compiler prohibits expressions of the form `(a = b) = c`, but expressions of the form `a = b = c` are valid. The effect of the last line of code in our example is to return the receiver object. To gain access to the object itself, we apply the *dereference operator* (*) to `this`. The receiver object will be returned as a constant l-value because the return type is specified as a reference to a class.

Class Templates

A *class template* in C++ allows client programs to specify the component types in a class when instances of that class are created. In the case of the vector class, this allows a client program to create a vector of integers, a vector of real numbers, and a vector of strings, using the angle bracket notation.

```
apvector<int> intVector;
apvector<double> doubleVector;
apvector<apstring> stringVector;
```

The angle brackets appear again in the class declaration for `apvector`, this time surrounding information about the component type. Following we use the notations `template <class itemType>` and `apvector<itemType>` to specify that the class can have any element type. The name `itemType` behaves like a formal type parameter in the class definition. It holds a place for any actual type parameter provided by the user, such as `int`, `double`, or `apstring`, when an instance of the class is created. Other than this new syntax, working with class templates is similar to working with ordinary C++ classes.

```
// Class declaration file: apvector.h

#ifndef _APVECTOR_H
#define _APVECTOR_H

template <class itemType> class apvector
{
    public:
```

```cpp
    // constructors
    apvector();
    apvector(int size);
    apvector(int size, const itemType &fillValue);
    apvector(const apvector<itemType> &vec);

    // destructor

    ~apvector();

    // assignment

    const apvector<itemType>& operator =
        (const apvector<itemType> &rhs);

    // accessor

    int length() const; // capacity of vector

    // indexing

    const itemType& operator [ ] (int index) const;
    itemType& operator [ ] (int index);

    // modifier

    void resize(int newSize);

    private:

    // Data members

  int mySize;     // # elements in array
  itemType *myList;  // array used for storage
};

#include "apvector.cpp"

#endif
```

Software Engineering Principles

UNIT 1

lesson 1
15 hrs.

Algorithm Analysis: Space and Time Considerations

lesson 2
15 hrs.

Data Abstraction and Object-Oriented Software Engineering

unit 1 review
2 hrs.

 Estimated Time for Unit 1: 32 hours

1

ALGORITHM ANALYSIS: SPACE AND TIME CONSIDERATIONS

OBJECTIVES

Upon completion of this lesson, you will be able to:

■ Identify criteria by which complex software is evaluated.

■ Develop a functional interface that can be used with a variety of sorting algorithms.

■ Understand the potential difference between the computer operations of comparing data items and interchanging them.

■ Trace in detail the comparisons and interchanges of data items that occur during execution of the bubble sort, selection sort, and insertion sort algorithms.

■ Understand the formal definition of big-O notation and use it to classify the time efficiency of algorithms involving nonrecursive, iterative control constructs.

■ Recognize often-used big-O categories and see the relationship between an algorithm's big-O classification and its expected run time on a computer.

■ Apply big-O notation in analyzing the time efficiencies of the bubble sort, selection sort, and insertion sort algorithms.

■ Understand the difference between physically sorting and logically sorting.

■ Understand the radix sort algorithm and analyze its time and space efficiency.

■ Understand and analyze the efficiency of the sequential search algorithm, the binary search algorithm, and key-to-address transformations.

🕐 **Estimated Time: 15 hours**

22

UNIT 1: SOFTWARE ENGINEERING PRINCIPLES

Vocabulary

big-O notation	insertion sort	polynomial algorithms
binary search	linear algorithm	quadratic algorithm
bubble sort	logarithmic algorithms	radix sort
cubic algorithm	logical order	selection sort
dominant term	order of magnitude	sequential search
exponential algorithm	pointer sort	time/space trade-off

Introduction

This lesson marks an important step in your exploration of computer science. Up to this point, it has been difficult to divorce your study of computer science from the learning of C++. You have developed problem-solving skills, but the problems we have encountered have been very focused. That is, the problems were chosen specifically to illustrate a particular feature of C++. This is the way problem-solving skills must be developed: Start with small problems and work toward large ones.

By now, you are familiar with many features of the C++ programming language. You are ready to direct your attention toward larger, more complex problems that require you to integrate many of the particular skills you have developed. Now our attention will be directed more toward issues of software design and less toward describing C++. If we need a particular feature of C++ that you have not yet learned, we will introduce it when appropriate. Our main objective, however, is to study more complex problems and the software design issues that arise out of them. From here on, we view C++ primarily as the vehicle to implement, test, and experiment with our solutions to problems. The techniques of software design we are about to explore will enable us to write programs that have the following characteristics:

■ *Large*. Actually, our programs can properly be called systems because they typically involve numerous modules that interact to solve one complex problem.

■ *Reliable*. The measure of the reliability of a system is that it can anticipate and handle all types of exceptional circumstances.

■ *Flexible*. The system should be easily modified to handle circumstances that may change in the future.

■ *Expandable and reusable*. If the system is successful, it will frequently spawn new computing needs. We should be able to incorporate solutions to these new needs into the original system with relative ease.

■ *Efficient*. The system should make optimal use of time and space resources.

■ *Structured*. The system should be divided into compact modules, each of which is responsible for a specific, well-defined task.

■ *User-friendly*. The system should be clearly documented so that it is easy to use. Internal documentation helps programmers maintain the software, and external documentation helps users use it.

In designing software to meet these criteria, one of the key skills you must develop is the ability to choose the appropriate tools for the job. You should not have to rediscover algorithms and techniques for information storage and retrieval each time you write a new program. As a computer scientist, you must have a detailed knowledge of algorithms and data storage techniques at your fingertips and apply this knowledge when designing software to solve a variety of problems. You should look into your storehouse of algorithms and data storage strategies, choose the most appropriate methods, and then tailor them to the application at hand.

As you expand your knowledge of computer science, you will find that a given problem frequently lends itself to more than one method of solution. Hence, in addition to knowing the individual principles, you must be able to evaluate them comparatively. This comparative evaluation must be conducted in as systematic and quantitative a fashion as possible. That is, you must justify your choice of a method by presenting cogent arguments based on facts and figures pertinent to the problem. Given this perspective on computer science, we turn our attention to a twofold task:

1. Stocking our algorithmic toolbox with methods that have become standards in computer science.

2. Developing criteria for knowing which tool to choose in a particular situation.

1.1 Introduction to Analyzing Algorithms: Simple Sorting

To begin this task, we consider some techniques for sorting and searching. We then evaluate these techniques for their efficiency in terms of execution time and use of space (memory) resources. To conduct such a time/space analysis, we introduce what has come to be known as big-O notation. In effect, big-O notation is the mathematical measuring stick by which computer scientists quantitatively evaluate algorithms. It allows us to place algorithms into categories based on their efficiency. Such categorization helps us determine whether a proposed solution is practical in terms of the real-world requirements and constraints dictated by the problem.

An Interface for Studying Sorting Algorithms

Our discussion in this section will use a vector (that is, an array) of objects that we want to sort in ascending order according to a given attribute for each object. The attribute on which the sort is based is known as the key attribute. For instance, we may wish to arrange a list of student objects in alphabetical order according to student last name or a list of inventory objects in order according to product identification numbers. To provide a suitable setting for our upcoming discussion of the sorting problem, we will make the following assumptions:

1. The objects being sorted are of type element. element is a synonym for whatever class of object we wish to place in a vector.

2. If necessary, the element class overloads the standard C++ operators =, ==, <, and > that are used by the sort algorithms. The operator = is used for copying elements, while ==, <, and > compare two elements with respect to the key attribute.

Under these assumptions, we wish to write a sort function that meets the following specifications:

```
// Function: sort
// Sorts a vector of elements into ascending order provided the type
// element implements the operators =, ==,  <, and >
//
// Inputs: a vector of elements in arbitrary order and the
//         number of elements currently in the vector
// Output: the vector of elements arranged in ascending order

template <class element>
void sort(apvector<element> &list, int n);
```

Two aspects of these declarations are worth noting. First, the fashion in which we have used a template for the function's interface will allow this function to sort a vector of any size and base type provided that the necessary operators are overloaded. This method of declaration represents an attempt to make the C++ function abstract: It embodies an algorithm that can sort a variety of data types.

Second, the measure of an algorithm's run-time efficiency is in direct proportion to the number of elementary machine operations that must be performed as the algorithm is executed. With sorting algorithms, these elementary machine operations compare and interchange two data items. Depending on the amount of data in the `element` type in the preceding declarations, it is entirely possible that interchanging two data items could be considerably more costly in machine time than comparing two items. Why? An interchange of large data items will generate a loop that moves a significant number of bytes at the machine language level.

Our analysis of run-time efficiency should take this factor into account. It may be more important to minimize data interchanges at the expense of comparisons. This complication does not apply when we are concerned with sorting vectors that contain only simple, unstructured data items.

Bubble Sort

Given a list of data objects stored in a vector, a ***bubble sort*** causes a pass through the vector to compare adjacent pairs of keys. Whenever two keys are out of order with respect to each other, the associated objects are interchanged. The effect of such a pass through a list of names is traced in Figure 1-1, which gives a "snapshot" of the vector after each comparison. Notice that after such a pass, we are assured the list will have the name that comes last in alphabetical order in the final vector position. That is, the last name will "sink" to the bottom of the vector, and preceding names will gradually "percolate" to the top.

FIGURE 1-1

Trace of bubble sort on a vector with four names

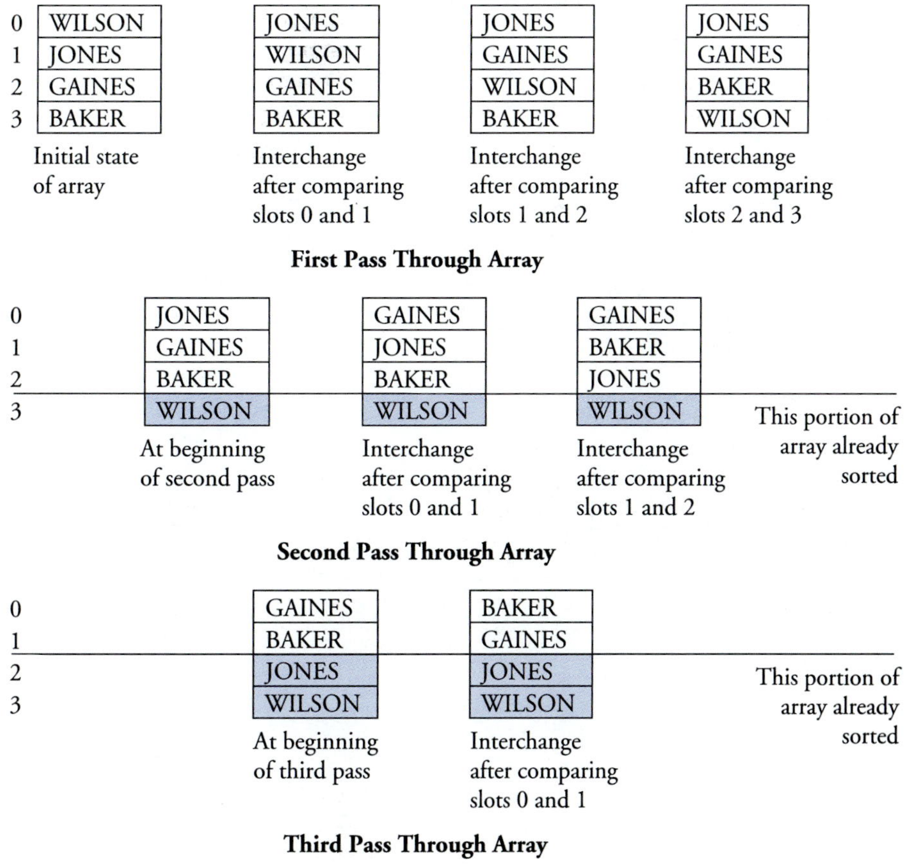

First Pass Through Array

Second Pass Through Array

Third Pass Through Array

If one pass through a vector of n keys guarantees that the key last in order appears in the appropriate position, then passing through the remaining $n - 1$ entries using the same logic will guarantee that the key second to last in order is in its appropriate position. Repeating the process for a total of $n - 1$ passes eventually ensures that all objects are in their appropriate positions. In general, on the kth pass through the vector, $n - k$ comparisons of pairs must be made.

Thus the bubble sort algorithm involves a nested loop structure. The outer loop controls the number of (successively smaller) passes through the vector. The inner loop controls the pairs of adjacent entries being compared.

If we ever make a complete pass through the inner loop without having to make an interchange, we can declare the vector sorted and avoid all future passes through it. A top-level pseudocode development of the algorithm is:

1. Initialize counter k to zero
2. Initialize Boolean exchangeMade to **TRUE**
3. While $(k < n - 1)$ and exchangeMade
    3.1. Set exchangeMade to **FALSE**
    3.2. Increment counter k
    3.3. For each j from 0 to $n - k$
        3.3.1. If entry in jth slot > entry in $(j + 1)$st slot
        3.3.1.1. Exchange these entries
        3.3.1.2. Set exchangeMade to true

The complete C++ function to implement this algorithm for a vector of objects follows. The function assumes the existence of appropriate data declarations.

```
template <class element>
void bubbleSort(apvector<element> &list, int n)
{
    int j, k;
    bool exchangeMade;
    element temp;
    k = 0;
    exchangeMade = true;

    // Make up to n - 1 passes through
    vector, exit early if no exchanges
    // are made on previous pass

    while ((k < n - 1) && exchangeMade)
    {
        exchangeMade = false;
        ++k;
        for (j = 0; j < n - k; ++j)
        // Number of comparisons on
        kth pass
            if (list[j] > list[j + 1])
            {
                temp = list[j];
                // Exchange must be made
                list[j] = list[j + 1];
                list[j + 1] = temp;
                exchangeMade = true;
```

```
            }
        }
    }
```

Although we provide only listings of the sort and search functions in the text itself, complete demonstration programs are available. See your instructor.

Example 1-1

Trace the action of the function `bubbleSort` if n is 5 and the vector `list` initially contains

```
0 | 43
1 | 20
2 | 24
3 | 31
4 | 36
```

First Pass Through Array

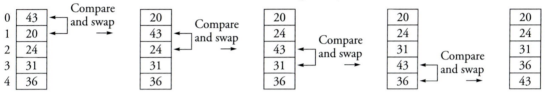

Second Pass Through Array

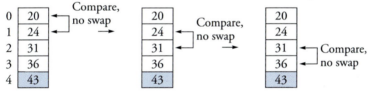

`exchangeMade` remained false throughout the inner loop, so the algorithm is done.

In Section 1.2, we will analyze in detail the run-time efficiency of the bubble sort. First, however, we should consider two other sorting algorithms to which the efficiency of bubble sort may be compared: *selection sort* and *insertion sort*.

Selection Sort

We have seen that the strategy of the bubble sort is to place the (current) largest vector value in the (current) last vector slot, then seal off that slot from future consideration, and repeat the process. The selection sort algorithm has a similar plan, but it attempts to avoid the multitude of interchanges of adjacent entries. To do so, on the *k*th pass through the vector, it determines the position of the smallest entry among

```
list[k], list[k + 1], ..., list[n-1]
```

This smallest entry is then swapped with the *k*th entry, k is incremented by 1, and the process is repeated. Figure 1-2 illustrates how this algorithm works on repeated passes through a vector with six entries. Asterisks are used to indicate the successively smallest (alphabetical) entries as they are correctly located in the vector.

FIGURE 1-2
Trace of section sort logic

Original Order of Keys	k = 0	k = 1	k = 2	k = 3	k = 4
DAVE	ARON*	ARON*	ARON*	ARON*	ARON*
TOM	TOM	BEV*	BEV*	BEV*	BEV*
PAM	PAM	PAM	DAVE*	DAVE*	DAVE*
ARON	DAVE	DAVE	PAM	PAM*	PAM*
BEV	BEV	TOM	TOM	TOM	SAM*
SAM	SAM	SAM	SAM	SAM	TOM*

As we see next, the C++ function for selection sort uses, as its inner loop, a simple algorithm to find the minimum entry and store its position in the variable `minPosition`. This inner loop avoids the potentially frequent interchange of vector elements that is necessary in the inner loop of `bubbleSort`.

```
template <class element>
void selectionSort(apvector<element> &list, int n)
{
    int minPosition;
    element temp;

    // Make n - 1 passes through successively smaller segments

    for (int k = 0; k < n - 1; ++k)
    {
        minPosition = k;
        // On each pass find index of the smallest element
        for (int j = k + 1; j < n; ++j)
            if (list[j] <  list[minPosition])
                minPosition = j;
        if (minPosition != k)
        {
            temp = list[minPosition];      // Exchange must be made
            list[minPosition] = list[k];
            list[k] = temp;
        }
    }
}
```

Example 1-2 indicates that the selection sort algorithm swaps no data values until exiting the inner loop. This approach apparently reduces the number of data interchanges and makes the selection sort more efficient than the bubble sort. Does it offer a significant improvement? Or have other subtle inefficiencies been introduced to offset this apparent gain? These are difficult questions to answer unless we have a better grasp of how to measure program efficiency. We'll explore efficiency in the next section. First, let's look at one more sorting algorithm for comparison purposes.

Example 1-2

Trace the action of the function `selectionSort` if n is 5 and the vector `list` initially contains

0	30
1	39
2	22
3	19
4	34

First Pass Through Array

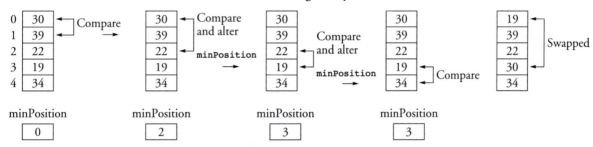

Second Pass Through Array

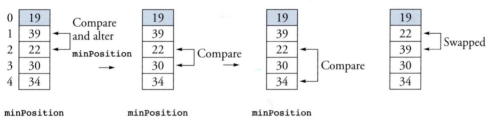

Third Pass Through Array

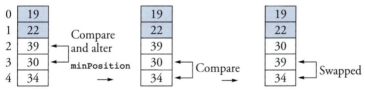

Fourth Pass Through Array

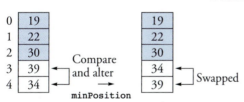

Insertion Sort

Although it reduces the number of data interchanges, the selection sort apparently will not allow an effective—and automatic—loop exit if the vector becomes ordered during an early pass. In this regard, the bubble sort is more efficient than the selection sort for a vector that is nearly ordered from the beginning. However, even with just one entry out of order, the bubble sort's early loop exit can fail to reduce the number of comparisons made.

The insertion sort attempts to take greater advantage of a vector's partial ordering. The goal is that on the kth pass through, the kth element among

```
list[0], list[1], ..., list[k]
```

should be inserted into its rightful place among the first k entries in the vector. Thus, after the kth pass (k starting at 1), the first k elements of the vector should be in sorted order. This sort works in a way analogous to the fashion in which many people pick up playing cards and order them in their hands. Holding the first (k - 1) cards in order, a person will pick up the kth card and compare it with cards already held until its appropriate spot is found. The following steps will achieve this logic:

1. For each k from 1 to n - 1 (k is the index of vector element to insert)
    1.1 Set `itemToInsert` to `list[k]`
    1.2 Set j to k - 1 (j starts at k - 1 and is decremented until the insertion position is found)
    1.3 While (insertion position not found) and (not beginning of vector)
        1.3.1 If `itemToInsert` < `list[`j`]`
            1.3.1.1 Move `list[`j`]` to index position j + 1
            1.3.1.2 Decrement j by 1
        1.3.2 Else
            1.3.2.1 The insertion position has been found
    1.4 `itemToInsert` should be positioned at index j + 1

In effect, for each pass, the index j begins at the (k - 1)st element and moves that element to position j + 1 until we find the insertion point for what was originally the kth element.

An insertion sort for each value of k is traced in Figure 1-3. In each column of this diagram, the data items are sorted in alphabetical order relative to each other above the item with the asterisk; below this item, the data are not affected.

FIGURE 1-3
Trace of repeated passes from insertion sort

Original Order of Keys	First Pass $k = 1$	Second Pass $k = 2$	Third Pass $k = 3$	Fourth Pass $k = 4$	Fifth Pass $k = 5$
PAM	PAM	DAVE	ARON	ARON	ARON
SAM	SAM*	PAM	DAVE	DAVE	BEV
DAVE	DAVE	SAM*	PAM	PAM	DAVE
ARON	ARON	ARON	SAM*	SAM*	PAM
TOM	TOM	TOM	TOM	TOM*	SAM
BEV	BEV	BEV	BEV	BEV	TOM*

To implement the insertion sort algorithm in C++, we have the following code:

```
template <class element>
void insertionSort(apvector<element> &list, int n)
{
   int j, k;
   element itemToInsert;
   bool stillLooking;

   // On the kth pass, insert item k into its correct position among
   // the first k entries in vector. }

   for (k = 1; k < n; ++k)
   {
      // Walk backward through list, looking for slot to insert A[K]
      itemToInsert = list[k];
      j = k - 1;
      stillLooking = true;
      while ((j >= 0) && stillLooking )
         if (itemToInsert  < list[j])
         {
            list[j + 1] = list[j];
            --j;
         }
         else
            stillLooking =
            false;
      // Upon leaving loop,
      J + 1 is the index
      // where itemToInsert
      belongs
      list[j + 1] =
      itemToInsert;
   }
}
```

Array at Beginning of the kth Stage

```
   0    1    2   ···  k – 1   k
 ┌────┬────┬────┬─··─┬────┬────┬────┬────┐
 │    │    │    │ ·· │    │    │    │    │
 └────┴────┴────┴────┴────┴────┴────┴────┘
 ╰───────────────────╯ ↑ ╰─────────────╯
        Sorted              Unsorted
```

kth element inserted in its rightful place
among first k entries on kth pass

Example 1-3

Trace the action of the function `insertionSort` if n is 5 and the vector `list` initially contains

```
0  80
1  40
2  32
3  54
4  61
```

First Pass (k = 2)

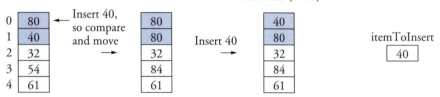

Second Pass (k = 3)

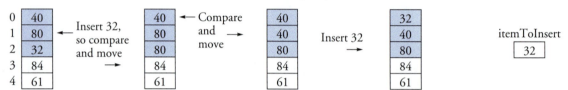

Third Pass (k = 4)

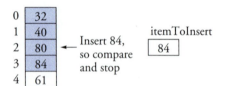

Fourth Pass (k = 5)

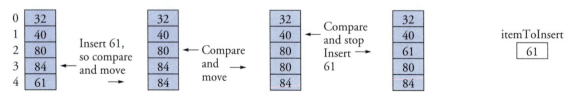

EXERCISES 1.1

1. Which of the sorting methods studied in this section allows a possible early exit from its inner loop? What is the potential advantage of using this early exit?

2. Which of the sorting methods studied in this section allows a possible early exit from its outer loop? What is the potential advantage of using this early exit?

UNIT 1: SOFTWARE ENGINEERING PRINCIPLES

3. Which of the sorting methods studied in this section does not allow for the possibility of an early exit from its inner or outer loops? What potential advantage does this method have over the other two methods that were presented?

4. Suppose that, initially, a vector contains seven integer entries arranged in the following order:

0	43
1	40
2	18
3	24
4	39
5	60
6	12

Trace the order of the vector entries after each successive pass of the bubble sort.

5. Repeat Exercise 4 for the selection sort.

6. Repeat Exercise 4 for the insertion sort.

7. Consider the following sort algorithm. Which of the methods studied in this section does this new algorithm most closely resemble? In what ways is it different from that method? Trace the action of this new sort algorithm on the vector from Exercise 4.

```
template <class element>
void sort(apvector<element> &list, int n)
{
    int j, k;
    bool exchangeMade = true;
    element temp;

    k = 0;
    while ((k < n - 1) && exchangeMade)
    {
        exchangeMade = false;
        ++k;
        for (j = n - 1; j > k + 1; --j)
            if (list[j] < list[j - 1])
            {
                temp = list[j];
                list[j] = list[j - 1];
                list[j - 1] = temp;
                exchangeMade = true;
            }
    }
}
```

8. Consider the following sort algorithm. Which of the methods studied in this section does this new algorithm most closely resemble? In what ways is it different from that method? Trace the action of this new sort algorithm on the vector from Exercise 4.

```
template <class element>
void sort(apvector<element> &list, int n)
{
    int j, k, position;
    element temp;

    for (k = 0; k < n - 1; ++k)
    {
        position = 0;
        for (j = 1; j < n - k + 1; ++j)
            if (list[j] > list[position])
                position = j;
        temp = list[n - k + 1];
        list[n - k + 1] = list[position];
        list[position] = temp;
    }
}
```

9. Consider the following sort algorithm. Which of the methods studied in this section does this new algorithm most closely resemble? In what ways is it different from that method? Trace the action of this new sort algorithm on the vector from Exercise 4.

```
template <class element>
void sort(apvector<element> &list, int n)
{
    int j, k;
    bool done;
    element temp;

    for (k = n - 1; k > 0; --k)
    {
        j = k;
        done = false;
        while ((j <= n - 1) && ! done)
            if (list[j] > list[j + 1])
            {
                temp = list[j];
                list[j] = list[j - 1];
                list[j - 1] = temp;
                ++j;
            }
            else
                done = true;
    }
}
```

10. Devise sample data sets to demonstrate the *best case* and *worst case* behavior of the bubble sort, insertion sort, and selection sort. That is, for each sorting algorithm, construct data sets that illustrate the minimum and maximum number of comparisons required for that particular algorithm.

11. Construct a data set in which just one value is out of order and yet the Boolean test of the `exchangeMade` variable never allows an early exit from the outer loop of bubble sort. How does the insertion sort perform on this same data set? Better, worse, or the same? Explain why.

12. Modify the sorting algorithms of this section so that they receive an additional argument indicating whether the sort should be in ascending or descending order.

13. The inner loop of an insertion sort can be modified merely to find the appropriate position for the *k*th vector entry instead of actually shifting items to make room for this entry. The shifting of items and placement of the original *k*th entry can then be achieved in a separate loop. Write a new insertion sort function that implements this modification. Intuitively, is your new version more or less efficient than the old version? Why?

14. Modify all of the sorting algorithms presented in this section to include counters for the number of comparisons and data interchanges that are made. Then run those sorting algorithms on a variety of data sets, maintaining a chart of the counters for each algorithm. Prepare a written statement to summarize your conclusions about the relative efficiencies of the algorithms.

1.2 *Which Sort Is Best? A Big-O Analysis*

Computers do their work in terms of certain fundamental operations: comparing two numbers, moving the contents of one memory word to another, and so on. It should come as no surprise to you that a simple instruction in a high-level language such as C++ may be translated (via a compiler) into many of these fundamental machine-level instructions. On most modern computers, the speeds of these fundamental operations are measured in microseconds—that is, millionths of a second—although some supercomputers are beginning to break the nanosecond (billionth of a second) barrier.

Let's assume, for the sake of argument, that we are working with a hypothetical computer that requires one microsecond to perform one of its fundamental operations. With execution speeds of this kind, it makes little sense to analyze the efficiency of those portions of a program that perform only initializations and final reporting of summary results. The key to analyzing a function's efficiency is to scrutinize its loops, especially its nested loops. Consider the following two examples of nested loops intended to sum each of the rows of an $N \times N$ `apmatrix` called `matrix`, storing the row sums in the one-dimensional vector `rows` and the overall total in `grandTotal`.

Example 1-4

```
grandTotal = 0;
for (k = 0; k < n - 1; ++k)
{
   rows[k] = 0;
   for (j = 0; j < n - 1; ++j)
   {
           rows[k] = rows[k] + matrix[k][j];
           grandTotal = grandTotal+ matrix[k][j];
   }
}
```

Example 1-5

```
grandTotal = 0;
for (k = 0; k < n - 1; ++k)
{
   rows[k] = 0;
   for (j = 0; j < n - 1; ++j)
         rows[k] = rows[k] + matrix[k][j];
   grandTotal = grandTotal+ rows[k];
}
```

If we analyze the number of addition operations required by these two examples, it should be immediately obvious that Example 1-5 is better in this respect. Because Example 1-4 incorporates the accumulating of `grandTotal` into its inner loop, it requires $2N^2$ additions. That is, the additions `rows[k] + matrix[k][j]` and `grandTotal + matrix[k][j]` are each executed N^2 times for a total of $2N^2$. Example 1=5, on the other hand, accumulates `grandTotal` after the inner loop; hence, it requires only $N^2 + N$ additions, which is less than $2N^2$ for any N after 1. Example 1-5 is seemingly guaranteed to execute faster than Example 1-4 for any nontrivial value of N.

But note that "faster" here may not have much significance in the real world of computing. Assume that our hypothetical computer allows us to declare a matrix that is 1000 by 1000. Example 1-4 would require two seconds to perform its additions; Example 1-5 would require slightly more than one second. On a larger 100,000 by 100,000 matrix, Example 1-4 would crunch numbers for slightly less than six hours, and Example 1-5 would take about three hours.

Although Example 1-5 is certainly better from an aesthetic perspective, it may not be good enough to be appreciably different from a user's perspective. That is, in situations where one version will respond within seconds, so will the other. Conversely, when one is annoyingly slow, the other will be as well. In terms of the **_order of magnitude_** of run time involved, these versions should not be considered significantly different. For the 1000 by 1000 matrix, both versions are fast enough to allow their use in an interactive environment. For the 100,000 by 100,000 matrix, both versions dictate an overnight run in batch mode because an interactive user is no more willing to wait three hours than six hours for a response. The essence of the difference between the run times of these two algorithms is that, no matter what the size of the matrix on which they operate, the first will always be approximately twice as slow as the second. In other words, the run times of the two algorithms are directly proportional to each other.

Because of the phenomenal execution speeds and very large amounts of available memory on modern computers, proportionally small differences between algorithms may often have little practical impact. Such considerations have led computer scientists to devise a method of algorithm classification that makes more precise the notion of order of magnitude as it applies to time and space considerations.

This method of classification, typically referred to as ***big-O notation*** (in reference to "on the order of"), hinges on the following definition: Suppose there exists a function $f(n)$ defined on the non-negative integers such that the number of operations required by an algorithm for an input of size n is less than or equal to some constant C multiplied by $f(n)$ for all but finitely many n. That is, the number of operations is at worst *proportional* to $f(n)$ for all large values of n. Such an algorithm is said to be an O[$f(n)$] algorithm relative to the number of operations it requires to execute. Similarly, we could classify an algorithm as O[$f(n)$] relative to the number of memory locations it requires to execute.

Figure 1-4 provides a graphic aid to understanding this formal definition of big-O notation. In general, we expect an algorithm's run time to increase as it manipulates an increasing number of data items—that is, as n increases. This increasing run time is depicted by the somewhat irregular, wavy curve in Figure 1-4. Now compare the wavy curve representing actual run time to the smoother curve of $C*f(n)$. Note that, for some small values of n, the actual number of operations for the algorithm may exceed $C*f(n)$. However, the graph indicates that there is a point on the horizontal axis beyond which $C*f(n)$ is always greater than the number of operations required for n data items. This is precisely the criterion that defines an algorithm's being O[$f(n)$].

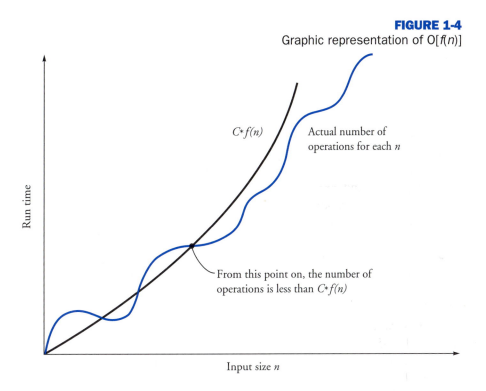

FIGURE 1-4
Graphic representation of O[$f(n)$]

$C*f(n)$

Actual number of operations for each n

Run time

From this point on, the number of operations is less than $C*f(n)$

Input size n

To say that an algorithm is O[$f(n)$] thus indicates that the function $f(n)$ may be useful in characterizing how the algorithm is performing for large n. For such n, we are assured that the operations required by the algorithm will be bounded by a constant multiplied by $f(n)$. The phrasing "for all large values of n" in the definition highlights the fact that there is little difference in the choice of an algorithm if n is reasonably small. For example, almost any sorting algorithm would sort 100 integers instantly.

We should also note that a given algorithm may be O[$f(n)$] for many different functions f. As Figure 1-5 shows, any algorithm that is O(n^2) will also be O(n^3).

Our main interest in classifying an algorithm with big-O notation is to find a relatively simple function $f(n)$ such that $C*f(n)$ parallels the number of operations as closely as possible. Hence, saying that an algorithm is O(n^2) is considered a better characterization of its efficiency than saying it is O(n^3).

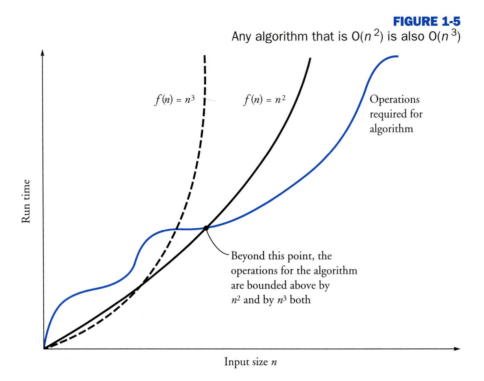

FIGURE 1-5

Any algorithm that is $O(n^2)$ is also $O(n^3)$

$f(n) = n^3$ $f(n) = n^2$ Operations
required for
algorithm

Run time

Beyond this point, the
operations for the algorithm
are bounded above by
n^2 and by n^3 both

Input size n

The importance of the constant C, known as the constant of proportionality, lies in comparing algorithms that share the same function $f(n)$; it makes almost no difference in the comparison of algorithms for which $f(n)$ is of different magnitude. It is therefore appropriate to say that the function $f(n)$ dominates the run-time performance of an algorithm and characterizes it in its big-O analysis. The following example should help clarify this situation.

Consider two algorithms L_1 and L_2 with run times equal to $2n^2$ and n^2, respectively. The constants of proportionality of L_1 and L_2 are 2 and 1, respectively. The dominating function $f(n)$ for both of these algorithms is n^2, but L_2 runs twice as fast as L_1 for a data set of n values. The different sizes of the two constants of proportionality indicate that L_2 is faster than L_1. Now suppose that the function $f(n)$ for L_2 is n^3. Then, even though its constant of proportionality is half of what it is for L_1, L_2 will be frustratingly slower than L_1 for large n. This latter comparison is shown in Figure 1-6.

Example 1-6

Use big-O analysis to characterize the two code segments from Examples 1-4 and 1-5, respectively.

Because the algorithm of Example 1-4 performs $2N^2$ additions, it is characterized as $O(N^2)$ with 2 as a constant of proportionality. We previously determined that the code of Example 1-5 performs $N^2 + N$ additions. However, $N^2 + N <= 1.1N^2$ for any $N >= 10$. Hence, we can characterize Example 1-5 as an $O(N^2)$ algorithm using 1.1 as a constant of proportionality. These two characterizations demonstrate that, although Example 1-5 is almost twice as fast as Example 1-4, they are in the same big-O category. Coupled with our earlier analysis of these two examples, this is an indication that algorithms in the same big-O category may be expected to have the same orders of magnitude in their run times.

How well does the big-O notation provide a way of classifying algorithms from a real-world perspective? To answer this question, consider Table 1-1. This table presents some typical $f(n)$ functions we will use to classify algorithms and their order of magnitude run times for inputs of various sizes on a hypothetical computer. From this table, we can see that an $O(n^2)$ algorithm will take hours to execute for an input of size 10^5. How many hours depends on the constant of proportionality in the definition of the big-O notation.

FIGURE 1-6
Graphic representation of two run times

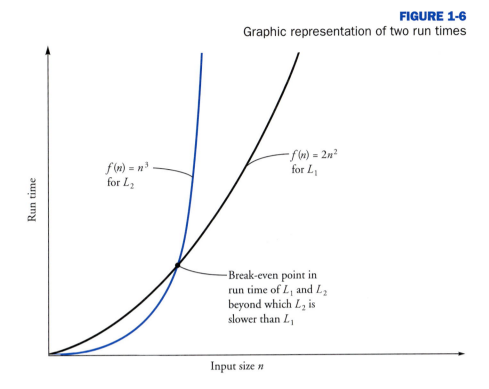

TABLE 1-1
Some typical $f(n)$ functions and associated run times

Assuming Proportionality Constant $K = 1$ and One Operation per Microsecond, Approximate Run Times for Input of Size			
$f(n)$	10^3	10^5	10^6
$\log_2 n$	0.000010 second	0.000017 second	0.000020 second
n	0.001 second	0.1 second	1 second
$n \log_2 n$	0.01 second	1.7 seconds	20 seconds
n^2	1 second	3 hours	12 days
n^3	17 minutes	32 centuries	3×10^4 centuries
2^n	10^{285} centuries	10^{104} years	10^{105} years

Regardless of the value of this constant of proportionality, a categorization of an algorithm as an $O(n^2)$ algorithm has thus achieved a very practical goal. We now know that, for an input of size 10^5, we cannot expect an immediate response for such an algorithm. Moreover, we know that, for a reasonably small constant of proportionality, we have an algorithm for which submission as an overnight job would not be impractical. That is, unlike an $O(n^3)$ algorithm, we could expect the computer to finish executing our algorithm in a time frame that would be acceptable if scheduled not to interfere with other uses of the machine. On the other hand, an $O(n^3)$ algorithm applied to a data set of this size would be completely impractical.

How does one determine the function *f(n)* that categorizes a particular algorithm? We give an overview of that process here and illustrate it by doing actual analyses for our three sorting algorithms. It is generally the case that, by analyzing the loop structure of an algorithm, we can estimate the number of run-time operations (or amount of memory units) required by the algorithm as a sum of several terms, each dependent on *n,* the number of items being processed by the algorithm. That is, typically we are able to express the number of run-time operations (or amount of memory) as a sum of the form

$$f_1(n) + f_2(n) + \ldots + f_k(n)$$

Moreover, we generally identify one of the terms in this expression as the **dominant term**. A dominant term is one that, for bigger values of *n,* becomes so large that it allows us to ignore all the other terms from a big-O perspective. For instance, suppose we had an expression involving two terms such as

$$n^2 + 50n$$

Here, the n^2 term dominates the $50n$ term since, for $n \geq 50$, we have

$$n^2 + 50n <= n^2 + n^2 = 2n^2$$

Thus, $n^2 + 50n$ would lead to an $O(n^2)$ categorization because of the dominance of the n^2 term.

In general, the problem of big-O categorization reduces to finding the dominant term in an expression representing the number of operations or amount of memory required by an algorithm.

Example 1-7

Use big-O notation to analyze the time efficiency of the following fragment of C++ code.

```
for (k = 1; k <= n / 2; ++k)
{
    .
    .
    .
    for (j = 1; j <= n * n; ++j)
    {
        .
        .
        .
    }
}
```

Because these loops are nested, the number of times that statements within the innermost loop are executed is the product of the number of repetitions of the two individual loops. Hence, the efficiency is $n^3/2$, or $O(n^3)$ in big-O terms, with a constant of proportionality equal to 1/2.

Note that the important principle illustrated by this example is that, for two loops with $O[f_1(n)]$ and $O[f_2(n)]$ efficiencies, the efficiency of the nesting of these two loops (in any order) is $O[f_1(n) * f_2(n)]$.

Example 1-8

Use big-O notation to analyze the time efficiency of the following fragment of C++ code.

```
for (k = 1; k <= n / 2; ++k)
{
    .
    .
    .
```

```
    }
    for (j = 1; j <= n * n; ++j)
    {
        .
        .
        .
    }
```

Because one loop follows the other, the number of operations executed by both of them is the sum of the individual loop efficiencies. Hence, the efficiency is $n/2 + n^2$, or $O(n^2)$ in big-O terms.

The important principle illustrated by Example 1-8 is that, for two loops with $O[f_1(n)]$ and $O[f_2(n)]$ efficiencies, the efficiency of the sequencing of these two loops (in any order) is $O[f_D(n)]$, where $f_D(n)$ is the dominant of the functions $f_1(n)$ and $f_2(n)$.

Example 1-9

Use big-O notation to analyze the time efficiency of the following fragment of C++ code.

```
    k = n;
    while (k > 1)
    {
        .
        .
        .
        k = k / 2;
    }
```

Because the loop control variable is cut in half each time through the loop, the number of times that statements inside the loop will be executed is $\log_2 n$. Note that the halving of a loop is central to the binary search algorithm, which will be explored further in Section 1.4. The principle emerging from Example 1-9 is that an algorithm that halves the data remaining to be processed on each iteration of a loop will be an $O(\log_2 n)$ algorithm.

Table 1-2, which lists frequently occurring dominant terms, will prove helpful in our future big-O analyses of algorithms. It is worthwhile to characterize briefly some of the classes of algorithms that arise due to the dominant terms listed in Table 1-2. Algorithms whose efficiency is dominated by a $\log_a n$ term [and hence are categorized as $O(\log_a n)$] are often called *logarithmic algorithms*. Because $\log_a n$ will increase much more slowly than n itself, logarithmic algorithms are generally very efficient.

TABLE 1-2

Common dominant terms in expressions for algorithmic efficiency, based on the variable n

n dominates $\log_a n$, a is often 2
$n \log_a n$ dominates n, a is often 2
n^2 dominates $n \log_a n$
n^m dominates n^k when $m > k$
a^n dominates n^m for any $a > 1$ and $m \geq 0$

Algorithms whose efficiency can be expressed in terms of a polynomial of the form

$$a_m n^m + a_{m-1} n^{m-1} + \ldots + a_2 n^2 + a_1 n + a_0$$

are called *polynomial algorithms*. Because the highest power of n will dominate such a polynomial, such algorithms are $O(n^m)$. The only polynomial algorithms we will discuss in this book have $m = 1, 2,$ or 3, and they are called *linear*, *quadratic*, or *cubic algorithms*, respectively.

Algorithms with efficiency dominated by a term of the form a^n are called *exponential algorithms*. Exponential algorithms are of more theoretical rather than practical interest, because they cannot reasonably be run on typical computers for moderate values of n.

Big-O Analysis of Bubble Sort

We are now ready to carry out some real comparisons between the three sorting methods we have discussed so far—bubble, insertion, and selection. To do so, we must determine functions $f(n)$ that allow us to make statements such as, "Sorting algorithm X requires $O[f(n)]$ comparisons." If it turns out that all three sorts share the same $f(n)$ function, then we can conclude that the differences between them are not approaching an order of magnitude scale. Rather, they would be more subtle distinctions, which would not appear as dramatic run-time differences.

We also realize that the key to doing a big-O analysis is to focus our attention on the loops in the algorithm. We do that first for the bubble sort. Recall the loop structure of the bubble sort.

```
k = 0;
exchangeMade = true;
while ((k < n - 1) && exchangeMade)
{
    exchangeMade = false;
    ++k;
    for (j = 0; j < n - k; ++j)

        if (list[j] > list[j + 1])
        {
            temp = list[j];
            list[j] = list[j + 1];
            list[j + 1] = temp;
            exchangeMade = true;
        }
}
```

Inner Loop

Outer Loop

Assume that we have the worst case possible for a bubble sort, in which the `exchangeMade` variable is always set to `true` so that an early exit is never made from the outer loop. If we then consider the comparison at the top of the inner loop, we note that it will be executed first $n - 1$ times, then $n - 2$ times, and so on down to one time for the final execution of the inner loop. Hence, the number of comparisons will be the sum of the sequence of numbers:

$$(n - 1)$$

$$(n - 2)$$

.

.

.

$$1$$

A formula from algebra will show this sum to be

$$n(n - 1) / 2$$

Thus we conclude that the bubble sort is an $O(n^2)$ algorithm in those situations for which the `exchangeMade` test does not allow an early loop exit.

PROGRAMMING SKILLS: Artificial Intelligence and the Complexity of Algorithms

Perhaps no area of computer science demands as much in terms of efficient algorithms as does *artificial intelligence* (AI). Those engaged in research in this field are concerned with writing programs that have the computer mimic intelligent human behavior in limited domains such as natural language understanding, theorem proving, and game playing. Why is efficiency so important in such programs? Typically, the strategy behind such a system is to have the computer search an enormous number of possibilities for the solution to the problem. These possibilities make up what is typically called the *state space* for the problem. For instance, for a computer program that plays a game such as checkers or chess, the state space would be a suitable representation of all game board configurations that could eventually be generated from the current state of the game. The computer's goal is to search through the state space, looking for a state in which it would win the game. The state space determined by the initial configuration of a chess game has been computed to be about 10^{120} different possible moves. The time required for a computer to examine each of these different moves, assuming it could examine one every microsecond, would be 10^{95} years. Even for a simpler game such as checkers, the time required for a computer to search all states in the game would require 10^{23} years.

The reason for these extraordinarily large and impractical time frames is that a "brute force" strategy of searching all states in such AI applications leads to exponential algorithms. To avoid exponential algorithms, researchers in artificial intelligence have attempted to follow the lead of human reasoning. That is, the human mind seems able to eliminate many of the possibilities in a search space without ever examining them. Similarly, AI programmers attempt to weed out large sections of the state space to be searched using *heuristics*. Heuristics are rules of thumb that enable one to rule out a vast number of possible states by doing some relatively simple computations. For instance, in checkers or chess, a heuristic might involve a mathematical formula that attached a positive or negative weight to a particular state of the game. Those states for which the heuristic value indicates a probable lack of success in future searching are simply eliminated from the state space. Because a heuristic is the computational equivalent of an educated guess, it runs the risk of making an error. However, it is often viewed as a worthwhile risk if it can enhance the efficiency of the search algorithm to a category that is no longer exponential.

Big-O Analysis of Insertion Sort

Recall that the loop structure of the insertion sort is given by

```
for (k = 1; k < n; ++k)

{
    itemToInsert = list[k];
    j = k - 1;
    stilllooking = true;
    while ((j >= 0) && stillLooking )
            if (itemToInsert < list[j])
            {
                    list[j + 1] = list[j];          Inner Loop        Outer Loop
                    —j;
            }
            else
                    stillLooking = false;
    list[j + 1] = itemToInsert;
}
```

Here, if the inner loop is never short-circuited by `stillLooking`, the comparison appearing as its first statement will be executed once for the first execution of the outer loop, then twice, and so on, reaching n - 1 executions on the final pass. We have a situation virtually identical to our preliminary analysis of the bubble sort. That is, the number of comparisons can be bounded by $n^2/2$, and the algorithm is therefore $O(n^2)$. Of course, with the insertion sort, the hope is that setting the Boolean variable `stillLooking` in the `else` clause can reduce the number of comparisons made by the inner loop. It is clear, however, that we can concoct many data sets for which this maneuver will have little or no effect. So, as with bubble sort, we are forced to conclude that insertion sort cannot guarantee better than $O(n^2)$ comparisons.

Big-O Analysis of Selection Sort

The loop structure of this algorithm was given by

```
for (int k = 0; k < length - 1; ++k)
{
    minPosition = k;
    for (int j = k + 1; j < length; ++j)
            if (list[j] < list[minPosition])          Inner Loop
                    minPosition = j;                                    Outer Loop
    if (minPosition != k)
    {
            temp = list[minPosition];
            list[minPosition] = list[k];
            list[k] = temp;
    }
}
```

A little investigation uncovers a familiar pattern to the nested loops of the selection sort. Observe that the first time the inner loop is executed, the comparison in the `if` statement will be made n - 1 times. Then it will be made n - 2 times, n - 3 times, and so on, then, finally, just one time. This is precisely the way the `if` statement in the bubble sort was executed in repeated passes. Thus, like the bubble and insertion sorts, the selection sort is an O(n^2) algorithm in terms of number of comparisons. The area in which the selection sort potentially offers better efficiency is that the number of interchanges of data in vector locations is guaranteed to be O(n) because the swap in the selection sort occurs in the outer loop. In both of the other sorts, the swap occurs in the inner loop but is subject to a conditional test. As a consequence, in their worst cases, both of the other algorithms require O(n^2) swaps as well as O(n^2) comparisons.

Despite the fact that a selection sort will usually fare better in the number of data interchanges required to sort a vector, it has a drawback not found in the other two sorts. It is apparently impossible to short-circuit the nested loop in a selection sort when it is given a list in nearly sorted order. So, for such data sets, the selection sort may be an order of magnitude worse than the other two options. This news is initially rather disheartening. It seems as if it is impossible to declare any of the sorts to be a decisive winner. Indeed, our big-O analyses indicate that there is little basis to distinguish between the bubble, insertion, and selection algorithms.

The fact that we were able to reach such a conclusion systematically, however, is significant. It reveals the value of a big-O analysis. After all, even knowledge of a negative variety can be valuable in choosing appropriate algorithms under certain circumstances. For instance, if a particular application usually involved adding a small amount of data at the end of an already sorted list and then resorting, we now know we should avoid a selection sort. Moreover, when we study more powerful sorting techniques in the next section (and again in Lesson 7), we will see that it is indeed possible to break the O(n^2) barrier limiting each of our three methods.

EXERCISES 1.2

1. Do a big-O analysis for those statements inside each of the following nested loop constructs.

   a.

```
for (k = 1; k <= n; ++k)
   for (j = 6; j <= m; ++j)
        .
        .
        .
```

   b.

```
 for (k = 1; k <= n; ++k)
{
   j = n;
   while (j > 0)
   {
        .
        .
        .
        j = j / 2;
   }
}
```

c.

```
k = 1;
do
{
    j = 1;
    do
    {
        .
        .
        .
        j = 2 * j;
    } while (j <= n);
    ++k;
} while (k <= n);
```

2. Suppose we have an algorithm that requires precisely

$$6 * \log_2 n + 34 * n^2 + 12$$

operations for an input of *n* data items. Indicate which of the following are valid big-O classifications of the algorithm.
   a. $O(n^3)$
   b. $O(n^2)$
   c. $O(n)$
   d. $O(n^2 * \log_2 n)$
   e. $O(n * \log_2 n)$
   f. $O(\log_2 n)$
   g. $O(1)$

Of those that you have indicated are valid, which is the best big-O classification? Why?

3. A certain algorithm always requires 32 operations, regardless of the amount of data input. Provide a big-O classification of the algorithm that reflects the efficiency of the algorithm as accurately as possible.

4. An algorithm has an efficiency $O(\ |n^2 \sin(n)|\ )$. Is it any better than $O(n^2)$ for a large integer *n*?

5. Suppose that each of the following expressions represents the number of logical operations in an algorithm as a function of *n*, the size of the list being manipulated. For each expression, determine the dominant term and then classify the algorithm in big-O terms.
   a. $n^3 + n^2\log_2 n + n^3\log_2 n$
   b. $n + 4n^2 + 4^n$
   c. $48n^4 + 16n^2 + \log_8 n + 2^n$

6. Consider the following nested loop construct. Categorize its efficiency in terms of the variable *n* using big-O notation. Finally, suppose the statements indicated by the ellipses required four main memory accesses (each requiring one microsecond) and two disk file accesses (each requiring one millisecond). Express in milliseconds the amount of time this construct would require to execute if *n* were 1000.

```
x = 1;
do
{
    y = n;
    while (y > 0)
    {
        .
        .
        .
            --y;
    }
    x = x + x;
} while (x < n * n);
```

7. Look back at the data set you constructed for Exercise 11 in Exercises 1.1. Evaluate the performance of insertion sort on that data set in terms of a big-O analysis.

8. You and a friend are engaged in an argument. She claims that a certain algorithm is $O(n^2 \log_2 n)$ in its efficiency. You claim that it is $O(n^2)$. Consider and answer the following questions:
   a. Are there circumstances under which both of you could be correct? If so, explain them.
   b. Are there circumstances under which both of you could be wrong? If so, explain them.
   c. Are there circumstances under which she could be right and you could be wrong? If so, explain them.
   d. Are there circumstances under which she could be wrong and you could be right? If so, explain them.

9. You and your friend are engaged in another argument. She claims that a certain algorithm is $O(n^2 + \log_2 n)$ in its efficiency. You claim that it is $O(n^2)$. Consider and answer the following questions.
   a. Are there circumstances under which both of you could be correct? If so, explain them.
   b. Are there circumstances under which both of you could be wrong? If so, explain them.
   c. Are there circumstances under which she could be right and you could be wrong? If so, explain them.
   d. Are there circumstances under which she could be wrong and you could be right? If so, explain them.

10. Is an $O(n^2)$ algorithm also an $O(n^3)$ algorithm? Justify your answer in a carefully written paragraph.

1.3 The Time/Space Trade-off: Pointer Sort and Radix Sort

Early in our discussion of efficiency considerations, we noted that true run-time efficiency was best measured in fundamental machine operations and that one instruction in a high-level language may actually translate into many such primitive operations. To illustrate this idea, suppose that the data being sorted by one of our algorithms consist of records, each of which requires 100 bytes of internal storage. Then, depending on your computer, it is entirely conceivable that one comparison or assignment statement in a high-level language could generate a machine language loop with 100 repetitions of such fundamental operations: one for each of the bytes that must be swapped. Those seemingly innocent portions of code, which swap two records using a temporary storage location, lead to the movement of 300 bytes inside the machine.

The first question we address in this section is whether, in such a situation, we can replace this large-scale internal transfer of entire records with the much swifter operation of swapping two integers. Although the solution we discuss does not achieve an order of magnitude speed increase in the big-O sense, it nonetheless reduces the number of actual machine-level swaps by a factor proportional to the record length involved, a factor that could produce a noticeable improvement in the function's run time.

Bubble Sort Implemented with Pointers

So far, our algorithms to sort data have implicitly assumed that the data are to be *physically sorted;* that is, the data are to be arranged in order within the vector being sorted. Hence, the data in the first index of our vector are the data that come first in order according to the key field, the data in the second index are second in key field order, and so on. However, if we are interested only in processing the data of a list in order by key field, is it really necessary that the data be arranged in physically ordered fashion in computer memory? No. It is possible to step logically through the data in order by key field without physically arranging it that way in memory. To do so, we must use another vector of pointers.

A *pointer* is a memory location in which we store the location of a data item as opposed to the data item itself. In the case of a vector, a pointer can be the index position of a data item in the vector.

Pointers can keep track of the *logical order* of the data without requiring them to be physically moved. At the end of our sorting routine, `pointer[0]` tells us the location of the data that should come first in our alphabetical listing, `pointer[1]` contains the location of the data that should come second, and so on. The sorting algorithm itself uses the logic of the bubble sort to interchange pointers instead of interchanging data. The actual data never move; they remain precisely where they were stored on initial input. Instead of the expensive, time-consuming swapping of potentially large records, we are able to swap integer pointers quickly.

A C++ function to implement this *pointer sort* technique follows. Besides the `list` vector, the function receives a vector of `int`s called `pointer`. These `int`s serve as the pointers, storing vector index positions. The function initializes the pointer vector to the state pictured in the "before" snapshot of Figure 1-7. Then, via repeated swaps of integer pointers, the vector is returned as shown in the "after" snapshot. As the figure indicates, the `list` vector itself is never altered.

FIGURE 1-7

"Before" (left) and "after" (right) snapshots of a pointer sort

	Key field of **list**		**pointer**
0	MAXWELL		0
1	BUCKNER		1
2	LANIER		2
3	AARON		3

Snapshot of **list** and **pointer** immediately after initialization

	Key field of **list**		**pointer**
	MAXWELL		3
	BUCKNER		1
	LANIER		2
	AARON		0

Snapshot of **list** and **pointer** returned by **pointerBubbleSort**

```
template <class element>
void pointerBubbleSort(apvector<element> &list,
                       apvector<int> &pointer, int n)
{
   int j, k, temp;
   bool exchangeMade;

   // Initialize pointer vector

   for (k = 0; k < n; ++k)
      pointer[k] = k;

   k = 0;
   exchangeMade = true;

   // Make up to n - 1 passes through vector, exit early if no
   // exchanges are made on previous pass

   while ((k < n - 1) && exchangeMade)
   {
      exchangeMade = false;
      ++k;
      for (j = 0; j < n - k; ++j)
         // Compare via pointers
         if (list[pointer[j]] > list[pointer[j + 1]])
         {
            temp = pointer[j];                // Swap pointers
            pointer[j] = pointer[j + 1];
            pointer[j + 1] = temp;
            exchangeMade = true;
         }
   }
}
```

Example 1-10

Given the physically ordered list of Figure 1-7, trace the action of the function `pointerBubbleSort` on the vector of pointers during each pass through the algorithm.

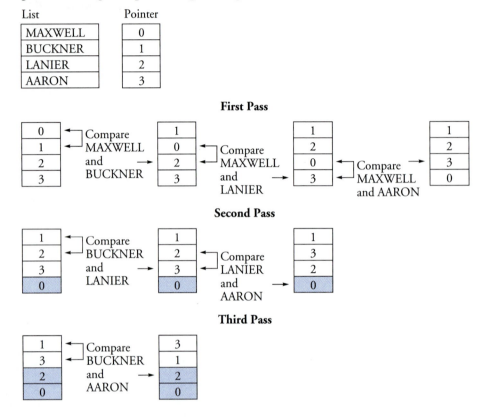

Example 1-11

Suppose that `pointerBubbleSort` was invoked from a main program or another function via the call

```
pointerBubbleSort (studentList, pointer, numberOfStudents);
```

where `numberOfStudents`, `studentList`, and `pointer` are of appropriate types. If the logical order established by the pointer vector is alphabetical by student name, explain how a report that listed students alphabetically could be printed after this invocation. Assume the existence of a function `printHeading` to print column headings for the report and a function `printStudent` to receive an individual student object and print it in formatted form as one detail line of the report.

After the call to `pointerBubbleSort`, `pointer[0]` contains the position of the object that is first in alphabetical order, `pointer[1]` contains the position of the object that is second, and so on. Hence, the following loop will step through all of the entries in the desired order:

```
printHeading();
for (k = 0; k < numberOfStudents; ++k)
    printStudent(studentList[pointer[k]]);
```

PROGRAMMING SKILLS: Virtual Memory and Program Performance

The more sophisticated operating systems of today often use what is known as ***virtual memory***. In such systems, a programmer is able to view main memory as virtually limitless. That is, such systems give the programmer the illusion of having "infinite" main memory. How is this possible? Virtual memory is not true main memory. Rather, it is memory divided into ***pages***—some of which actually reside in main memory while others reside on disk storage. When you write a program that accesses a virtual-memory page not presently in main memory, the operating system must execute a ***paging algorithm***. A paging algorithm is responsible for bringing into main memory the page requested by your program and deciding which page presently in main memory should be swapped out to disk storage to make room for the new page.

Virtual memory has made programmers' lives much easier. It means that we can now declare vectors in our programs that are much larger than vectors that could be declared in older systems that lacked virtual memory. Is any price paid for this convenience? Most definitely yes!

Paging is the hidden price paid for the programming convenience offered by virtual memory systems. A sorting algorithm applied to a vector that cannot fit in non-virtual main memory will work correctly, but it will also cause paging to occur. As paging represents a disk access, it will take much longer to execute than a pure memory access, which does not generate a page swap. An operation that generates a page swap can be slower than one that doesn't by a factor as large as 1000 (milliseconds as opposed to microseconds). The key to the efficiency of such a sorting algorithm not only is a factor of its big-O categorization, but also reflects whether the algorithm forces an excessive amount of paging to occur. Hence, even though we may know that the algorithm is $O(n^2)$ in the number of comparisons it uses, the real key to the amount of time it takes the algorithm to run is tied to how many of those comparisons force a page swap to occur. Many a programmer has been unpleasantly surprised to find out a program that should run in seconds according to a big-O analysis of its underlying algorithm actually ends up requiring minutes because of such paging.

Efficiency Analysis for Sorts Implemented with Pointers. The pointer technique illustrated here for the bubble sort may also be used with the insertion and selection sort algorithms. In any of these cases, the mere introduction of the pointer strategy will not reduce the big-O categorization of the sort. However, in cases where the data items being sorted use enough internal storage to slow down swapping times substantially, the pointer sort can attain a considerable savings in run time.

Is this run-time savings achieved without any sacrifice? An old saying that has been passed down by computer people since the days of the early vacuum tube machines is; "You get nothing for nothing." We have not escaped the consequences of that adage by using pointers to increase run-time efficiency. The pointers store *data about data;* this operation requires additional memory. If your application is not approaching the limits of memory, this cost may not be crucial. In certain situations, however, it could be the last straw for a program running short of memory. Thus, the pointer sort is essentially a trade-off; by using more memory, we get a program that runs more quickly.

This ***time/space trade-off*** continually recurs in the analysis of computer algorithms. Many sophisticated techniques to increase speed will need to store substantial data about data to achieve this goal. Those algorithms that solve a problem in a fashion that saves space *and* decreases run time are indeed worthy of special praise. We will be sure to note them.

Finally, the notion of a pointer, as defined and introduced here, plays an important role in our study of data structures beginning in Lesson 3. The time you spend exploring the details of the pointer sort technique will prove very valuable in your understanding of this topic in the future.

Radix Sort

The *radix sort* algorithm is also called the **bin sort**, a name derived from its origin as a technique used on (now obsolete) machines called card sorters. These machines would sort a deck of keypunched cards by shuffling the cards into small bins, then collecting the cards from the bins into a newly arranged deck, and repeating this shuffling–collection process until the deck was magically sorted. There was, as we shall see, a very clever algorithm behind this rapid shuffling.

For integer data, the repeated passes of a radix sort focus first on the ones digit of each number, then on the tens digit, the hundreds digit, and so on until the highest-order digit of the largest number is reached. For string data, the first pass hinges on the right-most character in each string, with successive passes always shifting their attention one character position to the left. To illustrate the algorithm, we will trace it on the following list of nine integers:

```
459 254 472 534 649 239 432 654 477
```

On each pass through these data, the radix sort will arrange them into ten sublists (bins)—one sublist for each of the digits 0 through 9. Hence, on the first pass, all the numbers with a ones digit equal to 0 are grouped in one sublist, all those with a ones digit equal to 1 are grouped in another sublist, and so on. The resulting sublists follow:

Digit	Sublist		
0			
1			
2	472	432	
3			
4	254	534	654
5			
6			
7	477		
8			
9	459	649	239

The sublists are then collected into one large list with the numbers in the sublist for 0 coming first, followed by those in the sublist for 1, and so on up to the sublist for 9. Hence, we have a newly arranged list:

```
472 432 254 534 654 477 459 649 239
```

This new list is again partitioned into sublists, this time keying on the tens digit. The result is shown below:

Digit	Sublist		
0			
1			
2			
3	432	534	239

4	649		
5	654	254	459
6			
7	472	477	
8			
9			

Note that in each sublist the data are arranged in order relative to their last two digits. The sublists would now be collected into a new master list:

```
432 534 239 649 654 254 459 472 477
```

Now, focusing on the hundreds digit, the master list is classified into ten sublists one more time. These final sublists are shown below. When the sublists are collected from this final partitioning, the data are arranged in ascending order.

Digit	Sublist			
0				
1				
2	239	254		
3				
4	432	459	472	477
5	534			
6	649	654		
7				
8				
9				

A pseudocode statement of the radix sort algorithm follows:

1. Begin with the current digit as the ones digit
2. While there is still a digit on which to classify data
 2.1 For each number in the master list
 2.1.1 Add that number to the appropriate sublist, keying on the current digit
 2.2 For each sublist (from 0 through 9)
 2.2.1 Append that sublist to a newly arranged master list
 2.3 Advance the current digit one place to the left

If the radix sort is applied to character strings instead of integers, this algorithm proceeds from the rightmost character to the leftmost character instead of from the ones digit to the highest order digit.

Efficiency of the Radix Sort. An analysis of the loop structure in the preceding pseudocode for radix sort indicates that, for each pass through the outer while loop, $O(n)$ operations must be performed. These $O(n)$ operations consist of doing the arithmetic necessary to isolate a particular digit within a number, appending that number to the proper sublist, and then collecting it again into a new master list. As the outer while loop will be executed only C times—where C is the number of digits (or characters) in the integer (or string)—the radix sort is an $O(n)$ sorting algorithm.

Although the radix sort is significantly faster than the other $O(n^2)$ algorithms we have studied in this lesson, there are again trade-offs to consider. The radix sort is potentially much less space efficient than the other sorting algorithms, due to the need for storing sublists for each of the possible digits in the number or characters in the string. Using vectors to store the sublists and lacking any prior knowledge about the distribution of the data, we would be forced to allocate an additional $10n$ storage locations when sorting a vector of n integers and $27n$ storage locations when sorting n strings of letters and blanks. We will alleviate this memory crunch somewhat when we study linked lists in Lesson 3; but even then, the radix sort will remain a space-inefficient algorithm compared to other sorting algorithms. Other factors negating the very good time efficiency of the radix sort are its inflexibility in handling data of varying size and the fact that, although $O(n)$ in time, its constant of proportionality in this regard is often large enough to make it less time efficient than the more sophisticated sorting algorithms we will study in Lesson 7.

Example 1-12

Assume the existence of the following declarations and functions to perform a radix sort on a vector of four-digit numbers. Here we use an `apmatrix` to represent the bin structure.

```cpp
int const MAX_LIST_SIZE = 100;

// Function: digit
// Computes the kth digit in number
//
// Inputs: integers number and k
// Output: the kth digit in number

int digit(int number, int k);

// Function: initializeCounters
// Initializes all bin counters to zero

void initializeCounters(apvector<int> &binCounters);

// Function: addToBin
// Insert number in bin structure, as indicated by place
//
// Inputs: a bin structure bins, a vector of bin counters,
//         a number, and a place
// Outputs: bin structure bins and its vector of counters
//          have been altered to reflect addition of number
//          in bin indexed by place

template<class element>
void addToBin(apmatrix<element> &bins,
        apvector<int> &binCounters, int number, int place);

// Function: collectBins
// Append numbers in bins to list
//
// Inputs: list, a bin structure, and a vector of counters for the
//         bin structure
// Outputs: a list
```

```
template<class element>
void collectBins(apvector<element> &list, apmatrix<element> &bins,
                 apvector<int> &binCounters);


// Function: radixSort
// Sorts numbers in list into ascending order
//
// Inputs: list and its length
// Outputs: the list with numbers sorted in ascending order

template<class element>
void radixSort(apvector<element> &list, int n);
```

Then the C++ code for this radix sort would be

```
template<class element>
void radixSort(apvector<element> &list, int n)
{
    int j, k;
    apmatrix<element> bins(10,MAX_LIST_SIZE);
    apvector<int> binCounters(10);


    initializeCounters(binCounters);

    // For k loop controls digit used to classify data.
    for (k = 1; k <= 4; ++k)
    {
        // For j loop iterates through all numbers, putting them into
        // bin determined by kth digit.
        for (j = 0; j < n; ++j)
            addToBin (bins, binCounters, list[j], digit(list[j], k));
        collectBins (list, bins, binCounters);
        initializeCounters(binCounters);
    }
}
```

EXERCISES ➩ 1.3

1. Suppose that you are given the following list of keys:

0	9438
1	3216
2	416
3	9021
4	1142
5	3316
6	94

Show what the contents of the pointer vector would be after each pass through the outer loop of function `pointerBubbleSort` discussed in this section.

2. Consider again the data set given in Exercise 1. How many passes would be made through the outer loop of the radix sort algorithm for these data? Trace the contents of the vector after each of these passes.

3. Consider the following list of strings:

0	CHOCOLATE
1	VANILLA
2	CARAMEL
3	PEACH
4	STRAWBERRY
5	CHERRY

How many passes would be made through the outer loop of the radix sort algorithm for these data? Trace the contents of the list after each of these passes.

4. Explain the difference between physical and logical ordering.

5. Cite an application in which the mere logical ordering of data, as achieved by the pointer sort technique, would not be sufficient; that is, give an application in which physical ordering of data is required.

6. What is the time/space trade-off? Define and discuss various contexts in which it may arise.

7. When the bubble sort was modified with a vector of pointers, did it improve its $O(n^2)$ run-time efficiency in a significant sense? Under what circumstances would you call the improvement in efficiency significant? Provide your answer to this question in a short essay in which you define "significant" and then explain why the circumstance you describe would lead to a significant improvement.

8. The bubble, insertion, and selection sort algorithms are all $O(n)$ in their space requirements. That is, each algorithm requires memory proportional to n to sort the items in a vector of n items. From a big-O perspective, what are the space requirements of these algorithms when the pointer sort technique is incorporated into their logic?

9. Would you expect the pointer strategy to have the *least* effect on the run-time efficiency of the bubble, selection, or insertion sort? Provide a rationale for your answer in a short essay.

10. Suppose you have 1000 objects to be sorted. Would the run-time efficiency of the pointer sort increase significantly if the 1000 objects were broken into four groups, each group sorted, and then merged together as one large sorted vector as compared to sorting the initial unsegmented vector? Why or why not?

11. Incorporate the pointer sort technique into the selection sort algorithm.

12. Incorporate the pointer sort technique into the insertion sort algorithm.

13. Write the functions assumed to exist in the version of `radixSort` given in Example 1-12.

14. Write a radix sort function to sort an arbitrary vector of integers. Analyze the space efficiency of your function.

15. Write a radix sort function to sort a vector of strings. Analyze the space efficiency of your function. Be sure to state carefully the assumptions you make about strings in performing your analysis of space efficiency.

16. Describe the complications in implementing the radix sort algorithm for a vector of real numbers. Discuss a strategy that could be used to overcome these complications.

1.4 Simple Search Algorithms

Many programs extensively employ algorithms that find a particular data item in a large collection of such items. Such algorithms, which are typically called *search algorithms,* are given the value of a key field that identifies the item being sought; they then return either all of the data associated with that particular key or a flag indicating that the data could not be found. We now explore search algorithms and subject them to an efficiency analysis using the big-O notation we have developed.

The search operation will look for an object in a list that is associated with a `target` key value. Thus, rather than comparing two objects of type `element`, the search algorithm will compare a key value and an object of type `element`. We will assume that the `element` type has overloaded the standard operators for comparing a key value and an object of the `element` type. The general setup for the search algorithms we discuss in this section is given by the following skeletal declarations:

```
// Function: search
// Find the object associated with the target key value
//
// Inputs: a list of objects, its length, and a target key value.  Assume
//     that the element type has overloaded the standard operators for
//     comparing a datum of type KeyType and an object of the element type
// Outputs: if the target key is found, return true and the object
//     associated with the target key; otherwise, return false

template<class element, class KeyType>
bool search(const apvector<element> &list,
        int n, KeyType target, element &object);
```

Figure 1-8 graphically portrays this setup.

5 7

FIGURE 1-8

General setup for search algorithm

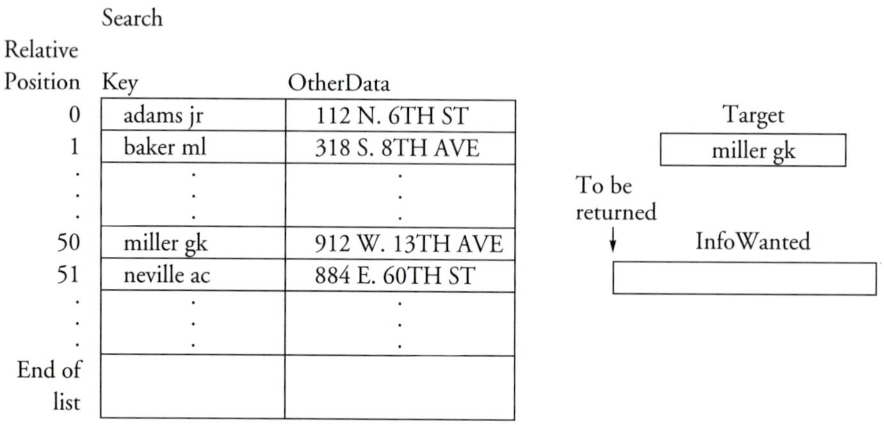

Relative Position	Search Key	OtherData
0	adams jr	112 N. 6TH ST
1	baker ml	318 S. 8TH AVE
.	.	.
.	.	.
50	miller gk	912 W. 13TH AVE
51	neville ac	884 E. 60TH ST
.	.	.
.	.	.
End of list		

Target

miller gk

To be returned

InfoWanted

Sequential Search Algorithm

The task of a computer scientist working with search algorithms may be compared to that of a librarian. Just as the librarian must devise a method of storing books on shelves in a fashion that allows patrons to easily find the books they want, so must a computer scientist devise methods of organizing large collections of electronic data so that records within that data can always be quickly found. Imagine the plight of the librarian who just throws books on shelves as they are unpacked from shipping boxes, without any consideration toward organizing the chaos! Unless the library had an artificially small collection, it would take patrons an impractical length of time to find their reading material. Because of the lack of any organizational order imposed on the books, the only search strategy available would be to pull books from the shelves in some arbitrary sequence until the desired book was found.

As a programmer given a completely unordered set of data, this is the same strategy you would have to follow. The logic of such a *sequential search* strategy is extremely simple and appears in the following function `sequentialSearch`.

```
template<class element, class KeyType>
bool sequentialSearch(const apvector<element> &list,
        int n, KeyType target, element &object)
{
    int k = 0;
    bool found = false;

    while ((k < n) && ! found)
        if (list[k] == target)
            found = true;
        else
            ++k;
    if (found)
        object = list[k];
    return found;
}
```

Efficiency of Sequential Search. Unfortunately, the simplicity of the sequential search is offset by its inefficiency as a search strategy. Obviously, the average number of probes into the list before the target key is found will be $n/2$, where n is the number of records in the list. For unsuccessful invocations of the function, all n records must be checked before we can conclude failure. Thus, in terms of a big-O classification, the method is clearly O(n). This may not seem bad when compared to the O(n^2) efficiency of our sorting methods, but searching is conceptually a much simpler operation than sorting: It should be significantly faster. Moreover, though O(n) may seem fast enough at microsecond speeds, there are many applications where an O(n) time factor can be unacceptably slow.

For instance, when a compiler processes your source program in C++, it must continually search a list of identifiers that have been previously declared. (This list is typically called a **symbol table**.) Hence, in such an application, the search operation merely represents the inner loop within a much more complex outer loop that is repeating until it reaches the end of your source file—an inner loop that, repeated at O(n) speeds, would make your compiler intolerably slow.

Another situation in which O(n) is not good enough for searching occurs when the list being searched is stored in a **disk file** instead of a main memory vector. Because accessing data on disk is a much slower operation than accessing data in main memory, each probe into the list might conceivably require approximately one millisecond (one-thousandth of a second) instead of a microsecond. Searching such a list of 1 million records at O(n) speed would require 1,000 seconds instead of just 1 second, which is too long to wait for one record and is certain to lead to angry users. We conclude that, although the sequential search may be fast enough for small and infrequently accessed lists stored in main memory, we need something that is better by an order of magnitude for many practical applications.

Binary Search Algorithm

By paying what may initially seem like a small price, we can dramatically increase the efficiency of our search effort using a **binary search** algorithm.

1. The list of objects with keys must be maintained in physically sorted order unless we are willing to use an additional list of pointers similar to that used in the `pointerBubbleSort` algorithm. (See the exercises at the end of this section.)

2. The number of objects in the list must be maintained in a separate variable.

3. We must be able to access randomly, by relative position, objects in the list. This is the type of access you have in C++ vectors.

For instance, suppose that the list of integer keys appearing in Figure 1-9 has the access facility of the third point just cited and that we wish to locate the randomly accessible data associated with the target key 1649. The strategy of the binary search is to begin the search in the middle of the list. In the case of Figure 1-9, this would mean beginning the search with the key found at position 4. Because the target we are seeking is greater than the key found at position 4, we are able to conclude that the key we want will be found among positions 5 through 9—if at all.

We will split those positions that remain viable candidates for finding the target by accessing the middle position:

$$(5 + 9) / 2 = 7$$

Because the key at position 7 is greater than `target`, we are able to conclude that the key being sought will be found in position 5 or 6—if it is to be found at all. Notice that, after only two accesses into the list, our list of remaining viable candidates for a match has shrunk to 2. (Compare this figure to a sequential search after two accesses into the same list.) We now split the distance between positions 5 and 6, arriving (by integer arithmetic) at position 5. Here we find the key being sought after a mere three probes into the list.

Crucial to the entire binary search algorithm are two pointers, `low` and `high`, to the bottom and top, respectively, of the current list of viable candidates. We must repeatedly compute the middle index of that portion of the list between `low` and `high` and compare the data at that middle index to the target using the following logic.

FIGURE 1-9

Physically ordered random access list of keys for binary search

Position Key

0	1119
1	1203
2	1212
3	1519
4	1604
5	1649
6	1821
7	2312
8	2409
9	3612

Number of Records $n = 10$

target = 1649

```
If list[middle] equals the target
     Search is done
     Target has been found in list
Else if list[middle] < target
     Low must be set to middle + 1
Else
     High must be set to middle - 1
```

Should these pointers ever cross—that is, if `high` were to become less than `low`—we would conclude that the target does not appear in the list. The entire algorithm is formalized in the following C++ function:

```
template<class element, class KeyType>
bool binarySearch(const apvector<element> &list,
          int n, KeyType target, element &object)
{
     int low, middle, high;
     bool found = false;

     low = 0;
     high = n - 1;
     while ((low <= high) && ! found)
     {
          middle = (low + high) / 2;
          if (list[middle] == target)
              found = true;
          else if (list[middle] < target) // Work with high end
              low = middle + 1;
          else
```

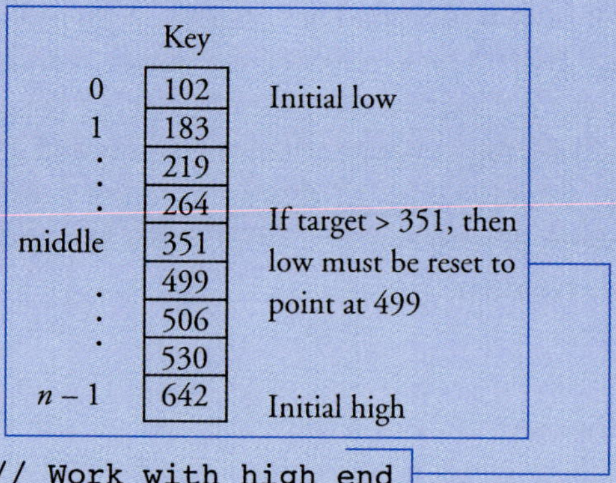

Key

0	102	Initial low
1	183	
.	219	
.	264	
middle	351	If target > 351, then
.	499	low must be reset to
.	506	point at 499
.	530	
$n-1$	642	Initial high

```
                    high = middle - 1;      // Work with low end
            }
        if (found)
            object = list[middle];
        return found;
    }
}
```

	Key	
0	102	Initial low
1	183	
·	219	
·	264	
middle	351	If target < 351, then high must be reset to point at 264
·	499	
·	506	
·	530	
$n - 1$	642	Initial high

Example 1-13

Trace the action of function `binarySearch` as it locates the record associated with target 1519 in the vector of Figure 1-9.

target

1519

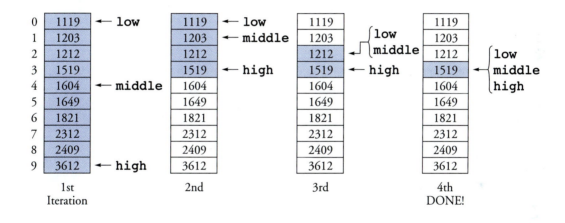

	1st Iteration	2nd	3rd	4th DONE!

Example 1-14

Trace the action of function `binarySearch` as it reports that target 2392 cannot be found in the vector of Figure 1-9.

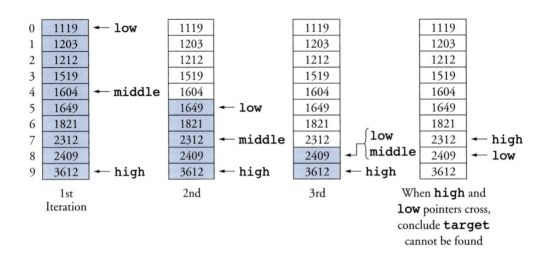

Efficiency of Binary Search. As indicated by the shaded portions of the lists in the preceding examples, the binary search continually halves the size of the list that must still be searched. This continual halving is critical to the effectiveness of the algorithm. When applied to the list of keys in Figure 1-9, the method in the worst case would require four different accesses. For an ordered list of 50,000 keys, the worst case efficiency is a mere 16 different accesses. (In case you do not believe this dramatic increase in efficiency as the list gets larger, try plugging 50,000 into a hand-held calculator and count how many times you must halve the displayed number to reduce it to 1.) The same list of 1,000,000 records stored on disk that would require approximately 1000 seconds to search sequentially will result in a virtually instantaneous response with the binary search strategy.

More formally, for a list of *n* items, the maximum number of times we would cut the list in half before finding the target item or declaring the search unsuccessful is

$$(\log_2 n) + 1$$

Thus the binary search is the first $O(\log_2 n)$ algorithm we have studied (see Example 1-10). In terms of the categorizations discussed in Section 1.2, it is a logarithmic algorithm. Expressions involving a $\log_2 n$ factor will arise frequently as we analyze other algorithms. They are extremely fast when compared to $O(n)$ algorithms, particularly for large values of *n*.

The drawback of the binary search lies not in any consideration of its processing speed but rather in a reexamination of the price that must be paid for being able to use it. For a volatile list (that is, one undergoing frequent additions and deletions), the requirement of maintaining the list in physical order can be quite costly. For large lists, it makes the operations of adding and deleting records so inefficient that the very fast search speed is all but negated. We will analyze this problem of list maintenance in more detail in future lessons.

Key-to-Address Transformations

A search technique so simple that it is often overlooked presents itself in certain situations where a record's key value can be transformed conveniently into a position within a list by applying a function to the key value. For instance, suppose that a school assigns its students five-digit identification numbers in which the first two digits indicate the student's year of matriculation and the last three digits are simply assigned in a sequential fashion among students matriculating in a given year. Hence the fourteenth student admitted in the class of 1999 would have the identification number

9 9   0 1 4
‿‿‿   ‿‿‿
year of matriculation   sequence number within that year

In such a situation, student records could be stored in a two-dimensional table in which rows were indexed by year of matriculation and columns indexed by sequence number within a given year. Then the integer arithmetic operations

```
key / 1000
```

and

```
key % 1000
```

would yield a given student's row and column index, respectively. The address of a student's record could therefore be obtained from the student's identification number using a mere two operations.

In such situations, the search efficiency to locate a student's record is O(1) in its big-O classification. The apparent restriction that must apply for this technique to work is that the transformation applied to a key to yield an address cannot yield the same address for two different students. As we shall see in Lesson 8, even this restriction can be relaxed somewhat if slightly more sophisticated search techniques are employed. Another drawback of the key-to-address transformation technique is its potentially inefficient use of space. You will perform such a space analysis for this strategy in this section's exercises.

EXERCISES 1.4

1. Suppose that a vector contains key values

```
18 40 46 50 52 58 63 70 77 90
```

   in index locations 0 through 9. Trace the index values for the low, high, and middle pointers in the binary search algorithm if the target 43 is being sought. Repeat for target values 40 and 90.

2. In Exercise 10 of Exercises 1.1, we defined the notions of best case and worst case behavior of an algorithm. Devise sample data sets to demonstrate the best case and worst case behavior of the binary search algorithm.

3. What is a compiler symbol table? Explain why a sequential search applied to such a table is not a practical strategy.

4. Explain the difference in run-time efficiency considerations for a program that manipulates data in a main memory vector versus one that accesses data stored in a disk file.

5. How many times would the while loop in the function binarySearch be executed if $n = 1,000,000$?

6. Consider the following modified version of the binary search algorithm. (Modifications are indicated by a comment highlighted by asterisks.) Will this new version of the binary search algorithm work correctly for all data? If not, specify a situation in which this version will fail.

```
template<class element, class KeyType>
bool binarySearch(const apvector<element> &list,
            int n, KeyType target, element &object)
{
    int low, middle, high;
    bool found = false;

    low = 0;
    high = n;
    while ((low <= high) && ! found)
    {
        middle = (low + high) / 2;
        if (list[middle] = target)
            found = true;
        else if (list[middle] < target)
            low = middle;          // *** Modification here ***
        else
            high = middle;         // *** Modification here ***
    }
    if (found)
        object = list[middle];
    return found;
}
```

7. Consider the following modified version of the binary search algorithm. (Modifications are indicated by a comment highlighted by asterisks.) Will this new version of the binary search algorithm work correctly for all data? If not, specify a situation in which this version will fail.

```
template<class element, class KeyType>
bool binarySearch(const apvector<element> &list,
            int n, KeyType target, element &object)
{
    int low, middle, high;
    bool found = false;

    low = 0;
    high = n;
    do                      // *** Use do. . .while instead of while ***
    {
        middle = (low + high) / 2;
        if (list[middle] = target)
            found = true;
        else if (list[middle] < target)
            low = middle + 1;
        else
```

```
            high = middle - 1;
     } while ((low <= high) && ! found); // *** Loop exit condition
     if (found)
         object = list[middle];
     return found;
  }
```

8. Consider the example of a key-to-address transformation for student identification numbers given in this section. Discuss the space efficiency of this strategy. On what factor is the space efficiency dependent?

9. Devise a key-to-address transformation to locate records in a data structure for employees of the East Publishing Company. Departments in the company are identified by a one-letter code A–Z. An employee's payroll identification number consists of a department code followed by another one-letter code representing the employee's pay rate classification, and a two-digit number assigned in sequential fashion to employees within a given department. Hence, the identification number DX40 is assigned to the 40th employee in department D; the X indicates the employee's pay rate category.

10. The requirement for the binary search that the data in a vector be physically ordered can actually be circumvented by keeping track of the logical order of the data via a pointer vector analogous to that used in the pointer sort. Rewrite the binary search algorithm under such an assumption. Explain why it might be advantageous to use this technique.

11. Implement the following modification to the sequential search algorithm. Temporarily insert the key for which you are searching at the end of the list. Search sequentially until you find this key; then examine the position where you found it to determine whether the search was successful. Note that this strategy requires your knowing the number of items in the list rather than a sentinel value stored at the end of the list. Comment on the run-time efficiency of this new strategy versus the sequential search algorithm discussed in this section.

12. Modify the insertion sort algorithm of Section 1.1 so that it finds the insertion point for the next vector entry using an appropriate modification of the halving strategy employed by the binary search algorithm. Once this insertion point is determined, other vector entries must be moved accordingly to make room for the entry being inserted. After completing this modified version of the insertion sort, perform a big-O analysis of its efficiency.

13. Imagine that you have been hired to write an information retrieval program for a company or organization. You must interview people within the organization to determine exactly their information retrieval needs. Construct questions that you could ask in such an interview to enable you to determine which search strategy would be most appropriate for the program you must write. Then, in an essay explain how answers to these questions would dictate your choice of search strategy.

CASE STUDY:
Empirically Measuring the Efficiency of an Algorithm

We will use this lesson's Case Study to examine how we can augment a program to help us analyze its own efficiency. This technique, known as *profiling*, consists of annotating the code for the algorithm with messages sent to objects that can monitor how much work the algorithm has done to that point in its execution. One of these monitoring objects is called a *watch* and measures work in terms of time. A watch is affected by the speed of the computer on which the algorithm is running. The other monitoring object is a *counter*. A counter measures work simply by counting specific kinds of operations performed by the algorithm. As such, it is independent of the computer on which the algorithm executes.

User Request

Write a complete program to empirically demonstrate (or refute) that the selection sort is an $O(n^2)$ algorithm.

Analysis

Empirically verifying the big-O category for a sorting algorithm requires a program that outputs information about its own run time. This information should take two forms: actual time as measured in seconds and implicit time as measured by the number of comparisons and exchanges performed by the algorithm. Moreover, such a program will have to randomly assign data to a vector whose size is initially input by the user. The random assignment of data to the vector will allow the user to gauge the average performance of the algorithm. The program should also make it convenient for the user to run multiple data sets of varying sizes through the algorithm. A run of the program should resemble the following interaction.

```
Enter the number of integers to be sorted: 40
Sorting ...
Running time = 0.062 seconds
Comparisons = 780
Exchanges = 39
Another list to sort? (Y/N) y

Enter the number of integers to be sorted: 80
Sorting ...
Running time = 0.266 seconds
Comparisons = 3160
Exchanges = 79
Another list to sort? (Y/N) y

Enter the number of integers to be sorted: 160
Sorting ...
Running time = 1.094 seconds
Comparisons = 12720
Exchanges = 159
Another list to sort? (Y/N) n
```

Design

The design of the main program should be kept rather simple, deferring complications to subordinate functions and classes. Two important subordinate functions will be (1) a function to generate a list of randomized data and (2) a function to perform a selection sort. The latter function must be annotated with messages sent to `watch` and `counter` objects that monitor the efficiency of the sort.

To generate random data, a `RandomGenerator` class will be used. The interface to members of this class is defined by the following excerpt from its header file. The protected and private data members in this header file are not shown because our profiling program will only use the `RandomGenerator` class as a client.

```cpp
// Class declaration file: random.h

// Objects of this class generate random numbers between specified
// lower and upper bounds.

class RandomGenerator
    {

    public:

    // Class constructors

    RandomGenerator();

    // Member functions

    // Given low and high, nextNumber returns a random integer
    // between low and high inclusive
    int nextNumber(int low, int high);

    // Private and protected data members omitted
    };
```

Similarly, interfaces to the `watch` and `counter` objects that will be used to monitor the selection sort follow:

```cpp
// Class declaration file: watch.h

// Objects of this class behave like
// stopwatches.  They can be started,
// stopped, and asked for the time passed
// in either seconds, minutes, or hours.

class watch
{
    public:

    // Class constructor
```

```
        watch();

        // Member functions

        // Start the timer for the stopwatch
        void start();

        // Stop the timer for the stopwatch
        void stop();

        // Introduce a delay.  During a delay the stopwatch
        // continues to accumulate time, but nothing else takes
        // place.  The duration of the delay is an artificial
        // measure that will have different effects on different machines.
        // Delays cause the stopwatch to artificially accumulate
        // time for monitoring an algorithm running on a relatively
        // small data set.  Without the delay, the granularity of the
        // stopwatch would not recognize any time as having passed
        // during the execution of the algorithm.
        void delay(int duration);

        // Return in seconds the time accumulated since the stopwatch
        // was started.
        float seconds();

        // Return in minutes the time accumulated since the stopwatch
        // was started.
        float minutes();

        // Return in hours the time accumulated since the stopwatch
        // was started.
        float hours();

        // Private and protected data members omitted
};
```

```
// Class declaration file: counter.h

// Objects of this class are used to count
// comparisons, exchanges, and one other
// operation in other algorithms.

class counter
{
    public:

        // Class constructor

        counter();

        // Member functions
```

```
            // Reset the counter for all operations to zero
            void reset();

            // Increment the counter that monitors comparisons
            void incComparisons();

            // Increment the counter that monitors data exchanges
            void incExchanges();

            // Increment the counter that monitors some other
            // operation as may optionally be needed by the
            // client program
            void incOther();

            // Return the accumulated number of comparisons
            int comparisons();

            // Return the accumulated number of data exchanges
            int exchanges();

            // Return the accumulated number of other operations
            int other();

            // Private and protected data members omitted
};
```

The main program, as a client of these classes, will have to iteratively:

1. Generate a randomized list of data

2. Reset the `counter` object.

3. Start the `watch` object.

4. Perform the profiled version of selection sort.

5. Stop the watch.

6. Output the empirical data obtained from the counter and watch objects.

The two crucial functions called by the main program, the randomization function and the selection sort, have the following specifications.

Module: Get random list.

Task: Determine from the user *n*, the number of values to put in the vector *list*, and then fill the first *n* indices of the vector with integer values between 1 and *n*.

Output: The vector *list* filled with randomized values.

Module: Selection sort.

Inputs: *n*, the number of items in the vector, and *list*, the vector itself.

Task: Sort the vector using the selection sort algorithm discussed in Section 1.1. Whenever values in the vector are compared or exchanged, send appropriate messages to the `watch` and `counter` objects.

Output: The sorted vector.

Implementation: The code for the main program and the randomization and sort functions is given in its entirety here. Where a message is sent to one of the profiling `watch` and `counter` objects, a comment of the form `//Profile` has been added. The implementation of the `watch`, `counter`, and `RandomGenerator` classes is not provided here. However, if you are curious about the implementations of these classes, their complete files have been provided. See your instructor.

```cpp
// Program file: select.cpp

// This program illustrates the gathering of data on the
// run-time performance of a sorting algorithm.

#include <iostream.h>
#include "counter.h"
#include "watch.h"
#include "list.h"
#include "apvector.h"

const int COMPARE_DELAY = 5000;        // Duration of a comparison
const int EXCHANGE_DELAY = 5000;       // Duration of an exchange

counter myCounter;      // Global counter for comparisons and exchanges.
watch myWatch;          // Global watch for recording running time.


template <class element>
void selectionSort(apvector<element> &list, int n);

int main()
{
    apvector<int> list(6000);
    int n;
    char again;

    do
    {
        getRandomList(list, n);
        cout << "Sorting ..." << endl;
        myCounter.reset();                              // Profile
        myWatch.start();                                // Profile
        selectionSort(list, n);
        myWatch.stop();                                 // Profile
        cout << "Running time = " << myWatch.seconds()
            << " seconds" << endl;
        cout << "Comparisons = " << myCounter.comparisons() << endl;
        cout << "Exchanges = " << myCounter.exchanges() << endl;
        cout << "Another list to sort? (Y/N) ";
```

```cpp
            cin >> again;
        } while (again != 'n' && again != 'N');
        return 0;
}


template <class element>
void selectionSort(apvector<element> &list, int n)
{
    int minPosition;
    element temp;

    for (int k = 0; k < n - 1; ++k)
    {
        // Find index of smallest element
        minPosition = k;
        for (int j = k + 1; j < n; ++j)
        {
            myCounter.incComparisons();   // Profile
            myWatch.delay(COMPARE_DELAY);  // Profile
            if (list[j] <  list[minPosition])
                minPosition = j;
        }
        // Exchange smallest element and element
        // at beginning of unsorted portion of list
        myCounter.incExchanges();               // Profile
        myWatch.delay(EXCHANGE_DELAY);          // Profile
        temp = list[minPosition];
        list[minPosition] = list[k];
        list[k] = temp;
    }
}


// A subordinate function from the list.cpp file …
void getRandomList(apvector<int> &list, int &n)
{
    RandomGenerator numbers;

    cout << "Enter the number of integers: ";
    cin >> n;
    if (n > list.length())
    {
        cout << "Using " << list.length() << " numbers." << endl;
        n = list.length();
    }
    for (int i = 0; i < n; ++i)
        list[i] = numbers.nextNumber(1, n);
}
```

Discussion

The profiling program presented here represents a starting point for an experimental tool that can be used to explore empirically the run-time behavior of algorithms. Consider, for example, the results of running the program that were presented in our analysis. From these results, we see that as the size of the data set progressed from 40 to 80 to 160:

■ the run time as profiled by the watch object increased from 0.062 to 0.266 to 1.094

■ the number of comparisons increased from 780 to 3160 to 12,720

■ the number of exchanges increased from 39 to 79 to 159

Suppose that we take the ratio of times, comparisons, and exchanges between each pair of successive runs, as shown in Table 1-3.

TABLE 1-3
Ratios between each pair of successive runs

Size of Data Sets in Two Runs	Ratio of Size of Data Sets	Ratio of Run Times	Ratio of Number of Comparisons	Ratio of Number of Exchanges
80 and 40	2	0.266 / 0.062 = 4.290	3160 / 780 = 4.051	79 / 39 = 2.026
160 and 80	2	1.094 / 0.266 = 4.113	12720 / 3160 = 4.025	159 / 79 = 2.013

Notice that, as the size of the data set doubles, the ratio of run times and numbers of comparisons increases by a factor of approximately 4. This is entirely consistent with an $O(n^2)$ algorithm. Why? The number of exchanges don't increase by this same factor. Why? Is this finding consistent with the algorithm's being $O(n^2)$? You will ponder these questions along with many others as you explore and expand the Case Study program in the projects at the end of the lesson.

Running, Debugging, and Testing Hints

■ When profiling a program that is also to be used as an application program above and beyond monitoring the efficiency of an algorithm, use a Boolean constant that can be set to TRUE or FALSE to turn profiling on or off, respectively.

■ When using integer counters in profiling a program, be careful to ensure that the number of operations executed by the algorithm does not overflow the capacity of integer storage. Most C++ implementations offer additional integer data types that can accommodate values too large for standard integers. Consult the local system's reference materials to find out what your version of C++ may offer in this regard.

■ A good way to keep profiling aspects of a program separate from the actual logic of algorithms in the program is to use classes specifically designed for profiling. The counter and watch classes discussed in this lesson are illustrative of such profiling tools.

Summary

In this lesson, you learned:

- An integral part of designing efficient software is the selection of appropriate algorithms to perform the task at hand.

- Two of the criteria used in selecting algorithms for a given task are time and space efficiency. An algorithm's time efficiency determines how long it requires to run. An algorithm's space efficiency is a measure of how much primary and secondary memory it consumes.

- Three simple sorting algorithms are the bubble sort, insertion sort, and selection sort. The selection sort minimizes the number of data interchanges that must be made at the expense of not being more efficient for data that are already partially ordered.

- The pointer sort and radix sort are techniques to enhance the time efficiency of a sort at the expense of increased space requirements.

- Three simple search algorithms are the sequential search, binary search, and key-to-address transformation technique.

- Profiling is an empirical technique that can be used to measure an algorithm's efficiency when a big-O analysis is inconclusive.

- Big-O analyses of sort and search algorithms discussed in this lesson are summarized in the following table:

Algorithms	Time Efficiency	Additional Comments
Bubble sort	$O(n^2)$ comparisons and interchanges in worst case	Can be faster if input data are already almost sorted.
Insertion sort	$O(n^2)$ comparisons and interchanges in worst case	Also can be faster if input data are already almost sorted.
Selection sort	$O(n^2)$ comparisons and $O(n)$ interchanges in worst case	Not significantly faster if input data are already almost sorted.
Pointer sort	Reflects number of comparisons of method on which it is layered	Although the number of interchanges is not reduced, the amount of data swapped for each interchange is potentially less. Drawback is additional memory required for pointers.
Radix sort	$O(n)$ comparisons and interchanges	Limited in types of data on which it works. $O(n)$ rating may have a large constant of proportionality, which can make the rating a misleading one. For vectors, it can have a large space requirement for storing sublists.

(continued on next page)

Algorithms	Time Efficiency	Additional Comments
Sequential search	$O(n)$ probes into list in worst case	Most inefficient of search algorithms we will study, but still appropriate for small lists stored in main memory.
Binary search	$O(\log_2 n)$ probes into list in worst case	Drawbacks are that we must continually maintain a count of number of records and that the list must be maintained in sorted order.
Key-to-address transformation	$O(1)$ list probes	Not applicable for many types

VOCABULARY REVIEW

Define the following terms:

big-O notation	insertion sort	polynomial algorithms
binary search	linear algorithm	quadratic algorithm
bubble sort	logarithmic algorithms	radix sort
cubic algorithm	logical order	selection sort
dominant term	order of magnitude	sequential search
exponential algorithm	pointer sort	time/space trade-off

LESSON 1 REVIEW QUESTIONS

FILL IN THE BLANK

Complete the following sentences by writing the correct word or words in the blanks provided.

1. The characteristic that indicates that software is easily modified to handle circumstances that may change in the future is _____.

2. When a program makes good use of time and space resources, it is said to be _____.

3. The sort algorithm characterized by some data sinking while other data percolates is the _____.

4. The sort characterized by first locating the smallest item in a list and moving it to the first location, then finding the second smallest item and moving it to the second location, and so forth, is called the _____ sort.

5. The method of analysis that uses order of magnitude as the comparison tool is the _____.

6. In the mathematical expression $f_1(n) + f_2(n) + \dots f_k(n)$, the term that becomes the largest as n increases in size is called the _____.

7. When you go through a list of names from beginning to end until you reach the one you need, you are performing a(n) _____ search.

8. When you locate a person's name in a directory by opening the book about at the middle, determining whether the name is before or after that page, then going to the approximate center of the remaining portion, and repeating this process until you find the page with the name, you are performing a(n) _____ search.

WRITTEN QUESTIONS

Write a brief answer to the following questions.

9. Trace the selection sort as it sorts the following values. List all values as any two values are swapped.

   11 66 44 33 99 77

10. Repeat Question 9 using the bubble sort.

11. Repeat Question 9 using the insertion sort.

12. Apply a simple big-O analysis to the following program segment:

```
for (k = 0; k < N; ++k)
    for (j = 6; j < N;  ++j)
    {
        ...
    }
```

13. Apply a simple big-O analysis to the following program segment:

```
for (k = 0;k < N; ++k)
{
    j = N
    while (j > 0)
    {
        ...
        j / = 2;
    }
}
```

14. Write a function that receives a list of floats called valuesList and an integer number that contains the size of the list. The function should use an insertion sort to place the list in order, from smallest to largest. Its declaration is

```
void insertionSort (ListType valuesList, int number);
```

15. Write a function that uses a sequential search to determine how many times a target value is found in a list of integers. The number of times that the value occurs should then be returned. The declaration for this function is

```
int countTargets (ListType list, int taget);
```

MATCHING

Match the correct big-O analysis in Column 2 to its algorithm in Column 1.

Column 1

_____ **16.** What is the big-O analysis for the algorithm $n^2 + 16n + \log_2 n + 400$?

_____ **17.** What is the big-O analysis for the algorithm $n^3 + 77n + 5\log_2 n + 400$?

_____ **18.** What is the big-O analysis for the algorithm $11n + 3\log_2 n + 400$?

_____ **19.** What is the big-O analysis for the algorithm $n^2 \times 47n - 4\log_2 n + 400$?

_____ **20.** What is the big-O analysis for the algorithm $n\log_2 n - 10,000$?

Column 2

a. $O(\log_2 n)$

b. $O(n)$

c. $O(n \log_2 n)$

d. $O(n^2)$

e. $O(n^3)$

LESSON 1 PROJECTS

PROJECT 1-1

SCANS

The Case Study program in this lesson presents a wide range of opportunities for expanding the program and then using it to explore the performance of sort and search algorithms. Here are some ideas:

1. The getRandomList function in the program allows a given value to appear more than once in the randomly generated vector. Modify the algorithm underlying this function so that it will *guarantee* the vector of *n* values contains each of the values 1, 2, ... , *n* exactly once. Make sure that your algorithm to do this is O(*n*).

2. Add a facility to the program that allows a user to input vector values interactively or from a file as well as having them generated randomly.

3. Add profiled versions of the insertion, bubble, and radix sorts to the program and allow the user to choose which sort algorithm to profile.

4. Add a facility that allows the user to save a particular data set to a file so that it can later be read using the option you programmed in part 1.

5. Add profiled versions of sequential and binary searches.

6. For each of the algorithms you added to the program in parts 3 and 5, use the profiling data accumulated from runs of the program to support (or refute) the formal big-O analysis of the algorithm that was presented in the lesson.

7. The watch class used to time the algorithms in the Case Study allows you to establish different times for the comparison and exchange operations. In certain contexts, it is reasonable to expect that one of these operations may take considerably longer than the other. Describe such a situation and explain why different times would arise for these two operations. Then adjust the times for comparisons and exchanges and use the data you collect from running the modified program to demonstrate which sorting algorithm performs best in that situation.

8. The Programming Skills special feature on *Virtual Memory and Program Performance* describes how a formal big-O analysis may not be truly reflected by program performance when paging occurs. Use the Case Study program to demonstrate this idea. Incrementally increase the size of the vector being sorted until one such increase causes an increase in time and/or number of operations that is not consistent with the increase in the size of the vector. In a carefully crafted written statement, explain how the profiling data output by the program gives evidence that paging has occurred.

PROJECT 1-2

SCANS

In this project, you will first write a function called listAllPrimes that will count and determine all primes less than or equal to a specified positive integer called number.

1. Use watches and counters to profile the prime number algorithm underlying listAllPrimes. Based on the empirical data output by these watches and counters, provide an appropriate big-O categorization for the listAllPrimes function.

2. The Greek mathematician Eratosthenes devised a "sieve" technique for finding all prime numbers between 2 and number. The sieve of Eratosthenes can be viewed as a Boolean vector indexed from 2 to number and initialized to true in all of its locations. Successive vector indices are then modified in the following fashion:

— Multiples of 2 greater than 2 are set to false.

— Multiples of 3 greater than 3 are set to false.

— Multiples of 4 can be ignored. Why?

— Multiples of 5 greater than 5 are set to false.

— Multiples of 6 can be ignored. Why?

— Multiples of 7 greater than 7 are set to `false`.

and so on.

The prime numbers are those vector indices where a true value remains. Redo the `listAllPrimes` function using this sieve of Eratosthenes algorithm. Then answer the following questions:

a. Which technique—the sieve or that used in the original function—produces the fastest runs?

b. Does either technique appear to be an order of magnitude better in its time efficiency? Cite results from profiling to back up your claims in this regard.

c. What are the time/space trade-offs involved in using these two techniques?

PROJECT 1-3

SCANS

Suppose that you know the keys in a list are arranged in increasing order. How could the sequential search algorithm presented in this lesson be improved with this knowledge? Rewrite the C++ function to incorporate this improvement and then test your new function in a complete program.

PROJECT 1-4

SCANS

Rewrite the binary search algorithm presented in this lesson with a splitting strategy other than halving. One possibility would be to use an interpolation strategy that would examine the target's distance from the current `low` and `high` pointers. This approach is more analogous to the way in which we look up names in a phone book. That is, for a name beginning with *S*, we do not open the phone book to the middle page but rather to a point approximately two-thirds of the way from the beginning of the book. Test run your program against a pure binary search and, through tracing and/or profiling the performance of each algorithm, determine whether there is any significant difference between the two techniques.

PROJECT 1-5

SCANS

Repeat Project 1-4, but change your algorithm so that, after the initial interpolative guess as to the location of the target, data locations are examined sequentially in an appropriate direction until the key is found or until it can be determined that the key does not appear in the list.

PROJECT 1-6

SCANS

Consider a list of records for students at a university. The list includes fields for student name, credits taken, credits earned, and total grade points. Write a program that, based on a user's request, will sort the list of records in ascending or descending order by keying on one of the four fields within the record. For instance, the user might specify that the sort should proceed in descending order according to credits earned. As much as possible, try to refrain from writing a separate sort function for each particular ordering and field. Experiment by developing different functions based on each of the sorting strategies discussed in this lesson.

PROJECT 1-7

Consider the same list of records as in Project 1-6. Now write a function to sort the records in descending order by credits earned. Records having the same number of credits earned should be arranged in descending order by total grade points. Those with the same number of credits earned and total grade points should be arranged alphabetically by name. Incorporate this function into the complete program that you wrote for Project 1-6. Experiment by developing different functions based on each of the sorting strategies discussed in this lesson.

PROJECT 1-8

Rewrite the pointer sort with the pointer vector as a local variable instead of as a global variable. How would this change affect a higher-level function that calls on the pointer sort? Illustrate by calling your new version of the pointer sort from a sample main program.

PROJECT 1-9

Merge the segmenting strategy described in Exercise 10 in Exercises 1.3 with the insertion sort, bubble sort, and selection sort algorithms. Empirically test how it affects the run time of the sort on a file of 1000 records. Does altering the number of segments affect the run time?

PROJECT 1-10

Implement the binary search algorithm for a disk file containing approximately 1000 records of the structure described in Project 1-6.

PROJECT 1-11

Design a complete program to load information into the database for employees of East Publishing Company described in Exercise 9 of Exercises 1.4. Then repeatedly call on a search function to retrieve the information associated with a given employee's identification key.

For any or all of Projects 1-12 through 1-16, design a program to answer the question posed. Then analyze the time efficiency of your program by using an appropriate combination of big-O analysis and profiling, using the watch and counter classes described in the Case Study. Run your program to try to see the relationship between big-O classification and actual run time as measured by a clock.

PROJECT 1-12

In the first century A.D. the numbers were separated into "abundant" (such as 12, whose divisors have a sum greater than 12), "deficient" (such as 9, whose divisors have a sum less than 9), and "perfect" (such as 6, whose divisors add up to 6). In all cases, you do not include the number itself. For example, the only numbers that divide evenly into 6 are 1, 2, 3, and 6, and $6 = 1 + 2 + 3$. Write a program to list all numbers between 2 and N; classify each as abundant, deficient, or perfect; and keep track of the numbers in each class.

PROJECT 1-13

In the first century A.D., Nicomachus wrote a book entitled *Introduction Arithmetica.* In it, the question "How can the cubes be represented in terms of the natural numbers?" was answered by the statement that "Cubical numbers are always equal to the sum of successive odd numbers and can be represented this way." For example,

$1^3 = 1 = 1$

$2^3 = 8 = 3 + 5$

$3^3 = 27 = 7 + 9 + 11$

$4^3 = 64 = 13 + 15 + 17 + 19$

Write a program to find the successive odd numbers whose sum equals k^3 for k having the values from 1 to N.

PROJECT 1-14

A conjecture, first made by the mathematician Goldbach, whose proof has defied all attempts, is that "every even number larger than 2 can be written as the sum of two prime numbers." For example,

$4 = 2 + 2$

$6 = 3 + 3$

$8 = 3 + 5$

$10 = 3 + 7$

$100 = 89 + 11$

Write a program that determines for every even integer N with $2 <= N$, two prime numbers P and Q such that $N = P + Q$.

PROJECT 1-15

A pair of numbers M and N are called "friendly" (or they are referred to as an "amicable pair") if the sum of all the divisors of M (excluding M) is equal to the number N and the sum of all the divisors of the number N (excluding N) is equal to M ($M \neq N$). For example, the numbers 220 and 284 are an amicable pair because the only numbers that divide evenly into 220 (1, 2, 4, 5, 10, 11, 20, 22, 44, 55, and 110) add up to 284, and the only numbers that divide evenly into 284 (1, 2, 4, 71, and 142) add up to 220. Write a program to find at least one other pair of amicable numbers. Be prepared to let your program search for some time.

PROJECT 1-16

A consequence of a famous theorem (developed by the mathematician Fermat) is the fact that

$$2^{(P-1)} \% P = 1$$

for every odd prime number P. An odd positive integer K satisfying

$$2^{(K-1)} \% K = 1$$

is called a pseudoprime. Write a program to determine a table of pseudoprimes and primes between 2 and N. How many pseudoprimes occur that are not prime numbers?

CRITICAL THINKING

ACTIVITY 1-1

The importance of communication skills in "selling" a program to those who will eventually use it should not be underestimated. Keeping this idea in mind, write a user's guide for the program you developed in Project 1-5. You should assume that the user is able to log onto (or boot) the system, but beyond that has no other knowledge of how to run this or any other program. Remember that unless the user's guide is very, very clear *and* very, very concise, it will probably be thrown in a file drawer—and your program never used.

ACTIVITY 1-2

(For the mathematically inclined.) Consider the claim that exponential algorithms will, *in general,* become practical on parallel processing machines. Provide a carefully constructed argument in which you show that adding more processors to a machine can never result in an exponential algorithm becoming practical for a wide variety of data sets. Your argument should explain the relationship between the number of processors used and the size of the data set that can be accommodated in reasonable time by the exponential algorithm. In essay form, justify the claim that the only real mathematical answer to solving a problem with an exponential algorithm in reasonable time is to discover a nonexponential algorithm that solves the same problem.

ACTIVITY 1-3

One of the drawbacks to the bubble sort algorithm is that a data set with just one item out of order can lead to worst case performance for the algorithm. First, explain how this situation can happen. Because of this phenomenon, a variation on the bubble sort called a *shaker sort* will, on alternative passes through the vector, put the largest entry into the last index and then the smallest entry into the first index. Explain how this idea can eliminate the worst case performance of the bubble sort on a vector with just one item out of order. Then implement the shaker sort algorithm. Using techniques from this lesson's Case Study, profile the number of comparisons and data interchanges in both the shaker sort and the bubble sort for a variety of data sets. Keep track of the empirical results you obtain from profiling these two algorithms. Finally, in a written report, compare the performance of these two algorithms based on your empirical data. Be sure that your report addresses situations in which the shaker sort will actually perform worse than the plain bubble sort.

ACTIVITY 1-4

An interesting variation on the insertion sort is to use a binary search strategy to find the index at which the insertion of the next vector element should occur. Implement this change in the algorithm. From a big-O perspective, has the efficiency of the algorithm changed? Profile the new algorithm using an appropriate driver program coupled with the `watch` and `counter` classes from this lesson's Case Study. Do your profiling statistics confirm your formal big-O analysis?

DATA ABSTRACTION AND OBJECT-ORIENTED SOFTWARE ENGINEERING

OBJECTIVES

Upon completion of this lesson, you will be able to:

■ Understand what is meant by data abstraction and what is involved in defining an abstract data type (ADT).

■ Understand the process of moving from the formal definition of an ADT to the implementation of that ADT as a C++ class.

■ Design and implement a new ADT, called an ordered collection, that prohibits references to uninitialized data elements in a vector.

■ Design an extension of the ordered collection, called a sorted collection, and implement this new ADT.

■ Formally define the one-key table ADT; compare and contrast several implementations of this ADT.

■ Formally define the two-key table ADT; compare and contrast several implementations of this ADT.

■ Enumerate the phases in the software engineering life cycle.

■ Understand more thoroughly what is done during the analysis phase of systems development.

■ Understand the responsibilities of the design phase of the software system life cycle.

■ Understand the CRC design methodology and transform user requirement specifications from the analysis phase into a CRC system design.

🕐 **Estimated Time: 15 hours**

Vocabulary

abstract data type (ADT)	dereference operator	ordered collection
ADT implementation rule	equivalence classes	physical size
ADT use rule	information hiding	software system life cycle
association	iterative prototyping	two-key table
black box testing	logical size	user requirements specification
boundary conditions	one-key table	white box testing
CRC modeling		

Introduction

It is important to design algorithms that manipulate larger data aggregates, such as vectors, efficiently. That need led to our study of algorithm analysis and big-O notation in Lesson 1. In this lesson, we will see how classes, vectors, and efficiency considerations fit into the software engineering process. In the first four sections of the lesson, we will define four classes that can serve as useful "containers" in which client programs can conveniently store objects. These containers—the ordered collection, the sorted collection, the one-key table, and the two-key table—will all be developed following a set of guidelines that form the foundation of a key concept known as data abstraction.

Developing classes in a "data abstract" fashion will enable us to conveniently experiment with many different ways of implementing the classes and to analyze the efficiency of each of these implementation techniques. In the final three sections of the lesson, we will see how these container classes fit naturally into the object-oriented software development process. By using this process, we will develop a Case Study significantly more complex than anything we have attempted previously. In future lessons, we will investigate ways in which the container classes defined in this lesson can be implemented in a more efficient fashion by using more sophisticated data structures.

2.1 The Ordered Collection Abstract Data Type

In almost any application that uses a vector, the user must distinguish between the *physical size* of the vector (its capacity or the number of memory locations available for data elements) and the *logical size* of the vector (the number of data elements currently stored in the vector). Failure to do so can cause errors when users attempt to access data locations in that portion of a vector where no data values have yet been stored.

For example, a vector `list` might be declared to store a maximum number of five integer elements, and three integers might be currently stored in positions 0 through 2. This situation is depicted in Figure 2-1. The data at index positions 3 and 4 are still unpredictable, so the references `list[3]` and `list[4]` for these values will likely lead to unreliable results.

FIGURE 2-1

Logical size of a vector may be different from physical size

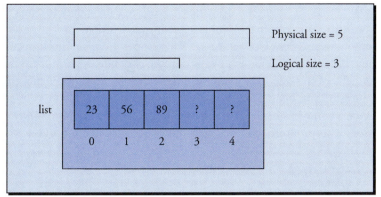

Users can keep track of the data within a physical vector in two ways:

1. The first method stores a special sentinel value at the index position immediately following the last data element currently in the vector. The cost of this method is that one location in the vector must be given up to store the sentinel value. Moreover, some data elements, such as bank account objects, might not be easily represented as sentinel values.

2. The second method maintains a separate integer variable as a counter of the number of data elements currently stored in the vector. Suppose that a variable called `length` maintains this value. When a new vector is declared or reinitialized, `length` is set to 0, to reflect the fact that there are no data elements stored in the vector. `length` is then passed with the vector variable to any function that processes the vector. Any indexed reference to a data element in a vector, either for accessing or for storing a value, should use an index that satisfies the condition `0 <= index < length`. The costs of this method are that a separate variable or parameter must be maintained for the number of data elements in the vector, and extra operations must be provided for adding or removing data elements.

We can use the second method to develop a new class called an ***ordered collection***. A class formalizes in C++ syntax the notion of an ***abstract data type (ADT)***. An ADT is an encapsulation of data objects that share a well-defined set of attributes and operations for processing the objects.

In providing a definition for an ADT such as an ordered collection, we must specify both the attributes and operations that all ordered collections have in common. Typically, we specify the attributes by describing the individual elements composing the ADT and the relationships among those individual elements. The operations may be specified using preconditions and postconditions.

Defining the Ordered Collection ADT

The ordered collection ADT is like a vector in that it provides indexed access to data locations. However, unlike a vector, the ordered collection provides indexed access just to those data locations where elements have been stored. It does so by maintaining its own logical size as a property. A user can access the logical size of an ordered collection, then determine whether indexing is allowed and, if so, what the legitimate range of an index should be. Finally, the ordered collection class provides a set of operations for adding or removing data elements. A test driver program that illustrates the use of an ordered collection of integers follows. We will discuss the use of such test driver programs later in this lesson as we take up the role of testing in the software engineering process.

Example 2-1

This program is merely a test driver that allows its user to exercise each of the operations provided with the ordered collection ADT. Source code files have been provided for this example—see your instructor. Notice from the sample run that values are initially stored in the ordered collection `list` using one of two operations, `addFirst` or `addLast`. These operations are used instead of a vector index operator because a new ordered collection is always empty. The index operator for an ordered collection will not allow assignment of a value to a location unless that location has been previously initialized using the `addFirst` or `addLast` operation. When each input value is added to the collection, its logical size grows by one. Once a value has been assigned to a location, index notation may be used to reference or modify that location. The program assumes that the ordered collection class is implemented in the library file `ordercol.h`.

```cpp
#include <iostream.h>
#include "ordercol.h"

int main()
{
    // Create an empty ordered collection
    // of integers

    OrderedCollection<int> list;
    int choice, value, index, k;

    cout << "[1] add first" << endl << "[2] add last" << endl
        << "[3] remove first" << endl << "[4] remove last" << endl
        << "[5] remove arbitrary" << endl << "[6] inspect index" << endl
        << "[7] change index" << endl << "[8] show collection" << endl
        << "[9] quit -->" << endl;
    do {
        cout << "Which operation should be tested? ";
        cin >> choice;
        switch (choice)
        {
            case 1:
                cout << "Enter value --> ";
                cin >> value;
                list.addFirst(value);
                break;
            case 2:
                cout << "Enter value --> ";
                cin >> value;
                list.addLast(value);
                break;
            case 3:
                cout << list.removeFirst() << " has been removed" << endl;
                break;
            case 4:
                cout << list.removeLast() << " has been removed" << endl;
                break;
```

```
            case 5:
                cout << "Enter value to remove --> ";
                cin >> value;
                if (list.remove(value))
                   cout << value << " has been removed" << endl;
                else
                   cout << value << " was not found" << endl;
                break;
            case 6:
                cout << "Enter index --> ";
                cin >> index;
                cout << "Value at index " << index << " is " << list[index];
                break;
            case 7:
                cout << "Enter index and new value --> ";
                cin >> index >> value;
                list[index] = value;
                break;
            case 8:
                for (k = 0; k < list.length(); k++)
                   cout << list[k] << " ";
                cout << endl;
                break;
            case 9:
                break;
            default:
                cout << "Invalid choice -- Please try again" << endl;
                break;
        }
    } while (choice != 9);

    return 0;
}
```

A *sample run of this program is:*

```
[1] add first
[2] add last
[3] remove first
[4] remove last
[5] remove arbitrary
[6] inspect index
[7] change index
[8] show collection
[9] quit
Which operation should be tested? 1
Enter value --> 20
Which operation should be tested? 1
Enter value --> 40
Which operation should be tested? 2
Enter value --> 10
```

```
Which operation should be tested? 8
40 20 10                                    Note: Entire collection shown here
Which operation should be tested? 7
Enter index and new value --> 1 50
Which operation should be tested? 8
40 50 10                                    Note: Entire collection shown here
Which operation should be tested? 5
Enter value to remove --> 50
50 has been removed
Which operation should be tested? 3
40 has been removed
Which operation should be tested? 4
10 has been removed
Which operation should be tested? 8
                                            Note: Entire collection shown here

Which operation should be tested? 9
```

To summarize the properties of an ordered collection that are illustrated by this example:

1. Range checking occurs during indexing.

2. A newly created ordered collection always has a logical length of 0. This length then grows or shrinks by 1 using appropriate operations.

3. When a data element is added to the beginning of an ordered collection, the positions of the remaining elements shift up by 1.

4. When a data element is removed from the beginning of an ordered collection, the positions of the remaining elements shift down by 1.

5. The use of ordered collections is safer than the use of vectors because references to uninitialized data elements are not allowed.

Formally Specifying the Operations for Ordered Collections

Now that we have an intuitive feel for how an ordered collection should behave, we need to provide a more specific, unambiguous definition of its operations. We start by defining the three attributes of an ordered collection:

1. Its logical length (the number of data elements currently stored)

2. Its data elements

3. The type E of each element in the collection

The formal specifications of the operations for an ordered collection follow:

Create Operation
Preconditions: The ordered collection is in an unpredictable state.
Postconditions: An ordered collection of length 0 is created.
Length Operation
Preconditions: The ordered collection is appropriately initialized.
Postconditions: The number of data elements in the ordered collection is returned.

Indexing Operation (for Observation or Modification of a Data Element)

Preconditions: The ordered collection is appropriately initialized.

The `index` parameter is an integer value in the range `0 <= index <` length of the ordered collection.

Postconditions: The location of the data element as specified by `index`, which can be used either to reference or to store a value, is returned.

Assignment Operation

Preconditions: The target is an ordered collection, appropriately initialized.

The source is an ordered collection, appropriately initialized.

Postconditions: The contents of the source object are copied into the target object, and the target's length is set to the source's length.

Add Last Operation

Preconditions: The ordered collection is appropriately initialized.

The parameter is an object of type `E`.

There is memory available to store the new item in the collection.

Postconditions: The length of the ordered collection is incremented by 1, and the parameter object is placed at the end of the ordered collection.

Remove Last Operation

Preconditions: The ordered collection is appropriately initialized, and the length of the ordered collection > `0`.

Postconditions: The length of the collection is decreased by 1, and what had been the last data element in the ordered collection is returned.

Add First Operation

Preconditions: The ordered collection is appropriately initialized.

The parameter is an object of type `E`.

There is memory available to store the new element in the collection.

Postconditions: The length of the ordered collection is incremented by 1, the data elements in the ordered collection are shifted up by one index position, and the parameter element is placed in the first position in the ordered collection.

Remove First Operation

Preconditions: The ordered collection is appropriately initialized, and the length of the ordered collection > `0`.

Postconditions: The length of the collection is decreased by 1, the data elements in the ordered collection that come after the first element are shifted down by one index position, and what had been the first element in the ordered collection is returned.

Remove Operation

Preconditions: The ordered collection object is appropriately initialized.

The parameter is the data element to be removed, the parameter must equal an element currently in the list, and the length of the ordered collection > `0`.

Postconditions: The length of the ordered collection is decreased by 1, and the data elements in the ordered collection that come after the parameter element are shifted down by one index position.

Declaring the Ordered Collection Class in C++

The separation of an ADT's specification from the declarations and instructions that implement the data type in a particular language is called data abstraction. An abstract data type may be viewed as a formal description of data elements and relationships that are envisioned by the software engineer; it is thus a conceptual model. Ultimately, however, this model will be implemented in C++ via declarations for the elements and relationships and instructions (often in the form of function calls) for the operations. At an even deeper level, the C++ compiler will then translate the implementation of the abstract data type in C++ into a physical electronic representation on a particular computer. This hierarchy of levels of abstraction is illustrated in Figure 2-2.

FIGURE 2-2

Hierarchy of levels of abstraction for implementing an ordered collection

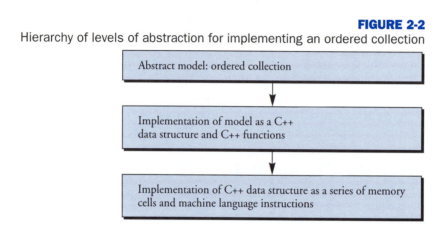

The first step in moving toward an ADT's implementation in an object-oriented language such as C++ is to restate the operations that act on ADT objects as declarations of public member functions in a class declaration module. We will call such a collection of function declarations the *interface for an ADT*. The class declaration module that specifies the interface for the ordered collection ADT closely adheres to the formal specifications that we presented earlier.

```
// Class definition file: ordercol.h

#include "apvector.h"

#ifndef ORDERCOL_H

const int MAX_VECTOR_SIZE = 50;

template <class E>
class OrderedCollection
{

    public:

    // Class constructors

    OrderedCollection();
    OrderedCollection(const OrderedCollection &oc);

    // Function members
```

```
   int length();

   // Assignment
   OrderedCollection& operator = (const OrderedCollection &oc);

   // Indexing
   E& operator [ ] (int index);

   // Modifiers
   void addLast(E e);
   E removeLast();
   void addFirst(E e);
   E removeFirst();
   bool remove(E e);

   protected:

   // Data members

   apvector<E> data;
   int cLength;

};

#define ORDERCOL_H
#endif
```

Note that in this implementation the data member for storing the data elements of an ordered collection is a vector of physical size MAX_VECTOR_SIZE. The length function will return the value stored in cLength—a variable that will keep track of the logical size of the collection. We declare both data members to be protected, so that any derived classes of OrderedCollection will have direct access to them, but client programs will not.

Implementing the Operations for an Ordered Collection

Default Constructor. The default constructor needs only initialize cLength to 0 to ensure that the length operation will return the correct value for an empty collection.

```
template <class E>
OrderedCollection<E>::OrderedCollection()
   : data(MAX_VECTOR_SIZE)
{
   cLength = 0;
}
```

Copy Constructor. The copy constructor assigns the vector and logical length contained in the collection it is given to the corresponding members of the object being constructed.

```
template <class E>
OrderedCollection<E>::OrderedCollection(const OrderedCollection &oc)
   : data(MAX_VECTOR_SIZE)
{
```

```
    for (int j = 0; j < oc.cLength; ++j)
        data[j] = oc.data[j];
    cLength = oc.cLength;
}
```

Length Operation. As long as the implementations of other operations are consistent in updating the value of `cLength`, the length function need only return the value of this protected data member.

```
template <class E>
int OrderedCollection<E>::length()
{
    return cLength;
}
```

Indexing Ordered Collections. The indexing operation for an ordered collection is the same as that for a vector. The only difference is that the logical size is used as an upper bound on the index value. By using `assert`, the indexing operation enforces the precondition that the index parameter is greater than or equal to 0 and less than the length of the collection. Put another way, this code guarantees that users can index only the data elements currently available in the collection.

```
template <class E>
E& OrderedCollection<E>::operator [ ] (int index)
{
    assert((index >= 0) && (index < cLength));
    return data[index];
}
```

Adding and Removing Elements. To add a new data element to the end of the collection, we store the data element in the vector location referenced by `cLength` and then increase `cLength` by 1 to reflect the new logical size of the collection. Because this implementation of an ordered collection uses a vector of physical size `MAX_VECTOR_SIZE`, `assert` is used to ensure that we do not exceed this physical size. You will explore other ways of handling this error condition in the exercises.

`addLast` performs the necessary steps to add a data element to the end of the collection.

```
template <class E>
void OrderedCollection<E>::addLast(E e)
{
    assert(cLength < MAX_VECTOR_SIZE);
    data[cLength] = e;
    ++cLength;
}
```

To remove a data element from the end of the collection, we must perform the inverse steps:

1. Save a copy of the removed data element for return to the caller.

2. Reduce by 1 the value of `cLength`.

    `removeLast` performs the necessary steps to remove a data element from the end of the collection.

```
template <class E>
E OrderedCollection<E>::removeLast()
```

```
{
    assert(cLength > 0);
    --cLength;
    E removedItem = data[cLength];
    return removedItem;
}
```

To add a new data element to the beginning of the collection, we must shift the existing data over one place to the right throughout the underlying vector. The new data element can then be stored in the first position in the vector. Finally, cLength must be increased by 1.

```
template <class E>
void OrderedCollection<E>::addFirst(E e)
{
    assert(cLength < MAX_VECTOR_SIZE);
    for (int i = cLength; i > 0; --i)
        data[i] = data[i - 1];
    data[0] = e;
    ++cLength;
}
```

Study the for loop in this function carefully to be sure that you understand the process of shifting the data in the vector.

To remove a data element from the beginning of an ordered collection, we must store the item to be removed, shift the existing data over one place to the left throughout the vector, and finally decrease cLength by 1.

```
template <class E>
E OrderedCollection<E>::removeFirst()
{
    assert(cLength > 0);
    E removedItem = data[0];
    for (int i = 0; i < cLength; ++i)
        data[i] = data[i + 1];
    --cLength;
    return removedItem;
}
```

The implementation of the remove operation is left as an exercise.

Evaluating the Implementation

In one sense, all implementations look the same to client programs because of the following two "rules" about ADTs:

1. **ADT use rule**: Algorithms that use an abstract data type should access or modify the ADT only through the operations provided in the ADT definition.

2. **ADT implementation rule**: An implementation of an abstract data type *must* provide an interface that is entirely consistent with the operations specified in the ADT's formal definition.

If users and implementers of ADTs comply fully with these rules, all high-level logic will be plug-compatible with all possible implementations of an ADT. The implementation is said to exhibit *information hiding*: It hides information about implementation details from higher-level logic. This behavior is the ideal.

9 3

In some situations, the syntax of C++ will force us into compromising the ideal. We will be careful to point out those situations and hold such compromises to a minimum.

Second, if high-level logic cannot tell the difference between two implementations, then why would we ever want more than one implementation of an ADT? Part of the answer to this question, lies in the different time and space efficiencies that various implementations provide. For instance, in the implementation of the ordered collection that we have discussed here, the `addFirst`, `removeFirst`, and `remove` operations all have an $O(n)$ efficiency. (Why?) If an implementation exists that could execute these operations in $O(1)$ or $O(\log n)$ time, then a client program using that implementation would run faster even though the code in the client program would look exactly the same regardless of which implementation was used. As we study more sophisticated data structures in later lessons, we will see that it is indeed possible to improve the efficiencies of these operations without violating the ADT implementation rule.

Another aspect to consider in evaluating the implementation of an ADT is the limitations that the implementation may impose as it attempts to model an abstraction. For instance, the vector-based implementation of the ordered collection ADT that we have discussed here imposes a maximum length limitation. When we study linked lists in Lesson 3, we will provide an implementation of the ordered collection that does not have this maximum length restriction.

The availability of different implementations of an ADT—all compatible from their outward interface—gives rise to some very exciting prospects for the software design endeavor. At a high level, we can design complex software by constructing a model that operates only on abstract data types. Once we have a high-level model with which we are satisfied, we can plug in the best implementation of the ADT for our particular application.

If formalized big-O analysis is inconclusive about which is the best implementation, it is relatively painless to experiment with several implementations. Different implementations can be plugged in, we can empirically profile their performance, and then we can choose the best. With the ADT approach, all of this experimentation can be done without any modification of the high-level model.

EXERCISES 2.1

1. Discuss the difference between the physical size of a vector and its logical size.

2. State two reasons why ordered collections are safer and more convenient to use than vectors.

3. Users complain that halting the program with an error message is too severe a price to pay for attempting to remove a data element from an empty ordered collection. They argue that a Boolean flag could be returned instead, indicating the success or failure of the operation. Discuss the relative merits of these two approaches.

4. Someone has proposed using an ordered collection rather than a vector to implement a string class. She claims that the new implementation will not have to waste a storage location on the null character. Discuss the merits of this proposal.

5. Implement the remaining operations for the ordered collection class and exercise it with the test driver program presented in Example 2-1.

6. Add an operation, `indexOf`, to the ordered collection class to search the collection for a given element.

If the element is found, the index position of the first instance of this element in the ordered collection should be returned. Otherwise, -1 should be returned.

7. Add an operation to the ordered collection class to sort the data elements in the collection.

8. Add an operation for output of ordered collections, overloading the << operator. Test the operation with an appropriate driver program.

9. Add an operation to concatenate two ordered collections. It should use the + operator in the same way as the `apstring` class. Discuss the limitations of this operation when using the implementation strategy presented in this section.

10. An alternative implementation strategy for an ordered collection is to store a special sentinel value at the index position immediately following the last data element currently in the vector. Clearly this approach eliminates the need to have the logical length of the collection as a protected data member. Implement each of the ordered collection operations using this strategy. Then, in a written statement, compare and contrast the efficiency and limitations of this alternative approach with the approach presented in this section.

11. Add two operations to the `OrderedCollection` class. The first should insert an element at position k, making what had been the kth element become the element at position $k + 1$. The second operation should remove the element at position k. Before writing code for these operations, provide a formal definition of their preconditions and postconditions.

2.2 *Sorted Collections*

Many applications demand that data values be kept in sorted order. For example, dictionaries and telephone books are two kinds of collections of data values that must be maintained in alphabetical order. One could use the ordered collection class to represent these kinds of data as long as a sort operation is provided to alphabetize the data after each insertion into the collection. However, the sort operation can be very expensive to use with large collections. Clearly, an ordered collection that could maintain its contents in sorted form without resorting to a sort operation would be very desirable for these applications.

We can design a new class, called a *sorted collection*, to fulfill these requirements. The new class inherits many of the characteristics of an ordered collection, such as a length and subscripting to look up a data element's value. However, to keep its data elements sorted, a sorted collection prohibits insertions at given positions in the collection. The sorted collection permits only one insertion operation, and that operation always puts a data element in its proper place in the collection. Additionally, for a data type to be stored in a sorted collection, that data type must have well-defined < and > operators.

Example 2-2

The following program provides a test driver for the sorted collection class that is similar to the driver program we used for the ordered collection class in Example 2-1. Source code files have been provided for this example—see your instructor. Examine the sample run following the program to gain a better understanding of the effect of the operations provided for this class.

```
// Program file: sortedcol_drv.cpp

#include <iostream.h>

#include "sortcol.h"

int main()
{
    // Create an empty ordered collection
    // of integers

    SortedCollection<int> list;
    int choice, value, index, k;

    cout << "[1] add " << endl << "[2] remove first" << endl
        << "[3] remove last" << endl << "[4] remove arbitrary" << endl
        << "[5] inspect index" << endl << "[6] show collection" << endl
        << "[7] quit " << endl;
    do {
        cout << "Which operation should be tested? ";
        cin >> choice;
        switch (choice)
        {
        case 1:
            cout << "Enter value --> ";
            cin >> value;
            list.add(value);
            break;
        case 2:
            cout << list.removeFirst() << " has been removed" << endl;
            break;
        case 3:
            cout << list.removeLast() << " has been removed" << endl;
            break;
        case 4:
            cout << "Enter value to remove --> ";
            cin >> value;
            if (list.remove(value))
                cout << value << " has been removed" << endl;
            else
                cout << value << " was not found" << endl;
            break;
        case 5:
            cout << "Enter index --> ";
            cin >> index;
            cout << "Value at index " << index << " is " << list[index];
            break;
        case 6:
            for (k = 0; k < list.length(); k++)
                cout << list[k] << " ";
            cout << endl;
            break;
```

```
        case 7:
            break;
        default:
            cout << "Invalid choice -- Please try again" << endl;
            break;
        }
    } while (choice != 7);

    return 0;
}
```

A sample run of this program is:

```
[1] add
[2] remove first
[3] remove last
[4] remove arbitrary
[5] inspect index
[6] show collection
[7] quit
Which operation should be tested? 1
Enter value --> 90
Which operation should be tested? 1
Enter value --> 80
Which operation should be tested? 1
Enter value --> 70
Which operation should be tested? 6
70 80 90
Which operation should be tested? 4
Enter value to remove --> 80
80 has been removed
Which operation should be tested? 6
70 90
Which operation should be tested? 7
```

Note the use of the operation add to insert a data element into the sorted collection. No position is specified, because the sorted collection figures this out automatically.

Formally Specifying the Operations for Sorted Collections

Because a sorted collection has so many of the attributes and behaviors of an ordered collection, it will be convenient to specify it as a derived class of an ordered collection. Sorted collections inherit all of the attributes of ordered collections: a length, a list of data elements, and a type E that is the data type of each element in the collection. We also assume that all of the operations on ordered collections can be used on sorted collections, except for adding a data element to the beginning or the end of the collection, and for indexing to modify a data element. We use an operation called add for insertions to enforce a sorted order in the collection. The formal specifications follow:

Create Operation
Preconditions: The sorted collection is in an unpredictable state.
Postconditions: A sorted collection of length 0 is created.

Length Operation

Preconditions: The sorted collection is appropriately initialized.

Postconditions: The number of data elements currently stored in the collection is returned.

Indexing Operation (for Observation of a Data Element Only)

Preconditions: The sorted collection is appropriately initialized.

The `index` parameter is an integer value in the range `0 <= index <` the length of the collection.

Postconditions: The object at the index position is returned.

Assignment Operation

Preconditions: The target is a sorted collection object, appropriately initialized.

The source is a sorted collection object, appropriately initialized.

Postconditions: The contents of the source object are copied into the target object, and the target's length is set to the source's length.

Add Operation

Preconditions: The sorted collection object is appropriately initialized, the parameter is an object of type E, and there is memory to store the new element in the collection.

Postconditions: The length of the collection is incremented by 1, and the parameter object is placed in its proper position in the sorted collection.

Remove Last Operation

Preconditions: The sorted collection is appropriately initialized, and the length of the collection `> 0`.

Postconditions: The length of the collection is decremented by 1, and what had been the last data element in the sorted collection is returned.

Remove First Operation

Preconditions: The sorted collection is appropriately initialized, and the length of the collection `> 0`.

Postconditions: The length of the collection is decremented by 1, the data elements in the ordered collection that come after the first element are shifted down by one index position, and what had been the first element in the sorted collection is returned.

Remove Operation

Preconditions: The sorted collection object is appropriately initialized.

The parameter is the data element to be removed, the parameter must equal an element currently in the list, and the length of the collection `> 0`.

Postconditions: The length of the collection is decremented by 1, and the data elements in the sorted collection that come after the parameter element are shifted down by one index position (effectively removing the parameter element from the collection).

Declaring the Sorted Collection Class in C++

The class declaration module for the sorted collection class is

```
// Class definition file: sortcol.h

#ifndef SORTCOL_H

#include "ordercol.h"
```

```
template <class E>
class SortedCollection : protected OrderedCollection<E>
{

    public:

    // Class constructors

    SortedCollection();
    SortedCollection(const SortedCollection<E> &sc);

    // Function members

    // These four are inherited from the base class
    OrderedCollection<E>::length;
    OrderedCollection<E>::removeFirst;
    OrderedCollection<E>::removeLast;
    OrderedCollection<E>::remove;

    // Assignment
    SortedCollection& operator = (const SortedCollection &sc);

    // Indexing (access only, no modification)
    const E& operator [ ] (int index);

    // Modifier
    void add(E e);

    // All data members are defined in base class

};

#include "sortcol.cpp"

#define SORTCOL_H
#endif
```

Note several things about this class declaration:

1. The sorted collection class inherits its attributes and behavior from the ordered collection class in protected mode. As a result, public and protected data members and member functions from the ordered collection cannot be used by clients of the sorted collection class, unless the sorted collection class redefines them. If inheritance were specified in public mode, all of the public members of the ordered collection class, such as addFirst, would also be available to users of the sorted collection class as well. A derived class should be declared in protected mode whenever we wish to deny other users access to some of the public members of the base class.

2. Users of the sorted collection are given access to four member functions of the ordered collection class by listing them in the following form in the public section:

<class name>::<member name>;

This kind of declaration is called an *access adjustment*. In general, an access adjustment broadens the scope of access no wider than the mode of access specified by the base class.

3. The remaining three member function declarations specify operations to be implemented by the sorted collection class. Note that the assignment and indexing operations are not inherited from the base class. In the case of the assignment, we must return the address of an object of a specific class (sorted collection, in this case). In the case of the index operator, we prohibit the use of the returned element as an l-value (that is, as the destination on the left side of an assignment operator) by specifying the function as constant.

Implementing the Sorted Collection Class

The constructors for the sorted collection class invoke the corresponding constructors in the base class:

```
template <class E>
SortedCollection<E>::SortedCollection()
   : OrderedCollection<E>()
{
}


template <class E>
SortedCollection<E>::SortedCollection(const SortedCollection &sc)
   : OrderedCollection<E>(sc)
{
}
```

The new operation to add a data element calls for some development. The logic of this operation must account for three possibilities:

1. The collection is empty. The new data element goes at the end.

2. The new data element is greater than the last element in the collection. The new data element goes at the end.

3. The new data element is less than or equal to some data element in the collection. We search for this place, shift the data elements over to the right from there, and put the new data element in that place.

The implementation reflects these alternatives as follows:

```
template <class E>
void SortedCollection<E>::add(E e)
{
   int place = 0;

   assert(cLength < MAX_VECTOR_SIZE);
   if ((cLength == 0) || (e > data[cLength - 1]))
      data[cLength] = e;
   else
   {
      while (e > data[place])
         ++place;
      for (int index = cLength; index > place ; --index)
         data[index] = data[index - 1];
      data[place] = e;
   }
   ++cLength;
}
```

The implementations of the assignment and index operations are left as exercises.

EXERCISES 2.2

1. Implement the assignment and index operations for sorted collections.

2. Design and test a program that attempts to use the index operator to assign a value to a position in a sorted collection. Explain the error that occurs.

3. Explain why the index operator for ordered collections cannot be used for sorted collections. What effect will this restriction have on client programs that use sorted collections?

4. Using big-O notation, analyze the efficiencies of each of the sorted collection operations for the implementation presented in this section.

5. Add an overloaded index operator to the sorted collection that will allow modification of the collection in the following fashion. When a new value is assigned to index k, if that value does not belong at location k, the sorted collection should store the new value at its appropriate position in the sorted order, shifting the positions of other values as needed to accomplish this goal. For example, if an sorted collection s contained 10 20 30 40 50 60 in indices 0 through 5, respectively, and a user made the assignment s[4] = 5, then the collection should be modified to contain 5 10 20 30 40 60. Note that 5 has replaced the 50 that was stored at index 4, but the 5 has been inserted into its correct position in the newly sorted collection. After implementing this operation, analyze the efficiency of your implementation using big-O notation.

6. Design and implement a member function merge for sorted collections. merge expects a sorted collection as a parameter. The function should build and return a sorted collection that contains the elements in the receiver collection and the parameter collection. After implementing this operation, analyze the efficiency of your implementation using big-O notation.

2.3 The One-Key Table Abstract Data Type

The ordered and sorted collections addressed one particular shortcoming of vectors: the lack of a safeguard to keep users from accessing uninitialized locations. In this section, we will examine an ADT designed to introduce another vector limitation: the inability of a vector to associate values with indices that are not of an integer type. As Example 2-3 will indicate, in many situations it is more natural to associate a value with an "index" that was a string. In the context of the ADT we are about to describe, this more general type of index is called a *key*.

Example 2-3

We have been storing a person's age in a database. Each year, we must increment the person's age by 1. We also wish to add information about the person's height and weight, and remove any information about the person's waistline. The database (called person) is represented so that we can add, retrieve, or remove information (all integer values) by specifying keys (all string values). The following pseudocode algorithm describes our task:

1. Retrieve the value at the "age" key from person.

2. Add 1 to this value.

3. Store the sum at the "age" key in person.

4. Store the person's height at the "height" key in person.

5. Store the person's weight at the "weight" key in person.

6. Remove the value at the "waistline" key in person.

The states of a sample *one-key table* before and after this process are depicted in Figure 2-3.

FIGURE 2-3

States of a one-key table before and after operations

person			person	
key	value		key	value
age	43	→	age	44
waistline	34		height	70
			weight	150

The solution presented in Example 2-3 is totally independent of considerations regarding how the one-key table will be represented in C++. Instead, the high-level pseudocode takes the perspective that a one-key table consists of abstract entities manipulated by abstract operations such as *retrieve* and *store*. As we did with ordered and sorted collections, before we move to any C++ code for the one-key table, it is first necessary to pin down exactly what we mean by these abstractions. That is, we must define the notion of a one-key table precisely enough to ensure that our pseudocode algorithm is unambiguous. Moreover, this definition must be entirely conceptual: It must be free from specifics about how a one-key table will be implemented in a programming language. Such a definition will allow us to refine our algorithm without worrying about details of how a one-key table will eventually be represented.

Formally Specifying the Operations for One-Key Tables

A one-key table is a collection of objects, each of which belongs to the same class. Each object in the collection is associated with a unique key value. The set of all key values must have a well-defined ordering in the sense that, for two different key values a and b, we can determine whether $a < b$ or $a > b$. Clearly, data values such as integers, real numbers, symbols of an enumerated type, and strings meet this ordering criterion. Some examples of one-key tables are shown in Figure 2-4. Note that the objects stored in these tables are of relatively simple types; objects with a more complex internal structure may be stored in one-key tables as well.

FIGURE 2-4

Some typical one-key tables

person		salaries		lineup		classRank	
key	value	key	value	key	value	key	value
age	44	ortiz	55000.00	C	Berra	1	Steinmetz
height	70	smith	45000.00	CF	Mantle	2	O'Leary
weight	150	vaselli	62000.00	SS	Kubek	3	Rakowski

The operations for a one-key table follow. In the specification of these operations, the term *receiver* refers to the object or the instance of the ADT being operated upon.

Create Operation

Preconditions:	Receiver is an arbitrary one-key table in an unpredictable state.
Postconditions:	Receiver is initialized to an empty table.

Empty Operation

Precondition:	Receiver is a one-key table.
Postcondition:	If receiver contains no objects, the Boolean value `true` is returned; otherwise, the Boolean value `false` is returned.

Length Operation

Precondition:	Receiver is a one-key table.
Postcondition:	The number of objects currently in the table is returned.

Store Operation

Preconditions:	Receiver is a one-key table. *target* is a key value. *item* is an object to be inserted in receiver. If *target* is not already a key in the table, there is memory available to store *item*.
Postconditions:	If an object is already associated with *target* in receiver, it is replaced by *item*. Otherwise, receiver has *item* inserted and associated with *target*.

Remove Operation

Preconditions:	Receiver is a one-key table. *target* is a key value associated with an object to be removed from the table.
Postconditions:	If the object with the *target* key can be found in the table, it is removed, *item* contains the object associated with *target*, and the operation returns `true`. Otherwise, the operation returns `false`, *item*'s contents are undefined, and the table is left unchanged.

Retrieve Operation

Preconditions:	Receiver is a one-key table, and *target* is a key value to be found in the table.
Postconditions:	If the *target* can be found in the table, then *item* contains the object associated with *target* and the operation returns `true`. Otherwise, the operation returns `false`, and *item*'s contents are undefined. In either case, the one-key table is left unchanged.

The effect of each operation is highlighted in Figure 2-5 for a one-key table in which the key is a string representing a name and the object is a real number representing a grade-point average.

FIGURE 2-5
Effects of the operations on a one-key table

Store 3.45 at key "Smith, Jane" ⟶ Smith, Jane | 3.45

Run the empty operation ⟶ FALSE

Store 2.86 at key "Woods, Bob" ⟶ Smith, Jane | 3.45
Woods, Bob | 2.86

Run the length operation ⟶ 2

Retrieve the value at key "Woods, Bob" ⟶ 2.86

Store 3.25 at key "Smith, Jane" ⟶ Smith, Jane | 3.25
Woods, Bob | 2.86

Remove the value at key "Woods, Bob" ⟶ Smith, Jane | 3.25

A C++ Interface for the One-Key Table ADT

Just as we did with ordered and sorted collections, the first step in moving toward an implementation of the one-key table ADT in an object-oriented language such as C++ is to restate the operations that act on ADT objects as declarations of public member functions in a class declaration module.

```cpp
// Class declaration file: onetable.h

#ifndef ONETABLE_H

#include "assoc.h"
#include "apvector.h"

// Declaration section

const int MAX_TABLE_SIZE = 50;

// Generic class for key type K and element type E.

template <class K, class E> class OneKeyTable
{

  public:

  // Class constructors

  OneKeyTable();
  OneKeyTable(const OneKeyTable<K, E> &table);

  // Function members

  int length();
  bool empty();
  void store(const K &target, const E &item);
  bool retrieve(const K &target, E &item);
  bool remove(const K &target, E &item);
  OneKeyTable<K, E>& operator = (const OneKeyTable<K, E> &table);

  protected:

  // Data members

  int tableLength;
  apvector <association<K, E> > data;

};

#include "onetable.cpp"

#define ONETABLE_H
#endif
```

Note several things about this class declaration module:

- The key and element types are template parameters called K and E, respectively. We have not previously seen a class that used more than one template parameter. However, there are no surprises in this regard. Wherever the C++ compiler would expect the key type, we use K; wherever the element type should appear, we use E.

- The protected data members in the class declaration section also provide a clue as to how we will be representing a one-key table in C++. We will maintain the current length of a table in a data member called `tableLength`. We will use a vector, called `data`, of *association* objects to store the data in the table. The association class, declared in the header file `assoc.h`, must therefore be included before the declaration of the one-key table class.

- The use of the association class to implement a one-key table class is completely hidden from users of the one-key table. They have awareness only of using keys, elements, and one-key tables. We will return to a discussion of the role of the association class in implementing one-key tables after the following example.

PROGRAMMING SKILLS: Association Lists and Dictionaries

The idea of associating data objects with key values in tables probably received its first expression in a programming language when LISP was developed more than 30 years ago. LISP (an acronym for LISt Processing Language) was designed to process lists of symbolic information in AI applications. These applications frequently need to associate information with a symbol. For example, a natural language processing application will have to maintain a dictionary of terms in a language. The keys for a dictionary would be symbols representing the words, and the values would be definitions or other information associated with the words. Every dialect of LISP recognizes a particular kind of list called an association list. An association list is a list consisting of key/value pairs. Once an association list has been defined, a LISP programmer can look up the value associated with a given key by using the LISP function `assoc`.

The object-oriented language Smalltalk, which is also used in many symbol processing applications, comes with a built-in hierarchy of collection classes. One subclass of the Smalltalk collection class is called a dictionary class. The dictionary class is similar to the association list in LISP. One difference is that the implementation of a dictionary in Smalltalk is geared toward very efficient retrievals, whereas a LISP association list supports only a linear search method.

Our one-key table ADT borrows much from these ideas in LISP and Smalltalk. In particular, the order of the data in the conceptual table is not specified for the user of the table, but it may be important for the efficiency of the implementation. One major difference is that we allow any key values that can be ordered, whereas LISP and Smalltalk usually allow only strings or symbols as keys. Another major difference is that all of the data values in our one-key table must be of the same type; LISP and Smalltalk allow objects of different types to be stored in the same association list or dictionary.

Example 2-4

Here is a test driver program to exercise the various operations for the one-key table. Source code files for this example and all one-key table examples have been provided—see your instructor. It is similar to what we did for the ordered and sorted collection classes in Examples 2-1 and 2-2, respectively. As you examine the sample run accompanying this program, make sure you understand how the program uses a string as the key for the table and an `int` for the value associated with a given key.

```cpp
// Program file: onekeytab_drv.cpp

#include <iostream.h>

#include "apstring.h"
#include "onetable.h"

int main()
{
    // Create an empty ordered collection
    // of integers

    OneKeyTable<apstring, int> intsByStrings;    // Create table
    int choice, value;
    apstring key;

    cout << "[1] length " << endl << "[2] empty" << endl
        << "[3] store " << endl << "[4] retrieve" << endl
        << "[5] remove" << endl << "[6] quit " << endl;
    do {
        cout << "Which operation should be tested? ";
        cin >> choice;
        switch (choice)
        {
        case 1:
            cout << "Table length is " << intsByStrings.length();
            break;
        case 2:
            if (intsByStrings.empty())
                cout << "Table is empty " << endl;
            else
                cout << "Table is not empty " << endl;
            break;
        case 3:
            cout << "Enter key followed by associated value --> ";
            cin >> key >> value;
            intsByStrings.store(key, value);
            break;
        case 4:
            cout << "Enter key to retrieve --> ";
            cin >> key;
            if (intsByStrings.retrieve(key, value))
                cout << "Associated value is " << value << endl;
            else
                cout << key << " not in table " << endl;
            break;
```

```
        case 5:
            cout << "Enter key to remove --> ";
            cin >> key;
            if (intsByStrings.remove(key, value))
                cout << key << " and its value " << value << " removed"
                    << endl;
            else
                cout << key << " not in table " << endl;
            break;
        case 6:
            break;
        default:
            cout << "Invalid choice -- Please try again" << endl;
            break;
        }
    } while (choice != 6);

    return 0;
}
```

A sample run of this program is:

```
[1] length
[2] empty
[3] store
[4] retrieve
[5] remove
[6] quit
Which operation should be tested? 3
Enter key followed by associated value --> foo 3
Which operation should be tested? 3
Enter key followed by associated value --> bar 7
Which operation should be tested? 3
Enter key followed by associated value --> baz 12
Which operation should be tested? 4
Enter key to retrieve --> bar
Associated value is 7
Which operation should be tested? 3
Enter key followed by associated value --> bar 1
Which operation should be tested? 4
Enter key to retrieve --> bar
Associated value is 1
Which operation should be tested? 5
Enter key to remove --> foo
foo and its value 3 removed
Which operation should be tested? 4
Enter key to retrieve --> foo
foo not in table
Which operation should be tested? 6
```

Example 2-5

This example illustrates that, *in one program*, it is possible to declare instances of one-key tables that have *different* key and element types. Here the table `intsByStrings` uses keys that are strings and elements that are `ints`, while the table `stringsByInts` reverses this process by declaring `ints` to be the key type and strings to be the elements.

```cpp
// Program file: test1key.cpp

#include <iostream.h>

#include "apstring.h"
#include "onetable.h"


void main()
{
   OneKeyTable<apstring, int> intsByStrings;    // Create tables
   OneKeyTable<int, apstring> stringsByInts;

   bool success;                                // Auxiliary variables
   int iElement;
   apstring sElement;

   intsByStrings.store("age", 40);              // Store some data
   stringsByInts.store(911, "emergency");

                                                // Retrieve the data
   success = intsByStrings.retrieve("age", iElement);
   if (success)
      cout << "Age = " << iElement << endl;
   success = stringsByInts.retrieve(911, sElement);
   if (success)
      cout << "911 = " << sElement << endl;
}

A sample run of this program is:

Age = 40
911 = emergency
```

Implementations of the One-Key Table ADT

We will consider two implementations of a one-key table in this section; each will have major shortcomings from an efficiency perspective. In future lessons, we will explore more sophisticated implementations that can improve on these inefficiencies. Before we examine the implementations, let us discuss the association ADT. Briefly, an association consists of two attributes: a key and a value. The only purpose of an association is to help us organize the data in a one-key table. We specify the interface for the association ADT as follows.

Create Operation

Preconditions:	Receiver is an association in an unpredictable state. *key* is a key value. *item* is the object to be associated with key.
Postconditions:	Receiver is initialized to associate *item* with *key*.

Get Key Operation

Preconditions:	Receiver is an association.
Postconditions:	*key* is returned.

Get Value Operation

Preconditions:	Receiver is an association.
Postconditions:	*value* is returned.

Set Value Operation

Preconditions:	Receiver is an association. *item* is an object to be inserted.
Postconditions:	*item* replaces the object currently in the association.

The C++ class declaration module for the association ADT is

```cpp
// Class declaration file: assoc.h

// Declaration section

// Generic class for key type K and element type E.

#ifndef ASSOC_H

template <class K, class E> class association
{
   public:

   // Class constructors

   association();
   association(const association<K, E> &a);
   association(const K &newKey, const E &newItem);

   // Member functions

   K getKey() const;
   E getValue() const;
   void setValue(const E &value);
   association& operator = (const association<K, E> &a);

   private:

   // Data members

   K theKey;
   E theValue;

};

#include "assoc.cpp"

#define ASSOC_H
#endif
```

Implementation 1: Physically Ordered Vector with Binary Search. The strategy of this implementation is to maintain the vector of associations in physical order by key. For example, the association at data[0] will have the smallest key, while the association at data[tableLength - 1] will have the largest key.

Example 2-6

The ordering for this implementation will support a binary search during the retrieve operation. The code is modeled after the algorithm we analyzed in Lesson 1:

```
template <class K, class E>
bool OneKeyTable<K, E>::retrieve(const K &target, E &item)
{
   int first, last, middle;
   K key;
   bool found = false;

   first = 0;
   last = tableLength;
   while ((first <= last) && !found)
   {
      middle = (first + last) / 2;
      key = data[middle].getKey();
      if (key == target)
         found = true;
      else if (key > target)
         last = middle - 1;
      else
         first = middle + 1;
   }
   if (found)
      item = data[middle].getValue();
   return found;
}
```

To store an object in the table in this implementation, we must do the following:

1. Search for the first association in the vector that has a key greater than or equal to that of the item we are adding.

2. If the association's key is equal to our target key, just replace the item in that association with our new item and quit.

3. Otherwise, examine the current length of the table to ensure that there is room to add a new association. In this implementation, use the C++ assert function to halt program execution if there is no memory available. Otherwise, beginning with the current association, move all associations down one slot in the vector.

4. Finally, create and insert a new association into the vector slot that has been vacated and increase by 1 the length of the table.

These actions are highlighted in Figure 2-6. Carefully study this figure in conjunction with examining the code in Example 2-7.

FIGURE 2-6

Storing an item at a new key in a one-key table

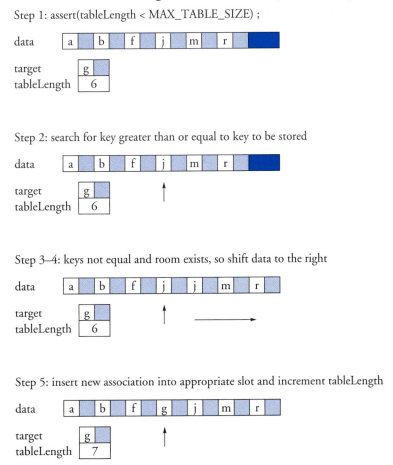

Step 1: assert(tableLength < MAX_TABLE_SIZE) ;

Step 2: search for key greater than or equal to key to be stored

Step 3–4: keys not equal and room exists, so shift data to the right

Step 5: insert new association into appropriate slot and increment tableLength

Example 2-7

Write complete C++ code for the `store` operation. This operation must maintain a correspondence between the physical order of the associations in the vector and the logical order of the keys in the associations.

```cpp
template <class K, class E>
void OneKeyTable<K, E>::store(const K &target, const E &item)
{
   int probe = 0;
   bool found = false;
   K key;

   while ((probe < tableLength) && ! found)        // Search for position
   {
      key = data[probe].getKey();
      if (key >= target)
         found = true;
      else
         ++probe;
   }
```

```
    if (found && (key == target))               // Key already in table
        data[probe].setValue(item);
    else if (tableLength < MAX_TABLE_SIZE)       // Room available for
    {                                            // new association?
        for (int i = tableLength; i > probe; --i)  // Yes, move them over
            data[i] = data[i - 1];
        association<K, E> a(target, item);
        data[probe] = a;
        ++tableLength;
    }
}
```

As you can see, the excellent efficiency of retrievals with this implementation is paid for by potentially expensive insertions and removals. The `create`, `remove`, `empty`, and `length` operations are left as exercises.

Implementation 2: Unordered Vector with Sequential Search. Our second implementation attempts to eliminate the inefficiency involved in moving a potentially large number of objects each time a `store` is performed. The encapsulation of the one-key table ADT still includes a vector of associations and a counter. However, now when an association is added, it is merely added after the last item currently stored in the vector. Figure 2-7 illustrates this strategy. As you can see, the increase in efficiency of the `store` operation is being traded for a decrease in efficiency for retrievals. The `retrieve` operation would now require a sequential search. The details of this implementation are left for you as exercises.

FIGURE 2-7
More efficient `store` operation

Physical order of keys in array does not correspond to logical order in table.

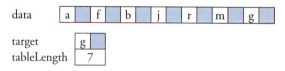

```
data        | a |   | f |   | b |   | j |   | r |   | m |   |   |
target      | g |   |
tableLength |   6   |
```

New data are always added to the right of the last data in the table.

```
data        | a |   | f |   | b |   | j |   | r |   | m |   | g |   |
target      | g |   |
tableLength |   7   |
```

These trade-offs in efficiency for various operations make the one-key table ADT particularly interesting to study. We will return to it often in future lessons.

EXERCISES ⟹ 2.3

1. Complete the implementation of the one-key table by developing code for the; `create`, `length`, `empty`, and `remove` operations. Be sure to obey the ADT implementation rule.

2. Provide a big-O efficiency analysis of the two implementations of the store operation. You should consider both the number of comparisons and data interchanges in this analysis.

3. Consider the second implementation of the `store` operation. Is there a way to take advantage of the fact that the vector is sorted when looking for the target key's appropriate position? If so, write an improved version of the function and provide a big-O analysis.

4. Provide a big-O efficiency analysis of the `remove` operation. You should consider both the number of comparisons and data interchanges in this analysis.

5. Is there a way to improve the efficiency of the `remove` operation for the second implementation? If so, write a new version and provide a big-O analysis.

6. Some applications may need to process all of the objects currently in a one-key table. For example, one might wish to output all of the objects in the order of their keys. It would be useful to provide two new operations called `keys` and `values`. `keys` returns a sorted collection of the keys currently in the table, and `values` returns an unsorted ordered collection of the objects currently in the table. First specify these operations as ADT operations with preconditions and postconditions, and then write the C++ code for them.

7. Describe the differences between the one-key table ADT and the ordered collection and sorted collection abstract data types discussed in Sections 2.1 and 2.2. Include in your discussion examples of applications for which each is most appropriate.

2.4 *The Two-Key Table Abstract Data Type*

Consider the problem of maintaining statistics for a baseball league. The statistics might be printed in a newspaper as follows:

	AB	Hits	2B	3B	HR	Ave
Alomar	521	192	25	6	29	.369
Brett	493	180	16	3	41	.365
Canseco	451	160	30	1	50	.354
McGwire	590	205	41	10	70	.347
Hubble	501	167	21	2	17	.333
Sosa	485	156	32	4	66	.321
Noguchi	562	180	24	2	32	.320
Perez	499	159	21	4	21	.318
Sokoloski	480	149	16	10	15	.310
Tanenbaum	490	150	14	0	23	.306

A database for storing this information should be organized so that we quickly obtain answers to queries such as, "How many home runs does Sosa have?" One way to conceptualize this organization is to imagine a table in which the desired data object is retrieved by specifying two keys: the name of the player and the category of the statistic. In the case of our example query, the answer might be obtained by running the abstract operation

retrieve the data at keys Sosa and HR

This manner of conceptualizing and using a database is so common that we will develop a new abstract data type, the two-key table, that can be used by any application. As with the one-key table, we first specify the attributes and behavior of the two-key table conceptually. Then we choose an implementation in C++. Finally, we do a big-O analysis of the behavior of our implementation and discuss the trade-offs of alternative implementations.

Two-Key Table: A *two-key table* is a collection of objects, each of which belongs to the same class. Each object in the collection is associated with two key values called *key1* and *key2*. Each *key1* value, called a **primary key**, is unique. Each *key2* value, called a **secondary key**, may be used with more than one primary key, but must indicate a unique data element when associated with a primary key. The set of all *key1* values must have a well-defined ordering in the sense that, for two different *key1* values *a* and *b*, we can determine whether $a < b$ or $a > b$. The same property holds for the set of all *key2* values.

The operations for a two-key table follow.

Create Operation
Preconditions: Receiver is an arbitrary two-key table in an unpredictable state.
Postconditions: Receiver is initialized to an empty table.

Empty Operation
Preconditions: Receiver is a two-key table.
Postcondition: If receiver contains no objects, the Boolean value `true` is returned; otherwise, the Boolean value `false` is returned.

Store Operation
Preconditions: Receiver is a two-key table. *key1* is the primary key value. *key2* is the secondary key value. *item* is an object to be inserted in receiver. If *key1* and *key2* do not specify an object already in the table, there is memory available to store *item*.
Postconditions: If an object is already associated with *key1* and *key2* in the table, it is replaced by *item*. Otherwise, the table has *item* inserted and associated with the *key1* and *key2* values.

Remove Operation
Preconditions: Receiver is a two-key table. *key1* and *key2* are the key values associated with an object to be removed from the table.
Postconditions: If the object with the key values *key1* and *key2* can be found in the table, it is removed from the table, item contains the object associated with the key values *key1* and *key2*, and the operation returns `true`. Otherwise, the operation returns `false`, *item*'s contents are undefined, and the table is left unchanged.

Retrieve Operation
Preconditions: Receiver is a two-key table. *key1* and *key2* are the key values associated with an object to be found in the table.
Postconditions: If the pairing of *key1* and *key2* can be found in table, then *item* contains the object associated with *key1* and *key2*, and the operation returns `true`. Otherwise, the operation returns `false`, and *item*'s contents are undefined. In either case, the table is left unchanged.

As you can see from these definitions, a two-key table is really an extension of a one-key table with an extra key. Note that we do not specify a `length` operation, however, because a two-key table is not a linear data structure.

A Class Template for the Two-Key Table ADT

In the spirit of our policy of making ADTs as general and flexible as possible, we will represent our conceptual definition of the two-key table ADT as a C++ class template. This approach will allow an application to specify the type of each key and the item type when a two-key table is created. For example, the table of baseball statistics discussed earlier could be declared as

```
TwoKeyTable<apstring, apstring, int> statistics;
```

where the last parameter is the type of data to be stored in the table, and the other parameters are the types of keys (first and second, respectively).

The C++ class declaration module for a two-key table class template is

```
// Class definition file: twotable.h

#ifndef TWOTABLE_H

template <class K1, class K2, class E> class TwoKeyTable
{

   public:

   // Class constructors

   TwoKeyTable();
   TwoKeyTable(const TwoKeyTable<K1, K2, E> &table);

   // Member functions

   TwoKeyTable<K1, K2, E> & operator = (const TwoKeyTable<K1, K2, E> &table);
   bool empty();
   void store(const K1 &key1, const K2 &key2, const E &item);
   bool retrieve(const K1 &key1, const K2 &key2, E &item);
   bool remove(const K1 &key1, const K2 &key2, E &item);

   protected:

   // Data members

   // Will be completed when we consider alternative implementations
};

#include "twotable.cpp"

#define TWOTABLE_H
#endif
```

Note that the interface to the class template, the function declarations, and component type parameters exactly mirror those given in our conceptual definition.

A Two-Dimensional Vector Implementation

Because a two-key table is a two-dimensional data structure at the conceptual level, we might try to represent it as a two-dimensional vector in C++. After all, we represented a one-key table as a one-dimensional vector. Each row of the vector would represent a `key1`, and each column would represent a `key2`. We could then choose between a direct mapping of keys to index positions along each dimension of the vector (supporting efficient retrievals) or a random mapping (supporting efficient insertions).

Because there are now two keys to map to two index positions in the vector, the association class must be extended to represent the association of a value with two keys. We do so by defining a derived class of association, `TwoKeyAssociation`, that contains the extra key. This approach has the effect of preserving the original association class for the use of one-key tables:

```
template <class K1, class K2, class E> class TwoKeyAssociation : public
        association
{
    public:

    // Class constructors

    TwoKeyAssociation();
    TwoKeyAssociation(const TwoKeyAssociation<K1, K2, E> &a);
    TwoKeyAssociation(const K1 &key1, const K2 &key2,
        const E &newItem);

    // Member functions

    K2 getKey2();
    TwoKeyAssociation<K1, K2, E>& operator =
        (const TwoKeyAssociation<K1, K2, E> &a);

    private:

    // Data members
    K2 theKey2;

};
```

Two other questions must be answered before we can write the definitions of the data members for the two-key table. First, what will be the maximum size of a two-key table? The answer to this question for one-key tables was specified by a constant, `MAX_TABLE_SIZE`, defined in the header file. For a two-dimensional vector, we will need two constants, `MAX_ROW_SIZE` and `MAX_COL_SIZE`, to define the maximum sizes of the two dimensions. Application modules will again specify these values, with the understanding that `MAX_ROW_SIZE` represents the maximum number of possible `key1` values in a two-key table and `MAX_COL_SIZE` represents the maximum number of possible `key2` values.

Second, how will we maintain the current number of objects stored in a two-key table? A one-key table used an integer data member, `tableLength`, representing the next available location in the vector for storing data. The situation in a two-dimensional vector is more complicated. We need to know both the position of the next available row (for a new `key1`) and the next available column in each row (for a new `key2`). Therefore, we will define two data members, an integer variable and a vector of integers, to represent these attributes.

The data members for the two-dimensional vector can now be added to the class declaration module of the two-key table:

```
// Data members

apmatrix <TwoKeyAssociation<K1, K2, E> > data; // constructed with
                                  // MAX_ROW_SIZE rows and MAX_COL_SIZE columns
int rowLength;
apvector<int> colLengths;        // constructed with MAX_ROW_SIZE entries
```

The next example shows how we would implement the `store` operation, assuming that we simply pick the next available row and column for a new object at `key1` and `key2`.

Example 2-8

Write the implementation of the member function that stores an object in a two-key table. We assume that if the `key1` is new, we enter at a new row, and if `key2` is new, we enter at a new column.

```
template <class K1, class K2, class E>
void TwoKeyTable<K1, K2, E>::store(const K1 &key1, const K2 &key2, const E &
item)
{
  int row, col;
  bool found = false;
  K1 rowKey;
  K2 colKey;

  row = 0;
  col = 0;
  while ((row < rowLength) && ! found)     // Search key1 in rows
  {
      rowKey = data[row][col].getKey();
      if (key1 == rowKey)
          found = true;
      else
          ++row;
  }
  if (found)                               // key1 already in table
  {
      found = false;                       // Search for key2 in column
      while ((col < columnLengths[row]) && ! found)
      {
          colKey = data[row][col].getKey2();
          if (key2 == colKey)
                found = true;
          else
                ++col;
      }
      if (found)                           // key2 also already in table
          data[row][col].setValue(item);
      else
      {
```

```
                assert(columnLengths[row] < MAX_COL_SIZE);    // Room available
                                                              // for column?
                TwoKeyAssociation<K1, K2, E> a(key1, key2, item);
                data[row][col] = a;            // Add a new key2
                ++columnLengths[row];
        }
    }
    else
    {
        assert(rowLength < MAX_ROW_SIZE);   // Room available for row?
        TwoKeyAssociation<K1, K2, E> a(key1, key2, item);
        data[row][0] = a;                            // Add a new key1
        columnLengths[row] = 1;
        ++rowLength;
    }
}
```

By now, you will probably have surmised that this implementation has some serious drawbacks. The most obvious one relates to the length and complexity of the `store` operation. With so many alternative cases to consider and data to maintain, this code will be very difficult to read, understand, and get correct. Moreover, the `retrieve` and `remove` operations will be almost as complicated.

As far as efficiency is concerned, the current implementation introduces a new data structure, the vector for maintaining the current lengths of the columns, that results in a linear growth of memory for the maximum number of secondary keys that an application needs in a table. The current version also forces us to add a data member to the association class to represent a second key. The only advantage is that binary searches for a target object might be very fast, assuming that one can get the code correct!

The choice of this implementation seems so unreasonable that we will not even leave its completion as an exercise but rather look for a simpler one.

Using One-Key Tables to Implement Two-Key Tables

Another way to think of a two-key table is as a one-key table. Each key in this table will represent a *key1* in the two-key table. At each of these keys, we store another one-key table. Each key in each of these tables will represent a *key2* in the two-key table. Thus the data elements stored at the keys in the nested one-key tables will be the data elements stored in the two-key table.

The advantage of this representation is that it allows us to use higher-level components to construct our two-key table ADT. This approach will allow us to use higher-level operations as well. For example, the operation for retrieving a data element at *key1* and *key2* in a two-key table can now be conceptualized as follows:

1. Retrieve the element at *key1* of the top-level one-key table

2. If the retrieval is successful, then

3. From this element (also a one-key table) retrieve the element at *key2*

The advantage of this implementation over the two-dimensional vector implementation is that its code for the search operations has already been written, so we just invoke the operations by name. In the two-dimensional vector implementation, we are forced to reinvent the wheel by rewriting this code. Source code files for the remaining two-key table examples have been provided—see your instructor.

Here is a class declaration module for a two-key table that uses one-key tables to support high-level implementations of two-key operations:

```
// Class definition file: twotable.h

#ifndef TWOTABLE_H

#include "onetable.h"

template <class K1, class K2, class E> class TwoKeyTable
{

   public:

   // Class constructors

   TwoKeyTable();
   TwoKeyTable(const TwoKeyTable<K1, K2, E> &table);

   // Member functions

   TwoKeyTable<K1, K2, E> & operator = (const TwoKeyTable<K1, K2, E> &table);
   bool empty();
   void store(const K1 &key1, const K2 &key2, const E &item);
   bool retrieve(const K1 &key1, const K2 &key2, E &item);
   bool remove(const K1 &key1, const K2 &key2, E &item);

   protected:

   // Data members

   OneKeyTable<K1, OneKeyTable<K2, E> > data;

};

#include "twotable.cpp"

#define TWOTABLE_H
#endif
```

The interface of the two-key table class stays the same, but the new implementation has just one data member. It is a one-key table whose key type is K1 and whose element type is another one-key table. The key type of this second one-key table is K2 and its element type is E. Carefully examine the line of code that defines this data member, especially the ordering of the angle brackets, so that you understand how the type parameters are passed to set up the data structure.

The next example shows how we can take advantage of the new data member definitions to implement the retrieve operation for two-key tables.

119

Example 2-9

Write the implementation of the `retrieve` operation for the two-key table class specified in the class declaration module given earlier.

```
template <class K1, class K2, class E>
bool TwoKeyTable<K1, K2, E>::retrieve(const K1 &key1, const K2 &key2,
    E &item)
{
    OneKeyTable<K2, E> table;

    if (data.retrieve(key1, table))
        return table.retrieve(key2, item);
    else
        return false;
}
```

After working through the code for the two-dimensional vector implementation, this code must seem almost magically simple. However, it represents a straightforward use of the one-key tables in the new data representation. Using the data member `data`, we attempt to retrieve a table at `key1`. If we are successful, we use this table to attempt to retrieve an item at `key2`. If we are successful here, the item is returned and the function returns `true`. If either of the retrievals fails, the function returns `false`.

Not only is this version easy to read, understand, and get correct, but we no longer need to consider the alternatives of linear search or binary search to implement a retrieval. These considerations have been resolved at a lower level, during the implementation of the one-key table. The next example shows how to implement a `store` operation for this version. Be sure to compare it to the other version in Example 2-8.

Example 2-10

Write the implementation of the `store` operation for the one-key table implementation of the two-key table ADT.

```
template <class K1, class K2, class E>
void TwoKeyTable<K1, K2, E>::store(const K1 &key1, const K2 &key2,
    const E &item)
{
    OneKeyTable<K2, E> table;

    data.retrieve(key1, table);
    table.store(key2, item);
    data.store(key1, table);
}
```

Comparing the Two Implementations

Our intuition in choosing a two-dimensional vector implementation for a two-key table seemed natural: One can think of each structure as consisting of a grid in which a data item is located by specifying a row and column. Moreover, because we were able to map a key in a one-key table to an index position in a one-dimensional vector, it seemed logical to try to map two keys to the two indices of a two-dimensional vector. However, when we turned to the actual data structures and algorithms for implementing this version, we quickly became lost in a welter of complexity. We found it necessary to introduce complex auxiliary data structures, such as a vector of column lengths and a two-key association class, and to write pages of code for each individual operation.

By reconceiving a two-key table as a one-key table whose data items are other one-key tables, we were able to simplify both the data structures used in the implementation and the code used in the operations. The one-key table ADT handles most of the work of representing the data and implementing the operations. We no longer have to think about using auxiliary ADTs such as the association, much less about inheriting from it to represent a second key. We no longer have to decide between an implementation that supports binary search (fast retrievals) or linear search (fast insertions).

On the other hand, the one-key table implementation gives us less control over the way a two-key table behaves than we might wish. If a client of the two-key table desires fast retrievals and the one-key table implements a linear search, the client is stuck with that choice. Moreover, clients can no longer specify separate maximum row and column sizes for two-key tables. This last factor can lead to a serious inefficiency in the use of memory, where storage would be allocated for rows or columns in the table that are not really needed by the application. We will see a way to remedy this last problem in later lessons.

The contrast between the two implementations can be viewed as a layered system versus an unlayered system. The one-key table implementation places a layer of high-level types and operations between the two-key table ADT and the underlying C++ data structures and operations. The two-dimensional vector implementation represents the two-key table ADT directly in terms of the underlying C++ data structures and operations. Layered systems are generally easy to design and maintain; unlayered systems may be more efficient but are usually much more difficult to design and maintain.

These considerations lead us to formulate one more principle for the design of abstract data types: Existing abstract data types should be used to implement new abstract data types, unless direct control over the underlying data structures and operations of the programming language is a critical factor. A well-designed implementation consists of layers of ADTs. This is known as the ***ADT layering rule***.

EXERCISES 2.4

1. Complete the one-key table implementation of the two-key table ADT.

2. Write a program that uses a two-key table to store and retrieve the baseball statistics described earlier in this section. Explain how you handle the data in the last column, which appear to be real numbers rather than integers.

3. A data item is located in a three-key table by specifying three keys. Write an abstract definition and an appropriate C++ class declaration module for this ADT. Remember to adhere to the ADT reuse and layering rules.

4. Example 2-4 presented a comprehensive test driver for the one-key table ADT. Write a similar test driver for the two-key table.

2.5 The Analysis Phase of the Software Engineering Life Cycle

Software engineering is the process by which large software systems are produced. As you might imagine, these systems need to be maintained and modified; ultimately, they are replaced with other systems. This entire process parallels that of an organism. That is, there is a development, maintenance, and subsequent demise. Thus this process is referred to as the *software system life cycle*. Specifically, a system life cycle can be viewed as consisting of the following phases:

1. Analysis

2. Design

3. Coding

4. Testing/verification

5. Maintenance

6. Obsolescence

It probably comes as a surprise to learn that computer scientists view this process as having a phase that precedes the design phase. However, it is extremely critical that a problem be completely understood before any attempt is made to design a solution. The analysis phase is complicated by the fact that potential users may not supply enough information when describing their intended use of a system. Analysis requires careful attention to items such as

■ Exactly what form of input is required.

■ Exactly what form of output is required.

■ How data entry errors (there will be some) should be handled.

■ How large the databases will become.

■ How much training in the use of the system will be provided.

■ What possible modifications might be required as the intended audience increases/decreases.

Clearly, the analysis phase requires an experienced communicator.

The design phase is where the solution is developed using a modular approach. Attention must be paid to techniques that include communication, algorithm development, writing style, teamwork, and so on. The key product of this phase is a detailed specification of the intended software product.

Coding closely follows design. Unfortunately, many beginning students want to write code too quickly. It can be a painful lesson if you have to scrap several days' worth of work because your original design was not sufficient. You must make sure your designs are complete before writing any code. In the real world, teams of designers work long hours before programmers ever get a chance to start writing code.

The testing phase of a large system is a significant undertaking. Early testing is done on individual modules to get them running properly. Larger data sets must then be run on the entire program to make sure the modules interact properly with the main program. When the system appears ready to the designers, it is usually field-tested by selected users. Each of these testing levels is likely to require changes in the design and coding of the system.

Finally, the system is released to the public and the maintenance phase begins. This phase lasts throughout the remainder of the program's useful life. During this phase, we are concerned with repairing problems that arise after the system has been put into use. These problems are not necessarily bugs introduced during the coding phases. More often they are the result of user needs that change over time. For instance, annual changes in the tax laws necessitate changes in even the best payroll programs. Or problems may arise as a result of misinterpretation of user needs during the early analysis phase. Whatever the reason, we must expect that a program will have to undergo numerous changes during its lifetime. During the maintenance phase, the time spent documenting the original program will be repaid many times over. One of the worst tasks imaginable in software development is to be asked to maintain an undocumented program. Undocumented code can quickly become virtually unintelligible, even to the program's original author. Indeed, one of the measures of a good program is how well it stands up to the maintenance phase.

Of course, no matter how good a program is, it will eventually become obsolete. At that time, the system life cycle starts all over again with the development of a new system to replace the obsolete one. Hence, the system life cycle is never-ending, being itself part of a larger repetitive pattern that continues to evolve with changing user needs and more powerful technology.

In each of the case studies in this book, we will develop a complete program by going through the analysis, design, and implementation phases. By using data abstraction wherever possible, software engineers have been able to somewhat control and manage the complexity inherent in developing large programs. The best way of understanding how data abstraction and other techniques can be used to advantage in the process is to illustrate how they are used in tackling a more substantial problem. That is what we propose to do in the rest of the lesson.

In this section, we will investigate some of the complications that can occur on the way to defining user requirements during the analysis phase. In Section 2.6, we will explore the design phase, focusing on how to progress from the user requirements document to a detailed definition of the ADTs needed by the software system. In Section 2.7, strategies for implementing and testing the system will be discussed. Finally, the Case Study will follow through on the material from the preceding sections to finish the system.

It has been said that the only simple problems in computing are those defined in textbooks. Perhaps a key to the truth of this statement is its use of the word *defined*. Once a problem has been specifically defined, the most difficult obstacle to solving it may have been surmounted. In the analysis phase you must define in detail the problem that you are charged with solving.

It is important to remember that in trying to provide such a definition, you are typically working with a problem originally posed by someone other than yourself. We will try to emphasize this fact in the following material by introducing the problem in the form of a memorandum from computer users. This is done to emphasize that programs are written not for computer scientists but for computer users. These computer users often know virtually nothing about the computer other than a vague (and often inaccurate) notion that it can magically take care of all of their record-keeping and computational needs. Bridging the gap between potentially naive users and the computer-oriented people who eventually are responsible for implementing the software system constitutes the first phase of the system life cycle.

Although many people are aware that systems analysts work with computers in some way, few know specifically what a systems analyst does. More than anything else, the systems analyst is responsible for the analysis phase of the system life cycle. A systems analyst talks to the users who initially request the system to learn exactly what they need. This task is accomplished not only by talking to users, but also by studying in detail what they do. For instance, a systems analyst working for a bank on an automated teller system would have to become an expert on the various duties and responsibilities of a teller. Having learned what the automated system is supposed to do, the systems analyst must then develop formal specifications describing the system and its requirements. The technical people who design and code the software will work from these specifications.

So, imagine yourself in the role of a systems analyst who receives the following memorandum from the principal at the world-renowned School of Hard Knocks. In it, she requests that you automate the school's record-keeping on its students.

MEMORANDUM
School of Hard Knocks

TO: Director of Information Systems
FROM: Principal
DATE: July 29, 2001
RE: Automation of record-keeping on students

As you know, we presently maintain our student records by manual methods. We believe the time has come to computerize this operation and request that you do so for us.

Here is what we need. Each student's record consists of his or her name, the total number of credits taken, the total number of credits earned, his or her cumulative grade-point average (GPA), and a list of grades received in each course taken. We maintain these records by a student's last name. Of course, at numerous times, we must add new students to our records and remove those who have graduated or withdrawn from school. Students often come into our office and request to see their current record, so we must be able to find that information quickly. At the end of each semester, we print a grade report for each student. This report consists of the items cited above, although we include only the grades of courses taken in the current term. At the end of the year, we need two lists of graduating seniors. One of these lists is to be printed in alphabetical order by student name. The other is printed in order by student grade-point average.

Certainly, the situation described in this memo is an oversimplification of any real grade-reporting system. However, even this relatively unsophisticated situation offers us some interesting food for thought. For one thing, the memo demonstrates the fact that your first contact with a user requesting the system will often leave gaps in your knowledge about the system that is actually needed. The principal's memo leaves unanswered the following questions:

1. What is the school's definition of grade points?

2. When grade reports are printed for each student, is it important that they be printed in any particular order?

3. Because grade reports are printed at the end of each semester, do you need some means of updating a student's record at the end of a semester?

4. What is the method used to compute a student's GPA?

5. What separates seniors who graduate from those seniors who don't graduate?

6. Is the list printed in order by student GPA arranged from best student to worst student, or vice versa?

7. What naming scheme is used for courses at the school?

You need to communicate these questions to the principal before the specifics of the system can be appropriately modeled. Suppose you do that and receive the following reply.

MEMORANDUM
School of Hard Knocks

TO: Director of Information Systems
FROM: Principal
DATE: August 2, 2001
RE: Responses to your questions

Question 1: Four grade points are assigned for a one-credit A grade, three for a B, two for a C, one for a D, and zero for an F. Courses worth more than one credit have their corresponding grade points multiplied accordingly.

Question 2: Grade reports should be printed in alphabetical order by student last name.

Question 3: At the end of each semester, faculty members turn in grades for each class they teach. We use the grades on these class rosters to update a student's academic information before printing a grade report.

Question 4: GPA is computed as the quotient of total grade points divided by credits taken.

Question 5: A graduating senior must have earned at least 120 credits.

Question 6: The list is to be printed from best student to worst student.

Question 7: Officially, our office identifies each course by a department code that is four characters or less and a course number. However, courses also have a longer descriptive title. This title should appear on the grade reports received by the student.

This process of give-and-take communication between the end users of the system and yourself as analyst continues until you conclude that you understand the school's operation in sufficient detail to write a formal *user requirements specification*.

User Requirements Specification for the Hard Knocks Grade Reporting System

After initially loading the student database, along with information on all of our courses, the system should present its user with a main menu that allows the following options:

- Enter a dialogue to add a new student to the database

- Enter a dialogue to delete a student from the database

- Enter a dialogue to update an existing student's record with the grades from the courses that he or she has completed in the current semester

- Enter a dialogue to inspect the complete academic record of a student

- Enter a dialogue to produce grade reports for all students in a specified semester

- Produce end-of-year reports of graduating seniors, first in alphabetical order and then in grade-point-average order

In the dialogue to add a new student to the database, that student should be identified by his or her full name—last name followed by first. Initially, that student will have an empty student record stored in the database. As that student accumulates courses, the student record should keep track of the total number of credits taken by the student, the total number of credits earned, the cumulative grade-point average, and a list of grade records for all courses that have been taken by the student. Each grade record consists of an identification of the course taken by the student, the year and semester (fall or winter) in which it was taken, the number of credits associated with that course, and the grade the student received in the course. Officially, two keys—its department code and its course number—identify a course in our database of courses. The former is a short string of four or fewer characters; the latter is a three-digit number. Unofficially, courses are identified by a title that is much longer and more descriptive than its two-key identification. This title must often be displayed in the output triggered by other dialogues in the system.

The dialogue to delete a student from the database merely requires that the user enter the full name of the student to be deleted. If the student exists in the database, he or she should be removed. Otherwise, an error message should be displayed, and the user should be returned to the main menu.

The dialogue to update an existing student's record starts with entering the student's full name. Assuming the student is found in the database, the user should then enter a succession of grade records for that student. In entering these grade records, it should not be necessary to enter the number of credits for the course since, for a given course, the number of credits will always be the same. Instead, once the user identifies the course, the system should be able to determine the number of credits from the course information that is stored within the student database.

The dialogue to inspect the complete academic record of a student should again be keyed by entry of the student's full name. If that student is found in the database, the information displayed should include the total number of credits taken by the student, the total number of credits earned, the cumulative GPA, and the list of grades for all courses that have been taken by the student. In this list, the information for each course should include the department, number, credits, grade, and full descriptive title.

The dialogue to produce grade reports for all students requires that the user enter the year and the semester. The former should be entered in 19XX or 20XX format. The latter should be entered as F or W, for the fall and winter semesters, respectively. The grade reports should appear in alphabetical order by student name. The information displayed for each student should include the total number of credits taken by the student, the total number of credits earned, the cumulative GPA, and the list of grades for all courses that have been taken by the student *in the specified semester only*.

The two end-of-year reports should include for each graduating student his or her full name, total number of credits taken, total number of credits earned, and cumulative GPA.

The user requirements specification is the most important document emerging from the analysis phase. It provides a complete and unambiguous definition of the system's input and outputs. It must be written in language nontechnical enough to allow the end users to "sign off" on the document—that is, give their official blessing that a system delivered in the form described will indeed satisfy their needs. At the same time, it must be stated in a form that is detailed enough to allow software designers to work from it during the design phase. These software designers want a complete statement of *what* the system must do, but not *how* it should be done. This distinction between *what* and *how* is critical and is the same distinction we encountered earlier when formally defining ADTs.

EXERCISES 2.5

1. Write a user requirements specification to give to the designers for a software system you will use each month to maintain your checking account at a local bank.

2. Write a user requirements specification to give to the designers for a software system you will use to keep track of the musical CDs that you own.

3. Write a user requirements specification to give to the designers for a software system you will use to maintain statistics for your favorite sports team.

4. For this task, you'll work with another student. Each of you should write a memorandum to specify what you view as the information-processing needs of an administrative office at your school (or any other office environment with which you may be familiar). Your memorandum should provide information similar to that provided by the principal at the School of Hard Knocks. Exchange your memoranda, study them, and then get together with the other person to resolve any questions you might have. Write a user requirements specification from what you have learned. Finally, have the other person critique the accuracy and completeness of your document.

5. Consider the following memorandum from the principal at the renowned American School of Basket Weaving—one of the main competitors of the School of Hard Knocks.

TO: Director of Information Systems
FROM: Principal
DATE: July 29, 2001
RE: Automation of record-keeping on students

Records for students at our school consist of an identification number, a last name, a first name, a middle initial, a Social Security number, a list of courses the student has taken along with the grade received in each course, and a list of extracurricular activities in which the student has indicated an interest. An identification number for a student consists of six digits. The first two digits represent the year a student entered the school. The remaining four digits are simply assigned on a sequential basis as students are admitted to the school. For instance, the student with ID number 990023 is the 23rd student admitted in the class that entered ASBW in 1999.

Given this database, we frequently need to work with it in the following ways:

- Find and display all data for a particular student.
- Add and delete student records from the database.
- Print records for all students.
- Add, change, or delete the information on a course for a particular student.
- Find all students with an extracurricular interest that matches a particular target interest.

Develop a set of questions that you would ask the principal to resolve what you feel are ambiguities in this memo. Give your set of questions to another student. That other student, acting as the principal, should answer the questions you've posed. Working from the original memo and the answers to questions provided by your classmate, write a user requirements specification for this software system

6. Write an essay in which you defend or attack the following position: To prepare for a career as a systems analyst, it is more important to develop interpersonal communication skills than it is to acquire a mass of technical knowledge about specific computer systems.

2.6 The Design Phase of the Software Engineering Life Cycle

You now need to change your hat and put yourself in the place of the systems designer. You have been given the user requirements specification from the analysis phase and now must develop a model from which programmers will write the actual code for the system. This model should divide the system into objects with well-defined behaviors. A hallmark of engineering as a discipline is to follow recognized methodologies in building a sequence of models that ultimately evolve into a finished product. The methodology that we will describe here is called ***CRC modeling.*** CRC stands for Classes-Responsibilities-Collaborators. You will find that it is a natural extension of the way in which we have already approached defining classes. However, what we have done previously has typically looked at a class as an isolated entity. In designing a complete system, we must additionally specify how each class will interact with the other classes in the system.

The first step in CRC modeling is to enumerate the classes that will compose the system. A good starting point is is to reread the requirements specification and identify the critical nouns in that document. Why? Objects are entities, not actions. As such they will correspond to nouns, not verbs, in the requirements specification. Using this heuristic, we again present the requirements specification for the Hard Knocks grade-reporting system. Now, however, we have underlined the important nouns.

User Requirements Specification for the Hard Knocks Grade Reporting System

After initially loading the <u>student database</u>, along with information on all of our courses, the system should present its user with a <u>main menu</u> that allows the following options:

- Enter a dialogue to add a new student to the database

- Enter a dialogue to delete a student from the database

- Enter a dialogue to update an existing student's record with the grades from the courses that he or she has completed in the current semester

- Enter a dialogue to inspect the complete academic record of a student

- Enter a dialogue to produce grade reports for all students in a specified semester

- Produce end-of-year reports of graduating seniors, first in alphabetical order and then in grade-point-average order

In the dialogue to add a new student to the database, that student should be identified by his or her full name—last name followed by first. Initially, that student will have an empty student record stored in the database. As that student accumulates courses, the <u>student record</u> should keep track of the total number of credits taken by the student, the total number of credits earned, the cumulative grade-point average, and a <u>list of grade records</u> for all courses that have been taken by the student. Each <u>grade record</u> consists of an identification of the <u>course</u> taken by the student, the year and semester (fall or winter) in which it was taken, the number of credits associated with that course, and the grade the student received in the course. Officially, two keys—its department code and its course number—identify a course in our <u>database of courses</u>. The former is a short string of four or fewer characters; the latter is a three-digit number. Unofficially, courses are identified by a title that is much longer and more descriptive than its two-key identification. This title must often be displayed in the output triggered by other dialogues in the system.

The dialogue to delete a student from the database merely requires that the user enter the full name of the student to be deleted. If the student exists in the database, he or she should be removed. Otherwise, an error message should be displayed, and the user should be returned to the main menu.

The dialogue to update an existing student's record starts with entering the student's full name. Assuming the student is found in the database, the user should then enter a succession of grade records for that student. In entering these grade records, it should not be necessary to enter the number of credits for the course since, for a given course, the number of credits will always be the same. Instead, once the user identifies the course, the system should be able to determine the number of credits from the course information that is stored within the student database.

The dialogue to inspect the complete academic record of a student should again be keyed by entry of the student's full name. If that student is found in the database, the information displayed should include the total number of credits taken by the student, the total number of credits earned, the cumulative GPA, and the list of grades for all courses that have been taken by the student. In this list, the information for each course should include the department, number, credits, grade, and full descriptive title.

The dialogue to produce grade reports for all students requires that the user enter the year and the semester. The former should be entered in 19XX or 20XX format. The latter should be entered as F or W, for the fall and winter semesters, respectively. The grade reports should appear in alphabetical order by student name. The information displayed for each student should include the total number of credits taken by the student, the total number of credits earned, the cumulative GPA, and the list of grades for all courses that have been taken by the student in the specified semester only.

The two end-of-year reports should include for each graduating student his or her full name, total number of credits taken, total number of credits earned, and cumulative GPA.

Extracting these key nouns from the requirements specification gives us a preliminary breakdown of the system into classes. Each of these classes should then be annotated with a brief comment as to its role in the system. Table 2-1 shows the result of doing this for the grade-reporting system.

TABLE 2-1
Preliminary breakdown of registrar's system into classes

Class	Role
student database	Maintains the records of all students at the school
main menu	Provides the interaction with users of the system
student record	Maintains data on each individual student
list of grade records	Maintains all of the grades associated with each individual student
grade record	Maintains the data on the grade a student receives in an individual course
course record	Maintains the data on an individual course at the school
database of courses	Maintains the collection of all course records

The first C in CRC modeling is now complete—we have defined the classes needed by the system. The next step is to define the responsibilities of each class (the R in CRC). The most essential aspect of this part of the process is one with which you are already familiar from our previous work in defining ADTs. That is, for each class, we must use preconditions and postconditions to define each of the operations belonging to that class. This step involves another careful reading of the requirements specification to better understand the details of the role each class will play in the system. As this task is done, the good designer will not only define the operations for each class but will also:

■ Recognize how preexisting ADTs may be used to help in the eventual implementation of the classes for this particular system.

- Begin to make some decisions about implementation strategies for the classes. In C++ vernacular, this statement means that the designer begins to make recommendations about what will ultimately become private or protected data members. Typically, these decisions will be made with an eye toward achieving a particular efficiency. The convention in CRC modeling is to use the word "knows" when making such a recommendation. The programmer who will carry out the implementation of this class should think of these recommendations as hints from the designer about effective ways to carry out the implementation.

- See how one class will have to rely on another class for help in carrying out a particular operation. The class that provides the help is called a collaborating class, and the designer should include notes about such collaborations in the design document that is passed on to the programmers. Doing so takes care of the second C in CRC.

Given this overview of the process, we will complete the CRC design of the system.

PROGRAMMING SKILLS: Object-Oriented Design and Productivity in Software Development

In 1986, renowned software engineer Frederick Brooks published an essay called "No Silver Bullet" (in *Proceedings of the IFIP Tenth World Computing Conference*, pp. 1069–1076). In it, Brooks predicted that over the ten-year span following the publication of the essay, there would be no programming technique that would lead to an order-of-magnitude improvement in the productivity of the software development process. Such a technique is what Brooks refers to as the "silver bullet." In effect, he is saying we will not discover a magical way to make easy something that is inherently hard.

In a 1995 essay called "No Silver Bullet Refired" appearing in *The Mythical Man-Month: 20th Anniversary Edition* (Reading, MA: Prentice Hall, 1995, p. 20), Brooks takes a retrospective look at his 1986 prediction. In it, he argues that his basic predictions have held and that we have not witnessed an order-of-magnitude improvement in the productivity of software developers. However, the picture he paints is not a bleak one. In many ways, he admits that we may be getting close to something significant. Much of the reason is tied to the progress that has and will be made in object-oriented development techniques. For example, he states that, whereas he once felt that *all* programmers should see *all* the code for a system, he now has come to be a firm believer in information hiding as a way of "raising the level of software design."

Brooks contends that we have just begun to scratch the surface of the advantages inherent in object-oriented design. Two things will happen in the near future. First, the designers of classes will learn to think bigger. They will develop classes with complete functionality to solve broad ranges of problems. Examples he cites are graphical user interface classes and classes for doing finite-element analysis. Second, those who write client programs will become more adept at using these high-powered classes in new and exciting ways. The combination will still not be the silver bullet, but Brooks now does go so far as to offer the following caveat: "Object-oriented programming—will a brass bullet do?"

CRC Design Specs for Main Menu Class

Knows: The student database

Create Operation

Preconditions: Main menu is in an arbitrary state. sd is a student database.

Postconditions: Main menu has been initialized with information in the student database *sd*.

Start Operation

Preconditions: Main menu has been created.

Postconditions: Main menu has been displayed, allowing the user the choice of adding a student, deleting a student, inspecting a student, updating a student's grade, displaying grade reports, displaying end-of-year reports, or quitting.

Add Dialogue Operation

Preconditions: None

Postconditions: User has been queried for information necessary to add a student to the database and the appropriate student record has been added.

Collaborators: Student database class

Delete Dialogue Operation

Preconditions: None

Postconditions: User has been queried for information necessary to remove a student from the database. The appropriate student record has been removed or the user has been informed that the student cannot be found in the database.

Collaborators: Student database class

Inspect Dialogue Operation

Preconditions: None

Postconditions: User has been queried for information necessary to inspect the record for a particular student in the database. The appropriate student record has been displayed or the user has been informed that the student cannot be found in the database.

Collaborators: Student database class

Update Dialogue Operation

Preconditions: None

Postconditions: User has been queried for a student name to update. If that student is not found in the database, an appropriate message is displayed. Otherwise, the user is repeatedly queried for grades in each of the courses taken by the student in the current semester.

Collaborators: Student database class

Report Dialogue Operation

Preconditions: None

Postconditions: User has been queried for the year and semester for which to produce grade reports. Grade reports for that semester have been printed.

Collaborators: Student database class

CRC Design Specs for Student Database Class

Knows: The course database, enabling it to access information on course titles and credits

Use Existing ADT: Extend the operations provided in the existing one-key-table class. Hence, all operations in the one-key table are available.

Create Operation

Preconditions: Student database object is in an unreliable state. A stream contains information on already existing students and courses.

Postconditions: Student database has been loaded from information in stream.

Add Student Operation

Preconditions: *studentName* contains the name of the new student to be added to the database.

Postconditions: *studentName* has been added to the database along with an empty student record.

Collaborators: Student record class

Student Exists Operation

Preconditions: *studentName* contains the name of the new student to be added to the database.

Postconditions: Returns `true` if *studentName* is in the database and `false` if it is not

Delete Student Operation

Preconditions: *studentName* contains the name of the student to be removed from the database.

Postconditions: *studentName* has been removed from the database along with a returned value of `true` to indicate success or `false` to indicate *studentName* cannot be found in the database.

Inspect Student Operation

Preconditions: *studentName* contains the name of the student whose record is to be displayed.

Postconditions: The record of *studentName* has been displayed along with a returned value of `true` to indicate success or `false` to indicate *studentName* cannot be found in the database.

Collaborators: Student record class

Add Course Operation

Preconditions: *studentName* contains the name of the student to whose list of grade records *newCourse* is to be added.

Postconditions: The record of *studentName* has been updated to contain the grade record *newCourse* and the Boolean value `true` is returned to indicate success or `false` to indicate *studentName* cannot be found in the database.

Collaborators: Student record class

Grade Reports Operation

Preconditions: *year* and *semester* contain the year and semester (F for fall or W for winter) for which grade reports are to be produced.

Postconditions: Grade reports have been printed in alphabetical order by student name.

Collaborators: Student record class

(continued on next page)

Graduation List by Name Operation

Preconditions: None
Postconditions: A list of all graduating seniors has been printed in alphabetical order.
Collaborators: Student record class

Graduation List by GPA Operation

Preconditions: None
Postconditions: A list of all graduating seniors has been printed in descending order by GPA.
Collaborators: Student record class

CRC Design Specs for Course Database Class

Use Existing ADT: Simply use the existing two-key-table class, with department as the primary key, course number as the secondary key, and course record objects as the elements stored in the table. This class will provide all the functionality that is needed for the course database.

CRC Design Specs for List of Grade Records Class

Use Existing ADT: Simply use the existing ordered collection class, with grade records being the elements stored in the collection. This class will provide all the functionality that is needed for the list of grade records.

CRC Design Specs for Student Record Class

Knows: The list of grade records for the courses that have been taken by this student
Knows: The course database (so it can look up course titles and credits)

Create Operation

Preconditions: Student record is in an arbitrary state. *courseDatabase* references the course database.
Postconditions: Student record has been initialized to know about *courseDatabase* and to have an empty list of grade records.

Get Credits Taken Operation

Preconditions: Student record has been created and perhaps acted upon by other operations.
Postconditions: Return the number of credits that this student has taken.
Collaborators: Course record class, grade record class, course database class, list of grade records class

Get Credits Earned Operation

Preconditions: Student record has been created and perhaps acted upon by other operations.
Postconditions: Return the number of credits that this student has earned.
Collaborators: Course record class, grade record class, course database class, list of grade records class

Get GPA Operation

Preconditions: Student record has been created and perhaps acted upon by other operations.
Postconditions: Return the student's cumulative grade-point average.
Collaborators: Course record class, grade record class, course database class, list of grade records class

Add Course Operation

Preconditions:	*gr* is a grade record.
Postconditions:	*gr* has been added to the list of grade records for this student.
Collaborators:	Grade record class, list of grade records class

Display Course History Operation (First Version)

Preconditions:	None
Postconditions:	Student's entire course history has been displayed.
Collaborators:	Course record class, grade record class, course database class, list of grade records class

Display Course History Operation (Second Version)

Preconditions:	*year* represents a year and *semester* represents a semester (F or W).
Postconditions:	Student's course history for *year* and *semester* has been displayed.
Collaborators:	Course record class, grade record class, course database class, list of grade records class

---

CRC Design Specs for Course Record Class

Knows:	The course title, the number of credits for the course

Create Operation

Preconditions:	Course record is in an arbitrary state. *title* is a course title and *credits* is the number of credits for the course.
Postconditions:	Course record has been initialized to know about *title* and *credits*.

Get Credits Operation

Preconditions:	Course record has been created.
Postconditions:	Return the number of credits for this course.

Get Title Operation

Preconditions:	Course record has been created.
Postconditions:	Return the title for this course.

CRC Design Specs for Grade Record Class

Knows:	The primary key (department) and secondary key (course number) to identify the course for which the grade was given, the year and the semester in which the course was taken, the letter grade received in the course.

Create Operation

Preconditions:	Grade record is in an arbitrary state. *dept*, *courseNum*, *year*, *semester*, and *grade* are parameters representing the five items the record must know.
Postconditions:	Grade record has been initialized to know about *dept*, *courseNum*, *year*, *semester*, and *grade*.

Get Department Operation

Preconditions:	Grade record has been created.
Postconditions:	Return the department code (primary key) associated with the course for which the grade was issued.

Get Course Number Operation

Preconditions:	Grade record has been created.
Postconditions:	Return the number (secondary key) associated with the course for which the grade was issued.

(continued on next page)

135

Get Year Operation
Grade record has been created.
Postconditions: Return the year in which this grade was issued.
Get Semester Operation
Preconditions: Grade record has been created.
Postconditions: Return the semester (F or W) in which this grade was issued.
Get Grade Operation
Preconditions: Grade record has been created.
Postconditions: Return the letter grade that was earned in the course.
Get Grade Points Operation
Preconditions: Grade record has been created.
Postconditions: Return the number of grade points associated with letter grade for this course.

The design phase is arguably the most creative phase of the software development life cycle. Decisions made during this phase determine not only whether the final system meets the needs described in the user requirements specification, but also whether those needs are met in a fashion that is efficient and easy to maintain in the future.

For example, two design decisions emerging from the preceding CRC model of the system point toward a concern with storing unnecessary and redundant information in the student database. First, we can see from the description of the "Knows" section of the student record class that we have chosen not to store as data the total number of credits taken and earned and the cumulative grade-point average of a student. Rather, when requested, these values must be computed and returned through operations provided by the class. Clearly, these operations will have to traverse the list of grades that is known to the student record. This traversal will require time, so here we have traded the time required to perform these computations for the space that would have been required to store the information permanently as part of the student record.

Second, we can see from the description of the grade record class that we have chosen not to store the number of credits and course title as part of each grade record. Rather, a student record is given a reference to the course database, allowing it to look up the title and number of credits in this database when needed. The potential for saving space is quite significant here. We store the title for a course only once instead of in each grade record. Imagine that a school had 500 courses, each with a course title that averaged 20 characters. In the course database, storing these titles will require $500 * 20 = 10,000$ characters of storage. If the school had 10,000 students, each of whom had completed an average of 25 courses and if we had chosen to store the course title (redundantly) in each grade record, the cost of storing all these titles is $10,000 * 20 * 25 = 5,000,000$ characters of storage. Thus this decision made during the design phase of development will result in a system that is more space efficient by a factor of 50. Considerations of this kind can ultimately make or break a system in the real world.

EXERCISES 2.6

1. In Exercise 1 of Section 2.5, you wrote a user requirements specification for a software system you will use each month to maintain your checking account at a local bank. Now follow up on this analysis by doing a complete CRC design for the system.

2. In Exercise 2 of Section 2.5, you wrote a user requirements specification for a software system you will use to keep track of your musical CDs. Now follow up on this analysis by doing a complete CRC design for the system.

3. In Exercise 3 of Section 2.5, you wrote a user requirements specification for a software system that will be used to maintain statistics for your favorite sports team. Now follow up on this analysis by doing a complete CRC design for the system.

4. In Exercise 4 of Section 2.5, you wrote a user requirements specification for a software system that will be used by an administrative office at your school. Now follow up on this analysis by doing a complete CRC design for the system.

5. In Exercise 5 of Section 2.5 you wrote a user requirements specification for a system requested by the principal at American School of Basket Weaving. Now follow up on this analysis by doing a complete CRC design for the system.

2.7 The Implementation and Testing Phases of the Software Engineering Life Cycle

In the implementation phase, you must churn out the code in C++ (or another appropriate language) necessary to put into effect the blueprint developed in the design phase. Although the terminology "churn out" may seem a bit degrading considering the amount of effort that must go into writing a program, we use it to stress the importance of the design phase. Given an appropriate set of formal specifications from the design phase, coding the programs really can be an easy task. The completeness of the design phase is the key to determining how easy coding is. Time spent in the design phase will be more than repaid by time gained in coding. This point cannot be overemphasized! The most common mistake made by many beginning programmers is jumping almost immediately into the coding phase, thereby digging themselves into holes they could have avoided by more thorough consideration of design issues.

What do the experts in software engineering see as the appropriate breakdown of time to spend in each of the phases of the software development life cycle? Frederick Brooks, in *The Mythical Man-Month: 20th Anniversary Edition*, recommends the following rule of thumb:

- Planning (analysis and design): one-third of the project development time

- Coding (implementation): one-sixth of the project development time

- Component testing: one-fourth of the project development time

- System testing: one-fourth of the project development time

The fact that coding consumes only one-sixth of development time is consistent with our earlier statement that coding should be relatively easy if you have a good design from which to work. What might be surprising in Brooks's recommendations is that *half of the development time should be devoted to testing the code*. The message should be clear: If you fail to schedule a considerable amount of time to verify the correctness of your program, your users (or instructor) will inevitably find bugs in it.

Moreover, Brooks breaks this testing down into two phases: *component testing* and *system testing*. During component testing you are concerned with testing the individual classes in your system. When you do component testing, you will be writing short driver main programs to exercise each of the operations that a class provides, similar to what we did in Examples 2-1, 2-2, and 2-4 for the ordered collection, sorted collection, and one-key table classes, respectively. Once each component class has been thoroughly tested, you may plug the classes into the final system. System testing can begin *after* you are sure that each component in the system works in a completely reliable fashion. Often, during system testing, you will go so far as to get end users involved in testing the software. By observing their reactions as they work with the system, you can fine-tune it to be sure that it does everything they want in a satisfactory fashion.

Given the heavy emphasis placed on component testing, we need to develop effective strategies for doing it. The first point to consider as you begin to test the classes that make up a system is the order in which they should be tested. Here's where the "collaborator" part of CRC modeling is very useful. Suppose that the operations for class X that are specified in a CRC model identify class Y as a collaborator. Then, clearly, we cannot test the operations for class X until class Y has been implemented and tested. Hence, the order in which classes should be implemented and tested may be extracted from the CRC model.

A much tougher question than establishing the order in which classes should be tested is, given a particular operation to be tested, how much should it be tested before we can conclude that it is correctly implemented? This question is critical because it cuts to the core of the software reliability issue. As this lesson's Programming Skills features will attest, software reliability is not only a technical issue but also a moral and ethical one. Just as we design software, we must also systematically design the test cases to verify that software is correct. When we design test cases for a module, we must be sure to exercise all the logical possibilities the module may encounter. Be aware that such test cases consist of more than just strategically chosen input data. Each set of input data must also include its expected result (sometimes called the *test oracle*) if it is truly to convince anyone of the module's correctness.

In designing test cases, programmers begin to mix methods of science and art. Every mathematician knows that we can never actually prove anything by testing examples (that is, input data). So how can we verify a module's correctness by merely concocting examples? One proposed answer is to classify input data according to possible testing conditions. Hence, a finite set of well-chosen **equivalence classes** of test cases can be sufficient to cover an infinite number of possible inputs. Deciding what such equivalence classes should be is the point at which the process becomes more of an art than a science.

Example 2-11

To illustrate these principles, consider the fee structure at the E-Z Park parking lot. Parking fees for vehicles are based on the following rules:

The module is given two data items: a character, which may be "C" or "T" indicating whether the vehicle is a car or truck, and an integer number indicating the number of hours the vehicle spent in the parking lot. Cars are charged $1.00 for each of their first three hours in the lot and $0.50 for each hour after that. Trucks are charged $2.00 for each of their first four hours in the lot and $0.75 per hour thereafter.

After computing the appropriate charge, a new module (computeParkingFee) is to call on another new module (prettyPrintTicket), which appropriately formats a parking fee ticket showing the vehicle type, hours parked, and resulting fee. The computeParkingFee module is given here:

```
// Function: computeParkingFee
//
// Task: computes charge for parking and calls prettyPrintTicket to
//       output ticket
// Inputs: vehicle type in vehicle category and time spent in hours

void computeParkingFee (char vehicleCategory, int hours)
{
    double charge;

    switch (vehicleCategory)
    {
        case 'C':   if (hours <= 3)
                            charge = hours;
                    else
                            charge = 3 + (hours - 3) * .5;
                    break;
        case 'T':   if (hours <= 4)
                            charge = hours * 2;
                    else
                            charge = 8 + (hours - 4) * .75;
    }
    prettyPrintTicket(vehicleCategory, hours, charge);
}
```

An appropriate driver main program would simply allow us to repeatedly send data to the computeParkingFee module to check its behavior in a variety of situations. An appropriate stub for the call to prettyPrintTicket would merely inform us that we reached this subordinate module and print the values received so that we could be sure they had been transmitted correctly. At this stage, the stub need not concern itself with detailed, formatted output; we are at the moment interested only in testing computeParkingFee.

In testing this module, we can begin by identifying the following six equivalence classes:

1. A car in the lot less than three hours

2. A car in the lot exactly three hours

3. A car in the lot more than three hours

4. A truck in the lot less than four hours

5. A truck in the lot exactly four hours

6. A truck in the lot more than four hours

Choosing one test case for each equivalence class, we arrive at the following set of test cases:

Vehicle Category	Hours	Expected Results
C	2	Charge = 2.00
C	3	Charge = 3.00
C	5	Charge = 4.00
T	3	Charge = 6.00
T	4	Charge = 8.00
T	8	Charge = 11.00

The test cases for exactly three hours for a car and exactly four hours for a truck are particularly important because they represent **boundary conditions** at which a carelessly constructed conditional check could easily produce a wrong result.

This parking lot example, although illustrative of the method we wish to employ, is artificially simple. The next example presents a more complex testing situation.

Example 2-12

Consider developing a strategy to test the sorting algorithms we discussed in Lesson 1. Recall that each of these algorithms—bubble sort, insertion sort, and selection sort—received a vector of physical size MAX_LIST_SIZE and an integer n to indicate the logical size of the vector—that is, the number of items currently stored in the vector.

Our criterion for choosing equivalence classes of test data for such a sorting algorithm is based on two factors:

1. The size of n, the number of items to be sorted

2. The ordering of the original data

The following table presents a partitioning of test data into equivalence classes for this example.

Size of n	Order of Original Data	Expected Results
n = 1	Not applicable	Vector to be arranged in
n = 2	Ascending	ascending order
n = 2	Descending	for all cases
n midsize and even	Descending	

(continued on next page)

Size of n	Order of Original Data	Expected Results
n midsize and even	Ascending	
n midsize and even	Randomized	
n midsize and odd	Ascending	
n midsize and odd	Descending	
n midsize and odd	Randomized	
n = physical vector size	Ascending	
n = physical vector size	Descending	
n = physical vector size	Randomized	

The module should be run for a minimum of 12 cases, one for each of the classes dictated by our table. Ideally, a few subcases should be run for each of the randomized cases. We cannot overemphasize the importance of testing seemingly trivial cases such as n = 1 and n = 2. These lower boundary conditions are typical examples of data that may cause an otherwise perfectly functioning loop to be incorrectly skipped. Similarly, it is important to test the upper boundary condition in which n reaches the physical vector size.

White Box/Black Box Testing

One factor that can influence the design of test cases is the knowledge you have of the design and implementation of the component being tested. If you have detailed knowledge of the design and implementation, you can engage in *white box testing.* That is, the module represents a "white box" because you are aware of the internal logic and data structure implementations in the module. In white box testing, test cases can be partitioned into equivalence classes that specifically exercise each logical path through a module. In *black box testing,* the module is approached without knowledge of its internal structure. You know what the module is supposed to do, but not how it does it.

Example 2-13

For instance, suppose that we want to test the retrieve operation for the one-key table class that we developed in Section 2.3. In both implementation strategies discussed for this class, we have used a vector of associations in which the physical size of the vector was established by the constant MAX_TABLE_SIZE. The physically ordered vector implementation maintained the vector by key so that a binary search algorithm could be used to find the data efficiently. The following table provides a set of test cases for the retrieve operation assuming that the physically ordered vector implementation has been used.

Test Case	Number of Keys in Table (Assume That Physical Capacity is 10)	Physical Ordering of Keys	Value to Retrieve	Expected Results	Rationale
I	10	ALLEN BAKER DAVIS GREEN HUFF MILLER NOLAN PAYTON SMITH TAYLOR	Try each key in the table	*true* should be returned as the value of the function. The data associated with the key should be returned in the element parameter.	Can we find everything in the physically full table?
II	10	Same as test case I	Try AARON NATHAN ZEBRA	*false* returned as the value of the function	Is *false* correctly returned when the table is physically full and the value being sought (1) precedes all keys in the table, (2) is interspersed with keys in the middle of the table, or (3) follows all keys in the table?
III	5	ALLEN DAVIS HUFF NOLAN SMITH	Same as test case I	Same as test case I	Can we find every thing in a mid-size table?
IV	5	Same as test case III	Same as test case II	Same as test case II	Same as test case II but for mid-size list
V	1	HUFF	HUFF	Same as test case I	Can we handle a successful search in a table with just one key?
VI	1	HUFF	Same as test case II	Same as test case II	Can we handle a successful search in a table with just one key?

(continued on next page)

Test Case	Number of Keys in Table (Assume That Physical Capacity is 10)	Physical Ordering of Keys	Value to Retrieve	Expected Results	Rationale
VII	0		HUFF	Same as test case II	Boundary condition. Will we always return *false* when the table is empty?

This set of values is a white box set of test data because in test cases II and IV we make explicit use of the knowledge that the data are physically ordered. Also, in test cases I and II, we make explicit use of knowledge that there is a physical limit on the amount of data that may be stored in the table. The situation in which the table is full to its physical capacity represents a boundary condition for the algorithm; we are aware of this condition because we are testing from a white box perspective. If we were testing from a black box perspective, it might not be possible to exercise all such boundary conditions.

PROGRAMMING SKILLS: Software Reliability and Defense Systems

The issue of software testing takes on great importance as we begin to rely increasingly on the computer as an aid in the decision-making process. In the late 1980s, a nationwide debate began about the degree to which computerized weapons should be used in military and defense systems. Perhaps the most famous aspect of this debate was the notorious "Star Wars" system, envisioned as a computer-controlled multilayer defense against nuclear ballistic missiles. Experience with much smaller weapons systems in the 1990s has illustrated the pitfalls that can occur when testing such systems.

For example, during the Persian Gulf war, Peter G. Neumann reports in *Computer-Related Risks* (ACM Press, 1995) that initial early reports of the success of computerized Patriot missile systems had to be downgraded from 95% successful to 13% successful. Part of the reason was that the system had been designed and tested to work under a much less stringent environment than that in which it was used in the war. According to Neumann, a clock drift error that surfaced when the Patriot systems were used for more than 100 consecutive hours resulted in tracking errors that were responsible for a Patriot missile missing a targeted Scud missile that eventually crashed into an American military barracks, killing 29 and injuring 97.

This clock drift problem resulted from something as obscure as software that used two different machine representations of the number 0.1. Because 0.1 cannot be represented with complete accuracy in the binary floating-point hardware of any computer, using two different representations resulted in two numbers being viewed as not equal when in fact they should have been equal. Although this discrepancy did not surface in the shorter usage times that were specified in the original requirements for the Patriot system, it resulted in serious clock problems when the systems were pushed beyond these requirements.

143

The problems in establishing the reliability of computerized military systems remain a thorny issue with serious ethical implications. According to Jeff Johnson in "The military impact of information technology," *Communications of the ACM*, vol. 40, no. 4, April 1997, pp. 20–22:

> *Computers and IT (information technology) are effective mainly when the application area is ordered and predictable (i.e., when the level of chaos and entropy is fairly low). War, however, is the epitome of a chaotic, highly entropic environment. It is a breakdown of rational human behavior. In short, war and armed conflict is one of the application areas to which IT is least applicable. Put crudely, when all hell breaks loose, computers are at their worst. That computer-controlled robot drone may work fine in the lab or on the testing range, but the situations encountered in battle are by the very nature of war new and unique.*

EXERCISES 2.7

1. Summarize what is involved in each of the phases of the software engineering life cycle. If you were to specialize your career in one of these phases, which would it be? Why? Provide your answer in essay form.

2. What is meant by the term *boundary conditions* for an algorithm?

3. Employees at the School of Hard Knocks are paid by the following rules:
   a. Employees who sign a contract for a total annual wage are paid 1/52 of that amount each week.
   b. Hourly employees receive a paycheck based on the number of hours they work in a given week and their hourly rate. They are paid this hourly rate for each of the first 40 hours they work. After 40 hours, they are paid time-and-a-half for each additional hour of work. Moreover, work on a holiday is a special case for hourly employees. They are paid double-time for all holiday work.

   Write a function to compute the pay for an employee of the School of Hard Knocks and then dispatch the appropriate information to a check printing module. Completely test the function you write by integrating it with appropriate driver and stub modules and by designing a complete set of test data for the module.

4. Develop a complete set of test data for each of the operations of the ordered collection ADT. Present your answers using tables in the style of those in Examples 2-11, 2-12, and 2-13.

5. Develop a complete set of test data for each of the operations of the sorted collection ADT. Present your answers using tables in the style of those in Examples 2-11, 2-12, and 2-13.

6. Develop a complete set of test data for each of the operations of the one-key table ADT. Present your answers using tables in the style of those in Examples 2-11, 2-12, and 2-13.

7. Develop a complete set of test data for each of the operations of the two-key table ADT. Present your answers using tables in the style of those in Examples 2-11, 2-12, and 2-13.

EXERCISES ⇨ 2.7 CONTINUED

8. This section has presented a strategy for testing that emphasized the design of equivalence classes of test cases to exercise all logical possibilities that a module may encounter. You are working on a software system with a friend who claims that such comprehensive testing is impossible. As evidence, the friend cites a module she has written with 20 `if` statements in it. Your friend points out that approximately 2^{20} logical paths through this module are possible and that comprehensive testing of the module is therefore, impossible. In a written essay, describe a strategy that your friend could follow to solve this dilemma.

CASE STUDY: Finishing the Hard Knocks Grade-Reporting System

In Sections 2.5 and 2.6, we made substantial progress in analyzing and designing the grade-reporting system. We will use the Case Study section of this lesson to finish that work. Source code files for the case study have been provided—see your instructor.

Analysis

To complete our analysis of the system, we will show some examples of the way in which we envision users interacting with the system. Showing end users such examples before the actual implementation of the system has proceeded too far is representative of an analysis technique known as *iterative prototyping.* Using this method, analysts construct a simplified model of a system that performs just the essential functions. Implementers then get this model up and running very quickly as a prototype of the entire system. Users can react to the prototype and work with the analysts to refine the requirements for the system. Data abstraction and object-oriented design make it relatively painless to change underlying implementations of operations that require refinements without disturbing other aspects of the system.

```
SAMPLE OF DIALOGUE TO INSPECT A STUDENT RECORD

[A]dd, [D]elete, [U]pdate, [I]nspect, [G]rades, [E]nd-of-year, [Q]uit -->i
Student name in form 'Last,First' --> Smart,Bea

                      Name    Taken   Earned   GPA
                  Smart,Bea     22      22     3.14

    DEPT   NUMBER                    COURSE TITLE  CREDITS   GRADE
    CHEM    101          Introductory Chemistry       5        B
    MATH    200                      Calculus I       5        A
    MATH    201                     Calculus II       5        A
     ENG    200            English Composition        3        C
    CMSC    100          Introductory Programming      4        C
```

SAMPLE OF DIALOGUE TO ADD AND UPDATE STUDENT RECORD

```
[A]dd, [D]elete, [U]pdate, [I]nspect, [G]rades, [E]nd-of-year, [Q]uit -->a
Student name in form 'Last,First' --> Sosa,Sammy

[A]dd, [D]elete, [U]pdate, [I]nspect, [G]rades, [E]nd-of-year, [Q]uit -->u
Student name in form 'Last,First' --> Sosa,Sammy
Enter department for course (**** to quit) --> MATH
Enter course number, year, semester (F or W), and letter grade -->202 1999
W B
Enter department for another course for this student (**** to quit) --> CMSC
Enter course number, year, semester (F or W), and letter grade -->342 1999
W C
Enter department for another course for this student (**** to quit) --> ****
```

SAMPLE DIALOGUE TO PRODUCE GRADE REPORTS

```
[A]dd, [D]elete, [U]pdate, [I]nspect, [G]rades, [E]nd-of-year, [Q]uit -->g
Enter year (19XX or 20XX) and semester (F or W) --> 1999 W
                        .
                        .
                        .
```

Name	Cum. Cr. Taken	Cum. Cr. Earned	Cum. GPA
Smart,Bea	22	22	3.14

For the semester 1999W the student's course record is:

DEPT	NUMBER	COURSE TITLE	CREDITS	GRADE
MATH	201	Calculus II	5	A
ENG	200	English Composition	3	C
CMSC	100	Introductory Programming	4	C

Name	Cum. Cr. Taken	Cum. Cr. Earned	Cum. GPA
Sosa,Sammy	8	8	2.63

For the semester 1999W the student's course record is:

DEPT	NUMBER	COURSE TITLE	CREDITS	GRADE
MATH	202	Calculus III	5	B
CMSC	342	Programming Languages	3	C

SAMPLE OF DIALOGUE TO REMOVE A STUDENT RECORD FROM THE SYSTEM

```
[A]dd, [D]elete, [U]pdate, [I]nspect, [G]rades, [E]nd-of-year, [Q]uit -->i
Student name in form 'Last,First' --> Egghead,Irma
```

```
                  Name    Taken   Earned    GPA
           Egghead,Irma     22      22      3.77

    DEPT   NUMBER                     COURSE TITLE  CREDITS    GRADE
     BIO    101          Introductory Biology          5        A
    MATH    200                    Calculus I          5        A
    MATH    201                    Calculus II         5        B
     ENG    200            English Composition         3        A
    CMSC    100       Introductory Programming         4        A
```

```
[A]dd, [D]elete, [U]pdate, [I]nspect, [G]rades, [E]nd-of-year, [Q]uit -->d
Student name in form 'Last,First' --> Egghead,Irma
[A]dd, [D]elete, [U]pdate, [I]nspect, [G]rades, [E]nd-of-year, [Q]uit -->i
Student name in form 'Last,First' --> Egghead,Irma
Student Egghead,Irma not found in database
```

<u>**PRODUCTION OF END-OF-YEAR REPORTS (10 CREDITS USED AS GRADUATION CUTOFF)**</u>

```
[A]dd, [D]elete, [U]pdate, [I]nspect, [G]rades, [E]nd-of-year, [Q]uit -->e

              Grad list in alphabetical order
                  Name    Taken   Earned    GPA
           Average,Joe      22      19      1.50
             Smart,Bea      22      22      3.14

                  Grad list in GPA order
                  Name    Taken   Earned    GPA
             Smart,Bea      22      22      3.14
           Average,Joe      22      19      1.50
```

Design

The CRC design that we developed in Section 2.6 has set the stage for providing the various C++ header files needed by the system.

Main Menu Class

```cpp
// Class declaration file: menu.h

#ifndef MENU_H

#include "apstring.h"
#include "studentDb.h"
#include "courseRec.h"
#include "gradeRec.h"
#include "studentRec.h"
#include <iostream.h>
#include <iomanip.h>
```

147

```
class menu
{
   public:

   // Constructors
   menu(studentDb & sd);
   menu(const menu &m);

   // Member functions

   menu& operator = (const menu &m);
   void start();

   protected:

   // Member functions
   void addDialogue();
   void deleteDialogue();
   void updateDialogue();
   void inspectDialogue();
   void reportDialogue();

   // Data members
   studentDb & studentRecords;
};

#define MENU_H
#endif
```

Student Database Class

```
// Class declaration file: studentDb.h

#ifndef STUDENTDB_H

#include <fstream.h>
#include <iostream.h>
#include <iomanip.h>
#include "apstring.h"
#include "apvector.h"
#include "studentRec.h"
#include "courseRec.h"
#include "onetable.h"
#include "twotable.h"
```

```
class studentDb : public OneKeyTable<apstring, studentRec>
{
  public:

  // Constructors
  studentDb();
  studentDb(const studentDb &db);

  // Member functions

  studentDb& operator = (const studentDb &table);
  void addStudent(const apstring &studentName);
  bool studentExists(const apstring &studentName);
  bool deleteStudent(const apstring &studentName);
  bool inspectStudent(const apstring &studentName);
  bool addCourse(const apstring &studentName, const gradeRec &newCourse);
  void gradeReports(int year, char semester);
  void graduationListByName();
  void graduationListByGpa();

  protected:

  // Data members

  TwoKeyTable<apstring, int, courseRec> courseDb;
};

#define STUDENTDB_H
#endif
```

Course Database Class

This class will just be a two-key table with an `apstring` (for the department code) as primary key, an `int` (for course number) as secondary key, and a `courseRec` as element type.

List of Grade Records Class

This class will just be an ordered collection, with each element of the collection being a member of the `gradeRec` class.

Student Record Class

```
// Class declaration file: studentRec.h

#ifndef STUDENTREC_H

#include "apstring.h"
#include "gradeRec.h"
```

```cpp
#include "ordercol.h"
#include "twotable.h"
#include "courseRec.h"
#include <iostream.h>
#include <iomanip.h>

// Declaration section
class studentRec
{

    public:

    // Class constructors

    studentRec();
    studentRec(TwoKeyTable<apstring, int, courseRec> * courseDatabase);
    studentRec(const studentRec &sr);

    // Function members

    studentRec& operator = (const studentRec &table);
    int getCreditsTaken();
    int getCreditsEarned();
    double getGpa();
    void addCourse(const gradeRec &gr);
    void displayCourseHistory();
    void displayCourseHistory(int year, char semester);

    protected:

    // Data members

    OrderedCollection<gradeRec> coursesTaken;
    TwoKeyTable<apstring, int, courseRec> * courseDb;

};

#define STUDENTREC_H
#endif
```

Course Record Class

```cpp
// Class declaration file: courseRec.h

#ifndef COURSEREC_H

#include "apstring.h"
```

```
// Declaration section
class courseRec
{

   public:

   // Class constructors

   courseRec();
   courseRec(const apstring &title, const int credits);
   courseRec(const courseRec &cr);

   // Function members

   courseRec& operator = (const courseRec &table);
   apstring getTitle();
   int getcredits();

   protected:

   // Data members

   apstring title;
   int credits;

};

#define COURSEREC_H
#endif
```

PROGRAMMING SKILLS: The (Lack of) Responsibility of Software Developers

If you have ever purchased software such as a word processor or spreadsheet for a microcomputer, you have probably signed a license agreement in which you agree not to copy the software except for your own backup protection. The fine print in such software licenses also typically contains disclaimers about the responsibility of the software developer should you eventually do something such as underpay your income tax because of a bug in the spreadsheet you used to keep your tax records.

For instance, the second page of the user's guide of a popular spreadsheet program provides the following disclaimer of warranties. The actual company name (designated here as X) is not given. This disclaimer is typical of that used by virtually all software companies.

The software and user manuals are provided "as is" and without express or limited warranty of any kind by either X or anyone who has been involved in the creation, production, or distribution of the software, including, but not limited to, the implied warranties of merchantability and fitness for a particular purpose.

The entire risk as to the quality and performance of the software and user manuals is with you. Should the software and user manuals prove defective, you (and not X or anyone

151

else who has been involved in the creation, production, or distribution of the software) assume the entire cost of all necessary servicing, repair or correction.

Compare such a disclaimer to the claims that appear in the software ads that adorn all popular computing magazines and you will see a real contradiction. Products that profess to do virtually everything guarantee absolutely nothing.

Perhaps the reservations that software developers have about guaranteeing the reliability of their products should not be surprising given what we have learned about the software system life cycle. The complexity of software design and testing makes it virtually impossible to develop software that is 100% free of bugs. To customers in the software marketplace, the message is clear: Caveat emptor (Let the buyer beware)!

Grade Record Class

```cpp
// Class declaration file: gradeRec.h

#ifndef GRADEREC_H

#include "apstring.h"

// Declaration section
class gradeRec
{

    public:

    // Class constructors

    gradeRec();
    gradeRec(const apstring &dept, const int courseNum,
        const int year, const char semester, const char grade);
    gradeRec(const gradeRec &gr);

    // Function members

    gradeRec& operator = (const gradeRec &table);
    apstring getDept();
    int getCourseNum();
    int getYear();
    char getSemester();
    char getGrade();
    int getGradePts();

    protected:

    // Data members

    apstring dept;
```

```
      int courseNum;
      int year;
      char semester;
      char grade;

};

#define GRADEREC_H
#endif
```

There should be no surprises in the public member functions for these classes. They are a direct reflection, in C++ syntax, of the operations we have specified in the CRC design of Section 2.6. Some of the private data members require a bit more explanation, and that will be provided in the following discussion of implementation details.

Implementation

One interesting aspect of the CRC design methodology is that is totally object-oriented. Because of this fact, the main program that we are used to writing becomes almost superfluous.

```
// program file: grades.cpp

#include "studentDb.h"
#include "menu.h"

void main()
{
   studentDb studentRecords;

   menu mainMenu(studentRecords);

   mainMenu.start();

}
```

The main program must only construct the database of student records and the main menu and then "start" the main menu. The iterative logic that continually queries a user for the next operation is embedded in the start method of the menu class.

```
void menu::start()
{
   char choice;

   do {
      cout << "[A]dd, [D]elete, [U]pdate, [I]nspect, [G]rades, "
         << "[E]nd-of-year, [Q]uit -->";
      cin >> choice;
      cin.ignore(10, '\n');
      switch (choice)
      {
```

```
            case 'A':
            case 'a':
               addDialogue();
               break;
            case 'D':
            case 'd':
               deleteDialogue();
               break;
            case 'U':
            case 'u':
               updateDialogue();
               break;
            case 'I':
            case 'i':
               inspectDialogue();
               break;
            case 'G':
            case 'g':
               reportDialogue();
               break;
            case 'E':
            case 'e':
               studentRecords.graduationListByName();
               studentRecords.graduationListByGpa();
               break;
            case 'Q':
            case 'q':
               break;
            default:
               cout << "Invalid choice -- Please try again" << endl;
               break;
         }
      } while (choice != 'Q' && choice != 'q');
}
```

In the student database class, the constructor is responsible for initially loading the course data and the data for each student. These data are loaded from a text stream. The structure of that stream is documented in the following code.

```
studentDb::studentDb()
{
   apstring dept, title;
   int num, credits;
   apstring name;
   int year;
   char semester, grade;
   ifstream academicRecords;

   academicRecords.open("acad.dat");
```

```
// First load course information. Each course's data are on four
// lines -- department code, number, title, and credits.
// Course information is terminated with a line containing
// the sentinel ****
academicRecords >> dept;
while (dept != "****")
{
   academicRecords >> num;
   academicRecords.ignore(10, '\n');
   getline(academicRecords, title);
   academicRecords >> credits;
   courseRec cr(title, credits);
   courseDb.store(dept, num, cr);
   academicRecords >> dept;
}
academicRecords.ignore(10, '\n');

// Now read the data for each student, terminated by
// the sentinel ****
getline(academicRecords, name);
while (name != "****")
{
   addStudent(name);
   // For each student read grade records in form dept, number,
   // year, semester, and grade. Grade records for this student
   // are terminated with **** as a sentinel department code.
   academicRecords >> dept;
   while (dept != "****")
   {
      academicRecords >> num;
      academicRecords >> year;
      academicRecords >> semester;
      academicRecords >> grade;
      gradeRec gr(dept, num, year, semester, grade);
      addCourse(name, gr);
      academicRecords >> dept;
   }
   academicRecords.ignore(10, '\n');
   getline(academicRecords, name);
}
academicRecords.close();
}
```

Most of the code that remains for implementing the student database class will be left for you to do in the projects at the end of the lesson. A member function that merits special consideration, however, is the one that produces the graduation list ordered by descending grade-point average. The one-key table from which the student database class is derived uses a vector of keys that is physically ordered. Here the keys are student names, so going through the table alphabetically by name presents no problem. However, to go through in grade-point order, we must use the pointer sort technique described in Lesson 1.

```cpp
void studentDb::graduationListByGpa()
{
    apvector<int> pointers(MAX_TABLE_SIZE);         // Used for pointer sort
    int j, k, temp;
    bool exchangeMade;
    studentRec s1(&courseDb), s2(&courseDb);

    // First we do a pointer sort on the one-key table, using
    // GPA as the basis for comparison

    // Initialize pointer vector
    for (k = 0; k < tableLength; k++)
        pointers[k] = k;

    k = 0;
    exchangeMade = true;

    // Next order the pointers, based on GPA
    while ((k < tableLength - 1) && exchangeMade)
    {
        exchangeMade = false;
        k++;
        for (j = 0; j < tableLength - k; j++)
        {
            s1 = data[pointers[j]].getValue();
            s2 = data[pointers[j + 1]].getValue();
            if (s1.getGpa() < s2.getGpa())
            {
                temp = pointers[j];      // Swap pointers
                pointers[j] = pointers[j + 1];
                pointers[j + 1] = temp;
                exchangeMade = true;
            }
        }
    }

    // Now follow the pointers through the data

    apstring stName;
    studentRec st(&courseDb);

    cout << setw(50) << "Grad list in GPA order" << endl;
    cout << setw(30) << "Name" << setw(10) << "Taken" << setw(10)
        << "Earned" << setw(10) << "GPA" << endl;
    cout << setiosflags(ios::fixed) << setprecision(2);
```

```
for (int i = 0; i < tableLength; i++)
{
    stName = data[pointers[i]].getKey();
    st = data[pointers[i]].getValue();
    if (st.getCreditsEarned() >= 120)
        cout << setw(30) << stName << setw(10) << st.getCreditsTaken()
            << setw(10) << st.getCreditsEarned() << setw(10)
            << st.getGpa() << endl;
}

}
```

One additional consideration in implementing the grade-reporting system is the course database object that is a data member of the student database.

```
class studentDb : public OneKeyTable<apstring, studentRec>
{
    public:

        .
        .
        .

    // Data members

    TwoKeyTable<apstring, int, courseRec> courseDb;
};
```

Not only does the student database need to know about the course database, but each student record object in the student database must also have access to the course database. For example, the displayCourseHistory function in the studentRec class will have to traverse the ordered collection of gradeRec objects for that student and display the title and number of credits attached to each course for which the student received a grade.

In Section 2.6, we made the design decision not to store the course title and number of credits along with each grade to save a considerable amount of storage. Instead, as this collection is traversed, the displayCourseHistory function will use the course department code and number to pull the necessary information from its central repository in the course database. Now we must consider the following question: As each student record must know the course database, do we really want to declare such an object in each student record? The course database is likely to require quite a bit of storage, and if we allocate such an object in each student record, we are likely to pay a stiff price in the amount of space used.

An alternative will give us the best of both worlds—that is, the capability for a student record to access the database without paying a large price in storage. That alternative is to give each student record a reference to the course database instead of a full-fledged copy of the course database. We can declare such a reference to an object by using a pointer. You were introduced to this notion in Section 1.3 and will continue to explore it at length in the next lesson. A pointer to an object is declared using the ***dereference operator*** (*). Compare the declaration of the course database in the `studentRec` class to that given earlier in the `studentDb` class. Notice the dereference operator in front of `courseDbPtr` in the `studentRec` class and the lack of that operator for the corresponding declaration in the `studentDb` class.

```
class studentRec
{

   public:
   .
   .
   .
   protected:

   // Data members

   OrderedCollection<gradeRec> coursesTaken;
   TwoKeyTable<apstring, int, courseRec> * courseDbPtr;


};
```

The difference between these two declarations is that the latter declares an actual instance of a course database object, whereas the former declares a pointer to such an object. Pointers store a memory address where the object can be found instead of the object itself. This concept is highlighted in Figure 2-8.

FIGURE 2-8

Each student record in the student database contains a pointer to the central course database

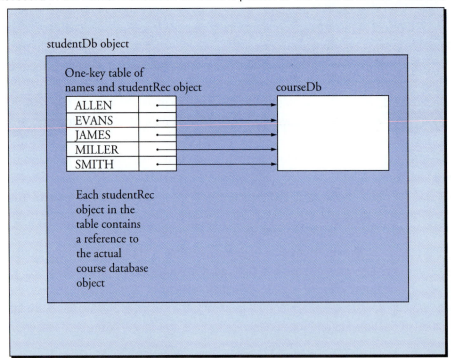

The next question that arises is: If `courseDbPtr` in the `studentRec` class is merely a reference to a course database object, what notation do we use to get at the contents of the object itself? That's where the dereference operator comes into play. The dereference operator takes a pointer to an object and returns the object referenced by that pointer. Here is another way of thinking about this notion: If `p` is a pointer to an object of type `P`, then `*p` is the object of type `P` to which `p` points.

In Figure 2-8, the `courseDbPtr` member in each `studentRec` object represents the address of the `courseDb` member of the `studentDb` class. Hence, for the `studentRec` object to get at the contents of `courseDb`, it must use the dereferencing notation `*courseDbPtr`. For the `courseDbPtr` member in each `studentRec` object to be "aimed at" the location where `courseDb` resides, `courseDbPtr` will have to be initialized with the memory address of `courseDb`. For this type of initialization, C++ provides the ampersand (`&`) in its role as the "address-of" operator. Here is how you should think about the address-of operator: If `p` is declared to be a pointer to an object of type `P` and `q` is declared to be an instance of an object of type `P`, then the assignment `p = &q` will make `p` point at where `q` resides. Thereafter, `*p` can be used to refer to the contents of `q`. For instance, the following code segment will output the number 5 twice.

```
int q = 5;
int * p;

p = &q;
cout << q << endl;
cout << *p << endl;
```

You will investigate pointers much more in the following lesson, but now we know enough to use them in the context of the grade-reporting system. First, consider the constructor for a `studentRec` object. Here, using an initializer list, `courseDbPtr` is initialized to the `courseDatabase` pointer that is passed to the constructor.

```
studentRec::studentRec(TwoKeyTable<apstring, int, courseRec> *
courseDatabase)
    : coursesTaken(), courseDbPtr(courseDatabase)
{
}
```

In the `studentDb` class, when a new student record is added to the database, the constructor for a `studentRec` is called, passing it the address of the `courseDb` object embedded in the `studentDb` class.

```
void studentDb::addStudent(const apstring &studentName)
{
  studentRec initialEmptyRec(&courseDb);    // Construct with
                                            // address of courseDb

  store(studentName, initialEmptyRec);
}
```

159

In the `studentRec` class, when we implement operations that must access the course database, the `*courseDbPtr` notation may be used. Here, code for the `displayCourseHistory()` and `getGpa()` functions is provided to illustrate use of this notation.

```
double studentRec::getGpa()
{
  int taken = 0;
  int gradePoints = 0;
  int numCourses = coursesTaken.length();
  courseRec cr;

  for (int k = 0; k < numCourses; k++)
  {
     (*courseDbPtr).retrieve(coursesTaken[k].getDept(),
                        coursesTaken[k].getCourseNum(), cr);
     taken += cr.getcredits();
     gradePoints += cr.getcredits() * coursesTaken[k].getGradePts();
  }
  if (taken != 0)
     return ((double) gradePoints) / ((double) taken);
  else
     return 0.0;
}

void studentRec::displayCourseHistory()
{
  int numCourses = coursesTaken.length();
  courseRec cr;

  cout << setw(8) << "DEPT" << setw(8) << "NUMBER" << setw(35)
     << "COURSE TITLE" << setw(8)
     << "CREDITS" << setw(8) << "GRADE" << endl;
  for (int k = 0; k < numCourses; k++)
  {
     (*courseDbPtr).retrieve(coursesTaken[k].getDept(),
                        coursesTaken[k].getCourseNum(),cr);
     cout << setw(8) << coursesTaken[k].getDept()
        << setw(8) << coursesTaken[k].getCourseNum()
        << setw(35) << cr.getTitle()
        << setw(8) << cr.getcredits()
        << setw(8) << coursesTaken[k].getGrade() << endl;
  }
}
```

The key statement in each of these functions is:

```
     (*courseDbPtr).retrieve(coursesTaken[k].getDept(),
                        coursesTaken[k].getCourseNum(), cr);
```

Here we want to retrieve a course record from the course database. `(*courseDbPtr).
retrieve` uses the `*` dereference operator to accomplish this task and invoke the `retrieve`
function for the course database two-key table. The first argument to `retrieve`—that is,
`coursesTaken[k].getDept()`—provides the primary key for this retrieve operation. The second
argument, `coursesTaken[k].getCourseNum()`, provides the secondary key. The third argument
`cr` stores the `courseRec` information that is retrieved. Although this notation may seem unusual
now, you will become more familiar with it as you work through the next lesson.

Running, Debugging, and Testing Hints

- When accessing an ADT, use only those operations specified in the ADT definition. This guideline is the ADT use rule. For instance, it is wrong to access an object in a one-key table by referring to its vector index. This approach assures that the implementor of the ADT is storing data in a vector. Such an assumption is not warranted according to the definition of this ADT.

- When writing the implementation of an ADT, be sure that the functions you develop obey the interface established by the ADT's definition. This guideline is the ADT implementation rule. For instance, if you, as implementor, need a counter to keep track of the number of objects in a one-key table, don't add the counter as an extra parameter in function calls. Instead, encapsulate it as a private or protected data member of the implementation.

- When providing the implementation of an ADT, be sure that each individual operation is thoroughly tested and debugged before it is used by higher-level logic. Then, if errors occur when higher-level modules execute, you know that these errors result from algorithms that use the ADT and are not in the implementation of the ADT.

- Do not underestimate the importance of the create operation for an ADT. From the implementor's perspective, this operation is where crucial initializations occur that will ensure the smooth functioning of other operations. From the perspective of the user of the ADT, you must be sure to call the create operation for each instance of a variable of that type. Failing to do so will usually lead to very bizarre program behavior.

- When testing a large program, always test modules individually before testing the entire system.

- When developing test cases, keep them in a file so that they can be readily used again after fixing errors.

- Be sure to design test data that exercise the boundary conditions of a module, which are where an error is most likely to occur.

Summary

In this lesson, you learned:

- Computer scientists engage in a modeling process as they develop software to satisfy users' needs. In this respect, the way in which a computer scientist works parallels the engineering profession. Consequently, this systematic approach toward the development of successful software is often called software engineering.

161

- Abstract data types are defined apart from considerations of their implementation in a particular programming language. A complete definition for an abstract data type must include a description of the individual elements, the relationship between these individual elements, and the operations that can be performed on them. These operations are conveniently specified as function and function declarations.

- The ADT use rule, the ADT implementation rule, and the ADT layering rule are guidelines governing the relationship between implementations of an ADT and higher-level algorithms using that implementation.

- We must often determine which of a variety of implementations is best in terms of time and space efficiency for a particular application.

- The logical size of a vector is the number of data elements currently stored in it; this size may differ from the vector's physical size.

- An ordered collection enables users to work with just the logical size of a vector of data elements.

- A sorted collection enables users to work with a vector of data elements whose alphabetical ordering is maintained automatically.

- The one-key table is an ADT characterized by operations that store, retrieve, or remove data. All of these operations are performed relative to a particular key value.

- A physically ordered vector with binary search and an unordered vector with pointer sort are two ways of implementing a one-key table.

- The two-key table is an ADT characterized by operations that store, retrieve, or remove data. All of these operations are performed relative to two particular key values.

- A two-dimensional vector and a one-key table of one-key tables are two ways of implementing a two-key table.

- During the analysis phase of the software system life cycle, you must determine the user's requirements. Typically, this effort involves considerable interaction between the systems analyst and the end user. A user requirements specification is one example of a document that is developed during this phase. Ultimately, the user's requirements must be described in a form suitable to pass on to the design phase.

- During the design phase, the user's requirements are examined, and the system that will ultimately meet these requirements begins to take shape. Software designers must turn out a blueprint of the eventual software system that can then be translated into program code. CRC modeling produces documents typical of those produced during the design phase.

- Testing and verification can consume up to 50% of the time spent in developing a software system. Each component should be tested as it is finished. Use drivers to feed inputs into the module and stubs to check the module's interactions with subordinate modules.

- System testing follows modular testing.

- The maintenance phase of a system follows its release to users. During this phase, adjustments must be made to the system in response to bugs and changes in user requirements.

VOCABULARY REVIEW

Define the following terms:

abstract data type (ADT)

ADT implementation rule

ADT use rule

association

black box testing

boundary conditions

CRC modeling

dereference operator

equivalence classes

information hiding

iterative prototyping

logical size

one-key table

ordered collection

physical size

software system life cycle

two-key table

user requirements specification

white box testing

LESSON 2 REVIEW QUESTIONS

FILL IN THE BLANK

Complete the following sentences by writing the correct word or words in the blanks provided.

1. The design methodology that determines the classes needed, the responsibilities of each class, and the classes with which it will collaborate is called _____ modeling.

2. The rule that states, "Algorithms that use an abstract data type should only access variables of that ADT through the operations provided in the ADT definition," is called the _____ rule.

3. The rule that states, "An implementation of an abstract data type must provide an interface that is entirely consistent with the operations specified in the ADT's definition," is called the _____ rule.

4. When you test the individual classes in your system, you are performing _____ testing.

5. When you test an entire software package as a single unit, you are performing _____ testing.

6. If you have detailed knowledge of the design and implementation, you can engage in _____ testing.

7. In _____ testing, the module is approached without knowledge of its internal structure.

8. Values that test the limits of a conditional test are called _____ conditions.

9. The test _____ lists the results expected from a specific set of test data.

10. In the last phase of the software engineering life cycle, the _____ phase, new features may be added to the system and bugs found by users may be fixed.

WRITTEN QUESTIONS

Write a brief answer to the following questions.

11. How does C++ support the concept of data abstraction? Explain with an example.

12. Explain how the ordered collection data type keeps track of the physical size of a vector.

13. List two characteristics that the sorted collection ADT inherits from the ordered collection ADT. List one characteristic that is different from the ordered collection.

14. Explain the difference between a primary key and a secondary key in the two-key table ADT.

15. Consider the ADT date with the following operations:

    setDate(m, d, y)   set a date with the given month, day, and year
    display()   display a date
    advance(n)   advance a date by n days

    Using these ADT operations and dot notation, write a statement for each of the following tasks:

    a. Display the date one week from yesterday, assuming today's date is X.

    b. Jerry was born on March 21, 1971, and his sister is 450 days younger. When was Jerry's sister born?

16. The Pascal language supports the subrange data types. A subrange is a subinterval of an already-defined type. For example, the subrange 35..80 is a data type for which a variable can only contain an integer between 35 and 80, inclusive. Define the subrange ADT and then implement it in C++ so that it supports the following:

```
int main(void)
   {
      IntSubrange x(1,80), y(60,170);
      IntSubrange z(x);
      x = 50;                  // ok
      y = x * 2;               // ok
      z = y;                   // out of range error, z is not changed
      x = x * 2;               // out of range error, x is not changed
   }
```

LESSON 2 PROJECTS

PROJECT 2-1

Complete the implementation of the School of Hard Knocks grade-reporting system as discussed in Sections 2.5, 2.6, and 2.7 and in this lesson's Case Study. Be sure that you test each component individually before you proceed to a complete system test.

PROJECT 2-2

A set is a collection of unique data values in no particular order. Operations on sets include the following:

    empty

    length

    add (an item)

    remove (an item)

    includes (an item)

    union (of two sets)

    intersection (of two sets)

    difference (of two sets)

No other modifications or access to sets is allowed. All of the data values in a set must be of the same type. This element type must support comparisons. The union of two sets is the set of elements in both sets combined. The intersection of two sets is the set of elements they have in common. The difference of two sets is the set of elements produced by combining the elements in the two sets and then removing the elements of the second set that are not contained in the first set. No other modifications or access to a set is allowed.

Write formal specifications for a set class, declare and implement these operations in a C++ library, and test the class with an appropriate driver program. Use the + operator for union, the * operator for intersection, and the - operator for difference. (*Hint:* Use another class developed in this lesson to represent the data within a set.) When you've completed your implementation, provide a big-O analysis of the efficiency of each set operation.

PROJECT 2-3

The radix sort algorithm, presented in Section 1.4, uses the notion of bins: data repositories that contain numbers or strings in a particular category as the algorithm progresses. Formalize the concept of a bin for the radix sort algorithm by providing an ADT definition for it. Then provide an implementation for your bin ADT and use the operations provided by the bin ADT to write a high-level version of the radix sort.

PROJECT 2-4

The definition of the one-key table ADT in Section 2.3 specifies that each object in the list must have a unique key value—that is, a key value shared by no other value in the list. Consider a variation on this ADT in which we allow multiple records to share the same key value (for example, several people may have identical names). Call this ADT a one-key table with duplicate keys.

1. Provide a complete definition for this ADT. Be very precise about what happens for each of the `store`, `remove`, and `retrieve` operations. Do you need to add any new operations because of the possibility of duplicate keys?

2. Translate your definition from part 1 into a C++ interface for a one-key table with duplicate keys.

3. Develop an implementation for this ADT. Discuss in a written statement any limitations of your implementation relative to the definition and interface of parts 1 and 2.

4. Test your implementation by plugging it into an appropriate test driver.

PROJECT 2-5

Invite the principal of your school to your class to discuss the type of data processing operations in which his or her office is typically engaged. After this discussion (which should include time for questions), describe the data involved in the operations of the office in terms of abstract data types. Write a user requirements specification and develop a CRC design model for your principal's system.

PROJECT 2-6

Consider the following data declaration and function declaration:

```
enum KindOfTriangle {SCALENE, ISOSCELES, EQUILATERAL, IMPOSSIBLE};...

// Function: triangleType
// Task: determines the type of triangle, given the lengths of the three sides
//
// Inputs: three integers representing the lengths of the three sides of a
// triangle
// Output:
//    EQUILATERAL, if all sides are equal
//     ISOSCELES, if two sides are equal
//     SCALENE, if all sides are different lengths
//     IMPOSSIBLE, if the integers do not constitute valid triangle sides

KindOfTriangle triangleType (double side1, double side2, double side3);
```

For this project, work with another student. Each of you should develop independently, first, the function just described and, second, a complete set of test data for the function. Next, jointly develop a driver program and test your functions. Have your partner use his or her test data on the function you developed. Then use your test data on your partner's function. The winner is the one whose function fails for the fewer number of test cases.

PROJECT 2-7

In Exercise 1 of Exercises 2.6, you designed a system for a software system you will use each month to maintain your checking account at a local bank. Implement and fully test that system.

PROJECT 2-8

In Exercise 2 of Exercises 2.6, you designed a system for a software system you will use to keep track of your musical CDs. Implement and fully test that system.

PROJECT 2-9

In Exercise 3 of Exercises 2.6, you designed a system for a software system that will be used to maintain statistics for your favorite sports team. Implement and fully test that system.

PROJECT 2-10

In Exercise 4 of Exercises 2.6, you designed a system for a software system that will be used by an administrative office at your school. Implement and fully test that system.

PROJECT 2-11

In Exercise 5 of Exercises 2.6 you designed a system for a system requested by the principal at American School of Basket Weaving. Implement and fully test that system.

CRITICAL THINKING

ACTIVITY 2-1

Suppose that you are computer operations manager for Wing-and-a-Prayer Airlines. In that role, you receive the following important memorandum:

MEMORANDUM
Wing-and-a-Prayer Airlines

TO: Computer Operations Manager
FROM: Vice President in Charge of Scheduling
DATE: August 28, 2001
RE: Matching flights and pilots

As you know, we presently have 1500 flights (uniquely identified by flight number) and employ 1400 pilots (uniquely identified by their last name and first initial) to fly them. However, because of factors such as type of airplane, amount of pilot experience, pilot geographic locations, and FAA regulations, each of our pilots qualifies to fly on only a relatively small percentage of flights. To help our schedulers, we frequently need to answer questions such as the following:

1. Given a flight, what are the names of the pilots qualified to fly it?

167

2. Given a pilot's name, what are the flight numbers that pilot is qualified to fly?
3. Given a flight's number and a pilot's name, do we have a match? In other words, is the specified pilot qualified for the particular flight?

Right now, our schedulers attempt to answer such questions by time-consuming manual methods. I'm sure that you can easily computerize this task for them. Thanks in advance for your help in this matter.

Carry out a complete analysis, design, implementation, and testing of the system requested in this memo. The document produced by your analysis should be a user requirements specification. Your design should produce a CRC model.

ACTIVITY 2-2

Design, implement, and test a program that takes a text file as input and displays an alphabetical list of unique words that appear in the file and their associated frequencies. The frequency of a word is the number of times that it occurs in the file. A word is any string of characters surrounded by white space characters. Case should be ignored in the spelling of words. As an added challenge, include a feature in your program that allows the user to select the sorted order for the list of words—alphabetically or in descending order by frequency of occurrence. (*Hint:* Your task will be much easier if you use one of the ADTs developed in this lesson.)

U N I T

1
REVIEW

UNIT 1 REVIEW QUESTIONS

TRUE/FALSE

Circle T if the statement is true or F if the statement is false.

T F **1.** When you go through a list of names, from beginning to end, until you reach the one you need, you are performing a binary search.

T F **2.** The sort characterized by first locating the smallest item in a list and moving it to the first location, then finding the second smallest item and moving it to the second location, and so forth, is called the selection sort.

T F **3.** When you locate a person's name in a directory by opening the book about at the middle, determining whether the name is before or after that page, going to the approximate center of the remaining portion, and repeating this process until you find the page with the name, you are performing a sequential search.

T F **4.** The sort algorithm characterized by some data sinking while other data percolates is the insertion sort.

T F **5.** The binary search has a worst case running time of $O(n)$.

T F **6.** White box testing approaches a module without knowledge of its internal structure.

T F **7.** An ordered collection tracks its logical size and makes this quantity available to users.

T F **8.** A sorted collection allows all of the operations to users that an ordered collection does.

T F **9.** During the analysis phase of the software system life cycle, reported bugs are fixed and new features are added to the software.

T F **10.** Integration testing occurs during the testing of each individual unit of a software system.

FILL IN THE BLANK

Complete the following sentences by writing the correct word or words in the blanks provided.

1. ADT stands for _____.

2. The logical size of an array can be different from its _____.

3. User requirements are formalized into a precise set of specifications during the _____ phase of the software system life cycle.

4. A bubble sort and a selection sort have an average running time of _____.

5. Of the selection sort, bubble sort, and insertion sort, the _____ behaves better as the list becomes more completely sorted.

6. Of the selection sort, bubble sort, and insertion sort, the fewest number of data exchanges in the worst case occurs in the _____ and is equal to _____.

7. The radix sort is _____ in running time.

8. A(n) _____ associates a set of keys and values.

9. The _____ method of implementation gets a simple model of a software system with just essential features up and running quickly.

10. The set of operations that are provided to users of an ADT is called its _____.

WRITTEN QUESTIONS

Write a brief answer to the following questions.

1. Explain the role of the constant of proportionality in the analysis of algorithms.

2. Explain why an algorithm with a running time of n^3 is no worse than an algorithm with a running time of n^2.

3. Decribe the differences between an ordered collection and a sorted collection.

UNIT 1 PROJECTS

PROJECT 1-1

Write constructors that build sorted collections from an array and from an ordered collection.

PROJECT 1-2

Write member functions that return the keys and values in a one-key table. Each function should return an ordered collection.

CRITICAL THINKING

ACTIVITY 1-1

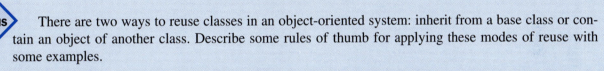

There are two ways to reuse classes in an object-oriented system: inherit from a base class or contain an object of another class. Describe some rules of thumb for applying these modes of reuse with some examples.

LINEAR DATA STRUCTURES

UNIT 2

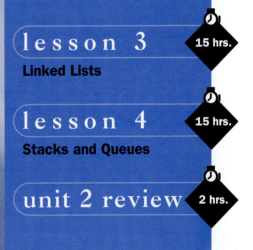

lesson 3 — 15 hrs.
Linked Lists

lesson 4 — 15 hrs.
Stacks and Queues

unit 2 review — 2 hrs.

Estimated Time for Unit 2: 32 hours

LINKED LISTS

OBJECTIVES

Upon completion of this lesson, you will be able to:

- Understand what kinds of problems require sophisticated methods of dynamic memory manipulation, and the properties of a data structure that can solve these types of problems.

- Understand the characteristics of a linked list that make it suitable for solving some kinds of problems, but not others.

- Visualize the logical structure of a linked list.

- Understand the operations on a linked list.

- Learn how to use pointers in C++ to manipulate dynamic data, and to represent a linked list.

- Understand the difference between the address of a memory location, and the value stored in a memory location.

- Understand how computer memory is organized to support different data types.

- Understand how the logical structure of a linked list can be independent of its structure in memory.

- Understand the costs and benefits of using linked lists.

 **Estimated Time: 15 hours**

Vocabulary

address-of operator (&)

arrow operator (->)

dereference

empty link (null pointer)

external pointers

garbage collector

heap store

heap underflow

link (pointer)

linked list

logical structure

memory leakage

random access data structure

run-time stack

sequential access data structure

sequential traversal

Introduction

In the previous lesson, we discovered that a vector implementation (with binary search) of a one-key table requires $O(n)$ data interchanges for the store and remove operations. Attempting to maintain, in order, such a vector-implemented list parallels the dynamics of waiting in a long line. When someone cuts into the middle of the line, a domino-like effect forces everyone behind that person to move back. When someone in the middle of the line decides to leave, the reverse effect occurs; everyone behind the departed person is able to move ahead one slot.

It is possible to draw an analogy between people waiting in a line and data items stored next to each other in computer memory. If the data items are arranged in some type of order and it becomes necessary to insert into or delete from the middle of the line, a considerable amount of data movement is involved. This data movement requires computer time and decreases program efficiency. A central motivation behind the linked list data structure is to eliminate the data movement associated with insertions into and deletions from such a list. Of course, by now we might suspect that efficiency in eliminating such data movement can come only by trading off other efficiency factors. One crucial question to ask yourself as we study linked lists is, what price are we paying to handle additions and deletions effectively?

In addition to optimizing the efficiency of insertion and deletion operations, studying linked lists will hone your skills in using dynamically allocated memory. In the Case Study for Lesson 2, you saw how strategically using pointers could help eliminate the need to store redundant copies of data. In this lesson, we explore more sophisticated ways in which dynamic memory can be manipulated to our advantage.

3.1 The Need for Linked Lists

To motivate our discussion of linked lists, let us consider two problems. The first problem is the file input problem. The second problem is the data movement problem. Both problems can be solved by using data structures that we have already studied. However, each problem reveals some shortcomings of those previous methods and points to the need for some new, more sophisticated techniques for dealing with dynamic memory.

The File Input Problem

The following sequence of operations is typical of many computer applications:

1. Input the data from a file into a structure in main memory.

2. Process the data.

3. Output the data back to the file.

The data in the file can be of any type, such as integers, strings, or personnel records. The processing step transforms these data in some way. For example, at the end of the year, each employee's salary might be adjusted. Because the data are written back to the same file, they must be saved in temporary locations for processing before output. A data structure that you have studied before, the `apvector`, can serve in this role.

First, consider an approach that uses a preallocated `apvector` as the temporary data structure for this problem. When the `apvector` variable is declared before the input step, the number of cells specified may be more than is needed to hold the data values from small files. This memory is consequently wasted. The number of cells may also be less than is needed to hold the data values from large files. This approach would cause a logic error because some data in the file would be missing from the list.

Assuming an element type called `element` and an input file stream called `inFile`, the following code segment illustrates this point:

```
// Declare data for a vector of 100 elements

const int MAX_LIST_SIZE = 100;
apvector<element> list(MAX_LIST_SIZE);
int length = 0;
element data;

// Input no more than 100 elements from a file

inFile >> data;
while (!  inFile.eof() && (length < MAX_LIST_SIZE))
{
    list[length] = data;
    ++length;
    inFile >> data;
}

// Display the consequences of the input operation

if (! inFile.eof() && (length == MAX_LIST_SIZE))
    cout << "Too bad, some data missing" << endl;
else if (length < MAX_LIST_SIZE)
    cout << "Too bad, some memory wasted" << endl;
else
    cout << "Lucky choice of size of vector" << endl;
```

The `resize` operation of the `apvector` class is an excellent choice to use in solving this problem because it takes advantage of dynamic memory. When the vector variable is declared, no memory is allocated for any cells. As each data value comes in from the file, the vector is resized and the data value is assigned to the last cell in the enlarged vector. At the end of the input process, no memory will have gone to waste and no data will be missing. The following code segment solves the file input problem using this strategy:

```
apvector<element> list;
element data;
inFile >> data;
while (!  inFile.eof())
{
    list.resize(list.length() + 1);
    list[list.length() - 1] = data;
    inFile >> data;
}
```

Each of the two solutions presented here comes with a potentially heavy price. The process of resizing a vector for each input value requires:

1. The allocation of memory for a new vector almost equal to the size of the old vector

2. The copying of all of the data from one vector to the other vector

For small files, these costs in processing time and memory are negligible. But for large files, the costs grow unreasonably. Merely adding one element to the structure is an $O(n)$ operation in its time efficiency despite the fact that the added element is appended to the end of the list. This $O(n)$ categorization arises from the n separate assignments that must be made from the old vector to the new vector. In its space efficiency, while the copying occurs from the old vector to the new vector, we are charged for $2*n$ memory locations even though we have only n values that we must store. In the worst case, the computer may run out of memory when a new vector is created during the input of a single data value. Alternatively, a process may not be completed on time because it took too long to copy a large number of data values from one vector to the other during an input operation.

Here is a case where the overall solution of a problem is correct, but the means of getting there is too costly. When faced with such a problem, a computer scientist focuses on the cause—the way dynamic memory is manipulated—and proposes a solution—a new way of manipulating this memory. An ideal data structure for the file input problem would do these tasks:

1. Start with an empty condition.

2. Create just one cell of memory during the insertion of each input value.

3. Require the copying of just one data value—the input value—to the new memory cell.

4. Allow the processing of each data value in sequence from the beginning to the end of the data structure.

We will soon examine a new ADT called a ***linked list*** that uses dynamic memory to meet these requirements.

The Data Movement Problem

Another common process in computer applications is the insertion or removal of a data value from a list. When a list is represented as a vector (or ordered collection), the insertion or removal of a data value can result in the movement of many other data values as well. An insertion requires all of the subsequent data values to be shifted to the right. A removal requires all of the subsequent data values to be shifted to the left. In the worst case, insertion or removal at the beginning of the list, the contents of the entire list must be moved. We have seen good examples of these cases with the addFirst and removeFirst operations of the ordered collection class that we investigated in Section 2.1. Because the ordered collection was implemented with a vector, both addFirst and removeFirst were $O(n)$ in their time efficiency.

A special case of this problem involves the insertion or removal of data from a file. We must first input all of the data from the file into a list (the file input problem). Then, we add or delete data from the list. Finally, we output the contents of the list back to the file. Clearly, from an efficiency perspective, a vector would be a poor choice of data structure to use in representing a list to solve this problem!

The ideal data structure for solving the data movement problem would allow insertions or removals without causing the physical movement of any other data values in the list. It turns out that the linked list ADT satisfies this requirement, as well as the others mentioned earlier. The use of dynamic memory allows a data value to be placed anywhere in a linked list with no physical movement of the other data in the list. We explore the concept of a linked list in the next section.

1. Suppose we have *n* data values stored in a file, and a program reads these values into an ordered collection implemented using the vector technique discussed in Section 2.1. Suppose also that, as a value is read in from the file, it is inserted at the beginning of the ordered collection; that is, the `addFirst` operation is called. Determine, using big-O notation, the running time for this program assuming that the file contains *n* data values.

2. Are there occasions for which we would still want to use a vector or an ordered collection implemented with a vector to receive file input, despite the problems we have discussed in this section? If so, discuss the reasons why.

3. Describe the case that causes the least amount of work during a data movement process in an ordered collection that is implemented with a vector. Does this case occur during insertion or removal, and where?

4. Suppose you sort a list of input values by reading them in one at a time and inserting them into a sorted collection object (see Section 2.2). Clearly, after you have read all of the input values, you will have a sorted list. Let's call this technique the *sorted collection sort algorithm*. Using big-O notation, analyze the time efficiency of this algorithm in terms of number of comparisons and number of data interchanges. Be sure that you take into account the underlying implementation strategy that we used for the sorted collection in Section 2.2. Compare the efficiency of this algorithm to the efficiencies of the other sort algorithms we have studied—insertion, bubble, selection, and radix sort.

3.2 The Concept of a Linked List

We have just seen two applications for which a linked list is ideally suited:

1. File input into a data structure in which the data can then be processed in sequence

2. Insertions or deletions of data from a data structure with minimal physical movement of data

A linked list works perfectly for these problems because it has the following characteristics:

1. It allows users to visit each data element in sequence from the first element to the last element.

2. It allows users to insert or remove a data element at a given position with no physical movement of the other data elements.

3. It uses only enough dynamic memory to store the data values inserted by the user.

To support these features, a linked list must have a special ***logical structure***. Its logical structure describes the organization of data independently of how it is stored in the physical memory of a computer. The primary organizational element of this structure is called a ***node***. In a linked list, a node contains two parts or ***members***:

1. A data element

2. A ***link*** or ***pointer*** to the next node in the list

The sequence of data elements in a linked list is thus linked by the sequence of nodes in which the elements are contained. Figure 3-1 shows a sequence of nodes in a linked list. Note that the data elements are labeled **D1** through **D4**. Each link is an arrow coming out of the back of a node and pointing at the next node. Note also that the link component of the last node in the list is a little box with no arrow. This designates an **empty link** or **null pointer**, indicating that there is no next node after this one in the list.

FIGURE 3-1
The nodes in a linked list

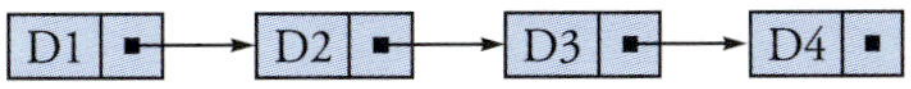

The logical structure of a linked list has four other components that support the implementation of operations on the list:

1. A first pointer to the first node in the list

2. A current pointer that can be moved to a desired node

3. A previous pointer that always points to the node before the current one

4. An integer representing the number of nodes in the list

The first three components are sometimes called **external pointers** because they are not links that hold the sequence of nodes together. Their purpose is to give users access to different nodes in the list. Figure 3-2 shows the linked list from Figure 3-1 with these additional components, after the current pointer has been moved to the second node in the list.

FIGURE 3-2
The external pointers of a linked list

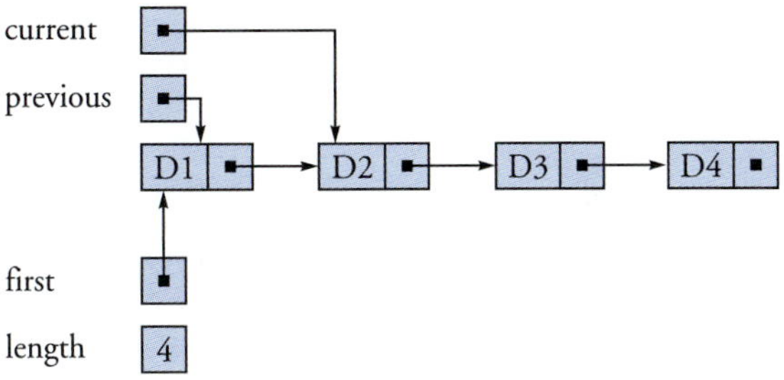

As we shall see shortly, this logical structure is just what we need to satisfy the requirements of a linked list mentioned earlier. Users can move through the list and visit each data element in sequence by moving the current pointer to the next node. Users can also insert or remove a data element from the list by redirecting some pointers at the appropriate nodes.

Linked List Operations

Let us now consider the abstract operations that the logical structure of a linked list makes possible. Each of these operations has a set of preconditions and postconditions. Most of these conditions concern the state of the external pointers in the linked list. In the following subsections, we provide an informal description of each operation, illustrate the operation with a figure, and state its preconditions and postconditions.

179

Creating a Linked List

When a linked list is created, it is empty and thus contains no nodes. However, the three external pointers and the length must all be initialized. Each of the pointers is set to null, as shown in Figure 3-3.

FIGURE 3-3

A newly created linked list

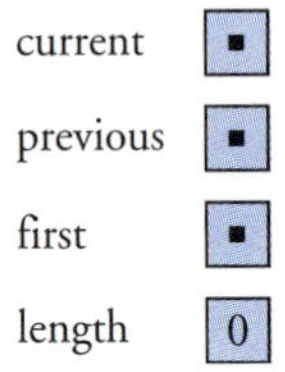

current   ▪

previous   ▪

first   ▪

length   0

The precondition of the `create` operation is that the linked list is in an unknown state. The postconditions are that each external pointer is null, and the length is 0.

Detecting an Empty Linked List

An empty linked list looks just like the list shown in Figure 3-3. The precondition of the `empty` operation is that the list has been appropriately initialized. The postcondition is that the operation returns `true` if there are no nodes in the list and `false` otherwise.

Moving to the Next Node

The `next` operation moves the current pointer to the next node after the current one. It also moves the previous pointer ahead one node. Figure 3-4 shows the states of a linked list before and after this operation, which moves the current pointer from the first node to the second node.

FIGURE 3-4

The effects of the `next` operation

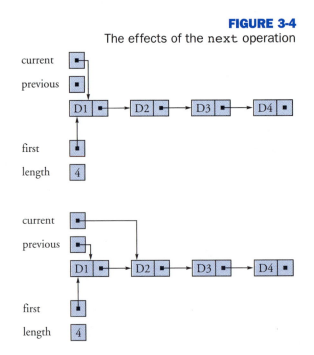

Note that the previous pointer was null before the operation and points to the first node afterward.

The `next` operation has one precondition. The current pointer must point to a node in the list. This will not be the case when the list is empty or after the `next` operation is executed with the current pointer referencing the last node. The postconditions of the `next` operation are as follows:

1. The previous pointer is moved to the next node.

2. The current pointer is moved to the next node, unless this component is null. In that case, the current pointer becomes null.

Figure 3-5 shows the states of a linked list during a series of `next` operations to move the current pointer as far as it can go in the list.

FIGURE 3-5
Running the `next` operation to the end of a list

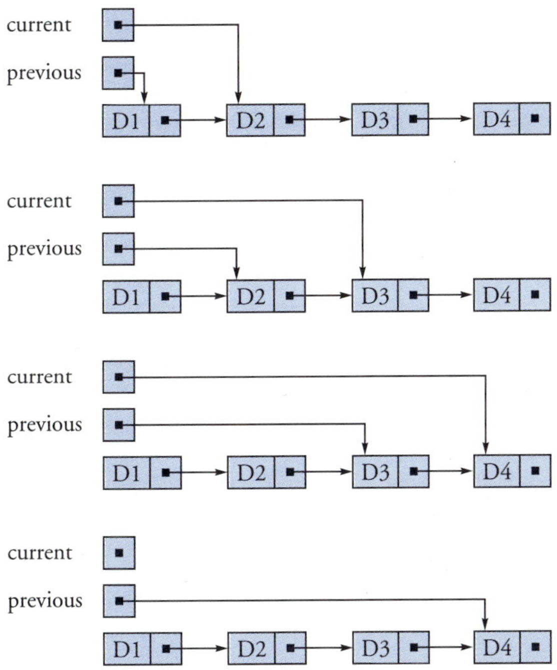

Detecting the End of the List

To avoid running off the end of a linked list, users need a means of detecting when the current pointer can advance no farther. For example, the `atEnd` operation returns `true` when a list is in the last state depicted in Figure 3-5. It also returns `true` when the list is empty. When neither of these conditions is true, `atEnd` returns `false`.

Accessing and Modifying the Data in the Current Node

A typical application will move the current pointer to a desired node in a linked list and then either access the data value in the node or modify it. These two operations, `access` and `modify`, assume that the current pointer is aimed at a node. In other words, `atEnd` must return `false`. `access` returns the data value in the current node. `modify` copies its parameter, a data value, into the data component of the current node. The result of an `access` operation to the contents of the last node is shown in Figure 3-6.

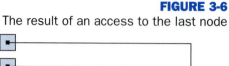

FIGURE 3-6

The result of an access to the last node

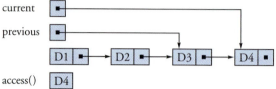

Moving to the First Node

Applications that process entire lists require an operation to move the current pointer to the first node in a list. The `first` operation assumes that the linked list has been appropriately initialized but has no other preconditions. If the list is not empty, the operation aims the current pointer at the first node and sets the previous pointer to null. If the list is empty, `first` does nothing. Figure 3-7 shows the states of a linked list before and after the `first` operation.

FIGURE 3-7

The effects of the `first` operation

Adding Data to the List

To add data to a linked list, a user moves the current pointer to the node before which the data should be inserted and then invokes the `insert` operation. The only precondition of this operation is that the list must be appropriately initialized. The postcondition is that the node containing the new data element becomes the current node. The linked list handles an insertion of data in different ways, depending on the position of the current pointer.

Case 1: If the list is empty, the new data element is placed in the first node. This process is shown in Figure 3-8.

FIGURE 3-8

Inserting data into an empty list

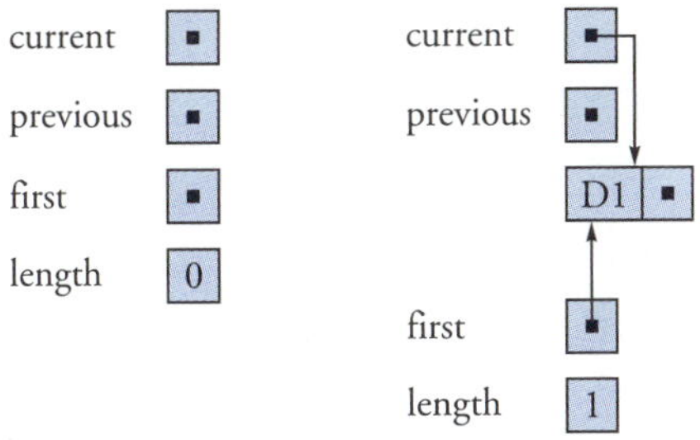

current ▪
previous ▪
first ▪
length 0

current ▪
previous ▪
D1 ▪
first ▪
length 1

Case 2: If the current pointer points to the first node, the new data element is placed in a new node and inserted before the first node, as shown in Figure 3-9. The new node becomes both the current node and the first node.

FIGURE 3-9

Inserting data at the beginning of a nonempty list

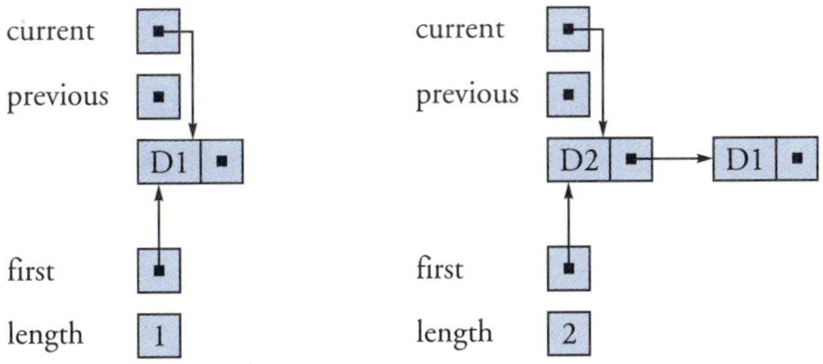

current ▪
previous ▪
D1 ▪
first ▪
length 1

current ▪
previous ▪
D2 ▪ → D1 ▪
first ▪
length 2

Case 3: If the current pointer points to a node after the first node, then the new data element is placed in a new node that is linked into the list between the current node and the previous node, as shown in Figure 3-10. Once again, the current pointer is aimed at the node just inserted.

FIGURE 3-10

Inserting data between the current node and the previous node

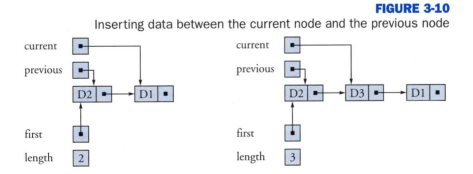

current ▪
previous ▪
D2 ▪ → D1 ▪
first ▪
length 2

current ▪
previous ▪
D2 ▪ → D3 ▪ → D1 ▪
first ▪
length 3

Case 4: If the current pointer has been moved past the last node in the list, the new data element is placed in a new node at the end of the list, as shown in Figure 3-11.

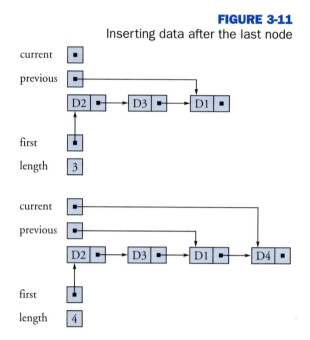

FIGURE 3-11
Inserting data after the last node

Note that in each case the external pointers and the length are updated appropriately.

The following algorithm describes in detail the process of creating a new node and linking it into a linked list:

1. Create a new node

2. Set the data component of the new node to the new data element

3. Set the next pointer of the new node to null

4. If the list is empty or the current node is the first node

   5. Aim the first pointer at the new node

   Else

   6. Aim the next pointer of the previous node at the new node

7. Set the next pointer of the new node to the current pointer

8. Aim the current pointer at the new node

9. Increment the length by 1

Figure 3-12 depicts the steps in this process for inserting a node into the middle of a linked list.

The order of steps 4 through 8 is critical. A different ordering of steps will result in the new node's not being properly linked, and the logical structure of the linked list will be corrupted. Also note that these are the only steps performed during an insertion, regardless of where it occurs in the list. No loop exists to adjust the positions of other data elements, as with vectors. That explains why a linked list solves the data movement problem in O(1) time.

FIGURE 3-12

The steps in the process of inserting a node into a linked list

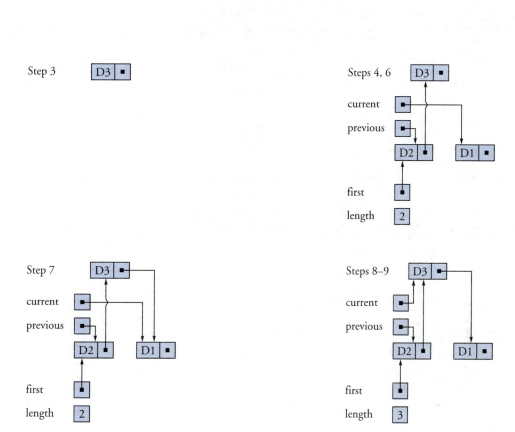

Removing Data from the List

To remove data from a linked list, the user moves the current pointer to the desired node and then invokes the `remove` operation. This operation assumes that the current pointer is pointing to a node (`atEnd` returns `false`). It unlinks the current node, returns its memory to the system, and returns the data element to the caller. At the end of the operation, the current pointer points to the node after the node just removed. The previous pointer remains unchanged. The first pointer may be updated as well.

The following algorithm describes in detail the process of unlinking a node to remove its data element from a linked list:

1. Save the data element in a temporary variable

2. Save a pointer to the current node

3. If the current node is the first node

4. Set the first pointer to the next pointer of the current node

   Else

5. Set the next pointer of the previous node to the next pointer of the current node

6. Set the current pointer to the next pointer of the current node

7. Use the saved pointer to return the old node to the system

8. Decrement the length by 1

9. Return the data element to the caller

Once again, the order of the operations is important. Figure 3-13 depicts the steps in this process for removing a node from the middle of a linked list. As with inserting a node, the operations are performed in O(1) time.

FIGURE 3-13
The steps in the process of removing a node from a linked list

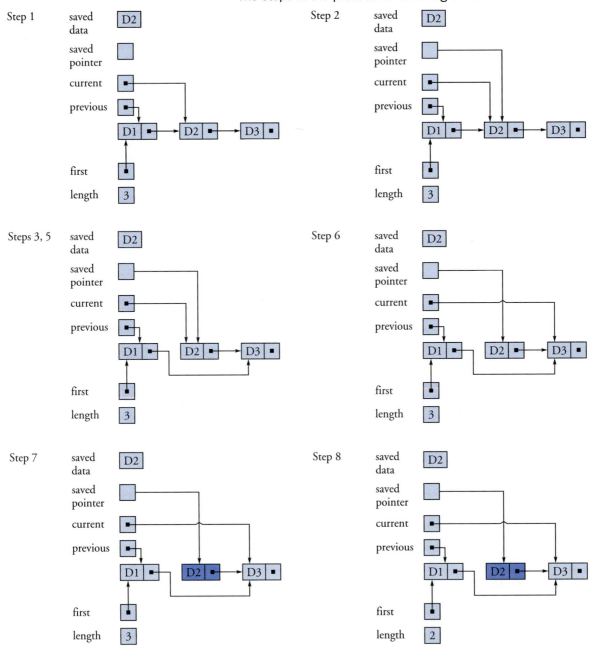

The operations on a linked list are summarized in Table 3-1.

TABLE 3-1

Operations on a linked list abstract data type

Operation	Preconditions	Postconditions
create	The list is in an unknown state.	The list is empty.
Empty	The list is initialized.	Returns true if empty, false otherwise.
atEnd	The list is initialized.	Returns true if the current pointer has run off the end of the list, false otherwise.
length	The list is initialized.	Returns the number of nodes in the list.
first	The list is initialized.	Moves the current pointer to the first node in the list.
next	The current pointer points to a node.	Advances the current and previous pointers ahead by one node.
access	The current pointer points to a node.	Returns the data element stored in the current node.
modify(newData)	The current pointer points to a node.	Sets the data in the current node to the new data.
insert(newData)	The list is initialized.	If atEnd is true, then inserts the new data into a new node at the end of the list. Otherwise, inserts the new data into a new node before the current one. Makes the new node the current one.
remove	The current pointer points to a node.	Removes the current node from the list, makes the node following this node the current one, and returns the removed data to the caller.

Using a Linked List to Solve Problems

Armed with a linked list abstract data type and knowing nothing about its implementation, we can now look at some examples of how it is used. We assume that the linked list ADT has been defined as a C++ class template. The type parameter for the linked list class is the type of the data stored in a list.

Example 3-1

The following program is a solution to an instance of the file input problem. The program reads integers from a file named _myfile.old_ into a linked list. It then increments each integer in the list. Finally, it writes the contents of the list back to the file _myfile.new_. Source code files for this example have been provided—see your instructor.

```
// Program file: fileprob.cpp

#include <iostream.h>
#include <fstream.h>
#include "linklist.h"

int main()
{
   ifstream inFile;
   ofstream outFile;
   LinkedList<int> list;
   int data;

   // Input phase - insert data at end of list

   inFile.open("myfile.old");
   inFile >> data;
   while (! inFile.eof())
   {
      list.insert(data);
      list.next();
      inFile >> data;
   }
   inFile.close();

   // Processing phase - increment all values
   //                    in the list

   list.first();
   while (! list.atEnd())
   {
      data = list.access();
      list.modify(data + 1);
      list.next();
   }

   // Output phase - write all values in the
   //                list back to the file

   outFile.open("myfile.new");
   list.first();
   while (! list.atEnd())
   {
      outFile << list.access() << endl;
      list.next();
   }
   outFile.close();
   return 0;
}
```

Let's examine the logic of each of the three main parts of the program of Example 3-1.

Input phase: In this part of the program, the input file is opened, and we enter a standard end-of-file `while` loop. The list is assumed to be empty at the beginning of the loop. Thus, when the first data value is inserted, it goes at the end of the list automatically. After the insertion, the `next` operation is run. It moves the current pointer beyond the last node in the list. Thus, on the next pass through the loop, the new data will continue to be inserted at the end of the list. At the end of the input phase, the data in the list will be in the same order as they were in the file and will be ready for sequential processing.

Processing phase: In this part of the program, the current pointer is moved to the first node to begin a *sequential traversal* of the list. Such a traversal visits each data item in the list, from beginning to end. The code for this traversal consists of an end-of-list `while` loop. In the body of the loop, we access the data in the current node, process the data, and modify the node with the result. Then we move on to the next node, continuing the process until we reach the end of the list. Note that the control condition is tested at loop entry to guard against the cases of the empty list and the end of the list.

Output phase: This part of the program is similar to the processing phase. In this case, however, we traverse the list and simply access the data in each node for output to the file.

Example 3-2

Users would like to have a function named `reverse` that expects a linked list as a parameter and returns a new linked list with the contents of the parameter in reverse order. This situation is another instance of the data movement problem. The following C++ function solves this problem:

```cpp
template <class E>
LinkedList<E> reverse(LinkedList<E> &list)
{
    LinkedList<E> result;

    list.first();
    for (int i = 1; i <= list.length(); ++i)
    {
        result.insert(list.access());
        list.next();
    }
    return result;
}
```

The function in Example 3-2 illustrates two new ideas:

1. A count-controlled `for` loop can be used to traverse a linked list. The loop assumes that the current pointer is at the first node. The loop counts from 1 to the length of the list and advances through the list by running the `next` operation.

2. The reversal of the data elements in the new list is automatically accomplished by inserting each value at the beginning of the list.

Note that the process of reversing the contents of a linked list is much more efficient than the process of reversing the contents of an ordered collection.

1. Based on the operations for a linked list discussed in this section, describe how the linked list ADT differs from the ordered collection ADT.

2. Describe two applications for which a linked list is a suitable data structure.

3. Explain why so many linked list operations assume that the `atEnd` operation returns `false`.

4. Draw a picture of a linked list with three nodes. The current pointer should be aimed at the first node. Now draw pictures that show each step during the process of removing this node from the list.

5. Suppose that the length of a linked list is not maintained as a separate component of the data structure. How does this change affect the behavior of the `length` operation?

6. Describe the method used by a new linked list operation called `insertLast`. This operation expects a data element as a parameter and inserts it at the end of a linked list. The only precondition is that the list must be initialized. Describe the efficiency of this operation using big-O notation.

7. Describe how to overload the assignment operator for vectors so that one can assign the contents in successive nodes of a linked list to the successive indices of a vector. Why would this operation be useful?

8. Overload the + operator to define a C++ function that concatenates two linked lists and returns the result. Describe the efficiency of this operation using big-O notation.

9. Given a linked list of `ints`, write a loop that starts at the beginning of the linked list and returns the position of the first list node with the value 0 in its data field. If no such node exists in the list, −1 should be returned.

10. Write a function `sum` to sum the integers in a linked list of integers.

11. Write a function to remove all of the nodes in a linked list.

12. Write a function called `merge` that receives two linked lists of integers arranged in ascending order. Your function should merge these two lists into a single list, also arranged in ascending order. The merged list should be returned from the function.

3.3 Defining the Linked List ADT as a C++ Class

In the previous section, we examined the definition and use of a linked list as an abstract data type. We assumed the existence of a C++ class template that corresponds to that definition and showed how that class can be used to solve some problems. Now it is time to develop the code for the C++ class template for a linked list.

IMPORTANT:

Source code for this section has been provided. See your instructor.

The first step, declaring the operations and data members for the class, results in the following file:

```cpp
// Class declaration file: linklist.h

#ifndef LINKLIST_H

template <class E> class LinkedList
{
   public:

   // constructors

   LinkedList();
   LinkedList(const LinkedList<E> &list);

   // destructor

   ~LinkedList();

   // assignment

   const LinkedList<E>& operator =
      (const LinkedList<E> &rhs);

   // accessors

   int  length() const;
   bool empty() const;
   bool atEnd() const;
   E access();

   // modifiers

   void first();
   void next();
   void modify(const E &item);
   void insert(const E &item);
   E remove();

   private:

   // Data members
```

```
struct node          // Definition of the node type
{
    E data;
    node * next;
};

// External pointers to the list

node * myFirst;
node * myCurrent;
node * myPrevious;

// The number of nodes in the list

int mySize;

// Member functions

node * getNode(const E &item);

};
```

The declarations of the operations call for no comment. They have been translated directly from the abstract operations listed in Table 3-1.

The data members `myFirst`, `myCurrent`, `myPrevious`, and `mySize` represent the four external components (first, current, previous, and length) of the logical structure of a linked list discussed in Section 3.2. Each of the pointer data members is of type `node *`. We now examine the definitions of this type and of the private member function `getNode`.

Defining a Pointer to a Node

As we saw in Section 3.2, each node in a linked list contains two parts: a data component and a pointer to the next node in the list. A struct is a logical choice for representing a node in C++. One component of the struct, the data element, is of type E. The other component of the struct must be a pointer to a node. As we saw in the Case Study in Lesson 2, C++ provides a special syntax for defining pointer types as follows:

<type of object pointed to> * <pointer variable name>

Thus, if we want a member of a struct of type `node` to be able to point at another struct of the same type, that member must be of type `node *`. The declaration of the `next` member in the struct `node` below meets this criterion:

```
struct node          // Definition of the node type
{
    E data;
    node * next;
};
```

Note in the `linklist.h` class declaration file, the type name `node` is declared as `private`. The struct `node` is, therefore, of use in the implementation of the linked list class only. Users of the linked list class will have no awareness of what a `node` is, nor will they be able to access data members of a `node` in any way.

Declaring the `getNode` Function

Each time a data element is added to a linked list, three things must be done:

1. Allocate dynamic memory for a new node.

2. Set the data part of the node to the new data element.

3. Set the next pointer part of the node to null.

This task is complex enough to warrant the definition of a function to perform it. Because the function will be used only within the implementation of the linked list class, we declare it as `private`. The function expects a data element as a parameter. It returns a pointer to a new node that contains the data element and a null pointer.

```
node * getNode(const E &item);
```

Now that we have completed the declaration of the linked list class, we can turn to its implementation.

Creating a Linked List

Recall from Section 3.2 that a new linked list is empty. Thus, its external pointers first, current, and previous should all be null, and its length should be 0. The default constructor does this:

```
template <class E>
LinkedList<E>::LinkedList()
: myFirst(0), myCurrent(0), myPrevious(0), mySize(0)
{
}
```

Note that the null pointer is represented in C++ as zero. This value looks like a number, but it is used here as a pointer value. The null value indicates that the pointer variable does not currently point to a node.

The Copy Constructor for a Linked List

The copy constructor copies all of the data from the parameter list into the receiver list. The function uses the temporary pointer `probe` to traverse the nodes in the parameter list. It uses `insert` and `next` to place each data value at the end of the receiver list.

```
template <class E>
LinkedList<E>::LinkedList(const LinkedList<E &list)
: myFirst(0), myCurrent(0), myPrevious(0), mySize(0)
{
   // Temporary pointer to first node in list

   node * probe = list.myFirst;

   // Loop until end of list is reached

   while (probe != 0)
   {
      // Insert data from node in list

      insert(probe->data);

      // Advance to end of receiver
```

```
        next();

        // Move probe to next node in list

        probe = probe->next;
    }
}
```

This code is heavily commented to clarify each step. Note the following points:

1. The `probe` pointer starts at the first node of `list`.

2. The loop control condition (`probe != 0`) returns `false` as long as `probe` points at a node in `list` but returns `true` when `probe` has reached the end of `list`.

3. The expression `probe->data` accesses the `data` component in the node pointed to by `probe`. This value is passed to `insert` to add it to the end of the receiver list.

4. The assignment statement `probe = probe->next;` sets `probe` to the value of the `next` component in the node pointed to by `probe`. It has the effect of advancing `probe` to the next node in `list`.

A pointer value can be compared to zero to determine whether or not it is null. The syntax for accessing a member of a node is new. Its form is

<pointer variable>-><node member name>

The *arrow operator* directs the computer to follow the arrow from the pointer variable to the designated member in the node as shown in our box and pointer diagrams. This process is accomplished in two steps:

1. A *dereference*, in which the node is located by using a pointer to refer to the contents of dynamic memory.

2. A *selection*, in which the designated member is located in the node

The same process could be accomplished by using the dereference operator (`*`) and the selector operator (`.`). For example, the expressions

`probe->next` and `*probe.next`

have the same effect. Obviously, the use of the arrow notation simplifies the expression, so we prefer it.

The Destructor for Linked Lists

The destructor makes use of the `first`, `empty`, and `remove` operations to return all of the nodes in the list to the system.

```
template <class E>
LinkedList<E>::~LinkedList()
{

    E item;

    first();
```

```
      while (! empty())
         item = remove();


   }
```

The first and next Operations

After the first operation, the current pointer points to the first node and the previous pointer is null. The first operation thus modifies the current and previous pointers appropriately.

```
template <class E>
void LinkedList<E>::first()
{
   if (myCurrent != myFirst)
   {
      myCurrent = myFirst;
      myPrevious = 0;
   }
}
```

The next operation moves the current and previous pointers ahead in the list by one node each. The precondition is that the current pointer must point to a node.

```
template <class E>
void LinkedList<E>::next()
{
   assert (myCurrent != 0);
   myPrevious = myCurrent;
   myCurrent = myCurrent->next;
}
```

Accessing and Modifying Data in a Node

Like the next operation, both the access and modify operations assume that the current pointer is pointing to a node.

```
template <class E>
E LinkedList<E>::access()
{
   assert(myCurrent != 0);
   return myCurrent->data;


}

template <class E>
void LinkedList<E>::modify(const E &item)
{
   assert(myCurrent != 0);
   myCurrent->data = item;


}
```

195

As you can see from the last three function implementations, it is the responsibility of the user to test for the end-of-list condition before running an operation that accesses the contents of a node. The assert function catches any failures to do so.

Testing for the End of the List

The atEnd operation should return true if the list is empty or if the current pointer has advanced to the end of the list. Otherwise, the operation returns false.

```
template <class E>
bool LinkedList<E>::atEnd() const
{
    return (empty() || myCurrent == 0);
}
```

Testing for an Empty List

The current pointer is null when the list is empty, but it is also null when it is at the end of a non-empty list. Thus the empty operation compares the length of the list to 0.

```
template <class E>
bool LinkedList<E>::empty() const
{
    return mySize == 0;
}
```

Inserting Data into a Linked List

The insert operation follows the algorithm presented in Section 3.2. The getNode function is used to create and initialize a new node with the new data element:

```
template <class E>
void LinkedList<E>::insert(const E &item)
{
    node *  newNode = getNode(item);

    if (empty() || (myFirst == myCurrent))
        myFirst = newNode;
    else
        myPrevious->next = newNode;
    newNode->next = myCurrent;
    myCurrent = newNode;
    ++mySize;
}
```

Implementing getNode

Whenever a new node is needed for a linked list, the implementation invokes the function getNode. To allocate dynamic memory for the new node, getNode employs the new operator. We use new in C++ to allocate memory for a data object dynamically, or as needed by a program. new is an operator that returns a pointer to a block of memory if memory is available. If memory is not available, new returns the pointer value 0.

In the context of linked lists, we want `new` to return a pointer to a node. Thus the form of the call to `new` should be `new node`. The `getNode` function verifies that memory was allocated for the node by asserting that the new node pointer is not null. `getNode` then uses the pointer to initialize the contents of the new node with the new data element and the null pointer, and it returns the pointer to the caller.

```
template <class E>
LinkedList<E>::node *  LinkedList<E>::getNode
   (const E &item)
{
   node *  newNode = new node;

   assert(newNode != 0);
   newNode->data = item;
   newNode->next = 0;
   return newNode;
}
```

Note a slight difference in the syntax of this function's heading from the headings of the other linked list functions. The scope specifier `LinkedList<E>::` must also appear at the beginning of the heading. The reason is that the privately declared return type, `node *`, would appear to be undefined if it were not preceded by the scope specifier of the class declaration module.

Removing Data from a Linked List

The `remove` operation follows the algorithm presented in Section 3.2:

```
template <class E>
E LinkedList<E>::remove()
{
   assert (myCurrent != 0);
   E data = myCurrent->data;
   node *  garbage = myCurrent;

   if (myFirst == myCurrent)
      myFirst = myCurrent->next;
   else
      myPrevious->next = myCurrent->next;
   myCurrent = myCurrent->next;
   delete garbage;
   —mySize;
   return data;
}
```

Note that the function uses the `delete` operator to return the memory for the node to the system. The `delete` operator is the inverse of `new`. It returns the memory pointed to by its operand to the system. In the present context, where we want to recycle just a node, we use the form `delete <pointer to a node>`.

XERCISES ⟹ **3.3**

1. Implement the remaining linked list member functions.

2. For each linked list member function implemented in this section and in Exercise 1, provide a big-O efficiency analysis.

3. Give an algorithm for an `addFirst` operation for linked lists and write the corresponding C++ member function. Then provide a big-O analysis for your implementation of this operation.

4. Give an algorithm for an `addLast` operation for linked lists and write the corresponding C++ member function. Then provide a big-O analysis for your implementation of this operation.

5. Compare the efficiencies of `addFirst` and `addLast`. Which is more expensive to run and why?

6. Give an algorithm and write a function for an index operation that allows access and modification of a data value at a given position in a linked list. Overload the operator `[ ]` for the function. After you've written the function, provide a big-O analysis of its efficiency.

7. Describe the differences between the index operation defined in Exercise 6 for linked lists and the index operation for vectors.

8. Suppose we drop the `mySize` data member from the definition of a linked list. Rewrite the function `length` so that it still returns the number of nodes in a list. What was the efficiency of `length` in the original implementation? What is the efficiency of the new implementation?

3.4 Pointers and the Management of Computer Memory

So far in this lesson, we have focused on the logical structure of a linked list and paid no attention to how the list is stored in computer memory. Even when we use the operators `new` and `delete` to manipulate dynamic memory, the operations are abstract, hiding any details of how the computer performs these tasks. In this section, we explore some of the concepts underlying memory management in C++ programs. In the process, you will gain a clearer understanding of the costs and benefits of using linked lists.

Addresses and Values of Simple Variables

You were introduced to the idea of a variable early in your study of computer science. We can illustrate the concept of a variable with little boxes and labels, as shown in Figure 3-14.

FIGURE 3-14

Visualizing variables and their values abstractly

```
int x = 3, y = 4;
double d = 5.6;
```

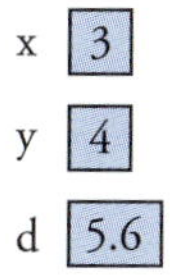

x [3]

y [4]

d [5.6]

As illustrated in Figure 3-14, variables in C++ are named memory locations where values can be stored and accessed. The picture is abstract, however, in that it suppresses the details of representing the memory cells and data at the machine level. When a program is loaded to run on a computer, each of the variable names is converted to a machine address, which is a binary number. The data stored in the memory cells are also represented as binary numbers. Thus the variables in Figure 3-14 might be more accurately depicted as shown in Figure 3-15.

FIGURE 3-15

Visualizing variables and their values at the machine level

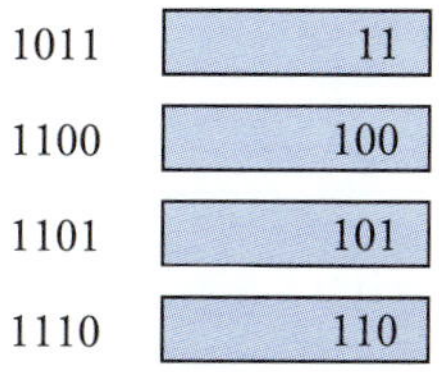

1011	11
1100	100
1101	101
1110	110

The binary numbers to the left of each memory cell in Figure 3-15 are called the ***addresses*** of the memory cells. The numbers inside the boxes are the data or values stored there. Note that one cell is reserved for each integer value, but two cells are needed for the real number. The whole part of the real number, 101 (5), is stored in cell 1101. The fractional part of the real number, 110 (6), is stored in the next cell. In general, the machine automatically computes the amount of memory needed for each type of data value and allocates that memory accordingly.

Addresses and Values of Vector Variables

The distinction between an address and a value stored at an address is one of the most important in computer science. This distinction also applies to vector variables. For example, we visualize a vector variable as a block of adjacent memory cells, as shown in Figure 3-16.

FIGURE 3-16
Visualizing a vector variable abstractly

```
int list[5];
for (int i = 0; i < 5; ++i)
        list[i] = i + 1;
```

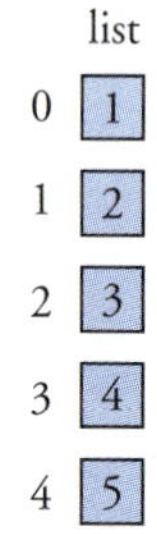

list

0	1
1	2
2	3
3	4
4	5

In the abstract view of a vector, the individual cells containing the data values are labeled with index values ranging from 0 to 4. The name list appears to label the entire block of cells.

At the machine level, the name list is translated into the binary address of the first cell appears in the vector. The address of each subsequent cell in the vector is 1 greater than the previous one, as shown in Figure 3-17.

FIGURE 3-17
Visualizing a vector at the machine level

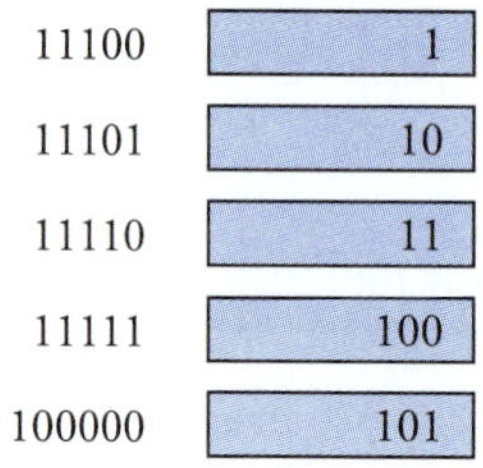

Address	Value
11100	1
11101	10
11110	11
11111	100
100000	101

This arrangement allows the address of a vector cell to be computed by adding its index value to the machine address of the first cell. (In cases where each data element requires several cells of memory, the index is first multiplied by this factor.) For example, if the machine address of list is 11100, the machine address of list[2] is 11100 + 10, or 11110 (using binary arithmetic). This method of computing the address of a vector cell is the reason vector indexing is so fast, no matter where the cell in the vector. In fact, a vector is called a ***random access data structure*** because the time needed to access a vector cell is independent of its position in the vector. Put another way, it takes no more time to access the cell at list[2] than it does to access the cell at list[0].

Addresses and Values of Pointer Variables

The distinction between an address and a value becomes even more obvious when we deal with pointer variables. A pointer variable is a special kind of memory cell capable of storing the address of another memory cell. Often a pointer variable contains either the null value (0) or a pointer to a chunk of dynamic memory returned by the new operator. However, as we saw in the Case Study in Lesson 2, we can use the ***address-of operator*** (&) to obtain the address of any C++ variable and store this value in a pointer variable. A restriction applies, however: The variable whose address is assigned to the pointer must be of the same type as the base type of the pointer. The following code segment accomplishes this goal for an integer variable:

```
// Declare an integer variable and set it to 2

int x = 2;

// Declare a pointer to an integer variable
// and set it to the address of x

int *intPtr = &x;
```

Figure 3-18 uses the abstract notation of boxes and arrows to distinguish between the pointer and integer values stored in the variables x and intPtr. Figure 3-19 shows what the contents of the memory cells might look like at the machine level.

FIGURE 3-18

An integer variable and a pointer to this variable

FIGURE 3-19

The variables of Figure 3-18 at the machine level

| 1000 | 10 |
| 1001 | 1000 |

Study the binary numbers stored in the memory cells in Figure 3-19 carefully. Both appear to be integer values. However, the value stored in cell 1001 is the address of cell 1000 and thus is a pointer value.

The dereference operator (*) is the inverse of the address-of operator. It expects a pointer value (an address) as an argument and returns the value stored at that address. Thus the following code segment displays the machine address of x (in decimal) and then the value stored at that address:

```
// Declare an integer variable and set it to 2

int x = 2;

// Declare a pointer to an integer variable
// and set it to the address of x

int *intPtr = &x;

// Display the address of x

cout << intPtr << endl;

// Dereference intPtr to display the value
// stored in x

cout << *intPtr << endl;
```

Using the memory shown in Figure 3-19, when the computer evaluates the expression `*intPtr`, it goes through these steps:

1. It looks up the value in memory cell 1001.

2. It uses the value from step 1, 1000, to look up the value in memory cell 1000.

3. It returns the value from step 2, 10.

PROGRAMMING SKILLS: Garbage Collection

Programs that make frequent use of dynamic memory can be error-prone. Such memory is located in a region called the *heap*. One kind of error that can occur is the failure to return pieces of dynamic memory to the heap when they are no longer needed. If this failure occurs often enough, the program will run out of memory, perhaps at a critical point in its task.

To avoid the problem of memory leakage, some programming languages have been designed so that the programmer does not have to worry about returning unused memory to the heap at all. The run-time system for these languages has a special module called a ***garbage collector*** that automatically recovers unused dynamic memory when it is needed.

Two such languages, Smalltalk and LISP, rely on dynamic memory for all of their data structures, so an automatic garbage collector is an essential part of their design. In Smalltalk, which is a pure object-oriented language, dynamic memory is used to create new objects. In LISP, which supports a linked list as a standard data structure, dynamic memory is used to add data elements to a list. When an application in either of these languages asks for a new piece of dynamic memory, the computer checks the heap to see whether the request can be satisfied. If it cannot, the garbage collector is invoked, and all of the unused memory locations are returned to the heap. The request is then granted if enough dynamic memory is available.

The garbage collection mechanism works roughly as follows: Every memory location is marked as either referenced by the application or not. A memory location is referenced if it is named by a variable or is part of a linked structure pointed to by such a variable. When memory is allocated for variables, it is marked as referenced. When memory becomes completely unlinked from any variable references in a program, it is marked as unreferenced. Thus only unreferenced memory locations will be candidates for return to the heap.

Garbage collection in early versions of LISP and Smalltalk sometimes degraded the performance of a program. During a collection, an application would appear to pause for a moment while the mechanism did its work. This delay is one reason why Smalltalk and LISP applications have not received much play in industry, where efficiency in time-critical tasks is a priority. However, much research and development have produced very efficient garbage collection algorithms so that LISP and Smalltalk programs now perform as well as programs written in languages without any garbage collector.

Pointers and Dynamic Allocation of Memory

In all of the code examples shown thus far in this section, the computer allocates memory automatically for the variables. When this memory is no longer needed, the computer deallocates the memory by returning it to the system. Another example of this process is a function call. If the function has value parameters and locally declared variables, the computer allocates memory for them each time the function is invoked. When the function returns, the computer returns this memory to the system for other uses. Because the computer manages this memory automatically, the programmer can focus on the syntax of variable declarations and the scope rules for referencing the variables without worrying about memory management.

As we have begun to see, however, the programmer can become involved in memory management by using the `new` operator to allocate dynamic memory for data structures such as vectors and linked lists. When this memory is no longer needed, the programmer is responsible for invoking the `delete` operator to return the memory to the system.

To understand how `new` and `delete` work, we must take a more global view of the organization of memory in a computer. We can think of this memory as a giant block of cells, as shown in Figure 3-20.

FIGURE 3-20
Computer memory

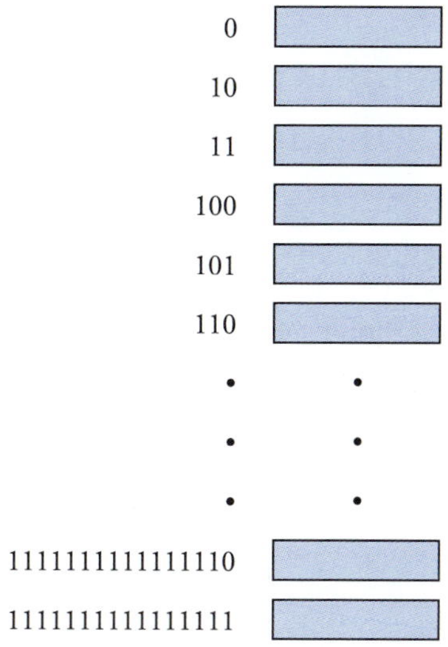

0	
10	
11	
100	
101	
110	
.	.
.	.
.	.
1111111111111110	
1111111111111111	

This block of cells resembles a giant random access data structure. In fact, it is treated in this way when the computer is asked to look up or store a value at a given memory location. That is why this memory is called *RAM* (random access memory).

To simplify our discussion, we assume that the computer has a single user running a single C++ program. The memory of the computer at run time is divided into the following components:

1. An area of cells for the instructions and data of the computer's operating system.

2. An area of cells for the instructions of the C++ program.

3. An area of cells for the variables and data necessary for function calls, including the main program function. This area is called a *run-time stack* and is discussed further in Lesson 4.

4. An area of cells for representing dynamic data. This area is called a *heap* or *free store*.
   Figure 3-21 depicts this organization of memory.

FIGURE 3-21

The four parts of computer memory

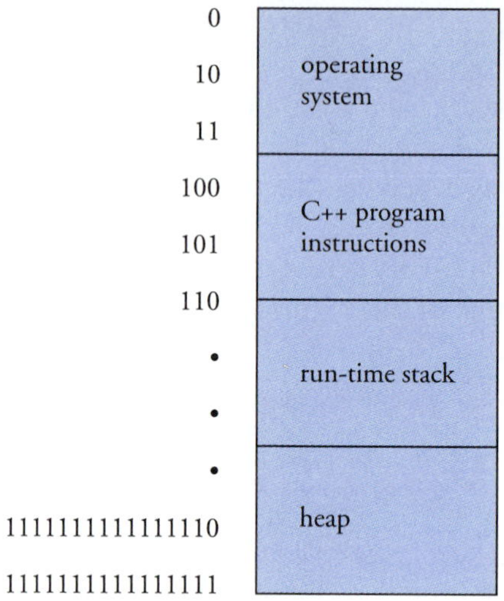

When a programmer uses the `new` operator to request a chunk of dynamic memory, the computer attempts to obtain the desired cells from the heap. If the heap cannot provide a block of these cells, the computer returns a null pointer to the caller of `new`. Otherwise, the computer returns a pointer to the first cell of the desired chunk of memory in the heap.

For example, consider the insertion of a new node into a linked list of integers. Each node requires a block of two cells, one for the integer and one for the pointer to the next node in the list. The `getNode` function asks for this memory and initializes it by running the statements

```
node * newNode = new node;
assert(newNode != 0);
newNode->data = item;
newNode->next = 0;
```

Assuming that `item` has the value 3, an abstract view of the memory allocated for the new node is shown in Figure 3-22.

FIGURE 3-22

An abstract view of a pointer to a node

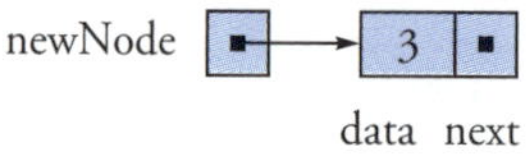

If the address of `newNode` is 1110 in the data area of computer memory and the address of the first available block of two cells in the heap is 1111111111111110, then the view of the node at the machine level matches that shown in Figure 3-23.

FIGURE 3-23
A pointer to a node at the machine level

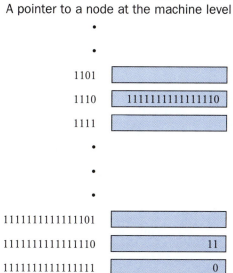

Now suppose that the values 1 and 2 are inserted, in that order, at the beginning of an empty linked list when the program begins execution. After these operations, the chunks of memory for the two nodes in the heap will be adjacent to each other, as shown in Figure 3-24.

FIGURE 3-24
Memory allocated for two nodes in a linked list

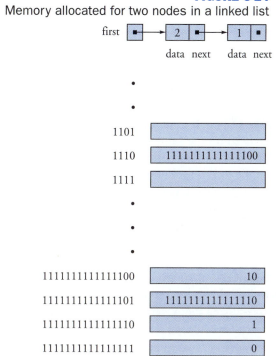

Note that the positions of the two nodes in the heap are similar to the positions of two structs in a vector. The positions are adjacent, and the physical order of the cells representing the nodes in memory is the same as the logical order of the nodes in the linked list. This situation might lead you to think that we could use indexing to access a data element at a given position in a linked list. However, this is true only in some cases.

Suppose the same program removed the first data element (2) from the linked list and reinserted it at the end of the list. Figure 3-25 shows the resulting situation.

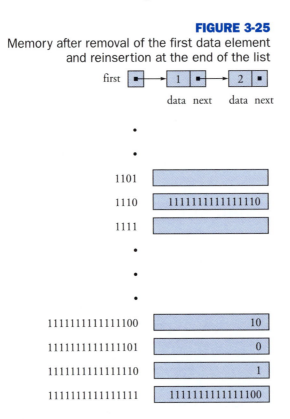

FIGURE 3-25
Memory after removal of the first data element
and reinsertion at the end of the list

The memory for the node containing the first data element is returned to the heap during the removal and reused for a new node to contain the data element during the insertion. Even though the same cells of physical memory are used for the same numbers in both cases, the logical order of the data elements in the linked list has been reversed. This situation is indicated by the changes in the pointer values stored in the external pointer of the linked list and in the next pointers within the nodes. The number 2 comes after 1 in the linked list from the user's perspective; in computer memory, however, 2 is stored before 1. Thus we cannot count on the physical order of cells in the heap to reflect the logical order of nodes in a linked list. For this reason, we must treat the logical order of the nodes in a linked list as independent of their order in computer memory.

The Costs of Using Linked Lists

Now that you understand how linked lists are represented in computer memory, you are in a position to more thoroughly assess the costs of using them. The first cost concerns the access time for a given data element in the list. Because the logical structure of a linked list is independent of its physical structure in memory, we cannot generally use random access indexing with linked lists. This restriction explains why a linked list is a *sequential access data structure*. To access a data element in this kind of data structure, we must start with a pointer to the first node and run a sequence of $n - 1$ `next` operations to reach the node at the nth position. The time needed to access a given data element in a linked list depends on its position in the list. The value at the end of a linked list of 1000 elements will take about 1000 times as long to access as the value at the second position. By contrast, the access to a data element at the end of a vector a, expressed as `a[length - 1]`, requires one or two machine instructions. The access to the last element in this vector would be just as fast as the access to the second data element, expressed as `a[1]`.

The low cost of random access with vectors plays a role in highly efficient search strategies, such as the binary search that was discussed in Lesson 1. The high cost of sequential access makes the linked list a poor choice of an ADT for applications that must perform many searches for given data elements or that must access data elements at specified positions. Also, some operations, such as insertion at the end of the list, require $n - 1$ `next` operations for a list of length n.

Another cost associated with linked lists is the use of memory. Each node in a linked list requires memory not only for a data element but also for a pointer to the next node. The memory needed to store one pointer value is not large (probably one cell). But a linked list of 1 million nodes requires 1 million such cells. By contrast, a vector of the same logical size requires 1 million fewer memory cells.

One final cost of using linked lists involves the likelihood of program errors. With dynamic data, the programmer carries the entire burden of memory management. It is easy to ask for dynamic memory with the `new` operator—but also easy to forget to return it with `delete` when it is no longer needed. The failure to recycle this memory is called *memory leakage*. If it is severe enough, memory leakage can lead to a condition known as *heap underflow*, in which new dynamic memory can no longer be obtained from the heap.

The Benefits of Using Linked Lists

As we saw in the first three sections of this lesson, the primary benefit of using linked lists is the low cost of inserting or removing a given data element. In each case, the process requires the rearrangement of at most three or four pointers. The number of these operations is close to the same regardless of whether the data element is at the beginning or at the end of the list. By contrast, a removal or insertion of a data element at position i in a vector of n data elements requires that $n - i$ data elements be shifted (copied) by one position. When the data elements are large and positioned near the beginning of the vector, insertions or removals can be very expensive.

Another benefit of using linked lists concerns the modeling of dynamic situations such as file input. In these situations, memory is allocated in a linked list for the incoming data incrementally, or node by node. By contrast, as we saw in Section 3.1, the use of vectors or ordered collections for these problems is expensive because n extra memory locations and n extra copy operations are necessary to accomplish each insertion into a list of length n.

To summarize, a linked list works very well for problems such as the file input problem or the data movement problem. In this class of problems, random access is unnecessary, but we need a data structure that can grow or shrink incrementally with the size of the data. A vector works much better when random access is needed, when we can predict how many data values will be input, and when the likelihood of movement of data within the vector is small.

EXERCISES ▷ 3.4

1. Discuss the difference between an address and the value stored at that address.

2. Draw pictures of the computer's memory, with binary addresses and data values, that show the memory cells for the following statements:

    a. `int x = 2, y = 3, z = 4;`

    b. `double a = 4.8, b = 7.6;`

    c. `char ch = 'a';`

d. `double list[5];`

e. `double * realPtr = 0;`

f.
```
struct
    {
    int first;
    double second;
    } aStruct;
```

3. Write a program to test for how many nodes can be allocated for a linked list of integers until the heap has no more memory. You can accomplish this task by writing a count-controlled loop whose upper bound is an input integer and which adds a new data element to the beginning of the list on each pass. Start with the input of a large integer. If an error occurs, try another integer of half that size. If an error does not occur, repeat the input with an integer half again the size of the previous input. When your inputs can alternate between an integer that causes an error and an integer that is 1 less but does not cause an error, you will have determined how many nodes can be obtained for storing integers from the heap.

4. Simon Seeplus recommends that we use a linked list rather than a vector to implement the data member of the ordered collection class (Section 2.1). He argues that the ordered collection class will then solve the data movement and file input problems very efficiently. Discuss his proposal. Does it violate any of the requirements of the ordered collection class?

Exercises 5–10 refer to the following data declaration:

```
struct node
{
    int data;
    node * next;
};
node * a;
node * b;
node * c;
```

5. Specify which of the following statements are syntactically correct. For those that are wrong, explain why they are wrong.

a. `a = b;`

b. `a = a->data;`

c. `a = a->nodeptr;`

d. `delete a;`

e. `delete b->data;`

f. `delete b;`

6. Show how the schematic below would be changed by each of the following:

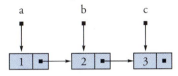

a. `a = a->next;`
b. `b = a;`
c. `c = a->next;`
d. `b->data = c->data;`
e. `a->data = b->next->data;`
f. `c->next = a;`

7. Write one statement to change

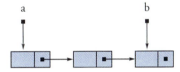

to

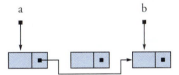

8. Consider the following list:

Write code to create a new linked list element with the value 12 and insert it at the beginning of the list headed by a.

9. Consider the following list:

Write code to remove the element at the head of the list and then add this element at the end of the list.

10. Indicate the output for each of the following:

a.

```
a = new node;
b = new node;
a->data = 10;
b->data = 20;
b = a;
a->data = 5;
cout << a->data << " " << b->data << endl;
```

b.

```
c = new node;
c->data = 100;
b = new node;
b->data = c->data % 8;
a = new node;
a->data = b->data + c->data;
cout << a->data << " " << b->data << " " << c->data << endl;
```

c.

```
a = new node;
b = new node;
a->data = 10;
a->next = b;
a->next->data = 100;
cout << a->data << " " << b->data << endl;
```

For Exercises 11–13, assume that the member names of a node are `data` and `next` and that the external pointers `first`, `probe`, and `trailer` and the integer variable `number` have been declared and initialized as follows:

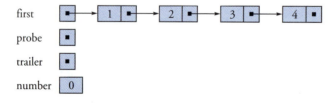

11. For the following statements labeled a through e, draw a picture of the state of these objects after the statements have been executed. Assume that the state of the objects carries over from one exercise to the next.

a.

```
probe = first;
trailer = first;
```

b.

```
while (probe != 0)
{
    trailer = probe;
    probe = probe->next;
}
```

c.

```
number = trailer->data;
```

d.

```
delete probe;
```

e.

```
trailer->next = 0;
```

12. Suppose that someone forgot to declare and implement a destructor for the linked list class. Describe a situation in which this omission is likely to cause problems.

13. Suppose that a bug has been introduced into the linked list implementation so that linked lists of the following form are created:

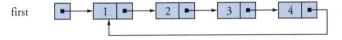

Describe the problems that this structure would cause for a sequential search for a given data element in the list.

3.5 *Using a Linked List to Implement a One-Key Table*

In Lesson 2, we analyzed the efficiency of a vector-based implementation of the one-key table ADT. We discovered that the principal trade-off is that this implementation supports fast retrievals (with binary search) but slow insertions and removals. The latter operations require a linear number of copy operations, which can be very expensive for large data elements. When the data are particularly volatile, requiring frequent insertions or removals, it might be best to choose the trade-off associated with a linked list implementation. With this option, we get linear search times but constant insertion and removal times (in the number of copies required). An additional factor in favor of a linked implementation has gone unnoticed until now. The vector implementation of a one-key table forces an application to settle for a fixed upper bound on the number of data elements that can be inserted. This constraint may cause a program to waste memory or not have enough memory to solve a problem. A linked list implementation, which provides memory for a table on an as-needed basis, uses only enough physical memory to accommodate the logical size of the table and no more.

The source code files supplied for this section have been provided—see your instructor. A short demo program, named **Tabdriv.cpp**, is also provided so that you can verify that the one-key table implementation works correctly.

Redefining the One-Key Table Class

We begin our new implementation of a one-key table by modifying the class declaration module from Lesson 2. We include the header file for the linked list class. The declarations of all public member functions (the interface to the class) remain the same. The only change in this module comes in the protected data members section. There we replace the vector and the integer data members with a single data member that is a linked list:

```
// Class declaration file: onetable.h

#ifndef ONETABLE_H

#include "assoc.h"
#include "linklist.h"

// Declaration section

// Generic class for key type K and element type E

template <class K, class E> class OneKeyTable
{

    public:

    // Class constructors

    OneKeyTable();
    OneKeyTable(const OneKeyTable<K, E> &table);

    // Member functions

    int length();
    bool empty();
    void store(const K &target, const E &item);
    bool retrieve(const K &target, E &item);
    bool remove(const K &target, E &item);
    OneKeyTable<K, E>& operator = (const OneKeyTable<K, E> &table);

    protected:

    // Data members

    LinkedList<association<K, E> > list;

};
```

```
#include "onetable.cpp"

#define ONETABLE_H
#endif
```

Note that the type of data in each node in the underlying linked list will be `association`. This type is specified by passing that type name to `LinkedList` as a parameter when the data member for the list is declared. Also, the `tableLength` data member is no longer needed, because the length of the table is just the length of the linked list.

Reimplementing the One-Key Table Class

Another benefit that we gain from representing a one-key table as a linked list rather than a vector is that our implementation becomes more abstract. Recall our discussion of the two-key table and the layering principle in Section 2.4. There we found that it is easier to work with high-level ADT operations than with low-level data structures such as vectors. The same ease of use occurs in the present case. We do not have to deal with vector indices or with C++ pointer manipulations; instead, we use high-level operations such as `first`, `next`, `insert`, and `remove`. A few examples will make this point clear.

Example 3-3

The simplest member functions are those that examine attributes of the one-key table. `empty` and `length` return the answers to the same questions asked of the linked list:

```
template <class K, class E>
bool OneKeyTable<K, E>::empty()
{
    return list.empty();
}

template <class K, class E>
int OneKeyTable<K, E>::length()
{
    return list.length();
}
```

Example 3-4

For retrievals, a linked list operation must perform a linear search for a datum stored by key value in the list. If we arrange the list so that the logical ordering of the keys maps directly to the ordering of the nodes in the list, then we can stop an unsuccessful search when a node's key value is greater than the target or when we examine the last node in the list. We begin by resetting the current pointer to the head of the list by invoking the `first` operation. We then iterate through the list, retrieve data from each node, and compare the key in the data with the target key. There are four cases to consider:

1. The key referenced from the list is less than the target—continue through the list.

2. The key referenced from the list equals the target—return `true`, along with the value associated with the key in the list.

3. The key referenced from the list is greater than the target—return `false` to signal an unsuccessful search.

4. The list's `atEnd` operation indicates that we have traversed the entire list—return `false` to signal an unsuccessful search.

213

The C++ code reflecting this logic follows:

```
template <class K, class E>
bool OneKeyTable<K, E>::retrieve(const K &target, E &item)
{

    list.first();        // Reset current pointer to head of list
    while ( (! list.atEnd()) && (list.access().getKey() < target) )
        list.next();        // Keep advancing

    // Did we go off the end of the list or advance past where
    // the target would be located if it were in the list?
    if (list.atEnd() || (list.access().getKey() > target) )
        return false;
    else                    // The key in the list must match the target
    {
        item = list.access().getValue();
        return true;
    }
}
```

Example 3-5

To store a data value in a table, we create a new association with the key and item. Then we iterate through the list, considering the same four cases as in Example 3-4, but this time taking different actions when the conditions of a particular case are satisfied.

1.   The key referenced from the list is less than the target—continue through the list.

2.   The key referenced from the list equals the target—use the list's `modify` operation to change the data associated with that key.

3.   The key referenced from the list is greater than the target—use the list's `insert` operation to add the new association in front of the key that is referenced.

4.   The list's `atEnd` operation indicates that we have traversed the entire list—use the list's `insert` operation to add the new association at the end of the list.
     The C++ code follows:

```
template <class K, class E>
void OneKeyTable<K, E>::store(const K &target, const E &item)
{
    association<K, E> newData(target, item);

    list.first();        // Reset current pointer to head of list
    while ( (! list.atEnd()) && (list.access().getKey() < target) )
        list.next();        // Keep advancing

    // Did we go off the end of the list or advance past where
    // the target should have been found?
    if (list.atEnd() || (list.access().getKey() > target) )
        list.insert(newData);
    else
        list.modify(newData);
}
```

As you can see, we have a linear amount of work to do in searching for the position of the data to be inserted in the table, but the linked implementation gives us a constant amount of work involved in moving data at that position.

E XERCISES 3.5

1. Perform a big-O analysis of each of the operations for a one-key table, assuming that the linked list implementation strategy is used.

2. Just as we have used a linked list instead of a vector to implement a one-key table, we can also use a linked list to implement an ordered collection (Section 2.1). Assuming such an implementation, perform a big-O analysis of each of the operations for an ordered collection.

3. Just as we have used a linked list instead of a vector to implement a one-key table, we can also use a linked list to implement a sorted collection (Section 2.2). Assuming such an implementation, perform a big-O analysis of each of the operations for a sorted collection.

4. In Section 2.4, we described an implementation of the two-key table ADT that was layered on one-key tables. Assuming a linked list implementation of the one-key tables on which the two-key table is layered, provide a big-O efficiency analysis of each of the operations for the two-key table.

5. Add `merge` and `append` operations to the interface of the one-key table and implement the operations.

PROGRAMMING SKILLS: Storage of Disk Files and Computer Security

Operating systems typically grant their users disk storage in units called blocks. On the magnetic disk itself, a block is a contiguous area capable of storing a fixed amount of data. For example, a block in DEC's well-known OpenVMS time-sharing system is 512 bytes. As a user enters data into a disk file, the system must grant additional blocks of storage as they are needed. In such a time-sharing environment, although each block represents physically contiguous storage area on the disk, it may not be possible for the operating system to give a user blocks that are physically next to each other. Instead, when a user needs an additional storage block, the operating system may put information into the current block about where the next block is located. In effect, it establishes a link from the current block to the next block. By the time a naive user has finished entering a four-block file, it may be scattered over the entire disk surface.

Although this approach may seem like an ingenious way of extending files indefinitely, one pays in several ways for such scattered blocks. Namely, the read-write head that seeks and puts data on the disk surface is forced to move greater distances, thereby slowing system performance. To combat such inefficiencies, shrewd users often take advantage of options that allow them to preallocate the contiguous disk storage that will be required for a file. Also, blocks may be released to users in clusters of contiguous blocks. In the event that file access remains sluggish despite such measures, systems managers may occasionally shut down the entire system to "defragment" disks, a process that entails copying all files that are presently scattered over the disk onto a new disk in physically contiguous form.

Another, more serious price that may be paid for storing disk files in this fashion revolves around the issue of data security and the operating system's treatment of blocks that are no longer needed by a user. The disk blocks used to store a file are returned to some type of available block list when a user deletes that file from his or her directory. This available list is not unlike the free store of memory that C++ maintains for you when `new` and `delete` are used to allocate and deallocate memory in a C++ program. When these "deleted" blocks are returned to that available space list, the data in them may remain intact until another user's request to extend a file results in the block's being reallocated to that new user. Consequently, if clever users ("hackers") know how to access the available space list, they may be able to scavenge through data that other users once owned and then released (assuming it was not destroyed upon being released).

One of the authors was actually involved in an incident in which a clever student was able to "find" old versions of a test that a professor had processed on the computer and then discarded to this available block list. Needless to say, the professor whose tests were being explored by the student was somewhat alarmed upon discovering what had happened. As a protection against this type of scavenging, many operating systems will, by default or as an option, actually destroy data returned to the available block list.

CASE STUDY: Optimizing A Radix Sort with Linked Lists

In this lesson, we've focused on presenting the linked list as an abstraction. However, as this Case Study will show, delving below that layer of abstraction and writing code for special purpose linked structures can sometimes greatly enhance the efficiency of a program. A file named **Radix.cpp** has been provided for you to use as the starting point for this Case Study—see your instructor.

User Request

A file containing a large number of integers (one per line) must be sorted into ascending order. Assume that all the integers in the file will fit into main memory at one time. The program should be optimized for speed, sorting the integers in the fastest way possible.

Analysis

The input and output of this program will be very simple, merely calling for input of the file name that contains the integers to be sorted and the file name to which the sorted list will be output. Given the user request to optimize the sort for speed and the fact that we will sort only integers, our analysis of sort efficiencies and limitations in Lesson 1 leads to the conclusion that the radix sort is the best algorithm (among those already studied) for this program.

Design

In addition to providing a very fast sorting algorithm, if we use the linked lists to implement the bin structures of the radix sort algorithm (see Section 2.4), we can achieve a very space-efficient version. Moreover, this situation will be one of those rare instances in which a space-efficient version is also more time efficient. To achieve this goal, we will specify that the algorithm receives a linked list of integers to be sorted rather than a vector. A top-level pseudocode description of radix sort is then given:

```
Set numberOfDigits to the number of digits in largest number in the list
For each k from 1 to numberOfDigits
    While the list to sort is not empty
        Transfer the first number in the sort list to the appropriate bin,
            keying on the kth digit (k = 1 corresponding to ones digit,
            k = 2 to tens digit, and so forth).
    For each j from 0 to 9
        Append the numbers in jth bin to the list to sort
```

In our discussion of the radix sort in Section 2.4, we were somewhat shackled by approaches that employed static allocation of the bins used to classify numbers. For instance, we determined that sorting n numbers by this algorithm would require $11n$ storage locations—n for the numbers being sorted and an additional $10n$ locations for the bins associated with the ten possible digits.

Linked lists and pointer variables provide a new implementation strategy for the bins needed by the radix sort. The dynamic allocation associated with these pointer variables will allow each bin to claim only the storage that it needs as the algorithm runs. We propose the following implementation for bins:

```
typedef LinkedList<int> BinStructureType[10];  // vector of 10 linked lists
…
BinStructureType bins;
```

We can now refine our high-level pseudocode for this new version of the radix sort. It will require the subordinate modules indicated in the structure chart shown in Figure 3-26.

FIGURE 3-26
Structure chart for radix sort

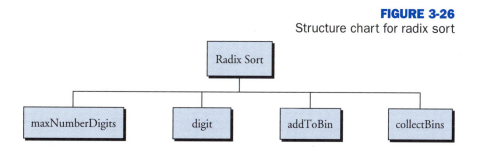

The specifications for each subordinate module follow.

Module: `maxNumberDigits`

Input: List of integers (assumed to be non-negative)

Output: The number of digits in the largest integer in list

Module: `digit`

Inputs: Non-negative integer number `k` representing a digit position in number,

with `k` = 1 corresponding to ones digit, 2 to tens digit, and so on

Output: Digit in position `k` of number

Module: `addToBins`

Inputs: A vector of bins,

Number to put into a bin,

Index indicating the bin to which to transfer the number

Outputs: Number has been put in appropriate bin

Module: `collectBins`

Inputs: A vector of bins,

List to sort (empty when received)

Output: Sublists in bin vector have been successively appended to sort list (order

of appending runs from bin 0 to bin 9)

Implementation

These module specifications give rise to the following C++ functions for the radix sort algorithm. We present only the top-level sort function and the `addToBins` and `collectBins` subordinate functions. You will complete the program and further investigate improving the efficiency of the radix sort in the end-of-lesson Projects.

```
void radixSort(LinkedList<int> &list)
{
    int k, temp;
    BinStructureType bins;
    int numberOfDigits;


    numberOfDigits = maxNumberDigits(list);

    // For k loop controls digit used to classify data.
    for (k = 1; k <= numberOfDigits; ++k)
    {
        list.first();

        // Inner loop iterates through all numbers, putting them into
        // bin determined by kth digit.
        while (! list.empty() )
        {
            temp = list.remove();
            addToBin (bins, temp, digit(temp, k));
        }
```

```
         collectBins (list, bins);
   }
}

void addToBin(BinStructureType bins, int number, int place)
{
   bins[place].insert(number);
   bins[place].next();
}

void collectBins(LinkedList<int> &list, BinStructureType bins)
{
   int place = 0;

   for (int i = 0; i < 10; ++i)          // Loop through all bins
   {
      bins[i].first();
      while ( !bins[i].empty() )          // Loop through numbers in a bin
      {
         list.insert(bins[i].remove()); // Append number from bin to list
         list.next();                    // Go to next place in list
      }
   }
}
```

Running, Debugging, and Testing Hints

- Be careful to initialize pointer variables to the null pointer with a statement such as `ptr = 0`.

- Be careful not to dereference a pointer that is null. If the assignment `ptr = 0;` is made, for example, a reference to `*ptr` or to `ptr->data` will result in an error.

- Always test a pointer to see whether it is null before attempting to dereference it. Use statements of the form

```
if (ptr != 0)
   process(ptr->data);
```

or

```
while (ptr != 0)
   ptr = ptr->next;
```

- When a piece of dynamic memory is no longer needed in a program, use `delete` so that the memory can be reallocated.

- After using `delete` with a pointer, its referenced memory is no longer available. If you use `delete ptr`, then `*ptr` and `ptr->data` give unpredictable results.

- When creating dynamic data structures, be careful to initialize properly by assigning the null pointer where appropriate and keeping track of the pointers as your structures grow and shrink.

- Operations with pointers require that they be of the same type. For this reason, exercise caution when comparing or assigning them.

- Values may become lost when pointers are inadvertently or prematurely reassigned. To avoid this problem, use as many auxiliary pointers as you wish. This approach is better than trying to use one pointer for two purposes.

- Be sure to declare and implement a destructor operation for a class that uses dynamic memory.

- An entry-controlled loop that tests for the end of a linked list is an important idiom in programming. It resembles an end-of-file `while` loop and describes a similar process. In both cases, we are testing for the presence of a sentinel, using the functions `atEnd` (lists) and `eof` (files). Also, in both cases, we advance to the next data value in a sequence by running the operations `next` (lists) and `>>` (files).

- The use of the arrow operator (`->`) with pointers is a bit like the use of the selector (`.`) with structs. However, you must exercise extreme caution when attempting to access the components of a node with the arrow operator. If the pointer variable is not initialized, or if the pointer variable is null, the use of the arrow operator could cause an error at run time. Remember that a pointer variable can point to a chunk of dynamic data (a node), but it need not do so. To protect your programs from bad pointer references, follow these guidelines:

  a. Set all pointers to null when they are declared.

  b. Test a pointer for the null condition before attempting to access the contents of a node with the arrow operator.

- You must be very careful when programming with pointers; one misplaced pointer can "lose" an entire data structure. Consequently, modular testing is more important than ever. Test the reliability of each module before releasing it for use in a large program.

- Be sure that you consider the boundary conditions when developing linked list algorithms. Does your logic cover the empty list, the first node on the list, and the last node on the list? For instance, if your insertion algorithm works for all lists except the empty list, it might as well not work at all because you will never be able to get any data on the list.

- Never reference the contents of the memory pointed to by `ptr` when `ptr` is a null pointer. The loop control structure

```
while ((ptr->getdata != target) && (ptr != 0))
```

  is asking for trouble. When `ptr` is null, the reference to `ptr->getdata` may cause a run-time error before the loop is exited. The positions of the two tests should be reversed to take advantage of short-circuit evaluation in C++.

- Programming with pointers is programming with logical pictures of linked lists. Draw a picture of what you want to do with a pointer and then write the code to make it happen. When debugging, verify and trace your code by drawing pictures of what it does with your data. For instance, an assignment to a pointer in your code corresponds to aiming an arrow somewhere in your corresponding snapshot of the data structure.

Summary

In this lesson, you learned:

- Values are stored in memory locations; each memory location has an address.

- A pointer variable contains the address of a memory location. It can be declared by

```
int *intPtr;
```

where the asterisk (*) is used after the predefined data type.

- Dynamic memory is memory that is referenced through a pointer variable. It can be used in the same context as any variable of that type. In the declaration

```
int *intPtr;
```

the dynamic memory is available after `intPtr = new int;` is executed.

- Dynamic memory is created by

```
ptr = new BaseType;
```

and destroyed (memory area made available for subsequent reuse) by

```
delete ptr;
```

- The success of dynamic memory allocation can be detected by examining the value returned by `new`. If it is 0, then no more dynamic memory is available.

- Assuming the definition

```
int *ptr;
```

the relationship between a pointer and its associated dynamic variable is illustrated by the code

```
ptr = new int;
*ptr = 21;
```

which can be envisioned as

ptr   *ptr

- 0 (the null pointer) can be assigned to a pointer variable; this tactic is used in a Boolean expression to detect the end of a list.

- Dynamic data structures differ from other data structures in that space for them is allocated under program control during the execution of the program.

- A linked list is a dynamic data structure formed by having each node contain a pointer that points to the next node.

- A node is a component of a linked list. Each node contains a member for storing a data element and a member for storing a pointer to the next node.

- References to the members of a node structure use the arrow operator -> as illustrated by

```
struct node
{
  int data;
  node *next;
};

node * ptr;

ptr = new node;
ptr->data = 45;
ptr->next = 0;
```

- When creating a linked list, the final component should have 0 assigned to its pointer member.

- Processing a linked list is accomplished by starting with the first node in the list and proceeding sequentially until the last node is reached.

- When a node is deleted from a linked list, it should be returned for subsequent use; this task is accomplished by using the standard operator delete.

VOCABULARY REVIEW

Define the following terms:

address-of operator (&)	garbage collector	logical structure
arrow operator (->)	heap store	memory leakage
dereference	heap underflow	random access data structure
empty link (null pointer)	link (pointer)	run-time stack
external pointers	linked list	sequential access data structure
		sequential traversal

LESSON 3 REVIEW QUESTIONS

FILL IN THE BLANK

Complete the following sentences by writing the correct word or words in the blanks provided.

1. In a linked list, each "package" of information is referred to as a(n) _____.

2. The value assigned to a pointer that points at nothing (or is empty) is _____.

3. You can use the _____ operator to find out where a C++ variable is stored.

4. The type of a pointer is called the _____ type.

5. A pointer that has been set to NULL (example: ptr = NULL) in C++ has the value _____.

WRITTEN QUESTIONS

Write a brief answer to the following questions. (For Questions 6–10 use the data declarations below. Indicate whether each of the statements in Questions 6–10 is syntactically correct or incorrect. You can assume that values for the pointers are defined. For those statements that are incorrect, explain why they are incorrect.)

```
struct node;
type node *nodePtrType;

struct node
{
     int  info;
      nodePtrType  next;
};
nodePtrType  p1, p2, p3;
```

6. `p1 = new nodePtrType;`

7. `p2 = 5;`

8. `p3  = new node;`

9. `p1 -> data = 5;`

10. `p1 -> next = p2 -> next;`

11. Draw a linked list that has four nodes. It should have three pointers: `first`, `current`, and `previous`. `current` should point to the third node and `previous` to the node in front of current. Use a variable named `length` to keep track of the number of nodes in the list.

12. Consider the ADT list that is a list of `dataItems` with the following operations:

`create`	create an empty list
`goFirst`	move to the first `dataItem` in the list
`currentValue`	value of the current `dataItem`
`advance`	move to the next `dataItem` in the list
`exhausted`	the "current `dataItem`" is off the list
`find(k)`	determines whether `dataItem` k is in the list
`insert(k)`	insert `dataItem` k into the list
`deleteItem(k)`	delete `dataItem` k from the list

Using these ADT operations and dot notation, write an algorithm (or a program segment in C++) to create a list that contains all the `dataItems` that are given in an array from index M to N, such that the list will have no duplicates.

13. Given the same ADT list as in Question 12, use the ADT operations and dot notation, and write an algorithm (or a program segment in C++) to delete from list x all dataItems that are in list y.

14. Assume that the class list has the public functions as defined in Questions 12 and 13, as well as a default constructor and copy constructor. Use list to implement another data structure set, which is an unordered collection of homogeneous items without duplicates. The set operations should include union (those items contained in either or both of two sets) and intersection (those items contained in both sets).

15. Assume that the class list has the public functions as defined in the previous questions. Write a C++ function printLots with the following declaration:

```
void printLots(list<char> S, list<int> P)
```

It should print those characters in S that are in positions specified by P. For example, if P = 3,7,1,5, the third, seventh, first, and fifth characters are printed. What is the running time of this function (in big-O notation)?

16. Suppose that the class list has been implemented using pointers. Now you are asked to add a new member function that sorts the list in increasing order (assuming the comparison operators are defined for the data stored in the list). The simple sorting algorithm looks like this:

```
for p1 pointing to the first node to the node preceding the last node
        for p2 pointing to the node following p1 to the last node
            if node's data of p1 is greater than that of p2
                swap the two nodes
```

17. Write a destructor for a pointer-based implementation of the class list. The destructor explicitly removes all elements from the list and frees the storage space allocated for the elements.

18. Write a member function that returns the location (a pointer) that points to the node containing the highest value among all numbers stored in a pointer-based list.

LESSON 3 PROJECTS

PROJECT 3-1

Complete the development of a linked list radix sort (see the Case Study) in the following stages.

1. Write the necessary subordinate modules.

2. Write a main program so that you can thoroughly test the algorithm.

3. Design test data that will exercise the various boundary conditions of the subordinate modules.

4. Perform a big-O analysis of the time and space requirements of this version of the radix sort. If you also implemented a vector version of the radix sort in Lesson 1, profile both versions by counting the number of operations that each must perform (use the profiling classes from the Case

Study in Lesson 1). Prepare a written report in which you compare the empirical performance of both versions.

5. You can further enhance the efficiency of the radix sort by using an implementation of linked lists in which the `collectBins` function appends successive bins to each other without removing each number from a bin and inserting it into the list to be sorted. Instead, by maintaining a pointer to the last node in the list as well as to the first, you can append one bin to another in O(1) time. Figure 3-27 depicts how this efficiency can be achieved. Implement this enhanced version of the radix sort along with the linked list operations it needs. After you have tested the new sort algorithm, profile it as you did for the version you wrote in part 4. Compare the performance of the new algorithm to the old one.

FIGURE 3-27

Appending one bin to another without removing and inserting items

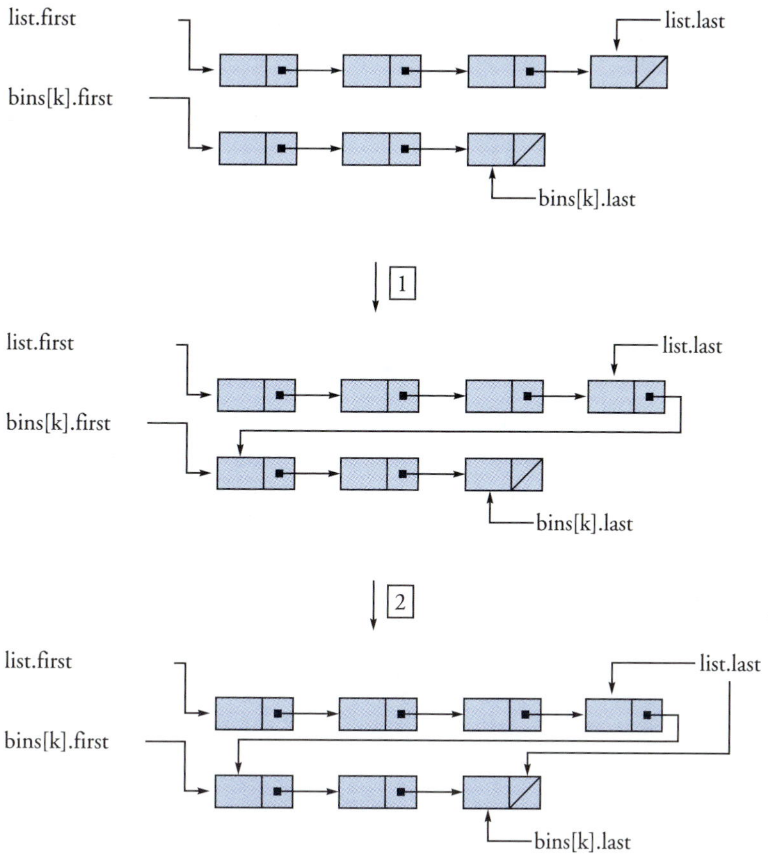

PROJECT 3-2

One problem faced by many businesses is how to best manage their lines of customers. One method is to have a separate line for each cashier or station. Another is to have one feeder line where all customers wait and the customer at the front of the line goes to the first open station. Write a program to help a manager decide which method to use by simulating both options. Your program should allow for customers arriving at various intervals. The manager wants to know the average wait in each system, average line length in each system (because of its psychological effect on customers), and the longest wait required.

PROJECT 3-3

Write a program to keep track of computer transactions on a mainframe computer. The computer can process only one job at a time. Each line of input contains a user's identification number, a starting time, and a sequence of integers representing the duration of each job. Assume that all jobs are run on a first-come, first-served basis. Output should include a list of identification numbers, starting and finishing times for each job, and the average waiting time for a transaction.

PROJECT 3-4

Several previous programming problems have involved keeping structures and computing grades for students in some class. If linked lists are used for the students' structures, such a program can be used for a class of 20 students or a class of 200 students. Write a record-keeping program that utilizes linked lists. Input is from an unsorted data file. Each student's information consists of the student's name, ten quiz scores, six program scores, and three examination scores. Output should include the following:

a. A list, alphabetized by student name, incorporating each student's quiz, program, and examination totals; total points; percentage grade; and letter grade

b. Overall class average

c. A histogram depicting class averages

PROJECT 3-5

Mailing lists are frequently kept in a data file sorted alphabetically by customer name. When they are used to generate labels for a bulk mailing, however, they must be sorted by ZIP code. Write a program to input an alphabetically sorted file and produce a list of labels sorted by ZIP code. The data for each customer follow:

a. Name

b. Address, including street (plus number), city, two-letter abbreviation for the state, and ZIP code

c. Expiration information, including the month and year

Use a linked list to sort the data by ZIP code. Your labels should include some special symbol for all expiring subscriptions.

PROJECT 3-6

A linked list limits users to movement in one direction through the list. Occasionally, it is useful to move backward to the previous node or start a process at the last node in the list. The operations `last`, `previous`, and `atBeginning`, which are the inverses of `first`, `next`, and `atEnd`, respectively, could be used with a doubly linked list having the following structure:

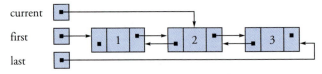

Note that a doubly linked list needs no external previous pointer. Write the specifications for the operations `last`, `previous`, and `atBeginning`, and declare and implement a doubly linked list class in C++. The operations on singly linked lists should also work with doubly linked lists, but they may be implemented differently. Test the new class with an appropriate driver program.

PROJECT 3-7

Wing-and-a-Prayer Airlines maintains four scheduled flights per day, which it identifies by the numbers 1, 2, 3, and 4. For each of these flights, the company keeps an alphabetized list of passengers. The database for the entire airline could hence be viewed as four linked lists. Write a program that sets up and maintains this database by handling commands of the following form:

Command ⟶ Add
Flight number ⟶ 3
Passenger name ⟶ BROWN
Command ⟶ Delete
From flight number ⟶ 1
Passenger name ⟶ JONES
Command ⟶ List
Flight number ⟶ 2
(List alphabetically all passengers for the specified flight.)

PROJECT 3-8

To take care of its growing business, the Fly-by-Night Credit Card Company would like to update its customer data file. Write a program in a high-level language that sets up a linked list that can support the following actions on a record:

a. Insert a record into the list in the correct place, sorted according to the Social Security number of the customer.

b. Update a record if the customer record exists.

c. Delete a record if the customer no longer wishes to patronize the company.

In the preceding data manipulation activities, the list should always remain in order sorted by Social Security number.

PROJECT 3-9

As a struggling professional football team, the Bay Area Brawlers have a highly volatile player roster. Write a program that allows the team to maintain its roster as a linked list in alphabetical order by player last name. Other data items stored for each player are:

Height
Weight
Age
University affiliation

As an added option, allow your program to access players in descending order of weight and age.

PROJECT 3-10

Develop a line-oriented text editor that assigns a number to each line of text and then maintains the lines in a linked list by line number order (similar to the fashion in which BASIC programs are maintained on many systems). Your program should be able to process the following commands:

I-line number 'text' (instruction to insert text at specified line number)
L-line1-line2 (instruction to list line1 through line2)
D-line1-line2 (instruction to delete line1 through line2)

If you feel really ambitious, extend your program by allowing the user to perform editing operations such as inserting and deleting characters within a given line.

PROJECT 3-11

Write a program that, given a file of text, will add to an index those words in the text that are marked by special delimiting brackets [ ]. The words in the index will be printed after the text itself has been formatted and printed. Words in this index should be listed in alphabetical order with a page number reference for each page of text on which they are delimited by the special brackets. Note that this program would be part of a word processing system that an author could use when developing a book with an index of terms.

PROJECT 3-12

Write a program that allows input of an arbitrary number of polynomials as coefficient and exponent pairs. Store each polynomial as a linked list of coefficient–exponent pairs arranged in descending order by exponent. Note that the coefficient–exponent pairs need not be input in descending order; it is the responsibility of your program to put them in that order. Your program should then evaluate each polynomial for an arbitrary argument X and output each polynomial in the appropriate descending exponent order. Be sure that your program works for all "unusual" polynomials, such as the zero polynomial, polynomials of degree one, and constant polynomials.

PROJECT 3-13

Write a program that uses the linked list class to solve the following problem. Imagine that a class of N students decided to choose one from among themselves to approach a curmudgeonly professor about postponing for a week an upcoming examination. They elect to arrange themselves in a circle and excuse the Mth person around the circle—with the size of the circle being reduced by one each time a person is excused. The problem is to find out which person will be the last remaining, or more generally, to find the order in which the people are excused. For example, if the circle contains JIM JANE JACK JUNE JASON JEAN JOE JEREMY JANELLE and $M = 5$, then the people are excused in the order JASON JIM JOE JUNE JACK JEAN JANELLE JANE, with JEREMY having to face the professor. To solve this problem, write a program that inserts the names of N persons into a circular list and then appropriately deletes them from the list until only one is left. Your program should output the name of each person as he or she is removed from the circle and finally output the name of the person left to face the professor.

PROJECT 3-14

Computers can store and do arithmetic only with integers of limited size. When integers surpass that limiting value, overflow occurs and the results will either be unreliable or cause your program to die with a run-time error. By altering the implementation of an integer, however, you can develop algorithms to do virtually limitless integer arithmetic. The basis of such an implementation is the storage of each digit of an integer in a list. That is, it represents an integer as a list of digits. You then develop algorithms to do integer arithmetic operations on a digit-by-digit basis, taking carries, borrows, and so forth into account as you would when performing these operations by hand. After carefully considering which list implementation best suits the problem, develop functions to perform extended integer addition, subtraction, multiplication, and division (quotient and remainder). As one test case, add the following integers and print the sum:

$$5643127821$$
$$+ \ 9276577159$$

CRITICAL THINKING

ACTIVITY 3-1

By consulting reference manuals for your version of C++ and by writing a variety of experimental programs, attempt to discover the details of how your C++ compiler manages the allocation of memory in the heap. Prepare a written report in which you describe your findings.

ACTIVITY 3-2

Your friend offers the following criticism of linked lists: "The problem with linked lists is that they cannot be used with large databases stored in files because pointers represent locations in main memory." Explain the fallacy in your friend's criticism. Then, in a detailed statement, discuss how linked lists could be implemented for data stored in random access files.

STACKS AND QUEUES

OBJECTIVES

Upon completion of this lesson, you will be able to:

- Define a stack as an ADT.

- Understand conceptually the role played by a stack in processing procedure and function calls.

- Implement a stack using a static vector.

- Implement a stack using a dynamically allocated linked list.

- Understand the differences between the infix, postfix, and prefix forms of algebraic expressions.

- Understand the computer algorithm that relies on a stack to convert infix expressions to their postfix equivalents, being particularly aware of the role of infix and in-stack priority functions in this algorithm.

- Understand the algorithm that uses a stack to evaluate a postfix expression.

- Understand the definition of the queue ADT.

- Understand what is meant by a computer simulation and use the queue ADT in a simulation program.

- Examine three implementations of the queue ADT: vector, circular vector, and linked list.

⏱ **Estimated Time: 15 hours**

Vocabulary

activation record	parsing	priority queue
first-in/first-out (FIFO)	popping	pushing
infix	postfix	queue
last-in/first-out (LIFO)	prefix	stack
		token

Introduction

In Lesson 3, we introduced the linked list as a data structure designed to handle conveniently the insertion and deletion of entries in a linearly ordered list. In this lesson we study two special types of linearly ordered lists: the stack and the queue. These lists are special because of the restrictions imposed on the way in which entries may be inserted and removed. Both structures may be implemented by vectors or by dynamically allocated linked lists.

The restriction placed on a stack is often described as *last-in/first-out (LIFO)*. Consider, for example, the order in which a smart traveler will pack a suitcase. To minimize shuffling, the last item packed should be the first worn. Another familiar example of such a storage strategy is that of the pop-up mechanism used to store trays for a cafeteria line. The first trays loaded into the mechanism may well have a long wait before they escape to a passing diner.

A list of data items processed via a LIFO scheduling strategy is called a *stack*. As we will see in this and later lessons, stacks are extremely useful data structures. They find extensive applications in the processing of subroutine calls, the syntactic checking and translation of programming languages by compilers, and the powerful programming technique of recursion (see Lesson 5).

In contrast to the linear order of a stack, a *queue* is a *first-in/first-out (FIFO)* list. This name comes close to completely characterizing the restricted types of adds and deletes that can be performed on a queue. Insertions are limited to one end of the list, whereas deletions may occur only at the other end. The conceptual picture that emerges from the notion of a queue is that of a waiting line—for example, jobs waiting to be serviced by a computer or cars forming a long line at a busy tollbooth.

4.1 The Stack Abstract Data Type and Its Implementation

The last-in/first-out nature of the stack implies that all additions and deletions occur at one designated end of the stack. That designated end is called the top, and the operations of adding to or deleting from the stack are referred to as *pushing* and *popping,* respectively. More formally, we define the stack ADT as a restricted list in which entries are added to and removed from one designated end called the top.

The operations to be performed on a stack are specified by the following preconditions and postconditions.

Create Operation
Preconditions: Receiver is an arbitrary stack in an unpredictable state.
Postconditions: Receiver is initialized to the empty stack.

Empty Operation
Preconditions: Receiver is a `previously` created stack.
Postconditions: Returns `true` if receiver is empty, `false` otherwise.

Push Operation
Preconditions: Receiver is a previously created stack. item is a value to be added to the top of the stack. There is memory available to store the new item in the stack.
Postconditions: Receiver is returned with item added to the top of the stack.

Pop Operation
Preconditions: Receiver is a previously created stack. The stack is not empty.
Postconditions: The stack has its top value removed, and this value is returned.

231

Figure 4-1 depicts the critical push and pop operations for the stack ADT. Conceptually, it is easiest to develop a mental image of the push and pop operations if you picture a stack as a vertical list with the first entry at the bottom and the last at the top. Then, as indicated in Figure 4-1, adding to the stack—that is, pushing—essentially makes this stack become taller, and removing from the stack—that is, popping—results in a shorter stack.

FIGURE 4-1
Pushing onto and popping from the stack

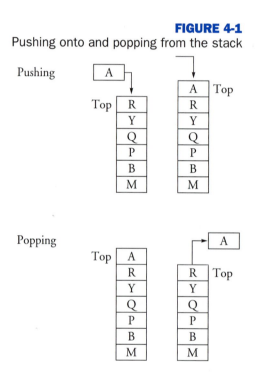

Stacks and Function Calls

Before we discuss methods of implementing a stack, we will hint at their importance in the processing of function calls. Of key importance to the processing of functions in any language is the fact that the return from a function must be to the instruction immediately following the call that originally transferred control to the function. For example, in the following partial coding,

```
int main()
{
   int q;
   .
   .
   .
   q = sub1(q);              // Call sub1
   cout << q;
   .
   .
   .
```

```
}

void sub3()
{
    .
    .
    .
}

void sub2(int q)
{
    .
    .
    .
    sub3();                     // Call sub3
    p = p - q;
    .
    .
    .
}

void sub1(int b)
{
    .
    .
    .
    b = sub2(a);                // Call sub2
    a = a + b;
    .
    .
    .
}
```

the order of operations is:

1. Leave `main` and transfer to `sub1`.

2. Leave `sub1` and transfer to `sub2`.

3. Leave `sub2` and transfer to `sub3`.

4. Return from `sub3` to the instruction `p = p - q` in `sub2`.

5. Return from `sub2` to the instruction `a = a + b` in `sub1`.

6. Return from `sub1` to the instruction `cout << q` in `main`.

7. End of `main`.

Each time a call is made, the machine must remember where to return upon completion of that function.

A stack is precisely the structure capable of storing the data necessary to handle calls and returns in this sequence. The data for each call of a function are stored in a data structure called an **activation record**. This record contains space for the return address (the address of the instruction following the call of the function), and for any values or addresses of actual parameters for that call of the function. Hence, the preceding partial coding would generate a stack that develops as illustrated in Figure 4-2. (The numbers in the figure correspond to the order of operations just shown on the preceding list.) Each time a call to a function is made, a return address is placed in an activation record, and this record is pushed on top of the stack. Each time a function is completed, the top record on the stack is popped to determine the memory address to which the return operation should be made. The nature of the leave-return sequence for functions makes it crucial that the first return address accessed be the last one that was remembered by the computer. Because data may enter or exit a stack at only one point, the top, the stack is the ideal data structure for this "last-stored, first-recalled" type of operation.

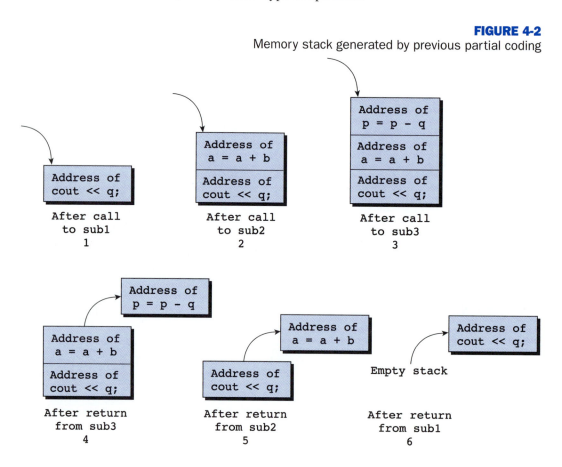

FIGURE 4-2
Memory stack generated by previous partial coding

This description of the method by which a compiler actually implements function calls is just one illustration of the utility of stacks. In Lesson 5, we'll discuss a different type of function usage called recursion and examine in detail the role of the stack in handling a recursive call.

C++ Interface for the Stack Abstract Data Type

The transition from defining a stack as an ADT to implementing this structure in a computer language requires, as usual, an interface to the ADT's operations. A C++ class declaration module for the stack ADT follows. Here we have used the class name `apstack` for consistency with the name of the stack structure in the Advanced Placement library of structures.

```
// Class declaration file: apstack.h

// Declaration section

#ifndef STACK_H
```

```
   // We assume that the constant MAX_STACK_SIZE is
   // already defined by the application in size.h

   #include "size.h"
   #include "apvector.h"

   template <class E> class apstack
   {

      public:

      // Class constructors

      apstack();
      apstack(const apstack<E> &s);


      // Member functions

      apstack<E>& operator = (const apstack<E> &s);
      bool isEmpty();        // return true if empty, else false
      int length();          // return number of elements in stack
      void push(const E &item);  // push item onto stack
      void pop(E & item);  // pop top stack value into item
      void pop();            // pop top stack value without returning it
      E onTop();             // return top stack value without popping it from
                             // stack

      private:

      // Data members

      int top;
      apvector<E> data;

   };

   #include "apstack.cpp"

   #define STACK_H
   #endif
```

We will discuss two implementations of the stack class in C++. The first uses a vector and, consequently, limits the size to which a stack may grow. The second employs a linked list with pointer variables, thereby allowing the stack to become as large as the free space in the C++ heap.

Vector Implementation of a Stack

Using a vector to implement a stack is relatively straightforward. Because insertions and deletions occur at the same end of a stack, only one pointer will be needed. We call that pointer `top`. The vector of elements will be called `data`, and its size is specified by the constant `MAX_STACK_SIZE`, defined in the application. Thus the C++ protected data members for the stack class are

```
int top;
apvector<E> data;
```

In Figure 4-3, we trace through the function example from Figure 4-2. As in Figure 4-2, the numbers below each vector correspond to the operations performed in our previous sequence of function calls and returns. The empty stack is signaled by the condition `top = -1`. If we think of `top` as pointing to the last entry pushed, then the two instructions

```
++top;
data[top] = item;
```

will push the contents of `item` onto the stack. Popping an entry from the stack into `item` requires

```
item = data[top];
--top;
```

FIGURE 4-3
Array implementation of stack from Figure 4-2

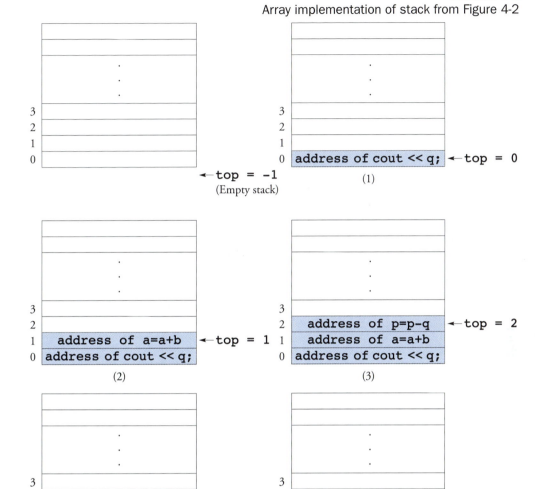

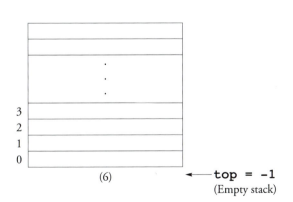

Complete functions for the push and pop operations follow in Example 4-1.

Example 4-1

Implement the push and pop operations for a vector implementation of a stack. Source code files for this example have been provided—see your instructor.

```
template <class E>
void apstack<E>::push(const E &item)
{
    assert(top < MAX_STACK_SIZE - 1);
    ++top;
    data[top] = item;
}

template <class E>
void apstack<E>::pop(E & item)
{
    assert(! isEmpty());
    item = data[top];
    --top;
}

template <class E>
void apstack<E>::pop()
{
    assert(! isEmpty());
    --top;
}
```

Note that the assert function is invoked to enforce the preconditions on each member function.

Linked List Implementation of a Stack

When we choose a linked list implementation of a stack, we are paying the price of a relatively small amount of memory space needed to maintain linking pointers for the dynamic allocation of stack space. A stack with the three integer entries 18, 40, and 31 would appear as follows:

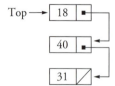

We also have the benefit of reusing an already developed class. The easiest way to use the linked list class to implement a stack class is to give the stack class a private data member that is a linked list.

```
// Class declaration file: apstack.h

// Declaration section

#ifndef STACK_H

#include "linklist.h"

template <class E> class apstack
{

    public:

    // Class constructors

    apstack();
    apstack(const apstack<E> &s);


    // Member functions

    apstack<E>& operator = (const apstack<E> &s);
    bool isEmpty();       // return true if empty, else false
    int length();         // return number of elements in stack
    void push(const E &item);  // push item onto stack
    void pop(E & item); // pop top stack value into item
    void pop();           // pop top stack value without returning it
    E onTop();            // return top stack value without popping it from
                          // stack

    private:

    // Data members

    LinkedList<E> stackData;

};

#include "apstack.cpp"

#define STACK_H
#endif
```

Note that the only data member of this stack class is a linked list called stackData. Functions to push and pop the stack now become nothing more than insertions into and deletions from the beginning of a linked list. As such, they use the high-level linked list operations that were developed in Lesson 3. You will write them as exercises at the end of this section.

Example 4-2

Source code files for this example, as well as the sample program presented, have been provided—see your instructor. To illustrate the use of stack operations in a program, let's consider a program that will check an arithmetic expression to make sure that parentheses are correctly matched (nested). Our program considers

```
(3 + 4  (5 % 3))
```

to make sure that each left parenthesis is paired with a following right parenthesis in the expression.

A first-level pseudocode for this problem follows:

Get a character from the keyboard
While the character does not equal end of line
    If it is a '('
        Push it onto the stack
    Else if it is a ')'
        Check for empty stack before popping previous '('
    Get a character from the keyboard
Check for empty stack

Figure 4-4 depicts the growing and shrinking of the stack. Assuming the existence of the basic stack operations, a program that examines an expression for correct use of parentheses is

```cpp
// Program file: parens.cpp

#include <iostream.h>
#include "apstack.h"

void main()
{
    apstack<char> s;
    char symbol;

    cin.get(symbol);
    while (symbol != '\n')
    {
        if (symbol == '(')
            s.push(symbol);
        else if (symbol == ')')
            if (s.isEmpty())
                cout << "The parentheses are not correct. " << endl;
            else
                s.pop(symbol);
        cin.get(symbol);
    }
    if (! s.isEmpty())
        cout << "The parentheses are not correct. " << endl;
}
```

FIGURE 4-4
Using a stack to check for balanced parentheses

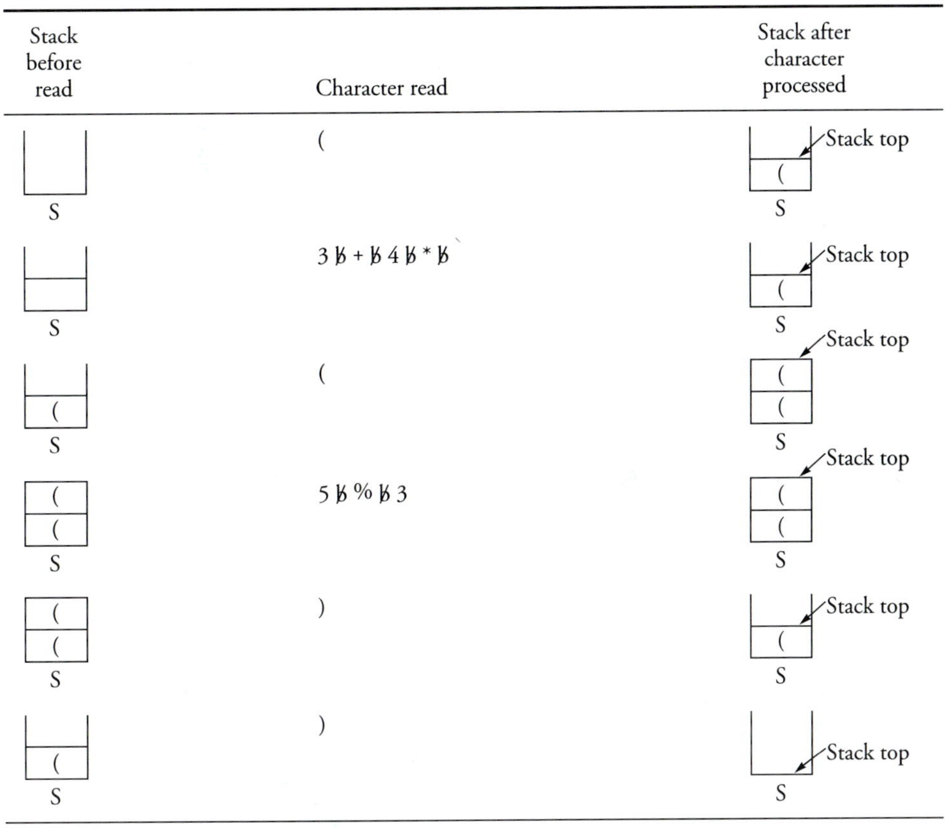

Stack before read	Character read	Stack after character processed
S	(	(← Stack top S
S	3 ƀ + ƀ 4 ƀ * ƀ	(← Stack top S
(S	(	((← Stack top S
((S	5 ƀ % ƀ 3	((← Stack top S
((S	)	(← Stack top S
(S	)	← Stack top S

*ƀ represents a blank page

This program will print an error message for an invalid expression and nothing for a valid expression. Several modifications of this short program are available and are suggested in the following exercises.

EXERCISES 4.1

1. Draw a picture of the stack of integers s after each of the following operations is performed:

```
int item;
apstack<int> s;

s.push(4);
s.push(10);
s.push(12);
s.pop(item);
s.push(3 * item);
item = s.onTop();
s.push (3 * item);
```

2. The `onTop` operation described in the definition of the stack as an abstract data type is actually unnecessary, because it can be defined in terms of other stack operations. Provide such a definition of the `onTop` operation.

3. Write functions to implement each of the following operations for a vector implementation of a stack. Be consistent with the operations already implemented in Example 4-1.
   a. `create` (do both the default constructor and the copy constructor)
   b. `empty`
   c. `onTop`

4. Write functions to implement each of the following stack operations for a linked list implementation of a stack.
   a. `create` (do both the default constructor and the copy constructor)
   b. `destroy`
   c. `empty`
   d. `push`
   e. `pop`
   f. `onTop`

5. Using the program for checking parentheses (Example 4-2), illustrate how the stack grows and shrinks when the following expression is examined:

   ```
   ( 5 / (3 - 2  (4 + 3) - (8 / 2)))
   ```

6. Modify the program in Example 4-2 so that several expressions may be examined. Also, provide more descriptive error messages.

7. Write a program that utilizes a stack to print a line of text in reverse order.

8. It is not necessary to use a stack to check expressions for matching parentheses. Write an algorithm that describes this task using a simple integer counter.

4.2 An Application of Stacks: Parsing and Evaluating Arithmetic Expressions

Often the logic of problems for which stacks are a suitable data structure involves the need to backtrack and return to a previous state. For instance, consider the problem of finding your way out of a maze. One approach is to probe a given path in the maze as deeply as possible. On finding a dead end, you need to backtrack to previously visited maze locations to try other paths. Such backtracking requires recalling these previous locations in the reverse order from which you visited them.

Not many of us need to find our way out of a maze. However, the designers of compilers are faced with an analogous backtracking situation in the evaluation of arithmetic expressions. As you scan the expression

$$A + B / C + D$$

in left-to-right order, it is impossible to tell upon initially encountering the plus sign whether you should apply the indicated addition operation to A and the immediately following operand. Instead, you must probe further into the expression to determine whether an operation with a higher priority occurs. While you undertake this probing of the expression, you must stack previously encountered operation symbols until you are certain of the operands to which they can be applied.

Further compounding the backtracking problem just described are the many different ways of representing the same algebraic expression. For example, the assignment statements

$$Z = A * B / C + D;$$
$$Z = (A * B) / C + D;$$
$$Z = ((A * B*) / C) + D;$$

should all result in the same order of arithmetic operations, even though the expressions involved are written in distinctly different forms. The process of checking the syntax of such an expression and representing it in one unique form is called *parsing* the expression. One frequently used method of parsing relies heavily on stacks.

Infix, Postfix, and Prefix Notation

Conventional algebraic notation is often termed *infix* notation—the arithmetic operator appears between the two operands to which it is being applied. Infix notation may require parentheses to specify a desired order of operations. For example, in the expression A / B + C, the division will occur first. If we want the addition to occur first, the expression must be parenthesized as A / (B + C).

Using *postfix* notation (also called reverse Polish notation after the nationality of its originator, the Polish logician Jan Lukasiewicz) eliminates the need for parentheses, because the operator is placed directly after the two operands to which it applies. Hence, A / B + C would be written as A B / C + in postfix form. This expression says

1. Apply the division operator to A and B.

2. To that result, add C.

The infix expression A / (B + C) would be written as A B C + / in postfix notation. Reading this postfix expression from left to right, we are told to

1. Apply the addition operator to B and C.

2. Then divide that result into A.

Although relatively short expressions such as the preceding ones can be converted from infix to postfix via an intuitive process, a more systematic method is required for complicated expressions. We propose the following algorithm for humans (and will soon consider a different one for computers):

1. Completely parenthesize the infix expression to specify the order of all operations.

2. Move each operator to the space held by its corresponding right parenthesis.

3. Remove all parentheses.

Consider this three-step method as it applies to the following expression, in which ^ is used to indicate exponentiation:

```
A / B ^ C + D * E - A * C
```

Completely parenthesizing this expression yields

```
(((A / (B ^ C)) + (D * E)) - (A * C))
```

243

Moving each operator to its corresponding right parenthesis, we obtain

$$(((A\ /\ (B\ {}^{\wedge}\ C))\ +\ (D\ *\ E))\ -\ (A\ *\ C\ )\ )$$

Removing all parentheses, we are left with

$$A\ B\ C\ {}^{\wedge}\ /\ D\ E\ *\ +\ A\ C\ *\ -$$

Had we started out with

$$A\ /\ B\ {}^{\wedge}\ C\ -\ (D\ *\ E\ -\ A\ *\ C)$$

our three-step procedure would have resulted in

$$(\ (\ A\ /\ (\ B\ {}^{\wedge}\ C\ )\ )\ -\ (\ (\ D\ *\ E\ )\ -\ (\ A\ *\ C\ )\ )\ )$$

Removing the parentheses would then yield

$$A\ B\ C\ {}^{\wedge}\ /\ D\ E\ *\ A\ C\ *\ -\,-$$

In a similar way, an expression can be converted into **prefix** form, in which an operator immediately precedes its two operands. The conversion algorithm for infix to prefix notation specifies that, after completely parenthesizing the infix expression according to order of priority, we move each operator to its corresponding left parenthesis. Applying the method to

$$A\ /\ B\ {}^{\wedge}\ C\ +\ D\ *\ E\ -\ A\ *\ C$$

gives us

$$(\ (\ A\ /\ (\ B\ {}^{\wedge}\ C\ )\ )\ +\ (\ (\ D\ *\ E\ )\ -\ (\ A\ *\ C\ )\ )\ )$$

and finally the prefix form

$$+\ /\ A\ {}^{\wedge}\ B\ C\ -\ *\ D\ E\ *\ A\ C$$

The importance of postfix and prefix notation in parsing arithmetic expressions is that both notations are completely free of parentheses. Consequently, an expression in postfix (or prefix) form is in unique form. In the design of compilers, this parsing of an expression into postfix form is crucial, because having a unique form for an expression greatly simplifies its eventual evaluation. Thus, in handling an expression, a compiler must:

1. Parse it into postfix form.

2. Apply an evaluation algorithm to the postfix form.

We limit our discussion here to postfix notation. The techniques we cover are easily adaptable to the functionally equivalent prefix form.

PROGRAMMING SKILLS: Logic Programming and Backtracking

In the 1960s, J. Robinson, a mathematical logician, discovered an algorithm for automating the process of proving theorems in first-order predicate logic. This discovery made the discipline of logic programming possible. A logic program consists of a set of assertions. Some of these describe particular facts, such as "Ken is over 40 years old." Other assertions describe general facts or rules, such as "All people over 40 years old have gray hair." A program consisting of these two facts can be used to prove other facts, such as "Ken has gray hair." The proof can be executed on a computer after one enters the known facts, expressed in the syntax of a logic programming language, into a database and inputs a request for the proof of the unknown fact to the computer.

PROLOG (an acronym for "Programming in Logic") is a logic programming language that provides a syntax for describing assertions and queries and an interpreter for user interaction and theorem proving. To return to our example, the known facts, expressed in the syntax of PROLOG, might be entered interactively at the -> prompt into the database as follows:

```
-> assert(over40(ken)).
OK

-> assert(grayhair(X) :- over40(X)).
OK
```

Queries for proofs of unknown facts might be entered as follows:

```
-> grayhair(ken).
Yes

-> over50(ken).
No
```

The PROLOG interpreter uses Robinson's algorithm to derive the unknown fact that Ken has gray hair from the fact that Ken is over 40 and the rule that if any individual is over 40, then he or she has gray hair. In our example, the algorithm starts with a goal of proving grayhair(ken). It finds a rule, grayhair(X) :- over40(X), whose consequent, grayhair(X), matches the goal. The algorithm then tries to prove the rule's antecedent, over40(X), with X = ken. A fact that matches this goal, over40(ken), is found in the database, so the query or unknown fact, grayhair(ken), has been proved.

Theorem proving is complicated by the fact that some rules may seem relevant but actually lead to dead ends. For example, suppose that the rules "All individuals with four children have gray hair" and "All individuals with weak backs have four children" are also facts in the database. These rules might be expressed in PROLOG as follows:

```
1. grayhair(X) :- has4children(X)
2. has4children(X) :- hasweakback(X)
```

245

If the algorithm happens to try rule (1) before the one discussed earlier, it will not be able to prove that Ken has gray hair. It will try to prove that Ken has four children and will fail when it cannot discover an assertion that Ken has a weak back.

To solve this problem, when a subgoal fails, the algorithm must backtrack to an earlier point in the process and try an alternative rule in the database. To support backtracking, the PROLOG interpreter maintains a stack of subgoals that are waiting to be proved. When a subgoal fails, the interpreter pops it off the stack and tries to prove the subgoal now at the top. In our example, the subgoals `hasweakback(ken)` and `has4children(ken)` would both be popped off the stack, and the interpreter would then try our other rule for `grayhair`. If the stack of subgoals becomes empty, then no proof of the given query can be found.

The use of a stack to implement the execution of a logic program is another example of the abstraction/implementation duality that we have emphasized throughout this book. At the abstract level, the logic programmer thinks in terms of first-order predicate logic and does not worry about how the computer proves theorems. At the implementation level, a backtracking algorithm supported by stack operations handles the real work of finding proofs.

Converting Infix Expressions to Postfix Notation

Let's consider the problem of parsing an expression from infix to postfix form. Our three-step method is not easily adaptable to machine coding. Instead, we will use an algorithm that has the following as its essential data structures:

1. A stream of characters containing the infix expression and terminated by the special delimiter #.

2. A stack named `opStack`, which may contain

    a. Arithmetic operators: +, −, *, and /.

    b. The left parenthesis, (. The right parenthesis,), is processed by the algorithm but never stored in the stack.

    c. The special delimiter #.

3. A string named `postfix` containing the final postfix expression.

To eliminate details that would merely clutter the main logic of the algorithm, we will assume that the string representing the infix expression contains **tokens** (that is, incoming symbols) consisting only of the arithmetic operators +, −, * , and /; parentheses; the delimiting character #; and operands that each consist of a single uppercase alphabetical character. We will also assume that these tokens may be read from a line without any intervening spaces. Later, we will consider some of the complications introduced by tokens of varying size and type and by the exponentiation operator ^. Thus, for the present, the algorithm we discuss will convert infix expressions of the form

```
A * B + (C - D / E) #
```

into their corresponding postfix notation.

The description of the algorithm follows:

1. Define a function `infixPriority`, which takes an operator, parenthesis, or # as its argument and returns an integer as

Character	*	/	+	−	(	)	#
Returned Value	2	2	1	1	3	0	0

This function reflects the relative position of an operator in the arithmetic hierarchy and is used with the function `stackPriority` (defined in step 2) to determine how long an operator waits in the stack before being appended to the postfix string.

2. Define another function `stackPriority`, which takes the same possibilities for an argument and returns an integer as

Character	*	/	+	−	(	)	#
Returned Value	2	2	1	1	0	Undefined	0

This function applies to operators in the operator stack, as their priority in the arithmetic hierarchy is compared to that of incoming operators from the infix string. The result of this comparison determines whether an operator waits in the stack or is appended to the postfix string.

3. Initialize `opStack` by pushing #.

4. Read the next character `ch` from the infix expression.

5. Test `ch` and

    5.1 If `ch` is an operand, append it to the postfix string.

    5.2 If `ch` is a right parenthesis, then pop entries from stack and append them to the postfix string until a left parenthesis is popped. This step ensures that operators within a parenthesized portion of an infix expression will be applied first, regardless of their priority in the usual arithmetic hierarchy. Discard both left and right parentheses.

    5.3 If `ch` is a #, pop all entries that remain on the stack and append them to the postfix string.

    5.4 Otherwise, pop from the stack and append to the postfix string operators whose `stackPriority` is greater than or equal to the `infixPriority` of `ch`. Stop this series of popping operations when you reach a stack element whose `stackPriority` is less than the `infixPriority` of `ch`. This comparison, keying on the priority of `ch` from the infix string and operators that have previously been pushed onto the operator stack, ensures that operators are applied in the right order in the resulting postfix string. After popping these operators, push `ch`.

6. Repeat steps 4 and 5 until `ch` is the delimiter #.

The key to the algorithm is the use of the stack to hold operators from the infix expression that appear to the left of another given operator, even though that latter operator must be applied first. The defined functions `infixPriority` and `stackPriority` specify this priority of operators and the associated pushing and popping operations. This entire process is best understood by carefully tracing through an example.

Example 4-3

Source code files for this example, as well as a demonstration program that includes the `infixToPostfix` function discussed in this example, have been provided—see your instructor.

Parse the infix expression

$$A * B + (C - D / E) \#$$

into its equivalent postfix form. Trace the contents of the operator stack and the postfix string as each character is read.

Table 4-1 gives the solution to this problem. In this table, the parenthesized numbers in the Commentary column refer to the subcases of step 5 in the preceding algorithm.

TABLE 4-1
Parsing of infix expression A * B + (C – D / E) #

ch	opstack	postfix	Commentary
	#		Push #
A			Read ch
		A	Append ch to postfix (5.1)
*			Read ch
	*		Push ch (5.4)
	#		
B			Read ch
		A B	Append ch to postfix (5.1)
+			Read ch
	+	A B *	Pop *, append * to postfix, push ch (5.4)
(			Read ch
	(+		Push ch (5.4)
	#		
C			Read ch
		A B * C	Append ch to postfix (5.1)
–			Read ch
	– (+		Push ch (5.4)
	#		
D			Read ch

(continued on next page)

UNIT 2: LINEAR DATA STRUCTURES

ch	opstack	postfix	Commentary
		A B * C D	Append ch to postfix (5.1)
/			Read ch
	/		Push ch (5.4)
	–		
	(		
	+		
	#		
E			Read ch
		A B * C D E	Append ch to postfix (5.1)
)			Read ch
	+	A B * C D E / –	Pop and append to postfix until (is reached (5.2)
	#		
#			Read ch
		A B * C D E / – + #	Pop and append rest of stack to postfix (5.3)

The following C++ function implements our algorithm for converting infix expressions of the form we have specified. You should study and thoroughly understand this algorithm before moving on to this chapter's Case Study section. There, the infix-to-postfix algorithm will be the focal point for an entire program that works with expressions of a slightly more complicated form.

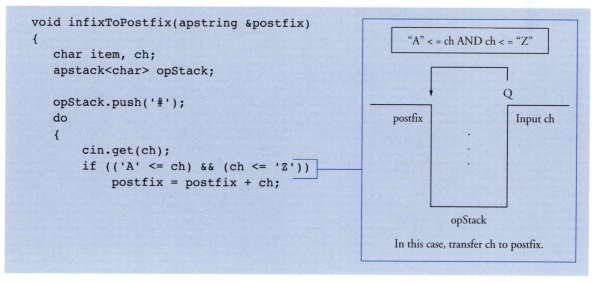

```
void infixToPostfix(apstring &postfix)
{
   char item, ch;
   apstack<char> opStack;

   opStack.push('#');
   do
   {
      cin.get(ch);
      if (('A' <= ch) && (ch <= 'Z'))
         postfix = postfix + ch;
```

"A" < = ch AND ch < = "Z"

Q

postfix   Input ch

opStack

In this case, transfer ch to postfix.

249

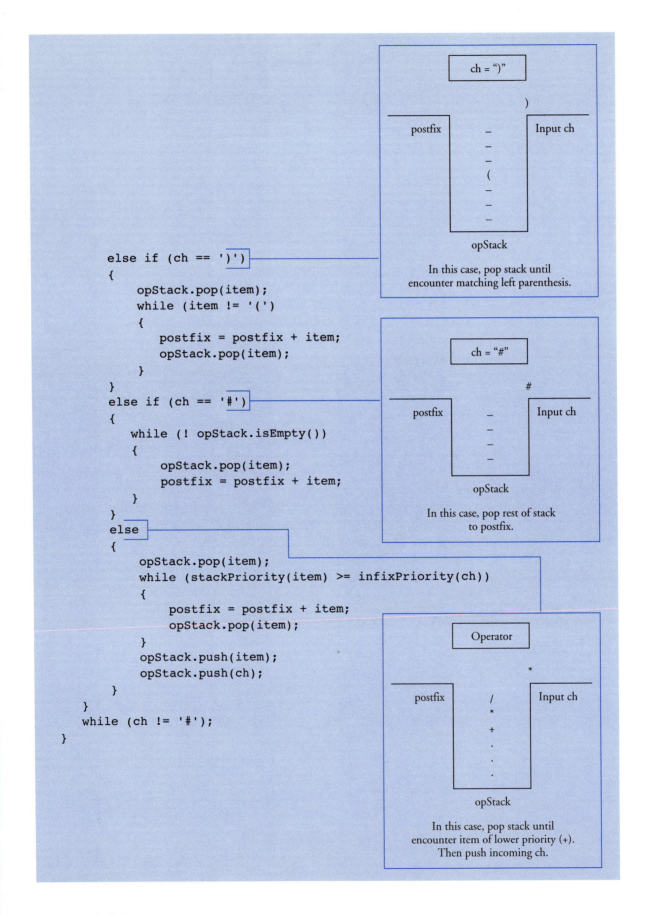

```
        else if (ch == ')')
        {
            opStack.pop(item);
            while (item != '(')
            {
                postfix = postfix + item;
                opStack.pop(item);
            }
        }
        else if (ch == '#')
        {
            while (! opStack.isEmpty())
            {
                opStack.pop(item);
                postfix = postfix + item;
            }
        }
        else
        {
            opStack.pop(item);
            while (stackPriority(item) >= infixPriority(ch))
            {
                postfix = postfix + item;
                opStack.pop(item);
            }
            opStack.push(item);
            opStack.push(ch);
        }
    }
    while (ch != '#');
}
```

ch = ")"

)

postfix — Input ch
—
—
(
—
—

opStack

In this case, pop stack until
encounter matching left parenthesis.

ch = "#"

#

postfix — Input ch
—
—
—

opStack

In this case, pop rest of stack
to postfix.

Operator

*

postfix / Input ch
*
+
.
.
.

opStack

In this case, pop stack until
encounter item of lower priority (+).
Then push incoming ch.

Evaluating Postfix Expressions

Once an expression has been parsed and represented in postfix form, another stack plays an essential role in its final evaluation. To evaluate a postfix expression, we repeatedly read characters from it. If the character read is an operand, we push the value associated with it onto the stack. If it is an operator, we pop two values from the stack, apply the operator to them, and push the result back onto the stack. After the last operand in the postfix expression has been processed, the value of the expression is the one entry on the stack. The technique is illustrated in the following example.

Example 4-4

Consider the postfix expression from Example 4-3.

A B * C D E / - + #

Let us suppose that the symbols A, B, C, D, and E had associated with them the following values:

Symbol	Value
A	5
B	3
C	6
D	8
E	2

The evaluation of the expression under this assignment of values proceeds as indicated in Figure 4-5. If we assume the functions `valueOf` (which will return the value associated with a particular symbol), `eval` (which will return the result of applying an operator to two values), and `nextToken` (which will return the next token to be read from the postfix expression), the C++ function to evaluate a postfix expression is given by the following code:

```
// Assume a suitable implementation of the string ADT,
// augmented by a nextToken operation.  nextToken(s) is
// a function that returns successive characters from a
// string s.  That is, the first time it is called, it returns the
// first character in s, then the second character in s, and so forth.

// Also, we assume the existence of a function valueOf that
// associates a character with its real value-similar to the
// way in which each variable in a program is associated with
// a value. As our tokens are only single characters, an easy way
// of implementing valueOf would be to use a vector of reals
// indexed by the subrange 0 .. 25. In effect, this would create a
// small, 26-location "memory." Finally, we assume the existence of
// an eval function that receives two real operands and the
// operator to apply to them. eval returns the result of applying
// that operator to the operands.

double evaluate(const apstring &postfix)
{
    char ch;
    double v, v1, v2;
    apstack<double> valueStack;
```

```
      ch = nextToken(postfix);
      while (ch != '#')
      {
         if (('A' <= ch) && (ch <= 'Z'))
            valueStack.push(valueOf(ch));
         else
         {
            valueStack.pop(v2);
            valueStack.pop(v1);
            v = eval(v1, v2, ch);
            valueStack.push(v);
         }
         ch = nextToken(postfix);
      }
      v = valueStack.onTop();
      return v;
   }
```

FIGURE 4-5

Evaluation of A B * C D E / - + #

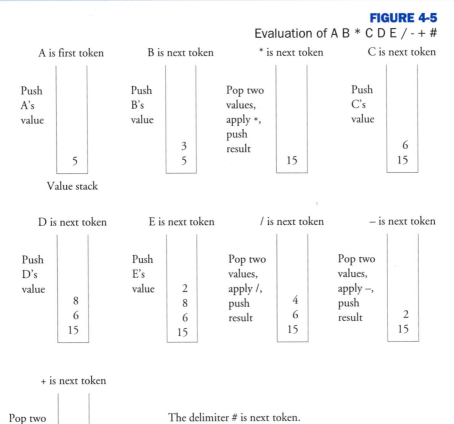

EXERCISES 4.2

1. What are the infix, postfix, and prefix forms of the following expression?

$$A + B * (C - D) / (P - R)$$

2. Trace the contents of the stack as the postfix form of the expression in Exercise 1 is evaluated. Assume the following assignment of values: $A = 6$, $B = 4$, $C = 3$, $D = 1$, $P = 12$, and $R = 11$.

3. Consider the expression with the infix notation

$$P + (Q - F) / Y$$

Using the algorithm discussed in this section to transform it into a postfix expression, trace the state of both the operator stack and postfix string as each character of the infix expression is processed. Conduct your trace following the style of Table 4-1.

4. Using the postfix expression you obtained in Exercise 3, trace the stack of real values that develops as the postfix expression is evaluated. You should indicate the numeric values on the stack as each character in the postfix expression is processed. Assume the values $F = 4$, $P = 10$, $Q = 18$, and $Y = 2$.

5. Parse the infix expression

$$P * (Q / Y) + A - B + D * Y \#$$

using the following definitions of `infixPriority` and `stackPriority`:

Priority	*	/	+	−	(	)	#
Infix	2	2	4	4	5	0	0
Stack	1	1	3	3	0	Undefined	0

Trace this parsing operation following the style of Table 4-1.

6. Using the postfix string you obtained in Exercise 5, trace the stack of real numeric values that develops as the postfix expression is evaluated. You should indicate the values on the stack as each character in the postfix expression is processed. Assume the values $A = 4$, $B = 3$, $D = 2$, $P = 1$, $Q = 4$, and $Y = 2$.

7. Write implementations of the `nextToken`, `valueOf`, and `eval` operations that are suitable for this section's evaluate function.

8. Explain how the relationship between the stack priorities and the infix priorities of (,), *, /, +, -, and # controls the parsing of the infix expression. Then explain how you would extend the definition of the stack and infix priority functions of this section to include an exponentiation operator ^. The exponentiation operator should be right associative; that is, in an expression such as

$$A \wedge B \wedge C$$

the exponentiations should occur in right-to-left order.

9. How could the functions `infixPriority` and `stackPriority` be extended to include the Boolean operators <, >, <=, > =, ==, ! =, &&, | |, and !? Justify your choices of priority values for these Boolean operators.

4.3 The Queue Abstract Data Type: Its Use and Implementations

The stack ADT that we have studied in the first two sections of this chapter is a last-in/first-out list. The next type of restricted list that we will examine, the queue, is a first-in/first-out list. All additions to a queue occur at one end, which we will designate as the rear of the queue. Items that enter the queue at the rear must move up to the front before they can be removed. `enqueue` is the name of the operation that adds an item to the rear of a queue, and `dequeue` is the name of the operation that removes an item from the front.

As noted earlier, the operations on a queue parallel the dynamics of a waiting line. The linear order underlying a queue is determined by the length of time an item has been in it. This concept is depicted in Figure 4-6. The analogy of a waiting line makes a queue the obvious ADT to use in many applications concerned with scheduling. Before we explore such applications, however, we must formally define a queue as an ADT.

FIGURE 4-6
Abstract data type queue as computer embodiment of waiting line

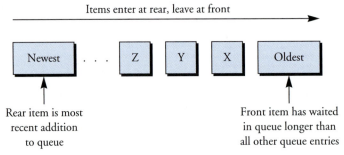

Queue. A queue is merely a restricted form of a list. In particular, the restrictions on a queue state that all additions to the queue occur at one end, the rear, and all removals from the queue occur at the other end, the front. These restrictions ensure that the earlier an item enters a queue, the earlier it will leave the queue. That is, items are processed on a first-in/first-out basis.

The five basic operations on a queue are specified by the following preconditions and postconditions.

Create Operation
Preconditions: Receiver is an arbitrary queue in unknown state.
Postconditions: Receiver is initialized to the empty queue.

Empty Operation
Preconditions: Receiver is a previously created queue.
Postconditions: Returns `true` if queue is empty, `false` otherwise.

Enqueue Operation
Preconditions: Receiver is a previously created queue. *item* is a value to be added to the rear of the queue. There is memory available to store the new item in the queue.
Postconditions: *item* is added to the rear of the queue.

Dequeue Operation
Preconditions: Receiver is a previously created queue. The queue is not empty.
Postconditions: Receiver has its front value removed, and `dequeue` returns this value.

AtFront Operation
Preconditions: Receiver is a previously created queue. The queue is not empty.
Postconditions: `atFront` returns the value at the front of the queue. Unlike the `dequeue` operation, the queue is left unchanged.

Example 4-5

To help conceptualize queue operations, consider the following sequence of actions on a queue of integers.

Create Q

Enqueue 6 onto Q

Enqueue 32 onto Q

Enqueue 18 onto Q

Dequeue from Q

Dequeue from Q

Enqueue 32 onto Q

Dequeue from Q

Dequeue from Q

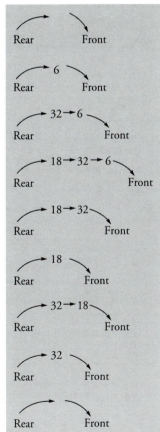

Application of a Queue in Computer Simulation

Before discussing implementations of a queue, we will examine how this ADT can be used in an application known as computer simulation. To introduce the notion of a simulation, consider the following question: The star car-washing team at Octopus Car Wash requires precisely 4 minutes to wash a car. A car arrives at Octopus on the average every 4 minutes. In a typical 10-hour day at Octopus, how long does a car have to wait between its arrival and beginning its wash?

It's tempting to answer this question by reasoning that the combination of 4 minutes to wash a car and 4 minutes between arrivals implies that no car should wait at all. However, such reasoning does not reflect the reality that cars arrive sporadically. Such sporadic arrival patterns are what can cause dreadful waiting lines.

That cars arrive, on the average, every 4 minutes really means that, in any given minute, there is a 25% chance that a car will arrive. We wish to reflect the notion of "chance" in a program that models the operation of Octopus Car Wash during a typical day. A computer simulation is a program that models a real-life event. To incorporate chance into simulations, a special function known as a random number generator is used.

A **random number generator** is a function that returns an unpredictable numerical value each time it is called. For our purposes, the value returned from a random number generator will be a real value greater than or equal to 0 but less than 1. We will approach a random number generator as a "black box" function. That is, we will not worry about the internal logic of how such numbers are generated. Many versions of C++ supply a random number generator; if yours doesn't, you might use the one given by the `RandomGenerator` class in Appendix E. Our only concern in using a random number generator is that if we call on the function `random` in a loop such as the following

```
for (int k = 0; k < 100; ++k)
    cout << random() << endl;
```

then we should see 100 values that obey statistical properties of randomness. Essentially these properties require that no pattern of values tends to recur and that values are evenly spread over the interval from 0 to 1.

How will a random number generator be used to reflect the "reality" of cars arriving at Octopus Car Wash? We will view each iteration through a loop as 1 minute in the daily operation of Octopus. On each iteration, we will call on `random` to generate a random number. If it is less than or equal to 0.25 (corresponding to the 25% chance of an arrival), our program will interpret it as a car arriving during that minute. If the random number is greater than 0.25, the program decides that no car arrived during that minute.

When a car does arrive, it will be added to the waiting queue of cars. So that we may accumulate some statistical results, the car will be time-stamped with the time that it entered the queue. This time-stamp will allow us to determine how long a car has been in the queue before it finally reaches the front. Conceptually, the queue at the core of this simulation is depicted in Figure 4-7. Pseudocode for the Octopus Car Wash simulation follows:

Initialize statistical counters
Create the queue of time-stamped cars
For each minute in the day's operation
    Call on the random number generator to determine whether a new car arrived
    If a new car arrived
        Time-stamp and enqueue it onto the queue of cars
    If no car is currently being washed and the queue of waiting cars is not empty
        Dequeue a car from the queue for washing
        Use the time-stamp for the car just dequeued to determine how long it waited
        Add that wait time to the accumulating total wait time
        Record that we have just begun to wash a car
    If a car is being washed
        Reduce by 1 minute the time left before we are done washing it

To refine this pseudocode into a C++ main program, we must establish a formal C++ interface for the queue ADT.

FIGURE 4-7

Cars waiting at Octopus Car Wash, time-stamped with the minute of their arrival

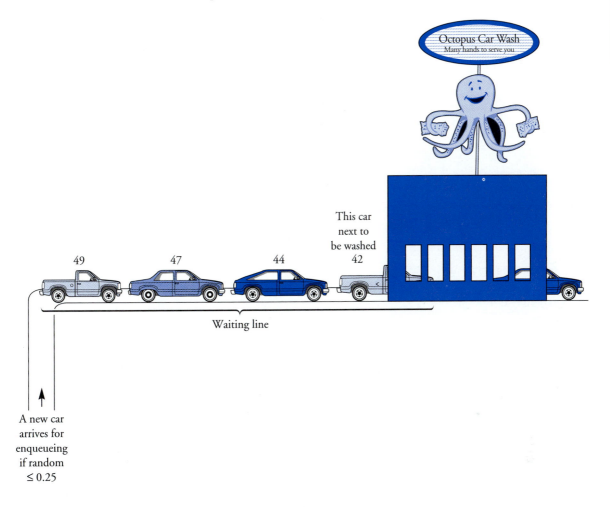

C++ Interface for the Queue ADT

As we did with the stack ADT, we add the prefix "ap" to our C++ class name for consistency with the naming conventions of the Advanced Placement data structures library.

```
// Class declaration file: apqueue.h

// Declaration section

#ifndef QUEUE_H

template <class E> class apqueue
{

public:

    // Class constructors
```

257

```
      apqueue();
      apqueue(const apqueue<E> &q);


      // Function members


      apqueue<E>& operator = (const apqueue<E> &q);
      bool isEmpty();
      int length();
      void enqueue(const E &item);    // add item to the queue
      void dequeue(E & item);         // remove from queue into item
      void dequeue();                 // remove from queue without returning
                                      // data removed

      E atFront();                    // return value at front of queue,
                                      // leaving queue unchanged


      protected:


      // Protected members appropriate to implementation technique
      // would be added here
};


#include "apqueue.cpp"


#define QUEUE_H
#endif
```

Example 4-6

Source code files for this example, as well as the sample program presented in this example, have been provided—see your instructor. Use the preceding C++ interface to write a main program for the Octopus Car Wash simulation. Assume the existence of a RandomGenerator class.

```
// Program file: octopus.cpp

// A program to simulate the operation of the Octopus Car Wash over
// 10 hours (600 minutes) of operation.  The variables timeForWash
// and probOfArrival represent the time it takes to run one car through
// Octopus's star car-washing team and the probability that a car
// arrives for a wash in any given minute.  This program assumes the
// existence of a queue data type and a random number generator invoked
// by a call to the parameterless function random.

#include <iostream.h>
#include <iomanip.h>

#include "apqueue.h"
#include "random.h"

RandomGenerator generator;

float random();
```

```
    void main()
    {
        int timeForWash,
            minute,
            timeEnteredQueue,
            carsWashed,
            totalQueueMin,
            timeLeftOnCar;
        float probOfArrival;
        apqueue<int> carQueue;

        cout << "Enter time to wash one car: ";
        cin >> timeForWash;
        cout << "Enter probability of arrival in any minute: ";
        cin >> probOfArrival;
        carsWashed = 0;
        totalQueueMin = 0;
        timeLeftOnCar = 0;
        for (minute = 1; minute <= 600; ++minute)
        {
            if (random() < probOfArrival)
                carQueue.enqueue(minute);
            if ((timeLeftOnCar == 0) && ! carQueue.isEmpty())
            {
                carQueue.dequeue(timeEnteredQueue);
                totalQueueMin = totalQueueMin + (minute -
                    timeEnteredQueue);
                ++carsWashed;
                timeLeftOnCar = timeForWash;
            }
            if (timeLeftOnCar != 0)
                —timeLeftOnCar;
        }
        cout << setw(4) << carsWashed << " cars were washed" << endl;
        cout << setiosflags(ios::fixed | ios::showpoint);
        cout << "Average wait in queue " << setw(8) << setprecision(2)
                << float(totalQueueMin) / carsWashed << endl;
    }

    float random()
    {
        return generator.nextNumber(1, 10) / 10.0;
    }
```

A sample run would appear as follows:

```
Enter time to wash one car 4
Enter probability of arrival in any minute 0.25
150 cars were washed
Average wait in queue 13.53
```

The files necessary for a linked list implementation of a queue ADT have been provided. In particular, the sample program used in Example 4-6 works equally well for both a vector and a linked list implementation of a queue.

The sample run of the program in Example 4-6 indicates how the sporadic arrival of cars can cause a backlog of work at Octopus Car Wash. One of the great values of simulation programs is that they allow cost-free experimentation with various scenarios to see whether a situation might improve or worsen. For instance, the program we have written for Octopus could be used to explore how adding more members to the car-washing team (and correspondingly reducing the amount of time it takes to wash a car) could affect the buildup of cars waiting for service. You will get a chance to explore further the use of queues for computer simulations in the exercises and projects in the remainder of this lesson.

Another noteworthy point about Example 4-6 is that it works with a queue even though we have no idea of how the queue of cars is actually implemented. Of course, this fact should not be surprising; it demonstrates the value of designing programs and data structures from an ADT perspective. However, given the high-level logic in our example, we should now turn our attention to ways in which we might implement the scheduling queue.

Vector Implementation of a Queue

From the definition of a queue, it is evident that two pointers will suffice to keep track of the data in a queue: one pointer to the front of the queue and one to the rear. This premise underlies all of the queue implementations we discuss in this section.

Let us consider computer jobs being scheduled in a batch processing environment, a good example of a queue in use. Suppose further that all job names are strings and that jobs are scheduled strictly in the order in which they arrive. Then a vector and two pointers can be used to implement the scheduling queue. We will encapsulate the vector and pointers in the class declaration module:

```
// Class declaration file: queue.h

#ifndef QUEUE_H

const int MAX_QUEUE_SIZE = 200;    // Determines maximum number of entries
#include "apvector.h"

template <class E> class apqueue
{

    public:

    // Class constructors

    apqueue();
    apqueue(const apqueue<E> &q);

    // Function members

    apqueue<E>& operator = (const apqueue<E> &q);
    bool isEmpty();
```

```
    int length();
    void enqueue(const E &item);   // add item to the queue
    void dequeue(E & item);        // remove from queue into item
    void dequeue();                // remove from queue without returning
                                   // data removed
    E atFront();                   // return value at front of queue,
                                   // leaving queue unchanged

  protected:

  // Data members

  int front, rear;
     int size;                     // size is used to implement the length function
  apvector<E> data;

  // Function member

bool full();

};

#include "apqueue.cpp"

#define QUEUE_H
#endif
```

If the front and rear pointers are initially set to 0 and -1, respectively, the state of the queue before any insertions or deletions appears as shown in Figure 4-8. Recalling that insertions may be made only at the rear of the queue, suppose that job NEWTON now arrives to be processed. The queue then changes to the state pictured in Figure 4-9. If job NEWTON is followed by PAYROLL, the queue's status must change to that of Figure 4-10, which shows that the addition of any item to the queue requires two steps:

```
++rear;
data[rear] = item;
```

FIGURE 4-8
Empty queue

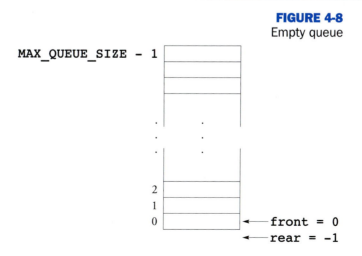

261

FIGURE 4-9

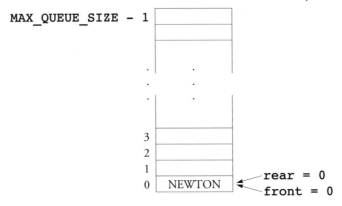

FIGURE 4-9
NEWTON added to the rear of the queue

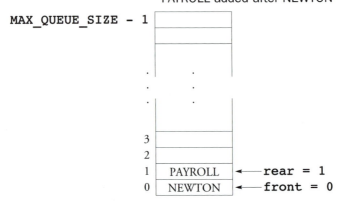

FIGURE 4-10
PAYROLL added after NEWTON

If the system is now ready to process NEWTON, the front entry must be removed from the queue to an appropriate location designated by `item` in Figure 4-11. Here the instructions

```
item = data[front];
++front;
```

achieve the desired effect.

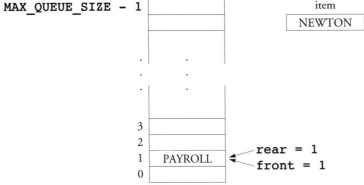

FIGURE 4-11
NEWTON removed from the queue

It should be clear that the conditions in Table 4-2 signal the associated boundary conditions for a vector implementation of a queue. The conditions allow us to develop our brief, two-line sequences for adding to and removing from a queue into full-fledged functions. These sequences, in turn, assume the existence of the Boolean-valued functions `empty` and `full` to check whether the `enqueue` and `dequeue` operations are possible. In the exercises, you will be asked to write the `create`, `empty`, and `full` operations.

TABLE 4-2
Boundary condition checks for array implementation of queue

Condition	Special Situation
rear < front	Empty queue
front = rear	One-entry queue
rear = MAX_QUEUE_SIZE	No more entries may be added to queue

Example 4-7

Source code files for this example have been provided—see your instructor. Write the `enqueue` and `dequeue` operations for a vector implementation of the queue ADT.

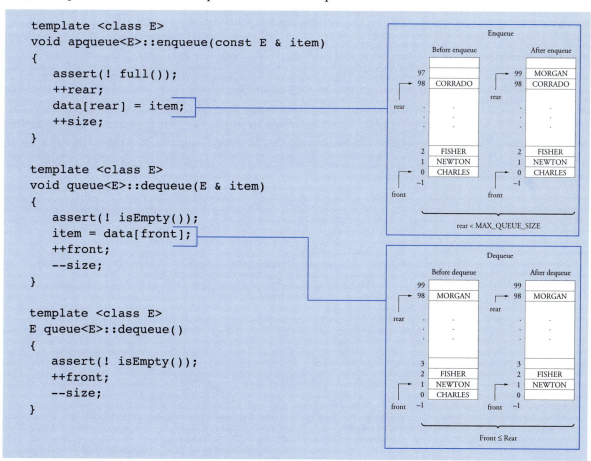

```
template <class E>
void apqueue<E>::enqueue(const E & item)
{
    assert(! full());
    ++rear;
    data[rear] = item;
    ++size;
}

template <class E>
void queue<E>::dequeue(E & item)
{
    assert(! isEmpty());
    item = data[front];
    ++front;
    --size;
}

template <class E>
E queue<E>::dequeue()
{
    assert(! isEmpty());
    ++front;
    --size;
}
```

263

As it now stands, our implementation of a queue as a scheduling structure for jobs in a batch environment functions effectively until `rear` matches `MAX_QUEUE_SIZE - 1`. Then a call to enqueue fails, even though only a small percentage of slots in the vector may actually contain data items currently in the queue structure. In fact, given the queue pictured in Figure 4-12, we should be able to use slots 0–996 again.

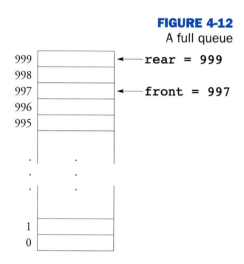

FIGURE 4-12
A full queue

This approach is not necessarily undesirable. For example, perhaps the mode of operation in a given batch environment is to process 1000 jobs, then print a statistical report on these 1000 jobs, and finally clear the queue to start another group of 1000 jobs. In this case, the queue in Figure 4-12 is the ideal structure, because data about jobs are not lost even after they have left the queue.

If the goal of a computer installation is to provide continuous scheduling of batch jobs without interruption after 1000 jobs, then the queue of Figure 4-12 would not be effective. One strategy that could be employed to correct this situation is to move the active queue down the vector upon reaching the condition `rear` matches `MAX_QUEUE_SIZE - 1`, as illustrated in Figure 4-13. If the queue contains a large number of items, however, this strategy is not satisfactory because it requires moving all of the individual data items. We will discuss two other strategies that allow the queue to operate in a continuous and efficient fashion: a circular implementation and a linked list implementation.

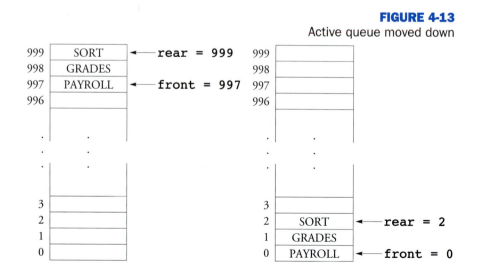

FIGURE 4-13
Active queue moved down

Circular Implementation of a Queue

A circular implementation of a queue essentially allows the queue to wrap around upon reaching the end of the vector. This transformation is illustrated by the addition of the item UPDATE to the queue in Figure 4-14. To handle the pointer arithmetic necessary for this implementation of a queue, we must make the front and rear pointers behave in a fashion analogous to an odometer in a car that has exceeded its mileage capacity. A convenient way of doing so is to use C++'s % operator. For instance, if we replace

```
++front;
```

in Example 4-7 with

```
front = (front + 1) % MAX_QUEUE_SIZE;
```

and

```
++rear;
```

with

```
rear = (rear + 1) % MAX_QUEUE_SIZE;
```

we will achieve the wraparound effect depicted in Figure 4-14. Unfortunately, it is clear from Figure 4-14 that `rear < front` will no longer suffice as a condition to signal an empty queue. To derive this condition, we must consider what remains after we remove an item from a queue that contains only a single item. There are two possible situations, as illustrated in Figure 4-15. An inspection of both cases reveals that after the lone entry has been removed, the relationship

```
( (rear + 1) % MAX_QUEUE_SIZE ) == front
```

holds between the pointers. There is a problem, however, with immediately adopting this strategy as a check for an empty queue. This same relationship between pointers also exists when the queue is full.

FIGURE 4-14

Queue wraps around when UPDATE is added

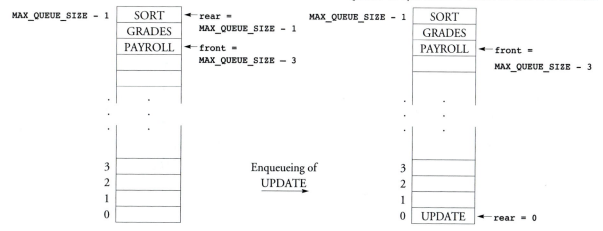

FIGURE 4-15
Removing from one-entry queue

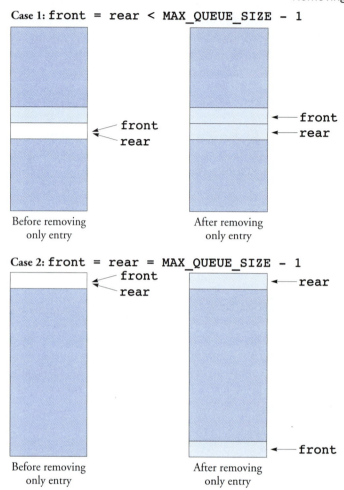

Case 1: `front = rear < MAX_QUEUE_SIZE - 1`

← front
rear

← front
← rear

Before removing
only entry

After removing
only entry

Case 2: `front = rear = MAX_QUEUE_SIZE - 1`

front
rear

← rear

Before removing
only entry

← front

After removing
only entry

We can easily avoid this apparent contradiction by adding a counter to our encapsulation of the queue to keep track of the number of items currently in the queue. Then, as Table 4-3 indicates, tests for empty and full conditions need merely check this counter.

TABLE 4-3
Boundary condition checks for circular queue with encapsulated counter

Condition	Special Situation
Counter is 1	One-entry queue
Counter is 0	Empty queue
Counter is MAX_QUEUE_SIZE	Full queue

The implementation of queue operations using a circular vector strategy is left for you to do in the exercises.

Linked List Implementation of a Queue

The linked list method allows a queue to be completely dynamic, with size restrictions imposed only by the pool of available nodes. Essentially, the queue is represented as a linked list with an additional rear pointer to the last node so that the list need not be traversed to find this node. We therefore define a queue as a new derived class of linked list, although we must be careful when we do so.

Up to this point, when we've used inheritance, the derived class has been in some sense "above and beyond" the base class. That is, the derived class provided its clients with all the operations of the base class plus new operations that were added specifically for the derived class. However, if a queue class is to inherit operations from the linked list class, we do not want client programs that use a queue to also have access to the linked list operations. Rather than extending the linked list class, the queue class is said to *adapt* the linked list class. When a derived class adapts a base class, it seals off users from operations provided by the base class and instead provides a new interface that restricts access to the base class in a form consistent with the new class.

PROGRAMMING SKILLS: Computer Simulations: Blessing or Curse?

The computer's ability to condense a large span of time (such as 600 minutes in Example 4-6) into the very short time frame required for a run of a simulation program is the blessing and the curse of computer simulations. It makes the computer a very valuable experimental tool. In addition to providing a much faster means of experimentation, simulation programs allow researchers and decision makers to set up initial conditions that would be far too risky if allowed in real life.

For example, consider the area of environmental studies. Here researchers can use simulation programs to create scenarios that would be far too time-consuming and dangerous if they were carried out in the environment. They could, for instance, use simulation software to see what might happen if pollution of a river were allowed to continue in an uncontrolled manner. If the results of the simulation indicate that all fish in the river would be gone within 10 years, nothing has really been lost. Moreover, valuable information has been gained; those who make decisions in the environmental arena would know that some sort of pollution controls are necessary. Further experimentation with the simulation could help

determine exactly what type and degree of controls should be imposed.

What can go wrong with decisions based on the result of computer simulation? Clearly, if the model on which the program is based is not an accurate reflection of the situation being simulated, results could be produced that would disastrously mislead decision makers. Additionally, we saw in Example 4-6, building the complex mathematical models used in simulation programs is a very sensitive process. Even models that seem to be relatively comprehensive can produce surprisingly inaccurate output. Hence, the real issue in using simulation results to support the decision-making process is the accuracy of the model on which the program is based. The history of simulation contains many examples of situations in which inaccurate models led to disastrous results:

■ In 1986, erroneous results during the simulation testing of a Handley-Page Victor aircraft resulted in the conclusion that there was no tail assembly flutter problem with the aircraft. In its first real flight, the tail assembly broke, killing the crew.

267

- In 1986, the collapse of the Salt Lake City Shopping Mall involved an incorrect simulation model. The roof caved in during the first big snowfall of the season—fortunately before the mall had been opened to the public.

- In 1991, a Titan 4 rocket booster blew up at Edwards Air Force Base because extensive three-dimensional computer simulations of the motor firing dynamics did not reveal subtle factors that led to the explosion.

If you're curious about these and other simulation disasters, see the article "Modeling and Simulation" by Peter G. Neumann in *Communications of the ACM*, Vol. 36, 6, June 1993, p. 124.

In our present example of a queue, the derived class adds functions for inserting, removing, and examining data in the linked list. However, we must prevent clients of the queue class from using any of the operations on linked lists, such as `first` or `next`. Defining the mode of inheritance as `protected` rather than `public` will allow the queue class to inherit all of the public and protected operations from the linked list class but prevent clients of the queue class from using them.

In addition to adapting the interface of the linked list class to a form more appropriate for queues, the queue class must maintain a rear pointer to the last node in the linked list. This will enable the `enqueue` operation to be done in O(1) time. Without the rear pointer, `enqueue` is an O(n) operation because we have to traverse the linked list to reach its end. Hence, the linked list implementation of the queue containing PAYROLL, GRADES, and SORT would appear as in Figure 4-16. We will follow the convention that the front pointer for the queue points at the first node, while the rear pointer points at the last node. We therefore access the first actual item in the queue through the head pointer of the linked list and the last actual item through the last pointer.

FIGURE 4-16
Queue with three data nodes

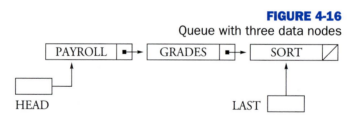

The class declaration module for a queue as a derived class of linked list (from Lesson 3) follows. Note in particular the addition of the `node *` pointer `myLast` to achieve the O(1) `enqueue` operation mentioned earlier.

```
// Class declaration file: apqueue.h

// Declaration section

#ifndef QUEUE_H

#include "linklist.h"

template <class E> class apqueue : protected LinkedList<E>
{

    public:

    // Class constructors
```

```
        apqueue();
        apqueue(const apqueue<E> &q);

        // Class destructor

        ~apqueue();

        // Member functions

        apqueue<E>& operator = (const apqueue<E> &q);
        bool isEmpty();
        int length();
        void enqueue(const E &item);    // add item to the queue
        void dequeue(E & item);         // remove from queue into item
        void dequeue();                 // remove from queue without returning
                                        // data removed
        E atFront();                    // return value at front of queue,
                                        // leaving queue unchanged

        protected:

        node * myLast;

    };

    #include "apqueue.cpp"

    #define QUEUE_H
    #endif
```

Appropriate functions for handling additions to and removals from the queue follow. Notice that from a calling module's perspective, it would make little difference whether these low-level functions used a vector or a linked list to implement the queue. For each implementation, we have bundled all of the information involved with the queue into a single object of class apqueue. Hence, the calling protocol for these modules is the same regardless of the implementation used. Remember the essence of data abstraction: The details of how a data structure is actually implemented are hidden as deeply as possible in the overall program structure.

PROGRAMMING SKILLS: Operating Systems and Scheduling Resource Use in a Time-Sharing Environment

One of the major problems facing designers of operating systems is the allocation and scheduling of resources that must be shared by a number of users. For instance, consider a simple time-sharing system that allows for multiple users, each on a video terminal, and has one shared printer. Suppose the currently running process, called process A, makes a request to use the printer. Before this process completes its task on the printer, its allotted time (often called a time burst) expires, and it is replaced by process B as the currently running process. If process B requests the printer while it is running, we have a clear problem. If process B is granted access to the printer, its output will be interspersed with that from Process A, which did not complete its printing before its time burst expired. Obviously, we cannot let process B continue to run.

The solution developed by operating system designers to honor both of these requests is to use multiple queues—one for processes that have cleared access to all resources they require to run and one for processes that have requested a resource currently owned by another process. The former of these queues is often called the **ready queue**; the latter is termed the **blocked queue.** Hence, the solution to the scenario described above involves two steps:

1. Move process A from its currently running state to the ready queue when its time burst expires (because it has all the necessary resources to start running again).

2. Move process B to the blocked queue when it requests the printer already owned by process A. Here it remains until process A is done with the printer, at which time the front entry in the blocked queue for the printer (B in this case) is moved to the ready queue.

In practice, the addition and removal of processes to and from these queues is controlled by special flags called *semaphores*. For a thorough exposition on operating system queues and semaphores, see Abraham Silberschatz and Peter B. Galvin, *Operating System Concepts*, 4th ed., Reading, MA: Addison-Wesley, 1994.

Example 4-8

Source code files for this example have been provided—see your instructor.

Code the `enqueue` and `dequeue` operations for a linked list implementation of a queue. `enqueue` will insert data at the end of the linked list. Therefore, we move the `previous` pointer to the last node, set the `current` pointer to null, and call `insert` with the data. After returning from `insert`, the `myLast` pointer is reset to the new final node on the list.

```
template <class E>
void apqueue<E>::enqueue(const E & item)
{
    myPrevious = myLast;
    myCurrent = 0;
    insert(item);
    myLast = myCurrent;
}
```

`dequeue` will remove data from the beginning of the linked list. Therefore, we call `first` to position the pointers and call `remove` to delete the data from the linked list. If `remove` has deleted the only node from a one-node list, the `myLast` pointer must be set to null to reflect the fact that the list is now empty.

```
template <class E>
void apqueue<E>::dequeue(E & item)
{
    assert(! LinkedList<E>::empty() );
    first();
    item = remove();
    if (LinkedList<E>::empty())
        myLast = 0;

}
```

Priority Queues

So far, we have used a batch scheduling application to demonstrate how a queue might be used in an operating system. Typically, such batch scheduling might also give higher priorities to certain types of jobs. For instance, at a university computer center, students in introductory computer science courses may receive the highest priority for their jobs to encourage a quick turnaround. Students in upper division courses may have the next highest priority, whereas jobs related to faculty research, which require a great deal of computation, get the lowest possible priority. These jobs could be classified as types A, B, and C, respectively. Any A job is serviced before any B or C job, regardless of the time it enters the service queue. Similarly, any B job is serviced before any C job. A data structure capable of representing such a queue requires just one *front pointer* but three *rear pointers*, one for each of the A, B, and C priorities.

A queue with eight jobs waiting to be serviced might appear as shown in Figure 4-17, which tells us that STATS, PRINT, and BANK are the A jobs awaiting service; COPY and CHECK are the B jobs; and UPDATE, AVERAGE, and TEST are the C jobs. If a new A job, PROB1, were to arrive for service, it would be inserted at the end of the A queue, between BANK and COPY. Because jobs can be serviced only by leaving the front of the queue, PROB1 would be processed before any B or C jobs.

FIGURE 4-17
Priority queue with eight jobs at three priority levels

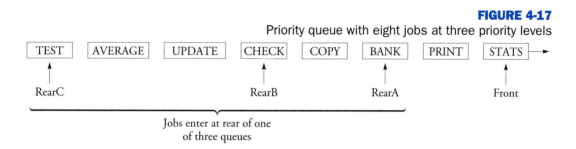

Because insertions in such a *priority queue* need not occur at the absolute rear of the queue, it is clear that a vector implementation may require moving a substantial amount of data when an item is inserted at the rear of one of the higher-priority queues. To avoid this problem, you can use a linked list to great advantage when implementing a priority queue. Whenever an item arrives to be inserted into a given priority level, the rear pointer for that priority gives us an immediately accessible pointer to the node after which the item is to be inserted. This strategy avoids a costly sequential search for the insertion point. If a dummy header is included at the beginning of the list, the empty conditions for any given priority are as shown in Table 4-4. The specifics of writing a formal ADT definition of a priority queue and providing an implementation for it are included as exercises at the end of this section.

TABLE 4-4
Empty conditions for a priority queue

Condition	Priority
Front = rear1	For priority 1, the highest priority
Rear1 = rear2	For priority 2
Rear $(n-1)$ = rear n	For priority n

271

In Lesson 6, we will see that priority queues may also be implemented using a special type of tree structure known as a heap (not to be confused with the heap maintained in C++ as described in Lesson 3). Unlike the implementation we have just discussed, the heap will conveniently allow an unrestricted number of different priorities.

EXERCISES 4.3

1. Suppose you are given a queue that is known to contain only positive integers. Use only the fundamental queue operations to write a function

```
void replace(apqueue<int> &q, int oldint, int newint);
```

that replaces all occurrences of the positive integer `oldint` in the queue with the positive integer `newint`. Other than performing this task, the queue is to remain unchanged. Avoid passing through the queue more than once.

2. Suppose you are given a queue of real numbers. Using only the fundamental queue operations, write a function that returns the average value of an entry in the queue.

3. Augment the simulation program of Example 4-6 by
   a. Counting the number of minutes during the day when the Octopus Car Wash team is idle; that is, there are no cars in the queue waiting to be washed.
   b. Counting how many cars are left waiting in the queue at the end of the day.

   Make no assumptions about how the `carQueue` might be implemented.

4. Consider a circular vector implementation of a queue in which the vector is declared to have an index range 0..4. Trace the status of the vector and the `front` and `rear` pointers after each of the following successive operations.

```
enqueue SMITH
enqueue JONES
enqueue GREER
dequeue
enqueue CARSON
dequeue
enqueue BAKER
enqueue CHARLES
enqueue BENSON
dequeue
enqueue MILLER
```

5. Implement the `create` and `empty` operations for a (noncircular) vector implementation of a queue. Be sure that your answers are consistent with the implementation of `enqueue` and `dequeue` in Example 4-7.

6. Provide data member declarations for a circular vector implementation of a queue. Then use these declarations to implement each of the basic queue operations.

7. Suppose we adopt the following conventions for the front and rear pointers associated with a queue. front is to point at the next item to be removed from the queue. rear is to point at the first available location—that is, the next location to be filled. Following these conventions, implement all queue operations for a noncircular vector representation of the ADT.

8. Repeat Exercise 7 for a circular vector representation.

9. In a queue used to schedule batch jobs on a computer system, it is often convenient to allow users to remove a job from the queue after submitting it. (They may, for example, realize that they accidentally submitted a job with an infinite loop.) Develop a function header for this removal operation. Be sure that you document it appropriately. Then implement this operation for a circular vector representation of a queue.

10. Repeat Exercise 9 for a linked list representation of a queue.

11. Provide a formal ADT definition for the priority queue. Then implement the ADT under the assumption that possible priority values are drawn from a set that could be used to index a vector. See if you can make your implementation of each operation O(1) in its efficiency.

12. Discuss ways in which the Octopus Car Wash simulation of Example 4-6 does not reflect the way in which a car wash really operates. Then discuss ways in which the pseudocode logic behind this example should be modified to overcome these shortcomings.

CASE STUDY: Integral Evaluation System

The application of the parsing algorithm described in Section 4.2 is not limited to compilers. Many of the programs typically used by scientists, engineers, and mathematicians can be greatly enhanced by allowing the user to enter an algebraic expression interactively as opposed to embedding the expression inside the program. Consider, for instance, the situation described in the following memorandum from the head of the physics department at the University of Hard Knocks.

Source code files for the case study have been provided—see your instructor.

User Request

MEMORANDUM
University of Hard Knocks

TO: Director of Computer Center
FROM: Head of Physics Department
DATE: November 22, 2001
RE: Making integration program more versatile

In physics, we find frequent application to take the integral of a function
$f(x)$ over the interval from a to b on the real number line. As you are aware,
this essentially means that we wish to find the area under the graph of the
function between endpoints a and b, as indicated in the following diagram:

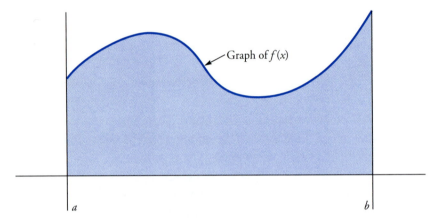

Graph of $f(x)$

We presently have a program that obtains a good approximation of this area
by adding up the areas of a large number of small rectangles, each with
base along the interval from a to b and top passing through the graph of
f(x). This concept is highlighted in the next diagram:

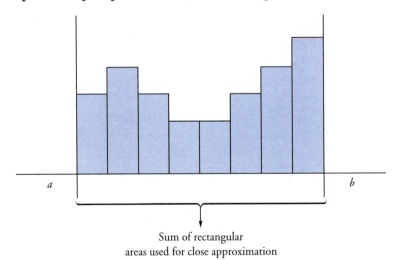

Sum of rectangular
areas used for close approximation

The user of our program can interactively enter the endpoints a and b and the number of rectangles. The result is a very good approximation when enough rectangles are used.

Our problem is not with the accuracy of the approximation but rather with the fact that, to change the function *f(x)*, the user must edit the definition of the function in the source program and then recompile. Can you help us by writing a program that will allow the user to enter the function *f(x)* interactively? The functions we integrate in this fashion can be defined in terms of the standard arithmetic operations of addition, subtraction, multiplication, division, and exponentiation. Thanks in advance for your prompt assistance.

Analysis

The physics department head has presented us with a substantial task in the preceding memorandum. Consider some of the subordinate problems that we will face in writing this program:

- The evaluation of integrals—that is, areas under graphs of functions. Obtaining numerical answers to mathematical problems of this type will introduce us to a subject known as *numerical analysis*.

- The interactive parsing and evaluation of a function will give us an opportunity to adapt the algorithms introduced earlier.

- For the type of functions described in the memorandum, the problem of finding the next token in the expression can become complicated. Consider, for instance, a function defined by the expression

$$3.14 * X \wedge 3 + X \wedge 2 \, \#$$

where $\wedge$ is used to denote exponentiation. Here, from a stream of incoming characters, we must be prepared to select a token that may be a real number, the variable *X*, or an arithmetic operator. The problem of recognizing tokens in an incoming stream of characters is called *lexical analysis*. To keep our situation relatively simple, we will assume that all tokens must be separated by a space and no other operations such as trigonometric functions may be used in defining the function *f*.

Given these requirements, a reasonable way for the user to interact with the final program is the following:

```
Enter left and right endpoints (left >= right to quit)--> 0 3
Enter number of rectangles for computing area--> 10
Enter function with spaces between tokens, then <ENTER>
3 #
Approximation to area is        9.000
```

```
Enter left and right endpoints (left >= right to quit)--> 0 3
Enter number of rectangles for computing area--> 10
Enter function with spaces between tokens, then <ENTER>
X ^ 2 #
Approximation to area is      8.977


Enter left and right endpoints (left >= right to quit)--> 0 3
Enter number of rectangles for computing area--> 100
Enter function with spaces between tokens, then <ENTER>
X ^ 2 #
Approximation to area is      9.000


Enter left and right endpoints (left >= right to quit)--> 0 1
Enter number of rectangles for computing area--> 100
Enter function with spaces between tokens, then <ENTER>
( X + 2 ) ^ 3 / ( X + 1 ) #
Approximation to area is      10.526


Enter left and right endpoints (left >= right to quit)--> 0 0
```

Design

Modular Structure for the Integral Evaluation System

With these comments in mind, we turn our attention toward designing a solution to the integration problem. Recall that the first step in this design process is to develop a modular structure chart reflecting the way in which we will partition the problem into subproblems (see Figure 4-18 on the next page). Because both the conversion from infix to postfix notation and the evaluation of a postfix expression require fundamental stack operations, we have located our stack processing modules at the deepest level of the structure chart. Here they will be accessible by both the parsing and evaluation algorithms.

Interestingly, our system will also make use of a queue. Because the tokens in the postfix expression are now more complicated objects than single characters, we need a data structure to which we can append tokens as they are processed by the infix-to-postfix algorithm. A queue emerges as a very nice ADT for this purpose. Hence, the structure chart also indicates the presence of fundamental queue operations at a level accessible by both the parsing and evaluation algorithms.

FIGURE 4-18

Lesson ④ Stacks and Queues

Modular structure chart of integration problem

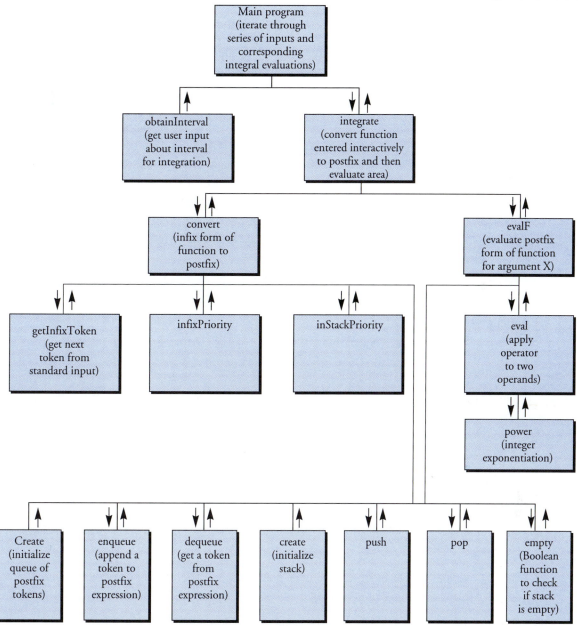

Data Structures for the Integral Evaluation System

We will need a queue to store the postfix expression that is built as the infix expression goes through our conversion algorithm. The data in this queue are more complex than characters, however. This complexity arises because the tokens needed from the infix string entered by the user are not necessarily individual characters. Rather, such tokens will fall into one of three categories:

1. *A real number:* If the token is a real number, the lexical analysis phase of our algorithm must convert it from the appropriate stream of digits and decimal point as typed by the user.

2. *The variable X:* The infix expression defines the function in terms of this general variable. When the function is evaluated, a particular value is then substituted for *X*.

3. *An operator:* We broadly include +, −, , /, ˆ, (,), and the special delimiter # in this category.

The problem with a token that may be either a real number or a character is that we essentially need a data type that can assume one of several identities, depending on the current token. In the abstract, we can think of each token as having two attributes: a *code* telling us which class of token it is (real number, operator, or variable) and a *value* that the particular token assumes (a particular, real number, operator, or variable name). To represent this information, we place the code attribute in a new class called *token*. Because the codes are of the same type, the code attribute will be treated as the *fixed part* of a C++ structure. Because the values can be of different types (double or char), the value attribute will be treated as the *variant part* of a C++ structure. Structure variants can be represented in C++ as *unions*. A union allows several data members of different types to be declared in a structure, although only one of them may be used at any given time. The currently used member is identified by examining the value of the fixed part of the structure. The structure definition that we will use for tokens follows:

```
enum TokenCode {REAL_VALUE, VAR_X, OPERATOR};

struct TokenRecord
{
    TokenCode code;
    union
    {
        double realValue;
        char op;
        char varX;
    };
};
```

The following points concerning variant parts or unions should now be made:

1. Each variant part or union should have associated with it a *tag member* in the fixed part of the structure.

2. The tag member should be an ordinal type, such as `int`, `char`, or an enumeration. This approach will allow examination of the tag member's value in a `switch` statement.

3. Only one member in a union can store a value at any given time.

4. Before storing a value in a member of a union, the programmer should set the corresponding tag member to the appropriate value. In our example, the tag member should be set to `REAL_VALUE` before storing a real number in the variant part or to `OPERATOR` or `VAR_X` before storing a character there.

5. Before using the value in a member of a union, the programmer should check whether the corresponding tag member has the appropriate value. This step is typically done with a `switch` statement. In our example, the programmer should use the value of the `realValue` member only if the tag member has the value `REAL_VALUE`.

6. Failure to adhere to the rules just specified can cause program errors. In our example, an attempt to access the `realValue` member of the variant part if the tag member contains the value `OPERATOR` may cause an error.

Variant parts or unions are defined by a form as follows:

```
union
{
 <type 1> <member 1>;
 <type 2> <member 2>;
 .
 .
 .
 <type n> <member n>;
};
```

`union` is a reserved word. The members of a union are indented for readability. The member names in a union lie in the same scope as the enclosing structure member names.

Here is the class declaration module for the `token` class:

```
// Class declaration file: token.h

#ifndef _TOKEN_H
enum TokenCode {REAL_VALUE, VAR_X, OPERATOR};

// Declaration section

class token
{

    public:

    // Class constructors:

    token(TokenCode code);
    token();
    token(const token &t);

    // Function members

    TokenCode code();
    double realValue();
    char op();
    char varX();
    void setCode(TokenCode code);
    void setRealValue(double value);
    void setOp(char op);
    void setVarX(char varX);
    token& operator = (const token &t);
    void print();
```

```
    protected:

    // Data members

    struct TokenRecord
    {
        TokenCode code;
        union
        {
            double realValue;
            char op;
            char varX;
        };
    };


    TokenRecord theToken;

};

#define _TOKEN_H
#endif
```

In processing any given token object, we first examine the code and then use the value appropriately. Moreover, we can use the token class as an element type in other data structures such as stacks and queues. For example, the three kinds of token used in parsing can be created, pushed onto a stack of tokens, and then popped off and output:

```
token number(REAL_VALUE);
token operator(OPERATOR);
token variable(VAR_X);
apstack<token> tokens;
token toOutput;

number.setRealValue(3.14);
operator.setOp('+');
variable.setVarX('X');

tokens.push(number);
tokens.push(operator);
tokens.push(variable);

while (! tokens.empty())
{
    tokens.pop(toOutput);
    switch (toOutput.code())
    {
            case REAL_VALUE:    cout << toOutput.realValue() << endl;
                                break;
```

```
        case OPERATOR:        cout << toOutput.operator() << endl;
                              break;
        case VAR_X:           cout << toOutput.varx() << endl;
   }
   cout << endl;
}
```

The preceding code will produce the following output:

```
X
+
3.14
```

Given this specification of a token type, an appropriate data structure for the postfix expression is a queue whose elements are of type `token`.

The final data structures needed by our program are stacks and queues. Actually, two conceptual stacks are needed: one for operator symbols during the parsing phase and one for values during the evaluation phase. However, by making `token` the class of items in the stack, we can use just one stack structure for both of the conceptual stacks. We will use a queue to store the collection of tokens that make up the postfix expression.

The module specifications for the integral evaluation problem posed by the head of the physics department follow.

1. **Module:** Main program

   Task: Repeatedly call on modules to obtain input specifications and then evaluate integral

2. **Module:** obtainInterval

   Task: Issue appropriate prompts and read user input; terminate when $a >= b$

   Outputs: Interval endpoints a and b, *numberOfRectangles* to use in approximating area

3. **Module:** integrate

   Task: Compute width of each rectangle as $(b - a)/numberOfRectangles$; call on module *convert* to convert infix expression read from standard input to postfix notation; initialize area to 0; repeatedly evaluate *f* at the midpoint of the base of the current rectangle, multiply it by the width of the base, and add resulting product to area accumulation

   Inputs: Endpoints a and b, and *numberOfRectangles* for which area is to be accumulated

   Outputs: Approximation to area under graph of function entered interactively by user

4. **Module:** infixToPostfix

   Task: Follow algorithm described in Section 4.2.

   Outputs: Postfix queue of tokens, delimited by #, corresponding to what user enters from standard input

281

5. Module: getInfixToken (*Note*: This module is responsible for lexical analysis.)

Task: Get the next token from the standard input stream

Inputs: Infix expression being read from standard input

Outputs: *fromInfix*, a token containing the next token read from standard input

Logic: (*Note:* We assume all tokens separated by one space.)

Initialize value field of fromInfix to 0 (in case token is a real number)
Do
    Let ch be next character read from standard input
    switch ch
        1. case ' ' : We are done
        2. case 'X' : Set fromInfix to ch
        3. case '+', '-', '*', '/', '^', '(', ')', '#' : Set fromInfix to ch
        4. case '.' : Set a multiplier to 0.1 for future accumulation
        5. case '0', '1', '2', ... '9':   if left of decimal
                                  Set value to 10 * value plus ch
                else
                                  Set value to value + multiplier * ch
                                  Divide multiplier by 10 for next
                                      iteration
While ch is not a space

6. Module: infixPriority

Task: See Section 4.2.

Inputs: *t,* a token

Outputs: Infix priority rank of *t*

7. Module: inStackPriority

Task: See Section 4.2.

Inputs: *t,* a token

Outputs: In-stack priority rank of *t*

8. Module: evalF

Task: See evaluation algorithm in Section 4.2.

Inputs: Postfix queue representation of function *f* and *x*, the real number at which *f* is to be evaluated

Outputs: The real number $f(x)$

9. Module: eval

Task: Select the appropriate C++ operation based on op

Inputs: *v1, v2*: the values of two operands and *op*, the character containing operator +, -, *, /, ^

Outputs: Numeric result of applying *op* to *v1* and *v2*

The complete C++ program for the integral evaluation system follows, with functions named in a fashion consistent with the module specifications. Also included are graphic documentation to give you a more detailed grasp of how the program functions at particular points.

```
// Program file: integral.cpp

// Program to compute area under curve of function entered
// interactively.  A stack is used to convert a function expression to
// postfix notation (which is stored in a queue) and then to
// evaluate it.  Valid function expressions can contain the variable X,
// numeric constants, operators +, -, *, /, ^ (for
// exponentiation), and appropriate parentheses.

#include <iostream.h>
#include <iomanip.h>
#include <math.h>
#include <ctype.h>

#include "token.h"
#include "apstack.h"
#include "apqueue.h"


const char END_TOKEN = '#';

void obtainInterval(double &a, double &b, int &numberOfRectangles);

void integrate(double a, double b, int numberOfRectangles, double &area);

void infixToPostfix(apqueue<token> &postfix);

void getInfixToken(token &fromInfix);

int infixPriority(token t);

int instackPriority(token t);

double evalF(apqueue<token> postfix, double x);

double eval(double v1, double v2, char op);
```

```cpp
bool isOp(char ch);

int main()
{
   double a, b, area;
   int numberOfRectangles;

   obtainInterval(a, b, numberOfRectangles);
   cout << setiosflags(ios::fixed | ios::showpoint) << setprecision(3);
   while (a < b)
   {
      integrate(a, b, numberOfRectangles, area);
      cout << "Approximation to area is " << setw(10) << area << endl;
      cout << endl;
      obtainInterval(a, b, numberOfRectangles);
   }

   return 0;
}

void obtainInterval(double &a, double &b, int &numberOfRectangles)
{
   cout << "Enter left and right endpoints (left >= right to quit)-> ";
   cin >> a >> b;
   if (a < b)
   {
      cout << "Enter number of rectangles for computing area-> ";
      cin >> numberOfRectangles;
   }
}

void integrate(double a, double b, int numberOfRectangles, double &area)
{
   apstack<token> tokenStack;
   apqueue<token> postfix;
   int count;
   double width, x;

   width = (b - a) / numberOfRectangles;
   count = 0;
   x = a;
   infixToPostfix(postfix);

   area = 0.0;
   while (count < numberOfRectangles )
   {
```

```
            area = area + evalF(postfix, x + width / 2.0) * width;
            x = x + width;
            ++count;
        }

    }


void infixToPostfix(apqueue<token> &postfix)
{
    token bottomStack(OPERATOR);
    token fromStack, fromInfix;
    apstack<token> tokenStack;
    char ch;


    // Must push END_TOKEN to correspond with algorithm in Section 14.2

    bottomStack.setOp(END_TOKEN);
    tokenStack.push(bottomStack);
    cout << "Enter function with spaces between tokens, then <ENTER>"
    << endl;
    cin.get(ch);
    do
    {
        getInfixToken(fromInfix);
        if ((fromInfix.code() == REAL_VALUE) ||
            (fromInfix.code() == VAR_X))
            //We have an operand — variable or number. }
            postfix.enqueue (fromInfix);
        else if (fromInfix.op() == ')')
        {
            tokenStack.pop(fromStack);
            while (fromStack.op() != '(')
            {
                postfix.enqueue (fromStack);
                tokenStack.pop(fromStack);
            }
        }
        else if (fromInfix.op() == END_TOKEN)
            while (! tokenStack.isEmpty())
            {
                tokenStack.pop(fromStack);
                postfix.enqueue(fromStack);
            }
        else
            // We have one of arithmetic operators +, -, *, /, ^, or )
        {
            tokenStack.pop(fromStack);
            while (instackPriority(fromStack) >=
                infixPriority(fromInfix))
            {
```

Graph of function f

This height is $f(x + Width/2)$

x Width

285

```
                postfix.enqueue(fromStack);
                tokenStack.pop(fromStack);
            }
            tokenStack.push(fromStack);
            tokenStack.push(fromInfix);
        }
    } while (! ((fromInfix.code() == OPERATOR) &&
        (fromInfix.op() == END_TOKEN)));
}


void getInfixToken(token &fromInfix)
{
    const char SPACE = ' ';
    char ch = ' ';
    double multiplier = 0.1;
    bool leftOfDecimal = true;
    int column = 0;

    do
    {
        ++column;
        cin.get(ch);
        if (isOp(ch))
        {
            fromInfix.setCode(OPERATOR);
            fromInfix.setOp(ch);
        }
        else if (isdigit(ch))
        {
            if (column == 1)
            {
                fromInfix.setCode(REAL_VALUE);
                fromInfix.setRealValue(0);
            }
            if (leftOfDecimal)
                fromInfix.setRealValue(fromInfix.realValue() *
                    10.0 + (ch - '0'));
            else
            {
                fromInfix.setRealValue(fromInfix.realValue() *
                    multiplier  + (ch - '0'));
                multiplier = multiplier / 10.0;
            }
        }
        else if (ch == '.')
        {
            leftOfDecimal = false;
            multiplier = 0.1;
        }
        else if (ch == 'X')
        {
```

23.14

For digits to left of decimal; must multiply accumulated value by 10 and add digit.

23.14

For digits to right of decimal; add digit scaled to appropriate decimal value by multiplier.

3.14

↑

We are currently here. Must prepare to accumulate digits to right of decimal.

```
                    fromInfix.setCode(VAR_X);
                    fromInfix.setVarX(ch);
            }
    } while ((ch != '\n') && (ch != SPACE) && (ch != END_TOKEN));
}


int infixPriority(token t)
{
    int priority = 0;

    switch (t.op())
    {
        case '^':          priority = 3;
                           break;

        case '*':
        case '/':          priority = 2;
                           break;

        case '+':
        case '-':          priority = 1;
                           break;

        case '(':          priority = 4;
                           break;

        case ')':
        case END_TOKEN:    priority = 0;
    }
    return priority;
}


int instackPriority(token t)
{
    int priority = 0;

    switch (t.op())
    {
        case '^' :         priority = 3;
                           break;

        case '*':
        case '/' :         priority = 2;
                           break;

        case '+':
        case '-':          priority = 1;
                           break;

        case '(':
        case END_TOKEN:    priority = 0;
    }
    return priority;
}


double evalF(apqueue<token> postfix, double x)
{
```

```
      token result(REAL_VALUE);
      token t1, t2, t3;
      apstack<token> tokenStack;

      // Because postfix is passed by value, a copy of the queue is made.
      // Hence these dequeue operations will not remove everything from
      // the queue in the calling function.
      postfix.dequeue(t1);

      while (! ((t1.code() == OPERATOR) && (t1.op() == END_TOKEN)))
      {
         if (t1.code() != OPERATOR)
            if (t1.code() == REAL_VALUE)
               tokenStack.push(t1);
            else
            {
               t1.setCode(REAL_VALUE);
               t1.setRealValue(x);
               tokenStack.push(t1);
            }
         else
         {
            tokenStack.pop(t2);
            tokenStack.pop(t3);
            result.setRealValue(eval(t3.realValue(), t2.realValue(),
               t1.op()));
            tokenStack.push(result);
         }
         postfix.dequeue(t1);
      }
      tokenStack.pop(result);
      return result.realValue();
}

double eval(double v1, double v2, char op)
{
   double result = 1;

   switch (op)
   {
      case '+' :   result = v1 + v2;
                   break;
      case '-':    result = v1 - v2;
                   break;
      case '*':    result = v1 * v2;
                   break;
      case '/':     result = v1 / v2;
                   break;
      case '^':    result = pow(v1, v2);
                   break;
   }
```

```
        return result;
    }

    bool isOp(char ch)
    {
        return (ch == '+') || (ch == '-') || (ch == '*') || (ch == '/') ||
            (ch == '^') || (ch == '(') || (ch == ')') || (ch == END_TOKEN);
    }
```

Running, Debugging, and Testing Hints

■   In applications in which it is difficult to predict the size to which a stack or queue may grow, use a linked list to implement the ADT. That way, you can take advantage of C++'s dynamic memory management and avoid having to worry about a full data structure.

■   Many scientific and mathematical application programs can be enhanced by allowing users to enter function definitions at run time. This lesson's Case Study provides an example of such run-time definitions of a function.

■   When debugging simulations, use a random number sequence that remains the same over different runs of the program. Without such a sequence, your program will behave differently on separate runs even though you provide it with identical inputs, because you are getting a different pattern of random numbers. Appendix E indicates how you can ensure a fixed sequence of random numbers from one run of the program to the next.

Summary

In this lesson, you learned:

- Conceptually, a stack is simpler than a queue because all additions and deletions are limited to one end of the structure, the top. For this reason, a stack is also known as a last-in/first-out (LIFO) list. Like a queue, a stack may be implemented using either a vector or a linked list.

- The simplicity of the stack as an abstract structure belies the importance of its application. Stacks play a crucial role in the parsing done by language compilers.

- Parsing, as we have studied it in this chapter, involves the conversion of an expression from infix to postfix notation. In infix notation, an algebraic operator is located between its two operands. In postfix notation, the operator follows its two operands.

- Expressions in postfix notation do not require parentheses to override the standard hierarchy of algebraic operations.

- Stacks process function calls when a program executes.

- A queue is a first-in/first-out (FIFO) data structure used in processing data such as job scheduling in a large university computer environment. Two basic pointers—front and rear—are associated with this structure. New data items are added to the rear of the queue, and the data item that is about to be processed is removed from the front of the queue.

- The relative advantages and disadvantages of three implementations of queues—vector, circular vector, and linked list—are summarized as follows:

Implementation	Advantages	Disadvantages
Vector	A record of queue entries remains even after they have been removed.	Static allocation of storage limits the overall queue size. Vector locations cannot be reused once entries are removed from queue.
Circular vector	Vector locations can be reused once entries are removed from queue.	Static allocation of storage limits the overall queue size.
Linked list	With C++ pointer variables, a queue can grow dynamically to take full advantage of all space available in C++'s heap.	Could be less space efficient than array implementations because each node in queue must include a pointer field as well as data fields.

- Primary applications of queues are in the areas of operating systems and computer simulation of events.

VOCABULARY REVIEW

Define the following terms:

activation record

first-in/first-out (FIFO)

infix

last-in/first-out (LIFO)

parsing

popping

postfix

prefix

priority queue

pushing

queue

stack

token

LESSON 4 REVIEW QUESTIONS

FILL IN THE BLANK

Complete the following sentences by writing the correct word or words in the blanks provided.

1. A(n) _____ is a restricted list in which entries are added and removed from one designated end, called the top.

2. LIFO stands for _____.

3. The stack ADT contains five operations: _____.

4. The notation that places the operations after the operands is referred to as _____.

5. The notation that places the operator prior to the operands is referred to as _____.

6. The notation that requires parentheses is referred to as _____.

7. A(n) _____ is a restricted list in which entries are added at one designated end, called the rear, and removed from the other designated end, called the front.

8. FIFO stands for _____.

9. The queue ADT contains five operations: _____.

10. A queue can be implemented using either _____ or _____.

WRITTEN QUESTIONS

Write a brief answer to the following questions.

11. Assume the class stack has been implemented with these public functions: default constructor, copy constructor, `isEmpty()`, `push(item)`, and `pop()`. Assume `pop()` removes the top item from the stack and returns it. Write a nonmember, nonfriend function concatenate (that is, the function does not have access to the internal implementation of stack) that takes two stack objects S and R as parameters, and returns a stack that is the concatenation of S and R. That is, the resulting stack contains all elements of S followed by all elements of R, in the original order.

12. In converting the following infix expression

    ```
    A * (D - B + ((C / E + A)))
    ```

    to postfix form, illustrate the conversion process by showing, at each step of the conversion algorithm, the input symbol, the contents of the operator stack, and the output string that represents the postfix expression.

13. Consider a line of customers at a candy store waiting to be served. The store has only one checkout counter. Each customer wants to buy different numbers of bags of candies for Halloween. Because of the low sale price of the candy, the store limits customers to three bags at a time. If the customer wants more bags, he or she must check out and come in again and wait at the end of line. Assume the data structure queue has been implemented (a class with operations `isEmpty`, `enqueue`, `dequeue`). Write a nonmember, nonfriend function that takes a queue having a fixed number of customers as parameters and simulates the process until all customers have been served.

14. Assume that the definition of the class queue is given that has only the following operations: `isEmpty()`, `operator=`, `enqueue(item)`, and `dequeue()`. Write a nonmember, nonfriend function in C++ that takes two parameters: Q of type queue and E of type elemType. The function should update the front element of Q with the value E.

15. Assume that a class queue has member functions `enqueue(item)`, `dequeue()`, `operator=`, and `length()`. Write a nonmember, nonfriend function reverse that takes a parameter, Q, of type queue and returns a queue whose elements are the same as those of Q but in reverse order. Do not use any functions other than those mentioned above.

16. Consider a vector implementation of a stack. Assume an application requires using two stacks whose elements are of the same type. A natural implementation of such a two-stack data structure would be to use two vectors. An alternative implementation is to use a single vector for the storage and let the stacks grow toward each other, as shown below:

    Write a C++ definition of the class twoStack, including the data members and the implementation of the member functions `push`, `pop`, `isEmpty`, and `isFull`. Note that each of the member functions needs an extra parameter, which is either a 1 or a 2, indicating which of the two stacks the operation is applied to. You don't need to supply constructors.

17. Comparing a vector implementation and a linked list implementation of stack, the vector implementation is simpler, uses less storage space, and perhaps runs faster, whereas the linked list implementation offers unlimited stack size. To take advantage of both implementations, we can use linked vectors to implement a stack. That is, we can use a vector for the stack storage as in the vector implementation. When it is full, however, we create an additional vector that is linked to the previous vector. This process can continue so that the size of stack will be unlimited. We are given the following outline of the class declaration:

```
template  <class T>
    class  stack
    {
            private:
                    . . . . . . . . .
            public:
                    stack();
                    void push(T);
                    T pop();
                    . . . . . . . . . .
    }
```

Answer parts a and b in implementing the stack using the linked-vectors method.

   a. Define the private data members.

   b. Write a definition of the template member function push.

18. A pointer-based circular linked list is a linked list in which each node contains a pointer pointing to the next node and the pointer in the last node is pointing to the first node. Using such a circular linked list to implement the queue data structure, the general situation of a queue would look like this:

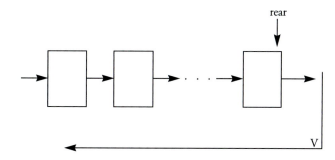

Use a circular linked list to implement the queue operations enqueue and dequeue.

PROJECT 4-1

SCANS

Write a program that will parse infix expressions into prefix form.

PROJECT 4-2

SCANS

Write a program to call for input of a decimal number and convert it to its binary equivalent using the method described in the following flowchart. Note that this method produces the binary digits for the given number in reverse order. Use a stack to print them in the correct order.

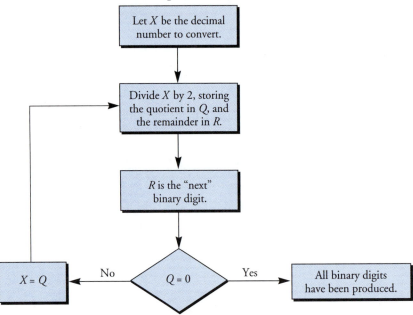

PROJECT 4-3

SCANS

Earlier you developed a passenger list processing system for the various flights of Wing-and-a-Prayer Airlines (see Project 3-7 in Lesson 3). Wing-and-a-Prayer management would now like you to extend this system so that it processes logical combinations of flight numbers. For example, the command

```
LIST 1 OR 2
```

should list all passengers whose names appear on the flight 1 or flight 2 list. Your program should also accept the logical operators AND and NOT and allow parenthesized logical expressions obeying the standard logical hierarchy

```
NOT
AND
OR
```

PROJECT 4-4

A tax form may be thought of as a sequence of items, each of which is either a number or defined by an arbitrary mathematical formula involving other items in the sequence. To assist the firm in its tax-planning strategy, top management at the Fly-by-Night Credit Card Company desires a program that would allow managers to enter interactively numbers or formulas associated with given lines of a tax form. Once all such lines have been defined, users of the program may redefine the number or formula associated with a particular line, and all other lines dependent on that one should be updated appropriately. Note that because formulas may be entered interactively, your program must use a stack to evaluate them. You will in effect, have written a small-scale spreadsheet program.

PROJECT 4-5

Write a program that will accept commands of the following form:

- `INPUT <variable name>`

- `<variable name> = infix expression involving variable names and arithmetic operators +, -, *, /`

- `PRINT <variable name>`

- `GO`

These commands are to be stored in a vector of strings until the GO command is entered. Once the GO command is entered, your program should execute the previously stored commands. "Execute" here means the following:

- **For an INPUT command:** Send a question mark to the terminal and allow the user to enter a real number; this real number is then stored in the variable name.

- **For an assignment statement:** Parse the expression into postfix form and then evaluate it, storing the results in the variable name on the left of the equality sign.

- **For a PRINT instruction:** Write to the terminal the numerical contents of the specified variable name.

To make things relatively easy, you may assume a syntax that

- Allows variable names consisting of one uppercase alphabetical character.

- Allows only one variable name following the commands for INPUT or PRINT.

- Allows one blank space after the commands for INPUT and PRINT and no blank spaces anywhere else.

For an additional challenge, design your program to handle successfully the exponentiation operator ^ within assignment statement expressions. The following example should illustrate the need for care in handling this exponentiation operator:

$$3^{2^3} = 3^8, \text{ not } 9^3$$

This project is an extension of Project 4-5 for a "compiler" for a primitive programming language. Write a program that will accept commands of the following form:

- ■ INPUT <variable name>

- ■ PRINT <variable name>

- ■ <variable name> = infix arithmetic expression involving variable names and arithmetic

- ■ operators +, -,* , /, ^

- ■ GOTO <line> ────┬── ALWAYS, or

    IF infix logical expression involving
        variable names and operators +, -, *,
        /, ^, & (for AND),| (for OR), !
        (for NOT), <, >, =

- ■ STOP

- ■ RUN

These commands are to be stored in a vector of strings until the RUN command is entered. Upon encountering the RUN command, your program should execute the previously stored commands. "Execute" here means the following:

- **For an INPUT command:** Send a question mark to the terminal and allow the user to enter a real number, which is stored in the variable name.

- **For a PRINT command:** Write to the terminal the numerical contents of the specified variable name.

- **For an assignment command:** Parse the expression into postfix form and then evaluate it. Store the result in the variable name on the left of the equality sign.

- **For a GOTO command:** Branch to the line number specified when the ALWAYS condition follows the line number or when the infix expression that follows the IF evaluates to true. Here "line number" refers to the relative position of the line in the sequence of lines that were entered prior to the RUN command. The first line number in this sequence is "00".

- **For a STOP command:** Halt execution.

To make things relatively easy, you may assume a syntax that

- Specifies that only one blank space follows INPUT, PRINT, GOTO, and the line number. No other blanks appear anywhere.

- Allows only one variable name to follow INPUT or PRINT.

- Allows only variable names consisting of one uppercase alphabetical character.

- Allows only line numbers consisting of two digits, 00 through 99.

The usual hierarchy for operators is assumed.

PROJECT 4-7

Modify the program in the Case Study section so that it integrates expressions involving the functions sin, cos, tan, exp, and ln. Test your modified program by having it evaluate the following integrals:

a. sin (X * 2) + cos X / 2 between 0 and 1
b. 3 * (X + 4) ^ 2 + tan (X / 2) between 0 and 1
c. 3 * (X + 4) ^ 2 + tan X / 2 between 0 and 1
d. exp ln X ^ 3 between 1 and 3
e. exp ln (X ^ 3) between 1 and 3

PROJECT 4-8

If you have access to a graphics library in your version of C++, write a program that allows a user to define interactively a function and then displays a graph of the function between two specified endpoints.

PROJECT 4-9

Develop a program to simulate the processing of batch jobs by a computer system. The scheduling of these jobs should be handled via a queue (or priority queue for more of a challenge). Examples of commands that your program should be able to process follow:

Command	Purpose
ADD	To add an entry to the queue
DELETE	To take an item out of the queue
STATUS	To report on items currently in the queue

PROJECT 4-10

Previously you developed a program to keep track of a bank's records. Now the bank has asked you to develop a program to simulate the arrival of customers in a waiting line at the bank. Factors to consider are the average time it takes to service one customer, the average number of customers who arrive in a given time period, and the number of service windows maintained by the bank. These factors should be provided as input to your program. Statistics such as the length of time the average customer has to spend in the waiting line could be very helpful in the bank's future planning.

PROJECT 4-11

Here is a problem typically encountered in text formatting applications. Given a file of text, text that is delimited by the special bracketing symbols [and] is to be considered a footnote. Footnotes, when encountered, are not to be printed as normal text but instead are stored in a footnote queue. Then, when the special symbol # is encountered, all footnotes currently in the queue are printed and the queue should be returned to an empty state.

What you learn in solving this problem will allow you to make good use of string processing techniques discussed in earlier lessons.

PROJECT 4-12

To improve its services, the Fly-by-Night Credit Card Company (see Project 3-8 in Lesson 3) has decided to give incentives to its customers for prompt payment. Customers who pay their bill two weeks before the due date receive top priority and a 5% discount. Customers who pay their bill within one week of the due date receive second priority and a 1% discount. Third priority is given to customers who pay their bill on or within two days after the due date. The customers who pay their bills thereafter are assigned the lowest priority. Write a program to set up a priority queue to access customer records accordingly.

PROJECT 4-13

The Bay Area Brawlers professional football team (see Project 3-9 in Lesson 3) has been so successful in recent weeks that the team management is considering the addition of several new ticket windows at the team's stadium. However, before investing a sizable amount of money in such an improvement, managers would like to simulate the operation of ticket sales with a variety of ticket window configurations. Develop a computer program that allows input of such data as number of ticket windows, average number of fans arriving each hour as game time approaches, and average length of time to process a ticket sale. Output from your program should include statistics such as the average waiting-line length each hour as game time approaches and the amount of time the average fan had to wait in line before having his or her ticket request processed. Use queues to represent each of the waiting lines.

PROJECT 4-14

Consider the design for an implementation of the radix sort algorithm and its associated bin (sublist) structure that was discussed in Lesson 3's Case Study. Note that queues could provide an alternative implementation for the bin structure needed by a radix sort. What queue implementation would provide the most space-efficient bin structure for a radix sort? Why? Develop a complete radix sort program that uses queues to implement the bins needed by the algorithm and then accesses these bins *only* through the defined ADT operations for a queue. Is this implementation of a radix sort more or less time efficient than that described in Lesson 3's Case Study? Justify your answer in a written memorandum.

PROJECT 4-15

SCANS

As director of computer operations for Wing-and-a-Prayer Airlines, you receive the following memorandum. Design and write a simulation program to satisfy the specifications in the memo.

MEMORANDUM
Wing-and-a-Prayer Airlines

TO: Director of Computer Operations
FROM: President, Wing-and-a-Prayer Airlines
DATE: September 30, 2000
RE: Wasted Fuel and Time

Wing-and-a-Prayer Airlines is becoming increasingly concerned about the amount of fuel being wasted as its planes wait to land at and take off from world-famous O'Hair Airport. Could you please help us write a program to simulate the operation of one day's activity at O'Hair and report on the times spent waiting to land and take off for each Wing-and-a-Prayer flight? Input data to the program should include:

- Average number of Wing-and-a-Prayer arrivals each hour

- Average number of other airline arrivals each hour

- Average number of Wing-and-a-Prayer departures each hour

- Average number of other airline departures each hour

- Number of available runways

- Average time a runway is in use for an arrival

- Average time a runway is in use for a departure

By appropriately adjusting these parameters, we hope to do some valuable "what-if" analyses regarding the time spent waiting for a runway by our arrivals and departures.

PROJECT 4-16

SCANS

If an arithmetic expression is written in prefix notation, then there is no need to use parentheses to specify the order of operators. For this reason, some compilers translate infix expressions (such as 2 + 8) to prefix notation (+ 2 8) first and then evaluate the prefix string. Write a program that will read prefix expressions and then compute and display the value of the indicated arithmetic expression. Assume that the operands are single-digit positive integers separated by blanks. The operators can be +, -, *, and /, also separated by blanks, with their usual meanings of add, subtract, multiply, and divide.

PROJECT 4-17

Implement the following user-friendly enhancements for the program in this lesson's Case Study.

1. Make the `getInfixToken` module more robust by allowing the user to separate individual tokens with an arbitrary number of zero or more spaces.

2. Make the `getInfixToken` module more robust by guarding against input of an invalid arithmetic operator.

3. Make the `getInfixToken` module more robust by guarding against an invalid character in a stream of characters intended to be a real number. When such an invalid character is detected, allow the user to recover from the point of error rather than forcing the user to retype the entire line.

CRITICAL THINKING

ACTIVITY 4-1

This lesson's special feature *Computer Simulations: Blessing or Curse?* cites some issues arising out of simulation. Research and prepare a more thorough written report on computer simulation. Your report could discuss any or all of the following:

- Examples of disciplines and industries in which simulation has been used to great advantage.

- Limitations and inaccuracies that arise in modeling a system by computer simulation. Techniques that can be used to measure and monitor such inaccuracies.

- The reliance of many simulation programs on the effective generation of random numbers.

- The potential danger in relying on the results of simulation programs without examining the validity of their underlying models.

ACTIVITY 4-2

This chapter's Case Study demonstrated how a computer program can be used to solve a mathematical problem in interactive fashion. In particular, the type of problem solved by this program is the evaluation of integrals. Explore other types of mathematical problems that can be solved interactively by software systems available at your school. (The Mathematica program from Wolfram Research is one example of such a system available at many universities.) Prepare a report on the results of your explorations. In keeping with the theme of this chapter's Case Study, be sure that your report includes a discussion of the types of mathematical expressions that can be parsed and evaluated by such systems.

UNIT 2 REVIEW QUESTIONS

TRUE/FALSE

Circle T if the statement is true or F if the statement is false.

T F **1.** In C++, the * operator is used to obtain the address of a variable.

T F **2.** In C++, the dereference operator is the & symbol.

T F **3.** In C++, the `new` operator is used to allocate cells for storing data.

T F **4.** In C++, the `dispose` operator is used to return memory cells to the system.

T F **5.** The computer can continue to allocate dynamic memory for data indefinitely.

T F **6.** C++ automatically returns unused dynamic memory to the system.

T F **7.** The memory cells for dynamic data objects are automatically allocated from the run-time stack.

T F **8.** A stack is a FIFO data structure.

T F **9.** You would use a queue to enforce a first-come, first-served processing schedule.

T F **10.** There is only one possible implementation of a queue, which uses a vector.

FILL IN THE BLANK

Complete the following sentences by writing the correct word or words in the blanks provided.

1. In C++, a(n) _____ variable contains the address of another cell in memory.

2. The area of memory from which cells are allocated for dynamic data is called a(n) _____.

3. The _____ value is used to initialize a variable to indicate that it does not contain the address of another memory cell.

4. A data structure that contains a data element and a link to the next item in a list is called a(n) _____.

5. The last link in a linked list contains the _____ value.

6. Items in a queue are added at the _____ and removed from the _____.

7. The operations to add and remove an item from a stack are called _____ and _____, respectively.

8. A stack is used in applications where one must return to the _____ visited state of a program.

9. Two implementations of stacks use _____ and _____.

10. The three possible notations for expressions are _____, _____ and _____.

WRITTEN QUESTIONS

Write a brief answer to the following questions.

1. Describe three ways to initialize a pointer variable in C++.

2. Assess the costs and benefits of using vectors or linked lists in an application.

3. Convert the following infix expressions to their equivalent postfix forms.
    a. (a + b) * c / d
    b. a + b − c / d
    c. a * b * c / d

4. Explain why a computer can more easily evaluate a postfix expression than an infix expression.

5. Describe two different applications in which a stack might be used.

6. Describe two different applications in which a queue might be used.

PROJECT 2-1

SCANS

Write a function `listToVector`. The function expects a linked list as a parameter and returns a vector of items in the list. The postconditions are that the parameter list is unchanged and the items in the vector are in the same positions as they are in the list.

PROJECT 2-2

SCANS

Write a function `stackToQueue`. This function expects a stack as a parameter and returns a queue constructed from the items in the stack. The postconditions are that the front item in the queue is the bottom item in the stack and the stack parameter is unchanged.

CRITICAL THINKING

ACTIVITY 2-1

SCANS

Describe the costs and benefits of two different implementation strategies for using a linked list to implement a stack. The first strategy defines a stack class as a derived class of a linked list class. The second strategy defines a stack class that contains a linked list object as a data member.

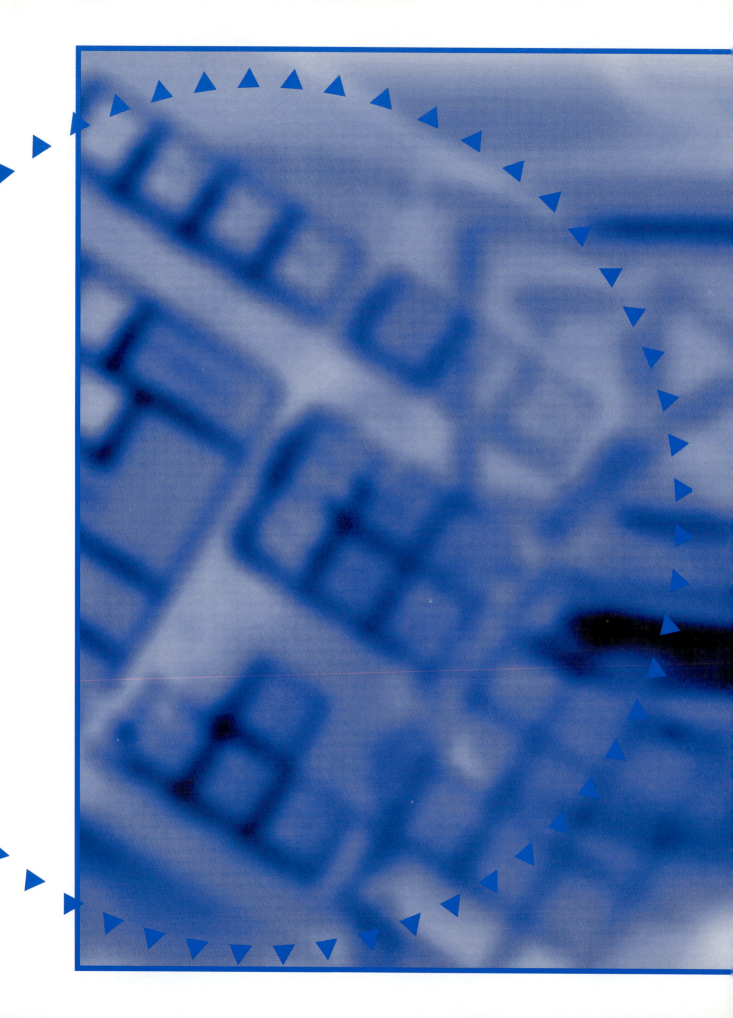

RECURSION AND RECURSIVE DATA STRUCTURES

RECURSION

OBJECTIVES

Upon completion of this lesson, you will be able to:

■ Recognize problems particularly suited to recursive solutions.

■ State the solutions to such problems as a simpler instance of the same problem.

■ Trace the performance of a recursive algorithm using a run-time trace diagram.

■ Use an algorithm's run-time trace diagram to estimate the time and space efficiency of the algorithm.

■ See how recursive algorithms that potentially involve more than one recursive call at each level may lead to an exponential time efficiency.

■ Develop an intuitive approach for developing recursive solutions to problems.

■ Use recursion in implementing a search strategy called trial-and-error backtracking.

🕐 **Estimated Time: 15 hours**

Vocabulary

binding time problem	nonterminals	stack frame
context-free grammar	parse tree	start symbol
generalized nested loops	recursion	tail recursive
grammar	recursive descent parsing	terminals
LISP	run-time trace diagram	trial-and-error backtracking

Introduction

In introductory programming courses, you have examined problems that are suited to iterative control by methods such as `while`, `do`, and `for` loops. Many of these problems can more easily be solved by designing functions that call themselves. In computer science, this form of self-reference is called *recursion*. We are now ready to embark on a detailed study of recursive problem solving.

In this lesson, we first examine the essentials of *recursive functions*. Now that we are familiar with stack operations, we will also be able to explain how recursion is implemented. The "invisible" data structure underlying recursive functions is a stack used by the system to process the call-and-return pattern of functions in a program (see Section 4.1). By examining the role of this system stack more closely, you will build confidence in your ability to express algorithms recursively. In time, you will use this technique without hesitation in your problem solving.

Next, we will begin to use recursion to explore problems for which nonrecursive solutions would be exceedingly difficult to fathom. We hope that you will be amazed at the ease with which recursion handles such problems. We will demonstrate that recursion is a natural and elegant way to solve many complex problems. We will also begin to explore the price paid for this elegance: The compactness of a recursive solution to a complex problem is not necessarily an accurate statement of its time or space efficiency.

We will then use recursion to develop a problem-solving methodology known as *trial-and-error*, or nondeterministic, *backtracking*. By "nondeterministic" we mean that the user cannot predict in advance what path a solution will take. In theory, this technique can solve a large variety of problems. Unfortunately, in practice, the technique is so computationally expensive that it can only be used to solve small instances of such problems in a reasonable amount of time.

Finally, we will look at how recursive techniques can be used to specify the syntax of languages by using a formalism called a *grammar*. The advantage of defining languages in this fashion is that it leads to a very natural way of writing parsers for such languages. The resulting methodology, called *recursive descent parsing*, will be demonstrated in the Case Study.

5.1 Controlling Simple Iteration with Recursion

Any recursive algorithm must have a well-defined stopping state, or *termination condition*. Without careful logical control by means of such conditions, recursive functions can fall prey to looping in endless circles. To illustrate this idea, let us suppose that we have access to an output device known as a pen plotter. Such a device is equipped with a pen held by a mechanical hand that is under control of the computer.

Typical functions to manipulate the pen could include the following:

Function	Action
`line(n)`	Draw a line of length *n* in the current direction.
`rightTurn(d)`	Alter the current direction by rotating *d* degrees in a clockwise direction.

Such functions are not unlike those found in the LOGO programming language or the "turtle" graphics toolkits that accompany many popular C++ compilers. If you have access to such a compiler, you may wish to explore developing some recursive graphic figures.

If we assume that the pen is initially set to draw a line toward the north—the top of the plotting page—then the following sequence of instructions will clearly draw a square with sides of length 10.

```
line(10);
rightTurn(90);
line(10);
rightTurn(90);
line(10);
rightTurn(90);
line(10);
```

Let us now try to predict what will happen when the following recursive function draw is invoked by the initial call draw(1).

```
void draw(int side)
{
    line(side);
    rightTurn(90);
    draw(side + 3)       // Recursive call
};
```

The initial call draw(1) will result in a line of length 1 in a northerly direction. We then rotate the pen toward the east and, via a recursive call, generate a line of length 4. This step is followed by a rotation to the south and a new invocation (invoke) for a line of length 7. The emerging pattern should now be clear; the resulting right-angled spiral is shown in Figure 5-1.

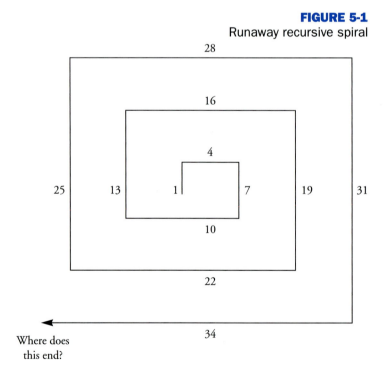

FIGURE 5-1
Runaway recursive spiral

Unfortunately, our spiral-producing function has tumbled into a vicious circle loop of self-reference. There is currently no way to turn off the *recursive calls* made to draw. Consider what happens, however, if we provide ourselves with a *recursive termination condition* (or recursive out) as in the following new version of draw:

```
void draw(int side)
{
  if (side <= 34)          // Recursive termination condition
  {
      line(side);
      rightTurn(90);
      draw(side + 3)       // Recursive call
  }
}
```

Now after drawing the line of length 34 in Figure 5-1, our draw function invokes itself once more, passing 37 for the parameter side. Because the recursive termination condition is now false, no line of length 37 will be drawn. More important, no further recursive invocation of draw will be made. Hence, we return immediately from the call to draw with side being 37. Moreover, that return triggers returns (in reverse order) from all the previous invocations of draw, eventually ending up at the instruction following our initial call—that is, draw(1).

The important point to stress here is that, to use recursion appropriately, we must use a recursive termination condition to avoid an infinite series of recursive calls. If we were to view each recursive call as a descent one level deeper into an algorithm's logic, we in effect must use a recursive termination condition to allow a corresponding ascent back to the level of the first call to the function. This concept is highlighted in Figure 5-2.

FIGURE 5-2
Unwinding from descent through recursive calls

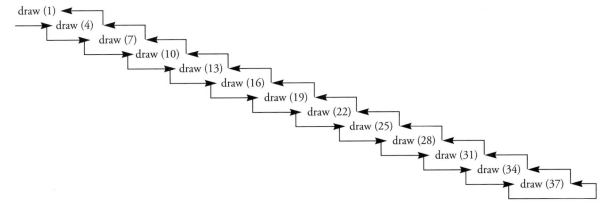

Linked Lists as Recursive Data Structures

In Section 3.1, we defined the linked list ADT. We can now reformulate that definition from a recursive perspective. The key to such a perspective is the realization that the pointer leading from each linked list node references another linked list. More formally, a linked list is a pointer that is either null (the recursive termination condition signaling an empty list) or references a node designated as the head node. The head node contains a data field and a pointer that satisfies the criteria for being a linked list.

Although an English composition teacher may find fault with our defining a linked list in terms of itself, our new definition is nonetheless completely free of ambiguity. For instance, to verify that the list in Figure 5-3 is a linked list, we note the following:

1. The head node in the three-item structure contains a pointer to an embedded two-item structure, which we must verify as a linked list.

2. The head node in the two-item structure contains a pointer to an embedded one-item structure.

3. The head node in the one-node structure contains a null pointer.

4. By the recursive termination condition, a null pointer meets the criteria for being a linked list.

5. Hence, the one-node structure in step 3 contains a pointer to a linked list and meets the criteria for being a linked list.

6. Similarly, we climb up the recursive ladder to verify that the two-node and, consequently, the three-node structures in steps 1 and 2 meet the criteria for being linked lists.

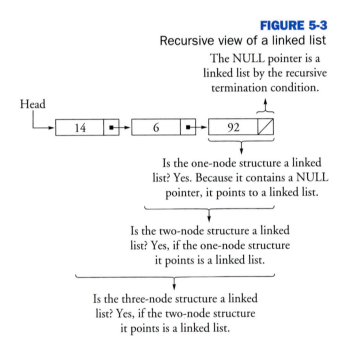

FIGURE 5-3
Recursive view of a linked list

Not only does our recursive definition unambiguously specify the linked list ADT, but it also provides a natural way to implement linked list operations by recursive functions. Consider the following example.

Example 5-1

A linked list of integers is implemented by C++ pointer variables in the following declarations:

```
struct node
{
  int data;
  node * next;
};
```

Develop a recursive implementation of a function that receives a pointer to the head node of the list and then traverses the list, printing the integer in each node.

The implementation of such a function literally flows from our recursive definition of the linked list structure. That is, if the list we are traversing is empty, there is nothing to do; otherwise, we must process the data in the head node and recursively traverse the linked list referenced by the next field in the head node. This logic is embodied in the following C++ function:

```
void traverse(node * head)
{
  if (head != 0)
  {
        cout << head->data << endl;
        traverse(head->next);
  }
}
```

A trace of the recursive function `traverse` for the list of Figure 5-3 is given in Figure 5-4. This trace shows that the function is initially called with a list pointer to the node containing 14. The data are processed, and the first recursive call then passes in a pointer to the node containing 6. Data item 6 is processed, and a pointer to the node containing 92 is recursively passed to the function. The node containing 92 is processed, and a null pointer is recursively passed to the function. Because the recursive termination condition (`head == 0`) is now met, we unwind from the series of recursive calls. As we return to each prior recursive level, there is nothing left to do since the recursive call is the last operation at that level.

FIGURE 5-4

Trace of recursive function traverse on the linked list of Figure 5-3

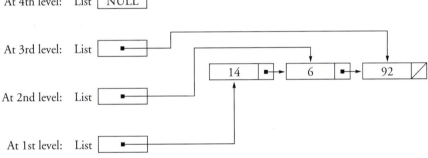

A recursive function is called **_tail recursive_** if only one recursive call appears in the function and that recursive call is the last operation performed at that procedural level. (That is, nothing else must be done after returning from a deeper recursive level.) The `traverse` function of Example 5-1 is clearly tail recursive. Typically, such a tail-recursive function can be easily recast in the form of a nonrecursive function using a `while` or `do` control structure.

How Is Recursion Implemented?

As we begin to examine recursive algorithms that are not tail recursive, we will need to understand in detail how a computer language implements recursion. Here again, we encounter the abstraction/implementation duality we have emphasized throughout the book. Recursion is a powerful conceptual tool. Unless you understand details of how recursion is implemented, however, your use of it will be limited to an intuitive approach that often employs a trial-and-error strategy to reach a solution.

In Section 4.1, we indicated that the stack is an essential data structure in a compiler's implementation of function calls. The role of a system stack being manipulated by the function calls in your program becomes even more crucial as we use recursion. To illustrate this idea, let us consider a problem more computationally oriented than our previous graphics and linked list examples. N factorial, denoted $N!$, is defined by

$$N! = N \times (N - 1) \times (N - 2) \times \ldots \times 2 \times 1$$

That is, $N!$ is the product of the first N integers. We note that an alternative way of defining N! is by means of using $(N - 1)!$

$$N! = \begin{cases} 1 \text{ if } N = 1 \text{ or } N = 0 \\ N \times (N\text{-}1)! \text{ otherwise} \end{cases}$$

This alternative definition is recursive because it uses the notion of a factorial to define a factorial. Despite this circularity, we have a perfectly valid definition because of the recursive termination condition in the special definition of 1!.

To see how recursion works for factorial computation, think of the preceding definition as a series of clues that will eventually allow us to unravel the mystery of how to compute $N!$. That is, to compute $N!$, the recursive definition tells us to

1. Remember what N is.
2. Compute $(N - 1)!$.
3. Once we've computed $(N - 1)!$, multiply that result by N to get our final answer.

Of course, when we use the definition to determine how to compute $(N - 1)!$, we find out that we must in turn compute $(N - 2)!$. Computing $(N - 2)!$ will involve finding $(N - 3)!$. This downward spiral will eventually end with 1!, allowing us to begin the actual series of multiplications that will bring us to the appropriate answer. Figure 5-5 illustrates the logic of the recursive method for computing N factorial. In particular, if N were 4, the sequence of recursive invocations of the definition and resulting computations would be as shown in Figure 5-6. The program in Example 5-2 calls a recursively defined `factorial` function. The associated run indicates the behavior of the program for an input of 4.

FIGURE 5-5
Recursive computation of *N*!

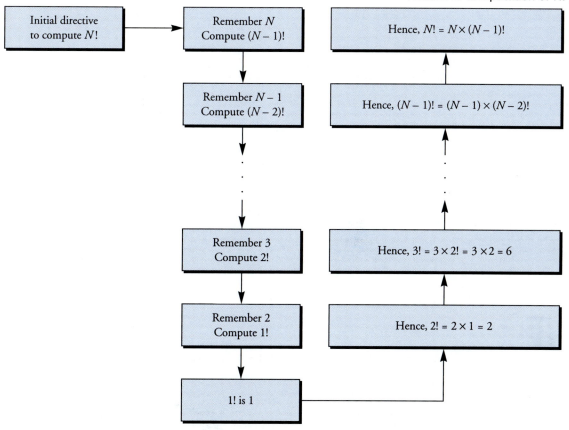

FIGURE 5-6
Recursive computation of 4!

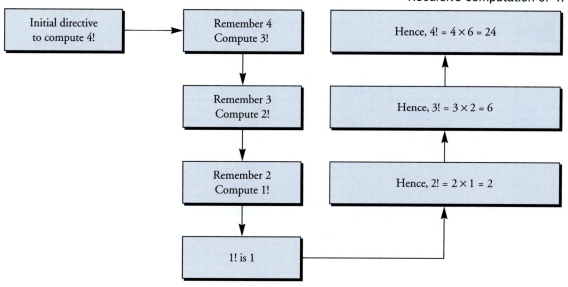

Example 5-2

```cpp
// Program file: factor.cpp

#include <iostream.h>
#include <iomanip.h>

int indent = 0;

int factorial(int n);

int main()
{
    int m;

   cout << "ENTER NUMBER for FACTORIAL COMPUTATION-> ";
   cin >> m;
   cout << factorial(m) << endl;     // Return Point 1
   return 0;
}

int factorial(int n)
{
   int result;

   cout << setw(indent) << "" << "ENTERING FACTORIAL WITH N = " << n << endl;
   if ((n == 1) || (n == 0))
   {
      cout << setw(indent) << "" << "LEAVING FACTORIAL WITH N = " << n;
      cout << ", FACTORIAL(N) = " << 1 << endl;
      --indent;
      return 1;
   }
   else
   {
      ++indent;
               // Return Point 2

      result = n * factorial(n - 1);
      cout << setw(indent) << "" << "LEAVING FACTORIAL WITH N = " << n;
      cout << ", FACTORIAL(N) = " << result << endl;
      --indent;
      return result;
   }
}
```

A sample run for the preceding code follows:

```
ENTER NUMBER for FACTORIAL COMPUTATION--> 4
ENTERING FACTORIAL WITH N = 4
 ENTERING FACTORIAL WITH N = 3
  ENTERING FACTORIAL WITH N = 2
   ENTERING FACTORIAL WITH N = 1
   LEAVING FACTORIAL WITH N = 1, FACTORIAL(N) = 1
  LEAVING FACTORIAL WITH N = 2, FACTORIAL(N) = 2
 LEAVING FACTORIAL WITH N = 3, FACTORIAL(N) = 6
LEAVING FACTORIAL WITH N = 4, FACTORIAL(N) = 24
24
```

The output statements used on entry to and exit from the function `factorial` in Example 5-2 are not necessary but have been included to demonstrate the precise call and return sequence triggered by the initial call of `factorial(4)` in the main program. Note that the output from `cout` statements implies that we must in some sense have multiple copies of the variable N—one copy for each descent to a recursively deeper level. As we shall see, a stack keeps track of these multiple copies of N in the appropriate fashion.

It is also important to emphasize that the function `factorial` would not be tail recursive even if the output statements were removed. The recursive call to `factorial` is not the last operation performed by the algorithm. After a return from the call to `factorial (N - 1)`, we must multiply by N. This multiplication is the final operation performed. The fact that we multiply by N after returning from a recursive call indicates that, for algorithms that are not tail recursive, we must have some means of preserving the values of parameters and local variables at each level of the recursive execution of the algorithm.

The comments `// Return Point 1` and `// Return Point 2` in Example 5-2 allow us to trace the role played by the stack as this program is run. We have already alluded to the existence of a general system stack onto which return addresses are pushed each time a function or function call is made. We will now explain this concept more fully. Each time a function or function call is made, an item called a stack frame or activation record will be pushed onto the system stack. The data in this **stack frame** consist of the return address and a copy of each local variable and parameter for the function. Figure 5-7 illustrates how stack frames are pushed and popped from the system stack when `factorial(4)` is invoked. Return addresses have been indicated by referring to the appropriate comments in the C++ code.

Although the function `factorial` of Example 5-2 provides an illustration of an algorithm that is not tail recursive, you could nevertheless argue that the computation of N! could be achieved more easily by a nonrecursive, iterative loop structure. To sense the real power and elegance of recursion, we must explore algorithms that more subtly manipulate the stack frames hidden below the surface of recursive processing. These stack frames provide us with a "free" stack data structure—that is, a structure that we need not declare formally and that we control completely by the recursive calling pattern of our algorithm.

FIGURE 5-7

Sequence of pushes and pops in computing 4!

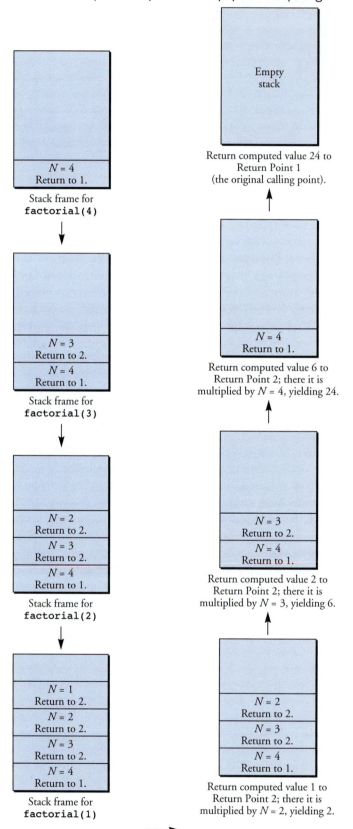

EXERCISES ⟹ 5.1

1. Stand between two parallel mirrors and see how recursion works for you.

2. Consider the following pair of functions to compute N!

```
int factorial(int n)
{
  return factHelper(n, 1);
}

int factHelper(int n, int result)
{

  if ((n ==0) || (n == 1))
      return result;
  else
      return factHelper(n - 1, n * result);
}
```

Is `factHelper` tail recursive? Will it work? Explain why or why not.

3. Each of the following functions offers a slight variation on the traverse function developed in Example 5-1. For each function, indicate what output would be produced if the function were called initially with the linked list of Figure 5-3 and the process function merely printed the data field of each node. If the function would crash with a run-time error for the data of Figure 5-3 or any other test case, explain why.

a.

```
void traverse(node * head)
{
  if (head != 0)
  {
      traverse(head->next);
      cout << head->data << endl;
  }
}
```

b.

```
void traverse(node * head)
{
  cout << head->data << endl;
  if (head->next != 0)
      traverse(head->next);
}
```

c.

```
void traverse(node * head)
{
  if (head->next != 0)
  {
      cout << head->data << endl;
      traverse(head->next);
  }
}
```

4. Which of the functions in Exercise 3 are tail recursive?

5. The following programs are intended to read a string character by character, put each character on the system stack, and then print the string of characters in reverse order. Which one(s) actually achieve the intent? Which one(s) don't? Why not? What will be the output of each program for input of "MADAM"?

a.

```
// Print out a string in reverse order to check if palindrome
#include <iostream.h>
void reverse();

int main()
{
    reverse();
    return 0;
}

// Keep recursively stacking characters until end of string.
// Then print it out in reverse by unstacking.
void reverse()
{
    char ch;         // Here ch is locally declared

    cin.get(ch);
    if (ch != '\n')
    {
            reverse();
            cout.put(ch);
    }
    else
            cout.put( '\n');
}
```

b.

```
// Print out a string in reverse order to check if palindrome
#include <iostream.h>
char ch;                    // Here ch is globally declared
void reverse();

int main()
{
    reverse();
    return 0;
}

// Keep recursively stacking characters until end of string.
// Then print it out in reverse by unstacking.
void reverse()
{
    cin.get(ch);
    if (ch != '\n')
    {
        reverse();
        cout.put(ch);
    }
    else
        cout.put('\n');
}
```

6. Given the declarations for the linked list structure in Example 5-1, write a recursive function to search the list for a particular item and return a pointer to the item in the list if it is found. If the item is not found in the list, a null pointer should be returned.

7. Suppose that numberVector is declared as follows:

```
typedef int numberVector[100];
```

Study the following function and determine what it computes. (*Hint:* Try to trace it for several small instances of the vector and N values.)

```
int compute(numberVector a, int n)
{
    if (n == 0)
            return a[n];
    else if (a[n] < compute(a, n - 1))
            return a[n];
    else
            return compute(a, n - 1);
}
```

8. Write a recursive function of two integer arguments M and N, both greater than or equal to 0. The function should return M^N.

9. Write a recursive function of two integer arguments M and N, $M > 1$ and $N > 0$. The function should return the integer log of N to the base M. This value is defined to be the least integer L such that $M^{L+1} > N$. (*Hint:* Although your function receives only two arguments, have it call an auxiliary function of three arguments—M, N, and L. Call on the auxiliary function initially with $L = 0$; the auxiliary function is then called recursively.)

10. Given the declaration of `numberVector` in Exercise 7, write a recursive function `product` that receives two arguments, one of type `numberVector` and another argument `N` that indicates the logical size of `numberVector`. Remember that the logical size of a vector is the number of indices that store well-defined data items. The recursive function `product` should return the product of the entries in the vector from indices 0 through $N - 1$.

11. Insert tracer output instructions at strategic points and use them to debug the following version of a function, which attempts to compute factorials recursively. After you've debugged the function, write a statement in which you explain the behavior of the function as originally coded and why the function did not work in its original form.

```
int factorial(int n)
{
    if ((n == 0) || (n == 1))
            return 1;
    else
    {
            --n;
            return n * factorial(n);
    }
}
```

5.2 Weaving More Complex Recursive Patterns

The recursive algorithms we have examined so far share the property that, at each level of recursive execution of the algorithm, at most one recursive call will be made. The pattern of operations on the system stack for such algorithms is that a series of stack frames is pushed, a recursive termination condition is reached, and then all stack frames are successively popped until we return to the execution level of the main program. More complex recursive algorithms involve multiple recursive calls at each level of execution. Correspondingly, the pattern of operations on the system stack will not be a series of uninterrupted pushes followed by a series of uninterrupted pops. Instead, the system stack will initially grow a bit, then shrink, then grow again, then shrink, and so forth.

Towers of Hanoi Problem

Legend has it that a group of monks was once given the painstaking task of moving a collection of *n* stone disks from one pillar, designated as pillar A, to another, designated as pillar C. Moreover, the relative ordering of the disks on pillar A had to be maintained as they were moved to pillar C. That is, as illustrated in Figure 5-8, the disks—all of different sizes—were to be stacked from largest to smallest, beginning from the bottom. Additionally, the monks were to observe the following rules in moving disks:

- Only one disk could be moved at a time.

- No larger disk could ever be placed on top of a smaller disk on any pillar.

- A third pillar B could be used as an intermediate to store one or more disks while they were being moved from their original source A to their destination C.

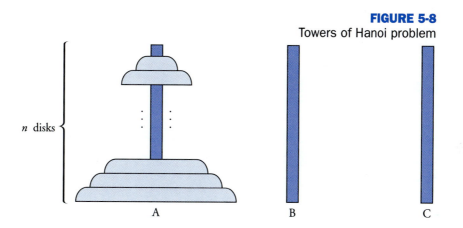

FIGURE 5-8
Towers of Hanoi problem

Consider the following recursive solution to this problem:

1. If *n* = 1, merely move the disk from A to C.

2. If *n* = 2, move the first disk from A to B. Then move the second disk from A to C. Then move the first disk from B to C.

3. If *n* = 3, call on the technique already established in step 2 to move the first two disks from A to B using C as an intermediate. Then move the third disk from A to C. Then use the technique in step 2 to move the first two disks from B to C using A as an intermediate

   .
   .
   .

n. For general *n*, use the technique in the previous step to move *n* - 1 disks from A to B using C as an intermediate. Next, move one disk from A to C. Then use the technique in the previous step to move *n* - 1 disks from B to C using A as an intermediate.

Notice that this technique for solving the Towers of Hanoi describes itself in terms of a simpler version of itself. That is, it describes how to solve the problem for *n* disks in terms of a solution for *n* - 1 disks. In general, any problem you hope to solve recursively must be approached in this fashion. This strategy is important enough to state as the principle of recursive problem solving: *When trying to solve a problem by recursion, always ask yourself, "What could I do if I had a solution to a simpler version of the same problem?"*

321

We have seen that the use of recursion has two costs: the extra time and extra memory required to manage recursive function calls. These costs have led some to argue that recursion should never be used in programs. However, as Guy Steele has shown in "Debunking the 'expensive procedure call' myth" (*Proceedings of the National Conference of the ACM*, 1977), some systems can run recursive algorithms as if they were iterative ones with no additional overhead. The key condition is to write a special kind of function called a tail-recursive function. A function is tail recursive if no work is done in it after a recursive call. For example, according to this criterion, the factorial function that we presented earlier is not tail recursive because a multiplication is performed after each recursive call. We can convert this version of the factorial function to a tail-recursive version by performing the multiplication before each recursive call. To do so, we will need an additional parameter that passes the accumulated value of the factorial down on each recursive call. In the last call of the function, this value is returned as the result:

```
int factIter(int n, int result)
{
    if (n == 1)
            return result;
    else
            return factIter(n - 1, n * result);
}
```

Note that the multiplication is performed before the recursive call of the function, when its parameters are evaluated. When the function is initially called, the value of `result` should be 1:

```
int factorial(int n)
{
    return factIter(n, 1);
}
```

Steele showed that a smart compiler can translate tail-recursive code in a high-level language to a loop in machine language. The machine code treats the function parameters as variables associated with a loop and generates an iterative process rather than a recursive one. There is no linear growth of function calls, and extra stack memory is not required to run tail-recursive functions on these systems.

The catch is that a programmer must be able to convert a recursive function to a tail-recursive function and find a compiler that generates iterative machine code from such functions. Unfortunately, some functions, such as the one used to solve the Towers of Hanoi problem, are difficult or impossible to convert to tail-recursive versions. Also, the compiler optimizations are not part of the standard definitions of many languages, including C++. If your C++ compiler supports this optimization, you should try converting some functions to tail-recursive versions and see whether they run faster than the original versions.

If you can see how to use the solution to a smaller version of the problem in solving the original problem, you have hurdled your toughest obstacle. All that remains is to determine the recursive termination conditions. This task can be accomplished by answering the question, "Under what circumstances is this problem so simple that a solution is trivial?" Your answer to this question will define parameter values that trigger an immediate return from the recursive algorithm.

Example 5-3

Implement a C++ solution to the Towers of Hanoi problem. Our earlier discussion indicated that the problem for *n* disks can be defined in terms of *n* - 1 if we switch the roles played by certain pillars. This switching can be achieved by altering the order in which parameters are passed when recursive calls are made. When a value of 1 is passed in for *n*, we have reached the recursive termination condition. The comments `// Return Point 1` and `// Return Point 2` in the following C++ code will be used in a later trace of the function `hanoi`.

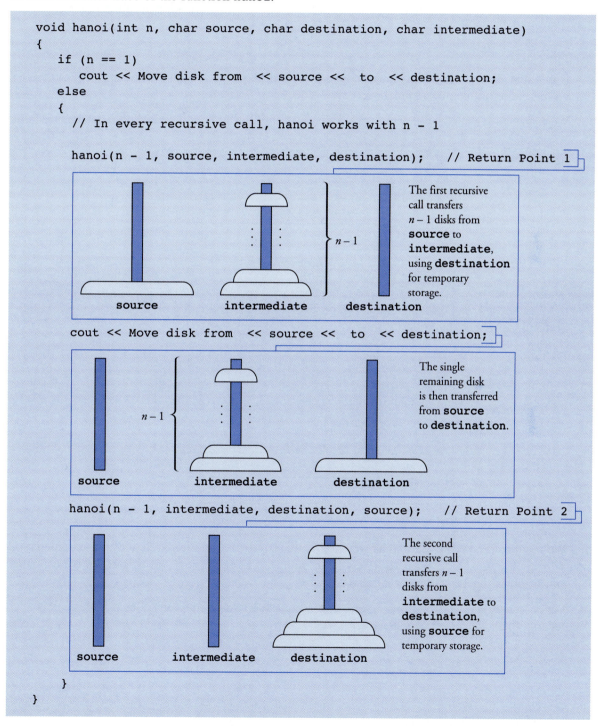

```
void hanoi(int n, char source, char destination, char intermediate)
{
   if (n == 1)
      cout << Move disk from  << source <<  to  << destination;
   else
   {
      // In every recursive call, hanoi works with n - 1

      hanoi(n - 1, source, intermediate, destination);   // Return Point 1
```

The first recursive call transfers *n* − 1 disks from **source** to **intermediate**, using **destination** for temporary storage.

source   intermediate   destination

```
      cout << Move disk from  << source <<  to  << destination;
```

The single remaining disk is then transferred from **source** to **destination**.

source   intermediate   destination

```
      hanoi(n - 1, intermediate, destination, source);   // Return Point 2
```

The second recursive call transfers *n* − 1 disks from **intermediate** to **destination**, using **source** for temporary storage.

source   intermediate   destination

```
   }
}
```

323

Unlike in the previously studied recursive algorithms in which only one recursive call was made each time the function was invoked, the function `hanoi` will reinvoke itself twice each time it is called with $n > 1$. The result is a more complicated algorithm that could not be implemented easily by using mere iterative control structures. Implicitly, through its recursive calls, `hanoi` is weaving an intricate pattern of push and pop operations on the system stack.

Example 5-4

To illustrate, we trace through the actions affecting the system stack when a call of the form

```
hanoi(3, 'A', 'C', 'B');
```

is initiated. The values in the return address portion of the stack are the documentary `// Return Point` labels in our `hanoi` function.

1. We enter `hanoi` with the following stack frame. `n` is not 1, so the condition in the `if` statement is false.

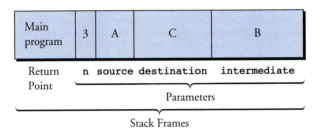

2. We encounter `hanoi(n - 1, source, intermediate, destination)` with A, B, and C as the first, second, and third arguments, respectively. Because this call represents a (recursive) function call, some stacking must be done.

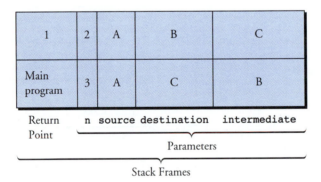

3. We reenter `hanoi`. Notice that as we enter it this time, the function's view of the parameters is `n = 2, source = A, destination = B`, and `intermediate = C`. Because `n` is not 1, the condition in the `if` statement is false.

4. We encounter `hanoi(n - 1, source, intermediate, destination)`. Because this call is a recursive call, stacking occurs.

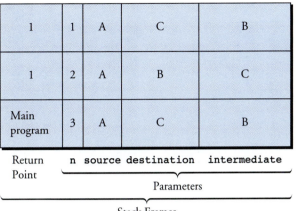

		n	source	destination	intermediate
1	1	A	C	B
1	2	A	B	C
Main program	3	A	C	B

Return Point | | Parameters

Stack Frames

5. We reenter `hanoi` with n = 1, source = A, destination = C, and intermediate = B. Because n = 1, the condition in the `if` statement is true.

6. Hence,

Move disk from A to C

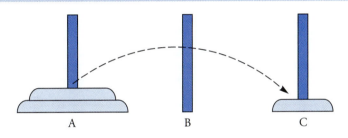

is printed and a return triggers a popping of a return address (1) and four parameters, leaving the system stack in the following state:

		n	source	destination	intermediate
1	2	A	B	C
Main program	3	A	C	B

Return Point | | Parameters

Stack Frames

7. Because the return address popped was 1

Move disk from A to B

is printed and

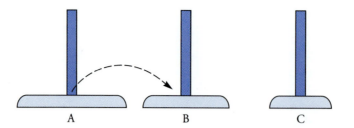

```
hanoi(n - 1, intermediate, destination, source)
```

is encountered with n = 2, source = A, destination = B, and intermediate = C.

8. The call pushes a return address and four parameters onto the system stack.

Return Point	n	source	destination	intermediate
2	1	C	B	A
1	2	A	B	C
Main program	3	A	C	B

Return Point   n   source   destination   intermediate

Parameters

Stack Frames

9. We reenter hanoi, this time with n = 1, source = C, destination = B, and intermediate = A.

10. Because n = 1, the if statement generates the output

```
Move disk from C to B
```

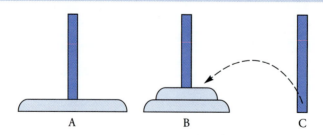

and a return.

11. The return pops a frame from the system stack. We return to the statement labeled by 2 with n = 2, source = A, destination = B, and intermediate = C.

12. Statement 2 triggers a return, so a stack frame is popped again. We return to the statement labeled 1 with n = 3, source = A, destination = C, and intermediate = B.

13. Statement 1 triggers the output

```
Move disk from A to C
```

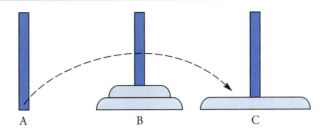

and we are immediately at another call

```
hanoi(n - 1, intermediate, destination, source)
```

Hence, the status of the system stack is changed to

2	2	B	C	A
Main program	3	A	C	B
Return Point	n	source	destination	intermediate

Parameters

Stack Frames

14. We reenter hanoi with n = 2, source = B, destination = C, and intermediate = A. Because n is not 1, another call is executed and more values are stacked.

1	1	B	A	C
2	2	B	C	A
Main program	3	A	C	B
Return Point	n	source	destination	intermediate

Parameters

Stack Frames

15. We reenter hanoi with n = 1, source = B, destination = A, and intermediate = C. Because n = 1, we print

```
Move disk from B to A
```

327

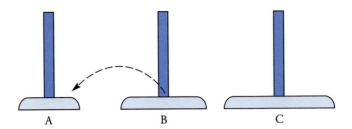

and return.

16. The return prompts the popping of the system stack. The return address popped is the statement labeled 1. Statement 1 triggers the output

```
Move disk from B to C
```

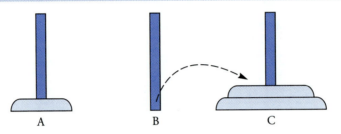

with the stack frames left at

Return Point	n	source	destination	intermediate
2	2	B	C	A
Main program	3	A	C	B

Parameters

Stack Frames

17. The output from statement 1 is followed by a recursive call

```
hanoi(n - 1, intermediate, destination, source)
```

Return Point	n	source	destination	intermediate
2	1	A	C	B
2	2	B	C	A
Main program	3	A	C	B

Stack Frames

Hence, another frame is pushed onto the stack.

18. We reenter `hanoi` (for the last time) with n = 1, source = A, destination = C, and intermediate = B. Because n = 1, we output

`Move disk from A to C`

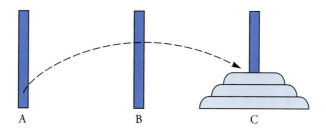

and return.

19. The return pops return address 2 from the stack, so we return to statement 2 with the system stack given by

Return Point	n	source	destination	intermediate
2	2	B	C	A
Main program	3	A	C	B

Stack Frames

20. Statement 2 is another return, so we pop the stack again. The return address popped is 2, the same return point. This time the return will transfer control back to the original calling location—so we are done!

Though this example may seem long-winded, it is essential that you understand it. Recursive functions are crucial to many of the algorithms used in computer science, and you can acquire the necessary familiarity with recursion only by convincing yourself that it really works. If you have some doubt or are not sure whether you understand this example, we recommend that you trace through the `hanoi` function with n = 4 (be prepared to go through a lot of paper).

Efficiency Analysis of the Recursive Towers of Hanoi Algorithm

An analysis of the time and space efficiency of a recursive algorithm depends on two factors. First is the depth—that is, the number of levels—to which recursive calls are made before reaching the recursive termination condition. Clearly, the greater the depth, the greater the number of stack frames that must be allocated and the less space efficient the algorithm becomes. It is also clear that recursive calls to a greater depth will consume more computer time and hence make the algorithm less time efficient. The second factor affecting efficiency analyses (particularly time efficiency) of recursive algorithms is the amount of resource (time or space) consumed at any given recursive level.

Figure 5-9 portrays this leveled view of a recursive algorithm as a hierarchy of the recursive calls that are (potentially) made as the algorithm executes. Such a hierarchy can be used as a diagrammatic model of the run-time behavior of a recursive algorithm. Consequently, we will call the hierarchy associated with the execution of a particular recursive program a **_run-time trace diagram_** for that algorithm. Figure 5-10 presents a run-time trace diagram for the Towers of Hanoi algorithm with n = 4 disks.

FIGURE 5-9
Generalized hierarchy of calls by recursive algorithm

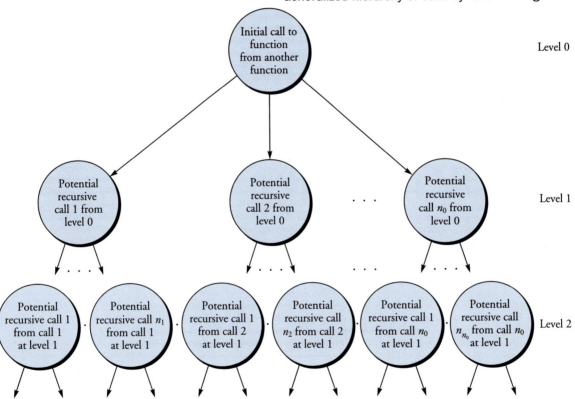

Descent continues from each potential call until recursive termination condition is reached.

Total time is sum of times spent processing at each level.

FIGURE 5-10
Run-time trace of function `hanoi` with *n* originally 4 (numbers next to circles indicate order of recursive calls)

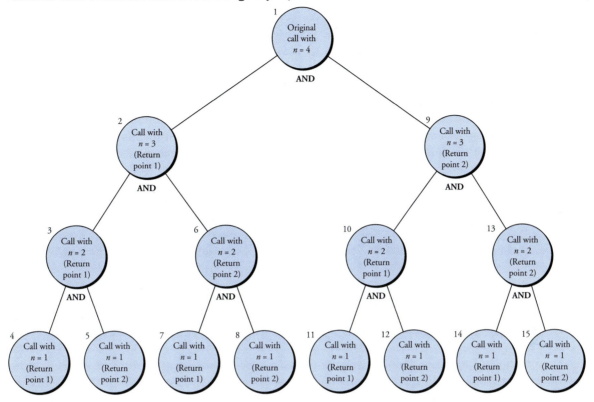

A run-time trace diagram can often be used in analyzing the time and space efficiency of an algorithm. We will provide two general principles for carrying out such analyses and then illustrate them in the context of the Towers of Hanoi algorithm.

Space efficiency of a recursive algorithm: Because a stack frame must be allocated at each level of recursive execution, the space efficiency of a recursive algorithm will be proportional to the deepest level at which a recursive call is made for a particular set of values—that is, the deepest level in its run-time trace diagram.

Time efficiency of a recursive algorithm: Because processing time is associated with each recursive call, the time efficiency of a recursive algorithm will be proportional to the sum, over all levels, of the times spent processing at each level.

Example 5-5

Use the run-time trace diagram of the function `hanoi` to analyze the time and space efficiency of the algorithm.

A graphic representation of this diagram for four disks is given in Figure 5-10. Note that the two calls descending from each call are linked by AND. This usage emphasizes that, when n is not 1, both potential recursive calls in the function `hanoi` will be made. The fact that both potential calls are made has a rather dramatic effect on the time efficiency of the algorithm. In particular, calling `hanoi` initially with n = 4 results in a total of 15 calls in the run-time trace diagram. The numbers outside the circles in Figure 5-10 indicate the order in which these 15 calls are made. Increasing n to 5 in this figure adds an additional level with 16 calls to the run-time trace. In general, adding one disk adds only one level to the run-time trace diagram but doubles (plus 1) the number of calls in the diagram. This principle implies that the space efficiency of `hanoi` relative to the system stack is $O(n)$ but, because every call in the run-time trace diagram will be made, the time efficiency is $O(2^n)$.

The analysis carried out in Example 5-5 demonstrates that the `hanoi` algorithm falls into the class of exponential algorithms defined in Section 1.3. It is the first exponential algorithm we have encountered. Recall from our discussion of algorithm efficiency in Section 1.3 that such algorithms are impractical to run even for moderate values of n. We will conclude our discussion of the Hanoi legend by noting that, if the monks of Hanoi use the recursive algorithm that we have described here, the exponential efficiency of the algorithm ensures that the world will exist for many more centuries.

Recursive Implementation of the Binary Search Algorithm

Do not let our solution to the Towers of Hanoi problem mislead you into thinking that every recursive algorithm having more than one recursive call will be exponential in its efficiency. Consider, for example, a recursive formulation of the binary search algorithm. Recall the interface to this algorithm that we developed in Section 2.5:

```
// Function: binarySearch
// If data are found in list, return position of data; otherwise, return -1
//
// Inputs: A sorted list of data elements, the length of the list, and a
//            target key
// Outputs: Function returns target's position if target is found in
//            list, and -1 otherwise

int binarySearch(apvector <int> &list, int n, KeyType target);
```

The principle of recursive problem solving (stated in our discussion of the Towers of Hanoi problem) directs us to solve the binary search problem in terms of a simpler version of itself. Toward this end, we employ a perspective often used in recursive algorithms that act on a vector: We view the algorithm as occurring between a certain subrange of vector indices. For the binary search, that subrange is specified by `low ... high`, where `low` is initially `0` and `high` is initially n. The "simpler version" of the binary search needed for a recursive statement of the algorithm is then a version that works on a smaller subrange of vector indices. This subrange ultimately may become so small that it triggers the recursive termination condition for an unsuccessful search.

An intuitive recursive statement of the binary search logic then becomes:

If (recursive termination for unsuccessful search)
    Return -1 (and recursion terminated)
Else
    Compute middle index between low and high
    If (target is found at middle index)
      Search is successful (and recursion terminated by returning middle index)
    Else if (target is less than data at middle index)
        Recursively call with same low and middle - 1 as high
      Else
        Recursively call with middle + 1 as low and same high

According to this logic, the recursive calls result in a continual narrowing of the range to be searched until either the target is found or a recursive termination condition for an unsuccessful search is reached.

To identify this unsuccessful recursive termination condition, consider Figure 5-11. It portrays successive recursive calls on a vector in which the target does not exist. The shaded regions of these vector snapshots indicate the index subrange in which `target = 152` could possibly be found on successive recursive calls. Note that, on the fourth recursive call, no portion of the vector is shaded; the condition `low > high` exists. This condition is therefore the recursive termination check for an unsuccessful search. The following example presents the code for the recursive binary search in its entirety.

FIGURE 5-11

Unsuccessful search for a vector with 15 key values

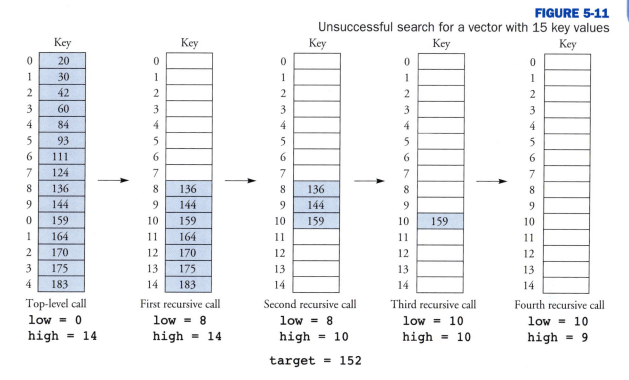

Top-level call
`low = 0`
`high = 14`

First recursive call
`low = 8`
`high = 14`

Second recursive call
`low = 8`
`high = 10`

Third recursive call
`low = 10`
`high = 10`

Fourth recursive call
`low = 10`
`high = 9`

`target = 152`

Example 5-6

Developing a recursive version of the binary search requires that we use an auxiliary function to work with the index subrange `low ... high`. Using this auxiliary function will allow us to preserve the interface to the function `binarySearch`. This interface should not require its user to pass in an initial low value of 0. Instead, the user need pass in only n, the number of objects in the list. From there, the front-end portion of `binarySearch` need merely call on its auxiliary function, passing in 0 for `low` and `n - 1` for `high`.

```
int binarySearch(apvector <int> &list, int n, KeyType target)
{
    return binarySearchAux(list, 0, n - 1, target);
}

int binarySearchAux(apvector <int> &list, int low, int high, KeyType
target)

{
    int middle;

    if (low > high)
        return -1;
    else
    {
```

333

```
        middle = (low + high) / 2;
        if (list[middle] == target)
            return middle;
        else if (list[middle] > target)
            return binarySearchAux(list, low, middle - 1, target);
        else
            return binarySearchAux(list, middle + 1, high, target);
    }
}
```

Efficiency Analysis of the Recursive Binary Search

As we did for the Towers of Hanoi problem, we will use a run-time trace diagram of potential recursive calls to analyze the efficiency of the recursive implementation of the binary search algorithm. This diagram appears in Figure 5-12. For the specific case of a vector with 15 data items, the run-time trace stops at level 3, as indicated in Figure 5-13. The ORs that appear in these two figures are indicative of the fact that, at any given level, we will make at most one recursive call or the other, but not both. This restriction is important and, as we have seen, different from the AND pattern of recursive calls in the Towers of Hanoi problem. It implies that the work done at any given level is simply the work done at one node along that level.

FIGURE 5-12
Run-time trace diagram of potential calls for recursive binary search algorithm

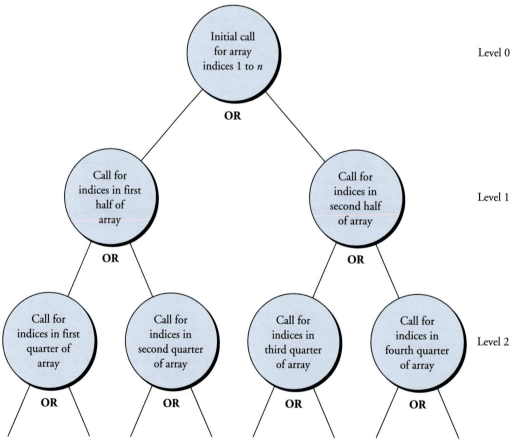

And so forth for eighths, sixteenths, . . .

FIGURE 5-13
Trace of Figure 5-12 for the specific case of a vector with 15 data items

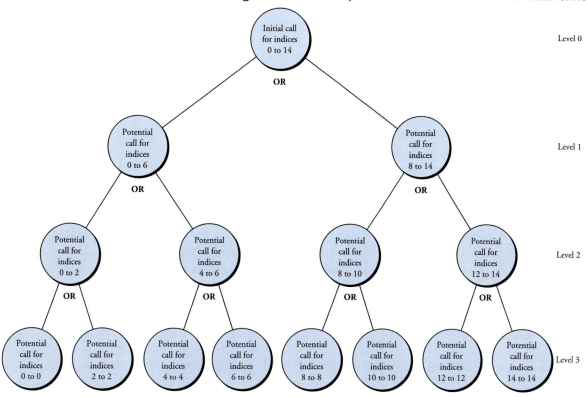

In the binary search, the work done at any node is O(1) , as we are comparing the `target` item to the data at the `mid` position. Hence, the time efficiency of the recursive version of this algorithm will be proportional to the number of levels in the run-time trace diagram for a vector with n items. In Figures 5-12 and 5-13, doubling the number of items in the vector will merely add one level to the run-time trace diagram. That is, the number of levels in the diagram is $\log_2 n + 1$ (truncated). With the O(1) work done at each level, we can conclude that the time efficiency of a recursive binary search is $O(\log_2 n)$. Similarly, because a stack frame will be allocated for each recursive level, the additional space requirements of the algorithm (beyond the vector itself) are $O(\log_2 n)$. Note that our earlier, nonrecursive implementation of the binary search algorithm did not incur this additional cost in space efficiency.

Recursive Computation of "N Choose K"

The preceding discussion of the binary search algorithm has honed our ability to use the run-time trace diagram to measure the efficiency of a recursive algorithm. It did not, however, represent a solution to a problem that would be difficult to conceptualize without recursion. We close this section with an example in the latter category.

The phrase "N choose K" is often used in the combinatorics branch of mathematics to refer to the number of ways that we could choose K objects from among N different objects. For instance, "52 choose 13" represents the number of ways that you could be dealt a bridge hand (that is, 13 cards out of 52). We seek a recursive function to compute N choose K for arbitrary N and K, K <= N.

Our principle of recursive problem solving asks us to consider how we could use a solution to a simpler version of the same problem. For N choose K, a simpler version of the same problem could mean a solution for a smaller value of N or K. Let us designate our N objects as object #1, object #2, . . . , object #(N - 1), object #N. Figure 5-14 indicates that we can partition selections of K objects from these N objects as those groups of K objects that come strictly from objects #1, #2, . . . , #N - 1 and those groups of K objects that include object #N in addition to K - 1 chosen among objects #1, #2, . . . , #N - 1. In other words,

$$\text{choose}(N, K) = \begin{cases} \text{choose}(N\text{-}1, K) & \text{(Ways of selecting } K \text{ objects from among the first } N\text{-}1) \\ + \text{choose}(N\text{-}1, K\text{-}1) & \text{(Ways of selecting } K\text{-}1 \text{ objects from among the first} \\ & N\text{-}1 \text{ and then including object } \#N) \end{cases}$$

This equation appears to be the recursive key we need to write our function. We need merely develop recursive termination conditions to complete the puzzle. Note from the preceding equation that one of the terms being summed, choose(N - 1, K), will recursively reduce N until it eventually equals K. In such a case, we are merely asking for the number of combinations of N objects selected N at a time—and there is trivially only one such combination. Hence, our first recursive termination condition is when $N = K$, for which we immediately return the value 1.

FIGURE 5-14

Formulating choose (N, K) in terms of choose (N − 1, K) and choose (N − 1, K − 1)

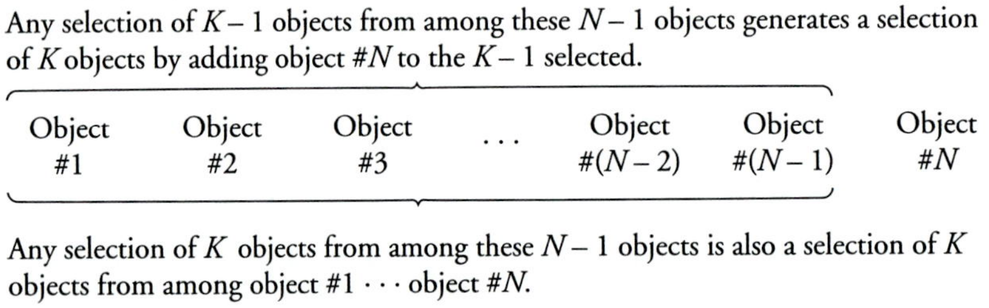

Any selection of $K - 1$ objects from among these $N - 1$ objects generates a selection of K objects by adding object #N to the $K - 1$ selected.

Object #1	Object #2	Object #3	. . .	Object #($N-2$)	Object #($N-1$)	Object #N

Any selection of K objects from among these $N - 1$ objects is also a selection of K objects from among object #1 $\cdots$ object #N.

To develop the second recursive termination condition, we examine the second term, choose(N - 1, K - 1), in the sum. Because both N and K will be reduced by this recursion, K will eventually reach 0. The number of ways of choosing 0 objects from among N, however, is again trivially 1. Consequently, the second recursive termination condition is when $K = 0$; this condition flags the immediate return of the value of 1.

Example 5-7

Implement a recursive N choose K function based on the preceding discussion.

```
// Function: choose
// Computes N choose K, the number of ways of selecting
//          K objects from N
//
// Inputs: N, the number of objects being selected from,
//              and K, the number of objects being selected
// Outputs: The value of N choose K

int choose(int n, int k)
{
    if ((k == 0) || (n == k))
            return 1;
    else
            return choose(n - 1, k) + choose(n - 1, k - 1);
}
```

Example 5-8

Trace the `choose(n, k)` function by developing the run-time trace diagram for `choose(4, 2)`.

This diagram is provided in Figure 5-15. The numbers next to the circles indicate the order in which calls are made.

FIGURE 5-15

Run-time trace diagram for `choose(4, 2)`

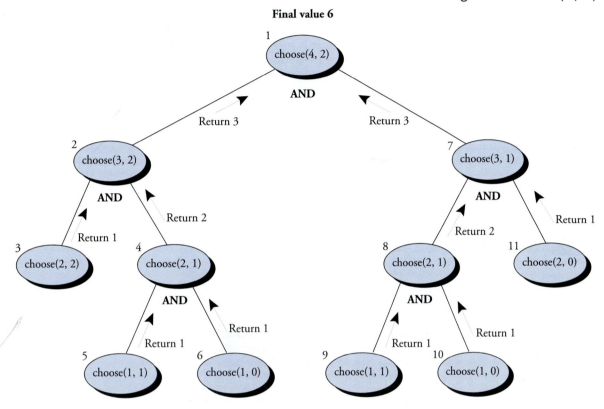

EXERCISES 5.2

1. Trace the stack frames that are pushed and popped from the system stack as the Towers of Hanoi algorithm executes for n = 4 disks.

2. Is the recursive binary search algorithm presented in this section tail recursive? Provide a written rationale for your response.

3. Construct run-time trace diagrams in the style of Example 5-8 for a variety of values of n and k in the function `choose(n,k)`. Judging from the run-time trace diagrams you construct, make conjectures about the time and space efficiency of this algorithm. Support these conjectures in a written statement.

4. Consider the following version of the function `binarySearchAux` from Example 5-6 to which a tracer output statement has been added. What output would be produced from this tracer output if we were to call on the function `binarySearch` from Example 5-6 with a list of 16 integers containing the key values

```
12 34 67 89 113 125 169 180 191 201 225 237 256 270 299 304
```

and a `target` of 191?

```cpp
int binarySearchAux(apvector <listType> &list, int low, int high,
    KeyType target)
{
    int middle;

    cout << low <<   << high << endl;         // Tracer output added here
    if (low > high)
          return -1;
    else
    {
          middle = (low + high) / 2;
          if (list[middle] == target)
                return middle;
          else if (list[middle] > target)
                return binarySearchAux(list, low, middle - 1, target);
          else
                return binarySearchAux(list, middle + 1, high, target);
    }
}
```

5. Repeat Exercise 4, this time with a `target` of 6.

6. Consider the following recursive function and associated top-level call. Comments of the form `// Return Point N` label possible return points from recursive calls. What would a stack frame for this function contain? Show by a series of stack "snapshots" how the stack would be manipulated for the calls indicated. Finally, provide the output produced by these calls.

```cpp
#include <iostream.h>

int weird(int m, int n);

int main()
{
    cout << weird(1, 3) << endl;              // Return Point 1
    return 0;
}

int weird(int m, int n)
{
```

```
cout << m <<   << n << endl;
    if (m == 0)
           return n + 1;
    else if (n == 0)
           return weird(m - 1, 1);                    // Return Point 2
    else
           return weird(m - 1, weird(m, n - 1));   // Return Points 3 and 4
}
```

7. The function `hanoi` developed in this section specified the sequence of disk moves that would have to be performed to complete the Towers of Hanoi problem for n disks. Now write a recursive function that computes the exact number of disk moves needed to solve the Towers of Hanoi problem for n disks. (*Hint:* Express the number of individual moves necessary to transfer *n* disks in terms of the number of moves necessary to transfer *n* - 1 disks.)

8. Write a recursive function to determine the minimum entry in a vector of *n* integers.

9. Write a recursive implementation of the insertion sort algorithm.

10. Suppose we have an amount of money *M* that is divisible evenly by 10 cents. Write a recursive function that computes the number of ways that *M* can be broken down into half dollars, quarters, and dimes. (*Hint:* Study Example 5-7.)

11. In essay form, discuss some of the trade-offs in terms of time and space efficiency that are made when recursion is used.

12. Both a modular structure chart and a run-time trace diagram reflect a hierarchical pattern of how functions are called in a program. In a carefully written statement, explain the differences between these two diagrammatic techniques.

5.3 Recursion, Trial-and-Error Backtracking, and Generalized Nested Loops

In the previous section, we saw examples of recursive algorithms in which the number of recursive calls at each recursive level is (potentially) more than 1. In this section, we consider what happens when the number of recursive calls made on any given level is under the control of an iterative control structure such as a `for`, `while`, or do loop.

As an example of the class of problems we will study in this section, consider the notion of a permutation. A permutation of the integers 1, 2, . . . , *N* is an ordered arrangement of these integers in which each integer appears exactly once. For instance, two possible permutations of the integers 1, 2, 3, 4 are 3 2 1 4 and 2 4 3 1.

The Permutations Problem

We now pose the following problem: For input of N, devise a program that outputs all permutations of the integers $1, 2, \ldots, N$.

Example 5-9

The following program solves this problem, but only for the special case where $N = 4$.

```cpp
#include <iostream.h>

int main()
{
    for (int k1 = 1; k1 <= 4, k1++)
        for (int k2 = 1; k2 <= 4; k2++)
            if (k1 != k2)
                for (int k3 = 1; k3 <= 4; k3++)
                    if ((k2 != k3) && (k1 != k3))
                        for (int k4 = 1; k4 <= 4; k4++)
                            if ((k3 != k4) && (k2 != k4)
                                && (k1 != k4))
                                cout << setw(2) << k1 << " "
                                    << setw(2) << k2 << " "
                                    << setw(2) << k3 << " "
                                    << setw(2) << k4 << " "
                                    << endl;
    return 0;
}
```

The strategy of this program is to use a `for` loop to control a variable that runs through the four possibilities for each of the four permutation positions. Four loops emerge, nested within each other. When an inner loop generates a number that matches one at a previously generated position, the `if` statement is used to reject that number.

The program in Example 5-9 constitutes a simple and straightforward approach to the permutation problem. Unfortunately, it falls far short of solving the general problem as originally posed, because it works only for the number 4, not for a general N to be input when the program runs. The requirement that N be entered at run time causes the major complication. Certainly, the strategy of using nested loops allows us to write one program that works for $N = 2$, another that works for $N = 3$, another for $N = 4$, and so on. However, in addition to having a ridiculous number of nested `for` loops for reasonably large N, the decision as to which permutations to generate would instead be made at the time the appropriate program is compiled and not when it runs. Computer scientists typically call this dilemma a ***binding time problem***. Here we would prefer to bind a value to N when our program runs instead of when it compiles. Clearly, the later the binding time, the more versatile the program. To solve this problem, we need some means of simulating arbitrarily deep nested loops when the program runs.

To see how we can use recursion to achieve such a simulation, consider the diagram of permutation possibilities in Figure 5-16. This diagram bears a resemblance to what we called a run-time trace diagram of recursive calls in the preceding section. We interpret the diagram by viewing any given path from the node labeled Start down to the base level of the diagram as a potential candidate for a permutation of $1, 2, \ldots, N$. As we progress from one level to the next along a path, we encounter the next digit in this potential permutation.

Conceptually, we must use recursion to generate all the paths that appear in the figure. As soon as we generate a path containing two equal numbers, we abandon that dead-end path and backtrack one level to continue the path along a potentially more fruitful route. If we ever complete one entire permutation along a path, we will output it, backtrack a level, and continue looking for more permutations that share the beginning of this path. At a given point in our search for a permutation, we need store only the current path. For this task, a simple global vector will suffice. Thus the vector `currentPermutation` of Figure 5-17 will store in its *j*th subscript the number in the jth position of the permutation currently being generated. The limiting factor on the size of permutations generated by our program will be the dimension of this vector.

FIGURE 5-16
Candidates for permutations

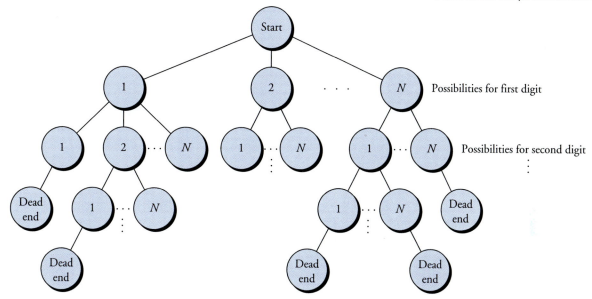

FIGURE 5-17
Current exploration of permutations beginning with 2 1 4

currentPermutation   maxPermutation

1	2	3	4	5	· · ·	Size
2	1	4	Undefined	Undefined	· · ·	Undefined

A complete program to solve our permutation problem follows. The heart of this program is the recursive function `attempt`. This function receives three parameters:

Parameter	Explanation
n	The number of numbers to be permuted in the current run.
level	The level in the tree of Figure 5-16; that is, the position in `currentPermutation` at which attempt is to `attempt` placement of a new value.
possibility	The new value to be placed at this level.

The function `attempt` initially calls on a function `addToCurrentPath` to place `possibility` at the appropriate level. Once this placement is made, the `currentPermutation` vector could be in any of three states.

1. The placement of the value `possibility` at the designated level could have completed a successful permutation. In this case, we call on a function to print the permutation and then remove `possibility` from `currentPermutation` at the given `level` so that we may continue seeking additional permutations.

2. The placement of the value `possibility` at the designated level did not complete a permutation but does represent a valid beginning of length `level` for a potential permutation. For instance, this case would occur if n, `level`, and `possibility` were 6, 4, and 5, respectively, and we called `attempt` with `currentPermutation` as pictured in Figure 5-17. The `currentPermutation` vector would be extended to contain 2 1 4 5. Here we must test the possible candidates for a value at the next position— that is, at depth (`level` + 1). This testing is done by an iterative series of recursive calls to attempt, passing a variety of values for `possibility` at (`level` + 1). This iterative series of recursive calls achieves the desired simulation of nested looping. After all of these deeper-level possibilities (that is, those below the beginning of the current permutation in Figure 5-16) have been explored, we return and can remove `possibility` from `currentPermutation` at position `level` because (recursively) all permutations with this beginning arrangement will have been generated.

3. The placement of the value `possibility` at `level` destroys the viability of the current path by adding a number that appeared earlier in the permutation. For instance, calling on `attempt` with n = 6, level = 4, and `possibility` = 1 would cause an invalid path for the state of `currentPermutation` given in Figure 5-17. In this case, we do nothing but retract from the placement of this invalid possibility before attempting to place other possible values.

You should carefully study how these three cases are handled in our recursive function `attempt` in the example program. The modular structure chart presented in Figure 5-18 indicates how `attempt` invokes other functions. Following the program, we adapt the technique illustrated here to a broader class of problems.

FIGURE 5-18
Modular structure chart for permutations program

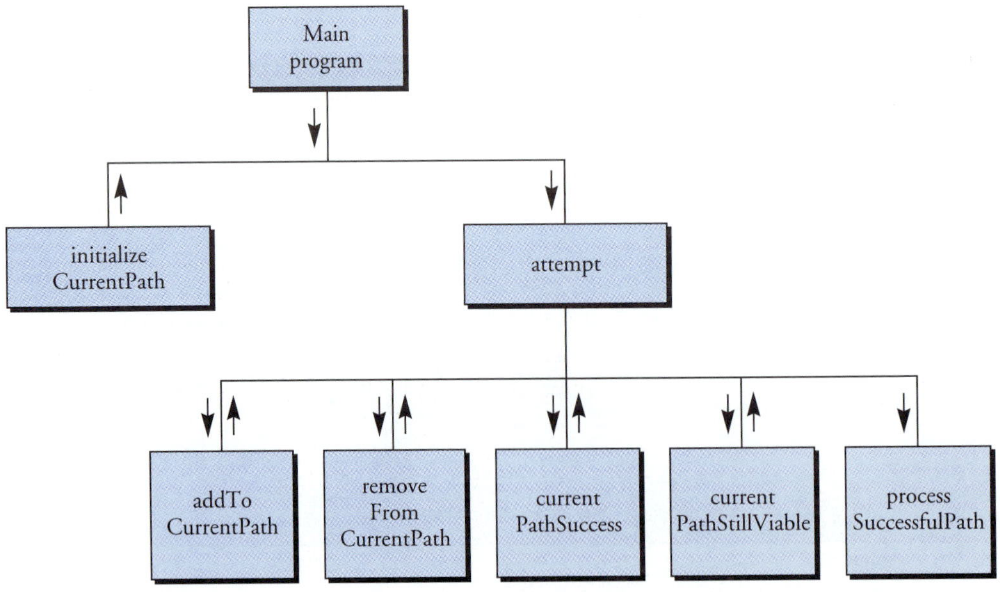

```
// Program file: permute.cpp

// Use recursion to find all permutations of 1,2, ..., N.

#include <iostream.h>
#include <iomanip.h>
#include <limits.h>
#include "apvector.h"


const int MAX_PERMUTATION_SIZE = 100;
const int UNDEFINED = INT_MAX;


apvector<int> currentPermutation(MAX_PERMUTATION_SIZE + 1);

// Function: initializeCurrentPath
// Initializes all indices in vector to the UNDEFINED flag.
//
// Inputs: The currentPermutation vector in an unreliable state
// Outputs: The initialized vector

void initializeCurrentPath();

// Function: attempt
// After locating possibility at the specified level, check if we have a
// permutation.
// If so, print it.  If not, check whether a permutation is still possible
// for this placement of possibility.  If so, attempt placement at a deeper
//   level by a recursive call.
//
//
// Inputs: n, the number of numbers we are attempting to permute;
//       level, the current depth of the solution path as portrayed in
//       Figure 5-16; possibility, the number we wish to place at that level
//
// Outputs: Relative to this level, the vector is returned unaltered.
//       However, if a permutation was found, the contents of this vector
//       are printed.


void attempt(int n, int level, int possibility);

// Function: addToCurrentPath
// Assign possibility to this level.
//
// Inputs:  level, the current depth of the solution path;
//       possibility, the number we wish to place at that level

void addToCurrentPath(int level, int possibility);

// Function: removeFromCurrentPath
// Remove value at that level.
```

```
//
// Inputs:  The deepest level to which solution path has grown
// Outputs: Suitably altered vector

void removeFromCurrentPath(int level);


// Function: currentPathSuccess
// Check if contents of vector through index level constitute a complete
// permutation of the first n numbers.
//
// Inputs:  level, the depth to which the solution path has grown
// Outputs: true if we have a permutation; false otherwise

bool currentPathSuccess(int n, int level);


// Function: currentPathStillViable
// Check if contents of vector through index level constitute a viable
// beginning for the permutation of the first n numbers.
//
// Inputs:  level, the depth to which the solution path has grown;
//          n, the number of numbers we are attempting to permute
// Outputs: true if the current path is still viable; false otherwise

bool currentPathStillViable(int level);


// Function: processSuccessfulPath
// Write out the first n indices of the vector.
//
// Inputs:  n, the number of numbers we are attempting to permute

void processSuccessfulPath(int n);


int main()
{
   int n;

   initializeCurrentPath();
   cout << "Permutation  of integers from 1 to ? ";
   cin >> n;
   for (int k = 1; k <= n; ++k)
      attempt(n, 1, k);
   return 0;
}


void initializeCurrentPath()
{
   for (int k = 1; k < MAX_PERMUTATION_SIZE; ++k)
      currentPermutation[k] = UNDEFINED;
}


void attempt(int n, int level, int possibility)
```

```
{
    addToCurrentPath(level, possibility);
    if (currentPathSuccess(n, level))
        processSuccessfulPath(n);
    else if (currentPathStillViable(level))
        for (int k = 1; k <= n; ++k)
            attempt(n, level + 1, k);
    removeFromCurrentPath(level);
}

void addToCurrentPath(int level, int possibility)
{
    currentPermutation[level] = possibility;
}

void removeFromCurrentPath(int level)
{
    currentPermutation[level] = UNDEFINED;
}

bool currentPathSuccess(int n, int level)
{
    bool success = true;
    int k = 1;

    if (n > level)
        success = false;
    else
        while ((k <= level - 1) && success)
        {
            success = currentPermutation[k] != currentPermutation[level];
            ++k;
        }
    return success;
}

bool currentPathStillViable(int level)
{
  bool viable = true;
  int k = 1;

  while ((k <= level - 1) && viable)
    {
        viable = currentPermutation[k] != currentPermutation[level];
        ++k;
    }
    return viable;
}

void processSuccessfulPath(int n)
{
```

345

```
    for (int k = 1; k <= n; ++k)
        cout << setw(3) << currentPermutation[k];
    cout << endl;
}
```

PROGRAMMING SKILLS: Fractal Geometry and Recursive Patterns

Fractal geometry as a serious mathematical endeavor began with the pioneering work of Benoit Mandelbrot, a Fellow of the Thomas J. Watson Research Center, IBM Corporation. Fractal geometry is a theory of geometric forms so complex that they defy analysis and classification by traditional Euclidean means. Yet fractal shapes occur universally in the natural world. Mandelbrot has recognized them not only in coastlines, landscapes, lungs, and turbulent water flow, but also in the chaotic fluctuation of prices on the Chicago commodity exchange.

The c-curve below is an instance of a fractal shape. It represents a series of recursive patterns of increasing levels of complexity. When the level is zero, the c-curve is a simple line specified by the endpoints $<x1, y1>$ and $<x2, y2>$. A level N c-curve is composed of two level $N - 1$ c-curves connected at right angles. Thus a level 1 c-curve is composed of two perpendicular lines, and a level 2 c-curve is three quarters of a square, which begins to resemble the letter C.

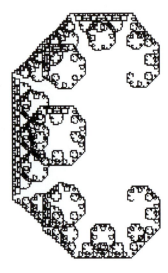

Our level 12 c-curve was generated on a graphics workstation by running a recursive function written in C++:

```
void cCurve(int x1, int y1, int x2, int y2, int level)
{
    int xm, ym;

    if ( level == 0)
        drawLine (x1, y1, x2, y2);
    else
    {
        xm = (x1 + x2 + y1 - y2)/2;
        ym = (x2 + y1 + y2 - x1)/2;
        cCurve(x1, y1, xm, ym, level - 1);
        cCurve(xm, ym, x2, y2, level - 1);
    }
}
```

You may have noticed that certain efficiency considerations have not been taken into account in writing the previous program. For example, the initialization of the `currentPermutation` vector is unnecessary in this particular implementation. Also, the call to `removeFromCurrentPath` could have been eliminated because the undefined flag that this function assigns is quickly replaced without ever being explicitly used. Finally, additional global data could be used to keep track of information that would eliminate the necessity of using loops in the `currentPathSuccess` and `currentPathStillViable` functions. You will be asked to rewrite the program taking these economies into account in the exercises.

Our purpose in the preceding discussion has not been to present the most compact version of a permutations program, but rather to illustrate how recursion can be used to simulate generalized nested loops whose nesting depth can be established at run time. Such generalized nested loops can then be used in situations where trial-and-error backtracking is an appropriate strategy in searching for a problem's solution. In this context, the permutations program is meant to be illustrative of a general problem-solving approach rather than a solution to a particular problem.

Consider what we must abstract from the permutations program to view it as a general template for trial-and-error backtracking instead of a mere permutation printer. Figure 5-16 presents the problem of finding permutations as a problem in finding certain types of paths through a maze. We probe deeper and deeper along a given path (that is, add new numbers to the current permutation) until we reach a predefined goal or reach a dead end. As we take a new step along the current path, we must analyze the state in which it has placed us:

1. Have we reached a goal state?

2. Have we reached a state that, although not itself a goal, is still a viable start toward that goal?

3. Have we reached a dead end?

For each of the three cases, we take appropriate action such as:

1. Processing a goal state—for example, printing it out, tallying a counter, or setting a flag signaling that we are done.

2. Probing further along a viable path by recursively taking another step.

3. Taking no action in the case of a dead end.

After taking the appropriate action, we retract from the step that led us to the current state, possibly returning to a higher recursive level where we may find ourselves in the midst of a similar three-state analysis. The essence of this trial-and-error backtracking logic is illustrated in Figure 5-19. Upon reaching a dead end for path A, you must retrace steps 9→8→7→6→5 before you can attempt the new path B. The retracing of states that have been visited previously is conveniently done by unwinding from recursive calls.

FIGURE 5-19
Backtracking problem illustrated by maze solution

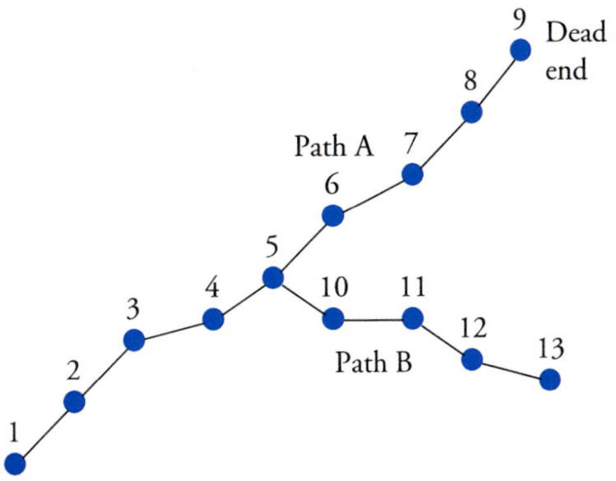

347

Artificial intelligence—the science of implementing on computers the problem-solving methods used by human beings—is one of the most rapidly expanding fields within computer science. Research efforts in this field include enabling computers to play games of strategy, to understand natural languages, to prove theorems in logic and mathematics, and to mimic the reasoning of human experts in fields such as medical diagnosis. Only recently has artificial intelligence become a commercially viable area of application, capable of solving some real-life problems apart from the idealized setting of a pure research environment. More and more, we are seeing artificial intelligence systems that perform such practical functions as aiding business executives in their decision-making processes and providing a "near-English" user interface language for database management software.

What has sparked the sudden emergence of artificial intelligence? Why wasn't it possible to produce commercially feasible programs in this field until recently? One answer to these questions is tied to the language in which most artificial intelligence programming is done—LISP (for LISt Processor). Interestingly, the control structures of LISP are based almost entirely on recursion. What a C++ programmer would view as normal iterative control structures (for example, `while`, `do`, and `for` loops) appear in various versions of LISP only as infrequently used, nonstandard extensions to the language.

One reason that a recursively based language such as LISP is so ideally suited to this field is that most problem-solving methods in artificial intelligence involve searching for a particular goal state. That is, they search for a path leading to a complete problem solution. This strategy is similar to the approaches we have taken in the permutations problem and the Eight Queens problem in this section.

The complexity of the problems studied in artificial intelligence leads to run-time trace diagrams of enormous size. Interestingly, LISP has been available as a recursive language ideally suited to such problems for a long time. It is one of the oldest high-level programming languages, having been developed by John McCarthy in the late 1950s.

Researchers who work in artificial intelligence have realized since LISP's introduction that its ability to process general data structures recursively is, on a theoretical basis, exactly what they need. The problem through the years has been that, because of the very high overhead associated with recursion (and some other features built into LISP), computer hardware has not been fast enough to run LISP programs in practical applications. Thus researchers have been restricted not by LISP itself but rather by the inability of computer hardware to execute LISP programs in reasonable times. One of the major reasons for the recent emergence of artificial intelligence has been the increase in the speed of computing hardware and the decrease in cost of this same hardware. These trends have made it possible for users to have dedicated computer resources capable of meeting the demands of LISP's recursive style. As hardware continues to improve, applications in LISP and artificial intelligence will become increasingly sophisticated.

If you are curious about LISP and the important role that it plays at some of the frontiers of research in programming languages, consult the September 1991 and November 1995 issues of the *Communications of the ACM*, vol. 34, no. 9, and vol. 38, no. 11, respectively. Each of these issues was devoted to LISP and its application in artificial intelligence.

We will now indicate the power of this abstract approach to trial-and-error backtracking by sketching a solution to another problem that could be tackled via the same methodology. You will then complete the solution in the end-of-lesson Projects.

The Eight Queens Problem

The Eight Queens problem has long intrigued chess fanatics. It requires determining the various ways in which eight queens could be configured on a chessboard so that none of them could capture any other queen. (The rules of chess allow a queen to move an arbitrary number of squares in a horizontal, vertical, or diagonal fashion.) Figure 5-20 illustrates one such configuration.

FIGURE 5-20

One successful Eight Queens configuration

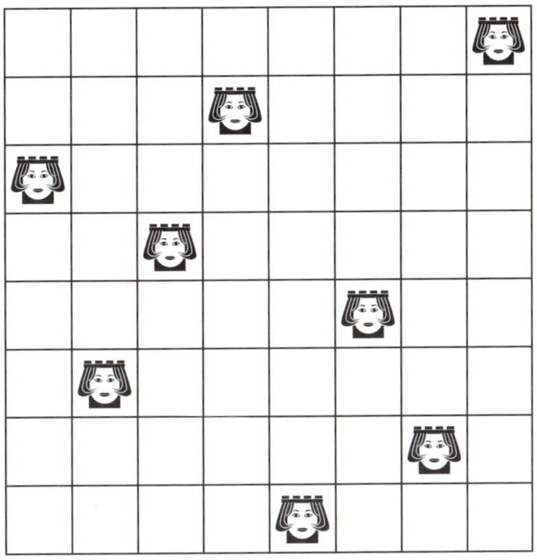

Applying backtracking logic to this problem, we could attempt to find a path to a configuration by successively placing a queen in each column of a chessboard until we reach a dead end: a column in which the placement of queens in prior columns makes it impossible to place the queen being moved. This situation is pictured in Figure 5-21. Here, the sixth queen cannot be placed due to the placement of the first five queens.

When we reach such a dead end, we must backtrack one column (to column 5 in Figure 5-21) and attempt to find a new placement for the queen in that column. If placement in the previous column is impossible, we must backtrack yet another column to attempt the new placement. This backtracking through previous columns continues until we are finally able to reposition a queen. At that point, we can begin a new path by again attempting to position queens on a column-by-column basis until another dead end is reached or until a fully successful configuration is developed.

FIGURE 5-21

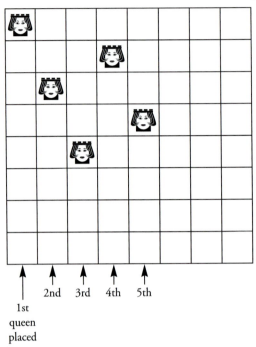

The key to a program that finds all possible configurations for the eight queens is a function that attempts to place a queen in a given square and, if successful, recursively calls itself to attempt the placement of another queen in the next column. Such a function in skeletal pseudocode form follows:

```
void tryQueen (K, J)

// Place a queen in row K, column J.
// Analyze state reached by this placement.
// If appropriate, recurse to place queen in next column.


Actually put queen at position K, J
If this results in successful configuration
    Tally this configuration
Else if no queen in immediate danger
    For each L from 1 to 8
            tryQueen(L, J + 1)
Retract from position K, J
```

The similarities between this sketch of a solution to the Eight Queens problem and our complete solution to the permutations problem should convince you that, from an abstract perspective, both problems are really the same. We have intentionally left the Eight Queens problem unfinished. Still to be resolved are the following issues:

- The initial call(s) to tryQueen.

- The representation of the chessboard.

- Ways to check whether placing a queen at position K, J puts it in immediate danger—that is, how to determine whether another queen currently shares the same row, column, or diagonal.

The resolution of these issues is left for your enjoyment in the Projects at the end of the lesson. Additional problems given there further illustrate the far-reaching applicability of the trial-and-error backtracking method.

EXERCISES 5.3

1. Consider the permutations program discussed in Section 5.3. Suppose that $N = 3$ in a particular run of this program and that we printed out the contents of the `currentPermutation` vector each time the `attempt` function was invoked in this run. How many times would the vector be printed? What would be the overall output?

2. Suppose you used the permutations function of this section to compute all permutations of 1, 2, 3, and 4. What would the complete run-time trace diagram of recursive function calls look like for such a run? Can you generalize from this diagram of function calls the efficiency of the permutations function? State your answer in big-O terms with respect to both stack size and number of stack operations. Justify your answer in a written statement.

3. Rewrite the example program for permutations in a fashion that takes into account the efficiency considerations discussed in Section 5.3. These considerations are discussed in the paragraph that follows the program.

4. What is the output from the following program?

```
#include <iostream.h>

void y(int a, int b, int c);

int main()
{
    y(16, 1, 4);
    return 0;
}

void y(int a, int b, int c)
{
    int k;

    if (b <= c)
    {
        cout << a << endl;
        for (k = b; k <= c; ++k)
            y(k, b + 1, c);
    }
}
```

5. What is the output from the following program?

```
#include <iostream.h>

void tough(int b, int c, int d);

int main()
{
    tough(1, 4, 12);
    return 0;
}

void tough(int b, int c, int d)
{
    int k;

    if (b <= c)
    {
        cout << d << endl;
        for (k = b; k <= c; ++k)
            tough(b + 1, c, k);
    }
}
```

6. A car's odometer may be viewed as a physical implementation of a nested loop. Each loop cycles through the digits 0 . . . 9, with the 1s digit cycling the fastest, then the 10s digit, and so forth. Write a function to simulate an *N*-digit odometer (*N* determined at run time) by creating a generalized nested loop structure that will run through, in sequence, all possible settings for the odometer.

5.4 Recursive Descent Parsing

In Section 4.3, we studied the parsing of infix algebraic expressions by using a stack and appropriate infix and stack priority functions. That parsing algorithm emphasized the conversion of the infix expression into a postfix expression and assumed that it had been given a syntactically valid infix expression. A problem equally important in parsing is the detection of syntax errors in the expression to be processed. One method of error detection, called *recursive descent parsing*, relies heavily on recursive procedures. The inspiration for such recursive procedures comes from the linguistic concept of a context-free grammar, which provides a rigorous formalism for defining the syntax of expressions and other programming language constructs. This formalism is similar to that found in the syntax diagram of Appendix C. The scope of context-free grammars goes far beyond what we will cover in one section of this text. If your interest is aroused by the following discussion, we encourage you to consult Charles N. Fischer and Richard J. LeBlanc, *Crafting a Compiler*, Benjamin/Cummings, Menlo Park, CA, 1988.

A *context-free grammar* is composed of three elements:

1. A set of *terminals*. The terminals represent the tokens—characters or groups of characters that logically belong together, such as operator symbols, delimiters, keywords, and variable names—that ultimately form the expression being parsed. In the case of infix algebraic expressions, the terminals are variables, numeric constants, parentheses, and the various operators allowed.

2. A set of **nonterminals**. The nonterminals represent the various grammatical constructs within the language we are parsing. In particular, one nonterminal is designated as the **start symbol** for the grammar.

3. A set of **productions**. The productions are formal rules defining the syntactic composition of the nonterminals from point 2. The productions take the form:

$$\text{Nonterminal} \rightarrow \text{String of terminals and/or nonterminals}$$

We say that the nonterminal on the left of such a production **derives** the string on the right.

An example of a context-free grammar should help clarify this three-part definition.

Example 5-10

Provide a context-free grammar for infix algebraic expressions involving addition and multiplication and show how the particular expression A + B * C is derived from it.

1. Set of terminals:

$$\{ \text{'+', '*', '(', ')', identifier, number} \}$$

2. Set of nonterminals:

$$\{ \text{<expression>, <factor>, <add-factor>, <mult-factor>, <primary>} \}$$

where <expression> is designated as the start symbol. By convention, nonterminals are enclosed in angle brackets to distinguish them from terminals.

3. Set of productions:

   a.   <expression>   →   <factor><add-factor>

   b.   <factor>   →   <primary><mult-factor>

   c.   <add-factor>   →   ' +' <factor><add-factor>

   d.   <add-factor>   →   '-' <factor><add-factor>

   e.   <add-factor>   →   NULL

   f.   <mult-factor>   →   ' *' <primary><mult-factor>

   g.   <mult-factor>   →   '/' <primary><mult-factor>

   h.   <mult-factor>   →   NULL

   i.   <primary>   →   identifier

   j.   <primary>   →   number

   k.   <primary>   →   ' (' <expression> ')'

The symbol NULL is used to indicate the empty string. In effect, it implies that one defining option for < add-factor > and < mult-factor > is the empty string. We will see why this option is necessary in the derivation of A + B * C, which follows.

To derive a particular infix expression, we begin with the start symbol < expression >. The production that defines < expression > says that < expression > must be < factor > followed by < add-factor >. Hence, we must now try to derive these two nonterminals. This process of involving nonterminals in the definition of other nonterminals continues until we finally reach those nonterminals that are defined by the terminals in the infix expression being parsed. Thus a formal derivation of A + B * C is given by

<expression> →	<factor><add-factor>	By production a
→	<primary><mult-factor><add-factor>	By production b
→	A <mult-factor><add-factor>	By production i
→	A <add-factor>	By production h
→	A + <factor><add-factor>	By production c
→	A + <primary><mult-factor><add-factor>	By production b
→	A + B <mult-factor><add-factor>	By production i
→	A + B * <primary><mult-factor><add-factor>	By production f
→	A + B * C <mult-factor><add-factor>	By production i
→	A + B * C	By productions e and h

Note that the grammar of Example 5-10 contains a hint of recursion in that some of the productions defining <add-factor> and <mult-factor> use these same nonterminals in their definitional pattern on the right of the production being defined. As Example 5-11 will show, this recursive portion of the definition allows us to add arbitrarily many identifiers in one expression. That is, by the recursive appearance of <add-factor> and <mult-factor> in productions c and f, respectively, we are able to keep introducing '+' and '*' into the expression being parsed.

Example 5-11

Provide a derivation of the infix expression A + B + C.

< expression > →	<factor><add-factor>
→	<primary><mult-factor><add-factor>
→	A <mult-factor><add-factor>
→	A <add-factor>
→	A + <factor><add-factor>
→	A + <primary><mult-factor><add-factor>
→	A + B <mult-factor><add-factor>
→	A + B <add-factor>
→	A + B + <factor><add-factor>
→	A + B + <primary><mult-factor><add-factor>
→	A + B + C <mult-factor><add-factor>
→	A + B + C <add-factor>
→	A + B + C

You are encouraged to justify each step in the derivation by determining the production applied.

PROGRAMMING SKILLS: Language Definition and Natural Languages

The syntax of most computer languages can be recursively defined using grammars similar to that described in this lesson. This consideration is of tremendous importance in the writing of compilers, most of which rely heavily on stacks and recursion to parse source programs.

A broader question than the definition and parsing of programming languages is the ability of the computer to process natural languages such as English. Researchers in the field of artificial intelligence are attempting to use more general recursive techniques to define the syntax of natural languages and, consequently, program the computer to cope with this more complex type of language. To date, their work has met with success only in highly restricted domains of natural language, such as that used to express word problems in algebra or interact with databases in a structured query language.

Despite these present limitations, research in language definition and the consequent processing of that language by a computer should be one of the most intensely explored fields within computer science in the future. According to researchers Kenneth Church and Lisa Rau, the vast quantity and variety of text available on the Internet and in other electronic media are "moving natural language processing along the critical path for all kinds of novel applications." If you want to read about some of these novel applications, consult Kenneth Church and Lisa Rau, "Commercial Applications of Natural Language," *Communications of the ACM*, vol. 38, no. 11, November 1995, pages 71–79.

Just as we were able to describe recursive procedure processing with a run-time trace diagram, the formal derivation of an expression via the productions of a grammar can be represented by a diagram called a ***parse tree***. (Parse trees for the derivation in Examples 5-10 and 5-11 are given in Figures 5-22 and 5-23, respectively.) Implicit in parse trees is the order of operations in the algebraic expressions. That is, parse trees are constructed, top-down, starting at each nonterminal within the tree and, from that nonterminal, descending to those nodes containing the terminals and nonterminals from the right side of the production applied in the derivation of the original nonterminal. Eventually, as we descend deeper into the tree, only terminals are left, and no nodes descend deeper from these terminals. In Figure 5-22, because the < factor > node on level 2 of the tree encompasses all of B * C below it, we have an indication that B * C must be first evaluated as a < factor > and then added to A. On the other hand, in the parse tree of Figure 5-23, the < factor > node at level 2 encompasses only the B term. Hence, B is to be added to A, with C (below the < factor > node at level 3) then added to that result.

In the exercises and projects, you will continue to explore the relationships between context-free grammars, derivations, parse trees, and orders of evaluation in infix expressions. In the Case Study for this lesson, we will turn our attention to the problem of transforming the formal grammar that specifies the syntax of a language into a program that determines whether the tokens stored in an incoming queue constitute a valid string.

E XERCISES ⟩ 5.4

1. Using the context-free grammar of Example 5-10, provide formal derivations and parse trees for the following expressions:
  a. A * B * C * D + E
  b. A + B * C * (D + E)
  c. ((A + B) * C) * (D + E)

2. Extend the grammar of Example 5-10 to:
  a. Allow exponentiation (^) as an algebraic operator. Be sure that your grammar yields parse trees that imply that the order of consecutive exponentiations goes from right to left instead of from left to right (as it is with other operators).
  b. Allow or (|) , and (&), and not (!) as logical operators so that Boolean as well as algebraic expressions are allowed by the grammar.

FIGURE 5-22

Parse tree for A + B * C reflects that B * C is evaluated first

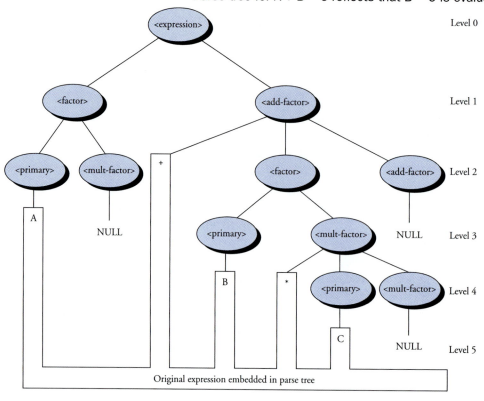

FIGURE 5-23

Parse tree for A + B + C reflects that B is added to A before addition of C

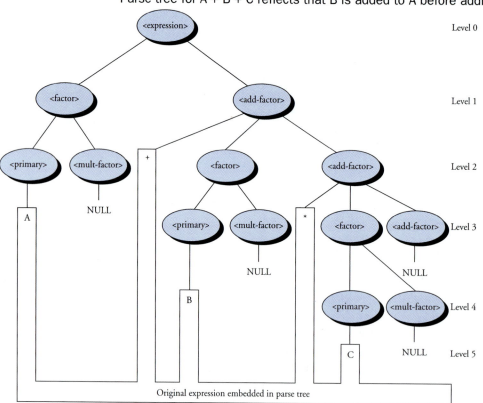

3. Consider the following alternative, context-free grammar for the expressions defined by the grammar of Example 5-10:

<expression>	→	<mult-factor>
<expression>	→	<mult-factor> ' + ' <expression>
<expression>	→	<mult-factor> '- ' <expression>
<mult-factor>	→	<primary>
<mult-factor>	→	<primary> '*' <mult-factor>
<mult-factor>	→	<primary> '/' <mult-factor>
<primary>	→	identifier
<primary>	→	number
<primary>	→	' (' <expression> ')'

  a. Does this grammar allow the same set of expressions as that in Example 5-10?

  b. Provide parse trees for any of the expressions in Exercise 1 that are accepted by the grammar of this exercise.

  c. What are differences in the parse trees produced by this grammar versus those produced by the grammar of Example 5-10?

  d. How would the differences you described in part c affect the order in which operators are applied?

  e. Which grammar—Example 5-10 or the one defined in this exercise—more accurately reflects the order of operations in standard programming languages?

4. (Left-Recursive Grammar) Consider the following alternative, context-free grammar for the expressions defined by the grammar of Example 5-10:

<expression>	→	<mult-factor>
<expression>	→	<expression> '+ ' <mult-factor>
<expression>	→	<expression> '- ' <mult-factor>
<mult-factor>	→	<primary>
<mult-factor>	→	<mult-factor> '*' <primary>
<mult-factor>	→	<mult-factor> '/' <primary>
<primary>	→	identifier
<primary>	→	number
<primary>	→	' (' <expression> ')'

This grammar is an example of a left-recursive grammar—one that admits a derivation of the form

$$< a > \rightarrow < a > X$$

where $< a >$ is a nonterminal and X is a string of terminals and/or nonterminals. For the grammar of this exercise, productions associated with the nonterminals <expression> and <mult-factor> fit this criterion, so the grammar is left-recursive.

  a. Does this grammar allow the same set of expressions as that of Example 5-10?

  b. Provide parse trees for any of the expressions in Exercise 1 that are accepted by the grammar of this exercise.

  c. What are differences in the parse trees produced by this grammar versus those produced by the grammars of Example 5-10 and Exercise 3?

  d. How do the differences you described in part c affect the order in which operators are applied?

  e. After reading the Case Study, discuss the difficulty arising when you attempt to implement a recursive descent parser that reflects directly the grammar given in this exercise.

5. Provide a context-free grammar for the `if` and `if-else` structures of a conventional programming language such as C++. Assume that nonterminals < condition > and < statement > are suitably defined elsewhere and, hence, can be used as primitives in your grammar. How many parse trees will your grammar allow for the following C++ statement?

```
if (a < b)
   if (c < d)
      a = d;
   else
      b = c;
```

Which, if any, of your parse trees correspond to the fashion in which standard C++ interprets this statement?

CASE STUDY: Parsing Expressions

In Section 5.4, we described context-free grammars as a way of recursively specifying the syntax of a language. This Case Study will demonstrate that, by using such a rigorous definitional tool for characterizing a language, the task of writing a program to parse expressions in that language is surprisingly easy.

User Request

Develop a program that will allow input of a stream of tokens corresponding to the grammar of Example 5-10. The stream should be parsed for syntactic correctness. That is, if the stream constitutes an acceptable expression in the language, the program should so indicate. Otherwise, the program should indicate that the stream is syntactically invalid. Assume that identifiers are uppercase letters, that tokens are separated by a space when entered, and that the end token # will be used to mark the end of the input stream.

Analysis

Based on this request, the program's interaction with a user should appear as follows:

```
Enter expression with spaces between tokens, then <ENTER>
( ( X + 14.3 ) / ( A * 2 ) ) #
Expression is valid

Enter expression with spaces between tokens, then <ENTER>
( ( X + 14.3 ) / ( A * 2 ) ) #
Expression is invalid
```

Design

At first consideration, writing this program may seem like a daunting task. However, we first note that we already have a token class from the Case Study in Lesson 4 that can be reused here. If necessary, you should reread the discussion of the token class in that Case Study to familiarize yourself with its use. In the program we are developing here, we will augment that token class with a few helper functions tied specifically to the grammar from Example 5-10.

```
// Get the next token from the input stream and return it in fromInfix
void getInfixToken(token &fromInfix);

// Read a sequence of tokens from the input stream, terminating with the
// END_TOKEN.  Return this stream of tokens in a queue.
void getInfixExp(queue<token> &infix);

// Return true if tok is an "add operator", that is, a + or -.
// Otherwise return false.
bool isAddOp(token tok);

// Return true if tok is an "mult operator", that is, a * or /.
// Otherwise return false.
bool isMultOp(token tok);

// Return true if tok represents a left parenthesis.
// Otherwise return false.
bool isLeftParen(token tok);

// Return true if tok represents a right parenthesis.
// Otherwise return false.
bool isRightParen(token tok);

// Return true if tok represents the END_TOKEN #.
// Otherwise return false.
bool isEndToken(token tok);
```

Given these helper functions for tokens, the process of writing a parsing function itself is surprisingly easy. It begins with a front-end function called from the main program. This front-end function receives the queue of tokens read from the input stream and will eventually return a Boolean value to indicate the success or failure of the parse.

```
// Given a queue of tokens called infix, representing an expression that is
// a candidate to satisfy the grammar of Example 5-10, return true if the
// expression is syntactically valid and false otherwise.

bool parse(apqueue<token> infix);
```

To do so, this function performs the necessary initializations and then calls on the first in a suite of "verifying" functions. The initialization that `parse` must do is to dequeue the first token from the `infix` queue and pass it along to the verifying function as the "current token." We write a separate verifying function for each nonterminal in the grammar. The responsibility of each function is simply to verify the particular grammatical construction after which it is named. To do so, it receives the `currentToken` and what remains of the `infix` queue. The verifying functions strips away enough of the `infix` queue to verify its particular grammatical construction and then returns the potentially altered `currentToken` and `infix` queue to its calling function, along with a Boolean value indicating whether it was successful. Formally, the specifications for these verifying functions are as follows:

```
//-----------------------------------------------------------------
// Function parseExpression:        verifies an expression

// Given the current token and what is left in the queue of tokens that
// originally contained the entire expression to be parsed, return true if
// an expression (according to the grammar of Example 5-10) can be
// verified and false otherwise.

bool parseExpression(apqueue<token> &infix, token& currentToken);


//-----------------------------------------------------------------
// Function parseFactor:    verifies a factor

// Given the current token and what is left in the queue of tokens that
// originally contained the entire expression to be parsed, return true if
// a factor (according to the grammar of Example 5-10) can be
// verified and false otherwise.

bool parseFactor(apqueue<token> &infix, token& currentToken);


//-----------------------------------------------------------------
// Function parseAddFactor:     verifies an addFactor

// Given the current token and what is left in the queue of tokens that
// originally contained the entire expression to be parsed, return true if
// an addFactor (according to the grammar of Example 5-10) can be
// verified and false otherwise.

bool parseAddFactor(apqueue<token> &infix, token& currentToken);


//-----------------------------------------------------------------
// Function parseMultFactor:        verifies a multFactor

// Given the current token and what is left in the queue of tokens that
// originally contained the entire expression to be parsed, return true if
// a multFactor (according to the grammar of Example 5-10) can be
// verified and false otherwise.

bool parseMultFactor(apqueue<token> &infix, token& currentToken);


//-----------------------------------------------------------------
// Function parsePrimary:       verifies a primary

// Given the current token and what is left in the queue of tokens that
// originally contained the entire expression to be parsed, return true if
```

```
// a primary (according to the grammar of Example 5-10) can be
// verified and false otherwise.

bool parsePrimary(apqueue<token> &infix, token& currentToken);
```

Implementation

The subordinate functions called on by a given function are dictated by the right sides of productions defining that function's associated nonterminal in the context-free grammar. As many of these productions will typically have the terminal defined on the left reappearing on the right, many of the associated functions will be recursive in nature. Consequently, the general algorithmic technique is termed *recursive descent parsing*. The run-time trace diagram of recursive calls will parallel the parse tree for the expression. Complete implementations of parse and all verifying functions follow. Study them closely; the accompanying graphic documentation will help clarify what is happening. You will get a chance to explore recursive descent parsing more deeply in the problems at the end of this lesson.

```
bool parse(apqueue<token> infix)
{
  token currentToken;

  if (infix.isEmpty())
    return(false);
  else
  {
    infix.dequeue(currentToken);
    if (parseExpression(infix, currentToken))
      return(infix.empty());
    else
      return(false);
  }
}

bool parseExpression(apqueue<token> &infix, token& currentToken)
{
  if (parseFactor(infix, currentToken))
   return(parseAddFactor(infix, currentToken));    <expression> → <factor><add-factor>
  else
    return(false);
}

bool parseFactor(apqueue<token> &infix, token& currentToken)
{
  if (parsePrimary(infix, currentToken))
    return(parseMultFactor(infix, currentToken));   <factor> → <primary><mult-factor>
  else
    return(false);
}
```

361

```
bool parseAddFactor(apqueue<token> &infix, token& currentToken)
{
  if (! isAddOp(currentToken))    // NULL production is satisfied
    return(true);
  else if (infix.isEmpty())              // Something should follow add operator
    return(false);
  else
  {
    infix.dequeue(currentToken);        ┌─────────────────────────────────────┐
    if (parseFactor(infix, currentToken)) │ <add-factor> → '+' <factor><add-factor> │
      return(parseAddFactor(infix, currentToken)); └─────────────────────────────┘
    else
      return(false);
  }
}


bool parseMultFactor(apqueue<token> &infix, token& currentToken)
{
  if (! isMultOp(currentToken))  // NULL production is satisfied
    return(true);
  else if (infix.isEmpty())              // Something should follow mult operator
    return(false);
  else
  {
    infix.dequeue(currentToken);        ┌──────────────────────────────────────┐
    if (parseFactor(infix, currentToken)) │ <mult-factor> → '.' <factor><multfactor> │
      return(parseMultFactor(infix, currentToken)); └────────────────────────────┘
    else
      return(false);
  }
}


bool parsePrimary(apqueue<token> &infix, token& currentToken)
{
  if ( currentToken.code() == VAR_X || currentToken.code() == REAL_VALUE )
  {
    if (!infix.isEmpty())               ┌───────────────────────────────┐
      infix.dequeue(currentToken);      │ <primary> → indentifier        │
    return(true);                       │ <primary> → number             │
  }                                     └───────────────────────────────┘
  else
    if (! isLeftParen(currentToken))
      return(false);
    else                        // We must have parenthesized expression
      if(infix.isEmpty())
        return(false);
      else
      {
        currentToken = infix.dequeue();  ┌───────────────────────────────┐
        if (parseExpression(infix, currentToken)) │ <primary> → '('expression')' │
          if ( isRightParen(currentToken)) └─────────────────────────────┘
          {
```

```
              if (!infix.isEmpty())
                  infix.dequeue(currentToken);
              return(true);
          }
          else
              return(false);
      else
          return(false);
  }
}
```

The large amount of code in this suite of functions belies the ease with which each function can be written, provided that we start with a sound grammatical description of the expressions being parsed. As indicated by the graphic documentation, each verifying function merely calls on subordinate verifying functions in the order dictated by the right side of a production in the context-free grammar. For nonterminals that have more than one defining production, the currentToken parameter is examined to determine which production to follow.

As easy as the process seems, some negatives are attached to the recursive descent parsing method. First, it applies only to context-free grammars that have their productions in a suitable form. The productions from Example 5-10 are in that form, but in Exercise 4 (Section 5.4), you explored a context-free grammar that is not appropriate for the recursive descent method. Thus, to use recursive descent parsing, you must write "correct" grammars.

A second negative is the rigidity of a recursive descent parser once it has been implemented. Should you have a change of heart about the syntax rules of the language being parsed, the resulting changes in productions may lead to widespread and dramatic changes in the code for the parser itself, because the code is directly tied to the productions. Hence, maintaining the code in a recursive descent parser can be a problem. This fact places a premium on getting the grammar right the first time, before you begin generating code from it. Compare this situation to the ease with which you can alter a parse by changing the priority functions in the parsing method discussed in Section 4.3.

Running, Debugging, and Testing Hints

- Recursion is an elegant and powerful tool. It combines iterative control with a built-in data structure, the system stack. To properly control that iteration, you should provide an appropriate recursive termination condition for your algorithms.

- Be sure that, when you invoke a function recursively, you are in some sense passing in a smaller, simpler version of the problem being solved. Otherwise, your algorithm will infinitely recur.

- The use of tracer output can be valuable in debugging recursive algorithms. You must, however, be careful not to insert so many tracer output statements that you become lost in the copious output they produce. Remember that recursive algorithms are often exponential in efficiency and, consequently, may be exponential in the amount of output produced by tracers. Insert tracer output statements judiciously. Where appropriate, use a Boolean constant that can be toggled to **true** or **false** to control whether the tracer output is produced.

Summary

In this lesson, you learned:

- Stacks process function calls when a program executes. Understanding the role of the stack in this application is essential to effective use of the programming technique known as recursion.

- A recursive function invokes itself with a simpler version of the same problem it was originally given. Ultimately, there must be a recursive termination condition to break a series of recursive function calls.

- In tail recursion, no further processing occurs at any level of recursion after a return from a recursive call is made.

- A function's stack frame contains memory locations for all parameters and local variables as well as the machine address of the point to which to return after the function completes execution at the current level.

- A run-time trace diagram can often be used to help analyze the efficiency of a recursive algorithm. If the diagram indicates that multiple recursive calls are made at each level, there is a good chance that an exponential algorithm is being used.

- Recursion can be used to solve a complex class of search problems by using a trial-and-error backtracking strategy. Often such solutions consume a tremendous amount of resources, particularly in terms of run-time efficiency.

- Do not be misled into thinking that recursion is necessarily the most efficient programming technique because the code that expresses it is often compact and lacking in any explicit loop control statements such as `while` or `do`. The very nature of a recursive call generates iteration without the need for a `while` or `do` loop. The iteration control mechanism in recursion is the recursive termination condition that triggers a series of returns before another recursive call is made. Hence, from a time-efficiency perspective, a recursive algorithm's measure of effectiveness is closely tied to the number of times it must iterate its recursive call-and-return pattern. Moreover, with recursion, we pay a price in memory efficiency that is not present in other iterative control structures. This price is system stack space.

- The value of recursion lies in the way it enables us to express algorithms compactly and elegantly for a certain class of problems. Because we will use recursion frequently throughout the rest of this text, you will learn to acquire a feel for the type of problems particularly suitable to this powerful technique. In the next lesson, we will see that recursion is an indispensable strategy for manipulating a data structure known as a tree. In later lessons, recursion will be explored as a means of sorting and searching.

VOCABULARY REVIEW

Define the following terms:

binding time problem	nonterminals	stack frame
context-free grammar	parse tree	start symbol
generalized nested loops	recursion	tail recursive
grammar	recursive descent parsing	terminals
LISP	run-time trace diagram	trial-and-error backtracking

LESSON 5 REVIEW QUESTIONS

FILL IN THE BLANK

Complete the following sentences by writing the correct word or words in the blanks provided.

1. The "invisible" data structure underlying recursive functions is a(n) _____.

2. To end recursive calls, there must be a(n) _____ condition.

3. If only one recursive call appears in the function and it is the last operation performed at the procedural level, it is called _____ recursion.

4. Asking yourself, "What could I do if I had a solution to a simpler version of the same problem?", is called the _____.

5. An ordered arrangement in which each element appears exactly once is called a(n) _____.

WRITTEN QUESTIONS

Write a brief answer to the following questions.

6. What will be the output of the following program?

```cpp
#include <iostream>
void go (int n);
int main( void )
{
    go(100);
    cout << endl;
    return 0;


}
void go (int n)
{
    if (n >= 50)
    {
        cout << n << "   ";
        go(n - 5);
    }
}
```

7. In Question 6, what must be true for the recursive calls to stop?

8. Assume when this function is called, a = 20 and k = 5. What will be the output?

```cpp
int findNum (int a, int k)
    {
        if (a <= 0)
```

365

```
        return 1;
    else
    {
        --a;
        k = k - 2;
        cout << setw(8) << a << setw(8) << k << endl;
        return a + findNum(a+k, k);
    }
}
```

9. Rewrite the function in Question 8 so that it is iterative rather than recursive.

10. A palindrome is a word or phrase that reads the same backward or forward, such as *level, today is si yadot,* and so on. Write a recursive C++ function to determine whether a given phrase (character string) is a palindrome.

11. Write a recursive C++ function to implement a search algorithm to search a vector for a given item.

12. Write a recursive function to determine whether a vector of integers is sorted in ascending order.

13. Write a recursive function to read one line of characters from a text file and display them in reverse order without using an auxiliary vector.

14. Assume that the class queue is given that has member functions enqueue(item), dequeue(), operator=, and length(). Write a nonmember, nonfriend recursive function that takes a parameter, Q, of type queue and returns a queue whose elements are the same as those of Q but in reverse order. Do not use any function other than those that were mentioned above.

LESSON 5 PROJECTS

PROJECT 5-1

SCANS

Write a program to call for input of a decimal number and convert it to its binary equivalent using the method described in the following flowchart:

This method produces the binary digits for the given number in reverse order. One strategy for printing the digits in the correct order is to store them in a vector as they are produced and then print the vector. This strategy has the drawbacks of allocating unnecessary storage for a vector and then limiting the size of the binary number to the size of the vector. Your program should not employ this strategy. Rather, it should call for input of the decimal number in the main program and then immediately transfer control to a function that is called recursively, stacking the binary digits as they are produced. Once division by 2 yields 0, the succession of returns can be used to print the digits one by one as they are popped from this stack.

Let x be the decimal number to convert.

↓

Divide x by 2, storing quotient in q and remainder in r.

↓

r is the "next" binary digit.

↓

$q = 0$ — No → $x = q$

$q = 0$ — Yes → All binary digits have been produced.

PROJECT 5-2

The Nth Fibonacci number is defined by

1 if N is 1

1 if N is 2
The sum of the previous two Fibonacci numbers otherwise

Write a recursive function to compute the Nth Fibonacci number. Then, using a run-time trace diagram, analyze the efficiency of your function.

PROJECT 5-3

Euclid devised a clever algorithm for computing the greatest common divisor (GCD) of two integers. According to Euclid's algorithm,

$$GCD\ (M,N) = \begin{cases} GCD(N, M) \text{ if } N > M \\ GCD(N, M\ \%\ N) \text{ if } N > 0 \\ M \text{ if } N = 0 \end{cases}$$

Write a recursive function to compute GCDs via Euclid's method.

PROJECT 5-4

Suppose you have N thousand dollars and can use this sum to buy a combination of Orange computers (which cost \$1000 each), HAL computers (which cost \$2000 each), or MAX computers (which cost \$4000 each). How many different combinations of Orange, HAL, and MAX computers could be bought with your N thousand dollars? Write a program that receives N as input and responds with the number of possible combinations.

Hint: If N were 100, then the number of combinations is

The number of combinations totaling $100,000 and involving Orange and HAL computers only

PLUS

The number of combinations totaling $96,000 and involving potentially all three brands

Think about this hint for a while and extend it to a recursive function that solves this problem.

PROJECT 5-5

Ackermann's function is defined recursively for two non-negative integers m and n as follows:

$$\text{Ackermann}(m, n) = \begin{cases} n + 1 \text{ if } m = 0 \\ \text{Ackermann}(m - 1, 1) \text{ if } n = 0 \\ \text{Ackermann}(m - 1, \text{Ackermann }(m, n - 1)) \text{ otherwise} \end{cases}$$

Write a recursive version of this function. Develop a run-time trace diagram for the function when $m = 2$ and $n = 3$. Attempt to deduce the big-O efficiency of the recursive version with respect to stack size and stack operations. Justify your answer in a written statement.

PROJECT 5-6

If you have access to an appropriate graphics device, write the functions `line` and `rightTurn` described in Section 5.1. Then, experiment by writing recursive functions that call on these functions (and others you may develop) to produce a variety of interesting figures.

PROJECT 5-7

Write a function that receives a set of N integers and then prints all subsets of this set.

PROJECT 5-8

Write a program that completes the solution of the Eight Queens problem as sketched in Section 5.3.

PROJECT 5-9

A K-permutation of the first N positive integers, $K <= N$, is a permutation of a K-element subset of $\{1, 2, \ldots, N\}$. Write a function to generate all possible K-permutations of the first N positive integers.

PROJECT 5-10

A continued fraction is a number of the form that follows (where each a_i is an integer):

$$a_1 + \cfrac{1}{a_2 + \cfrac{1}{a_3 + \cfrac{1}{a_4 + \cfrac{1}{\ddots \cfrac{1}{a_n}}}}}$$

Although a continued fraction is composed of integers a_i, it has a real value. For example, consider the following continued fraction and its indicated real value:

$$1 + \cfrac{1}{2 + \cfrac{1}{6 + \cfrac{1}{5}}} = 1 + \cfrac{1}{2 + \cfrac{1}{\frac{31}{5}}} = 1 + \cfrac{1}{2 + \cfrac{5}{31}} = 1 + \cfrac{1}{\frac{67}{31}} = \frac{98}{67} = 1.46$$

Provide a class declaration of your implementation of a continued fraction. Then, write a recursive function that receives a continued fraction and returns its associated real value. If you are really ambitious, write a complete suite of arithmetic operations on continued fractions.

PROJECT 5-11

There are five other teams in the same league as the Bay Area Brawlers (Project 3-9 in Lesson 3, and Project 4-13 in Lesson 4). Over a given 5-week period, the Brawlers must play each of the other teams exactly once. Using recursion, write a program to determine the ways in which such a 5-week schedule could be accomplished. For an added challenge, introduce more realistic scheduling considerations into this problem. For instance, have your program determine the ways in which a 15-game schedule could be constructed such that each of the six teams in the league plays each of the other teams exactly three times, but never consecutively.

PROJECT 5-12

Write a function that uses a random number generator to produce mazes. One way of viewing a maze is as a matrix of structures:

```
struct location
{
    bool
        northBlocked,
        eastBlocked,
        southBlocked,
        westBlocked;
};
```

At each square in the matrix, the Boolean attributes are set to indicate whether we can proceed in the indicated direction. After your maze-generating function is working, develop a function that uses trial-and-error backtracking to solve the maze.

PROJECT 5-13

A transportation network such as the following can be represented as a matrix with rows and columns indexed by the cities in the network. The number stored at position (K, J) of such a matrix represents the distance of the link between two cities. Zero indicates that two cities are not directly linked.

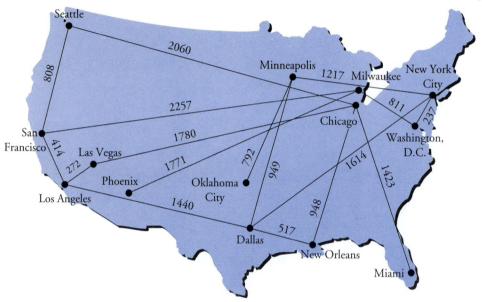

Write a program that, for input of two cities, outputs all possible paths connecting the two cities. Then modify the program so that it outputs only the shortest path linking the two cities. Use a trial-and-error backtracking strategy to solve this problem. We will discuss a more efficient algorithm for it in the next lesson.

PROJECT 5-14

SCANS

Another classic chess problem that can be solved by trial-and-error backtracking is known as the Knight's Tour. Given a chessboard with a knight initially placed at coordinates x_0, y_0, the problem is to specify a series of moves for the knight that will result in each board location being visited exactly once. From a given square on the chessboard, a knight may move to any of the eight numbered squares in the following diagram:

	3		2	
4				1
		♞		
5				8
	6		7	

Write a program to find a valid Knight's Tour.

PROJECT 5-15

SCANS

A famous theorem in mathematics states that four colors are enough to color any map in a fashion that allows each region on the map to be a different color from any of its adjacent neighbors. Write a program that initially allows input of a map. One way of doing so is to input each region followed by a list of its adjacent neighbors. This information can then be stored in a Boolean matrix with rows and columns indexed by region names. Store `true` at row K, column J, if region K and region J are neighbors; otherwise, store `false`. Once your program has appropriately stored the information associated with the input map, it should use trial-and-error backtracking to find a pattern for coloring the map with four colors. Note that the Four-Color Theorem from mathematics guarantees that such a pattern can be found.

PROJECT 5-16

SCANS

Write a program to find a solution to the following stable marriage problem (or indicate that no solution exists for the input data). According to this problem, we have N men and N women, each of whom has stated distinct preferences for their possible partners. The data regarding these preferences are the input for this problem. This information can be stored in two matrices: one in which each woman has rated each of the men as first choice, second choice, . . . , Nth choice, and another in which each man has similarly rated each of the women. Given this input, a solution to the stable marriage problem is to find N couples (marriages) such that

■ Each man is part of exactly one couple (marriage).

■ Each woman is part of exactly one couple (marriage).

■ There does not exist a man and a woman who are not married to each other but who would prefer each other to their current spouses.

If a pair as specified in the last requirement does exist, then the assignment of N couples is said to be unstable and should be avoided. Note that the stable marriage problem is representative of many real-life problems in which assignments have to be made according to preferences.

371

PROJECT 5-17

Write a program to analyze football scores by computing the point spread for any team A playing any team B. Your program should compute the point spreads as follows:

Level I analysis: Team A played B in the past
Level II analysis: Average point spreads for situations such as

```
A played C—point spread 3

C played B—point spread 7
```

Total point spread 10
Level III analysis: Average point spread for situations such as

```
A played C—point spread 3

C played D—point spread -14 (C lost)

D played B—point spread 7
```

Total point spread –4
Level IV analysis: Average point spreads for situations such as

```
A played C—point spread 3

C played D—point spread -14

D played E—point spread 21

E played B—point spread 4
```

Total point spread 14

All level II point spreads are then averaged for a final level II point spread figure. Point spreads are similarly averaged for levels III and IV. Items that potentially need to be stacked (via recursion) in this program include:

- Accumulated point spread at current position
- Number of scores reflected in the accumulated point spread at current position
- Current position—that is, team A playing team B
- Path to the current position—that is, teams played to get to the current position

PROJECT 5-18

Write a solution to the Towers of Hanoi problem in which you use a nonrecursive iterative control structure and a stack. In effect, your stack will simulate the role played by the system stack in the recursive version of the algorithm. In a written statement, compare the time and space efficiency of your nonrecursive solution to the recursive solution presented in this lesson. Is your solution faster than the exponential recursive solution? If so, explain why it is. Otherwise, explain why it is still exponential in its run time.

PROJECT 5-19

Extend the recursive descent parser from the Case Study in this lesson by:

1. Providing descriptive error messages when a syntax error is encountered

2. Returning a queue of tokens representing the postfix form of the expression

3. Allowing any or all of the additional operators suggested in Exercise 2 of Exercises 5.4

PROJECT 5-20

Repeat Project 5-19, but develop the recursive descent parser from the context-free grammar in Exercise 3 in Exercises 5.4.

CRITICAL THINKING

ACTIVITY 5-1

SCANS   If you have taken a course in discrete mathematics, then you may be familiar with recurrence relations and methods for explicitly solving them. Use your knowledge of recurrence relations to analyze the time and space efficiencies of the Towers of Hanoi and recursive binary search algorithms. Your analysis should be presented as a precise mathematical argument, citing any results that you use but do not prove.

BINARY TREES, GENERAL TREES, AND GRAPHS

OBJECTIVES

Upon completion of this lesson, you will be able to:

■ Define partially the general tree ADT and define completely the binary tree ADT.

■ Become familiar with some examples of binary trees, such as heaps, arithmetic expression trees, and binary search trees.

■ Develop algorithms for the three traversal operations on the linked implementation of a binary tree.

■ Understand the linear implementation of the binary tree ADT.

■ Recognize the advantages and disadvantages of the linear implementation versus the linked implementation.

■ See why the linear implementation is particularly well suited to representing a binary tree with the heap property.

■ Understand the definition and operations for the graph ADT.

■ Understand the definition and operations for the network ADT.

■ Understand traversal algorithms for graphs and networks.

 Estimated Time: 15 hours

Vocabulary

ancestor	digraph	leaf node
binary search tree	directional graph	network
binary tree	general tree	parent node
breadth-first traversal	graph	postorder traversal
child node	heap	preorder traversal
concordance	height balancing	root node
depth-first traversal	inorder traversal	

Introduction

Humans organize much of the world around them into hierarchies. We have emphasized throughout the text that computer scientists design a software system by breaking it down into modules and defining hierarchical client-server relationships among those modules. In Lesson 5, we used hierarchical run-time trace diagrams to analyze the efficiency of recursive algorithms. In Section 5.4, we introduced the notion of a parse tree as a way of diagrammatically representing the syntax of an expression. To continue this discussion, we now introduce the idea of trees as a data structure.

The familial parent–child relationship allows a natural breakdown of a family's history into a genealogical tree. In computer science, a tree is a data structure that represents such hierarchical relationships between data items.

To introduce some of the terminology of tree structures, consider the record of a student at a university. In addition to the usual statistical background information such as Social Security number, name, and address, a typical student record contains listings for a number of courses, exam and final grades in each course, overall grade-point average, and other data relating to the student's performance at the college. Figure 6-1 is a tree structure representing such a student record.

As in genealogical trees, at the highest level (0) of a tree is its *root* (also called the *root node*). Here STUDENT is the root node. The nodes NAME, ADDRESS, SSN, COURSE, and GPA, which are directly connected to the root node, are the *child nodes* of the *parent node* STUDENT. The child nodes of a given parent constitute a set of *siblings*. Thus NAME, ADDRESS, SSN, COURSE, and GPA are siblings. In the hierarchy represented by a tree, the child nodes of a parent are one level lower than the parent node. Thus NAME, ADDRESS, SSN, COURSE, and GPA are at level 1 in Figure 6-1. A link between a parent and its child is called a *branch* in a tree structure. Each node in a tree except the root must descend from a parent node via a branch. Thus LAST NAME, FIRST NAME, and MIDDLE NAME descend from the parent node NAME. The root of the tree is the *ancestor* of all the nodes in the tree.

A node with no children is called a *leaf node*. In Figure 6-1, GPA is a leaf node. LAST NAME, FIRST NAME, MIDDLE NAME, EXAM 1, and EXAM 2 are also leaf nodes.

A *subtree* is a subset of a tree that is itself a tree; the tree in Figure 6-2 is a subtree of the tree in Figure 6-1. This subtree has the root node NAME. Similarly, the tree in Figure 6-3 is another subtree of the tree in Figure 6-1. Notice that the tree in Figure 6-3 is a subtree of the tree in Figure 6-1 and the tree in Figure 6-4.

375

FIGURE 6-1

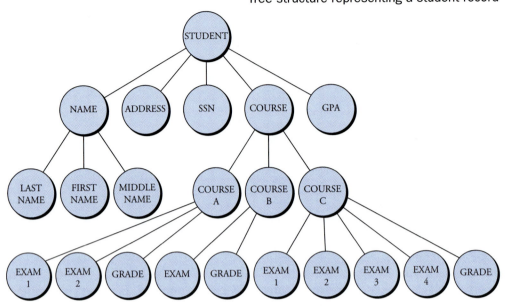

FIGURE 6-1
Tree structure representing a student record

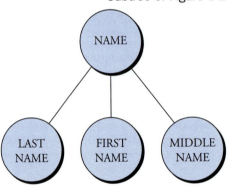

FIGURE 6-2
Subtree of Figure 6-1

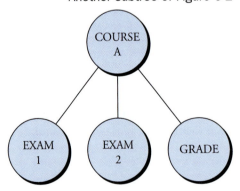

FIGURE 6-3
Another subtree of Figure 6-1

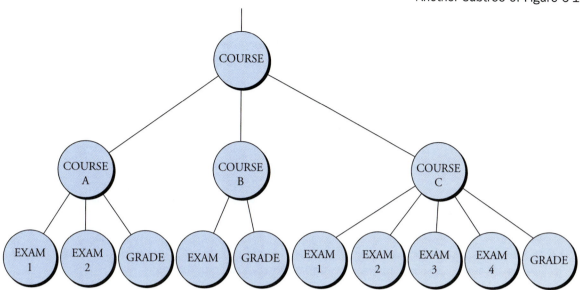

6.1 *General Trees and Binary Trees as Abstract Data Types*

It is evident from the preceding discussion that a tree has the following interesting property: Any given node within a tree is itself the root node of a completely analogous tree structure. That is, a tree is composed of a collection of substructures, each of which also meets the criteria for being a tree. This definition sounds dangerously circular. To formally describe a tree in this fashion, we must be sure to give ourselves an escape from the recursion. We therefore use the following definition of a tree as an abstract data type: A general *tree* is a set of nodes that is either empty (the recursive termination condition) or has a designated node called the root from which descend zero or more subtrees. No node is an ancestor of itself, and each subtree that descends from the root also satisfies the definition of a tree.

We'll elaborate on the definition of a general tree in Section 6.5, where we will more formally discuss the operations associated with this ADT.

Two points about this partial definition should be emphasized. First, the recursive fashion in which a tree is defined should provide a strong hint that most tree-processing algorithms will also be recursive. Second, most operations on the tree data structure are closely linked to the hierarchical relationship among nodes for that particular tree. This hierarchical relationship may vary greatly from tree to tree. To consider some examples of such relationships, which are found quite often in computer science applications, let us restrict our attention for the moment to an abstract data type called a *binary tree*. A binary tree is a tree in which each node has exactly two subtrees. These two subtrees are designated as the left and right subtrees, respectively. Note that either or both of these subtrees could be empty.

We specify the following operations on a binary tree in terms of preconditions and postconditions.

Create Operation
Preconditions: Receiver is a binary tree in an unpredictable state.
Postconditions: Receiver is initialized to the empty binary tree.

Empty Operation
Preconditions: Receiver is a previously created binary tree.
Postconditions: Returns `true` if the tree is empty, `false` otherwise.

Insert Operation
Preconditions: Receiver is a previously created binary tree based on a particular hierarchical property, and `item` is a value to be inserted in the tree. There is memory available in the tree for the new item.
Postconditions: `item` is added to the tree in a way that maintains the tree's hierarchical property.

preorderTraverse Operation
Preconditions: Receiver is a previously created binary tree, and `process` is an algorithmic process that can be applied to each node in the tree.
Postconditions: Each node of the tree is visited in the following order: First visit the root of the tree, then visit recursively all nodes in the left subtree, then visit recursively all nodes in the right subtree. As each node is visited, `process` is applied to it.

inorderTraverse Operation
Preconditions: Receiver is a previously created binary tree, and `process` is an algorithmic process that can be applied to each node in the tree.
Postconditions: Each node of the tree is visited in the following order: First visit recursively all nodes in the left subtree of the tree, then visit the root of the tree, then visit recursively all nodes in the right subtree. As each node is visited, `process` is applied to it.

postorderTraverse Operation
Preconditions: Receiver is a previously created binary tree, and `process` is an algorithmic process that can be applied to each node in the tree.
Postconditions: Each node of the tree is visited in the following order: First visit recursively all nodes in the left subtree of the tree, then visit recursively all nodes in the right subtree, then visit the root of the tree. As each node is visited, `process` is applied to it.

Several remarks are in order concerning this definition. First, the three traversal procedures require some clarification. With a linked list, there is only one obvious traversal because only one node can be reached from any given node. However, with a binary tree, at any node, some choices need to be made:

■ Should we apply `process` to the data field of the root before proceeding to the left and right subtrees?

■ Should we apply `process` to the nodes in the left subtree and right subtree before processing the data in the root?

■ Should we apply `process` to all the nodes in one of the subtrees, then to the root, and finally to all the nodes in the other subtree?

The answers to these questions determine the type of traversal. Figure 6-5 demonstrates the different orders in which nodes are visited under the three traversals.

FIGURE 6-5

Differences between preorder, inorder, and postorder traversals

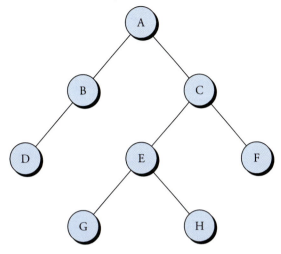

Order in which nodes are processed:

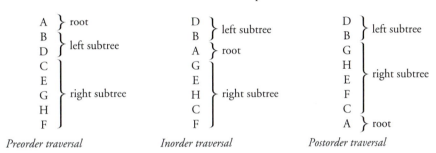

Preorder traversal   *Inorder traversal*   *Postorder traversal*

Second, the `insert` operation specified in our ADT definition for a binary tree provides a generic tree-building operation. That is, repeated applications of the `insert` operation on an initially empty binary tree typically lead to the construction of a binary tree. However, it is virtually impossible to define or implement the `insert` operation in a way that is general enough for all applications that will use a binary tree. Each instance of a binary tree is highly dependent on the hierarchical relationship between nodes that defines that particular binary tree. Therefore, we have linked our specification of the `insert` operation to the hierarchical relationship underlying a particular binary tree.

The following three examples provide illustrations of hierarchical relationships that can be used in defining binary trees. We will often use trees based on these hierarchical properties as examples in the remainder of the lesson. These three properties should by no means be considered exhaustive, however, because virtually every application that uses a binary tree will have its own essential property. The point to be emphasized now is that the `insert` operation must, in its implementation, always be tailored to the property that defines a tree.

Example 6-1

The tree of Figure 6-6 is a binary tree. Each node of this tree has two subtrees (null or non-null) designated as the left subtree and the right subtree. The particular hierarchical relationship underlying this tree is that the data in any given node of the tree are greater than or equal to the data in its left and right subtrees. A tree with this property is said to be a ***heap*** and to have the ***heap property***. (This notion is not to be confused with the heap maintained by C++ for allocating space to pointer variables, as described in Lesson 3.) We will discuss heaps in more detail in the next section. Also, they will prove particularly important in our discussion of more powerful sorting methods in Lesson 7. The end-of-lesson Projects also indicate how a heap may be used to implement the priority queue abstract data type introduced in Lesson 4. The heap property is one example of a hierarchical relationship that can underlie a tree and hence must be preserved when various operations are performed on the tree.

FIGURE 6-6
Binary tree with the heap property

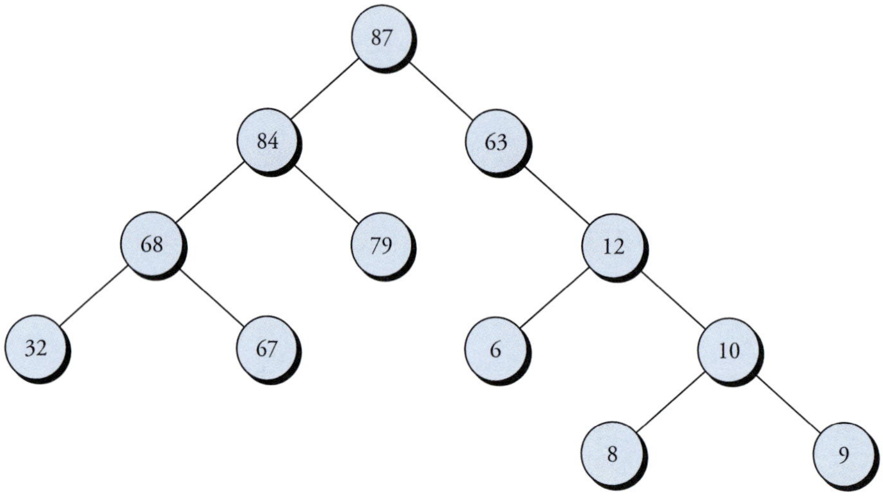

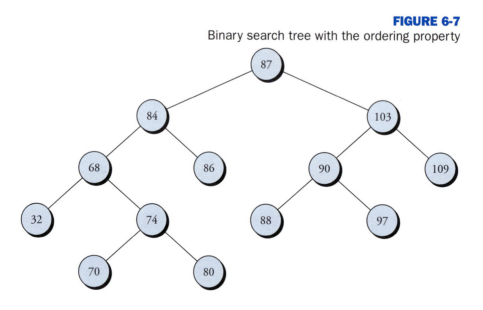

Example 6-2

A second example of a hierarchical relationship underlying a binary tree structure is shown in Figure 6-7. This binary tree exhibits the property known as the ordering property; the data in each node of the tree are greater than all of the data in that node's left subtree and less than or equal to all of the data in the right subtree. A binary tree with the ordering property is often called a ***binary search tree***. We will see the importance of trees possessing this property when we explore binary trees as a means of implementing a one-key table in Section 6.3.

FIGURE 6-7
Binary search tree with the ordering property

Example 6-3

As a final example of a hierarchical relationship that can determine the arrangement of data in a binary tree, consider Figure 6-8, in which we have a binary tree representation of the infix algebraic expression

$$(A - B) + C * (E / F)$$

Take a moment to make particular note of Figure 6-8. As we will refer back to it frequently throughout this lesson, you may want to clip the page or mark it with a bookmark.

FIGURE 6-8

Binary expression tree for `(A - B) + C * (E/F)`

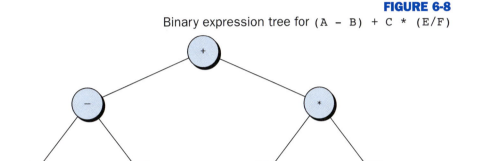

The hierarchical relationship of a parent to its children in this tree is that of algebraic operator to its two operands. Note that an operand may itself be an expression (that is, a subtree) which must be evaluated before the operator in the parent node can be applied. Note also that, if the order of evaluation in the expression changes, as in

$$(A - B) + C * E / F$$

then the corresponding binary expression tree must also change, as reflected in Figure 6-9. Contemporary compilers make use of tree structures in obtaining forms of an arithmetic expression for efficient evaluation. As we've seen, there are basically three forms for an arithmetic expression such as that corresponding to Figure 6-8: infix, prefix, and postfix.

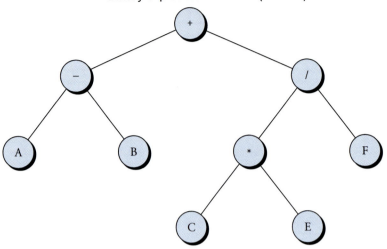

FIGURE 6-9
Binary expression tree for (A – B) + C * E/F

Expression	**Form**
(A – B) + C * (E / F)	infix
+ – A B * C / E F	prefix
A B – C E F / * +	postfix

All three of these forms are immediately available to us if we know exactly how the corresponding tree should be traversed. The ***inorder traversal*** of the binary tree for an arithmetic expression gives us the expression in unparenthesized infix form. The ***preorder traversal*** of the same tree leads us to the prefix form of the expression, whereas the ***postorder traversal*** of the tree yields the postfix form of the expression. We shall study procedures for these three traversals in Section 6.2, when we discuss a method of implementing a binary tree.

We close this section with a C++ interface for the binary tree ADT. In the sections that follow, we will analyze two implementations that adhere to this interface.

C++ Interface for the Binary Tree ADT

```
// Class declaration file: bintree.h

// Declaration section

#ifndef TREE_H
#define TREE_H

template <class E> class BinaryTree
    {

    public:

    // Class constructors
```

```
        BinaryTree();
        BinaryTree(const BinaryTree<E> &bt);

        // Class destructor

        ~BinaryTree();

        // Member functions

        bool empty();
        void insert(const E &item);
        void preorderTraverse(void (* process) (E &item));
        void inorderTraverse(void (* process) (E &item));
        void postorderTraverse(void (* process) (E &item));
        BinaryTree<E>& operator = (const BinaryTree<E> &bt);

        protected:

        // Protected declarations dependent on implementation would go here

        };

#endif
```

Note that the formal parameter list of each of the member function traverse operations has a parameter of type *pointer to function*. The syntax for declaring a parameter that is itself a (pointer to a) function is to provide the interface for any function that will be passed in this parameter slot. In the preceding traverse operations, this interface is given by void (* process) (E &item), which says that any function passed in this slot must return void (that is, no return value) and must have one formal reference parameter of type E. A client program having a binary tree of integers that it wanted to display via an inorder traversal must define the function to display one integer and then pass this function in as the actual parameter associated with process. The following code segment shows how this task is accomplished:

```
#include <iostream.h>

#include "bintree.h"

void print(int &x);        // Interface for the function that will
                           // display one of the ints in the tree

int main()
{
   BinaryTree<int> myTree;        // Tree of data

   // Here the client program would have code to load data into
   // the tree.

   ...
```

```
        myTree.inorderTraverse(print);      // Call on traversal with
                                            // function to display


     return 0;
}

void print(int &x)          // Implementation of the display function
{
   cout << x << " ";
}
```

The use of a parameter that is a pointer to a function allows the client program to decide what will be done at each node during the traversal. For instance, if the client program later wanted to display only those nodes that were even numbers during a traversal, it could define another display function

```
void printEvens(int &x)
{
   if (x % 2 == 0)
      cout << x << " ";
}
```

and then invoke the traversal with the following function:

```
        myTree.inorderTraverse(printEvens);
```

This method for allowing a client program to determine what a traversal will do at each node is limited to the constraints that the interface to the function allows. At times, this limitation greatly inhibits the use of the traversals. You will investigate ways of extending the basic binary tree class in the Case Study for this lesson.

EXERCISES 6.1

1. Draw a binary tree for the following expression:

$$A * B - (C + D) * (P / Q)$$

2. Represent the following information as a binary tree:

```
struct name
{
     apstring firstName, lastName;
};

struct year
{
     apstring firstSem, secondSem;
};
```

```
struct student
{
        name studentName;
         year yearOfStudy;
};
```

3. What, in an abstract sense, does a tree structure represent?

4. Indicate which of the following are binary search trees with the ordering property. Carefully explain what is wrong with those that are not.

a.

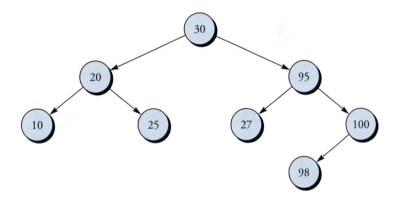

b.

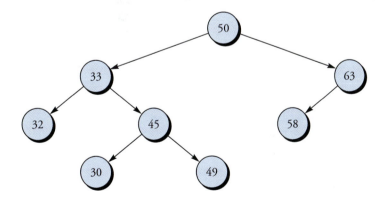

c.

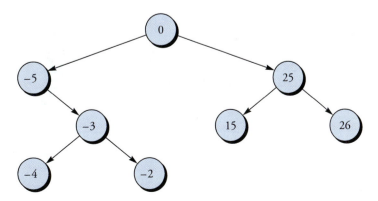

385

d.

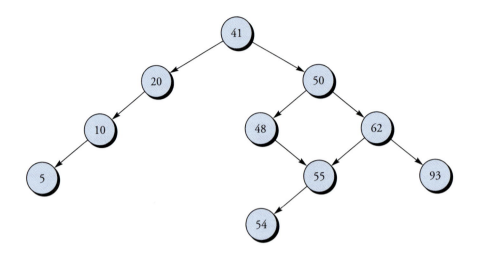

5. Indicate which of the following are binary trees with the heap property. Carefully explain what is wrong with those that are not.

a.

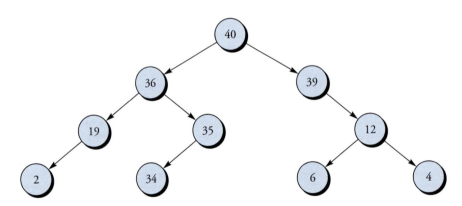

b.

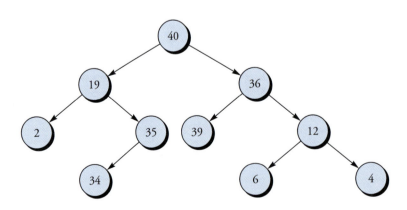

c.

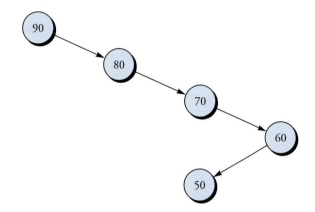

6. Given the following binary tree, indicate the order in which nodes would be processed in a preorder, postorder, and inorder traversal.

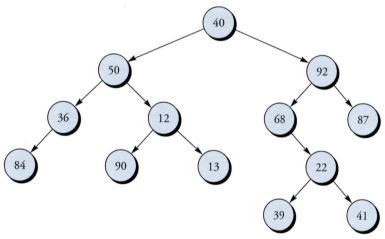

7. Construct some binary search trees with the ordering property, then do some inorder traversals of these trees. What do you observe about the order in which nodes are processed? Be as specific as possible in stating your answer.

8. Given the following postorder and inorder traversals of a binary tree, draw the tree.

Postorder: ABCDEFIKJGH

Inorder: CBAEDFHIGKJ

Attempt to deduce your answer in a systematic (and recursive) fashion, not by trial-and-error methods. After you have solved this problem, write a statement in which you describe the method you used to solve it and explain how this method could be applied to similar problems.

9. Draw binary expression trees corresponding to the algebraic expression whose
   a. infix representation is P / (Q + R) * X - Y.
   b. postfix representation is X Y Z P Q R * + /- *.
   c. prefix representation is + * - M N P / R S.

10. In a written statement, explain how the arrangement of data in a binary expression tree reflects the order of operations in the corresponding expression.

6.2 Linked Implementation of a Binary Tree

Consistent with the way in which we have studied other data structures, we now have a very good idea of what a tree is without any consideration of how we will implement it. We now explore this latter issue.

Two common methods are available for implementing binary trees. One method, known as **linked implementation**, uses dynamic allocation of nodes and pointers to these nodes. The other, which does not require the overhead of maintaining pointers, is called **linear implementation** or **vector implementation**. In this section and Section 6.3, we focus on the linked implementation. We will see how this implementation is particularly well suited for binary search trees and binary expression trees.

Because each node in a binary tree may have two child nodes, a node in a linked implementation has two pointer members, one for each child, and one or more members for storing data. When a node has no children, the corresponding pointer members are null. Figure 6-10 is a linked representation of the binary expression tree of Figure 6-8. The left and right members are pointers to (that is, memory addresses of) the left child node and the right child node of the current node.

FIGURE 6-10

Linked representation of the binary expression tree of Figure 6-8

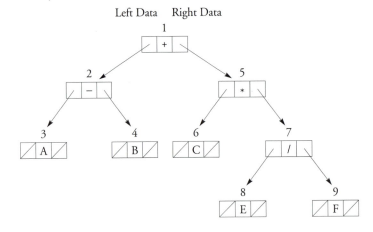

For the moment, let us give a detailed description of the linked representation of the binary tree of Figure 6-8. Once the concept is thoroughly understood, we will begin using C++ pointer variables for the actual implementation of binary trees. For example, we can implement the tree of Figure 6-10 as shown in Table 6-1 by building the left subtree for each node before considering the right subtree. The numbers on top of the cells in Figure 6-10 represent the addresses given in the left and right members.

TABLE 6-1
Implementation of Figure 6-10 using a vector of records

Node	Data	Left	Right
1	+	2	5
2	-	3	4
3	A	NULL	NULL
4	B	NULL	NULL
5	*	6	7
6	C	NULL	NULL
7	/	8	9
8	E	NULL	NULL
9	F	NULL	NULL

In the linked representation, insertions and deletions involve no data movement except the rearrangement of pointers. Suppose we wish to modify the tree in Figure 6-8 to match Figure 6-11. (This change might be needed due to some recent modification in the expression represented by Figure 6-8.) The insertion of the nodes containing – and P into the tree structure can be achieved easily by adding the nodes – and P in the next available spaces in the vector and adjusting the corresponding pointers.

FIGURE 6-11
Desired modification of Figure 6-8

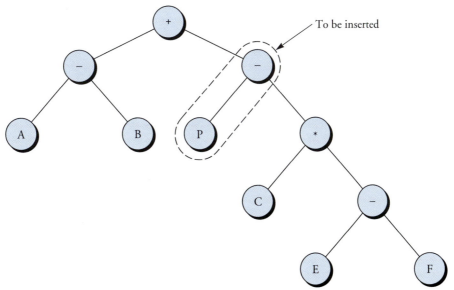

For the implementation of the tree shown in Figure 6-10, the effect of this insertion is given by Table 6-2. The adjusted pointers and data fields have been circled. Notice that the change in row 1 of the right column and the additional rows 10 and 11 are all that is necessary. No data were moved.

TABLE 6-2

Modification of Table 6-1 by insertions into the tree of Figure 6-8

Row	Data	Left	Right
1	+	2	5
2	-	3	4
3	A	NULL	NULL
4	B	NULL	NULL
5	*	6	7
6	C	NULL	NULL
7	/	8	9
8	E	NULL	NULL
9	F	NULL	NULL
10	-	11	5
11	P	NULL	NULL

Similarly, if we wish to shorten the tree in Figure 6-8 by deleting the nodes * and C, then all we must do is rearrange the pointers to obtain the altered tree, as shown in Figure 6-12. The effect of this deletion is given in Table 6-3. As before, the adjusted pointers and data fields have been circled.

FIGURE 6-12

Another modification of Figure 6-8

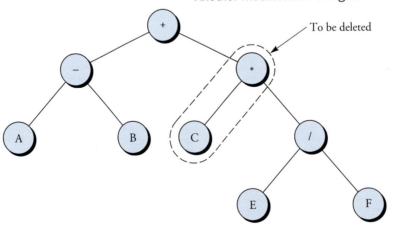

TABLE 6-3
Modification of the tree of Figure 6-8

Row	Data	Left	Right	Modified Tree
1	+	2	7	
2	-	3	4	
3	A	NULL	NULL	
4	B	NULL	NULL	
5	*			Unused space after deletion of "*" and "C"
6	C			
7	/	8	9	
8	E	NULL	NULL	
9	F	NULL	NULL	

A more formal statement of the algorithm underlying such insertions and deletions depends on the hierarchical property that forms the basis for the tree structure. We will soon examine in detail insertion and deletion algorithms for binary search trees.

Now that we have explained the linked representation of a binary tree by using pointer values that can be explicitly traced, we will use the following general structure description with C++ pointer variables to implement this structure in the remainder of this section and the next sections in this lesson:

```
struct node
{
    E data;
    node * left;
    node * right;
};
```

As we did for the pointer implementation of a linked list in Lesson 3, we embed this set of data definitions in the class definition for a binary tree, along with a data member for the root pointer:

```
// Class declaration file: bintree.h

// Declaration section
#ifndef TREE_H
#define TREE_H

template <class E> class BinaryTree
    {

    public:

    // Class constructors

    BinaryTree();
    BinaryTree(const BinaryTree<E> &bt);
```

391

```cpp
      // Class destructor

      ~BinaryTree();

      // Member functions

      bool empty();
      void insert(const E &item);
      void preorderTraverse(void (* process) (E &item));
      void inorderTraverse(void (* process) (E &item));
      void postorderTraverse(void (* process) (E &item));
      BinaryTree<E>& operator = (const BinaryTree<E> &bt);

   private:

      // Individual node structure

      struct node
      {
         E data;
         node * left;
         node * right;
      };

      // Data members

      node * tree;             // root pointer

      // Member functions

      // helper function to return pointer to a node with
      // data in it and left and right children NULL
      node * getNode(const E &data);

      // recursive helper functions for insert and traverse operations
      void insertAux(node * &tree, const E &data);
      void preorderAux(node * tree, void (* process) (E &item));
      void inorderAux(node * tree, void (* process) (E &item));
      void postorderAux(node * tree, void (* process) (E &item));

      // recursive helper functions for copying and destroying trees
      void copyAux(node * tree);
      void destroyAux(node * tree);

   };

#include "bintree.cpp"
#endif
```

Note the comments about helper member functions. Because we will use recursion to implement many of the tree-processing algorithms, we need a way of passing the tree data member as a parameter to each recursive function. This data member is protected, so it cannot be a parameter of the public functions. Therefore, each of the operations in question will consist of a public function calling a protected helper function that carries out the recursive algorithm on the tree. We will need one such function for `insert` and for each of the traversal operations.

Recall that we defined a utility function, `getNode`, in Lesson 3 to handle the details of creating and initializing a new node for a linked list. We can write a similar function for binary trees as well:

```
template <class E>
BinaryTree<E>::node * BinaryTree<E>::getNode(const E &data)
{
    BinaryTree<E>::node * temp = new BinaryTree<E>::node;

    assert(temp != 0);
    temp->data = data;
    temp->left = 0;
    temp->right = 0;
    return temp;
}
```

Note that `getNode` asks for new memory from the system heap and then checks for successful allocation before initializing the contents of a node. Now we have two pointers in a node to set to null. Therefore, if a pointer to a node is returned, the node is a leaf node.

Example 6-4

Using the linked representation of a binary tree, implement the `insert` operation for a binary search tree with the ordering property. The `insert` operation passes the new element and the protected data member tree to a helper function, `insertAux`:

```
template <class E>
void BinaryTree<E>::insert(const E &data)
{
    insertAux(tree, data);
}


template <class E>
void BinaryTree<E>::insertAux(BinaryTree<E>::node * &tree, const E &data)
{
    if (tree == 0)
    {
        tree = getNode(data);
        ++treeLength;
    }
    else if (data < tree->data)
        insertAux(tree->left, data);
    else
        insertAux(tree->right, data);
}
```

If data < 18, add it in left subtree; otherwise, add it in right subtree.

The `insertAux` function of this example implies that insertion of new nodes will always occur at the leaf nodes of a tree. As with insertion into a linked list, no data are moved; only pointers are manipulated. Unlike with the steps required by a linked list, however, we do not have to traverse the list sequentially to determine where the new node belongs. Instead, we use the insertion rule—if less than, go left; otherwise, go right—so that we traverse by subdividing the tree to determine the position for a new node. For example, if the `insert` function of this example is successively fed numeric items in the order:

16 8 -5 20 30 101 0 10 18

then the binary search tree that results can be traced by the sequence in Figure 6-13. Note that the shape of the binary search tree depends on the order in which data items are given to the `insert` operation. This dependence of the shape of the tree on the order in which data arrive for insertion complicates any attempt to analyze the efficiency of the insert function in this example. We will provide a more detailed analysis of binary search trees with the ordering property in Section 6.3.

FIGURE 6-13
Growth of search tree when data arrive in order 16 8 -5 20 30 101 0 10 18

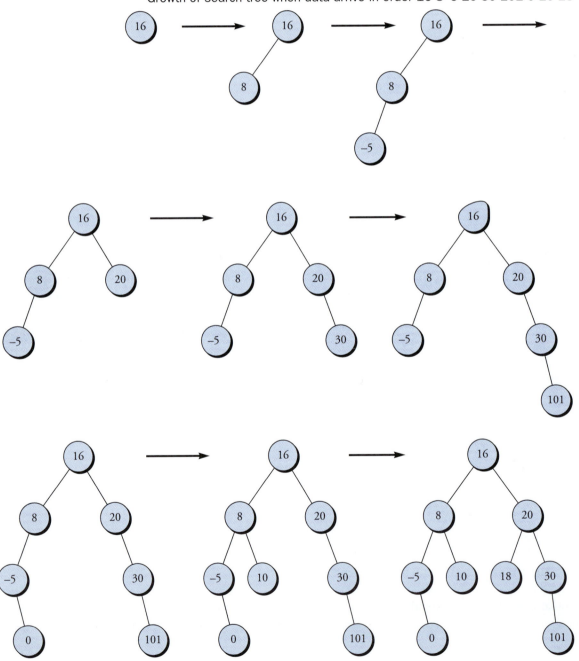

Implementing Traversal Operations on a Binary Tree

In Section 6.1, we described conceptually three different traversal operations on a binary tree: preorder, inorder, and postorder. In Example 6-3, we established correspondences between these three traversals and the prefix, infix, and postfix forms of the algebraic formula represented by a binary expression tree. It is important to reiterate that the three traversals apply broadly to all binary trees, regardless of the hierarchical relationship underlying their structure.

Recall from Section 6.1 the threefold dilemma facing us at each node we visit in a traversal of a binary tree:

1. Do we process the data contained in the node at which we are currently located?

2. Do we remember the location of the current node (so that we can return to process it) and visit (and process) all nodes in its left subtree?

3. Do we remember the location of the current node (so that we can return to process it) and visit (and process) all nodes in its right subtree?

Each of the three choices is valid. The route chosen out of the three-way dilemma dictates the order in which the nodes are visited and processed.

Preorder Traversal of a Binary Tree

In a preorder traversal, the three options are combined in the following order:

1. Process the root node.

2. Recursively visit all nodes in the left subtree.

3. Recursively visit all nodes in the right subtree.

These three ordered steps are recursive. Once the root of the tree is processed, we next go to the root of the left subtree, then to the root of the left subtree of the left subtree, and so on until we can go no farther. Following these three steps, the preorder traversal of the tree of Figure 6-8 would process nodes in the order

$$+ - A\ B * C / E\ F$$

This order is the prefix form of the expression

$$(A - B) + C * (E / F)$$

Hence, we conclude that if to process a node means to print it, then a preorder traversal of a binary expression tree will output the prefix form of the expression.

The preorder traversal of an existing binary tree implemented via the linked representation can be accomplished recursively using the following pair of functions, where `preorderAux` is the helper function for the public member function `preorderTraverse`:

```cpp
template <class E>
void BinaryTree<E>::preorderTraverse(void (* process) (E &item))
{
    preorderAux(tree, process);
}


template <class E>
void BinaryTree<E>::preorderAux(BinaryTree<E>::node * tree,
                                void (* process) (E &item))
```

395

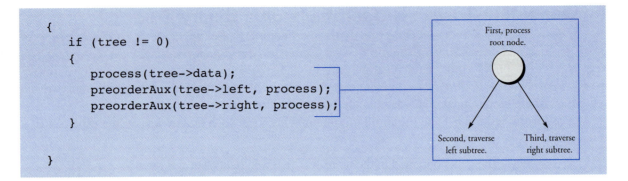

```
{
    if (tree != 0)
    {
        process(tree->data);
        preorderAux(tree->left, process);
        preorderAux(tree->right, process);
    }

}
```

First, process root node.

Second, traverse left subtree.

Third, traverse right subtree.

Inorder Traversal of a Binary Tree

The inorder traversal of a binary tree proceeds as outlined in the following three ordered steps:

1. Recursively visit all nodes in the left subtree.

2. Process the root node.

3. Recursively visit all nodes in the right subtree.

By carefully following these steps for the tree of Figure 6-8 and assuming "process" means "print," we obtain the readily recognizable infix expression

$$A - B + C * E / F$$

Unless we add parentheses, this infix expression is not equivalent to the order of operations reflected in the tree of Figure 6-8. The fact that prefix and postfix notations do not require parentheses to avoid such ambiguities makes them distinctly superior to infix notation for evaluation purposes.

An implementation of the recursive algorithm for an inorder traversal is given in the following pair of functions for a linked representation of a binary tree:

```
template <class E>
void BinaryTree<E>::inorderTraverse(void (* process) (E &item))
{
    inorderAux(tree, process);
}

template <class E>
void BinaryTree<E>::inorderAux(BinaryTree<E>::node * tree,
                               void (* process) (E &item))
{
    if (tree != 0)
    {
        inorderAux(tree->left, process);
        process(tree->data);
        inorderAux(tree->right, process);
    }

}
```

Second, process root node.

First, traverse left subtree.

Third, traverse right subtree.

Postorder Traversal of a Binary Tree

The third standard traversal of a binary tree, the postorder traversal, entails an arrangement of options that postpones processing the root node until last.

1. Recursively visit all nodes in the left subtree of the root node.

2. Recursively visit all nodes in the right subtree of the root node.

3. Process the root node.

Applying these three steps to the binary expression tree of Figure 6-8 yields the postfix form of the underlying expression:

$$A\ B - C\ E\ F\ /\ *\ +$$

The actual implementation of the postorder traversal operation is completely analogous to the inorder and preorder operations. Consequently, we will leave it as an exercise.

Although we have illustrated the three traversal algorithms using binary expression trees, we emphasize that the traversals apply in general to any binary tree. Indeed, as we will see in the next section, the inorder traversal when used in combination with a tree exhibiting the hierarchical ordering property of a binary search tree will neatly allow us to implement a one-key table using a binary tree.

Copying and Destroying a Binary Tree

Two of the binary tree class operations that require traversals are the copy constructor and the destructor. The copy constructor should copy all of the data elements in the original (parameter) tree to the new (receiver) tree. Not only should this operation preserve the ordering of the data in the new binary tree, but the structure of the nodes should also exactly match that in the original tree. Thus the root node of the new tree should contain the same data element as the root node of the original tree, and so on for each subtree. To guarantee both ordering and structure, we perform a preorder traversal of the original tree. When a node in the original tree is visited, its data element is inserted into the new tree with `insert`. The left and right subtrees are then copied in the same manner. Unfortunately, we cannot use the `preorderTraverse` operation for copying the original tree because the `process` function would have no access to the new tree. Therefore, a new helper function must be written that performs the preorder traversal directly. The code for the copy constructor and the helper function follows:

```
template <class E>
BinaryTree<E>::BinaryTree(const BinaryTree<E> &bt)
{
    tree = 0;
    // Pass the original tree's data member to the helper function
    copyAux(bt.tree);
}


template <class E>
void BinaryTree<E>::copyAux(BinaryTree<E>::node * tree)
{
    if (tree != 0)
    {
        // Copy from original to new (receiver) tree
        insert(tree->data);
        copyAux(tree->left);
        copyAux(tree->right);
    }
}
```

397

Note that the identifier `tree` in the helper function refers to the data member of the original tree, not to the receiver tree's data member. The receiver tree's data member is accessed with the same identifier within the implementation of `insert`.

Recall from Lesson 3 that any class that uses dynamic memory in its implementation should have a class destructor operation. This function returns any memory used for nodes to the system heap. The class destructor is run automatically by the computer when a variable or parameter that is bound to an instance of the class goes out of scope. Given these requirements, we need a traversal algorithm that visits the leaf nodes of a tree first, deletes them from the tree, and then visits the leaf nodes at the next level up. Clearly, a preorder traversal will not work because it deletes root nodes first. An inorder traversal deletes the left subtree before the root node, but the root node is lost before we could visit the leaves of the right subtree. A postorder traversal is appropriate because it first deletes the left subtree, then deletes the right subtree, before deleting a root node. The recursive process guarantees that the leaf nodes at any level in the tree are deleted first. Once again, we cannot use an established traversal operation because of scope problems. We therefore present the code for the class destructor and a new helper operation that carries out a mass deletion in postorder:

```
template <class E>
BinaryTree<E>::~BinaryTree()
{
    destroyAux(tree);
    tree = 0;
}


template <class E>
void BinaryTree<E>::destroyAux(BinaryTree<E>::node * tree)
{
    if (tree != 0)
    {
        destroyAux(tree->left);
        destroyAux(tree->right);
        delete tree;                // Return leaf node to system heap.
    }
}
```

In both of these functions, the identifier `tree` refers to the receiver's data member. After `destroyAux` has returned any nodes to the system heap, the top-level destructor operation sets the data member to null to indicate an empty binary tree.

EXERCISES ⟩ 6.2

1. Using a preorder traversal of the tree you derived in Exercise 1 in Exercises 6.1, obtain the prefix form of the expression in that exercise.

2. Sketch the binary search tree that would result when the `insert` function of Example 6-4 is used for data that arrive in the following orders:
   a. 100 90 80 70 60 50 40 32 20 10
   b. 60 80 30 90 70 100 40 20 50 10
   c. 0 50 70 40 80 30 90 20 100 10

Provide a brief written description of how the shape of the binary search tree is related to the order in which data arrive for insertion into the tree.

3. Consider the following search trees with the ordering property. For each, specify an order of arrival of data items that would result in that particular tree if the `insert` function of Example 6-4 is used.

a.

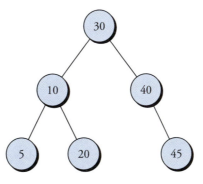

b.

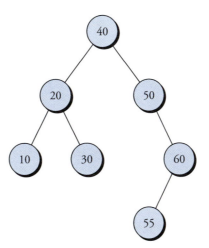

c.

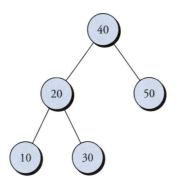

4. What is the output produced by the following function for the pictured tree?

399

```
void treeWalk(node * tree)
{
    if (tree == 0)
        cout << OOPS << endl;
    else
    {
        treeWalk(tree->right);
        treeWalk(tree->left);
        cout << tree->data << endl;
    }
}
```

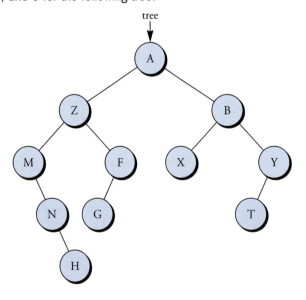

5. How does the output from Exercise 4 change if the statement

```
cout << tree->data << endl;
```

is moved ahead of the recursive calls to `treeWalk`?

6. How does the output from Exercise 4 change if the statement

```
cout << tree->data << endl;
```

is located between the recursive calls to `treeWalk`?

7. Repeat Exercises 4, 5, and 6 for the following tree:

8. A ***ternary tree*** is a one in which each node may have at most three children. A pointer/record structure for a linked implementation of such a tree could thus be given by the following declarations:

```
struct node
{
   E data;
   node * left;
   node * middle;
   node * right;
};
```

What would be the output produced by the following `treeWalk` function

```
void treeWalk(node * tree)
{

   if (tree != 0)
      {
         cout << tree->data << endl;
         treeWalk(tree->right);
         treeWalk(tree->middle);
         treeWalk(tree->left);
      }
}
```

if it were initially called with the root pointer to the tree in the following diagram?

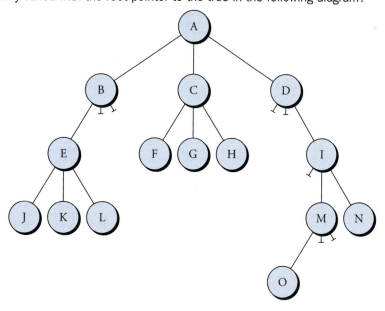

9. Write implementations of the `create` and `empty` operations for a binary search tree with the ordering property using the linked representation method.

10. Write an implementation of the postorder traversal operation for a linked representation of a binary tree.

401

11. Write a function that reads an algebraic expression in prefix notation and builds the binary tree corresponding to the expression (see Example 6-3). Assume that all tokens in the expression are individual characters.

12. Write a function that reads an algebraic expression in postfix notation and builds the binary tree corresponding to the expression (see Example 6-3). Assume that all tokens in the expression are individual characters.

13. Implement one of the traversal algorithms in a nonrecursive fashion by using a stack to keep track of pointers to nodes that must be visited when you finish processing the current subtree. Your stack will approximate the role played by the system stack in the recursive version of the algorithm.

14. Suppose that you have a binary tree representation of an algebraic expression consisting of the operators +, –, *, and /, and operands that are uppercase letters. Suppose also that you have a function value that, given an operand, will return the numeric value associated with that operand. Write a recursive function to evaluate the expression tree.

15. Write a function to solve the following puzzle. Assume that the element type stored in tree nodes is char. Your function receives two strings of the same length. The first represents the order in which the nodes of a tree would be visited by a preorder traversal. The second represents the order in which nodes from the same tree would be visited by an inorder traversal. Your function should construct the tree from these two traversals.

16. Write a Boolean-valued function that receives two binary trees composed of the same type of data. The function should return true if the two trees are identical—that is, if they have precisely the same shape and have the same values in each node. Otherwise, it should return false.

17. How could the inorder traversal of a binary tree be used to sort data logically? Provide your answer in the form of a precise written statement.

6.3 Binary Search Tree Implementation of a One-Key Table

The implementations we have considered for the one-key table have been found lacking in certain respects. The physically ordered vector implementation of Lesson 2 allowed for the fast inspection of objects via the binary search algorithm but necessitated excessive data movement when objects were added to or deleted from the list. The linked list implementation suggested in Lesson 3 handled insertions and removals nicely but presented us with an undesirable O(n) search efficiency due to the lack of random access.

In this section, we shall see that by implementing a one-key table using a binary tree with the ordering property, we can achieve efficiency in both searching and adding or deleting while at the same time keeping the list in order. Moreover, we do not have to pay too great a price in other trade-offs to achieve this best of both worlds. Indeed, binary trees with the ordering property are called binary search trees precisely because of their frequent application in efficiently implementing one-key tables.

A binary search tree is organized via the hierarchical ordering property discussed in Example 6-2 in Section 6.1. Recall that this ordering property stipulates:

For any given data item X in the tree, every node in the left subtree of X contains only items that are less than X with respect to a particular type of ordering. Every node in the right subtree of X contains only items that are greater than or equal to X with respect to the same ordering.

For instance, the tree of Figure 6-14 illustrates this property with respect to alphabetical ordering. You can quickly verify that an inorder traversal of this tree (in which the processing of each node consists merely of printing its contents) leads to the following alphabetized list:

ARPS
DIETZ
EGOFSKE
FAIRCHILD
GARTH
HUSTON
KEITH
MAGILLICUDDY
NATHAN
PERKINS
SELIGER
TALBOT
UNDERWOOD
VERKINS
ZARDA

FIGURE 6-14
Ordering property with respect to alphabetical ordering

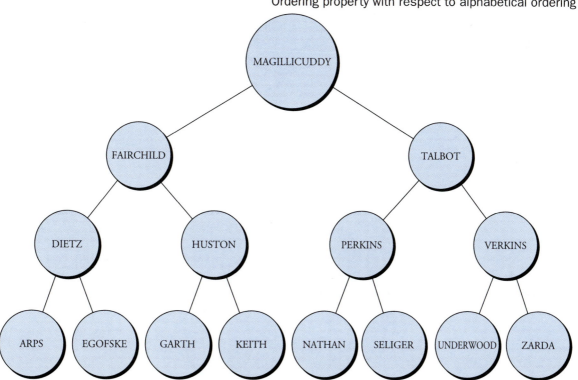

This knowledge allows us to reach the important conclusion that an inorder traversal of a binary search tree will visit nodes in ascending order. Hence such a tree may be viewed as an ordered table. The first table element is the first item visited by the inorder traversal. More generally, the *n*th element visited by the inorder traversal corresponds precisely to the *n*th element in the table. Given this view of a binary search tree as an implementation of a one-key table, let us now consider the operations of adding, deleting, and finding (retrieving) nodes in the table.

Adding Nodes to the Binary Search Tree Implementation of a One-Key Table

Insertion of a new key into such a tree is a fairly easy process that may require significantly fewer comparisons than insertion into a linked list. The specifics of the insert operation were developed in Example 6-4. Consider, for example, the steps necessary to insert the key "SEFTON" into the tree of Figure 6-14 in such a fashion as to maintain the ordering property. We must

1. Compare SEFTON to MAGILLICUDDY. Because SEFTON is greater than MAGILLICUDDY, follow the right child pointer to TALBOT.

2. Compare SEFTON to TALBOT. Because SEFTON is less than TALBOT, follow the left child pointer to PERKINS.

3. SEFTON is greater than PERKINS. Hence follow the right child pointer to SELIGER.

4. SELIGER is a leaf node, so SEFTON may be added as one of its children. The left child is chosen because SEFTON is less than SELIGER.
    The resulting tree for the sample insertion is shown in Figure 6-15.

FIGURE 6-15
Tree in Figure 6-14 with the insertion SEFTON

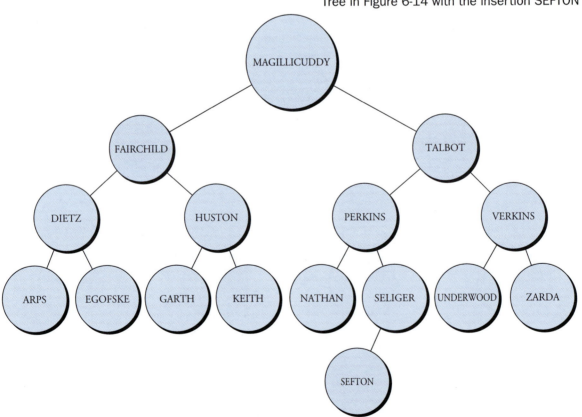

Provided that the tree maintains a full shape, the number of nodes on a given branch will be at most $(\log_2 n + 1)$ where n is the total number of nodes in the tree. By full we mean that all nodes with fewer than two children must occur at level m or $m - 1$ where m is the deepest level in the tree. In other words, all nodes above level $m - 1$ must have exactly two children. Hence, adding ROBERTS to the tree of Figure 6-15 by the insertion rule would destroy its fullness.

Given this definition of "full," the $(\log_2 n + 1)$ figure for the maximum number of nodes on a branch emerges immediately upon inspection or, more formally, using a proof by mathematical induction. Our purpose here, however, is not to give the details of such a proof but rather to emphasize that a binary search tree presents an alternative to a linked list structure for the type of processing involved in maintaining ordered lists. Moreover, it is a particularly attractive alternative when the tree is full, because substantially fewer comparisons are needed to locate where in the structure an insertion is to be made. For instance, if n is 1024, the linked list may require as many as 1024 comparisons to make an insertion. Because $\log_2 1024$ is 10, the full binary search tree method will require at most 11 comparisons. This difference becomes even more dramatic as n gets larger. For an ordered list with 1 million entries, a linked list may require 1 million comparisons, but the full binary search tree requires a mere 21.

What happens when the tree is not full? We will comment on that situation at the end of this section, when we discuss the overall efficiency considerations for this implementation of a one-key table. Before that, however, consider the operations of finding and deleting data in a binary search tree.

PROGRAMMING SKILLS: Hypertext

Hypertext is a technology that allows users to browse through any kind of information that can be stored electronically (text, images, sound, and video). Users experience hypertext associatively as a set of one-key tables. Each entry in a table is a chunk of information presented to the user by some output device. Where the output device is a visual display, the keys for locating other entries in the tables are embedded as hot spots in the currently visible chunk of information. The user retrieves a desired entry by targeting a hot spot with a mouse or cursor device. This entry, in turn, may have other embedded keys. Each entry also has a hot spot for returning to the entry from which its key was triggered. More structured queries for entries can be executed by entering key terms into a search engine, which returns a list of all the entries that satisfy a query. Hypertext also has the feel of a graph in that users can freely move back and forth in a nonlinear fashion among the entries or nodes.

As an example, one might begin with a query for Beethoven's Ninth Symphony. From the answer list one might then select a biography of the composer (text and images). After reading a couple of pages, one might next point at a hot spot referencing the last movement of the Ninth Symphony to listen to a few bars (sound). Returning to the biography, one might finally hit another hot spot to play a bit of *Immortal Beloved*, a film about Beethoven's life (video).

According to John B. Smith and Stephen F. Weiss, "Hypertext," *Communications of the ACM*, vol. 31, no. 7, July 1988, this unrestricted associativity among hypertext nodes parallels the flexibility of human memory. Smith and Weiss cite the following quotation from Vannevar Bush, a well-known electrical engineer who speculated as early as the 1940s about the way in which humans think:

The human mind . . . operates by association. With one item in its grasp, it snaps instantly to the next that is suggested by the association of thoughts, in accordance with some intricate web of trails carried by the cells of the brain.

Selection by association, rather than indexing may yet be mechanized. One cannot hope . . . to equal the speed and flexibility with which the mind follows an associative trail, but it should be possible to beat the mind decisively in regard to the permanence and clarity of the items resurrected from storage.

Early hypertext systems were implemented as a set of files residing on a single disk in the user's personal computer. With the growth of the Internet and networking technology, most hypertext systems are now distributed among many different physical sites. The World Wide Web, the best known of these systems, supports public browsing by Internet users from thousands of sites around the world. The nodes of information in the Beethoven example mentioned earlier might each be located at different sites in different parts of the world, although from the user's perspective the information seems connected in a seamless way.

If the notion of electronic hypertext intrigues you, begin by consulting the *Communications of the ACM* issue cited above. Then check out some more recent publications, such as *Communications of the ACM*, vol. 37, no. 2, February 1994, and *Communications of the ACM*, vol. 38, no. 8, August 1995, each of which has been dedicated to this revolutionary and rapidly growing field.

Searching for Data in a Binary Search Tree Implementation of a One-Key Table

The insertion rule also dictates the search path followed through a binary search tree when we are attempting to find a given data item. Interestingly, if we trace the nodes visited on such a search path for a full tree, we will probe exactly the same items that we would in conducting a binary search on a physically ordered vector containing the same data. For instance, if we are searching for SMITH in the tree of Figure 6-14, we will have to probe MAGILLICUDDY, TALBOT, and PERKINS. These are precisely the items that would be probed if the binary search algorithm were applied to the physically ordered list associated with Figure 6-14. Our analysis of such a tree has allowed us to conclude that, as long as the binary search tree remains full, the search efficiency for this method of implementing a one-key table matches that of the physically ordered vector implementation. That is, the search efficiency is $O(\log_2 n)$.

Deleting Data in a Binary Search Tree Implementation of a One-Key Table

The deletion algorithm for a binary search tree is conceptually more complex than that for a linked list. Suppose, for instance, that we wish to remove TALBOT from the list represented by the tree of Figure 6-14. Two questions arise:

1. Can such a deletion be achieved merely by manipulating pointers?

2. If so, what does the resulting tree look like?

To answer these questions, begin by recalling that what is necessary to represent a one-key table with a binary search tree. That is, for each node in the tree

1. The left subtree must contain only items less than it.

2. The right subtree must contain only items greater than or equal to it.

With the preservation of this ordering property as the primary goal in processing a deletion, one acceptable way of restructuring the tree of Figure 6-14 after deleting TALBOT appears in Figure 6-16; essentially, SELIGER moves up to replace TALBOT in the tree. The choice of SELIGER to replace TALBOT is made because SELIGER represents the greatest data item in the left subtree of the node containing TALBOT. As long as we choose this greatest item in the left subtree to replace the item being deleted, we guarantee preservation of the crucial ordering property that enables the tree to represent the list accurately.

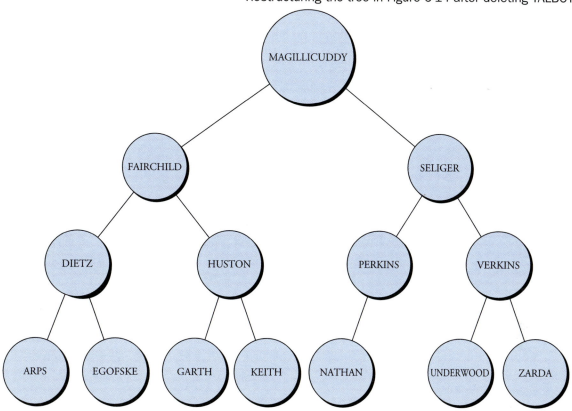

Given this general motivation for choosing a node to replace the one being deleted, let us now outline a case-by-case analysis of the deletion algorithm. Throughout this analysis, we assume that we have a pointer P to the item we wish to delete. The pointer P may be one of the following:

1. The root pointer for the entire tree.

2. The left child pointer of the parent of the node to be deleted.

3. The right child pointer of the parent of the node to be deleted.

Figure 6-17 highlights these three possibilities; the algorithm applies whether 1, 2, or 3 holds.

FIGURE 6-17
Three possibilities for the pointer P

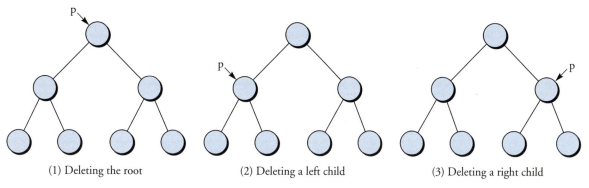

(1) Deleting the root   (2) Deleting a left child   (3) Deleting a right child

We now examine three cases of node deletion on a binary search tree:

1. The node to be deleted has no children.

2. The node to be deleted has a right child but no left child.

3. The node to be deleted has a left child.

Case 1. The node pointed to by **p**—that is, the node to be deleted—has no children. This situation is the easiest of all the cases. It can be compactly handled as follows:

```
x = p;
p = 0;   // make the pointer null
delete x;
```

Case 2. The node pointed to by **p**—that is, the node to be deleted—has a right child but no left child. This case poses no more problems than case 1 and is described in Figure 6-18. The node to be deleted is merely replaced by its right child. The necessary C++ coding is

```
x = p;
p = x->right;
delete x;
```

FIGURE 6-18
In case 2 the node pointed to by p has a right child but no left child

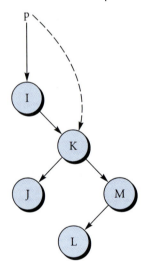

Case 3. The node pointed to by **p**—that is, the node to be deleted—has a left child. In Figure 6-19, node M is to be deleted, and it has left child K. In this case, because we have a non-null left subtree of the node to be deleted, our previous discussion indicates that we must find the greatest node in that left subtree. If the node pointed to by p->left (node K in the figure) has no right child, then the greatest node in the left subtree of **p** is p->left itself. Figure 6-19 illustrates this situation; the dotted lines indicate new pointer values.

FIGURE 6-19

Case 3 with `P->left` (node K) having no right children

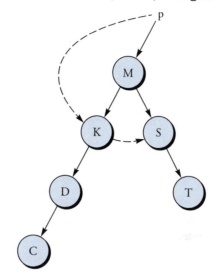

The partial coding to achieve this pointer manipulation is

```
x = p;
p = x->left;
p->right = x->right;
delete x;
```

If the node pointed to by `p->left` does have a right child, then to find the greatest node in the left subtree of **p** we must follow the right branch leading from `p->left` as deeply as possible into the tree. In Figure 6-20, node R is the one chosen to replace the deleted node. This figure gives the schematic representation, with the pointer changes necessary to complete the deletion. The coding necessary for this slightly more complicated version of case 3 is

```
x = p;
q = x->left->right;
qParent = x->left;

// q will eventually point to a node that will replace p.
// qParent will point to q's parent.
// The following loop forces q as deep as possible
// along the right branch from p->left.

while (q->left != 0)  // while not null
{
    q = q->right;
    qParent = qParent->right;
}
```

```
// Having found node q to replace p, adjust pointers
// to appropriately link it into the tree.

q->right = x->right;
p = q;
qParent->right = q->left;
q->left = x->left;
delete x;
```

FIGURE 6-20

Case 3 with `P->left` having a right child

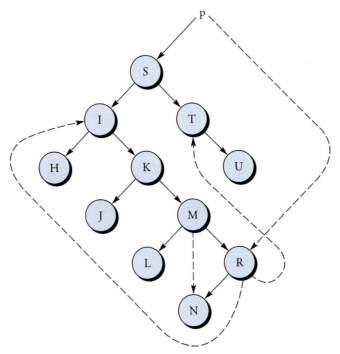

Efficiency Considerations for Binary Search Tree Implementation of a One-Key Table

In all three cases, the deletion of a node from the tree involved only pointer manipulation and no actual data movement. Hence, in a one-key table maintained with a binary search tree, we are able to process both insertions and deletions by the same pure pointer manipulation that makes linked lists so desirable. Moreover, the binary search tree approach apparently allows us to locate data for retrieval, insertion, or deletion much faster than a linked list representation does. However, some aspects of the binary tree method tarnish its performance in comparison to a linked list. These aspects are discussed next.

The binary search tree implementation requires more memory in two respects. First, each node has two pointers instead of the one required in a singly linked list. This proliferation of pointers is particularly wasteful because many of the pointers may be null. Second, we currently can traverse the tree in order only by using recursive techniques. A substantial amount of overhead may be needed to maintain the stack used by recursive calls.

The $O(\log_2 n)$ efficiency of the binary search tree method is only an optimal efficiency, not a guaranteed. It is contingent on the tree remaining nearly full. The tree remaining full is, in turn, contingent on the order in which the data are added and deleted. In the worst possible case, data entering the tree structure in the wrong order can cause the tree to degenerate into a glorified linked list with a corresponding $O(n)$ efficiency. (The exercises at the end of this section have you explore this relationship between the order in which data arrive for insertion and the resulting search efficiency of the binary search tree.)

Both of these drawbacks can be overcome. We can avoid the overhead associated with recursion if we use a technique (known as threading) that puts to good use the pointers that are otherwise wasted as null.

Moreover, by using a technique known as ***height balancing,*** the binary search tree can be maintained in a fashion that approaches fullness at all times, regardless of the order in which data arrive for entry. This nearly full form is enough to completely guarantee the $O(\log_2 n)$ search efficiency. Originally devised by G. M. Adelson-Velskii and Y. M. Landis, the height-balancing algorithm is sufficiently complex to be beyond the scope of this book. In-depth treatments of it and the threading technique just cited are given in *Data Structures in C++* by Ellis Horowitz and Sartaj Sahni (New York: Computer Science Press, 1990) and in *Introduction to Data Structures and Algorithm Analysis with C++* by George J. Pothering and Thomas L. Naps (St. Paul, Minnesota: West Publishing, 1995).

Overall, the binary search tree implementation of a one-key table seems the best of the three implementations we have studied for situations in which additions, deletions, and searches must all be processed efficiently. Even when steps are not taken to correct the two disadvantages we have cited, it offers the addition/deletion advantages of a linked list with a search efficiency that is bounded between $O(\log_2 n)$ and $O(n)$.

EXERCISES 6.3

1. Which of the following binary search trees are full?

    a.

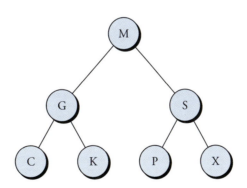

b.

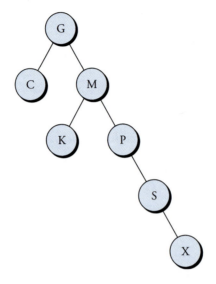

c.

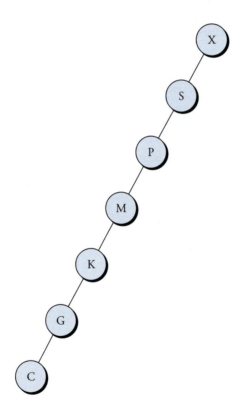

2. The key values 1 through 10 are to be inserted in a binary search tree. Specify orders of arrival for these values to create trees that correspond with each of the following shapes.

a.

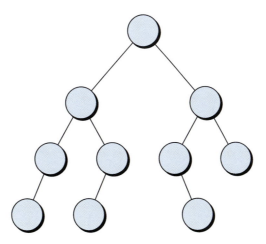

b.

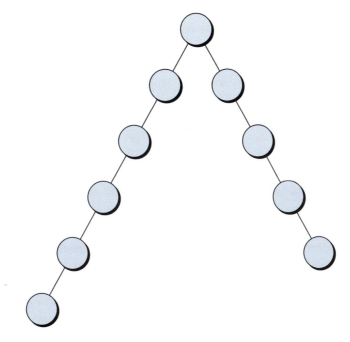

c.

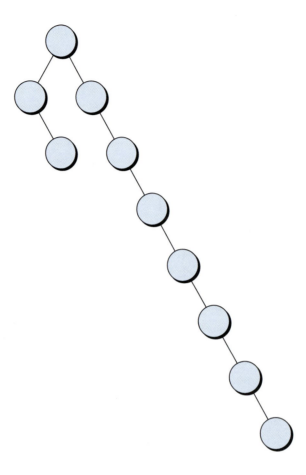

3. In an essay, discuss the relative merits of maintaining a one-key table by a binary search tree, a singly linked list, and a doubly linked list.

4. In an essay, discuss how the order in which data are entered into a binary search tree affects the fullness of the tree. Be sure to identify the best and worst possible cases. Analyze the efficiency of tree operations to add, delete, and find data for each of these cases.

5. The node containing 46 is to be deleted from each of the following binary search trees. Assuming the deletion algorithm described in this section is used, draw the tree after the deletion of 46.

a.

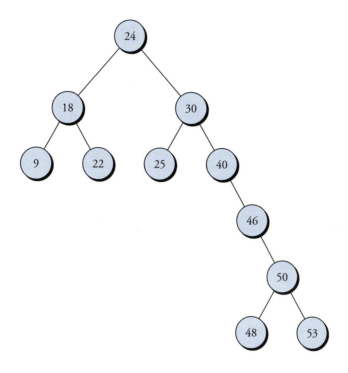

b.

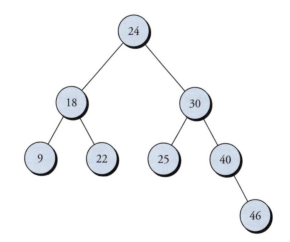

c.

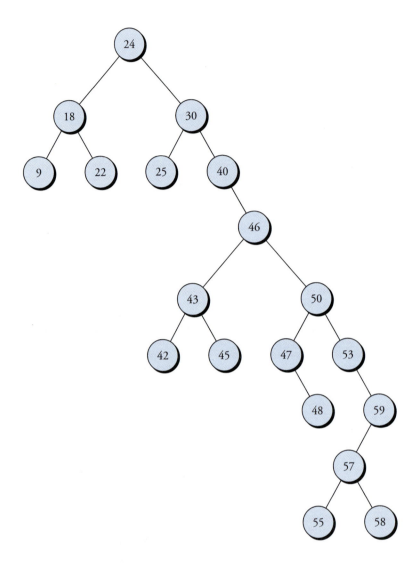

6. In Example 6-4 we provided an implementation of the insert operation for a binary search tree. What does the function in that example do when we try to insert a key value that already exists in the tree? Modify the function so that, when we try to insert such a key value, the tree is left unaltered.

7. The implementation of the insert operation for a binary search tree in Example 6-4 is recursive. Write a nonrecursive implementation of this operation.

8. Develop recursive and nonrecursive implementations of the algorithm to search for a particular data item in a binary search tree.

9. Develop a complete implementation of the algorithm to delete an item from a binary search tree. This implementation will essentially require that you combine into one module the three cases discussed in this section. For an added challenge, try writing the function so that it handles deletion by using the "mirror image" of these three cases.

10. Look back to the definition of the one-key table ADT in Lesson 2. Provide a complete implementation of the table operations using a binary search tree as the underlying data structure. (*Hint:* You should provide comparison operations for the association class so that associations can be the objects stored in binary trees.)

11. Suppose you are given a list of data in increasing order of keys. Develop a C++ algorithm that will load this list into an optimal binary search tree.

12. A binary search tree could itself be considered an ADT that is derived from the more generic binary tree ADT defined in Section 6.1. Write a complete definition and a C++ interface for the binary search tree as an ADT. Be sure that the set of operations you describe will allow your binary search tree ADT to be used as an implementation strategy for the one-key table ADT.

6.4 Linear Implementation of the Binary Tree Abstract Data Type

The linear implementation of a binary tree uses a vector of size $[2^{(d+1)} - 1]$, where d is the depth of the tree—that is, the maximum level of any node in the tree. In the tree of Figure 6-8, the root + is at the level 0, the nodes - and * are at level 1, and so on. The deepest level in this tree is the level of E and F, level 3. Therefore, $d = 3$ and this tree will require a vector of size $2^{(3+1)} - 1 = 15$. Once the size of the vector has been determined, the following method is used to represent the tree:

1. Store the root in the first location of the vector.

2. If a node is in location n of the vector, store its left child at location $(2n + 1)$, and its right child at location $(2n + 2)$.

With the aid of this scheme, the tree of Figure 6-8 is stored in the vector tree of size 15 shown in Figure 6-21. Locations `tree[7]` through `tree[12]` are not used.

FIGURE 6-21
Tree of Figure 6-8 stored in a linear representation using a vector

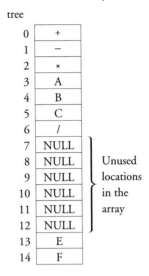

An encapsulated definition of the binary tree ADT for this linear representation is given by the following code:

```
// Class declaration file: bintree.h (linear implementation)

// Declaration section

// This constant establishes the size of the underlying vector
const int MAX_TREE_NODES = // To be filled in with appropriate size

template <class E> class BinaryTree
{

  public:

  // Nothing changes here

  ...

  protected:

  // Protected data members

  struct node                    // Either null or a node
  {
    bool null;
    E data;
  };
```

```
apvector<node> tree(MAX_TREE_NODES);     // Vector of nodes
int numberNodes;                 // Number of nodes in tree

// Protected function members, declared as needed

};
```

The `create` operation simply sets the `numberNodes` data member to zero and initializes the null member of all nodes in the vector locations to `true`. The `null` flags are necessary to detect whether a given tree node has children. A tree node at location n has a left subtree if and only if the node at location $2n + 1$ contains a `null` flag that is `false`. A similar consideration applies to the right subtree of the tree node at location n.

Efficiency Considerations for the Linear Representation

The main advantages of this method lie in its simplicity and the fact that, given a child node, its parent node can be determined immediately. If a child node is at location n in the vector, then its parent node is at location $(n - 1)/2$. In spite of its simplicity and ease of implementation, the linear representation method has all the costs that come with physically ordering items. Insertion or deletion of a node in a fashion that maintains the hierarchical relationships within the tree may cause considerable data movement up and down the vector and hence use an excessive amount of processing time. Also, depending on the application, memory locations (such as locations 7 through 12 in Figure 6-21) may be wasted due to partially filled trees.

Using the Linear Implementation for a Heap

One type of binary tree for which the linear implementation of a binary tree proves to be ideal is the heap, as defined in Example 6-1. The data in a heap can be embedded in a vector without ever wasting any locations. To prove this claim, we will show that, given a heap with $N - 1$ nodes embedded in a vector with no gaps, we can add an Nth node and maintain the dense packing of data in the vector.

To illustrate the algorithm for doing this, consider the heap with eight nodes pictured in Figure 6-22. The numbers outside the circular nodes in this figure indicate the vector indices where data would be stored in the linear representation of a binary tree.

Now suppose we want to add 40 to the heap of Figure 6-22. We will begin by comparing 40 to the data in the smallest index that does not yet have two children: 20 at index 3 in Figure 6-22. Figure 6-23 shows a series of data interchanges that "walk 40 up" a path until the tree is transformed into a heap. The algorithm to achieve this "walking up" is given in the following example.

FIGURE 6-22
A heap with eight nodes

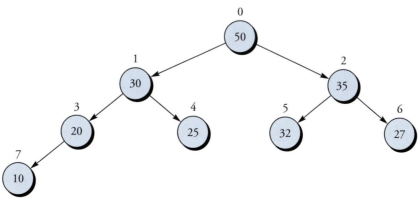

419

FIGURE 6-23

Transforming a heap to accommodate the insertion of 40 (numbers outside circles indicate vector index positions)

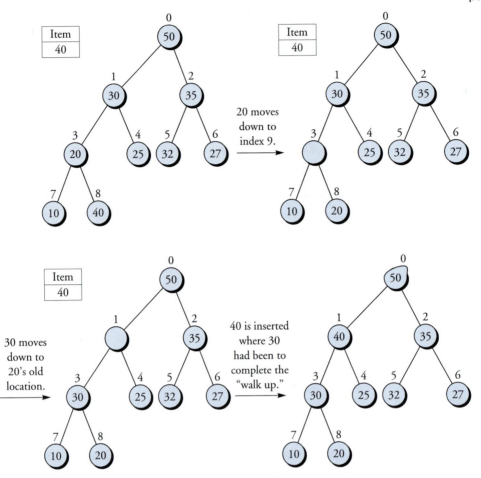

Example 6-5

Implement the `insert` operation for a linear representation of a binary tree with the heap property.

```
template <class E>
void heap<E>::insert(const E &item)
{
    int location, parent;

    assert(numberNodes < MAX_TREE_NODES);

    // Now walk the new item up the tree, starting at location

    location = numberNodes;
    parent = (location - 1) / 2;
```

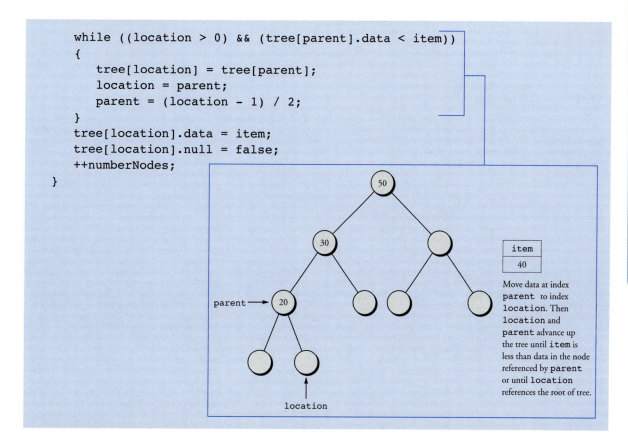

```
    while ((location > 0) && (tree[parent].data < item))
    {
        tree[location] = tree[parent];
        location = parent;
        parent = (location - 1) / 2;
    }
    tree[location].data = item;
    tree[location].null = false;
    ++numberNodes;
}
```

item
40

Move data at index parent to index location. Then location and parent advance up the tree until item is less than data in the node referenced by parent or until location references the root of tree.

Efficiency Analysis of `insert` for Linear Representation of a Heap

Clearly, the time efficiency of adding an item to the heap is directly proportional to the length of the path that the item must "walk up" as its appropriate position is determined. Because the linear representation of a heap leaves no unused gaps between values stored in the vector, doubling the number of items in the heap will add only one level to the resulting binary tree. Thus a heap with n nodes will have $\log_2 n$ levels using the linear representation. In other words, the length of the path that a new item will follow, and hence the efficiency of the `insert` operation, is $O(\log_2 n)$.

In the exercises at the end of this section, you will explore an algorithm to delete a node from a heap. That exploration will show how a heap could be used to implement the priority queue ADT defined in Lesson 4.

Example 6-6

In this example, we illustrate how the postorder traversal algorithm may be implemented for a linear vector implementation of a binary tree. The algorithm is slightly more difficult for this representation because the tree is the encapsulation of a vector and a count of the number of nodes. Unlike with the linked implementation, there is not an explicit root pointer for the tree; instead, the root of the entire tree is understood to be at index 0. The following function, `postorderTraverse`, compensates for this omission by acting as a mere "front end" for a local auxiliary function, which is where the actual recursion takes place. Our front-end function `postorderTraverse` simply passes a root pointer value of 0 to the auxiliary function to start the recursion. We must also assume that a flagging null value of `true` occupies vector locations that are not currently storing data in the tree. This approach allows the auxiliary function to detect when the equivalent of a null pointer is passed.

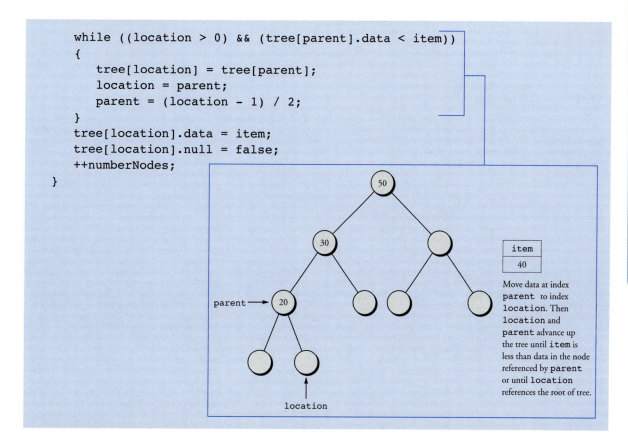

```
template <class E>
void BinaryTree<E>::postorderTraverse(void (* process) (E &item))
{
   if (numberNodes > 0)
      postorderAux(0, process);
}


template <class E>
void BinaryTree<E>::postorderAux(int location, void (* process) (E &item))
{
   if (location < MAX_TREE_NODES)
      if (! tree[location].null)
      {
         postorderAux(2 * location + 1, process);
         postorderAux(2 * location + 2, process);
         process(tree[location].data);
      }
}
```

Third, process
root node.

First, traverse
left subtree.

Second, traverse
right subtree.

EXERCISES ▷ 6.4

1. Suppose that items arrive for insertion into a heap in the following order:

   10 20 30 40 50 60 70 80 90 100

   Using the algorithm of Example 6-5, trace the contents of the tree vector after each item is added to the heap.

2. Write implementations of the `create` and `empty` operations for a binary tree with the heap property using the linear vector implementation. Be sure that your `create` operation is consistent with the postorder traversal algorithm of Example 6-6.

3. Write implementations of the preorder and inorder traversal operations for a linear vector implementation of a binary tree.

4. Implement the following operation for a linear representation of a binary tree with the heap property.

```
void remove(E &item);
```

(*Hint:* When the root is removed, temporarily replace it with the tree node in the last active index of the vector. Then develop an algorithm to walk this new root down a branch of the tree until the tree becomes a heap again.) In a written statement, indicate how the `insert` function of Example 6-5 and the `remove` function that you have written for this exercise could be used to implement a priority queue (Lesson 4) using a heap.

5. In a written statement, discuss the relative advantages and disadvantages of the linear vector implementation of a binary tree versus the linked implementation described in Section 6.2.

6.5 *General Trees*

We began this lesson with a discussion of the many ways in which hierarchical structures are used to organize information around us. We then quickly dictated that at most two children could be used, which focused all of our attention on the seemingly restricted case of the binary tree. What about all of those applications requiring a hierarchical relationship where a parent may have an unrestricted number of children? You may have become suspicious that we are avoiding such considerations because they are too difficult.

Fortunately, we have a much more educationally sound reason. That is, we may use a binary tree to implement a *general tree*. The nice implication of this rather surprising statement is that we will not have to spend a significant amount of time discussing general trees because we have unknowingly studied them in our thorough analysis of binary trees. Moreover, the formal operations on a general tree may be viewed as operations derived from those associated with a binary tree.

The real key to using a restricted type of tree such as a binary tree to implement a more general type of tree is to adjust our perspective. For example, consider the general genealogical tree of Figure 6-24. Here BILL is the first child of the JONES family, with KATY, MIKE, and TOM as BILL's siblings. Similarly, LARRY is the first child of MARY, with PAUL and PENNY as siblings. In a linked representation of a binary tree, we have two pointer fields associated with each node. We have called these pointer fields `left` and `right` because it suited our perspective at the time. Now, however, we will switch that perspective in the following way. One of the pointer fields is to be viewed as a pointer to the leftmost child of a node in a general tree. The second pointer identifies the next sibling to the right of the node under consideration in the general tree. Because the children of a node taken in this context form an ordered set of nodes, we can regard the leftmost child of a node as first and the sibling to the right of this node as sibling. We will henceforth adopt this terminology for the two link fields involved with the binary tree representation of a general tree. Figure 6-25 gives the binary representation of the general genealogical tree shown in Figure 6-24.

FIGURE 6-24
Genealogical tree

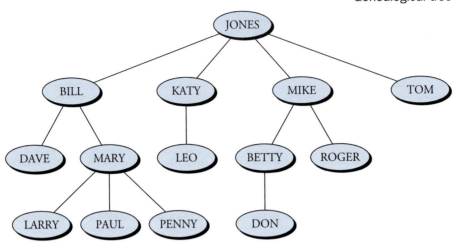

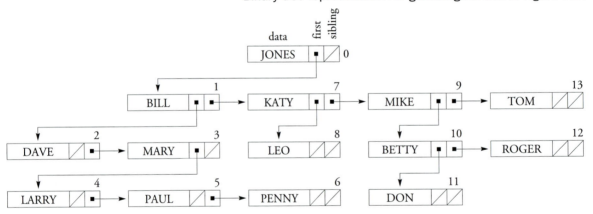

Note that we number the pointers in the tree of Figure 6-24. This numbering is reflected in Table 6-4. You should carefully check all first and sibling values to convince yourself that the scheme used to fill this vector was to store a node before any of its children and then recursively store the leftmost child.

TABLE 6-4
Tree in Figure 6-24 stored in vector of records for data and pointers

Location	Data	First	Sibling
0	JONES	1	0
1	BILL	2	7
2	DAVE	0	3
3	MARY	4	0

(continued on next page)

Location	Data	First	Sibling
4	LARRY	0	5
5	PAUL	0	6
6	PENNY	0	0
7	KATY	8	9
8	LEO	0	0
9	MIKE	10	13
10	BETTY	11	12
11	DON	0	0
12	ROGER	0	0
13	TOM	0	0

The representation in terms of C++ pointer variables (and the representation we will use from this point forward) requires the following type declarations:

```
protected:

// Protected data members

 struct node
 {
     E data;
     node * first;
     node * sibling;
 };

 node * tree;          // Root pointer for entire tree
```

Traversals of a General Tree Implemented via a Binary Tree

As this implementation scheme for a general tree is nothing more than a special interpretation of a binary tree, all of the traversals defined for a binary tree clearly exist for the general tree. A more relevant question than the mere existence of a traversal, however, is the significance of the order in which the nodes of a general tree are visited when its corresponding binary tree is traversed. Of particular interest in this regard are the preorder and postorder traversals.

You should verify that the preorder traversal algorithm for a binary tree applied to Figure 6-24 visits nodes in the following order:

JONES
       BILL
              DAVE
              MARY
                     LARRY
                     PAUL
                     PENNY
KATY
              LEO
MIKE
              BETTY
                    DON
              ROGER
TOM

PROGRAMMING SKILLS: Computer Security and Tree-Structured File Systems

One of the prime concerns in developing operating systems for multiuser computers is to ensure that a user cannot, in an unauthorized fashion, access system files or the files of other users. A convenient data structure to implement such a file directory system is a tree such as that pictured here:

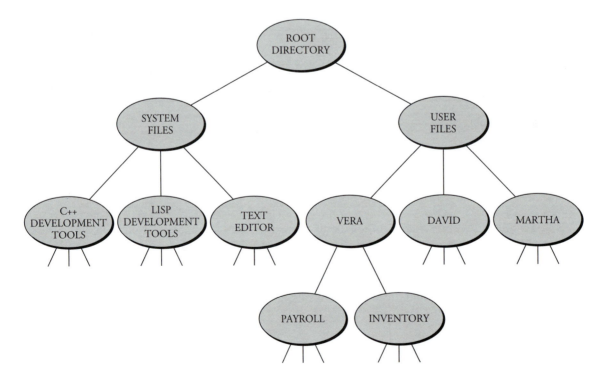

Each interior node of the tree can be viewed as a directory containing various system information about those files or subdirectories that are its descendants. Leaf nodes in the tree are the actual files. Hence, in the diagram, files can be broken down into system files and user files. System files consist of the C++ DEVELOPMENT TOOLS, the LISP DEVELOPMENT TOOLS, and the TEXT EDITOR. User directories are called VERA, DAVID, and MARTHA. One of the very convenient features of such a system is that it allows the user to extend this tree structure as deeply as desired. For instance, in the given tree directory structure, we see that user VERA has created subdirectories for files related to PAYROLL and INVENTORY. DAVID and MARTHA could have similarly partitioned subdirectories to organize their work.

In addition to offering users the convenience of being able to group their files into appropriate subdirectories, such a file system offers a very natural solution to the problem of file security. Because each individual user is, in effect, the root of a miniature subordinate file system within the overall system, a user is given, by default, free access to every node in his or her subtree. That is, the user is viewed as the owner of every node in the subtree. To jump outside of this subtree of naturally owned files and directories requires that special permissions be given the user by other users or by the operating system itself. Thus the tree structure offers convenience as well as a means of carefully monitoring the integrity of the file system.

AT&T's UNIX operating system, developed at Bell Laboratories in the early 1970s, was one of the first to use such a tree-structured directory system. The widespread popularity of UNIX today and the adoption of this scheme by a significant number of other operating systems are evidence of the attractive way it combines user convenience with system security. Of course, such systems are not completely free of security problems. Once the security of such a system is slightly compromised, the tree structure lends itself to a cascade of far-reaching security breaks. Brian Reid's "Reflections on Some Recent Widespread Computer Break-ins," *Communications of the ACM*, vol. 30, no. 2, February 1978, provides an interesting account of how such security problems surfaced at Stanford University and spread to an entire network of computers. An entertaining narrative of another security incident is presented by Clifford Stoll in *The Cuckoo's Egg* (New York: Doubleday, 1989).

The indentation here has been added to highlight the fact that the preorder traversal will recursively process a parent node and then process the child nodes from left to right.

Relative to the general tree pictured in Figure 6-24, we see that the effect of the preorder traversal is to fix on a node at one level of the tree and then run through all of that node's children before progressing to the next node at the same level (the sibling). There is a hint here of a generalized nested loop situation that, as you will see, has some interesting applications in the end-of-lesson projects.

The other traversal of interest in a binary tree representation of a general tree is the postorder traversal. In this regard, it should first be verified that the postorder traversal applied to Figure 6-24 (and its binary tree implementation in Figure 6-25) yields the following listing:

PENNY
PAUL
LARRY
MARY
DAVE
LEO
DON
BETTY
ROGER
TOM
MIKE
KATY

BILL
JONES

In general, the postorder traversal works its way up from the leaf nodes of a tree, ensuring that no given node is processed until all nodes in the subtree below it have been processed.

EXERCISES 6.5

1. How would you implement a preorder traversal to print nodes in a fashion that has children indented under their parents?

2. Consider the following abstract graphic representation of a general tree:

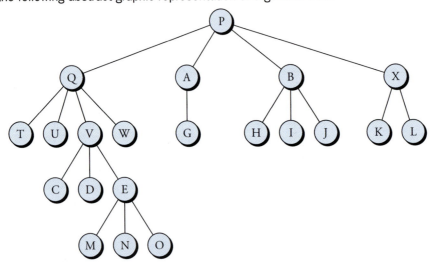

Provide a specific C++ record description for a node in this tree as you would represent it. (Do not make any assumption about a maximum possible number of children.) Then draw a specific picture of how this tree would actually be stored using the record description you have chosen.

3. Given the tree from Exercise 2, in what order would nodes be visited by a preorder traversal? A postorder traversal?

4. For this exercise, you are to assume a linked binary tree representation of a general tree. Write a function that meets the following specification:

```
// Function: addChild
// Insert a tree as the kth subtree of another tree.
// If the root node of the tree already has k or more subtrees, the new
// tree becomes the kth subtree and the former kth subtree becomes
// the (k + 1)st subtree.
// If the root node of the tree has fewer than k subtrees,
// then the new tree is inserted as the last subtree of the root node.

template <class E>
void generalTree<E>::addChild(node * &gt, node * st, int k)
```

5. Use the function you developed for Exercise 4 in another function to generate the following tree. Verify that you have generated the correct tree with a traversal function that outputs the tree in appropriate fashion.

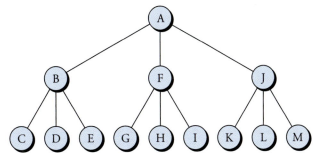

6. Is a binary tree a special case of a general tree? Provide a written rationale to justify your answer.

6.6 Graphs and Networks: Bidirectional Trees

The key defining characteristic of a tree is the hierarchical relationship between parent and child nodes. In a tree, this hierarchical relationship is one-way. That is, within the tree, pointer information allows us to descend from parent to child. There is generally no pointer information within the tree that allows us to ascend from a child node to its parent. In many information storage applications, such a one-way relationship is not sufficient. Consider, for instance, the relationship between students and courses at a university. Each student is enrolled in several courses and could thus be viewed as a parent node with children consisting of the courses he or she is taking. Conversely, each course enrolls many students and could thus be viewed as a parent node with children consisting of the students enrolled in that particular course. The data structure that emerges from this type of bidirectional relationship is pictured in Figure 6-26.

FIGURE 6-26
Bidirectional relationship between students and courses

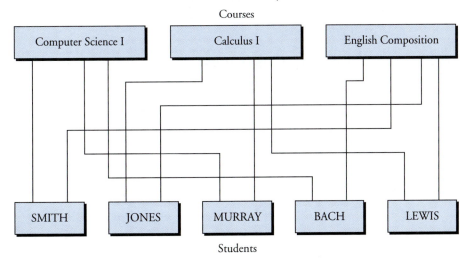

429

In terms of an abstract data type, the representation of such a bidirectional relationship between nodes is called a *graph*. A graph consists of two sets. One set is a fixed set of objects called nodes. The other is a set of *edges*, the contents of which vary depending on the operations that have been performed on the graph. A node is a data element of the graph, and an edge is a direct connection between two nodes. A node may also be called a *vertex* of the graph. If an edge exists between two nodes, we say that the second node is adjacent to the first node.

The operations associated with the graph ADT are specified in terms of the following preconditions and postconditions:

---

create Operation

Preconditions: Receiver is a graph in an unpredictable state.

Postconditions: Graph is initialized to a state with no edges. That is, no nodes are connected to any other nodes, including themselves.

addEdge Operation

Preconditions: Receiver is an arbitrary graph that has been initialized by `create` and, potentially, affected by other operations. `node1` and `node2` are two nodes in the graph.

Postconditions: Receiver is returned with an edge from `node1` to `node2`. If an edge already existed from `node1` to `node2`, the graph is not affected.

removeEdge Operation

Preconditions: Receiver is an arbitrary graph that has been initialized by `create` and, potentially, affected by other operations. `node1` and `node2` are two nodes in the graph.

Postconditions: If there is an edge from `node1` to `node2`, it is removed. Otherwise, the graph is not affected.

edge Operation

Preconditions: Receiver is an arbitrary graph that has been initialized by `create` and, potentially, affected by other operations. `node1` and `node2` are two nodes in the graph.

Postconditions: `edge` returns `true` if there is an edge from `node1` to `node2`, and `false` otherwise.

traverse Operation

Preconditions: Receiver is an arbitrary graph that has been initialized by `create` and, potentially, affected by other operations. `start` is a node at which the traversal is to start. `process` is an algorithmic process that can be applied to each graph node.

Postconditions: Receiver is returned with each node that can be reached from `start` affected by `process`. A given node can be reached from `start` if the given node is the start node or if there is a sequence of edges $E_0, E_1, \ldots,$ E_n such that (1) E_0 begins at the `start` node, (2) the node at which E_{i-1} ends is the node at which E_i begins, and (3) E_n ends at the given node. In effect, the sequence of edges determines a path from `start` to the given node. The path is composed of edges between adjacent nodes. `process` is not applied to any node more than once.

As it relates to Figure 6-26, the formal definition of a graph does not rule out the possibility of an edge connecting two courses or connecting two students. It is merely the nature of this course–student relationship that makes the existence of such a course-to-course edge or student-to-student edge impractical. In other applications, such as the transportation network pictured in Figure 6-27, it may be entirely feasible for any node in the graph to have an edge connecting it to any other node.

FIGURE 6-27

Transportation network as graph in which edges represent flights between cities

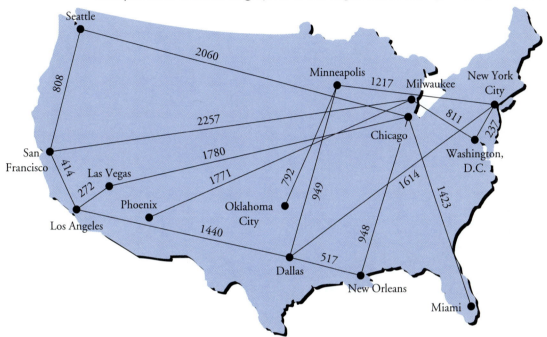

To illustrate how a graph grows from an initial state with no edges, suppose that we start with a set of nodes labeled A, B, C, and D. Figure 6-28 traces the effect of a sequence of `addEdge` and `removeEdge` operations on a graph with these nodes. Note from this figure that the concept of an edge carries with it the notion of a direction. That is, it is possible to have an edge from `node1` to `node2` in a graph G without there being a corresponding connection in the opposite direction. Figure 6-28 (8) also illustrates that it is possible to have an edge from a node to itself.

By convention, when we draw a graph without arrows on the edges, it is implicit that all edges run in both directions. Thus, in Figure 6-27, the line connecting San Francisco and Los Angeles implicitly represents two edges—the one from San Francisco to Los Angeles and the one from Los Angeles to San Francisco.

FIGURE 6-28

Graph affected by sequence of `addEdge` and `removeEdge` operations

D   A

C   B

create G
(1)

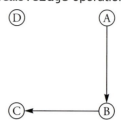

addEdge A → B
(2)

addEdge B → C
(3)

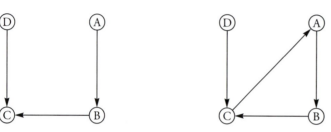

addEdge D → C
(4)

addEdge C → A
(5)

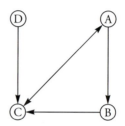

addEdge A → C
(6)

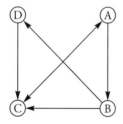

addEdge B → D
(7)

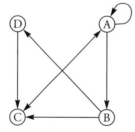

addEdge A → A
(8)

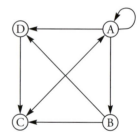

addEdge A → D
(9)

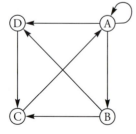

removeEdge A → C
(10)

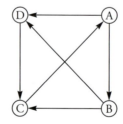

removeEdge A → A
(11)

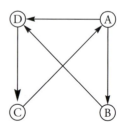

removeEdge B → C
(12)

We will sometimes use the terminology *directional graph*, or *digraph*, to emphasize that a particular graph has some edges that exist in only one direction. Figure 6-29 illustrates a digraph. In a digraph, arrows specify the direction of an edge between nodes.

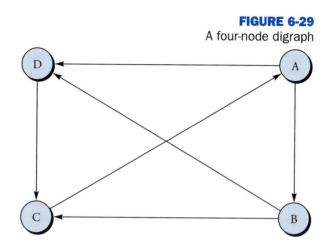

FIGURE 6-29
A four-node digraph

Before providing a C++ interface for the graph ADT, we should clarify a point of ambiguity in the definition of the traversal operation. In particular, this operation does not establish a unique order of visiting nodes that can be reached from the start node. The following examples illustrate two potential orders in which nodes can be visited starting at A in the graph of Figure 6-29.

Example 6-7

Consider a traversal from start node A in the digraph of Figure 6-29 guided by the following strategy: A given path starting at A should be explored as deeply as possible before another path is probed. If we assume that B is the first node adjacent to A, then the traversal will proceed from A to B. If we then assume that C is the first node adjacent to B, the traversal will continue from B to C. From C, it is not possible to visit any nodes that have not already been visited. Hence, we will backtrack to B and, from there, continue the traversal to D since D is adjacent to B. Hence, the overall order in which nodes are visited by a traversal under the strategy and assumptions of this example is

```
A, B, C, D
```

The strategy exemplified here is often called a *depth-first traversal* because a given path is probed as deeply as possible before we backtrack and explore another path.

Example 6-8

Next, we will indicate the order in which nodes would be visited in a traversal starting at node A in the digraph of Figure 6-29 following a strategy that does not probe one path as deeply as possible but rather "fans out" to all nodes adjacent to a given node. In this case, we would proceed from A to B and then to D, because both B and D are adjacent to A. As all nodes adjacent to A have been exhausted, we would fan out from B, the first node we visited from A. This step takes us to C by the edge B → C, completing the traversal in the overall order

```
A, B, D, C
```

The fan-out strategy exemplified here is often termed a *breadth-first traversal*.

Examples 6-7 and 6-8 just begin to scratch the surface of the variety of graph traversal strategies that exist. We will soon examine the implementation of these traversal strategies more closely. At this time the point to emphasize is that the graph traversal operation is open to a variety of implementation techniques.

C++ Interface for the Graph ADT

Before we can develop graph algorithms in detail, we must provide a C++ interface for this ADT. This task is accomplished in the following class declaration module. The interface makes the assumption that the data in graph nodes are drawn from a range of values that can serve both as keys for tables and as values over which a `for` loop can iterate, such as `int`, `char`, or an enumerated type. Our reasons for making this assumption will become apparent when we discuss ways of implementing graphs.

```
// Class declaration file: graph.h

#ifndef GRAPH_H
#define GRAPH_H

// Definition section

template <class Node> class graph
    {

    public:

    // Class constructors

    graph();
    graph(const graph<Node> &g);

    // Member functions

    void addEdge(const Node &node1, const Node &node2);
    void removeEdge(const Node &node1, const Node &node2);
    bool edge(const Node &node1, const Node &node2);
    void traverse(Node &start, void (*process) (Node &item));
    graph<Node>& operator = (const graph<Node> &g);

    // Protected data and member functions pertaining to
    // the implementation would be located here.

    };

#endif
```

The Network ADT

Graphs such as that shown in Figure 6-27 are somewhat special in that the edges have weights associated with them, here representing distances between nodes (cities). Such a graph is an example of the **network** abstract data type. A network is a graph in which each edge has a positive numeric *weight*. The operations associated with the network ADT are the same as those for the graph ADT with the exceptions that the `addEdge` operation must now specify the weight of the edge being added and we must add an operation that, given two nodes, returns the weight of the edge that may exist between them.

These two new operations are specified by the following preconditions and postconditions.

---

addEdge Operation

Preconditions: Receiver is an arbitrary network that has been initialized by `create` and, potentially, affected by other operations. `node1` and `node2` are two nodes in the network. `weight` is a positive number representing the weight of an edge to be added from `node1` to `node2`.

Postconditions: Receiver has an edge of weight `weight` from `node1` to `node2`. If an edge already existed from `node1` to `node2`, the weight of that edge is now `weight`.

edgeWeight Operation

Preconditions: Receiver is an arbitrary network that has been initialized by `create` and, potentially, affected by other operations. `node1` and `node2` are two nodes in the network.

Postconditions: `edgeWeight` returns 0 if there is no edge from `node1` to `node2` and the numeric value of the edge if it exists.

Graphs and networks provide excellent examples of how a theoretical area of mathematics has found very relevant application in computer science. It is beyond the scope of this text to provide a comprehensive treatment of graphs and networks. Rather, our purpose in the rest of this section is to provide you with an overview of a data structure that you will no doubt encounter again as you continue your study of computer science. More in-depth treatments of graphs and networks can be found in numerous advanced texts on data structures, such as *Data Structures in C++* by Ellis Horowitz and Sartaj Sahni (New York: Computer Science Press, 1990) and *Introduction to Data Structures and Algorithm Analysis with C++* by George J. Pothering and Thomas L. Naps (St. Paul, Minnesota: West Publishing, 1995).

Implementation of Graphs and Networks

A graph may be conveniently implemented using a matrix of Boolean values. For instance, the information in Figure 6-26 is contained in Table 6-5, a two-dimensional table. In this table, the value `true` indicates the presence of an edge between two nodes and the value `false` indicates the absence of such an edge. In the case of a network, the two-dimensional table implementation still applies. Now, however, the data stored in the table are of a type compatible with edge weights. Such a two-dimensional table implementation of the transportation network from Figure 6-27 is given in Table 6-6. Note that the data are mirrored across the diagonal of the table because all edges are bidirectional. Table 6-6 illustrates a quality typically found in two-dimensional table implementations of large graphs and networks: the sparseness of nontrivial data. Hence, the methods we have discussed for implementing sparse two-key tables actually provide alternative implementation strategies for graphs and networks.

PROGRAMMING SKILLS: Computer Networks: Their Use and Potential Abuse

It's a rare student who doesn't take advantage of electronic mail to stay in touch with friends at distant campuses. It could easily be argued that, more than any other single factor, interaction among distant users on the Internet has been responsible for making nearly everyone aware of the potential of computing. But the Internet is merely one part of the information superhighway. According to Haruhisa Ishida and Lawrence H. Landweber, "Internetworking," *Communications of the ACM*, vol. 36, no. 3, August 1993:

> *The National Information Infrastructure (NII) and the Electronic Superhighway are two of the titles used by the Clinton/Gore administration to describe plans for an enhanced communications environment. Video conferencing and telephony, entertainment, access to libraries and information repositories, and support for medical consultations are just some of the services to be available to homes, offices, and schools. All of this has been made possible by rapid advances in communications and networking technology over the last decade.*

The potential for uses of information networks is unlimited. For example, Janet Murray provides details of how the K12 Network is finding growing use in elementary and secondary education in "K12 Network: Global Education Through Telecommunications," *Communications of the ACM*, vol. 36, no. 3, August 1993. Some of the opportunities within the K12 Network include language exchanges with native speakers in French, German, Japanese, Spanish, and Russian; cooperative physics experiments, such as attempts of students in Oregon, California, Nova Scotia, and Maryland to replicate Eratosthenes' experiment in Alexandria to determine the size of the earth by measuring the length of a shadow cast by a stick; and the "MathMagic" challenge in which students post a variety of solutions to nontrivial problems.

For all of the wonders of networks, there is also a downside. As we begin to rely increasingly on networks, a variety of privacy-related problems arise. An excellent overview of these problems is presented in a series of articles under the heading "Internet Privacy: The Quest for Anonymity," *Communications of the ACM*, vol. 42, no. 2, February 1999.

TABLE 6-5

Two-dimensional table implementation of graph from Figure 6-26

Course	Smith	Jones	Murray	Bach	Lewis
Computer Science	true	false	true	true	false
Calculus I	false	true	true	false	true
English Composition	true	true	false	true	true

TABLE 6-6
Two-dimensional table implementation of network from Figure 6-27

	NY	Wash	Miam	Milw	Chi	NOrl	Mpls	OklC	Dals	LVeg	Phex	StL	SFra	LA
Ny		237		811			1217		1614					
Wash														
Miam					1423									
Milw	811										1771		2257	
Chi			1423			948				1780		2060		
NOrl					948				517					
Mpls 1217	1217							792	949					
OklC							792							
Dals 1614	1614					517	949							1440
LVeg					1780									272
Phex				1771										
StL					2060								808	
SFra				2257								808		414
LA										272			414	

In the discussion of the two-graph/network algorithms that follow, we do not tie ourselves to a particular implementation strategy for representing the underlying data structure. Rather, we discuss the algorithms in terms of the operations associated with the abstract data type involved and leave implementation considerations for the exercises at the end of this section and the end-of-lesson projects.

Examples of Graph Algorithms: Depth-First and Breadth-First Traversals

In many practical applications of graphs, there is frequently a need to visit systematically all the nodes on a graph from a designated starting node. One such application occurs when the organizers of a political campaign are interested in having their candidate visit all important political centers. The presence or absence of direct transportation routes (that is, edges) between such centers will determine the possible ways in which all the centers can be visited. At the moment, our only concern is the development of an algorithm that ensures that all possible nodes are visited. Such an algorithm will provide an implementation for the graph traversal operation. Later in the lesson, we investigate how to determine the shortest possible distances from one node to all others.

Depth-First Traversal. This technique was illustrated in Example 6-7. The main logic of the depth-first algorithm is analogous to the preorder traversal of a tree. It is accomplished recursively as follows:

1. Designate the starting node as the search node and mark it as visited.

2. Find a node adjacent to the search node (that is, connected by an edge from the search node) that has not yet been visited. Designate it as the new search node (but remember the previous one) and mark it as visited.

3. Repeat step 2 using the new search node. If no nodes satisfying step 2 can be found, return to the previous search node and continue from there.

4. When a return to the previous search node in step 3 is impossible, the search from the originally chosen search node is complete.

This algorithm is called a depth-first traversal because the search continues progressively deeper into the graph in a recursive manner.

To illustrate this function more clearly, consider Figure 6-30; its table implementation is shown in Table 6-7. Suppose we have a function called `searchFrom`, which is invoked to begin a depth-first traversal from a given node on the graph. The steps followed by the algorithm are:

1. Begin by marking node 1 as visited and invoking `searchFrom(1)`.

2. Both nodes 2 and 3 are adjacent to node 1 according to the matrix implementation of the graph, but node 2 is encountered first on a left-to-right scan of the row for 1, thus the search goes to node 2. We invoke `searchFrom(2)`, and node 2 is marked as visited.

3. As node 3 is the first unvisited node adjacent to node 2, the search now goes to node 3, `searchFrom(3)` is invoked, and node 3 is marked as visited.

4. As there is no unvisited node adjacent to node 3, we say that this node has exhausted the search; the search goes back to its predecessor—that is, to node 2.

5. From node 2, we visit node 4.

6. From node 4, we proceed to node 5. All nodes have now been visited, and the depth-first traversal is complete.

FIGURE 6-30
Graph to illustrate depth-first search

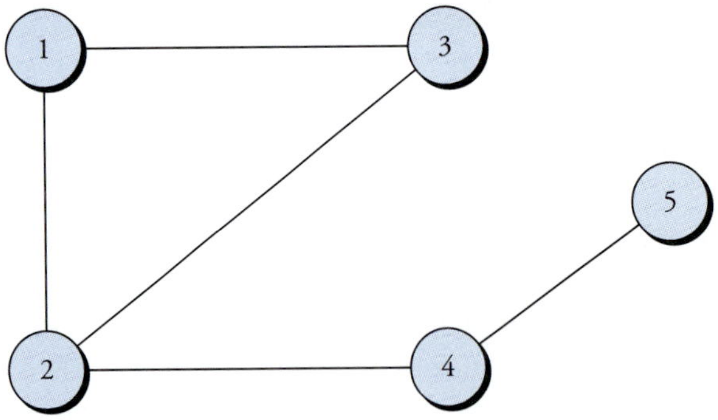

Use Table 6-7 to verify these steps.

	1	2	3	4	5
1	false	true	true	false	false
2	true	false	true	true	false
3	true	true	false	false	false
4	false	true	false	false	true
5	false	false	false	true	false

The order in which nodes are visited in a depth-first traversal is not unique, because the order depends on the manner in which "adjacent" nodes are chosen. That is, given two unvisited nodes adjacent to another node, which one should be chosen to invoke the searchFrom function? In practice, this choice will usually be determined by the ordering of the data type used to implement the nodes in the graph.

Example 6-9

Implement the depth-first traversal algorithm under the assumption that the node data type is an appropriate enumeration type.

As with our implementation of the postorder traversal operation for a binary tree in Example 6-6, we use an auxiliary function as the real recursive workhorse. The traverse function is itself merely a front end, which appropriately sets the stage for the auxiliary function searchFrom.

We can now see the reason for the restriction placed on the node type in our C++ interface for the graph ADT. It must be a type capable of keying a table and controlling an iterative loop structure. Both of these properties are assumed in the code of this example.

```
// Assumption:  Type Node represents an enumeration with a designated
// firstValue and lastValue.  This allows values of type Node
// to correspond to indices in an bool vector visited that is
// used to keep track of graph nodes that have already had
// process applied to them.

template <class Node>
void graph<Node>::traverse(Node &start, void (*process) (Node &item));
{
    // Allocate a vector of bool
    bool * visited = new bool [lastValue - firstValue + 1];
    Node k;
```

```
    // Initially nothing is processed
    for (k = firstValue, k <= lastValue, ++k)
       visited[k - firstValue] = false;
    // Make the top-level call to searchFrom
    searchFrom(start, process, visited);
    delete [] visited;
}


template <class Node>
void graph<Node>::searchFrom(Node &start, void (*process) (Node &item),
                             bool * visited)

{
   Node k;

   // Process the start node and mark it in the vector of visited nodes
   process(start);
   visited[start - firstValue] = true;


   // Then proceed deeper into the graph
   for (k = firstValue, k <= lastValue, ++k)
      if ( (!visited[k - firstValue]) && edge(start, k))
         searchFrom(k, process, visited);

}
```

The recursive call will successively pass in as **start** graph nodes along this path, ensuring that this path is completely probed before any other nodes adjacent to the original **start** are visited.

Breadth-First Traversal. An alternative to the depth-first graph traversal strategy is the breadth-first traversal. Instead of proceeding as deeply as possible along one path from the current node in the graph, the breadth-first traversal examines all nodes adjacent to the current node before proceeding more deeply along any given path. Hence, for the graph of Figure 6-31, implemented by Table 6-8, a breadth-first traversal starting at node 1 visits nodes in the order 1, 2, 3, 4, 5 (as opposed to the order 1, 2, 4, 5, 3 dictated by a depth-first traversal).

PROGRAMMING SKILLS: The Traveling Salesperson and NP-complete Problems

A well-known problem of classical graph theory, which is easy to state but difficult to solve, is the traveling salesperson problem. The problem essentially tries to minimize the round-trip cost of visiting once and only once every city on the business route of the salesperson. This problem was first described by the Irish mathematician Sir William Rowan Hamilton (1805–1865).

The problem can be viewed as a network such as we have discussed in Section 6.6. The cities to be visited are the nodes in the network, and the weighted edges are the distances between the cities. Unlike the shortest distance algorithm discussed in Section 6.6, the only known algorithm to solve the traveling salesperson problem is to examine *all possible* round trips that visit exactly once every city in the network.

Although this algorithm solves the traveling salesperson's problem, it is slow because of the exponential number of possible round trips. When the number of cities on the salesperson's tour is moderately large (even as large as 20), the solution is annoyingly slow, but nothing better is known that will guarantee finding a solution to the problem.

The complexity of the traveling salesperson problem places it in a class of problems known as NP-complete problems. This theoretical class of problems has the following interesting property. If we can even find for any one such problem a solution that has a polynomial time efficiency, then we will automatically have polynomial time solutions to all other problems in this class and an even larger theoretical class of problems known as NP problems. A thorough discussion of NP and NP-complete problems may be found in Thomas Cormen, Charles Leiserson, and Ronald Rivest, *Introduction to Algorithms* (New York: McGraw-Hill, 1989).

FIGURE 6-31
Graph to illustrate breadth-first traversal

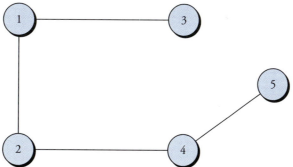

TABLE 6-8
Table implementation of Figure 6-31

	1	2	3	4	5
1	false	true	true	false	false
2	true	false	false	true	false
3	true	false	false	false	false
4	false	true	false	false	true
5	false	false	false	true	false

A breadth-first traversal of a graph involves the following steps:

1. Begin with the start node and mark it as visited.

2. Proceed to the next node having an edge connection to the node in step 1. Mark it as visited.

3. Come back to the node in step 1, descend along an edge toward an unvisited node, and mark the new node as visited.

4. Repeat step 3 until all nodes adjacent to the node in step 1 have been marked as visited.

5. Repeat steps 1 through 4 starting from the node visited in step 2 and then starting from the nodes visited in step 3 in the order visited. Continue as long as possible before starting a new scan.

You will be asked to explore this strategy in the end-of-lesson projects.

Example of a Network Algorithm: Finding Shortest Paths

If the graph under consideration is a network in which edge weights represent distances, then an appropriate question is: From a given node called source, what is the shortest distance to all other nodes in the network?

For instance, the network of Figure 6-32 could be thought of as showing airline routes between cities. An airline would be interested in finding the most economical route between any two given cities in the network. The numbers listed on the edges in this case represent distances between cities. Thus the airline wishes to find the shortest path that can be flown from node 3 to reach nodes 1, 2, 4, and 5.

FIGURE 6-32
Network with edge weights representing distances

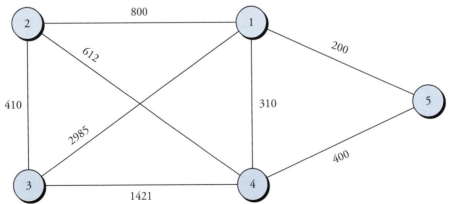

Suppose we want to find the shortest path from node 1 to node 3. From Figure 6-32, we note that this path is $1 \rightarrow 2 \rightarrow 3$, yielding a total weight of $800 + 410 = 1210$. An algorithm to find such a path was discovered by E. W. Dijkstra. For convenience in discussing Dijkstra's algorithm, often called the shortest path algorithm, let us assume that the nodes in the network under consideration are numbered 1, 2, . . . numberOfNodes. That is, the node type is the subrange of the integers given by 1 . . . numberOfNodes.

Given such a collection of nodes, Dijkstra's algorithm requires three vectors in addition to a suitable implementation of the network M. These three vectors are identified as follows:

```
int distance[MAX_DISTANCE_SIZE];
int path[MAX_PATH_SIZE];
apvector<bool> included(MAX_INCLUDED_SIZE);
```

Identifying one node as source, the algorithm proceeds to find the shortest distance from source to all other nodes in the network. At the conclusion of the algorithm, the shortest distance from source to node j is stored in distance[j], whereas path[j] contains the immediate predecessor of node j on the path determining this shortest distance. While the algorithm is in progress, distance[j] and path[j] are being continually updated until included[j] is switched from false to true. Once this switch occurs, it is known definitely that distance[j] contains the shortest distance from source to j. The algorithm progresses until all nodes have been so included. Hence, it gives us the shortest distance from source to every other node in the network.

Given the source node in the network M, the algorithm may be divided into two phases: an initialization phase and an iteration phase, in which nodes are included one by one in the set of nodes for which the shortest distance from source is known definitely.

During the initialization phase, we must

1. Initialize included[source] to true and included [j] to false for all other j.

2. Initialize each index j in the distance vector via the rule:

if j == source

distance[j] = 0

else if M.edgeWeight(source, j) != 0

distance[j] = M.edgeWeight(source, j)

else if j is not connected to source by a direct edge (that is, if

M.edgeWeight(source, j) == 0)

distance[j] = Infinity

3. Initialize each index j in the path vector via the rule:

if M.edgeWeight (source, j) != 0

path[j] = source

else

path[j] = Undefined

Given this initialization, the iteration phase may be expressed in a generalized pseudocode form as follows:

Do

  Find the node J that has the minimal distance among those nodes not yet included

  Mark J as now included

  For each R not yet included

    If there is an edge from J to R

      If distance[J] + M.edgeWeight (J, R) < distance[R]

        distance[R] = distance[J] + M.edgeWeight (J, R)

        path[R] = J

While all nodes are not included

The crucial part of the algorithm occurs within the innermost `if` of the `for` loop. Figure 6-33 provides a pictorial representation of the logic involved here. The nodes included with the circle represent those nodes already included prior to a given iteration of the `do` loop. Node J in Figure 6-33 represents the node found in the first step of the `do` loop; R represents another arbitrary node, which has not yet been included. The lines emanating from `source` represent the paths corresponding to the current entries in the distance vector. For nodes within the circle—that is, those already included—these paths are guaranteed to be the shortest distance paths. If J is the node having the minimal entry in distance among those not yet included, we will add J to the circle of included nodes and then check to see if J's connections to other nodes in the network that are not yet included may result in a newly found shorter path to such nodes.

FIGURE 6-33

`do . . . while` loop logic in shortest path (Dijkstra's) algorithm

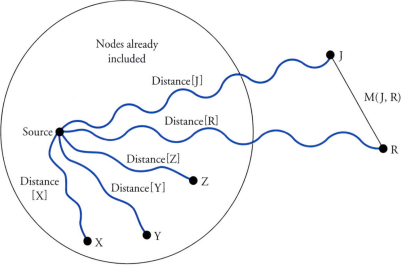

Referring to Figure 6-33 again, the sum of two sides of a triangle

```
distance[J] + M.edgeWeight(J, R)
```

may in fact be shorter than the third side,

`distance[R]`

This geometric contradiction is possible because these are not true straight-sided triangles, but "triangles" whose sides may be very complicated paths through a network.

It is also apparent from Figure 6-33 why Dijkstra's algorithm works. As the node J in this figure is found to have the minimal distance entry from among all those nodes not yet included, we may now include it among the nodes whose minimal distance from the `source` node is absolutely known. Why? Consider any other path P to J containing nodes that are not yet included at the time J is included. Let X be the first such nonincluded node on path P. Then clearly, as the first nonincluded node on the path P, X must be adjacent to an included node. However, as Figure 6-34 indicates, the criterion that dictated the choice of J as an included node ensures that

$$distance[J] \qquad \leq \textit{The total edge weight through node X on the path P}$$
$$\leq \textit{Total edge weight of path P}$$

This inequality demonstrates that, once J is included, there exists no other path P to J through a nonincluded node that can yield a shorter overall distance. Hence we have verified our claim that including a node guarantees our having found a path of shortest possible distance to that node.

FIGURE 6-34

Guaranteeing the minimality of distance to J once it is included

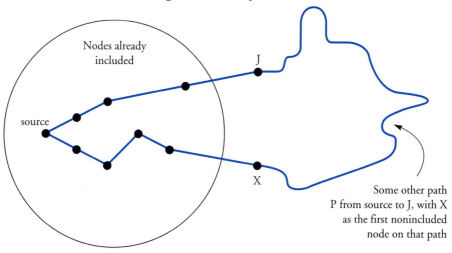

Criterion for including J ensures
Distance [J] ≤ Distance [X] ≤ Length of path P

Example 6-10

To be sure that you understand Dijkstra's algorithm before you attempt to implement it, trace it through on the network of Figure 6-32 with `source = 1`.

Initially, we would have

distance[2] = 800   path[2] = 1
distance[3] = 2985   path[3] = 1
distance[4] = 310   path[4] = 1
distance[5] = 200   path[5] = 1

445

in accordance with steps 2 and 3 of the initialization phase. According to the iteration phase of the algorithm, we would then, in order, perform these steps:

1. Include node 5; no change in `distance` and `path` needed.

distance[2] = 800   path[2] = 1
distance[3] = 2985 path[3] = 1
distance[4] = 310   path[4] = 1
distance[5] = 200   path[5] = 1

2. Include node 4; update `distance` and `path` to

distance[2] = 800   path[2] = 1
distance[3] = 1731 path[3] = 4
distance[4] = 310   path[4] = 1
distance[5] = 200   path[5] = 1

(Note that it is shorter to go from node 1 to node 4 to node 3 than to follow the edge directly connecting node 1 to node 3.)

3. Include node 2; update `distance` and `path` to

distance[2] = 800   path[2] = 1
distance[3] = 1210 path[3] = 2
distance[4] = 310   path[4] = 1
distance[5] = 200   path[5] = 1

(Now we find that traveling from node 1 to node 2 to node 3 is even better than the path determined in step 2.)

4. Finally, node 3 is included with (obviously) no changes made in `distance` or `path`.

EXERCISES ⟩ 6.6

1. Indicate the order in which nodes would be visited if a depth-first traversal of the network in Figure 6-27 were initiated from Seattle. Use the adjacency relationships from Table 6-6.

2. Repeat Exercise 1 but initiate the traversal from Miami.

3. Repeat Exercise 1 for a breadth-first traversal.

4. Repeat Exercise 2 for a breadth-first traversal.

5. Trace the contents of the `distance`, `path`, and `included` vectors as Dijkstra's shortest path algorithm is applied to the transportation network of Figure 6-27. Use Phoenix as the `source` node.

6. Repeat Exercise 5 with Milwaukee as the `source` node.

7. Using a matrix, write functions to implement each of the basic operations for the graph abstract data type. Then provide a big-O time efficiency analysis of each of the operations. How is this analysis affected by a particular sparse matrix technique that may be underlying the matrix? Be as specific as possible in stating your answer.

8. Using a matrix, write functions to implement each of the basic operations for the network abstract data type.

9. In a written statement, discuss the implications of eliminating the requirement that type `node` be a sub-range of an ordinal type in the C++ interface for the graph ADT. Your statement should identify problems that this approach would cause and outline strategies for solving such problems.

CASE STUDY: A Concordance Problem

The declarations for our binary tree class are intentionally less complete than those for other data structures we have discussed. Why? The organizational structure of a binary tree is highly dependent on the data stored in the tree and the way in which an application program wants to manipulate those data. Consequently, we have presented only a "bare bones" set of generic operations that all binary trees have in common. It is almost inevitable that any applications program using a binary tree will have to extend those operations in a fashion appropriate to its needs. Fortunately, object-oriented inheritance makes this task very easy to do. We will demonstrate such inheritance in this Case Study. Source code/data files for the Case Study have been provided—see your instructor.

User Request

Write a program that reads a file of text representing a work of literature. Produce a ***concordance*** of the words in this file—that is, an alphabetical listing of the words along with a count of how many times each word appears in the work. Assume that, prior to your program reading the file, all punctuation has been stripped out and all letters have been converted to lowercase. After displaying the concordance, output the word that occurs most often, along with its frequency.

447

Analysis

Ideally, the program will call for input of the name of the file from which the words are read, so a sample run will appear as follows:

```
Name of file to read words from? tea_party.txt


a 48
about 5
above 1
accounts 1
added 5
advantage 1
...
yawning 2
year 2
yes 3
yet 3
you 50
young 1
your 4
yourself 1


Occurring most is — the — 159 times
```

Design

We could have solved this particular problem earlier by using a vector, linked list, or sorted collection as the data structure in which to store the words (and their counts) as they are read from the file. However, all of these data structures would have led to an $O(n^2)$ efficiency, where n is the number of words in the file. With a binary search tree as the underlying data structure, there is a good chance that the processing time for each word as it is read from the file will be $O(\log_2 n)$. Hence, barring an unbalanced tree, the overall efficiency of our program will be $O(n * \log_2 n)$.

The `BinaryTree` class developed in Section 6.2 provides a good start toward solving the problem at hand. For the templated data type in each tree node, we can use a `struct` containing a word and the count of how many times that word appears in the file.

```
struct WordStruct
{
   apstring word;
   int count;
};
```

Once the tree is filled with words from the file, calling on the `inorderTraverse` function for the `BinaryTree`, with an appropriate display function, will produce the concordance output. Two tasks, however, will require extending the `BinaryTree` class by adding two new methods—one to take care of inserting words and their counts into the tree and another to determine the word that occurs most frequently.

The logic to insert a word into the tree is described in the following pseudocode:

If the tree is empty
 Insert the word along with a count of 1

Else if the word to be inserted matches the word in the root of the tree
 Increase the count for that word by 1

Else if the word to be inserted precedes the word in the root of the tree
 Recur with the left subtree

Else
 Recur with the right subtree

To determine the word that occurs most frequently (once the tree is built), we must use a recursive version of a standard champion–challenger algorithm:

Initialize the champion to a value, such as 0, that is updated upon its first challenge.

If the count associated with the word at the root of the tree beats the champion
 Update the champion to this count

Recur with the champion and the left subtree

Recur with the champion and the right subtree

Implementation

The specialized insertion and maximum-finding algorithms described in the design are found in the following `WordTree` class derived from the `BinaryTree` class:

```
class WordTree : public BinaryTree<WordStruct>
{
  public:

  // Class constructor

    WordTree();

  // Member functions

    void insert(const apstring &theWord);
    WordStruct mostFrequent();

  protected:

    // Recursive helper for top-level insert
    void insertAux(BinaryTree<WordStruct>::node * &tree,
                const apstring &theWord);

    // Recursive helper for top-level mostFrequent
    void mostFrequentAux(BinaryTree<WordStruct>::node * &tree,
                WordStruct & w);
};
```

```
void WordTree::insert(const apstring &theWord)
{
    insertAux(tree, theWord);
}


void WordTree::insertAux(BinaryTree<WordStruct>::node * &tree,
                         const apstring &theWord)
{
    WordStruct ws;


    ws.word = theWord;
    ws.count = 1;
    if (tree == 0)                                  // word occurs for first time
        tree = getNode(ws);
    else if (theWord == tree->data.word)  // word appeared before
        ++(tree->data.count);
    else if (theWord < tree->data.word)
        insertAux(tree->left, theWord);
    else
        insertAux(tree->right, theWord);
}

WordStruct WordTree::mostFrequent()
{
    WordStruct w;

    w.word = "";                        // Initialize the struct
    w.count = 0;
    mostFrequentAux(tree, w);       // Call recursive helper
    return w;
}

void WordTree::mostFrequentAux(BinaryTree<WordStruct>::node * &tree,
WordStruct & w)
{

    if (tree != 0)
    {
        if (tree->data.count > w.count)         // Did challenger beat champion?
        {
            w.count = tree->data.count;
            w.word = tree->data.word;
        }
        mostFrequentAux(tree->left, w);
        mostFrequentAux(tree->right, w);
    }
}
```

Running, Debugging, and Testing Hints

- Trees are inherently recursive data structures, so learn to think recursively when devising algorithms that process trees.

- When using the linear vector representation of a binary tree, remember that all vector locations must be initialized to a flagging null value if the implementations of other operations are to work correctly.

- The use of a preorder traversal to print a tree with indentation to reflect the depth of a node is a handy tracing tool when debugging a tree program that has gone awry. Keep such a function in your library, so it is readily available when the need arises. For more information, see this lesson's Case Study.

- When using a binary search tree to implement a one-key table, some experimentation may be necessary to determine the efficiency of this technique for the particular data of your application.

Summary

In this lesson, you learned:

- Trees are a data structure used to reflect a hierarchical relationship among data items. Indicative of this hierarchy is the parent–child terminology used to express the relationship between items on successive levels of the tree. Trees are by nature recursive structures, with each node of a tree being itself the root of a smaller embedded subtree.

- Binary trees are trees in which each parent may have at most two child nodes. Although this limitation seems like a major restriction, binary trees find a wide range of applications. Three such applications are the representation of algebraic expressions, one-key tables, and priority queues.

- Two ways of implementing a binary tree are the linear representation and the linked representation. The former method uses a vector and requires no pointers but is prone to wasting a large number of vector locations. The latter uses pointers and consequently is able to take advantage of C++'s dynamic memory allocation.

- Three standard ways of traversing a binary tree—that is, three ways of visiting all nodes exactly once—exist: the preorder, postorder, and inorder traversals.

- In a preorder traversal, the current root node is processed, followed recursively by the nodes in the left subtree and then the right subtree.

- In a postorder traversal, all nodes in the left subtree of the current root are recursively processed. Then all nodes in the right subtree are processed, and the root itself is processed last.

- In an inorder traversal, the nodes in the left subtree are processed first, followed by the root node, and finally the nodes in the right subtree of the root. The inorder traversal is critical in the binary tree implementation of a one-key table because the order in which it visits nodes corresponds precisely to the ordering of items as first, second, third, . . . , within the list represented by the tree.

- The binary search tree implementation of a one-key table is the third such table implementation we have studied. The other two were the vector implementation (Lesson 2) and the linked list implementation (Lesson 3). The following table summarizes the relative advantages and disadvantages of the three methods.

Method	Search	Additions/Deletions	Other Comments
Physically ordered vector	$O(\log_2 n)$ with binary search	Excessive data movement	Data must be physically ordered
Linked list	Requires sequential search; $O(n)$	Only pointer manipulation required	
Binary search tree	Bounded between $O(\log_2 n)$ and $O(n)$, although advanced methods can guarantee the former	Only pointer manipulation required	May necessitate the overhead associated with recursive traversals

- The binary tree may be used to implement the general tree structure. The preorder and postorder traversals emerge as the most important for this particular application.

- Graphs and networks are abstract data structures that are more complex than trees because they reflect bidirectional rather than hierarchical relationships. Depth-first and breadth-first traversals and finding the shortest path are examples of algorithms that manipulate graphs and networks.

VOCABULARY REVIEW

Define the following terms:

ancestor	digraph	leaf node
binary search tree	directional graph	network
binary tree	general tree	parent node
breadth-first traversal	graph	postorder traversal
child node	heap	preorder traversal
concordance	height balancing	root node
depth-first traversal	inorder traversal	

LESSON 6 REVIEW QUESTIONS

FILL IN THE BLANK

Complete the following sentences by writing the correct word or words in the blanks provided.

1. The starting node of a tree is called the _____ node.

2. The nodes of a tree that are one level below a specific node are the _____ of that node.

3. Nodes at the same level are called _____.

4. A node with no children is called a(n) _____ node.

5. A tree whose nodes can have at most two children is a(n) _____ tree.

6. A tree where each root node is greater than all of the data in the node's left subtree and less than or equal to all of the data in the right subtree is said to have the _____ property.

7. A tree where each node is greater than or equal to the values of the nodes in the right and left subtrees is said to have the _____ property.

8. Traversing a tree by considering the contents of each node before examining its right and left subtrees is called a(n) _____ traversal.

9. To print the contents of a binary search tree in a sorted order, print the contents of the tree using a(n) _____ traversal.

10. A tree can be implemented using a(n) _____ implementation or a(n) _____ implementation.

11. In a(n) _____ tree, one node can have any number of children.

12. A graph is composed of _____, which are a set of fixed objects, and a set of _____, which can vary depending on the operations that have been performed on the graph.

WRITTEN QUESTIONS

Write a brief answer to the following questions.

13. Recreate a binary search tree that has had a preorder traversal result in the following output:

    24 11 6 2 14 29 26 37 50

14. Draw a binary search tree of integers such that the inorder traversal display will produce

    3 8 14 19 22 28 30 32 35 48 51 57 63

    whereas the preorder traversal display will produce

    48 14 8 3 30 22 19 28 35 32 57 51 63

15. Draw the binary search tree after 48 is deleted from the tree in Question 14 and show the postorder traversal display of the resulting tree.

16. Write a member function `sameShape` of the class `binaryTree` that determines whether the shapes of the two binary trees are the same. (The nodes do not have to contain the same values.)

17. Indicate whether the following tree is a binary tree with the ordering property. If it is not, indicate why not.

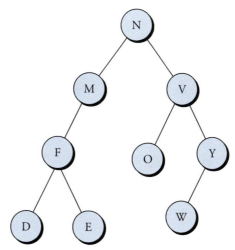

18. Perform a depth-first traversal of the following tree:

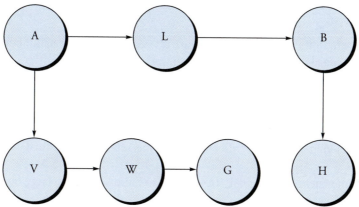

PROJECT 6-1

Discrepancies frequently arise between a user's projection of his or her computer needs and the unforeseen demands that materialize once the software system is put into use. A good systems analyst can hold those discrepancies to a minimum but not totally eliminate them. Elements of chance and probability are inherent in many algorithms.

An example of this final point is the order of arrivals for insertion into a binary search tree. We can guarantee that the search efficiency in a binary search tree will be between O(n) and O($\log_2 n$). We can specify best and worst cases. But what happens in between? When do we cross over from response times that are acceptable to those that are not? Real-life data are rarely the best case or worst case. Hence, the "in-between" question is often of vital importance. Yet it is also the one that a pure big-O analysis leaves relatively unanswered.

Design and implement a program that can serve as a start toward further exploration of the questions just posed. The program should initially read a list of unordered integers from a file, create a binary search tree containing those integers, and then print the binary search tree using indentation to reflect the levels at which various nodes occur in the tree.

a. Use the program in its initial form to acquire a feel for the relationship between the order of input data and the shape of the binary search tree that results.

b. Instead of reading data from a file, randomly generate the data being inserted in the tree.

c. After a tree has been generated, add the capability to delete nodes selectively from the tree. Reprint the tree after deleting a node as verification that it has retained the critical ordering property.

d. Use the random generation capability from part b to build some very large trees. Instead of printing out these trees after they have been generated, compute the length of the average path that must be followed to find a node in the tree. Do the results of your experiment indicate that, for random data, binary search trees yield a search efficiency that is O($\log_2 n$) or O(n)? Justify your conclusion with a written statement that is backed up by empirical data provided from your experimental runs.

e. Extend part d by computing the maximal path length in each randomly generated tree. What percentage of randomly generated trees have a maximal path length that is O(n)?

f. Depending on the availability of graphics functions in your version of C++, change the character-based tree printout into a more appealing graphic representation.

PROJECT 6-2

Use a binary tree to implement the sorted collection ADT defined in Section 2.2.

PROJECT 6-3

Modify the airline reservation system you developed for Wing-and-a-Prayer Airlines (Project 3-7,

Lesson 3) so that the alphabetized lists are maintained with binary trees instead of linked lists.

PROJECT 6-4

Write a program that sorts the records of the Fly-by-Night Credit Card Company file (Project 3-8, Lesson 3) in alphabetical order by the last name and then the first name of the customer. Use a binary tree and its inorder traversal to accomplish the sort.

PROJECT 6-5

Recall the roster maintenance system that you wrote for the Bay Area Brawlers (Project 3-9, Lesson 3). The system has been so successful that the league office would like to expand it to include all the players in the league. The goal is to maintain the list of players in alphabetical order, allowing for frequent insertions and deletions as players are cut, picked up, and traded among teams. In addition to storing each player's height, weight, age, and university affiliation, each record should be expanded to include team affiliation, years in league, and annual salary. Because the database for the entire league is many times larger than that for just one team, maintain this list as a binary search tree to increase its efficiency.

PROJECT 6-6

Write a program that reads an expression in its prefix form and builds the binary tree corresponding to that expression. Next, write functions to print the infix and postfix forms of the expression using inorder and postorder traversals of this tree. Finally, try to extend the program to evaluate the expression represented by the tree.

PROJECT 6-7

Here is a problem you will encounter if you write statistical analysis software. Given an arbitrarily long list of unordered numbers with an arbitrary number of different values appearing in it, determine and print the marginal distribution for this list of numbers. That is, count how many times each different value appears in the list and then print each value along with its count (frequency). The final output should be arranged from smallest to largest value. This problem can be solved in elegant fashion using trees. An example of such output as produced by COSAP (Conversationally Oriented Statistical Analysis Package) of Lawrence University follows:

```
Command? Marginals Judge
              Pine County Criminal Cases

MARGINAL FREQUENCIES
Variable Judge              JUDGE BEFORE WHOM CASE BROUGHT (2)
Value label                 Value          Absolute        Relative
                                           Frequency       Frequency

   ALLEN                    1              677             80.8%
   JONES                    2              88              10.5%
   KELLY                    3              26              3.1%
   MURCK                    5              47              5.6%
        838 Valid 0 Missing 838 Total Observations
```

Here the data file contained 838 occurrences of the values 1, 2, 3, and 5. Each value was a code number assigned to a particular judge.

PROJECT 6-8

Many compilers offer the services of a cross-referencing program to aid in debugging. Such a program will list in alphabetical order all the identifiers that appear in a program and the various lines of the program that reference them. Write such a cross-reference for your favorite language using a binary tree to maintain the list of identifiers that are encountered.

PROJECT 6-9

A relatively easy game to implement with a binary tree is to have the computer try to guess an animal about which the user is thinking by asking the user a series of questions that can be answered with yes or no. A node in the binary tree to play this game could be viewed as Yes/No pointers leading to

1. Another question.

2. The name of the animal.

3. Null.

If null, have your program surrender and then ask the user for a new question that uniquely defines the animal. Then add this new question and animal to the growing binary tree database.

PROJECT 6-10

Write a program that will differentiate expressions in the variable X. The input to this program will be a series of strings, each representing an infix expression to be differentiated. Each such expression is to be viewed as a stream of tokens. Valid tokens are integers, the variable X, the binary operators (+, -, *, /, ^), and parentheses. To make scanning for tokens easy, you may assume that each token is followed by exactly one space, with the exception of the final token, which is followed by the end-of-line character.

First your program will have to scan the infix expression, building up an appropriate binary tree representation of it. For this effort, you should be able to borrow significantly from the work you did in parsing expressions in Lessons 4 and 5. The major difference here is that the end result of this parse is a binary tree instead of a postfix string.

Once the binary expression tree is built, traverse it, building up another binary expression tree, which represents the derivative of the original expression. The following differentiation rules should be used in this process:

Suppose C is a constant, and S and T are expressions in X:

```
Diff(C) = 0
Diff(X) = 1
Diff(S + T) = Diff(S) + Diff(T)
Diff(S - T) = Diff(S) - Diff(T)
Diff(S * T) = S * Diff(T) + T * Diff(S)
Diff(S / T) = ((T * Diff(S)) - (S * Diff(T))) / (T ^ 2)
Diff(S ^ C) = (C * S ^ (C - 1)) * Diff(S)        { Remember the infamous chain
rule? }
```

Finally, once the binary expression tree for the derivative has been built, print the expression. Print it in completely parenthesized infix notation to avoid ambiguity.

Note that there are three distinct phases to this problem:

- Parsing of the original infix expression into a binary tree representation

- Building a binary tree representation of the derivative

- Printing the derivative in completely parenthesized infix notation

For an added challenge, simplify the expression for the derivative before printing it according to the following rules:

```
S + 0 = S
0 + S = S
S - 0 = S
S * 0 = 0
0 * S = 0
S * 1 = S
1 * S = S
0 / S = 0
S


0 = 1
S ^ 1 = S
S - S = 0
0 / S = 0
S / S = 1
S / 0 = DIVISION BY ZERO
0 / 0 = UNDEFINED
```

PROJECT 6-11

Wing-and-a-Prayer Airlines (Project 6-3) is expanding its record-keeping database. This database may now be pictured hierarchically as

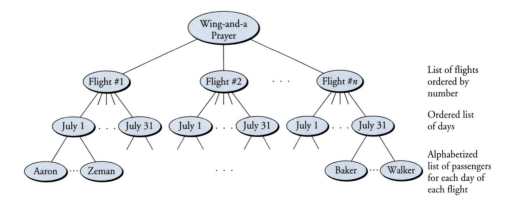

Write a program to maintain this database. Your program should process requests to add, delete, or list the following:

- Specified flight number

- Specified day of the month (for a given flight number)

- Specified passenger or all passengers (for a given flight number and day of the month)

PROJECT 6-12

Many statistical analysis packages support a "cross-tabulation" command designed to explore the relationship between statistical variables. A cross-tabulation between two variables produces a two-dimensional table containing a frequency count for each possible ordered pair of values of the two variables. These statistical packages typically allow this type of analysis to proceed even further than merely exploring two variables. For instance, in a legal system database, we might be interested in cross-tabulating a defendant's age with the judge before whom the defendant stood trial. We may then wish to cross-tabulate this result with the sex of the defendant. Sex in this case is called the control variable. We would output one such cross-tabulation table for each possible value of sex. Note that this type of output is not limited to just one control variable. There may be an arbitrary number of control variables and tables to cycle through. Moreover, the variables have an arbitrary number of observations and are all in arbitrary order. Yet for each variable, the list of possible values is always printed in smallest-to-largest order. The general tree structure that emerges for handling cross-tabulation is:

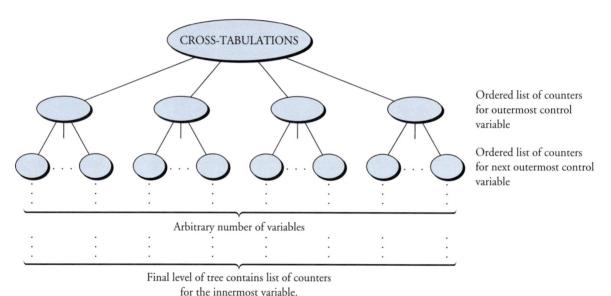

Ordered list of counters for outermost control variable

Ordered list of counters for next outermost control variable

Arbitrary number of variables

Final level of tree contains list of counters for the innermost variable.

Write a program to handle the task of producing statistical cross-tabulations.

PROJECT 6-13

Write a program to print the nodes of a tree level by level—that is, all level 0 nodes, followed by all level 1 nodes, followed by all level 2 nodes, and so on. (*Hint:* This program will afford an excellent opportunity to practice using a queue in addition to a tree.)

PROJECT 6-14

Operating systems often use general trees as the data structure on which their file directory system is based. Leaf nodes in such a system represent actual files or empty directories. Interior nodes represent nonempty directories. For instance, consider the following situation:

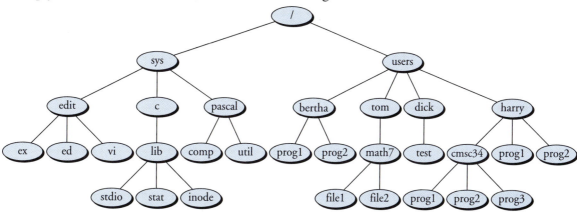

A directory entry is specified by its path name. A path name consists of tree node names separated by slashes. Such a path name is absolute if it starts at the root—that is, if it starts with a slash (/). It is relative to the current directory if it does not start with a slash.

In this assignment, you are to write a command processor that will allow a user to manipulate files within such a directory structure. The commands accepted by your processor will be in the form of numbers associated with particular operations and path names, as shown in the following table:

Number	Operation	Path Name
1	Change directory	Absolute path name, relative path name, or ". ." for parent
2	Make a new directory	Absolute or relative path name
3	Make a new file	Absolute or relative path name
4	Remove a file	Absolute or relative path name
5	Remove a directory, but only if it is empty	Absolute or relative path name
6	Remove a directory and, recursively, everything below it	Absolute or relative path name
7	Print directory entries in alphabetical order	Absolute or relative path name
8	Recursively print directory entries in alphabetical order	Absolute or relative path name
9	Print current directory name	Not applicable
10	Quit processing commands	Not applicable

As even intelligent tree-walking users can easily get lost, your command processor should be prepared to trap errors of the following variety:

- Specifying a nonexistent path name

- Specifying a path name that is a file when it should be a directory

- Specifying a path name that is a directory when it should be a file

Upon detecting such an error, your command processor should print an appropriate error message and then return to accept the next user command.

PROJECT 6-15

Trees have significant applications in the area of artificial intelligence and game playing. Consider, for instance, the game of FIFTEEN. In this game, two players take turns selecting digits between 1 and 9 with the goal of selecting a combination of digits that add up to 15. Once a digit is chosen, it may not be chosen again by either player. Rather than immediately considering a tree for the game of FIFTEEN, let us first consider a tree for the simpler game of SEVEN with digits chosen in the range 1 to 6. A tree that partially represents the states that may be reached in this game is:

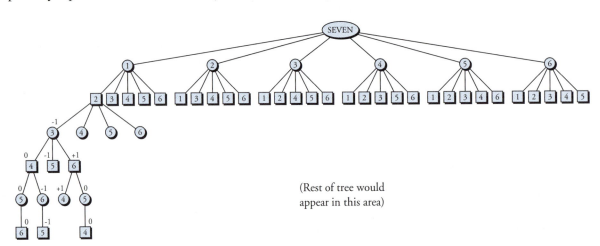

(Rest of tree would appear in this area)

In this tree, circular nodes represent the states that may be reached by the player who moves first (the computer), and square nodes represent the states that may be reached by the player who moves second (a human opponent). The +1, 0, or -1 attached to each node represents a weighting factor designed to help the computer choose the most advantageous move at any given stage of the game. The rules used to compute these weighting factors follow:

- If the node is a leaf node, its weight is determined by some static weighting function. In this case, the static weighting function used was to assign +1 to a leaf node representing a computer win, 0 to a leaf node representing a draw, and -1 to a leaf node representing a human win.

- If the node is one in which the computer will move next (that is, a state occupied by the human opponent), then the weighting factor of the node is the maximum of the weighting factors of its children.

- If the node is one in which the human opponent will move next, then the weighting factor of the node is the minimum of the weighting factors of its children.

In its turn, the computer should always choose to move to the node having the maximum possible weighting factor. The rationale behind this technique, called the minimax technique, is that the computer will move in such a way as to always maximize its chances of winning. The human opponent, if playing intelligently, will always move to a node having a minimum weighting factor. Thus, in the partial game shown, the computer would choose 4 if the human had been naive enough to select the 6 node with the weighting factor of +1.

Write a program to build a weighted game tree for the game of FIFTEEN and then have the computer play against a human opponent. Note that this game is really the game of tic-tac-toe if one considers the following matrix:

4 9 2
3 5 7
8 1 6

All winning tic-tac-toe paths add up to 15. Give some consideration as to the time and efficiency of your algorithm. Many games simply cannot be completely represented via a general tree because of space limitations. Consequently, a partial game tree is built in which the leaf nodes may not be the final moves made in the game. In such situations, the static weighting function applied to the leaf nodes in the game tree requires a bit more insight to develop.

PROJECT 6-16

Consider a priority queue (see Section 4.3) in which each item is assigned a different priority. Discuss how a binary tree with the heap property could be used to maintain such a priority queue. Write functions for a heap implementation of the basic priority queue operations:

```
create
empty()
enqueue(item)
dequeue()
```

Categorize the run-time efficiency of the dequeue and enqueue operations in big-O terms. Is a linear implementation or a linked implementation of the binary tree more advantageous for this application? Explain why.

Finally, use your priority queue implementation to solve a problem such as Project 4-12 in Lesson 4 or to simulate the servicing of priority-rated jobs on a time-sharing computing system.

PROJECT 6-17

Implement Dijkstra's shortest path algorithm using a suitable two-key table representation scheme to store the network data. Test your program with the transportation network pictured in Figure 6-27. Note that this same problem appeared in Project 5-13 (Lesson 5). There you used a different algorithm for solving it. In a written statement, compare the efficiencies of the two algorithms.

PROJECT 6-18

A breadth-first traversal of a graph was discussed in Section 6.6. Implement this algorithm as a C++ function. (*Hint:* Use a queue.)

463

ACTIVITY 6-1

In the binary tree class presented in this lesson, our traversal operations have allowed the client program to pass a function as an actual parameter to the traversal. That function dictated what was to be done at each node during the traversal. This approach has limitations. In the Case Study, we demonstrated one way around these limitations—derive a new class from the generic `BinaryTree` class and then implement specialized traversals in this subclass. Another approach makes the `BinaryTree` class even more "powerful" and often allows a client program to use the `BinaryTree` class without having to subclass from it. This approach is to provide operations that allow the client program to write a loop that iterates through all tree nodes in the order dictated by a particular traversal. Notice the difference in perspective here: the client program has iterative logic to walk through the tree nodes one at a time instead of calling a traversal algorithm that uses recursion to process all the nodes for the client program. To illustrate how a client program would proceed through tree nodes in an inorder fashion using such iterator operations, suppose we add the following two operations to our `BinaryTree` class:

```
template <class E> class BinaryTree
  {

public:

// Class constructors

BinaryTree();
BinaryTree(const BinaryTree<E> &bt);

…

// Other operations appear as before

// Return pointer to first datum in the tree that would be
// processed by an inorder traversal
E * inorderBegin();

// Return pointer to next datum in the tree that would be
// processed by an inorder traversal.  If a null pointer
// is returned, there are no additional data to be processed
// via an inorder traversal.
E * inorderNext();

protected:

// Implementation-dependent declarations appear here
};
```

Given these new `inorderBegin` and `inorderNext` functions, a client iterates through an inorder traversal of a binary tree containing integers as its data by using the following loop:

```
int * k;

for (k = tree.inorderBegin(); k != 0; k = tree.inorderNext())
   cout << *k << " ";
```

Note that this approach is very similar to the way we allowed a client program to iterate through a linked list. For this program, add such iterator operations to the `BinaryTree` class for each of the three traversals we studied. Test them with an appropriate driver program. (*Hint:* You will have to add a new protected node pointer for each traversal. That pointer will point at the node currently being accessed in the particular traversal. You will also find it convenient to add a "parent" pointer to each node so that you can ascend from a node to its parent as well as descend to its children.)

ACTIVITY 6-2

Explore some additional graph and network algorithms in one of the advanced texts cited earlier in this lesson, such as Horowitz and Sahni, *Data Structures in C++* (New York: Computer Science Press, 1990) or Pothering and Naps, *Introduction to Data Structures and Algorithm Analysis with C++* (St. Paul, Minnesota: West Publishing, 1995). Then prepare a written or oral report in which you explain the logic behind one of the algorithms you explore.

UNIT 3 REVIEW QUESTIONS

TRUE/FALSE

Circle T if the statement is true or F if the statement is false.

T F   1. It is possible to rewrite any recursive function as a function that uses a loop.

T F   2. A recursive function that does not have a well-defined termination state will run forever.

T F   3. In tail recursion, there is more work to be done after each recursive call.

T F   4. Some compilers translate tail-recursive functions to object code that uses simple iteration.

T F   5. Recursive functions generally have the same running time and memory usage as the corresponding loops.

T F   6. Each node in a tree can have at most one parent node.

T F   7. A tree is a special case of a graph.

T F   8. In a binary search tree, the datum in a given node is less than the datum in its left child.

T F   9. In a heap, the datum in a given node is less than the data in either of its children.

T F 10. There is only one possible implementation of a tree, which uses a linked structure.

FILL IN THE BLANK

Complete the following sentences by writing the correct word or words in the blanks provided.

1. A correctly written recursive function requires at least two parts, a(n) _____ and a(n) _____.

2. The hidden data structure that the computer uses to support recursion is called a(n) _____.

3. A(n) _____ contains memory for the parameters and return value of each recursive call.

4. The type of recursion in which there is no more work to be done after a recursive call is called _____ recursion.

5. Some recursive functions can be translated to functions that use a loop and a(n) _____.

6. Nodes in a tree that have no children are called _____ nodes.

7. A(n) _____ tree is a tree whose nodes have at most two children.

8. Two basic components of graphs are _____ and _____.

9. A(n) _____ traversal visits all the nodes in one level of a graph before visiting nodes at the next level.

10. A(n) _____ is a graph whose edges have weights associated with them.

WRITTEN QUESTIONS

Write a brief answer to the following questions.

1. Describe what is needed in the design of a recursive function.

2. Give a definition and list two applications of an expression tree.

3. Describe the heap property and how it supports a heap sort.

4. Describe the costs and benefits of using a binary search tree.

5. Explain the difference between a depth-first search and a breadth-first search.

UNIT 3 PROJECTS

PROJECT 3-1

Write a recursive function to raise a number to a given exponent. The function assumes that both parameters are positive integers. The implementation should take advantage of the fact that when the exponent is even, the result is the square of the number raised to that exponent divided by 2.

PROJECT 3-2

Here is the code for member functions that accomplish an inorder traversal of a binary tree:

```
void BinaryTree<E>::inorderTraverse(void (* process) (E &item))

{
    inorderAux(tree, process);
}

template <class E>
void BinaryTree<E>::inorderAux(BinaryTree<E>::node * tree,
                                   void (* process) (E &item))
{
    if (tree != 0)
    {
        inorderAux(tree->left, process);
        process(tree->data);
        inorderAux(tree->right, process);
    }
}
```

Write member functions that build and return a linked list of the data items in a binary tree by making an inorder traversal of the tree.

CRITICAL THINKING

ACTIVITY 3-1

A level order traversal of a binary tree visits nodes from left to right on each level before descending to the next level. Describe an algorithm for accomplishing a level order traversal. (*Hint*: The algorithm uses two queues.)

ADVANCED SORT AND SEARCH ALGORITHMS

UNIT 4

lesson 7
15 hrs.

More Powerful Sorting Methods

lesson 8
15 hrs.

More Powerful Search Methods

unit 4 review
2 hrs.

Unit 4 Estimated Time: 32 hours

MORE POWERFUL SORTING METHODS

OBJECTIVES

Upon completion of this lesson, you will be able to:

- Understand the logic behind advanced sorting algorithms.
- Develop C++ functions to represent advanced sorting algorithms.
- Analyze the efficiency of advanced sorting algorithms.

 Estimated Time: 15 hours

Vocabulary

diminishing increment sort	merge sort	relatively prime
external sort	partition	shell sort
heap sort	pivot	
internal sort	quick sort	

Introduction

In Lesson 1, we analyzed three simple sorting algorithms: bubble sort, insertion sort, and selection sort. We also discussed a technique, called a pointer sort, that can be combined with any of these three algorithms to minimize data movement when large records are being sorted by a particular key field. The essence of the pointer sort is to maintain a vector of pointers that dictates the logical order of the records in a vector of records. When the sorting algorithm dictates a swap, only the pointers must be interchanged, not the actual records.

With all three of our sorting algorithms, however, we ran into a barrier. This barrier was a run-time efficiency of $O(n^2)$ comparisons. Because the pointer sort technique reduces data movement but not the number of comparisons, this barrier exists whether or not we incorporate the pointer sort idea into the sorting algorithm. Our goal in this lesson is to study sorting algorithms that break the $O(n^2)$ comparisons barrier. These new algorithms will use what we have learned since Lesson 1. In particular, both recursion and a conceptual understanding of trees are essential prerequisites to analyzing these more powerful methods.

The general setup for the sort algorithms of this lesson is the same as the one we used in Lesson 1.

We wish to write a sort function that meets the following specifications:

```
// Function: sort
// Sorts a list of elements into ascending order
//
// Inputs: a list of elements in arbitrary order and its current length
// Output: the list of elements arranged in ascending order

void sort(apvector<int> &list);
```

Although our algorithms for this lesson are presented in the context of sorting vectors in ascending order, they apply more generally to any list whose elements can be directly accessed (for example, vectors or one-key tables) and they can be easily modified to sort in descending order. Moreover, some of the methods we discuss (quick sort and merge sort) do not require direct access into the list. Hence, with relatively minor modifications, these algorithms can be applied to lists that are just sequentially accessible, such as sequential files and linked lists.

7.1 The Shell Sort Algorithm

The *shell sort,* named after its inventor, D. L. Shell, incorporates the logic of the insertion sort to a certain extent. However, instead of sorting the entire vector at once, it first divides the vector into smaller noncontiguous segments, then separately sorts these segments using the insertion sort.

The advantages of this approach are twofold. First, where a comparison dictates a swap of two data items in a segment, this swap within a noncontiguous segment of the vector moves an item a greater distance within the overall vector than the swap of adjacent vector entries in the usual insertion sort. As a consequence, one swap is more likely to place an element closer to its final location in the vector when using a shell sort than when using the simple insertion sort. For instance, a large-valued entry that appears near the front of the vector will more quickly move to the end of the vector, because each swap moves it a greater distance in the vector.

The second advantage of dividing the vector into segments is tied to the first; that is, because early passes tend to move elements closer to their final destination than do early passes in a straight insertion sort, the vector becomes partially sorted quite rapidly. The fact that the vector is likely to become partially sorted relatively early allows the embedded insertion sort logic to make more frequent use of its check for an early exit from its inner loop. (Recall that this check makes the insertion sort particularly efficient for vectors that are partially sorted.) An example will help clarify this shell sort rationale.

Example 7-1

Suppose we have a vector containing the following integers:
80 93 60 12 42 30 68 85 10
We first divide this vector into three segments of three elements each.

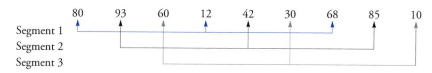

80	12	68	→	Segment 1
93	42	85	→	Segment 2
60	30	10	→	Segment 3

Next, sort each of the segments:

```
12   68   80
42   85   93
10   30   60
```

The original vector, partially sorted, now appears as

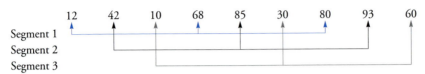

We divide this partially sorted vector as

```
12   10   85   80   60   →   Segment 1
42   68   30   93        →   Segment 2
```

These segments are then sorted and the vector takes the form

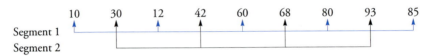

Finally, this vector is sorted as one segment; 12 and 30, and 93 and 85, are swapped to give us the sorted vector

10 12 30 42 60 68 80 85 93

The key to the shell sort algorithm is that the whole vector is first fragmented into K segments for some number K, where K is preferably a prime number. These K segments are given by

a[0], a[K], a[2 * K], ...

a[1], a[K + 1], a[2 * K + 1], ...

.

.

.

a[K - 1], a[2 * K - 1], a[3 * K - 1], ...

Because each segment is sorted, the whole vector is partially sorted after the first pass. For the next pass, the value of K is reduced, which increases the size of each segment, thereby reducing the number of segments. Preferably, the next value of K is also chosen so that it is prime relative to its previous value, or *relatively prime*. (Two integers are said to be relatively prime to each other if they have no common factor greater than 1.) This process is repeated until K = 1, at which point the vector is sorted. The insertion sort is applied to each segment, so each successive segment is partially sorted. Consequently, the later applications of the insertion sort become very efficient, dramatically increasing the overall efficiency of the shell sort.

To emphasize the fashion in which the shell sort algorithm relies on the logic of insertion sort, we present a `segmentedInsertionSort` function, which arranges each of k segments in an n-element vector into ascending order. Compare this function with the function for an insertion sort that was given in Lesson 1. You will see that `segmentedInsertion Sort` moves an item from position j to position j + k. When k = 1, this algorithm exactly matches the original insertion sort algorithm.

```
void segmentedInsertionSort(apvector<int> &list, int k)
{
   int j;
   int itemToInsert;
   bool stillLooking;

   for (int i = k; i < list.length(); ++i)
   {
      itemToInsert = list[i];
      j = i - k;
      stillLooking = true;
      while ((j >= 0) && itemToInsert < list[j])
      {
         list[j + k] = list[j];
         j = j - k;
      }
      list[j + k] = itemToInsert;
   }
}
```

| 80 | 93 | 60 | 12 | 42 | 30 |

With *n* = 6 and *k* = 3, the array is divided into three segments of two elements each.

80 12 → Segment 1
93 42 → Segment 2
60 30 → Segment 3

Sort each of the segments:
12 80
42 93
30 60

Given the `segmentedInsertionSort` function, we now merely call on it with values of k that become successively smaller. Eventually, `segmentedInsertionSort` must be called with K = 1 to guarantee that the vector, viewed as one segment, is completely sorted.

The function `shellSort` that follows illustrates these successive calls to `segmentedInsertionSort` for values of k that are repeatedly halved.

```
void shellSort(apvector<int> &list)
{
   int k = list.length() / 2;

   while (k > 0)
   {
      segmentedInsertionSort(list, k);
      k = k / 2;
   }
}
```

Efficiency of the Shell Sort

The shell sort is also called the *diminishing increment sort* because the value of k (the number of segments) continually decreases. The method becomes even more efficient if the successive values of k are kept relatively prime to each other, thereby helping to ensure that a pair of values previously compared to each other are not compared again. D. E. Knuth has mathematically estimated that, with relatively prime values of k, the shell sort will execute in an average time proportional to $O[n(\log_2 n)^2]$ (see Donald E. Knuth, Searching and Sorting, in The Art of Computer Programming, Volume 3 [Menlo Park, California: Addison-Wesley, 1973]). However, the sort will work for any values of k, as long as the last value of k is 1. For instance, in the version of shellSort given earlier, the successive values of k will not often be relatively prime. When the values of k are not relatively prime, then the efficiency of the shell sort is of the order $O(n^r)$, where $1 < r < 2$. The particular value of r makes the sort less efficient than $O[n(\log_2 n)^2]$ for large values of n, but better than the $O(n^2)$ methods of Lesson 1. The shell sort is most efficient with vectors that are nearly sorted. In fact, the first chosen value of k is large to ensure that the whole vector is fragmented into small individual vectors, for which the insertion sort is highly effective. Each subsequent sort causes the entire vector to be more nearly sorted, so that the efficiency of the insertion sort as applied to larger partially sorted vectors is increased. Trace through a few examples to convince yourself that the partially ordered status of the vector for one value of k is not affected by subsequent partial sorts for a different value of k.

The value of k with which the shell sort should start is not known, but Knuth suggests a sequence of values such as 1, 3, 7, 15, . . . , for reverse values of k; that is, the (j + 1)st value is two times the jth value plus 1. Knuth suggests other possible values of k, but generally the initial guess at the first value of k is all that you need. The initial guess will depend on the size of the vector and, to some extent, the type of data being sorted.

EXERCISES 7.1

1. Consider the shellSort function given in this section. Suppose we were to trace the contents of the vector being sorted after each call to the function segmentedInsertionSort. What would we see as output if we called shellSort with the following vector?

   60 12 90 30 64 8 6

2. Repeat Exercise 1 for a six-element vector that initially contains

   1 8 2 7 3 6

3. Where did the shell sort get its name?

4. Why is the shell sort most efficient when the original data are in almost sorted order?

5. What advantage do the relatively prime values of the increments have over other values in a shell sort? Formulate your answer in a precise written statement that explains why relatively prime values are better.

6. What property must the sequence of diminishing increments in the shell sort have to ensure that the method will work?

7. Provide examples of best case and worst case data sets for the shell sort algorithm presented in this section. Justify your data sets by explaining why they generate best case and worst case performance.

8. In Lesson 1, `pointerSort` used an index of pointers to sort data logically without rearranging them. Identify the sort algorithm that was behind the C++ `pointerSort` function. Adapt the pointer sort function to the shell sort algorithm.

9. The version of a shell sort presented in this section uses the following sequence of diminishing increments:

$n/2, n/4, \ldots , 8, 4, 2, 1$

Rewrite the shell sort so that the following sequence of diminishing increments is used:

$k, \ldots , 121, 40, 13, 4, 1$

Here k represents the largest member of this sequence, which is $<=n$ where n is the logical size of the vector being sorted.

7.2 The Quick Sort Algorithm

Even though the shell sort provides a significant advantage in run time over its $O(n^2)$ predecessors, its average efficiency of $O[n(\log_2 n)^2]$ may still not be good enough for large vectors. The next group of methods, including the ***quick sort***, has an average execution time of $O(n \log_2 n)$, which is the best that can be achieved. Compared to $O[n(\log_2 n)^2]$ or $O(n^r)$ for $1 < r < 2$, an $O(n \log_2 n)$ sort is often a good choice as the main vehicle for large sorting jobs.

The essence of the quick sort algorithm, which was originally devised in 1961 by C. A. R. Hoare, is to rely on a subordinate algorithm to partition the vector. The process of partitioning involves moving a data item, called the ***pivot,*** in the correct direction just far enough for it to reach its final place in the vector. The partitioning process, therefore, reduces unnecessary interchanges and potentially moves the pivot a great distance in the vector without forcing it to be swapped into intermediate locations. Once the pivot item is chosen, moves are made so that data items to the left of the pivot are less than (or equal to) it, whereas those to the right are greater (or equal). The pivot item is thus in its correct position. The quick sort algorithm then recursively applies the partitioning process to the two parts of the vector on either side of the pivot until the entire vector is sorted.

In the next example, we illustrate the mechanics of this partitioning logic by applying it to a vector of numbers.

Example 7-2

Suppose the vector contains integers initially arranged as follows:

15 20 5 8 95 12 80 17 9 55

Table 7-1 shows a partitioning pass applied to this vector. The following steps are involved:

1. Remove the first data item, 15, for use as the pivot, mark its position, and scan the vector from right to left, comparing data item values with 15. When you find the first smaller value, remove it from its current position and put it in position a[0]. (This is shown in line 2.)

2. Scan line 2 from left to right, beginning with position a[1], comparing data item values with 15. When you find the first value greater than 15, extract it and store it in the position marked by parentheses in line 2. (This is shown in line 3.)

3. Begin the right-to-left scan of line 3 with position a[7], looking for a value smaller than 15. When you find it, extract it and store it in the position marked by the parentheses in line 3. (This is shown in line 4.)

4. Begin scanning line 4 from left to right at position a[2]. Find a value greater than 15, remove it, mark its position, and store it inside the parentheses in line 4. (This is shown in line 5.)

5. Now, when you attempt to scan line 5 from right to left beginning at position a[4], you are immediately at a parenthesized position determined by the previous left-to-right scan. This is the location in which to put the pivot data item, 15. (This is shown in line 6.) At this stage, 15 is in its correct place relative to the final sorted vector.

Notice that all values to the left of 15 are less than 15, and all values to the right of 15 are greater than 15. The method will still work if two values are the same. The process can now be applied recursively to the two segments of the vector on the left and right of 15. Notice that these recursive calls eventually sort the entire vector. The result of any one call to function quickSort is merely to partition a segment of the vector so that the pivotal item is positioned with everything to its left being less than or equal to it and everything to its right being greater than or equal.

TABLE 7-1
Each call to quickSort partitions a vector segment

Line Number	a[0]	a[1]	a[2]	a[3]	a[4]	a[5]	a[6]	a[7]	a[8]	a[9]
										←
1	15*	20	5	8	95	12	80	17	9	55
			→							
2	9	20	5	8	95	12	80	17	( )	55
								←		
3	9	( )	5	8	95	12	80	17	20	55
			→							
4	9	12	5	8	95	( )	80	17	20	55
					←					
5	9	12	5	8	( )	95	80	17	20	55
6	9	12	5	8	15	95	80	17	20	55

*Indicates the pivot value (here 15).

The function `partition` that follows achieves one partitioning pass in the overall `quickSort` algorithm as described in Example 7-2. The indices `lo` and `hi` represent the pointers that move from the left and right, respectively, until they meet at the appropriate location for the pivot. The pivotal value is initially chosen to be `a[lo]`. Later, we will discuss the implications of choosing a different pivotal value. Note that it is crucial for `partition` to return in `pivotPoint` the position where the pivotal value was finally inserted. This information will allow the `quickSort` function that calls on `partition` to determine whether a recursive termination condition has been reached.

```
// Partition vector between indices lo and hi.
// That is, using list[lo] as the pivotal value, arrange
// entries between lo and hi indices so that all
// values to left of the pivot are less than or equal
// to it and all values to right of the pivot are
// greater than or equal to it.
//
// Input: vector and lo and hi
// Output: Partitioned vector, and pivotPoint
//         containing final location of pivot.

void partition(apvector<int> &list, int lo,
               int hi, int &pivotPoint)
{
   int pivot = list[lo];

   while (lo < hi)
   {
      while ((pivot < list[hi]) && (lo < hi))
         --hi;
      if (hi != lo)
      {
         list[lo] = list[hi];
         ++lo;
      }

      while ((pivot > list[lo]) && (lo < hi))
         ++lo;
      if (hi != lo)
      {
         list[hi] = list[lo];
         --hi;
      }
   }
```

Right-to-left scan until smaller value found here

pivot = 12

| 12 | 8 | 7 | 6 | 14 | 20 | 30 | 5 | 19 | 13 | 15 | hi = 7 |
| 0 | 1 | 2 | 3 | 4 | 5 | 6 | 7 | 8 | 9 | 10 | |

Left-to-right scan until larger value found here

pivot = 12

| 5 | 8 | 7 | 6 | 14 | 20 | 30 | 5 | 19 | 13 | 15 | lo = 4 |
| 0 | 1 | 2 | 3 | 4 | 5 | 6 | 7 | 8 | 9 | 10 | |

```
        list[hi] = pivot;
        pivotPoint = hi;
    }
```

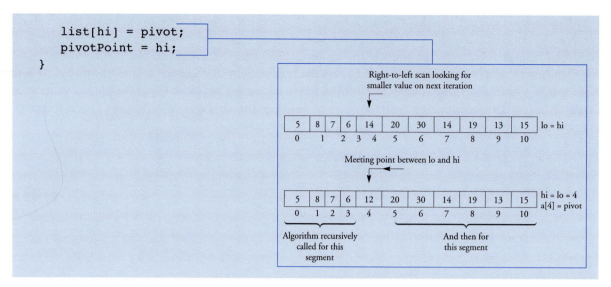

Given the previous `partition` function, `quickSort` itself must call `partition` and then use the returned value of `pivotPoint` to decide whether recursive calls are necessary to perform more refined partitioning of the segments to the left and right of `pivotPoint`. The recursive logic for this decision is given in the following function, `quickSort`:

```
void quickSort(apvector<int> &list, int lower, int upper)
{
    int pivotPoint;

    partition(list, lower, upper, pivotPoint);
    if (lower < pivotPoint)
        quickSort(list, lower, pivotPoint - 1);
    if (upper > pivotPoint)
        quickSort(list, pivotPoint + 1, upper);
}
```

For instance, after the first call to `quickSort` for a partitioning pass on the data in Table 7-1, we recursively call on `quickSort` with `lower = 1` and `upper = 4`. This action triggers deeper-level recursive calls from which we ultimately return, knowing that the segment of the vector between indices 1 and 5 is now sorted. This return is followed by a recursive call to `quickSort` with `lower = 6` and `upper = 10`. Figure 7-1 gives the run-time trace diagram of recursive calls to `quickSort` for the data of Table 7-1. You should verify this call–return pattern by walking through the preceding function.

FIGURE 7-1

Run-time trace diagram of (recursive) calls to `quickSort` data in Table 7-1

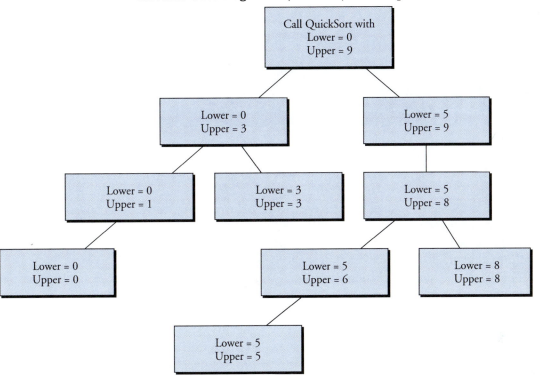

Efficiency of the Quick Sort

As mentioned earlier, the average run-time efficiency of the quick sort is $O(n \log_2 n)$, which is the best that has been achieved for a large vector of size n. In the best case, it is quite easy to provide a rationale for this $O(n \log_2 n)$ value. This best case occurs when each vector segment recursively passed to `quickSort` is partitioned at its midpoint; that is, the appropriate location for each pivotal value in the series of recursive calls is the midpoint of the segment being partitioned. In this case, we find that:

One call to `quickSort` (the first) is made with a segment of size *n*.
Two calls to `quickSort` are made with segments of size *n*/2.
Four calls to `quickSort` are made with segments of size *n*/4.
Eight calls to `quickSort` are made with segments of size *n*/8.
.
.
.
n calls to `quickSort` are made with segments of size 1.

Overall $\log_2 n$ levels

Because each call with a segment of size m requires $O(m)$ comparisons, it is clear that k calls with segments of size n/k will require $O(n)$ comparisons. Hence, the total number of comparisons resulting from the preceding sequence of calls will be $O(n \log_2 n)$.

If segments are partitioned away from the midpoint, the efficiency of the quick sort begins to deteriorate. In the worst case situation, when the vector is already sorted, the efficiency of the quick sort may drop to $O(n^2)$ due to the continuous right-to-left scan all the way to the last left boundary. In the exercises at the end of the section, you will explore how the worst case situation is affected by your choice of the pivotal element.

You may wonder how large a stack is needed to sort a vector of size n. (Remember that this stack is implicitly created even when you use recursion.) In situations where the depth of the run-time trace diagram is $O(n \log_2 n)$, the maximum stack size will also be $O(n \log_2 n)$. However, in the worst case, it will be $O(n)$.

PROGRAMMING SKILLS: Privacy Issues Kill Microsoft's Registration System

What are the social responsibilities that go along with state-of-the-art capabilities to sort and search through gigabytes of information? Advances in computers are making it easier to gather and piece together minutely detailed portraits of households, and marketers are gobbling this information up to help choose targets for direct-mail and telephone marketing campaigns. A recent incident involving Microsoft illustrates the importance of having a social conscience in computing.

In early 1999, John Smith, a programmer and president of PharLap Software of Cambridge, Massachusetts, discovered that the Microsoft Office suite of business software was creating unique numbers identifying a user's personal computer and embedding these numbers in spreadsheet and word processing documents. Smith notified Microsoft that he believed this capability created a potential privacy threat. Why? This same number, related to the Ethernet adapter address of the computer, was apparently being sent to Microsoft when a user went through the online registration process for Microsoft Office. According to Smith, quoted in the March 7 Milwaukee Journal, "Microsoft never asked me if it was OK to send them this number, and they never said it was being sent. They are apparently build-

ing a database that relates Ethernet adapter addresses to personal information."

In the same article, Jason Catlett, president of a consumer privacy organization, maintained that "Microsoft is tattooing a number into each (Office) file. Think of the implications. If some whistle-blower sends a file, it can be traced back to the person himself. It's an extremely dangerous feature. Why did they do it?"

To its credit, Microsoft demonstrated belated sensitivity to the ethical issues that had been raised by the incident. Robert Bennett, Microsoft's product manager for Windows, said, "We're definitely sensitive to any privacy concerns. The software was not supposed to send this information unless the user checked a specific option." Bennett went on to say that Microsoft would alter the way that the registration software worked and also that information already collected as a result of the process would be expunged from the company's database.

Although Microsoft may have exercised poor judgment in the original policy, its decision to pull the plug after making a sizable investment in the enterprise illustrates a commendable sense of social responsibility. Such ethical dilemmas are likely to play an increasing role in the careers of many computing professionals.

EXERCISES ⟩ 7.2

1. Consider the `quickSort` function given in this section. Suppose we inserted the following tracer output at the beginning of this function:

```
cout << lower <<   << upper << endl;
for (k = lower; k <= upper; ++k)
    cout << a[k];
cout << endl;
```

   What would we see as output from these tracers if we called `quickSort` with the key vector initially containing the following seven entries?

   60 12 90 30 64 8 6

2. Repeat Exercise 1 for a six-element vector that initially contains

   1 8 2 7 3 6

3. When is a bubble sort better than a quick sort? Explain your answer in a written statement.

4. Under what circumstances would you not use a quick sort? Explain your answer in a written statement.

5. How does the choice of the pivotal value affect the efficiency of the quick sort algorithm? Suppose the middle value or the last value in a segment to be partitioned was chosen as the pivotal value. How would this choice alter the nature of the best case and worst case data sets? Give examples to illustrate your answer.

6. Develop run-time trace diagrams of function calls to `quickSort` for a variety of test data sets (analogous to what was done in Figure 7-1). Use these diagrams to analyze the efficiency of `quickSort`. What types of data sets yield $O(n\log_2 n)$ efficiency? What types yield $O(n^2)$ efficiency?

7. In Lesson 1, `pointerSort` used an index of pointers to sort data logically without rearranging the data. Adapt the pointer sort function to the quick sort algorithm.

8. Implement `quickSort` in a nonrecursive fashion by using a stack.

9. Implement a variation on the quick sort algorithm presented in this section, in which the pivot is chosen to be the median of the following three values:

   ```
   a[lo], a[(lo + hi) / 2], a[hi]
   ```

   In a carefully written statement, explain why this variation should be more efficient than the version that chooses the pivot to be `a[lo]`.

7.3 The Heap Sort Algorithm

The *heap sort* is a sorting algorithm that is roughly equivalent to the quick sort; its average efficiency is $O(n \log_2 n)$ for a vector of size n. The method, originally described by R. W. Floyd, has two phases. In the first phase, the vector containing the n data items is viewed as equivalent to a full binary tree. That is, the vector to be sorted is viewed as the linear representation of a full binary tree containing n items (see Lesson 6). (If you want to read Floyd's description of this method, see "Algorithm 245: Tree Sort 3," Communications of the ACM, vol. 7, 1964, page 701.) As an example, suppose we want to sort the following vector:

11 1 5 7 6 12 17 8 4 10 2

The tree now appears as shown in Figure 7-2. The goal of phase 1 is to sort the data elements along each path from leaf node level to the root node. If we wish to sort in ascending order, then the numbers along any path from leaf node to root should be in increasing order. Eventually, after phase 1, the tree will be a heap (as described in Lesson 6). That is, the data item at each node will be greater than or equal to both of its children. To achieve this goal, we take the following steps:

1. Process the node that is the parent of the rightmost node on the lowest level as follows: If its value is less than the value of its largest child, swap these values; otherwise, do nothing.

2. Move left on the same level. Compare the value of the parent node with the values of the children. If the parent is smaller than the largest child, swap them.

3. When the left end of this level is reached, move up a level and, beginning with the rightmost parent node, repeat step 2. Continue swapping the original parent with the larger of its children until it is larger than its children. In effect, the original parent is being walked down the tree in a fashion that ensures all numbers will be in increasing order along the path.

4. Repeat step 3 until the root node has been processed.

FIGURE 7-2
Full binary tree corresponding to vector

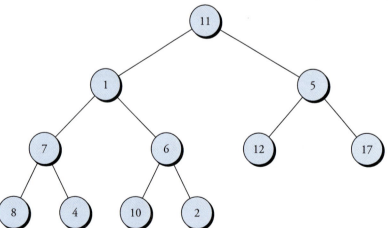

Figure 7-3 shows these steps applied to Figure 7-2.

Phase 2 of the heap sort finds the node with the largest value in the tree and cuts it from the tree. This step is then repeated to find the second largest value, which is also removed from the tree. The process continues until only two nodes remain in the tree; they are then exchanged if necessary. The precise steps for phase 2 are as follows:

1. Swap the root node with the bottom rightmost child and sever this new bottom rightmost child from the tree. This is the largest value.

2. Continue swapping the new root value with the larger of its children until it is not exceeded by either child. In effect, this new root value is being walked down a path in the tree to ensure that all paths retain values arranged in ascending order from leaf node to root node. That is, the tree is being restored to a heap.

3. Repeat steps 1 and 2 until only one element is left.

FIGURE 7-3

Phase 1 of heap sort applied to the binary tree in Figure 7-2

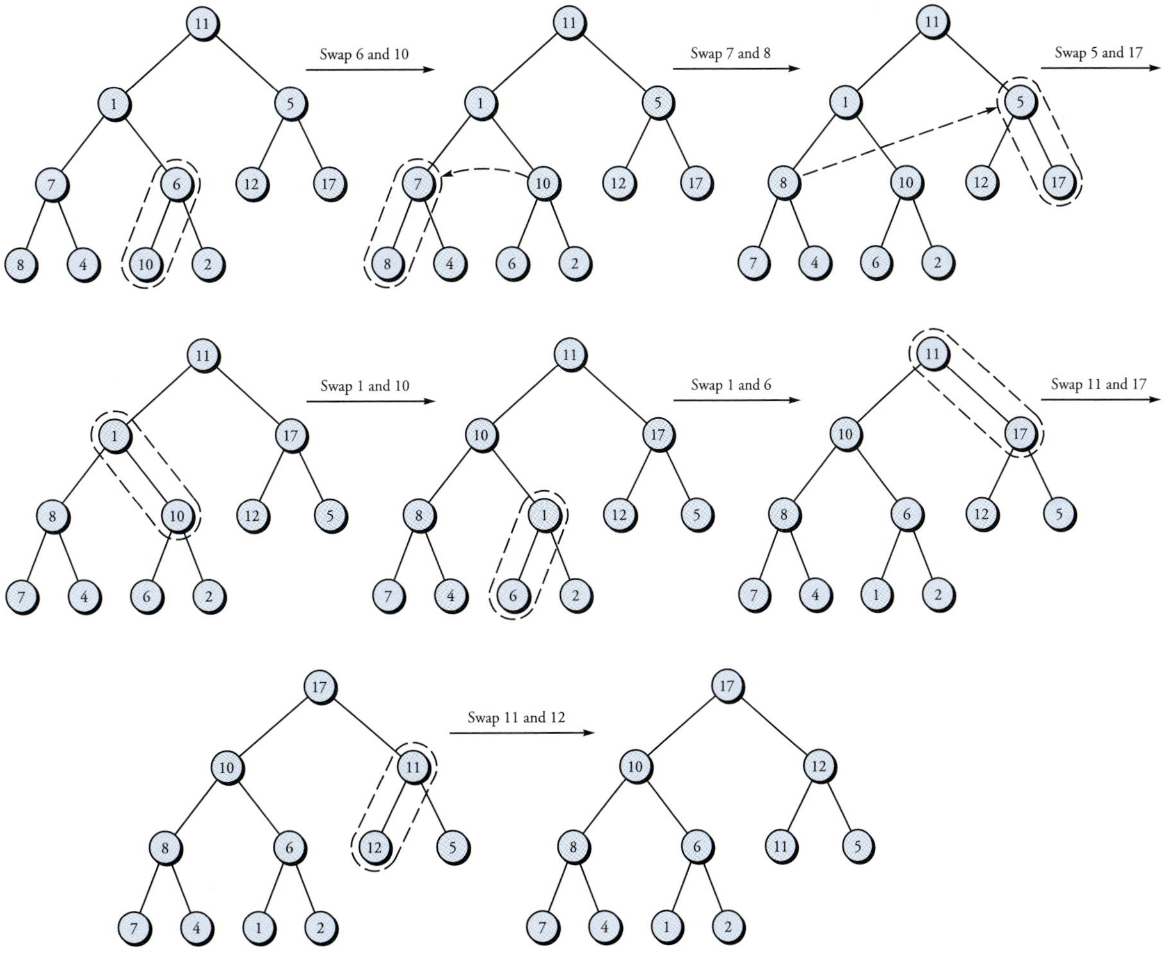

Phase 2 of the heap sort begun in Figure 7-3 is shown in Figure 7-4 for the three highest values.

FIGURE 7-4
Phase 2 of heap sort for three values

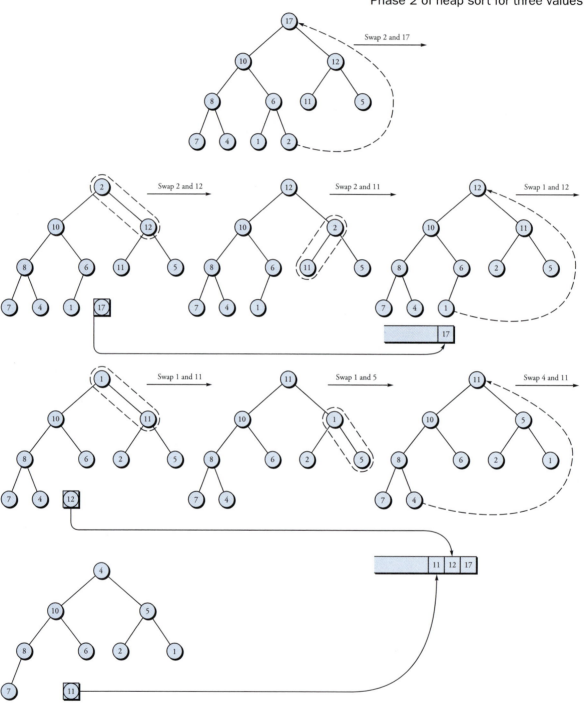

Both phase 1 and phase 2 use the same strategy of walking a parent down a path of the tree via a series of swaps with its children. The following function, walkDown, isolates this crucial subordinate algorithm. In the linear representation of a tree assumed by walkDown, the assignment statement k = 2 * i will make k reference the left child of the node indicated by i. That is, this statement will allow us to descend a level deeper into the tree.

```
// Function: walkDown
// Repeatedly exchange this parent with the child of
// greatest value until the original parent is
// greater than both of its children
//
// Inputs: Vector to be viewed as full binary tree.
// n, the number of entries in the vector.
// j, the index of a parent node within the tree.
// Outputs: Tree vector, as altered by this task.

void walkDown(apvector<int> &list, int j, int n)
{
    int i, k;
    int ref;
    bool foundSpot = false;

    i = j;
    ref = list[i];

    // list[i] will move along the appropriate path in the tree

    k = 2 * i + 1;

    // Initially k references left child of list[i]

    while ((k < n) && ! foundSpot)
    {
        if (k < n - 1)                    // Make k reference largest child
            if (list[k + 1] > list[k])
                ++k;
        if (list[k] > ref)               // Child must move up
        {
            list[i] = list[k];
            i = k;
            k = 2 * i + 1;
        }
```

ref

list[k]
larger
of

if list[k] > ref

```
        else                        // Appropriate spot has been found
            foundSpot = true;
    }
    list[i] = ref;
}
```

With the essential `walkDown` logic isolated in a separate function, phases 1 and 2 of `heapSort` may now be developed easily. The loop for phase 1 repeatedly calls `walkDown` to form the tree into a heap. A loop for phase 2 then repeatedly swaps the root of the tree with the last child and calls `walkDown` to allow this new root to find an appropriate position in the heap.

```
void heapSort(apvector<int> &list)
{
    int y;
    int temp;

    // First phase arranges the tree into a heap

    y = list.length() / 2 - 1;   // y starts at last node to have child
    while (y >= 0)
    {
        walkDown(list, y, list.length());
        --y;
    }

    // End of first phase; y is now used to point at the
    // current last vector slot.

    y = list.length();
    while (y > 0)
    {
    // Interchange root with bottom right leaf node.
        temp = list[0];
        list[0] = list[y - 1];
        list[y - 1] = temp;
        --y;
        walkDown(list, 0, y);
    }
}
```

Swap these two and then remove leaf node from further consideration.

Efficiency of the Heap Sort

It is relatively easy to deduce that the heap sort requires $O(n \log_2 n)$ comparisons. To see this fact, note that the phase 1 loop in the preceding C++ function will execute $n/2$ times. Inside this loop we call `walkDown`, which in turn has a loop that will execute at most $\log_2 n$ times (because it merely follows a path down a full binary tree). Hence, phase 1 requires at most

$$(n/2) * \log_2 n$$

iterations at its deepest level.

Phase 2 may be similarly analyzed. The phase 2 loop iterates n times. Within each iteration, `walkDown` is called, again resulting in at most $\log_2 n$ operations. Thus phase 2 requires at most n * $\log_2 n$ iterations at its deepest level. Overall, we get

$$1.5n * \log_2 n$$

as an upper bound for the number of iterations required by the combination of phases 1 and 2.

Thus both the quick sort and the heap sort yield $O(n \log_2 n)$ efficiencies. In Searching and Sorting, referenced in Section 7.1, Knuth has shown that, on average, the quick sort will be slightly faster because its big-O constant of proportionality will be smaller than that for a heap sort. However, a heap sort offers the advantage of guaranteeing an $O(n \log_2 n)$ efficiency regardless of the data being sorted. As we have already noted for the quick sort, worst case data can cause its performance to deteriorate to $O(n^2)$.

EXERCISES 7.3

1. Consider the `heapSort` function given in this section. Note that `walkDown` is called at two points in the function: once in phase 1 and again in phase 2. Suppose we traced the contents of the vector being sorted after each call to `walkDown`. What would we see as output if we called `heapSort` with a vector that initially contained the following?

   60 12 90 30 64 8 6

2. Repeat Exercise 1 for a six-element vector that initially contains

   1 8 2 7 3 6

3. Where did the heap sort get its name?

4. What is a heap sort?

5. Is a heap sort always better than a quick sort? When is it better? When is it worse? Explain your answer in a written essay.

6. What is the worst case and average case efficiency of the heap sort algorithm?

7. Give examples of vectors that generate the best and worst performances, respectively, for the heap sort algorithm. Explain why these vectors generate the best and worst performances.

8. In Lesson 1, `pointerSort` used an index of pointers to sort data logically without rearranging them. Adapt the pointer sort function to the heap sort algorithm.

7.4 The Merge Sort Algorithm

The essential idea behind *merge sort* is to make repeated use of a function that merges two lists, each already in ascending order, into a third list, also arranged in ascending order. The merge function itself requires only sequential access to the lists. Its logic is similar to the method you would use if you were merging two sorted piles of index cards into a third pile. That is, you start with the first card from each pile. You then compare the cards to see which one comes first, transfer that one over to the third pile, and advance to the next card in that pile. You repeat the comparison, transfer, and advance operations until one of the piles runs out of cards. At that point, you merely move what is left of the remaining pile over to the third merged pile.

This logic is reflected in the generalized merge function that follows. For reasons that will become apparent when we incorporate it into a full sorting function, this version of a merge begins with the two sorted lists stored in one vector. The first list runs from subscript `lower` to `middle` of vector `source`. The second runs from subscript `middle + 1` to `upper` of the same vector. The merged result of the two lists is stored in a second vector `destination`.

```
// Function: merge
// Merge the two ordered segments of source into
// one list arranged in ascending order.
//
// Inputs: Vector source arranged in ascending order between
//         indices lower..middle and middle + 1..upper, respectively.
// Outputs: The complete ordered list in destination.

void merge(apvector<int> &source,
           apvector<int> &destination,
           int lower, int middle, int upper)
{
   int s1 = lower;
   int s2 = middle + 1;
   int d = lower;

   // Repeat comparison of current item from each list.

   do
   {
      if (source[s1] < source[s2])
      {
         destination[d] = source[s1];
         ++s1;
      }
      else
      {
         destination[d] = source[s2];
         ++s2;
      }
```

```
      ++d;
   } while ((s1 <= middle) && (s2 <= upper));

   // Move what is left of remaining list.

   if (s1 > middle)
      do
      {
         destination[d] = source[s2];
         ++s2;
         ++d;
      } while (s2 <= upper);
   else
      do
      {
         destination[d] = source[s1];
         ++s1;
         ++d;
      } while (s1 <= middle);
}
```

Clearly, merge is an O(n) algorithm where n is the number of items in the two lists to be merged. A question remains: How can merge be used to sort an entire vector? To answer this question, we need another function called order that will take the values in the indices lower through upper of a vector source and arrange them in ascending order in the subscripts lower through upper of another vector called destination. Notice that order is itself almost a sorting function except that it produces a sorted list in a second vector instead of actually transforming the vector it originally receives. We will use order to obtain two sorted half-length sequences from our original vector.

Afterward, we will use the merge function we have already developed to merge the two sorted half-length sequences back into the original vector. Of course, this approach merely defers our original question of how to use merge to sort, because now we are faced with the question of how order will be able to produce two sorted half-length sequences. Here is where recursion enters the picture. To produce a sorted half-length sequence, we use order to produce two sorted quarter-length sequences and apply merge to the results. Similarly, the quarter-length sequences are produced by calling order to produce sorted eighth-length sequences and applying merge to the results. The recursive termination condition for this descent into shorter and shorter ordered sequences occurs when order receives a sequence of length 1.

Given the crucial order function, the mergeSort function itself is almost trivial. It need merely create a copy of the vector to be sorted and then call order to sort the elements of the copy into the original. Because order continually calls merge and merge cannot do its work within one vector, the need to create a copy of the original vector is unavoidable. Complete C++ versions of mergeSort and order follow:

```
void mergeSort(apvector<int> &list)
{
   apvector<int> listCopy;

   listCopy = list;       // Make copy for call to order.

   order(listCopy, list, 0, list.length() - 1);
}
```

```
// Function: order
// Transfer source in ascending order to destination,
// between indices lower..upper.
//
// Inputs: source and destination, two vectors that are
//         initially identical between indices lower..upper.
// Outputs: destination arranged in order between lower and upper.

void order(apvector<int> &source,
           apvector<int> &destination, int lower, int upper)
{
   int middle;

   if (lower != upper)
   {
      middle = (lower + upper) / 2;
      order(destination, source, lower, middle);
      order(destination, source, middle + 1, upper);
      merge(source, destination, lower, middle, upper);
   }
}
```

Recursively call order to get two sorted segments in source, which are then merged into destination. This approach requires destination originally to be a copy of source.

The run-time trace diagram of function calls in Figure 7-5 highlights the interaction between order and merge triggered by calling mergeSort with a sample vector of size n = 11. The leaf nodes in this trace diagram represent the recursive termination condition reached when lower = upper.

FIGURE 7-5
Run-time trace of function calls to `order` and `merge`

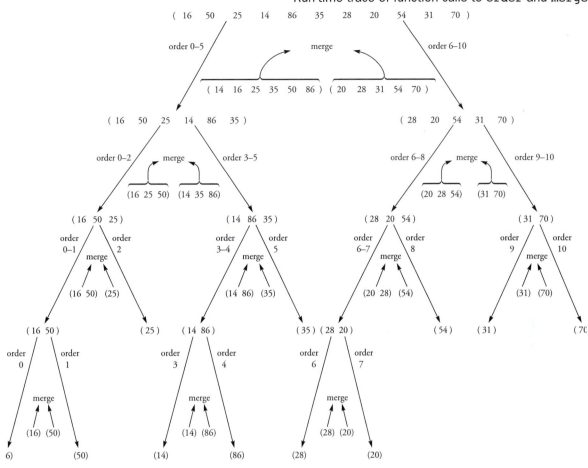

Analysis of the Merge Sort

From a run-time trace of function calls such as that appearing in Figure 7-5, it is quite easy to deduce that merge sort requires $O(nlog_2n)$ comparisons. The reasoning is as follows. All of the merge operations across any given level of the trace diagram will require $O(n)$ comparisons. There are $O(log_2n)$ levels in the trace diagram. Hence, the overall efficiency is the product $O(nlog_2n)$. Notice that, like the heap sort, the merge sort can guarantee this efficiency regardless of the original data. That is, there is no worst case that can cause its efficiency to deteriorate (as for the quick sort).

The price paid for using a merge sort relates to the memory space it requires. Of course, stack space is associated with recursion. More important, however, is the need for a duplicate copy of the vector being sorted. In applications where the original vector barely fit in memory, this space requirement made the merge sort totally impractical, particularly in the days when the cost of memory was high. As the cost of memory has declined, so has the cost of using memory-intensive algorithms such as the merge sort.

There is an added benefit to the merge sort that makes it the only possible choice for certain applications: a merge sort may be written in a way that necessitates only sequential access to the lists being manipulated. As we have presented the algorithm here, random access is required at only one point—namely, in the `merge` function to access the second list beginning at the index (`middle + 1`) of `source`. The need for this access could have been eliminated by having `merge` work with two separate source vectors. That is, we could merge the ordered vectors `source1` and `source2` into `destination`. This, however, is very costly with vectors because it necessitates using three vectors to sort one vector. Nevertheless, it is less costly when the lists being manipulated are being implemented not by vectors but

491

rather by dynamically allocated linked lists or sequential files. In both of these latter situations, the need to use sequential access would make the merge sort strategy the only appropriate sorting method.

In the exercises at the end of the section and the Projects at the end of the lesson, you will be asked to adapt mergeSort to such sequential implementations of a list. In particular, when the list exists in a file instead of main memory, the sorting method employed is said to be an **external sort** (as opposed to the **internal sorts** we have studied in this lesson).

PROGRAMMING SKILLS: Public-Key Cryptography

The manner in which computers can sort through and in other ways manipulate information gives rise to concern over the security of electronic information. Cryptography is the science of encoding information to protect it from being viewed by unauthorized parties. Today, as an increasing amount of sensitive information is transmitted in electronic and magnetic form via Web servers and the Internet, cryptography is becoming an increasingly important field.

A conventional encryption system works much like a mailbox with a combination lock. Anyone knowing the combination can open the box to leave a message or to read any of the messages in the box. In computerized information systems, the "combination" to the mailbox is a digital key—a particular bit pattern that is applied to an electronic message to encode or decode it. In conventional systems, anyone knowing the digital key has access to the information in the electronic mailbox. Hence such systems are best suited to a small number of users and not to the networking of information among many computer installations that is possible with today's technology.

An interesting development in cryptography occurred in the early 1970s with the development of a theory for public-key encryption systems. Such systems work on two different digital keys: one for writing information into the electronic mailbox and another for reading encoded information that has been left in the mailbox. As a user of such an encryption system, you could freely give out the write key to your mailbox (the public key), allowing anyone to send you an encoded letter. However, you would keep the read key (the decoding key)

secret so that only you would be able to make sense out of your mail.

The best-known public-key encryption scheme is the RSA algorithm (named after Rivest, Shamir, and Adleman, the mathematicians who developed it). This algorithm is based on the difficulty of factoring large numbers that are the product of two prime numbers. For instance, the number $51 = 3 \times 17$ would satisfy this criterion except that it is not nearly large enough.

In the RSA system, the product of the two prime factors would be linked to your public key. However, this public key would include only the product, not the prime factors that make the product. Your private key would include each of the individual prime factors. Why should such numbers be large? The answer to this question lies in the present limitations of the area of mathematics known as number theory. It turns out that, given the product of two such prime factors without being told the factors themselves, number theory provides no known way of factoring the number into its prime factors in a reasonable amount of time, even using the most advanced supercomputers. From a security perspective, this consideration means that your code could not be broken by outside agencies, even if they were using a computer to assist them.

The role of public-key cryptography in electronic data systems will no doubt become increasingly important in the future. For an excellent description of the details underlying this technique, see Thomas Cormen, Charles Leiserson, and Ronald Rivest, *Introduction to Algorithms* (New York: McGraw-Hill, 1989). A broader overview of the entire field of cryptography and ethical issues arising out of it may be found in *Applied Cryptography* by

Bruce Schneier (Wiley, 1996). In a shorter article entitled "Cryptography, Security, and the Future," Communications of the ACM, vol. 40, no. 1, January 1997, page 138, the same Bruce Schneier forcefully presents the importance of cryptographic systems:

Present-day computer security is a house of cards; it may stand for now, but it can't last. Many unsecure products have not yet been *broken because they are still in their infancy. But when these products are widely used, they will become tempting targets for criminals. The press will publicize the attacks, undermining public confidence in these systems. Ultimately, products will win or lose in the marketplace depending on the strength of their security.*

EXERCISES 7.4

1. Consider the mergeSort function given in this section. Note that this function contains a subordinate function called order. Suppose we inserted the following tracer output at the beginning of the order function.

```
cout << lower <<    << upper << endl;
for (int k = lower; k < upper; ++k)
     cout << source[k] <<   ;
cout << endl;
```

What would we see as output from these tracers if we called mergeSort with a vector that initially contained the following?

60 12 90 30 64 8 6

2. Repeat Exercise 1 for a six-element vector that initially contains

1 8 2 7 3 6

3. Implement mergeSort in a nonrecursive fashion by using a stack.

4. In Lesson 1, pointerSort used an index of pointers to sort data logically without rearranging the data. Adapt the pointer sort function to the merge sort algorithm.

5. Identify and give an example of best case and worst case data sets for the merge sort algorithm. Explain why your data sets generate best and worst case performance.

6. A sorting method is said to be *stable* if two data items with matching values are guaranteed not to be rearranged with respect to each other as the algorithm progresses. For example, in the four-element vector

$60\ 42_1\ 80\ 42_2$

a stable sorting method guarantees a final ordering of

$42_1\ 42_2\ 60\ 80$

493

Classify each of the sorting algorithms studied in this lesson and in Lesson 1 as to their stability. (To see why stability may be important, consider Projects 7-5 and 7-9 at the end of this lesson.)

7. You are asked to sort a vector in a program in which the following considerations are to be taken into account. First, the amount of data to be sorted is so large that frequent $O(n^2)$ run times will prove unsatisfactory. The amount of data will also make it impossible for your program to use a large amount of overhead data (for example, stack space) to make the sort efficient in its run time. This situation arises because the space required by the overhead data potentially takes up space needed by the vector to be sorted. Second, you are told that the vector to be sorted is often nearly in order initially. For each of the seven sorting methods indicated, specify whether that method is appropriate for this application and, in a brief statement, explain your answer.

a. Bubble sort

b. Insertion sort

c. Selection sort

d. Shell sort

e. Quick sort

f. Heap sort

g. Merge sort

CASE STUDY: Efficiently Sorting a Linked List

User Request

A program has a linked list with a large number of doubles that must be sorted into ascending order. An algorithm is needed to handle this task. Because the list contains a large number of values, it should be an $O(n\log_2 n)$ algorithm.

Analysis

In the Case Study for Lesson 3, we were faced with a similar problem except that the list contained integers instead of doubles. With a list of integers, we chose a radix sort as the appropriate algorithm. A radix sort will not work when the data types of the elements in the list are doubles. (Why?) Instead, for the problem now at hand, we will adapt the quick sort algorithm to linked lists.

Design

Recursively, we can specify the logic of the quick sort for linked lists by the following pseudocode:
If the list L to be sorted is not empty
        Partition the list L into three components:
                (1) The PIVOT element, taken to be the first element in L
                (2) A list called SMALLS consisting of those values in L, after
                        the first element, that are less than PIVOT

(3) A list called BIGS consisting of those values in L, after

the first element, that are greater than or equal to PIVOT

Recursively sort the list SMALLS

Recursively sort the list BIGS

Now that the SMALLS and BIGS are sorted, form the sorted list

by "gluing together" the values in SMALLS, followed by

the PIVOT, followed by the values in BIGS

This algorithm mirrors the logic we used in Section 7.2 for quick-sorting a vector—that is, the pivot element is taken as the first element in the list to be sorted.

Implementation

Because we don't have direct access to a linked list, the partitioning logic used for linked lists will differ significantly from that developed earlier for vectors. Because the nodes in linked lists are dynamically allocated, however, we have the luxury of being able to remove values from one list (the list ultimately to be sorted) and attach them to the lists of small and big values. In doing so, our algorithm will manipulate three lists at each level of recursion, but we will never be charged for more space than that required for all values in the original list. To use this approach with vectors (that is, to allocate two vectors in addition to the original) would have been very wasteful. With linked lists, however, it works out beautifully! The partitioning algorithm is given by the following code:

```
// Partition nonempty list into:
//      (1) pivot element at front of list
//      (2) the list smalls — those values < pivot
//      (3) the list bigs — those values >= pivot
//

void partition(LinkedList<double> &list, double & pivot,
            LinkedList<double> &smalls, LinkedList<double> &bigs)
{
   list.first();
   smalls.first();
   bigs.first();

   // Grab the pivot from the front of the list
   pivot = list.remove();

   // Rest of the list gets partitioned into smalls and bigs
   while (!list.empty())
   {
      if (list.access() < pivot)
      {
         smalls.insert(list.remove());
         smalls.next();
      }
```

```
            else
        {
            bigs.insert(list.remove());
            bigs.next();
        }
    }
}
```

The quick sort, in turn, uses `partition` as follows:

```
void quickSort(LinkedList<double> &list)
{

    LinkedList<double> smalls;
    LinkedList<double> bigs;
    double pivot;

    // if the list is empty, it's trivially sorted
    if (! list.empty())
    {
        partition(list, pivot, smalls, bigs);
        // Recursively sort smalls and bigs
        quickSort(bigs);
        quickSort(smalls);
        // Glue everything back together
        smalls.first();
        while ( !smalls.empty() )
        {
            list.insert(smalls.remove());
            list.next();
        }
        list.insert(pivot);
        list.next();
        bigs.first();
        while ( !bigs.empty() )
        {
            list.insert(bigs.remove());
            list.next();
        }
    }
}
```

Running, Debugging, and Testing Hints

■ To describe and understand the more complex sorting algorithms, it is helpful to present them via subordinate algorithms and stepwise refinement. To this end, we have found it convenient initially to focus on subalgorithms (`segmentedInsertionSort` for `shellSort`, `partition` for `quickSort`, `walkDown` for `heapSort`, and `merge` for `mergeSort`). Our method is illustrative of the stepwise refinement approach to problem solving: Break a complex problem down into smaller problems, solve these smaller problems, and then tie their solutions together to solve the original large problem.

- Describing and understanding algorithms are separate issues from their actual implementation in a specific programming language on a real machine. One implication of this separation of algorithm description and algorithm implementation is the run-time cost associated with a function call. We must consider the hidden costs of making a function call and determine how deeply embedded the function call is in the iterative structure of the calling module.

- Depending on the machine you are using, calling a function instead of directly inserting the code necessary may mean that your program spends more run-time handling the hidden cost of function calls than it does interchanging data items. If large data sets are being sorted and if run-time efficiency is of primary importance, then we should implement our algorithm without actually calling a function.

- Keep in mind the distinction between algorithm description and algorithm implementation when making decisions about whether to transform a given sequence of instructions into a procedure. What may be appropriately isolated as a trivial subalgorithm at the time when a designer is concerned with describing an algorithm may carry a steep price if implemented as a trivial function that is called many times when the resulting program is put into use.

- In making the decision whether to use functions or in-line code when implementing an algorithm, carefully weigh run-time considerations with respect to the clarity and readability of code. A useful rule of thumb is that only in exceptional circumstances should the code associated with a module exceed one printed page in length. This guideline allows in-line insertion of code for simple algorithmic units and ensures that the overall software system does not become unwieldy.

Summary

In this lesson, you learned:

■ The four sorting algorithms introduced in this lesson give us a large variety of tools from which to choose when we need to perform a sorting job. The following comparison table summarizes the pros and cons of each sorting method we've covered.

Sorting Method	Lesson	Number of Comparisons in Terms of the Number of Data Items Being Sorted (n)	Space Requirement	Additional Comments
Binary tree	6	Between $O(n^2)$ and $O(n\log_2 n)$ depending on original data and whether tree is height-balanced	Pointers for tree and possible stack space for recursive traversals	
Bubble	1	$O(n^2)$	No additional overhead	Loop check allows early exit as soon as vector is ordered.
Heap	7	$O(n\log_2 n)$	No additional overhead	
Insertion	1	$O(n^2)$	No additional overhead	Loop check allows early exit as soon as item is correctly placed.
Merge	7	$O(n\log_2 n)$	Requires duplicate vector and stack space for recursion	Requires only sequential access, so it can be used for linked lists and sequential files.
Pointer	1	Depends on the method with which it is combined	Requires list of pointers to maintain logical order	Can be combined with any method to substantially reduce the size of data items being interchanged.
Quick	7	$O(n\log_2 n)$ on the average but $O(n^2)$ for worst cases	Stack space for recursion	
Radix	1, 3	$O(n)$	Space for bins	Although $O(n)$, in its efficiency, has a large constant of proportionality. Not applicable to all types of data—for example, real numbers.
Selection	1	$O(n^2)$	No additional overhead	
Shell	7	Between $O[n(\log_2 n)^2]$ and $O(n^{1.5})$ depending on increments used	No additional overhead	

VOCABULARY REVIEW

Define the following terms:

diminishing increment sort

external sort

heap sort

internal sort

merge sort

partition

pivot

quick sort

relatively prime

shell sort

LESSON 7 REVIEW QUESTIONS

FILL IN THE BLANK

Complete the following sentences by writing the correct word or words in the blanks provided.

1. The shell sort is also called the _____ sort.

2. The sort that uses a pivot to make a pass through the data is called the _____ sort.

3. The act of separating the data about a pivot is called _____.

4. The average run-time efficiency of the quick sort is _____.

5. The worst case run-time efficiency for the quick sort is _____.

6. The sort that uses a tree with the heap property is referred to as the_____ sort.

7. The heap sort can most efficiently be implemented using a(n) _____ as the data structure.

8. The heap sort has an average run-time efficiency of _____.

9. The sort that combines two already sorted lists is referred to as the _____ sort.

WRITTEN QUESTIONS

Write a brief answer to the following questions.

10. Show the process of sorting the following vector of integers using the shell sort:

    0, 35, 13, 100, 84, 6, 9 19, 51

499

11. Given the following vector of integers

14, 3, 24, 65, 6, 8, 18, 43, 12, 20

show the vector after each swap during the process of sorting the vector using the quick sort algorithm described in the text.

12. Assume that the elements 8, 20, 7, 2, 16, 4, 35, 13, 21, 6 have been inserted, in that order, into an initially empty binary heap (a priority queue with the smallest value at the front) that is implemented using a vector. Draw a diagram of the resulting heap and show the contents of the vector. A deleteMin operation is then performed on the heap just constructed. Trace the steps of this operation by either showing the contents of the vector or drawing the diagram of the heap for each movement of heap elements during the operation.

LESSON 7 PROJECTS

PROJECT 7-1

In the Case Study of Lesson 1, we presented tools and techniques for profiling sorting algorithms. In particular, we developed a complete program that helped us empirically explore the efficiency of a selection sort. Now apply the same tools and techniques to develop a profiling program for each of the sorting algorithms studied in this lesson—shell, quick, heap, and merge. Write a report on the exploration that you do with your profiling program.

PROJECT 7-2

Modify your profiled version of a shell sort from Project 7-1 so that it uses a variety of sequences of diminishing increments. In a written report, compare the performance of the algorithm for these differing sequences. Which sequence performs the best?

PROJECT 7-3

Modify the shell sort so that it employs bubble sort logic on segments instead of an insertion sort. Incorporate this change into the program you wrote for Projects 7-1 and 7-2. Compare the observed efficiency of this new version of a shell sort with the original on a variety of data sets. Which performs better? Explain your answer in a carefully written statement.

PROJECT 7-4

Modify the profiled version of a quick sort that you wrote for Project 7-1 so that you can experiment with the selection of a pivot element or try invoking an insertion sort when the size of the vector segment to be partitioned becomes sufficiently small. For whatever experimentation you choose to do, write a report on your exploration. In your report, draw conclusions about the efficiencies of various strategies. Support your conclusions with empirical data obtained from your exploratory runs.

PROJECT 7-5

SCANS

The Bay Area Brawlers professional football team (Project 3-9 in Lesson 3 and Project 6-5 in Lesson 6) has stored the records of all players who have played on the team during its history. Each player's record consists of the following information:

- Name

- Total points scored

- Number of touchdowns

- Number of field goals

- Number of safeties

- Number of extra points

Write a program that lists players in order from the most points scored in the team's history to the fewest points scored. Players who have scored the same number of points should then be arranged in alphabetical order.

PROJECT 7-6

SCANS

Take n randomly generated integers. Now apply a bubble sort, a shell sort, a quick sort, a heap sort, and a merge sort. Observe, compare, and plot their execution time for n = 100; n = 1,000; n = 10,000; n = 100,000, ...

PROJECT 7-7

SCANS

Put some hypothetical data in an external file and apply a modified merge sort to them.

PROJECT 7-8

SCANS

Write a C++ program to complete the following steps:

- Artificially create a file with a large number of randomly chosen names.

- Read into a vector all names that begin with A through some letter—say G—chosen so that all the names will fit in the vector.

- Sort this vector with one of the sorting algorithms from this lesson and store the sorted vector into another file.

- Read into the vector all names from the file that begin with H through another appropriate letter.

- Sort the vector and append it to the end of the new file.

Repeat this process until all names from the original file have been processed. The new file will be the sorted version of the original. Observe the execution time of your program. Analyze its efficiency in big-O terms.

PROJECT 7-9

Consider a list of records, each containing four fields:

- Name
- Month of birth
- Day of birth
- Year of birth

Write a program to sort this list in order from oldest to youngest. People with the same birth date should be arranged alphabetically. One strategy you could employ would be to concatenate strategically the four fields into one, and then sort just that one field. Another strategy would be to sort the list four times, each time by a different field. (Think carefully about which field to sort first.) Which of the strategies require you to choose a stable sorting algorithm? (See Exercise 6 in Exercise 7.4.)

PROJECT 7-10

Modify `mergeSort` so that it will sort a linked list instead of a vector.

CRITICAL THINKING

ACTIVITY 7-1

Given a sequential file containing an unordered list of passengers and their flight numbers for Wing-and-a-Prayer Airlines (Project 3-7 in Lesson 3 and Project 6-3 in Lesson 6), produce a listing arranged in flight-number order. Passengers on the same flight should be ordered by last name. The easy version of this program assumes that all information will fit in memory, allowing the use of an internal sort. For an added challenge, write the program using an external sort algorithm. (Hint: Adapt `mergeSort` along the lines discussed in the text.)

ACTIVITY 7-2

A variation of the merge sort is called the natural merge sort. This algorithm looks for natural "runs" of ordered data within the original vector. For instance, the following vector of 16 items shows eight natural runs (indicated by brackets).

```
0 [503]
1 [ 87]
2 [512]
3 [ 61]
4 [908]
5 [170]
6 [897]
7 [275]
8 [653]
9 [426]
```

```
10 ┌154┐
11 │509│
12 │612│
13 │677│
14 └765┘
15 [703]
```

These eight runs are arranged in a new vector with the first run positioned at the top of the new vector, the second run reversed and moved to the bottom of the vector, the third run positioned after the original first run, the fourth run reversed and positioned above the original second run, and so forth. The pattern in this new vector is as follows:

```
 0 ┌503┐ ← Original 1st run
 1 ┌ 61 ┐ ← Original 3rd run
 2 └908┘
 3 ┌275┐ ← Original 5th run
 4 └653┘
 5 ┌154┐
 6 │509│
 7 │612│ ← Original 7th run
 8 │677│
 9 └765┘
10 └703┘ ← Original 8th run reversed
11 └426┘ ← Original 6th run reversed
12 ┌897┐ ← Original 4th run reversed
13 └170┘
14 ┌512┐ ← Original 2nd run reversed
15 └ 87 ┘
```

The runs in this new vector are now merged back into the original vector, resulting in the following pattern of data:

```
0 ┌ 87 ┐
1 │503│ ← Merged data from original 1st and 2nd runs
2 └512┘
3 ┌275┐
4 │426│ ← Merged data from original 5th and 6th runs
5 └653┘
```

```
 6  ┌765┐
 7  │703│
 8  │677│
 9  │612│  ← Merged data from original 7th and 8th runs
10  │509│
11  └154┘
12  ┌908┐
13  │897│
14  │170│  ← Merged data from original 3rd and 4th runs
15  └ 61┘
```

This merging pattern then cascades back and forth from between the original and new vector until only one run remains. Discover this merging pattern and implement the natural merge sort. Describe circumstances under which the natural merge algorithm is likely to perform better and worse than the merge sort algorithm described in Section 7.4.

MORE POWERFUL SEARCH METHODS

OBJECTIVES

Upon completion of this lesson, you will be able to:

- Understand what is meant by a key-to-address transformation—that is, a hashing function.

- Develop techniques for constructing hashing functions.

- Understand what the term "collision" means relative to hashing.

- Develop methods for processing collisions: linear probing, quadratic probing, rehashing, linked (chained) probing, and bucket hashing.

- Discuss how hashing could be used to implement the one-key table ADT.

- Discuss how hashing could be used to implement the two-key table ADT.

- Study how the indexed sequential search methodology is implemented.

- Understand how the B-tree data structure may be used to implement an index for a random access file.

- Understand how the trie data structure may be used to implement the index for a random access file keyed by strings of variable length.

 **Estimated Time: 15 hours**

Vocabulary

boundary folding

bucket

clustering

hashing

linear collision processing

linked collision processing

quadratic collision processing

rehashing

shift folding

Introduction

In earlier lessons, we analyzed three methods of searching for items within a list: sequential search, binary search, and binary search tree. The sequential search, although easy to implement and applicable to short lists, is limited in many practical situations by its O(*n*) search efficiency. The binary search offers a much faster $O(\log_2 n)$ search efficiency but also has limitations. Foremost among these limitations are the need to maintain the list in physically contiguous order and the need to maintain a count of the number of records in the list. Both of these limitations are particularly restrictive for volatile lists—that is, lists in which insertions and deletions are frequently made. In Lesson 6, we learned that a binary search tree offers the best of both worlds. Insertions and deletions can be done on a binary search tree by merely manipulating pointers instead of moving data, and an $O(\log_2 n)$ search efficiency can be achieved if the tree remains nearly full. Unfortunately, to guarantee that the tree remains nearly full and hence preserve the $O(\log_2 n)$ efficiency, a sophisticated technique known as height balancing (see Lesson 6) is required. The complications involved in implementing this technique frequently dictate that it not be used. Essentially, you must weigh the significant cost in development time needed to implement a height-balanced tree against the risk that the order in which data arrive for insertion may cause search efficiency to deteriorate from $O(\log_2 n)$ to O(*n*). If data items arrive in a relatively random order, then taking that risk may be prudent.

The efficiency of all three of these techniques depends on the number of items in the list being searched. In this lesson, we will study another alternative, called *hashing.* Its efficiency is measurable in terms of the amount of storage you are willing to waste. In this sense, hashing can achieve phenomenally fast search times regardless of how much data you have, provided that you can afford to keep a relatively large amount of unused list space available.

We will also explore some of the special considerations that enter into searching for data stored in a disk file instead of main memory. These considerations lead to a variety of search schemes, all of which employ some variation of a data structure known as an *index.*

8.1 Density-Dependent Search Techniques

In an ideal data processing world, all identifying keys, such as product codes, Social Security numbers, and so on, would start at 0 and follow in sequence thereafter. Then, in any given list, we would merely store the key and its associated data at the position that matched the key. The search efficiency for any key in such a list would be one access to the list, and all data processors could live happily ever after! Unfortunately, in the real world, users (not being concerned with the happiness of data processing personnel) desire keys that consist of more meaningful characters, such as names, addresses, and region codes. For instance, in a given inventory-control application, product codes may be numbered in sequence beginning with 10,000 instead of 0. A moment's reflection should indicate that this scenario is still a highly desirable situation because, given a key, we need merely locate the key at position

```
KeyValue - 10000
```

in the list, and we still have a search efficiency of 1. What we have done here is to define ***key-to-address transformation***, or ***hashing*** function. The idea behind a hashing function is that it acts on a given key in such a way as to return the relative position in the list where we expect to find the key.

Most hashing functions are not as straightforward as the preceding one, and present some additional complications that we can quickly illustrate. Suppose we use the following hashing function:

```
hash(keyValue) = keyValue % 4
```

Then the set of keys 3, 5, 8, and 10 will be scattered as illustrated here.

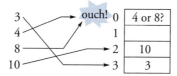

If we happen to have 3, 4, 8, and 10 as keys instead of 3, 5, 8, and 10, a problem arises: 4 and 8 hash to the same position. They are said to be synonyms, and the result is termed a collision. This situation—here a collision at position 0—is shown in the following illustration.

Clearly, one goal of the hashing functions we develop should be to reduce the number of collisions as much as possible.

The Construction of Hashing Functions

The business of developing hashing functions can be quite intriguing. The essential idea is to build a mathematical black box that will take a key value as input and issue as output the position in the list where that key value should be located. The position output should have a minimal probability of colliding with the position that would be produced for a different key. In addition, the black box we create must ensure that a given key will always produce the same position as output. You should begin to note a similarity between some of the properties possessed by a good hashing function and a good random number generator, such as that used in our simulation application in Lesson 4. Indeed, list access via a hashing function is sometimes called ***randomized storage,*** and the first type of hashing function we discuss makes direct use of a random number generator.

Method 1: Use of a Random Number Generator. Many high-level languages, including C++, provide a random number generator to produce random sequences of real values between 0 and 1. (For readable discussions of other methods of random number generation, see Chapter 7 in William H. Press, Brian P. Flannery, Saul A. Teukolsky, and William T. Vetterling, *Numerical Recipes* [Cambridge, United Kingdom: Cambridge University Press, 1986].) Typically, all of these methods rely on a global seed to start the process of generating random numbers. Computations done on this seed produce the random number. At the same time, the computations alter the value of the seed so that the next time the random number generator is called, a different random number will almost surely be produced.

In typical applications of random number generation, you need merely initialize the seed to some arbitrary value to start the random sequence. Once the seed is supplied, the random sequence is completely determined. If you have access to a system function that returns the current time, day, month, and year, this value can be called to initialize the seed in a fashion that ensures there is only a very small likelihood of generating the same random sequence twice.

How does this discussion relate to hashing? For a hashing application, we must slightly alter the definition of our random number generator so that the seed is supplied as a value parameter. Then we supply the values of search keys as the seeds. The nature of the random number algorithm ensures that

- Each time the same key is passed to the function, the same random value will be returned.

- Two different keys are unlikely to yield the same random value.

The random number between 0 and 1 that is correspondingly produced can then be appropriately multiplied, truncated, and shifted to produce a hash value within the range of valid positions.

Method 2: Folding. In situations where the key to be positioned is not a pure integer, some preliminary work may be required to translate it into a usable form. Take, for instance, the case of a Social Security number such as

387- 58 -1505

Viewed as one integer, this value would cause overflow on many machines. By a method known as *shift folding*, this Social Security number would be viewed as three separate numbers to be added

387

58

+ 1505

producing 1950. This result could be regarded either as the hash position itself or, more likely, as a pure integer that now could be further acted on by method 1 or 4 to produce a final hash position in the desired range.

Another common folding technique is called *boundary folding.* The idea behind boundary folding is that, at the boundaries between the numbers making up the key under consideration, every other number is reversed before being added to the accumulated total. Applying this method to our Social Security number example, we would have

387

85

+ 1505

yielding 1977. Clearly, the two methods do not differ by much, and a choice between them must often be made on the basis of some experimentation to determine which will produce more scattered results for a given application.

Regardless of whether shift or boundary folding is used, one of the great advantages of the folding method is its ability to transform noninteger keys into integers suitable for further hashing action. For keys such as names that contain alphabetical characters, the type of folding just illustrated may be done by translating characters into their ASCII (or other appropriate) codes.

Method 3: Digit or Character Extraction. In certain situations, a given key value may contain specific characters that are likely to bias any hash value arising from the key. The idea in digit or character extraction is to remove such digits or characters before using the result as a final hash value or passing it on to be transformed by another method. For instance, a company may choose to identify the various products it manufactures by using a nine-character code that always contains either an A or B in the first position and either 1 or 0 in the fourth position. The rest of the characters in the code tend to occur in less predictable fashion. Character extraction would remove the biased first and fourth characters, leaving a seven-character result to pass on to further processing.

Method 4: Division-Remainder Technique. All hashing presupposes a given range of positions that can be valid outputs of the hash function. In the remainder of this section, we assume the existence of a global constant RECORD_SPACE, which represents the upper limit of our hashing function. That is, the function should produce values between 0 and RECORD_SPACE - 1. It should then be evident that

```
hash(keyValue) = keyValue % RECORD_SPACE
```

is a valid hashing function for integer keyValue.

To begin examining criteria for choosing an appropriate RECORD_SPACE, let us load the keys 41, 58, 12, 92, 50, and 91 into a list with RECORD_SPACE = 15. Figure 8-1 shows the results. In this vector, zeros are used to denote empty positions. However, if we keep RECORD_SPACE the same and try to load the keys 10, 20, 30, 40, 50, 60, and 70, we have many collisions, as shown in Figure 8-2. Hence a different set of keys can cause disastrous results even though the list seemingly has plenty of room available. On the other hand, if we choose RECORD_SPACE to be 11, we have a list with considerably less room but no collisions. Figure 8-3 indicates the hashing positions when the same set of keys is acted on by 11 instead of by 15. Although these examples of the division-remainder technique are far from conclusive, they suggest that choosing a prime number for RECORD_SPACE may produce a more desirable hashing function. The exercises at the end of this section have you explore this question more deeply. Apart from considerations of whether RECORD_SPACE should be prime, it is clear that the nature of a particular application may dictate against the choice of certain RECORD_SPACE values. For instance, in a situation where the rightmost digits of key values happen to follow certain recurring patterns, it would be unwise to choose a power of 10 for RECORD_SPACE. (Why?)

FIGURE 8-1

Vector with RECORD_SPACE = 15 loaded using
a division-remainder hashing function

Position	Key
0	0
1	91
2	92
3	0
4	0
5	50
6	0
7	0
8	0
9	0
10	0
11	41
12	12
13	58
14	0

FIGURE 8-2
Vector from Figure 8-1, loaded differently, with several collisions

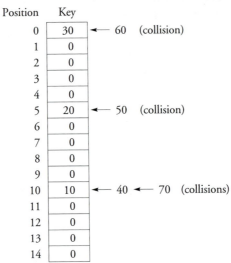

FIGURE 8-3
Vector with same keys as Figure 8-2, but with
RECORD_SPACE = 11; no collision results

Position	Key
0	0
1	0
2	0
3	0
4	70
5	60
6	50
7	40
8	30
9	20
10	10

Despite such considerations, a hashing function usually cannot rule out the possibility of collisions; it can only make them less likely. You should quickly be able to imagine a key value that will produce a collision for the hashing function used in determining the list of Figure 8-3. Notice that, as the list approaches the full state, the probability that collisions will occur increases. Hence, when using hashing as a search strategy, one must be willing to waste some positions in the list; otherwise, search efficiency will deteriorate drastically. How much space to waste is an interesting question that we will soon discuss. Furthermore, because hashing functions generally cannot eliminate collisions, we must be prepared to handle them when they occur.

Collision Processing

The essential problem in collision processing is to develop an algorithm that will position a key in a list when the position dictated by the hashing function itself is already occupied. Ideally, this algorithm should minimize the possibility of future collisions; that is, the problem key should be located at a position that is not likely to be the hashed position of a future key.

The nature of hashing makes the latter criterion difficult to meet with any degree of certainty, because a good hashing function does not allow prediction of where future keys are likely to be placed. We will discuss five methods of collision processing: linear, quadratic, rehashing, linked, and bucket. In all of the methods, it will be necessary to detect when a given list position is not occupied. To signify this state, we use a global constant EMPTY to distinguish unoccupied positions. As you read, give some thought to the question of how deletions could be processed from a list accessed via one of these hashing methods. In particular, will the EMPTY flag suffice to denote positions that have never been occupied and positions previously occupied but now vacant? This question is explored in the exercises and in the Projects at the end of this lesson.

Linear Collision Processing

The linear method of resolving collisions is the simplest to implement (and, unfortunately, the least efficient). *Linear collision processing* requires that, when a collision occurs, we proceed down the list in sequential order until a vacant position is found. The key causing the collision is then placed at this first vacant position. If we come to the physical end of our list in the attempt to place the problem key, we merely wrap around to the top of the list and continue looking for a vacant position. For instance, suppose we use a hashing function of

```
hash(keyValue) = keyValue % RECORD_SPACE
```

with RECORD_SPACE equal to 7. We then attempt to insert the keys 18, 31, 67, 36, 19, and 34. The sequence of lists in Figure 8-4 shows the results of these insertions. When a collision occurs at the third insert, it is processed by the linear method; 67 is thus loaded into position 5.

FIGURE 8-4

Insertion with linear collision processing

0	0	0	0	0	0	0	0	0	0	0	34
1	0	1	0	1	0	1	36	1	36	1	36
2	0	2	0	2	0	2	0	2	0	2	0
3	0	3	31	3	31	3	31	3	31	3	31
4	18	4	18	4	18	4	18	4	18	4	18
5	0	5	0	5	67	5	67	5	67	5	67
6	0	6	0	6	0	6	0	6	19	6	19

First insert	Second insert	Third insert	Fourth insert	Fifth insert	Sixth insert
hash(18) = 4	hash(31) = 3	hash(67) = 4	hash(36) = 1	hash(19) = 5	hash(34) = 6

Example 8-1

Suppose a vector has been loaded with data using the linear collision processing strategy illustrated in Figure 8-4. Write a C++ algorithm to seek a target key in this vector. We assume that `ListType` has been defined as a vector of records that contain key/value pairs.

```
// Function: linearHash
// Use linear hashing algorithm to search for target.
//
// Inputs:      List of objects loaded by linear
//              hashing method.
//              target, the key of an object to be found.
// Outputs:     If key matching target is found,
//              return true and the index at the key;
//              otherwise, return false.

bool linearHash(ListType list, KeyType target, element &item)
{
  int k = hash(target);
  int j = k;
  bool traversed = false;
  bool found = false;

  while (! list[j].empty() && ! (found || traversed))
     if (target == list[j].getKey())
     {
        item = list[j].getValue();
        found = true;
     }
     else
     {
        j = (j + 1) % RECORD_SPACE;
        traversed = (j == k);
     }
  return found;
}
```

		target = 419
0	419	hash(419) = RECORD_SPACE – 3
.	.	
.	.	
.	.	
RECORD_SPACE – 3	511	Repeated applications of
RECORD_SPACE – 2	312	**else** clause ensure eventual
RECORD_SPACE – 1	705	wraparound to first slot.

Several remarks are in order concerning the function in Example 8-1. First, note that the function as it stands does not handle list processing that requires deletions to be processed. In such a situation, an additional flagging value is needed to indicate a list position that had once been occupied but is now vacant because of a deletion. Without this distinction, we do not know whether to exit the search loop upon encountering an empty slot. You will explore the problem of deletions from a list maintained by hashing in greater detail in the exercises and end-of-lesson Projects. Second, note that the linear method is not without its flaws. In particular, it is prone to a problem known as *clustering.* Clustering occurs when a collision processing strategy relocates keys that have a collision at the same initial hashing position to the same region (known as a cluster) within the storage space. This choice usually leads to further collisions with other relocated values until everything is resolved. With linear collision processing, the clustering problem is compounded because, as one cluster expands, it can run into another cluster, immediately creating a larger cluster. This one large cluster ultimately causes collision resolutions to be drawn out longer than they would otherwise be. Hence, linear hashing is more likely to result in the clustering phenomenon pictured in Figure 8-5 than the other methods we discuss.

FIGURE 8-5

Clustering due to biased hashing function and linear processing

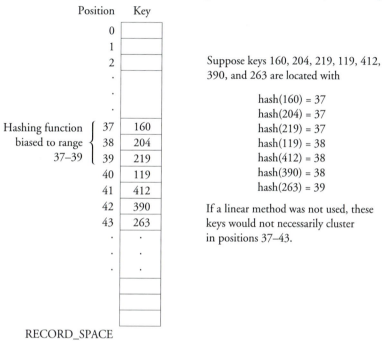

Suppose keys 160, 204, 219, 119, 412, 390, and 263 are located with

hash(160) = 37
hash(204) = 37
hash(219) = 37
hash(119) = 38
hash(412) = 38
hash(390) = 38
hash(263) = 39

If a linear method was not used, these keys would not necessarily cluster in positions 37–43.

Efficiency Considerations for Linear Hashing. A final point to note about the linear hashing method is its search efficiency. Knuth has shown that the average number of list accesses for a successful search using the linear method is

$$(1/2)\ [1 + 1/(1 - D)]$$

where

```
D = (number of currently active records)/RECORD_SPACE
```

(See Donald E. Knuth, *The Art of Computer Programming*, vol. 3, "Searching and Sorting," [Menlo Park, California: Addison-Wesley, 1973].) An interesting fact about this search efficiency is that it is not solely dependent on the number of records in the list but rather depends on the density ratio of the number of records currently in the list divided by the total record space available. In other words, no matter how many records exist, a highly efficient result can be obtained if one is willing to waste enough vacant records. This is what is meant by a ***density-dependent search technique.*** In the case of searching for a key that cannot be found, Knuth's results indicate that the average search efficiency will be

$$(1/2)\ [1 + 1/(1 - D)^2]$$

Table 8-1 illustrates the effectiveness of linear collision resolution by showing the computed efficiencies for a few strategic values of *D*.

TABLE 8-1
Average search efficiency for linear collision processing

D	Efficiency for Successful Search (Number of Accesses)	Efficiency for Unsuccessful Search (Number of Accesses)
0.15	1.06	1.18
0.50	1.50	2.50
0.75	2.50	8.50
0.90	5.50	50.50

Quadratic and Rehashing Methods of Collision Processing

Both the *quadratic* and *rehashing collision processing* methods attempt to correct the problem of clustering. They force the problem-causing key to immediately move a considerable distance from the initial collision. With the rehashing method, an entire sequence of hashing functions may be applied to a given key. If a collision results from the first hashing function, a second is applied, then a third, and so on until the key can be successfully placed.

The quadratic method has the advantage of not requiring numerous hashing functions for its implementation. Suppose that a key value initially hashes to position k and a collision results. Then, on its first attempt to resolve the collision, the quadratic algorithm attempts to place the key at position

$$k + 1^2$$

If a second attempt is necessary to resolve the collision, position

$$k + 2^2$$

is probed. In general, the rth attempt to resolve the collision probes position

$$k + r^2$$

(with wraparound taken into account). Figure 8-6 highlights this scattering pattern. At this point you should verify that, if the hashing function

```
hash(keyValue) = keyValue % RECORD_SPACE
```

is used with RECORD_SPACE equal to 7, the keys 17, 73, 32, and 80 will be located in positions 3, 4, 5, and 0, respectively.

FIGURE 8-6
Quadratic collision processing

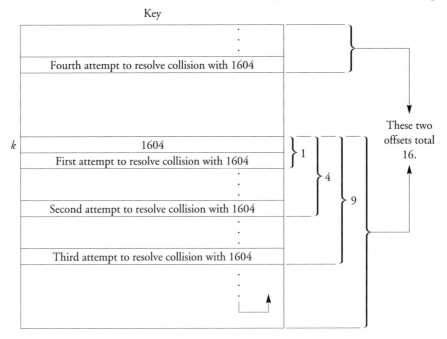

Efficiency Considerations for the Quadratic and Rehashing Methods. Knuth's results (see "Searching and Sorting," cited earlier in this section) demonstrate the effectiveness of the rehashing and quadratic methods versus the linear method. For the quadratic method, average search efficiencies improve to

$$1 - \log_e(1 - D) - (D/2)$$

for the successful case and to

$$1/(1 - D) - D - \log_e(1 - D)$$

for an unsuccessful search, where D is the density ratio as defined earlier in this section and e is the base for the natural logarithm function.

Rehashing with a completely random sequence of rehashing locations for each key slightly improves the efficiencies of the quadratic method to

$$-(1/D) * \log_e(1 - D)$$

for the successful case and to

$$1/(1 - D)$$

for an unsuccessful search. Compare the numbers presented in Table 8-2 for quadratic collision processing and (ideal) random rehashing to those in Table 8-1 for linear collision processing.

TABLE 8-2

Average search efficiency for quadratic and rehashing collision processing

D	Efficiency for Successful Search (Number of Accesses)		Efficiency for Unsuccessful Search (Number of Accesses)	
	Quadratic	Rehashing	Quadratic	Rehashing
0.10	1.05	1.05	1.11	1.11
0.50	1.44	1.39	2.19	2.00
0.75	2.01	1.84	4.64	4.00
0.90	2.85	2.56	11.40	10.00

You may have surmised that the increased efficiency of the quadratic method entails at least some drawbacks. First, the computation of a position to be probed when a collision occurs is somewhat more obscure than it was with the linear method. We leave it for you to verify that the position for the rth probe after an initial unsuccessful hash to position k is given by

```
(k + r2) % RECORD_SPACE
```

A more significant problem is that the quadratic method seemingly offers no guarantee that we will try every position in the list before concluding that a given key cannot be inserted. With the linear method, as the list became relatively dense when keys and insertions were attempted, the only way that the insertion could fail was for every position in the list to be occupied. The linear nature of the search, although inefficient, ensured that every position would be checked. With the quadratic method applied to the RECORD_SPACE of Figure 8-7, you can confirm that an initial hash to position 3 will lead to future probing of positions 3, 4, and 7 only; the method will never check positions 0, 1, 2, 5, or 6. A satisfactory answer to the question of what portion of a list will be probed by the quadratic algorithm was fortunately provided by Radke for values of RECORD_SPACE that are prime numbers which satisfy certain conditions. Radke's results and their application to the quadratic algorithm are explored in the exercises at the end of the section. (If you wish to read Radke's results, see C. E. Radke, "The Use of Quadratic Residue Research," *Communications of the ACM*, vol. 13, no. 2, February 1970, pages 103–105.)

FIGURE 8-7

Quadratic probing after initial hash to 3

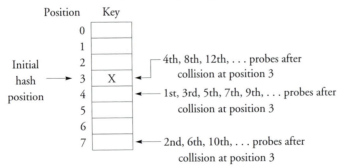

Linked Method of Collision Processing

The logic of *linked collision processing* eliminates the possibility that one collision begets another. It requires a storage area divided into two regions: a ***prime hash area*** and an ***overflow area.*** Each record requires a link field in addition to the `key` and `otherData` fields. The global constant `RECORD_SPACE` is applicable to the prime hash area only. This storage concept is illustrated in Figure 8-8. Initially, the hashing translates function keys into the prime hashing area. If a collision occurs, the key is inserted into a linked list with its initial node in the prime area and all following nodes in the overflow area. Figure 8-9 shows how this method loads the keys 22, 31, 67, 36, 29, and 60 for a `RECORD_SPACE` equal to 7 and hashing function

```
hash(keyValue) = keyValue % RECORD_SPACE
```

FIGURE 8-8

Storage allocation for linked collision processing

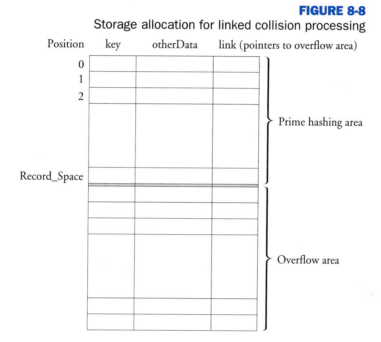

517

FIGURE 8-9

Loading keys with `keyValue % RECORD_SPACE`
and linked collision processing

Position	Key	Link
0	0	NULL
1	22	7
2	0	NULL
3	31	NULL
4	67	9
5	0	NULL
6	0	NULL
7	36	8
8	29	NULL
9	60	NULL
10	0	NULL
11	0	NULL
12	0	NULL
13	0	NULL
14	0	NULL
15	0	NULL
16	0	NULL

Example 8-2

Suppose a vector has been loaded with data using the linked collision processing strategy illustrated in Figures 8-8 and 8-9. Write a C++ function to find a target key in this vector.

We have made the link fields be integer pointers to other vector locations instead of C++ dynamic memory pointers to facilitate using the algorithm with a random access file. As written, the function assumes that all key locations in the prime area have had their corresponding key and link fields initialized to appropriate constant flags for EMPTY and NULL, respectively. The assumption is also made that no keys will be deleted.

```
// Function: linkedHash
// Use linked hashing algorithm to search for target.
//
// Inputs:     List of objects loaded by linked hashing method.
//             target, the value of a key to be found in list.
// Outputs:    If record with key field matching target is found,
//                 return true and object;
//             otherwise, return false

bool linkedHash(ListType list, KeyType "target" element & item)
{
    int k = hash (target);
    boolean found = false;

    do
    {
        if (target == list[k].getKey())
        {
            item = list[k].getValue();
            found = true;
        }
```

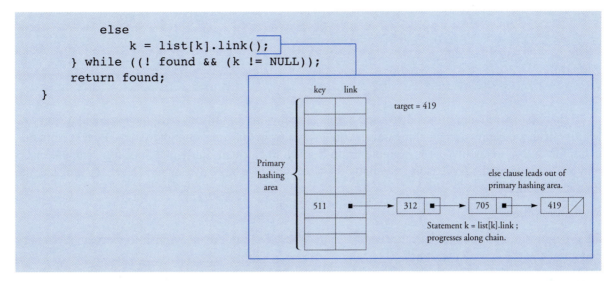

```
        else
            k = list[k].link();
    } while ((! found && (k != NULL));
    return found;
}
```

Efficiency Considerations for Linked Hashing. Knuth's efficiency results for the linked hashing method depend on a density factor D, which is computed using the RECORD_SPACE in the prime hashing area only. Unlike the other hashing methods we have discussed, the linked method allows a density factor greater than 1. For example, if the RECORD_SPACE for the primary hash area is 200 and the overflow area contains space for 300 additional records, then 400 active records yield a density factor of 2. Given this variation, average search efficiencies for the successful and unsuccessful cases are $1 + D/2$ and D, respectively. Table 8-3 shows computations of this search efficiency for selected values of D, and should be compared to the corresponding results for the linear and quadratic methods, which were presented in Tables 8-1 and 8-2, respectively.

TABLE 8-3
Average search efficiencies for the linked method

D	Efficiency for Successful Search (Number of Accesses)	Efficiency for Unsuccessful Search (Number of Accesses)
2	2	2
5	3.5	5
10	6	10
20	11	20

When the search algorithms discussed in this lesson were first discovered, they sparked a flurry of activity in an area known as machine translation. Programs in this area attempt to translate text from one natural language to another—for example, from English to German. Early attempts at machine translation tended to view the process as essentially the searching of a large dictionary. Hence, to translate the English sentence

The sun is yellow,

the program simply found each of the words in a disk-based version of an English-to-German dictionary and arrived at the German sentence

Die Sonne ist gelb.

The complexities of semantics (meanings) in natural language soon slowed machine translation activity. The translation of some sentences by these early systems produced some rather humorous results. According to computer folklore cited in William M. Bulkeley, "Computers Gain as Language Translators Even Though Perfect Not They Always," *Wall Street Journal*, February 6, 1985, page 25, the following translations occurred in an early English-to-Russian system.

English Phrase	Russian Translation
The spirit is willing but the flesh is weak.	The vodka is good but the meat is rotten.
Out of sight, out of mind.	Invisible maniac.

The difficulty in performing such translations is that, when a human hears a sentence like those in the left column, he or she has a wealth of experiential knowledge that enable him or her to make the correct decisions about how to translate the sentence. This experiential knowledge was totally missing in early language processing systems and, in large part, is still missing today. However, researchers now recognize the problem and are taking steps to correct it. Foremost among these researchers is Douglas Lenat, founder of Cycorp. Lenat's CYC project is an attempt to construct a database of "common sense" knowledge in such a way that other programs, such as machine translation systems, can interface with it to gain the deeper understanding necessary to function as intelligent agents. The article by Daniel Lyons, "Artificial Intelligence Gets Real," *Forbes*, November 1998, summarizes Lenat's project as requiring the encoding of millions of common-sense rules into an electronic data retrieval system. Lenat has already spent 15 years on this project and figures that it won't be completed until 2035. When it is, we may well have what Lenat calls "a generally intelligent artifact" and what Stanford AI pioneer Edward Feigenbaum calls "the big enchilada."

Bucket Hashing

In the bucket hashing strategy of collision processing, the hashing function transforms a given key into a physically contiguous region of locations within the list to be searched. This contiguous region is called a **bucket**. Thus, instead of hashing to the *k*th location, a key would hash to the *k*th bucket of locations. The number of locations contained in this bucket would depend on the bucket size. (We assume that all buckets in a given list are the same size.) Figure 8-10 illustrates this concept for a list with 7 buckets and a bucket size of 3. Having hashed to a bucket, the target must then be compared in sequential order to all of the keys in that bucket. On the surface, it seems that this strategy could do no better than duplicate the efficiency of the linked hash method discussed earlier. Indeed, because a sequential search is conducted in both cases after the initial hash is made, the average number of list accesses for a successful or unsuccessful search cannot be improved by using buckets. Moreover, provisions for linking to some sort of overflow area must still be made in case a series of collisions consumes all of the space in a given bucket.

FIGURE 8-10

Storage allocation for bucket hashing

	Position	Key
	0	
Bucket #1	1	
	2	
	3	
Bucket #2	4	
	5	
	6	
Bucket #3	7	
	8	
	9	
Bucket #4	10	
	11	
	12	
Bucket #5	13	
	14	
	15	
Bucket #6	16	
	17	
	18	
Bucket #7	19	
	20	

What could be a possible advantage of using buckets? If the list to be searched resides entirely in main memory, there is no advantage. If the list resides in a disk file, the bucket method will allow us to take advantage of some of the physical characteristics of the storage medium itself. To see this point, we must realize that a one-surface disk is divided into concentric tracks and pie-shaped sectors as indicated in Figure 8-11.

The bucket hashing strategy may take advantage of the organization of the data on a disk in two ways. First, when records in a contiguous random access file are stored on a disk, they are generally located in relative record number order along one track, then along an adjacent track, and so on. The movement of the read/write head between tracks is generally the cause of the most significant delays in obtaining data from a disk. The farther the movement, the greater the delay. Hence, if our knowledge of the machine in question allows us to make a bucket coincide with a track on the disk, then hashing to the beginning of a bucket and proceeding from there using a sequential search within the bucket (that is, the track) will greatly reduce head movement. A linked hashing strategy, on the other hand, could cause considerable movement of the read/write head between tracks on the disk, thereby slowing program execution. This consideration is an excellent example of how one must examine more than just the number of list accesses when measuring the efficiency of a program involving disk files.

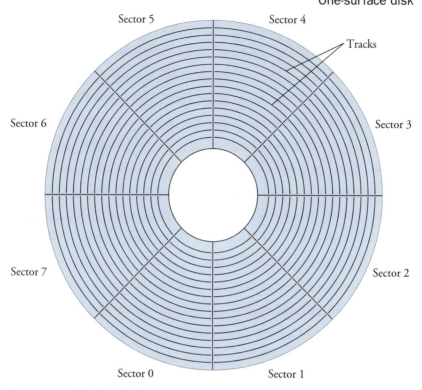

FIGURE 8-11
One-surface disk

Sector 5

Sector 4

Tracks

Sector 6

Sector 3

Sector 7

Sector 2

Sector 0

Sector 1

A second advantage of the bucket hashing algorithm when disk files are being searched relates to the way in which records are transferred between the disk and main memory. Frequently, programming languages create the illusion that each record accessed requires a separate disk access. However, records are frequently blocked—that is, positioned in contiguous regions on a track of the disk—so that a fixed number of them are brought into main memory when a record in that block is requested. If the record requested happens to be part of the block presently in main memory, a program statement that requests a record may not even require a disk access but rather just a different viewing window applied to the block already in main memory. Because main memory manipulations are orders of magnitude faster than the rate of data transfer to and from a disk, positioning our buckets to coincide with a disk block will necessitate only one disk access each time an entire bucket is sequentially searched. Here again, the more scattered nature of a purely linked hashing algorithm does not allow this disk-oriented efficiency consideration to be taken into account.

EXERCISES 8.1

1. Assume a hashing function has the following characteristics:

   Keys 459 and 333 hash to 0.

   Key 632 hashes to 1.

   Key 1090 hashes to 2.

Keys 1982, 379, 238, and 3411 hash to 9.

Assume that insertions into a hashed file are performed in the order 1982, 3411, 333, 632, 1090, 459, 379, and 238.

a. Indicate the position of the keys if the linear method is used to resolve collisions.

Record No.	Key
0	
1	
2	
3	
4	
5	
6	
7	
8	
9	
10	

b. Indicate the position of the keys if the quadratic method is used to resolve collisions.

Record No.	Key
0	
1	
2	
3	
4	
5	
6	
7	
8	
9	
10	

c. Indicate the position of the keys and the contents of the link fields if the chaining (that is, linked) method is used to resolve collisions. Use zeros to represent null links and assume that the first record used in the overflow area is 11, then 12, then 13, and so on.

Record No.	Key	Link
0		
1		
2		
3		
4		
5		
6		
7		
8		
9		
10		

Prime Area

Record No.	Key	Link
11		
12		
13		
14		
15		
16		
17		
18		
19		
20		
21		

Overflow Area

523

2. Repeat Exercise 1 with the order of insertion of keys reversed.

3. Write functions to search for a key via
   a. Quadratic hashing
   b. Bucket hashing

4. Devise strategies to delete keys from a list maintained by each hashing strategy in Exercise 3. Write C++ versions for each algorithm. Given your deletion strategy, describe in detail the modifications (if any) that must be made in the various search and insertion functions of Exercises 3 and 4.

5. In Section 8.1, we mentioned a result by Radke that answered the question of how many vector slots would be probed by the quadratic hashing algorithm for certain values of RECORD_SPACE. In particular, Radke showed that if RECORD_SPACE is a prime number of the form $4m + 3$ for some integer m, then half of the vector slots would be probed by the sequence of probes

$$k, k + 1^2, k + 2^2, k + 3^2, \ldots$$

where k is the original hash position. Radke also showed that the other half would be probed by the sequence

$$k - 1^2, k - 2^2, k - 3^2, \ldots$$

Rewrite your insertion and search functions for the quadratic method in Exercises 3 and 4 to take Radke's result into account.

6. a. Given the arrival of integer keys in the order 67, 19, 4, 58, 38, 55, 86 and RECORD_SPACE = 9 with

```
hash(keyValue) = keyValue % RECORD_SPACE
```

trace the insertion steps of linearly processing collisions.

Index	keyValue	
0	0	(0 indicates empty position)
1	0	
2	0	
3	0	
4	0	
5	0	
6	0	
7	0	
8	0	

b. Given the arrival of integer keys in the order 32, 62, 34, 77, 6, 46, 107 and RECORD_SPACE = 15 with

```
hash(keyValue) = keyValue % RECORD_SPACE
```

trace the insertion steps of quadratically processing collisions.

```
Index  keyValue
  0  |   0   |        (0 indicates empty position)
  1  |   0   |
  2  |   0   |
  3  |   0   |
  4  |   0   |
  5  |   0   |
  6  |   0   |
  7  |   0   |
  8  |   0   |
  9  |   0   |
 10  |   0   |
 11  |   0   |
 12  |   0   |
 13  |   0   |
 14  |   0   |
```

c. Given the arrival of integer keys in the order 5, 3, 16, 27, 14, 25, 4 and RECORD_SPACE = 11 with initial hashing function

```
hash1(keyValue) = keyValue % RECORD_SPACE
```

trace the insertion steps of the rehashing collision processing method where the secondary hashing function is

```
hash2(keyValue) = 5 * keyValue % RECORD_SPACE
```

Assume that if the secondary hashing function is not successful in locating a position for the key, then linear collision processing is used from the address indicated by the secondary hashing function.

```
Index  keyValue
  0  |   0   |        (0 indicates empty position)
  1  |   0   |
  2  |   0   |
  3  |   0   |
  4  |   0   |
  5  |   0   |
  6  |   0   |
  7  |   0   |
  8  |   0   |
  9  |   0   |
 10  |   0   |
```

Comment on the effectiveness of rehashing with this particular secondary hashing function. Can you think of a better one? Explain why yours is better.

7. In a written statement, explain how hashing could be used to search for keys that were not unique. For instance, you might have several people identified by the same name.

8.2 Two Abstract Data Types Revisited

We can analyze hashing from a pragmatic perspective by considering how it might be used to implement two ADTs introduced in Lesson 2: the one-key table and the two-key table. You will be asked to carry out these implementations in the exercises and in the end-of-lesson Projects.

The One-Key Table ADT Implemented by Hashing

In this context, hashing emerges as yet another list maintenance strategy to be evaluated and compared to the strategies we have already discussed: vector with binary search, linked list, and binary tree. Hence, we must examine its performance with respect to the same `insert`, `retrieve`, `remove`, and `traverse` operations that were introduced in Lesson 2 and then used to evaluate these other one-key table implementation techniques. Additionally, should an application want to extend the one-key table to allow an operation that traverses the table in ascending order by key, we will consider the efficiency of this operation when hashing is used as an implementation strategy. Assuming the existence of an appropriate hashing function to act on the key and a willingness to waste enough storage to allow for fast searching, hashing will clearly perform very well in all of these areas with the exception of ordering data. Here is where we have to pay a price for the scattered storage of records that are located via a hashing function.

Nonetheless, strategies can be used to allow hashing and ordering of data to coexist. One such strategy is to use a pointer sort algorithm (see Lesson 1) to sort the data logically when an ordered list is needed. This approach has the drawback of not maintaining the list in order but actually performing a potentially costly sort algorithm each time an ordering is requested. Clearly, it would not be a wise choice if such an ordering is requested frequently and unpredictably.

In situations where requests for ordering come frequently enough to make maintaining the list in order (as opposed to sorting) a necessity, we could follow a strategy that combines the search speed of hashing with the ordered list advantages offered by a linked list implementation. This combination uses hashing to search for an individual record but adds link fields to each record so that a linked list for each desired ordering could be woven through the collection of hashed records. Implementing this combination of hashing and linked lists entails the following considerations with respect to the one-key table operations:

`insert`: In effect, the hashing/collision processing algorithm provides us with an available node in which to store data. Each linked list involved then has to be traversed to link the node into each ordering in the appropriate logical location.

`retrieve`: There is no problem here because the hash algorithm should find the desired record quickly.

`remove`: This operation is similar to the `retrieve` operation. We use hashing to find the record to be deleted and then adjust the link field appropriately. A doubly linked list could prove to be particularly valuable here. (Why?)

`traverseInOrder`: There is no problem here because the linked lists constantly maintain the appropriate orderings.

The Two-Key Table ADT Implemented by Hashing

We have already covered two implementation strategies for two-key tables.

1. In Section 2.4, we described a strategy that simply creates a list of the rows and columns corresponding to nontrivial values in the table. Determining the value of the data at a conceptual row/column location is then simply a matter of searching this list.

2. Using linked lists (Lesson 3), we could form a linked list of the nontrivial columns in each row. Determining the value of the data at a conceptual row/column location is then reduced to the problem of sequentially searching a relatively small linked list.

At the time we explored these two strategies, the first one appeared to be less attractive. Because the data in the list of row/column coordinates corresponding to nontrivial values are likely to be volatile, physically ordering the data for a binary search would not be practical. Yet, without a binary search, requests to inspect the value at any given location are met with the $O(n)$ response time of a sequential search. Hashing allows us to search for a row/column coordinate in the list of the first strategy in a very efficient fashion—probably faster than the sequential search along the linked list representing a given row required by the second strategy. Moreover, because the order of the data in the list is not important for this application, the scattered nature of hashed storage does not present any obstacle.

The considerations we have discussed with respect to these two ADTs make it evident that hashing is a very attractive table implementation technique. It will be extremely efficient in regard to the `insert`, `retrieve`, and `remove` table operations if we are willing to pay the price of wasting enough storage to get a reasonably low density ratio. The only other drawback to hashing, in addition to this wasted storage, is the price that must be paid if various orderings of the data are frequently needed.

EXERCISES 8.2

1. Suppose we combine hashing with a linked list in the fashion described in this section so that all one-key table operations can be efficiently performed. Which of the variations on a linked list structure would be most effective in this context? Explain why in a carefully worded statement. (*Hint:* Think about the `retrieve` and `remove` operations.)

2. Give an example of an application where the hashing implementation of a two-dimensional table described in this section would be less efficient (overall) than the linked list implementation. Explain why in a carefully worded statement.

3. Provide implementations of all one-key table operations using the hashing strategy described in this section. Provide alternative implementations of the `traverse` operations: One should invoke a pointer sort and another should combine hashing with a linked list.

4. Provide implementations of all two-key table operations defined in Lesson 2 using the hashing strategy described in this section.

5. We have covered binary search, linked lists, binary trees, and hashing as methods of implementing a one-key table ADT. Choose the method you would use to implement the data list involved for each of the following three real-world applications. In each case you should choose the most appropriate implementation technique. "Most appropriate" refers here to efficient handling of all required operations while not being too powerful—that is, not doing something that should be easy in an overly complicated way. Then provide a written rationale as to why yours would be the appropriate method.
   a. The list to be maintained is the card catalog of a library. The library makes frequent additions to and deletions from this catalog. Additionally, users frequently search for the data associated with a given book's key. The library rarely prints out an ordered list of all its holdings; so ordering the list is not a high priority.

b. You are writing a program that maintains the lists of passengers on flights for an airline company. Passengers are frequently added to these lists. Quite often, passengers cancel flight plans and must be removed from a list. The airline frequently wants alphabetized listings of the passengers on a given flight and often needs to search for a particular passenger by name when inquiries are received from individuals.

c. You are writing a program to access a large customer database and build up counts for the numbers of customers from each of the 50 states plus the District of Columbia. You will use a list of records consisting of the two-character state abbreviation and an integer representing the count of customers from that state. For each customer you read in from the database, you must find the customer's home state in your list and increase the corresponding count field. At the end, print out the counts in order alphabetized by the two-character state abbreviation.

8.3 Indexed Search Techniques (Optional)

All of the search strategies we have studied up to this point could be applied to lists implemented in main memory or on a random access disk. However, with the exception of bucket hashing, none of the methods we have studied takes into account the physical characteristics of disk storage in an attempt to enhance its efficiency. In practice, because retrieval of data from a disk file is orders of magnitude slower than retrieval from main memory, we often cannot afford to ignore these special characteristics of disk files if we want reasonable response time for our searching efforts. The indexing schemes that we will discuss in this section are primarily directed toward file-oriented applications and, therefore, take into account the operational properties of this storage medium. We encourage you to reread the discussion of bucket hashing at the end of Section 8.1 for a summary analysis of file storage considerations.

The idea behind the use of an index is analogous to the way in which we routinely use an address book to find a person whom we are seeking. That is, if we are looking for a person, we do not knock on the doors of numerous houses until we find the one where that person lives. Instead, we apply a search strategy to an address book. There we use the name of the person as a key to find a pointer—that is, an address—to lead us swiftly to where the person can be found. Only one actual "house access" must be made, although our search strategy may require numerous accesses into the address book index.

In a computer system, records (or, more precisely, blocks) could play the role of houses in the search scenario just described. Compared with main memory, data records on disk are terribly slow and awkward creatures to access. One reason for this problem is that much data must often be moved from disk to main memory every time a record is accessed. As a consequence, the conceptual picture for the general setup of an indexed search must be revised. The list of keys is no longer parallel to the actual data with which they are logically associated; rather, it is parallel to a list of pointers, which will lead us to the actual data. The revised picture is presented in Figure 8-12.

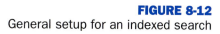

FIGURE 8-12

General setup for an indexed search

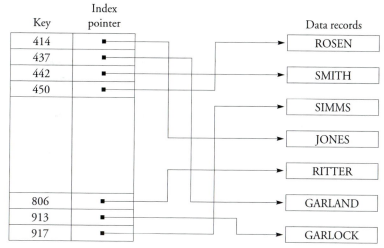

The general strategy of an indexed search is to use the key to search the index efficiently, find the relative record position of the associated data, and from there make only one access into the actual data. Because the parallel lists of keys and relative record positions require much less storage than the data, the entire index frequently can be loaded and permanently held in main memory, necessitating only one disk access for each record being sought. For larger indices, it remains true that large blocks of keys and associated pointers may be manipulated in main memory, thereby greatly enhancing search efficiency.

Indexed Sequential Search Technique

The *indexed sequential search* technique is also commonly recognized by the acronym ISAM, which stands for *indexed sequential access method*. Essentially, it involves carefully weighing the disk-dependent factors of blocking and track size to build a partial index. The partial index, unlike some other index structures we will study, does not reduce to one the number of probes that must be made into the actual data.

To continue the analogy between searching for data and searching for a person, the indexed sequential strategy resembles an address book that leads us to the street on which a person lives but makes us check each house on that street. The ISAM method correspondingly leads us to an appropriate region (often a track or a cylinder containing multiple tracks within a disk pack) and then leaves it to us to search sequentially within that region.

As an example, let us suppose that we can conveniently fit the partial index, or directory, pictured in Figure 8-13 into main memory and that the organization of our disk file allows six records per track. This directory is formed by choosing the highest key value in each six-record track along with a pointer indicating where that track begins. Here our pointers are simply relative record numbers; in practice, they could be a more disk-dependent locator. The strategy to conduct an indexed sequential search is:

1. Search the main memory directory for a key that is greater than or equal to the target.

2. Follow the corresponding pointer to the disk and search there sequentially until we find a match (success) or the key that the directory maintains as the high key within that particular region (failure).

FIGURE 8-13

One-level indexed sequential file

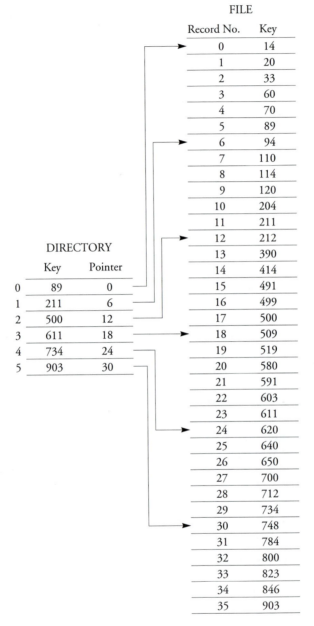

FILE

Record No.	Key
0	14
1	20
2	33
3	60
4	70
5	89
6	94
7	110
8	114
9	120
10	204
11	211
12	212
13	390
14	414
15	491
16	499
17	500
18	509
19	519
20	580
21	591
22	603
23	611
24	620
25	640
26	650
27	700
28	712
29	734
30	748
31	784
32	800
33	823
34	846
35	903

DIRECTORY

	Key	Pointer
0	89	0
1	211	6
2	500	12
3	611	18
4	734	24
5	903	30

For the data in Figure 8-13, this technique means that the 36-record file requires no more than six main memory index accesses plus six disk accesses, all of which are located in the same track.

For larger files, it may be advantageous to have more than one level of these directory structures. Consider, for instance, the two-level directory structure for a file with 216 records given in Figure 8-14. Here we might suppose that storage restrictions allow the entire primary directory to be kept in main memory, the secondary directory to be brought in from a disk file in blocks of six key–pointer pairs each, and the actual data records to be stored six per track. The primary directory divides the file into regions of 36 records each. The key in the primary directory represents the highest-valued key in a given 36-record region, but the pointer leads us into the subdirectory instead of the actual file. We then search the primary directory for a key greater than or equal to the target we are seeking. Once this task is done, we follow the primary directory pointer into the secondary directory. Beginning at the position indicated by the primary directory's pointer, we again search for a key greater than or equal to the target. Notice that fetching one block of six key–pointer pairs from the subdirectory has necessitated one disk access in our hypothetical situation. In return for this single disk access, we are able to subdivide the 36-record region determined by the primary directory into six 6-record regions, each of which will lie entirely on one track by the time we get to the actual disk file. Following the subdirectory's pointer to the file, we end up with a relatively short sequential search on the storage medium itself. In this example, the maximum number of disk accesses required to find any record would be seven, and six of those would be isolated on one track of the disk.

PROGRAMMING SKILLS: Data Integrity, Concurrent Updates, and Deadlock

The problems of finding and allowing a user to access a particular record in a file are complicated somewhat in a system that allows several users to access the same file simultaneously. To see why, recall that when you manipulate a record or part of an index from a file, you really have a copy of that portion of the file in your main memory area. Suppose that two users are accessing not only the same file simultaneously but also the same record in that file simultaneously. A scenario such as the following could emerge:

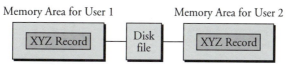

User 1 requests a record associated with key XYZ.
User 2 requests a record associated with key XYZ.
User 1 updates the address field of that record.
User 2 updates the inventory field of that record.
User 1 makes changes in the file by writing that record to disk.
User 2 makes changes in the file by writing that record to disk.

What will be wrong with the new record that exists in the disk file? Clearly, the address change made by User 1 will have been destroyed when User 2's copy of the record is written back to the disk. This *data integrity* problem is caused by the *concurrent updating* of the same record by two users. The situation can become much worse than merely losing an address change. Imagine the havoc created if one user deleted the record while another user was processing it, or what would happen if the portion of the file being simultaneously updated by two users was not a data record but instead part of the file index.

The concurrent updating problem must be avoided in any multiuser system if data integrity is to be ensured. The solution used in many systems is that of a *record lock facility.* With such a facility, the user who has a file record in main memory for updating is considered the owner of that record to the exclusion of any other users accessing that record. That lock on the record exists until the user writes the (perhaps altered) record back to the disk file. Hence, in our scenario, User 2 would not have been able to obtain the record for key XYZ immediately. Instead, that user would sit idle in a wait state until the record became available.

(Continued on page 533.)

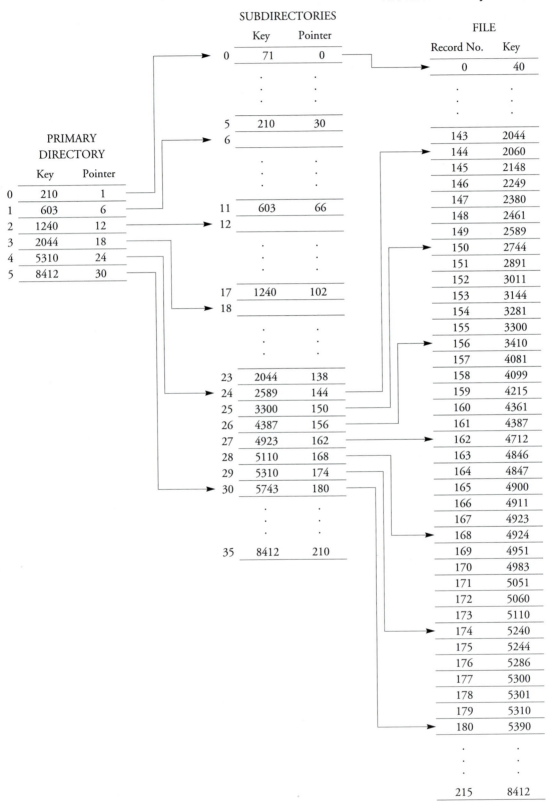

FIGURE 8-14
Two-level directory structure

SUBDIRECTORIES

	Key	Pointer
0	71	0
	.	.
	.	.
	.	.
5	210	30
6		
	.	.
	.	.
	.	.
11	603	66
12		
	.	.
	.	.
17	1240	102
18		
	.	.
	.	.
23	2044	138
24	2589	144
25	3300	150
26	4387	156
27	4923	162
28	5110	168
29	5310	174
30	5743	180
	.	.
	.	.
35	8412	210

PRIMARY DIRECTORY

	Key	Pointer
0	210	1
1	603	6
2	1240	12
3	2044	18
4	5310	24
5	8412	30

FILE

Record No.	Key
0	40
.	.
.	.
.	.
143	2044
144	2060
145	2148
146	2249
147	2380
148	2461
149	2589
150	2744
151	2891
152	3011
153	3144
154	3281
155	3300
156	3410
157	4081
158	4099
159	4215
160	4361
161	4387
162	4712
163	4846
164	4847
165	4900
166	4911
167	4923
168	4924
169	4951
170	4983
171	5051
172	5060
173	5110
174	5240
175	5244
176	5286
177	5300
178	5301
179	5310
180	5390
.	.
.	.
.	.
215	8412

Although the record-locking approach guarantees data integrity, it is not without its own set of problems. For instance, consider the following scenario:

User 1 requests and gets a record for key XYZ.
User 2 requests and gets a record for key ABC.
To process record XYZ, User 1 needs data associated with record ABC.
Because record ABC, is owned by User 2, User 1 must wait in an idle state.
To process record ABC, User 2 needs data associated with record XYZ.

Because record XYZ is owned by User 1, User 2 must wait in an idle state.

Although data integrity has been maintained, we now have two users in an infinite wait state known as a **deadlock** or, more glamorously, **fatal embrace**. The avoidance and/or detection of deadlock situations in a multiuser environment is a nontrivial problem. If you are interested in exploring it more deeply, see Harvey M. Deitel, *An Introduction to Operating Systems*, 2nd ed. (Reading, Massachusetts: Addison-Wesley, 1990).

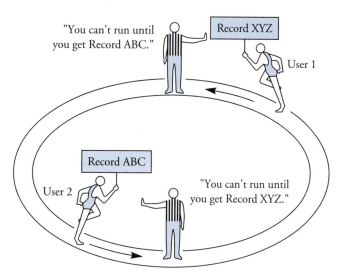

Two Users in a Deadlock Situation

Efficiency Considerations for the Indexed Sequential Search. It should be clear from the preceding discussion that the search efficiency of the indexed sequential technique depends on a variety of factors:

- The degree to which the directory structures are able to subdivide the actual file

- The degree to which the directory structures are able to reside in main memory

- The relationship of data records to physical characteristics of the disk such as blocking factors, track size, and cylinder size

It should also be clear that the indexed sequential method may not be ideal for a highly volatile file. As implicitly indicated in Figures 8-13 and 8-14, the actual data records must be physically stored in increasing (or decreasing) key order. The requirement for physical ordering is obviously not conducive to frequent insertions and deletions. In practice, the solution to this problem is that each file subregion, which is ultimately the subject of a sequential search, is equipped with a pointer to an overflow area. Insertions are located in this overflow area and linked to the main sequential search area. As the overflow area builds up, the search efficiency tends to deteriorate. In some applications, this deterioration can become so severe that data processing personnel have been known to refer to ISAM as the "intrinsically slow access method."

To avoid deterioration, you can reorganize the file periodically into a new file with no overflow. However, such reorganization cannot be done dynamically. It requires going through the file in key sequential order and copying it into a new one. Along the way, the indices must be rebuilt, of course. These types of maintenance problems involved with the ISAM structure have led to the development of several more dynamic indexing schemes.

Binary Search Tree Indexing

The concept of a binary search tree was covered in Lesson 6. The only twist added when the binary tree plays the role of an index is that each node of the tree contains a key and a pointer to the record associated with that key in some larger data aggregate. The advantages of using a binary search tree as an index structure include:

- A search efficiency potentially proportional to $\log_2 n$

- The ability to traverse the list indexed by the tree in key order

- Dynamic insertion and deletion capabilities

These qualities make the binary search tree the ideal index structure for situations in which the entire tree can fit in main memory. If the data collection is so large that the tree index must itself be stored on disk, the efficiency of the structure is less than optimal. This situation arises because each node of the index may lie in a disk block separate from the other nodes and hence require a separate disk access. Using an example of 50,000 keys, a search of a binary tree index could require 16 disk accesses. To solve this problem, we would like to cluster those nodes along a given search path into one or at least relatively few disk blocks. The B-tree index structure is a variation on the tree index that accomplishes this goal.

B-Tree Indexing

We begin this discussion of **B-trees** by reminding you that one index entry requires nothing more than a key and a pointer. Moreover, we have assumed that both the key and the pointer are integers, and we continue to operate under this assumption during our discussion of B-trees. We emphasize this point here because, in a B-tree, a tree node will contain many such key–pointer pairs. A B-tree node will in fact, coincide with one disk block. The idea behind a B-tree is that we will somehow group key–pointer pairs that are related in the search algorithm into a few strategic B-tree nodes—that is, disk blocks. At this point, we make a formal definition; later, we'll clarify this definition with some examples. A **B-tree of order** **n** is a structure with the following properties:

1. Every node in the B-tree has sufficient room to store $n - 1$ key–pointer pairs.

2. Every node also has room for n pointers to other nodes in the B-tree (as distinguished from the pointers within key–pointer pairs, which point to the position of a key in the file).

3. Every node except the root must have at least $(n - 1)/2$ key–pointer pairs stored in it.

4. All terminal nodes are on the same level.

5. If a nonterminal node has m key–pointer pairs stored in it, then it must contain $m + 1$ non-null pointers to other B-tree nodes.

6. For each B-tree node, we require that the key value in key–pointer pair KP_{i-1} be less than the key value in key–pointer pair KP_i, that all key–pointer pairs in the node pointed to by P_{i-1} contain keys that are less than the key in KP_i, and that all key–pointer pairs in the node pointed to by P_i contain key values that are greater than the key in KP_i.

According to property 5 of the definition, we can think of a B-tree node as a list

$$P_0, KP_1, P_1, KP_2, P_2, KP_3, \ldots, P_{m-1}, KP_m, P_m$$

where P_i represents the ith pointer to another B-tree node and KP_i represents the ith key–pointer pair. Note that a B-tree node will always contain one more pointer to another B-tree node than it does key–pointer pairs. With this picture in mind, the sixth and final property of our definition makes sense. Figure 8-15 illustrates how this rather involved definition applies to a B-tree node with three key–pointer pairs.

FIGURE 8-15

Example of a B-tree node with three key–pointer pairs

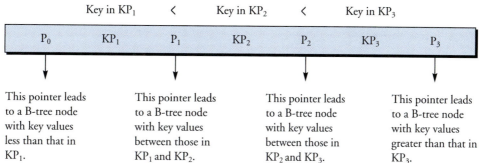

As a further illustration of this definition, a complete B-tree of order 6 serving as an index structure for the 36-record file of Figure 8-13 appears in Figure 8-16. (In this figure, the slash between numbers denotes a key–pointer pair; | denotes a null pointer.) Carefully verify that all six defining properties are satisfied.

Order 6 was chosen for Figure 8-16 only for the purpose of fitting the figure on a page of text. In practice, the order chosen would be the maximum number of B-tree pointers and key–pointer pairs that we could fit into one disk block. That is, the choice should be made to force a disk block to coincide with a B-tree node. It is also worth noting that B-trees of order 3 have special application as a data structure apart from indexing considerations. This application is covered in the end-of-lesson projects.

Efficiency Considerations for B-Tree Indexing. Let us now consider what is involved in searching a B-tree for a given key. Within the current node (starting at the root), we must search sequentially through the key values in the node until we come to a match, a key value that is greater than the one being sought, or the end of the key values in that particular node. If a match is not made within a particular B-tree node, we have a pointer to follow to an appropriate follow-up node. You should verify this algorithm for several of the keys appearing at various levels of Figure 8-16. The sequential search on keys within a given node may at first seem unappealing. However, the important fact to remember here is that each B-tree node is a disk block that is loaded entirely into main memory. Hence, it may be possible to search sequentially on hundreds of keys within a node in the time it takes to load one new node from disk. Our main concern is to minimize disk accesses, and here we have achieved a worst case search for our 36-entry file in three disk accesses.

What, in general, is the search efficiency for a B-tree index? It should be clear from the nature of the structure that the maximum number of disk accesses for any particular key will simply be the number of levels in the tree. Thus the efficiency question really amounts to knowing the maximum number of levels that the six defining criteria allow for a B-tree containing n key–pointer pairs. This number is the worst case search efficiency and, to determine it, we use the minimum number of nodes that must be present on any given level. Let l be the smallest integer greater than or equal to $k/2$ where k is the order of the B-tree in question. Then

Level 0 contains at least 1 node.
Level 1 contains at least 2 nodes.
Level 2 contains at least $2l$ nodes.
Level 3 contains at least $2l^2$ nodes.
.
.
.
Level m contains at least $2l^{m-1}$ nodes.

FIGURE 8-16

B-tree index of order 6 for file in Figure 8-13

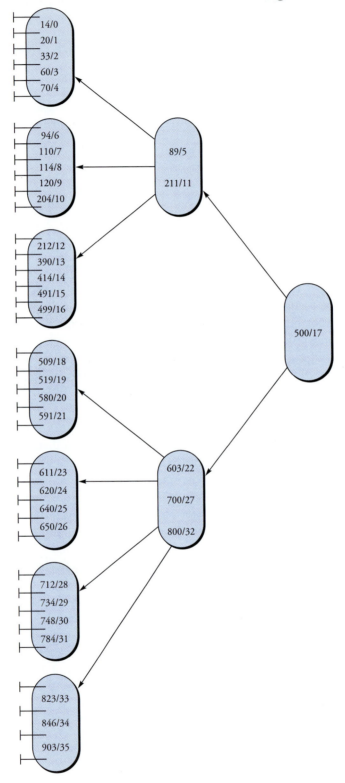

An argument based on Knuth's research (see "Searching and Sorting", cited in Section 8.1) uses this progression to show that the maximum number of levels (and thus the worst case search efficiency) for n key–pointer pairs is

$$\log_k[(n+1)/2]$$

Thus a B-tree search has an $O(\log_k n)$ efficiency, where n is the number of records and k is the order of the B-tree. Note that this value can be considerably better than an $O(\log_2 n)$ search efficiency. For example, the index for a file of 50,000 records, which would require on the order of 16 disk accesses using a binary tree structure, could be searched with 3 disk accesses using a B-tree of order 250. Given the typical block sizes for files, the choice of order 250 for this example is not at all unrealistic.

Unlike ISAM, the B-tree index can dynamically handle insertions and deletions without a corresponding deterioration in search efficiency. We next discuss how B-tree insertions are handled; deletions are left as an exercise. The essential idea behind a B-tree insertion is that we must first determine which bottom-level node should contain the key–pointer pair to be inserted. For instance, suppose we want to insert the key 742 into the B-tree of Figure 8-16. By allowing this key to walk down the B-tree from the root to the bottom level, we could quickly determine that this key belongs in the node presently containing

712/28
734/29
748/30
784/31

By the definition of a B-tree of order 6, this node is not presently full. Thus no further disk accesses are necessary to perform the insertion. We merely need to determine the next available record space in the actual data file (36 in this case) and then add the key–pointer pair 742/36 to this terminal node, resulting in

712/28
734/29
742/36
748/30
784/31

A slightly more complex situation arises when we find that the key–pointer pair we wish to add should be inserted into a bottom-level node that is already full. For instance, this case would occur if we attempted to add the key 112 to the B-tree of Figure 8-16. We would load the actual data for this key into file position 37 (given the addition already made in the preceding paragraph) and then determine that the key–pointer pair 112/37 belongs in the bottom-level node

94/6
110/7
114/8
120/9
204/10

The stipulation that any B-tree node except the root has at least $(n-1)/2 = 2$ key–pointer pairs allows us to split this node, creating one new node with two key–pointer pairs and one with three key–pointer pairs. We also have to move one of the key–pointer pairs up to the parent of the present node. The resulting B-tree is given in Figure 8-17 on the next page.

FIGURE 8-17
B-tree of Figure 8-16 after insertion of 112/37 and 742/36

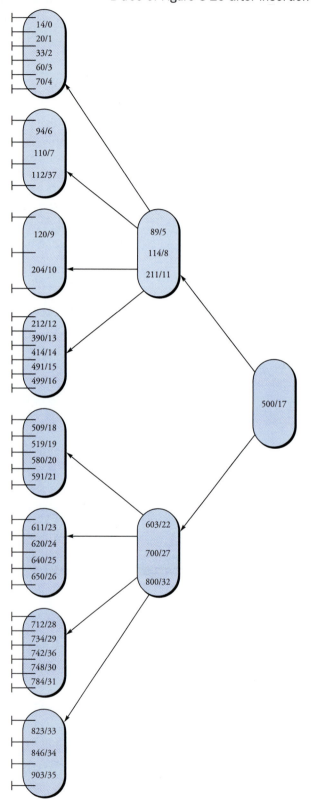

Although it does not happen in this particular example, it is entirely possible that the movement of a key–pointer pair up to a parent node that is already full would necessitate a split of this parent node, using the same function. Indeed, key–pointer pairs could be passed all the way up to the root and cause a split of the root. This is, in fact, how a new level of the tree is introduced. A split of the root forces the creation of a new root, which has only one key–pointer pair and two pointers to other B-tree nodes. However, at the root level, this number of pointers is sufficient to retain the B-tree structure. Because the insertion algorithm for a B-tree requires checking whether a given node is full and potentially moving back up to a parent node, it is convenient to allow space within a node to store both of the following:

- A count of the number of key–pointer pairs in the node

- A pointer back to the node's parent

Trie Indexing

In all of the indexing applications we have discussed so far, the keys involved have been integers. In the real world, we must be prepared to deal with keys of different types. Perhaps the worst case is that of keys that are variable-length character strings. *Trie indexing* has developed as a means of retrieving keys in this worst case. (The term itself is derived from the four middle letters of "retrieve," although it is usually pronounced "try.")

Let us suppose that the strings in the following list represent a set of keys. Each string may be thought of as a last name followed by initials and a delimiting $.

```
ADAMS BT$
COOPER CC$
COOPER PJ$
COWANS DC$
MAGUIRE WH$
MCGUIRE AL$
MEMINGER DD$
SEFTON SD$
SPAN KD$
SPAN LA$
SPANNER DW$
ZARDA JM$
ZARDA PW$
```

An individual node in a trie structure for these keys follows:

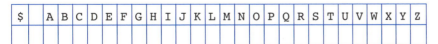

This node is essentially a fixed-length vector of 28 pointers: one for each letter of the alphabet, one for a blank, and one for the delimiter. Each pointer within one of these nodes can lead to one of two entities—either another node within the trie or the actual data record for a given key. Hence, it may be convenient to embed a Boolean flag in each pointer indicating the type of entity to which it is pointing. The trie structure for the preceding list of keys is given in Figure 8-18. In the figure, pointers to nodes labeled as data records lead us outside of the trie structure itself.

FIGURE 8-18
Trie index structure

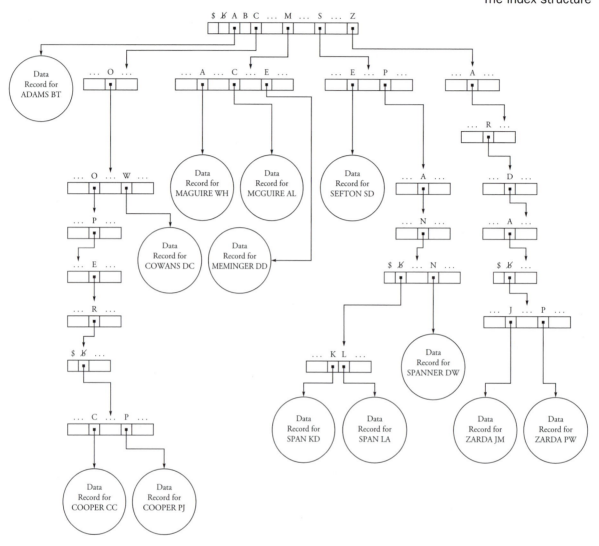

The logic behind a trie structure may best be seen by tracing through an example. This search algorithm involves examining the target key on a character-by-character basis. Let us begin by considering the easy case of finding the data record for ADAMS BT$. In this case, we look at A, the first character in the key, and follow the A pointer in the root node to its destination. From what we have previously said, we know that its destination will be either another node within the trie structure or an actual data record. If it is a node within the trie, it is a node on the search path for all keys that begin with A. In this case, only one key in our list begins with A, so the A pointer in the root node leads us directly to the actual data record for ADAMS BT$.

On the other hand, the search path to find the key COOPER CC$ in the trie is somewhat longer. We follow the C pointer from the root node down a level to a node shared by all keys starting with C. From there, the O pointer is followed to a trie node shared by all keys that start with CO. The process continues down level by level, following the O pointer to a trie node shared by all keys starting with COO, then the P pointer to a node for all keys starting with COOP, the E pointer to a node for all keys starting with COOPE, the R pointer to a node for all keys starting with COOPER, and the blank pointer to a node shared by all keys starting with COOPER followed by a blank. Notice that, as each character is read in, we must continue following these pointers from trie node to trie node (instead of from trie node to actual data record) until we finally reach a point where the next character to be read will uniquely define the key. At this point, the key in question need no longer share its pointer with other keys that match it on an initial substring. The pointer may now lead to an actual data record, as happens when we read in the next C to form the uniquely defined substring COOPER C.

Efficiency Considerations for Trie Indexing. The search efficiency for the trie index is quite easily determined. The worst case occurs when a key is not uniquely defined until its last character is read. In this case, we may have as many disk accesses as there are characters in the key before we finally locate the actual data record. You may have observed, however, that another efficiency consideration applies when you are using the trie method: the amount of wasted storage in the trie nodes. In our example using a short list of keys, only a small percentage of the available pointers are ever used. In the real world, a trie is used only for an extremely large file, such as the list represented by a phone book with names as keys. In such a situation, a much larger number of character combinations occurs, and the resulting trie structure is correspondingly much less sparse.

A final point to consider relative to trie indexes is their ability to handle insertions and deletions dynamically. Here we discuss insertions; deletions are left as an exercise. Insertions may be broken down into two cases. For both, we must begin by reading the key to be inserted, character by character, and following the appropriate search path in the trie until

- We come to a trie node that has a vacant pointer in the character position corresponding to the current character of the insertion key, or

- We come to an actual data record for a key different from the one that is being inserted.

The first case is illustrated by trying to insert the key COLLINS RT$ into the trie of Figure 8-18. We follow the search path pointers until we come to the trie node shared by all keys starting with CO. At this point, the L pointer is null. The insertion is completed by merely aiming the presently null L pointer to a data record for the key COLLINS RT$. The second case is illustrated by trying to insert the key COOPER PA$ into the trie of Figure 8-18. Here, following the search path of the trie would eventually lead us to the data record for the key COOPER PJ$. The dynamic solution is to get a new trie node, aim the P pointer presently leading to the data record for COOPER PJ$ to this new trie node, and use the A and J pointers in the new trie node to lead us to data records for COOPER PA$ and COOPER PJ$, respectively. Both the COLLINS RT$ and COOPER PA$ insertions are shown with the resulting trie in Figure 8-19 on the next page.

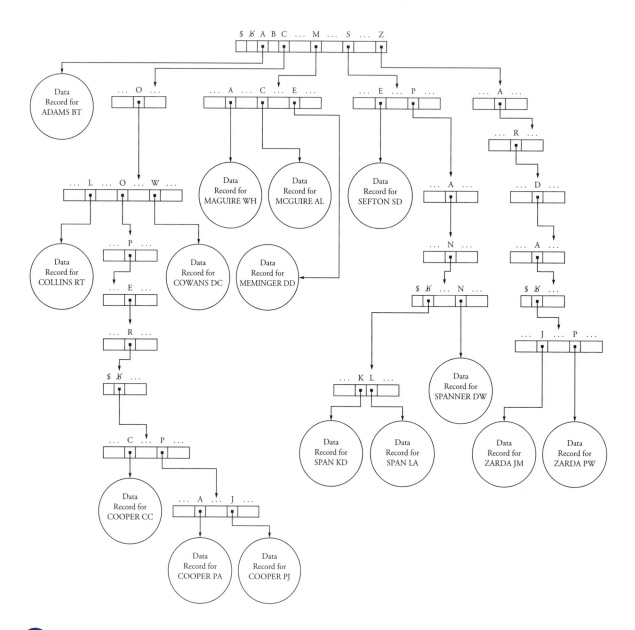

EXERCISES 8.3

1. a. Suppose the records associated with keys 810, 430, 602, 946, 289, 106, and 732 are stored in positions 0, 1, 2, 3, 4, 5, and 6, respectively, of a file. Draw a B-tree index of order 8 for this file.

b. Suppose the key 538 then arrives for insertion in position 8. Redraw your B-tree of order 8 after this insertion.

2. Suppose the following strings arrive for insertion into a trie index:

CARTER

HERNANDEZ

HERMAN

HERMANSKI

HERSCHEL

HALL

CARSON

CARSWELL

CARSEN
   a. Draw the trie index.
   b. Draw the index after CARSWELL and HERMANSKI have been deleted.

3. Discuss a key deletion strategy for B-trees. Write a function to implement your strategy.

4. Discuss a key deletion strategy for trie indexes. Write a function to implement your strategy.

5. Carefully read your system reference material concerning the specifics of how disk file records are blocked. Then explain how this knowledge would influence your decisions in the construction of
   a. A B-tree index structure
   b. A trie index structure
   c. A bucket hashing structure
   d. An ISAM index structure

6. All of the search strategies we have discussed assume a key that is uniquely valued. That is, no two records have the same value for their key field. In practice, this situation will not always be the case: We may have duplicate keys. For instance, a list of personnel records may contain two records for different people with the same name. In a carefully worded statement, discuss how each of the search strategies we have covered would have to be modified to perform a duplicate key search. What effect would these modifications have on the performance of the algorithm?

7. Devise functions to handle insertions into and deletions from a list maintained by the indexed sequential method. Do the strategies reflected by these functions require any modifications in your answers to Exercise 6? If so, explain the nature of these modifications.

8. Write an algorithm to insert a key and its data record into a trie.

CASE STUDY: Testing Hashing Strategies

In the Case Study for Lesson 1, we introduced the idea of developing a program to profile an algorithm—that is, to monitor the performance of an algorithm empirically. In doing the Projects in other lessons, you may have written similar programs to analyze the efficiency of binary search trees and more sophisticated sort algorithms. Such programs are extremely useful for algorithms whose analysis relies on somewhat random factors and therefore defies purely mathematical techniques. Insertions into binary search trees and the shell sort are prime examples of this type of algorithm. Certainly, the strategy of hashing, presented in Section 8.1, also falls into this category. The efficiency of hashing depends on a variety of factors: the randomness with which your hashing function scatters keys into the record space, the amount of space you are willing to sacrifice to empty storage locations, and the effectiveness of your collision-processing strategy in reducing clustering.

Because of hashing's dependence on these factors, an experimental tool for testing various hashing strategies can be very valuable in predicting how effective hashing will be for a particular application. In this Case Study, we discuss the design of such an experimental program for situations in which we wish to study the effectiveness of hashing on keys that are strings.

User Request

Develop a profiling program to experiment with hashing strategies. The program should allow us to choose between three forms of input to the hash table:

1. A sequence of randomly generated string keys

2. A sequence of string keys that are entered interactively, so that we can enter specific data sets particularly relevant to our experimentation

3. A sequence of string keys read one per line from a file

The program should also have the facility to save a particularly interesting data set in a text file form that can later be read by the program. This option will allow us to fine-tune the algorithm by altering the hashing function or selecting a different collision-processing method and then testing the new program with the same set of data.

When randomly generated keys are chosen as the method for loading the table, the program should prompt the user to specify the size of the hash table and the number of active records contained within that record space. Once the table is loaded, the program should report the average number of probes needed for successful and unsuccessful searches. To determine the average for a successful search, it should exercise the table's search strategy for each key occurring in the table, profiling the total number of probes made into the table as these searches are carried out. To determine the average for an unsuccessful search, the program should randomly generate a collection of keys that do not occur in the table and then profile the number of probes made as these keys are fed to the search algorithm.

Analysis

The sample runs below, annotated with italicized comments, define how the final program should interact with its user.

```
          1 - Load a random table
          2 - Interactively load a table
          3 - Load table from a file
          4 - Save table to a file
          5 - Display table
          6 - Test performance
          7 - Quit program

     Enter 1, 2, 3, 4, 5, 6, or 7 --> 1
     Enter record space size: (<= 500) 40
     Enter the number of records to insert: 30    { Table density is 75% }

          1 - Load a random table
          2 - Interactively load a table
          3 - Load table from a file
          4 - Save table to a file
          5 - Display table
          6 - Test performance
          7 - Quit program

     Enter 1, 2, 3, 4, 5, 6, or 7 --> 5

     0 wSGy 11
     1 Ut 21
     2 tqDV 9
     3 FbBU 29
     4 TYG 30
     5 sZ 4
     6 gg 8
     7  0
     8 gzSA 28
     9  0
     10  0
     11 oZd 18

     … { Here the contents of table indices 0 through 39 are displayed.
       Each table entry is a random string, 2-4 characters, along with
       an integer datum. }

     33 zxso 15
     34 HUQ 23
     35 HQS 7
     36 MHv 12
     37 da 17
     38 sy 19
     39 UD 25
     Record space = 40
     Active records = 30

          1 - Load a random table
          2 - Interactively load a table
          3 - Load table from a file
```

```
    4 - Save table to a file
    5 - Display table
    6 - Test performance
    7 - Quit program

    Enter 1, 2, 3, 4, 5, 6, or 7 --> 6

Average length of successful search = 2.03333
Average length of unsuccessful search = 5.2

    1 - Load a random table
    2 - Interactively load a table
    3 - Load table from a file
    4 - Save table to a file
    5 - Display table
    6 - Test performance
    7 - Quit program

    Enter 1, 2, 3, 4, 5, 6, or 7 --> 4
    Enter output file name: test.dat          { Table saved for later use }
    Number of active records = 30
    Record space = 40

    1 - Load a random table
    2 - Interactively load a table
    3 - Load table from a file
    4 - Save table to a file
    5 - Display table
    6 - Test performance
    7 - Quit program

    Enter 1, 2, 3, 4, 5, 6, or 7 --> 7
```

Now we could modify the hashing function and/or collision-processing strategy and see if any improvement occurs.

```
    1 - Load a random table
    2 - Interactively load a table
    3 - Load table from a file
    4 - Save table to a file
    5 - Display table
    6 - Test performance
    7 - Quit program

    Enter 1, 2, 3, 4, 5, 6, or 7 --> 3
    Enter record space size: (<= 500) 40      { Load the table from last run }
    Enter input file name: test.dat
    30 records input from file test.dat

    1 - Load a random table
    2 - Interactively load a table
    3 - Load table from a file
```

```
      4 - Save table to a file
      5 - Display table
      6 - Test performance
      7 - Quit program

      Enter 1, 2, 3, 4, 5, 6, or 7 --> 6        { Notice slight improvement! }
      Average length of successful search = 1.92481
      Average length of unsuccessful search = 4.92667

      1 - Load a random table
      2 - Interactively load a table
      3 - Load table from a file
      4 - Save table to a file
      5 - Display table
      6 - Test performance
      7 - Quit program

      Enter 1, 2, 3, 4, 5, 6, or 7 --> 7
```

Design

A modular structure chart for the program appears in Figure 8-20. The specifications for the functions called by the main program are given as documentation accompanying the following function protocols.

FIGURE 8-20
Structure chart for profiling program

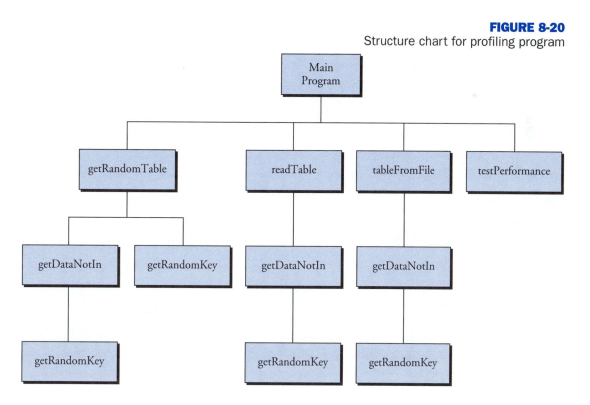

```
typedef HashTable<int> IntTable;
typedef OrderedCollection<apstring> ApstringList;

// Module:    testPerformance
//
// Task:    Display average number of probes for successful and unsuccessful
//          searches
// Inputs:    The hash table,
//          An ordered collection of string keys that are in the table,
//          An ordered collection of string keys that are not in the table,
//              to be used for profiling unsuccessful searches

void testPerformance(IntTable &table, ApstringList &dataIn,
                     ApstringList &dataNotIn);


// Module:    getRandomTable
//
// Task:    Determine from the user the record space and number of active
//          records to store in the hash table.  Then build the hash table
//          using random string keys.  Also build ordered collections of keys
//          to be used for profiling successful and unsuccessful searches.
// Outputs:   The hash table with appropriate number of random keys,
//          An ordered collection of string keys that are in the table,
//          An ordered collection of string keys that are not in the table,
//              to be used for profiling unsuccessful searches

void getRandomTable(IntTable &table, ApstringList &dataIn,
                    ApstringList &dataNotIn);


// Module:    getRandomKey
//
// Task:    Construct a random string to be used as a key for entry into
//          hash the table.  Size of string is at least half of and does not
//          surpass the local constant MAX_STRING_SIZE.

apstring getRandomKey();


// Module:    readTable
//
// Task:    Determine from the user the record space and number of active
//          records to store in the hash table.  Then build the hash table
//          using keys sentered intreactively.  Also build ordered
//          collections of keys to be used for profiling successful and
//          unsuccessful searches.
// Outputs:   The hash table with appropriate number of random keys,
//          An ordered collection of string keys that are in the table,
//          An ordered collection of string keys that are not in the table,
```

```
//                    to be used for profiling unsuccessful searches

void readTable(IntTable &table, ApstringList &dataIn, ApstringList
          &dataNotIn);

// Module:    tableFromFile
//
// Task:      Determine from the user the record the space for the hash table,
//            then build the hash table using keys that are read from the file.
//            Also build ordered collections of keys to be used for
//            profiling successful and unsuccessful searches.
// Outputs:   The hash table with appropriate number of random keys,
//            An ordered collection of string keys that are in the table,
//            An ordered collection of string keys that are not in the table,
//                to be used for profiling unsuccessful searches

void tableFromFile(IntTable &table, ApstringList &dataIn,
          ApstringList &dataNotIn);

// Module:    tableToFile
//
// Task:      Save the hash table to a file so it can be reloaded in future
//            runs
// Inputs:    The hash table

void tableToFile(IntTable &table);

// Module:    getDataNotIn
//
// Task:      Build the list of (random) keys not in the table to use for
//            profiling an unsuccessful search
// Inputs:    The hash table
// Outputs:   The ordered collection of keys not in the table

void getDataNotIn(IntTable &table, ApstringList &dataNotIn);
```

To accumulate the statistics, the program generates two ordered collections of keys—one containing all keys that are in the table and another containing additional random keys that are not in the table. The performance of the hash table is then exercised by sending the keys in each of these ordered collections through the search algorithm. A profiling accumulator for unsuccessful searches is maintained as these keys are processed.

The program will use a hash table class with the following declarations:

```
// Class declaration file: hashtab.h

#ifndef HASHTAB_H
#define HASHTAB_H
```

```
#include <fstream.h>
#include "assoc.h"
#include "ordercol.h"
#include "apstring.h"

const int MAX_HASH_SIZE = MAX_VECTOR_SIZE;   // MAX_VECTOR_SIZE in ordered
                                             // collection class

// Class declaration for hash table with string keys and data
// elements of type E
template <class E> class HashTable
{
   public:

   HashTable();
   HashTable(const HashTable<E> &h);

   // Reset the hash table to an empty table
   void reset();

   // Return number of active records in the hash table
   int length();

   // Display contents of the table to cout
   void display();

   // Allow the user to interactively set the record space to a value
   // not to exceed MAX_HASH_SIZE
   void setRecordSpace();

   // Return the record space set by the user
   int recordSpace();

   // Reset the probe counter used to profile performance
   void resetCounter();

   // Return the accumulated count of number of probes made
   // into the table
   int counter();

   // Insert keyValue and item into the table.  If table
   // is full, return false and leave table unaltered.  If
   // keyValue is already in table, use item to update its
   // associated data and return false.  Return true
   // when keyValue is successfully added as a new value in the table.
   bool add(const apstring &keyValue, const E &item);

   // Given keyValue, search the hash table for it.
   // If found, return found as true and return in index the
   // location of keyValue in the table.  If not found, return
   // found as false.  When found is false, return empty as true
   // if an empty slot was found in the table while searching
```

```
// for keyValue.  index then stores the location of that empty
// slot.  If both found and empty are returned as false, it means
// that keyValue was not found and the table is completely
// full.  In this case, the value of index is unreliable.
void search(const apstring &keyValue, int &index,
            bool &found, bool &empty);

// Output the hash table to a stream
void toFile(ofstream &outfile);

HashTable& operator = (const HashTable<E> &h);


private:

// -- PRIVATE DATA MEMBERS

// The hash table is implemented as a vector of associations.
// Each association has a string as its key and a datum of type E
association<apstring, E> table[MAX_HASH_SIZE];

// Record space used for profiling
int RECORD_SPACE;

// Number of active associations stored within RECORD_SPACE
int tableLength;

// Probe counter for performance measurement
int probes;

// -- PRIVATE MEMBER FUNCTIONS

// The hash function
int hash(const apstring &keyValue);

// Given that index has produced a collision, return the next location
// to try in the hash table
int processCollision(int index);

// Return true if a represents an empty association in hash table
bool emptySlot(const association<apstring, E> &a);

};

#include "hashtab.cpp"

#endif
```

The hash table is represented as a vector of associations. An empty slot in the table is detected by the presence of an empty string in an association.

Implementation

Given the specifications in our design, the main program must control the loop that was portrayed in our analysis.

```cpp
int main()
{
   IntTable table;
   ApstringList dataIn, dataNotIn;

   char choiceOfLoad;

   do
   {
      cout << endl << endl << endl;
      cout << " 1 - Load a random table" << endl;
      cout << " 2 - Interactively load a table" << endl;
      cout << " 3 - Load table from a file" << endl;
      cout << " 4 - Save table to a file" << endl;
      cout << " 5 - Display table" << endl;
      cout << " 6 - Test performance" << endl;
      cout << " 7 - Quit program" << endl;
      cout << endl;
      cout << " Enter 1, 2, 3, 4, 5, 6, or 7 --> ";
      cin >> choiceOfLoad;
      switch (choiceOfLoad)
      {
         case '1':   getRandomTable(table, dataIn, dataNotIn);
                     break;
         case '2':   readTable(table, dataIn, dataNotIn);
                     break;
         case '3':   tableFromFile(table, dataIn, dataNotIn);
                     break;
         case '4':   tableToFile(table);
                     break;
         case '5':   table.display();
                     break;
         case '6':   testPerformance(table, dataIn, dataNotIn);
                     break;
         case '7':   break;
         default:    cout << choiceOfLoad << " is not a valid "
                          << "response - try again" << endl;
      }
   } while (choiceOfLoad != '7');

   return 0;
}
```

Rather than show the complete implementations of all other functions in the program, we will concentrate on the four hash table functions to (1) compute the hashed position of a key, (2) add a key to the table, (3) search for a key or empty slot, and (4) process collisions. The entire implementation is available in the source code that accompanies the book. Most of your experimentation with this profiling program in the Programming Problems and Projects will require you to modify only these four functions, however.

The `hash` function adds together the ASCII values at the beginning and end of the key and returns the remainder from dividing this value by the record space. You may feel that this operation is not a good hash function. You're right! It is one of the first things you will want to change in your experimentation.

```cpp
template <class E>
int HashTable<E>::hash(const string &keyValue)
{
   return (keyValue[0] + keyValue[keyValue.length() - 1])
      % RECORD_SPACE;
}
```

The `processCollision` function implements the linear method.

```cpp
template <class E>
int HashTable<E>::processCollision(int index)
{
   return (index + 1) % RECORD_SPACE;
}
```

The `search` function calls the `hash` function to get an initial position for the key value. The function then enters a loop that stops when a matching key is found, an empty slot is found, or no empty slots are left in the table. In the first two cases, the index position of the key's slot in the table is returned. Note that this loop advances through the table by calling `processCollision`, which in its present form either increments the position or wraps around the end of the table.

```cpp
template <class E>
void HashTable<E>::search(const apstring &keyValue, int &index,
      bool &found, bool &empty)
{
   int initial = hash(keyValue);
   int current = initial;
   bool checkedAll = false;
   found = false;
   empty = false;

   ++probes;
   while ((! empty) && (! found) && (! checkedAll))
   {
      if (table[current].getKey() == keyValue)
         found = true;
      else if (emptySlot(table[current]))
         empty = true;
      else
```

```
      {
          current = processCollision(current);
          checkedAll = initial == current;
          ++probes;
      }
   }
   index = current;
}
```

The add function calls search with the key. If the slot is found (a duplicate key) or is empty, the key and the associated data item are inserted at the index position. If the slot is empty, the length of the table is also incremented by 1:

```
template <class E>
bool HashTable<E>::add(const apstring &keyValue, const E &item)
{
   bool found, empty;
   int index;

   search(keyValue, index, found, empty);
   if (found || empty)
   {
      association<apstring, E> a(keyValue, item);
      table[index] = a;
      if (empty)
         ++tableLength;
   }
   else
      cout << "Table full—cannot add new item." << endl;
   return found;
}
```

Running, Debugging, and Testing Hints

- When using hashing as a search strategy, provide yourself with a means of experimenting with your hashing function and collision-processing strategy. This approach will allow you to tailor your program to the particular kind of keys that are stored in the hash table.

- Searching for data in a random access file involves different criteria than searching for data in main memory. Programs that search for data in random access files should minimize file accesses at the expense of main memory accesses. Indexed searches provide ways of accomplishing this goal.

- If a search program must handle duplicate keys—that is, different records associated with the same key value—the search algorithm must be adjusted appropriately. Be sure you know and decide in advance whether this added complexity is necessary.

Summary

In this lesson, you learned:

■ The following table gives a concise synopsis of the search strategies that have been discussed in this and earlier lessons. Additional comments emphasize particular strengths or weaknesses of the strategy in terms of the one-key table operations we have considered throughout the text.

Method	Efficiency (N = number of records)	Other Components Regarding One-Key Table Operations
Binary	$O(\log_2 n)$	Data must be maintained in physical order, making insertions and deletions inefficient
Binary tree index	$O(\log_2 n)$ index probes, 1 file probe	Guaranteeing this efficiency requires height balancing
B-tree index order k	Worst case requires $1 + \log_k[(n + 1)/2]$	Choose k so that the index node coincides with the disk block
Indexed sequential	O(size of index) index probes, $O[n/(\text{size of index})]$ file probes	Index and file require physical ordering to maintain efficiency
Linear hashing	Average successful: $(1/2) * [1 + 1/1 - D)]$ Average unsuccessful: $(1/2) * [1 + 1/(1 - D)^2]$ where density $D = n/\texttt{RECORD\_SPACE}$	Data not maintained in any order
Linked hashing	Average successful: $1 + D/2$ Average unsuccessful: D (where $\texttt{RECORD\_SPACE}$ used in computation of D is that in the primary hash area)	Data not maintained in any order
Quadratic hashing	Average successful: $1 - \log_e(1 - D) - (D/2)$ Average unsuccessful: $1/(1 - D) - D - \log_e(1 - D)$	Data not maintained in any order
Rehashing	Average successful: $-(1/D) * \log_e(1 - D)$ Average unsuccessful: $1/(1 - D)$	Data not maintained in any order
Sequential trie index	$O(n)$ O(number of characters in target)	Specifically suited for character strings

■ In addition to hashing, other search strategies specifically oriented toward file structures include indexed sequential search, B-trees, and tries.

■ As an implementation strategy for one-key tables, hashing fares very well in all of the operations except ordering. It therefore represents a very viable addition to the list of implementation strategies discussed in earlier lessons: vector or random files with binary search, linked lists, and binary trees.

Define the following terms:

boundary folding	hashing	quadratic collision processing
bucket	linear collision processing	rehashing
clustering	linked collision processing	shift folding

LESSON 8 REVIEW QUESTIONS

FILL IN THE BLANK

Complete the following sentences by writing the correct word or words in the blanks provided.

1. The process of using a key-to-address transformation is called _____.

2. If two keys map to the same location when using a hash function, we say a(n) _____ has occurred.

3. The method of breaking a number into parts and adding the parts to form a key is called _____.

4. Eliminating parts of a number that may produce bias is called _____.

5. When large numbers of keys tend to be grouped together in some regions while other regions are left relatively empty, this phenomenon is known as _____.

WRITTEN QUESTIONS

Write a brief answer to the following questions.

6. What are three basic criteria for a hash function?

7. What is the primary advantage of hashing? What is a disadvantage of hashing?

8. How does linked collision processing eliminate the problem of clustering?

9. Which of the methods of collision processing discussed in this lesson is the simplest? Explain how it works.

10. Suppose the input keys 399, 287, 408, 527, 370, 961, 253, and 932 are to be inserted, in that order, into a hash table of size 10 (index from 0 to 9). Show the resulting hash table after all input keys have been inserted using:

    a. Linear probing with the hash function $h(x) = x$ mod 10. How many collisions have occurred?

    b. Quadratic probing with the hash function $h(x) = x$ div 100. How many collisions have occurred?

11. Assuming the same input keys as given in Question 10, give a hash function that will create no collisions using linear probing.

12. You are to insert the integers from 1 to 100, in that order, into a bucket-chaining hash table of size 10 (indexed 0, 1, . . . , 9). How many collisions will occur during the insertions using the hash function $h(x) = x$ mod 10? What is the load factor after all 100 integers have been inserted?

13. How is the ISAM method used to store data on disk?

14. In binary search tree indexing, what two items are contained in each node of the tree?

LESSON 8 PROJECTS

PROJECT 8-1

SCANS   Use the program from the Case Study as a means of conducting experiments on hashing. Source code files for this lesson's Case Study have been provided—see your instructor. Be as creative as you want, but here are some suggestions to guide you:

1. Run the program. Enter a record space of 400 and load 300 randomly generated keys. Save the keys for later experiments. What do you observe for the average search length for successful and unsuccessful searching? Are your observations consistent with the results from Knuth cited earlier in this lesson? If not, explain why. Examine the hash function, look at the data file saved, and consider the range of ASCII codes for the letters that appear in this file.

2. Modify the hash function so that it is not biased toward a particular region of the table. Run the program with this new hash function with the data set from step 1. In a written statement, summarize the effectiveness of your modifications.

3. Conduct a controlled experiment with four different hashing functions on five different data sets. The data sets should have the same large record space (about 400 records) but different density factors (or numbers of actual records). Use the ASCII values in the keys to develop four different hashing functions, each representing an improvement on the biased hashing function provided with the program. Record your results in a table. Also, plot each hash function's successful and unsuccessful search efficiencies where the axes of the graph represent the search efficiency and the density factor. In a written statement, characterize the efficiencies of the four hash functions. Is one function always better? If so, why? If not, can you explain the inconsistencies in performance? Are your observed results consistent with Knuth's theoretical results presented earlier in the lesson?

4. Determine whether minor changes in the size of the record space affect the performance of the best hash function you devised in step 3. Using that function and four of the data sets from step 3, run each data set with record spaces of 396, 397, 398, 399, and 400. Record the results in a table and present them in the same graphical form you used in step 3. Do your results indicate that a larger record space always produces a better efficiency than a smaller one? If not, describe the discrepancies and give a possible reason for them. Does it appear that a smaller record space could be consistently better than a larger one?

5. Implement the rehashing method (described in Section 8.1) by using the four functions you developed in step 3. If the collision is not resolved after using all four functions, then resort to linear collision processing. Run the program with the same data sets used in step 3, and plot its performance. Compare the performance of rehashing to that of the best hashing function developed in step 3. Also, address how your implementation of rehashing conforms to the theoretical results described by Knuth.

PROJECT 8-2

Implement the registrar's system described in Lesson 2 using hashing as the implementation technique for the student database. Recall that this database was derived from a one-key table. The difficult part of this problem will be to implement the sorted data that the registrar wants when hashing is used as the search strategy for the one-key table.

PROJECT 8-3

Implement the Wing-and-a-Prayer Airlines flight/pilot database (Project 3-7) using the implementation technique described in Section 8.2 for the two-key table.

PROJECT 8-4

A B-tree of order 3 is often called a 2-3 tree because each node has two or three children. Because of its low order, a 2-3 tree is not particularly applicable as a file index. However, if we store up to two actual data records in each node instead of up to two key–pointer pairs, then a 2-3 tree becomes an alternative to an ordered binary tree for implementing a list. Develop search, insertion, and deletion algorithms for such a 2-3 tree structure. Compare its performance characteristics with those of an ordered binary tree.

PROJECT 8-5

Implement the registrar's system of Project 8-2 using a 2-3 tree representation of a list (see Project 8-4).

PROJECT 8-6

Wing-and-a-Prayer Airlines has the records of all its customers stored in the following form:

■ Last name

■ First name

- Address

- Arbitrarily long list of flights on which reservations have been booked

Using a trie index, write a search-and-retrieval program that will allow input of a customer's last name (and, if necessary, the first name and address to resolve conflicts created by matching last names) and then output all flights on which that customer has booked reservations.

PROJECT 8-7

SuperScout, Inc., is a nationwide scouting service for college football talent to which the Bay Area Brawlers professional team subscribes (see Project 3-9). As the pool of college talent increases in size, SuperScout has found that its old record-keeping system has deteriorated considerably in its ability to locate quickly the scouting record associated with a given player in its file. Rewrite the scouting record system using a trie to look up the record location of the data associated with a given player's name.

PROJECT 8-8

Using a large collection of randomly generated keys, write a series of programs that will test various hashing functions you develop. In particular, your programs should report statistics on the number of collisions generated by each hashing function. This information could be valuable in guiding future decisions about which hashing functions and techniques are most effective for your particular system.

PROJECT 8-9

Consider a student data record that consists of the following items:

- Student identification number

- Student name

- State of residence

- Sex

Choose an index structure to process a file of such records. Then write a program to maintain such a file as a one-key table.

PROJECT 8-10

Suppose data records for a phone book file consist of a key field containing both a name and an address and a field containing the phone number for that key. Devise an appropriate index for such a file. Then write a program that calls for input of

1. A complete key

2. If a complete key is not available, as much of the initial portion of a key as the inquirer is able to provide

In case 1, your program should output the phone number corresponding to the unique key. In case 2, have your program output all keys (and their phone numbers) that match the provided initial portion.

PROJECT 8-11

SCANS

Consider the following problem faced in the development of a compiler. The source program contains many character-string symbols such as variable names, function names, and so on. Each of these character-string symbols has associated with it various attributes such as memory location, data type, and so on. However, it is too time-consuming and awkward for a compiler to manipulate character strings. Instead, each string should be identified with an integer that is viewed as equivalent to the string for the purpose of compiler manipulation. In addition to serving as a compact equivalent form of a string symbol within the source program, this integer can serve as a direct pointer into a table of attributes for that symbol. Devise such a transformation that associates a string with an integer, which in turn serves as a pointer into a table of attributes. Test the structures you develop by using them in a program that scans a source program written in a language such as C++. You will, in effect, have written the symbol table modules for a compiler.

PROJECT 8-12

SCANS

Write a spell checker program. Such a program must scan a file of text, looking up each word it finds in a dictionary of correctly spelled words. When a word cannot be found in the dictionary, the spell checker should convey this fact to its user, giving the user the opportunity to take one of the following steps:

1. Skip the word

2. Change the spelling of the word in the text file

3. Add the word to the dictionary so that it will not be reported as incorrectly spelled in the future
   Because the dictionary for such a program will be searched frequently and is likely to become quite large, an efficient search algorithm is a necessity. One possibility in this regard is to use a trie index with pointers into a large string buffer instead of the pointers to data records described in Section 8.3. Test your program with a text file and dictionary large enough to handle all of the possibilities that your algorithm and data structure may encounter.

CRITICAL THINKING

ACTIVITY 8-1

SCANS

If you solved one of the problems from Lesson 2 that involved maintaining a one-key table, redo that problem using hashing combined with linked lists as an implementation technique. When you are finished, write a report in which you empirically compare the performance of your two implementations.

ACTIVITY 8-2

SCANS

If you solved one of the problems from Lesson 2 that involved maintaining a two-key table, redo that problem using hashing of row and column indices as an implementation technique. When you are finished, write a report in which you empirically compare the performance of your two implementations.

UNIT 4 REVIEW QUESTIONS

TRUE/FALSE

Circle T if the statement is true or F if the statement is false.

T F **1.** The quick sort is also called the diminishing increment sort.

T F **2.** The heap sort uses a pivot to subdivide a list during the sorting process.

T F **3.** The worst case running time of a quick sort or merge sort is O($n$log$n$).

T F **4.** A merge sort combines two lists that are already sorted.

T F **5.** The best case of a pivot value in a quick sort is the median of the list.

T F **6.** Hashing can result in constant time searches, insertions, and removals.

T F **7.** Folding occurs when a large number of keys hash to one area, leaving other areas relatively empty.

T F **8.** Linear collision processing is simpler than rehashing.

T F **9.** Quadratic collision processing results in quadratic running times.

T F **10.** The division-remainder technique is a commonly used method for computing a hash value.

FILL IN THE BLANK

Complete the following sentences by writing the correct word or words in the blanks provided.

1. ISAM is short for _____.

2. When a collision occurs, linear collision processing places the new key in _____.

3. When a collision occurs, linked collision processing places the new key in _____.

4. The shell sort uses a helper function called _____.

5. The heap sort first builds a(n) _____ and then traverses it.

6. The worst case running time of a merge sort is _____.

7. The quick sort has a running time of _____ in the best case and _____ in the worst case.

8. The worst case running time of hashing is _____.

9. Two methods of determining a hash value are _____ and _____.

10. A(n) _____ may be used to implement the index for a random access file keyed by strings of variable length.

WRITTEN QUESTIONS

Write a brief answer to the following questions.

1. Describe a method for finding a pivot value for a quick sort that lies near the median of a list.

2. Describe a situation in which it would be advantageous to mix various sorting methods in one sort routine.

3. Describe how the problem of clustering arises and describe a solution to this problem.

4. Why does hashing potentially yield constant access times?

5. Explain the how the technique of folding works to yield a hash code.

UNIT 4 PROJECTS

PROJECT 4-1

Write a hash function that uses the technique of folding to generate a hash code.

PROJECT 4-2

Write a hash function that uses the quadratic method of resolving collisions. You may assume that there is room available in the record space for a new key.

CRITICAL THINKING

ACTIVITY 4-1

Hashing and sorting presuppose two radically different approaches to the access and manipulation of data for searches. Discuss the tradeoffs in these approaches and explain the situations in which one might prefer one or the other.

RESERVED WORDS

The following words have predefined meanings in C++ and cannot be changed. The words in boldface are discussed in the text. The other words are discussed in Stanley B. Lippman, *C++ Primer*, Third Edition (Reading, Massachusetts: Addison-Wesley, 1998).

Asm	continue	**float**	**new**	signed	try
Auto	**default**	**for**	**operator**	sizeof	**typedef**
Break	**delete**	friend	**private**	static	union
Case	**do**	goto	**protected**	**struct**	**unsigned**
Catch	**double**	**if**	**public**	**switch**	virtual
Char	**else**	inline	register	**template**	**void**
Class	enum	**int**	**return**	**this**	volatile
Const	extern	**long**	**short**	throw	**while**

APPENDIX B

SOME USEFUL LIBRARY FUNCTIONS

Some of the most commonly used library functions in the first course in computer science come from the libraries `math`, `ctype`, and `string`. Descriptions of the most important functions in each of these libraries are presented in the following three tables.

MATH

Function Declaration	Purpose
`double acos(double x);`	Returns arc cosine for *x* in range -1 to +1
`double asin(double x);`	Returns arc sine for *x* in range -1 to +1
`double atan(double x);`	Returns arc tangent of *x*
`double atan2(double y,` `        double x);`	Returns arc tangent of *y/x*
`double ceil(double x);`	Rounds *x* up to next highest integer
`double cos(double x);`	Returns cosine of *x*
`double cosh(double x);`	Returns hyberbolic cosine of *x*
`double exp(double x);`	Returns *e* to the *x*th power
`double floor(double x);`	Rounds *x* down to next lowest integer
`double fmod(double x,` `        double y);`	Returns remainder of *x/y*
`double ldexp(double x,` `        double exp);`	Returns *x* times 2 to the power of exp
`double log(double x);`	Returns natural logarithm of *x*
`double log10(double x);`	Returns base-10 logarithm of *x*
`double pow(double x,` `        double y);`	Returns *x* raised to the power of *y*

(continued on next page)

MATH

Function Declaration	Purpose
`double sin(double x);`	Returns sine of x
`double sinh(double x);`	Returns hyberbolic sine of x
`double sqrt(double x);`	Returns square root of x
`double tan(double x);`	Returns tangent of x, in radians
`double tanh(double x);`	Returns hyperbolic tangent of x

CTYPE

Function Declaration	Purpose
`int isalnum(int ch);`	ch is a letter or digit
`int isalpha(int ch);`	ch is a letter
`int iscntrl(int ch);`	ch is a control character
`int isdigit(int ch);`	ch is a digit (0–9)
`int isgraph(int ch);`	ch is a printable but not ' '
`int islower(int ch);`	ch is a lowercase letter
`int isprint(int ch);`	ch is a printable
`int ispunct(int ch);`	ch is a printable but not ' ' or alpha
`int isspace(int ch);`	ch is a white space character
`int isupper(int ch);`	ch is an uppercase letter
`int isxdigit(int ch);`	ch is a hexadecimal digit
`int tolower(int ch);`	Returns lowercase of ch
`int toupper(int ch);`	Returns uppercase of ch

APPENDIX C

SYNTAX DIAGRAMS

The following syntax diagrams correspond to the syntax forms used to describe the features of C++ discussed in the text. Two points of caution are in order. First, the diagrams in this appendix by no means represent an exhaustive description of C++. Second, many of the features discussed in this text have more than one syntactically correct construction (for example, `main` can be preceded by either `int` or `void`, but the C++ programming community prefers `int`). By confining your attention to preferred ways of using a small subset of features, we hope to place your focus on concepts rather than syntax. Students wanting to learn more features of C++ or other ways of expressing them are referred to Stanley B. Lippman, *C++ Primer*, Third Edition (Reading, Massachusetts: Addison-Wesley, 1998). The terms enclosed in ovals in the diagrams refer to program components that literally appear in programs, such as operator symbols and reserved words. The terms enclosed in boxes refer to program components that require further definition, either by another diagram or by reference to the text. The syntax of terms for which there are no diagrams, such as `identifier`, `number`, `string`, and `character`, should be familiar to anyone who has read this text.

Main program module

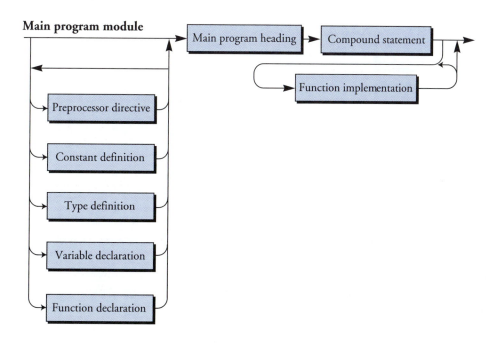

Preprocessor directive

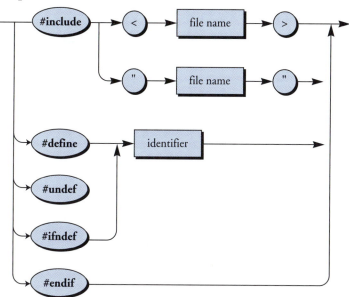

Constant definition

Type definition

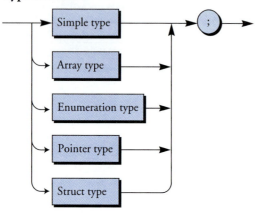

Simple type

Array type

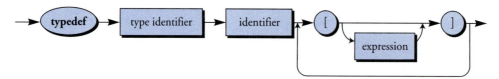

Enumeration type

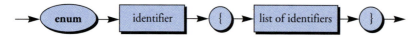

Pointer type

Struct type

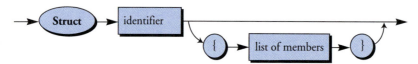

List of members

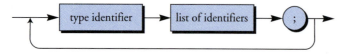

Variable declaration

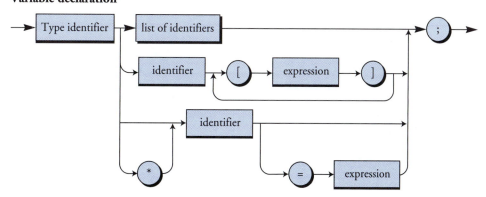

List of identifiers

Function declaration

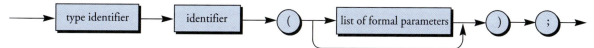

Main program heading

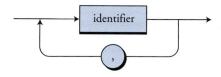

Compound statement

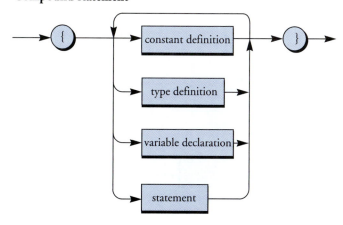

Statement

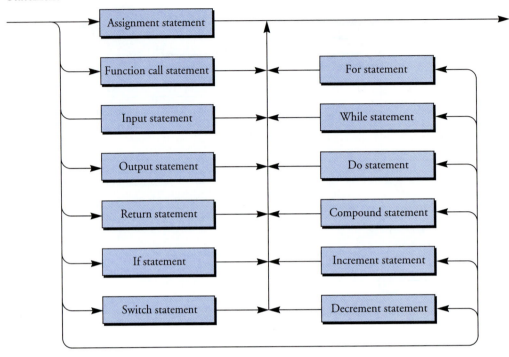

Assignment statement

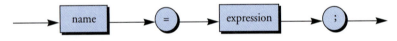

Function call statement

Input statement

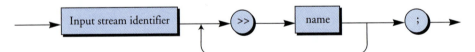

Output statement

Return statement

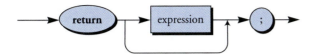

If statement

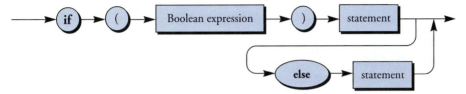

Switch statement

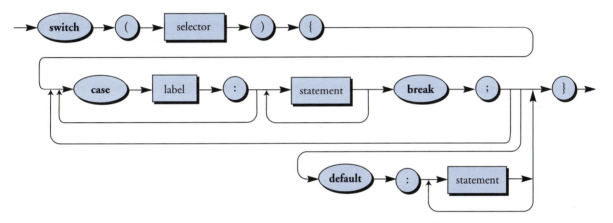

For statement

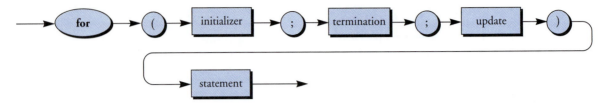

While statement

Do statement

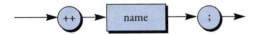

Increment statement

Decrement statement

Function implementation

Function heading

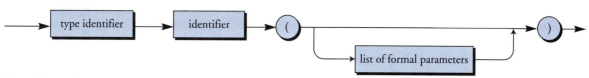

List of formal parameters

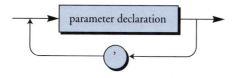

Parameter declaration

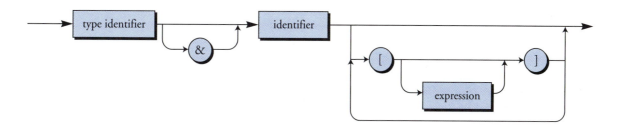

Expression

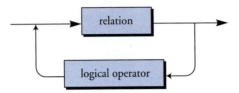

Relation

Simple expression

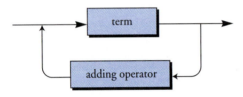

Term

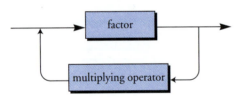

Factor

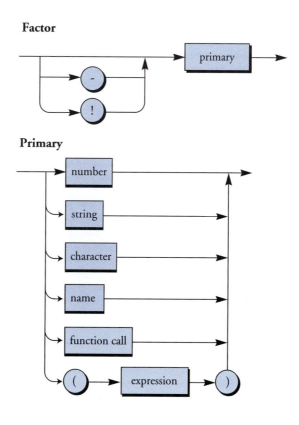

Primary

Name

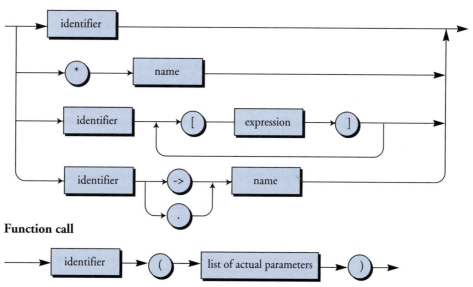

Function call

List of actual parameters

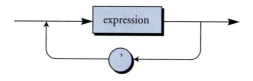

Logical operator

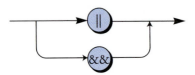

Adding operator

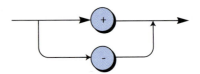

Comparison operator

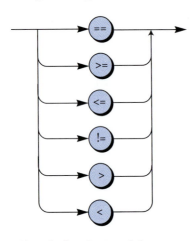

Multiplying operator

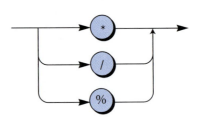

Class declaration module

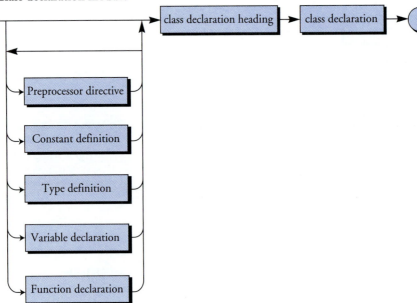

Class declaration heading

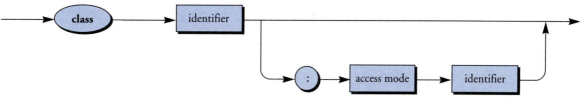

Class declaration

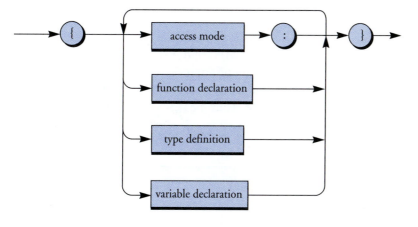

Access mode

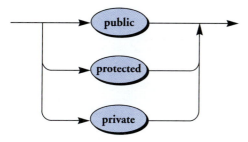

APPENDIX D

THE ASCII CHARACTER SET

The following table shows the ordering of the ASCII character set. The printable characters range from ASCII 33 to ASCII 126. The values from ASCII 0 to ASCII 32 and ASCII 127 are associated with white space characters, such as the horizontal tab (HT), or nonprinting control characters, such as the escape key (ESC). The digits in the left column represent the leftmost digits of the ASCII code, and the digits in the top row are the rightmost digits in the ASCII code. Thus the ASCII code of the character 'R' at row 8, column 2, is 82.

	0	1	2	3	4	5	6	7	8	9
0	NUL	SOH	STX	ETX	EOT	ENQ	ACK	BEL	BS	HT
1	LF	VT	FF	CR	SO	SI	DLE	DC1	DC2	DC3
2	DC4	NAK	SYN	ETB	CAN	EM	SUB	ESC	FS	GS
3	RS	US	SP	!	"	#	$	%	&	`
4	(	)	*	+	,	-	.	/	0	1
5	2	3	4	5	6	7	8	9	:	;
6	<	=	>	?	@	A	B	C	D	E
7	F	G	H	I	J	K	L	M	N	O
8	P	Q	R	S	T	U	V	W	X	Y
9	Z	[	\	]	^	_	'	a	b	c
10	d	e	f	g	h	i	j	k	l	m
11	n	o	p	q	r	s	t	u	v	w
12	x	y	z	{	|	}	~	DEL		

APPENDIX E

RANDOM NUMBER GENERATION

Many applications, such as the queue simulation in Lesson 4, require the use of random numbers. For example, a computerized game of backgammon requires the roll of two dice on each move. The results can be computed by selecting two random numbers between 1 and 6. C++ provides a library function, rand, that returns an integer between 0 and the compiler-dependent constant RAND_MAX, inclusive. Both the function and the constant are declared in the library header file stdlib.h. Unfortunately, the numbers generated by rand are not as random as we would like. The reason is that the number returned by rand depends on an initial value, called a seed, that is the same for each run of a program. Thus the sequence of random numbers generated by a program that uses this method will be exactly the same on each run of the program.

To help solve this problem, another function, srand(seed), also declared in stdlib.h, allows an application to specify the initial value used by rand at program start-up. Using this method, two runs of a program that use different values for seed will receive different sequences of random numbers. The problem then becomes one of providing an arbitrary seed value. Rather than force a user to enter this value interactively, most applications obtain it by reading the current time from the computer's internal clock. The C++ data type time_t and the function time, both declared in the time.h library header file, can be used to obtain the current time on the computer's clock. When converted to an unsigned integer, the current time can serve as a fairly arbitrary seed for a random number generator in most programs.

To summarize the discussion so far, the following program would display three random numbers between 0 and RAND_MAX, depending on the current time on the computer's clock at program start-up:

```cpp
// Displays three random numbers

#include <iostream.h>
#include <stdlib.h>
#include <time.h>

int main()
{
   time_t seconds;

   time(&seconds);
   srand((unsigned int) seconds);
   cout << rand() << endl;
   cout << rand() << endl;
   cout << rand() << endl;
   return 0;
}
```

Users of a random number generator might desire a narrower or a wider range of numbers than rand provides. Ideally, a user would specify the range with integer values representing the lower and upper bounds. To see how we might use rand to accomplish this goal, first consider how to generate a number between 0 and an arbitrary upper bound, high, inclusive. For any two integers, *a* and *b*, *a* % *b* is between 0 and $b - 1$, inclusive. Thus the expression `rand() % high + 1` would generate a random number between 0 and `high`, inclusive, where `high` is less than or equal to `RAND_MAX`. To place a lower bound other than 0 on the result, we can generate a random number between 0 and `high - low + 1`, and then add `low` to the result. The complete expression for computing a random number between a lower bound and an upper bound would then be `rand() % (high - low + 1) + low`.

The following complete program uses constants and random numbers to display the results of two rolls of dice:

```cpp
// Program file: dice.cpp
// This program displays the results of two rolls of dice.

#include <iostream.h>
#include <stdlib.h>
#include <time.h>

const int LOW = 1;
const int HIGH = 6;

int main()
{
    int first_die, second_die;
    time_t seconds;

    time(&seconds);
    srand((unsigned int) seconds);
    first_die = rand() % (HIGH - LOW + 1) + LOW;
    second_die = rand() % (HIGH - LOW + 1) + LOW;
    cout << "Your roll is (" << first_die << ", "
         << second_die << ")" << endl << endl;
    first_die = rand() % (HIGH - LOW + 1) + LOW;
    second_die = rand() % (HIGH - LOW + 1) + LOW;
    cout << "My roll is (" << first_die << << ", "
         << second_die << ")" << endl << endl;
    return 0;
}
```

A sample run might produce the following output:

```
Your roll is (1, 4)

My roll is (6, 6)
```

Note that the use of constants and the complete expressions for computing random numbers are not really necessary for this program. We could have used the expression `rand() % 6 + 1` for simplicity. To encapsulate the production of random numbers into a C++ class, the following header file is used:

```cpp
// Class declaration file: random.h

// Declaration section

#ifndef RANDOM_H
```

580

```
class RandomGenerator
{

    public:

    // Class constructors

    // Construct a random number generator object
    RandomGenerator();

    // Member functions

    // Return a random integer between low and high,
    // inclusive
    int nextNumber(int low, int high);

    // Reset the seed for the generator
    void reset();

};

#define RANDOM_H
#endif
```

The implementation of the RandomGenerator class is:

```
// Class implementation file: random.cpp

#include <stdlib.h>
#include <time.h>
#include <assert.h>
#include "random.h"

RandomGenerator::RandomGenerator()
{
        srand(int(clock()));
}


int RandomGenerator::nextNumber(int low, int high)
{
        assert((low < high) && (high <= RAND_MAX));
        return rand() % (high - low + 1) + low;
}

void RandomGenerator::reset()
{
        srand(int(clock()));
}
```

GLOSSARY

A

abstract data type (ADT) A form of abstraction that arises from the use of defined types. An ADT consists of a class of objects, a defined set of properties of those objects, and a set of operations for processing the objects.

abstraction The description of data structures at a conceptual level, apart from their implementation using a particular technique and language.

abstract syntax tree *See* **parse tree**.

access adjustment A method of changing the access mode of an inherited member from within a derived class. For example, a derived class may inherit all members from a base class in protected mode, and then make some members public by means of access adjustments. *See also* **access mode**, **derived class**, and **inheritance**.

access mode A symbol (**public**, **protected**, or **private**) that specifies the kind of access that clients have to a server's data members and member functions. *See also* **private member**, **protected member**, and **public member**.

activation record A group of memory cells, allocated for each function call, that keeps track of the values of the function's parameter, local variables, return value, and return address.

address Often called address of a memory location, this is an integer value that the computer can use to reference a location.

address-of operator The & symbol, which is used to obtain the address of a variable.

ADT *See* **abstract data type**.

ADT generality rule An abstract data type should not be limited by the types of its components. Wherever possible, users should be able to specify the component types of a generic abstract data type.

ADT implementation rule An implementation of an ADT must provide an interface that is entirely consistent with the operations specified in the ADT's definition.

ADT layering rule Existing abstract data types should be used to implement new abstract data types, unless direct control over the underlying data structures and operations of the programming language is a critical factor. A well-designed implementation consists of layers of ADTs.

ADT use rule An algorithm that uses an ADT should access variables of that abstract data type only through the operations provided in the ADT definition.

alias A situation in which two or more identifiers in a program come to refer to the same memory location. An alias can become the cause of subtle side effects.

analysis phase The first phase of the software system life cycle in which the systems analyst determines the user's needs and develops formal specifications describing the proposed system and its requirements.

ancestor A tree node that is hierarchically related to another tree node at a lower level in the tree.

array index The relative position of the components of an array.

arrow operator The arrow operator (->) directs the computer to follow the arrow from the pointer variable to the designated member in the node.

artificial intelligence (AI) The field of computer science in which the goal is to program the computer to mimic intelligent human behavior.

assertion Special comments used with selection and repetition that state what you expect to happen and when certain conditions will hold.

association A key/value pair that is used in a table.

Backus-Naur grammar A standard form for defining the formal syntax of a language.

best case The arrangement of data items prior to the start of a sort function to finish in the least amount of time for that particular set of items. *See also* **worst case**.

big-O analysis A technique for estimating the time and space requirements of an algorithm in terms of order of magnitude.

big-O notation Saying that an algorithm is $O(f(n))$ indicates that the function $f(n)$ may be useful in characterizing how efficiently the algorithm performs for large n. For such n, we are assured that the operations required by the algorithm will be bounded by the product of a constant and $f(n)$.

binary search The process of examining a middle value of a sorted array to see which half contains the value in question and halving until the value is located.

binary search tree A binary tree with the ordering property.

binary tree A tree such that each node can point to at most two children.

binary tree search A search algorithm driven by the hierarchical relationships of data items in a tree with the ordering property.

binding time The time at which a program variable is bound to a particular value. This can occur either at compile time or at run time.

binding time problem A problem that occurs at run time, which involves nested loops.

bin sort *See* **radix sort**.

black box testing The method of testing a module whereby the tester is aware of only what the module is supposed to do, not the method of implementation or the internal logic. *See also* **white box testing**.

blocked queue In an operating system, the queue of processes that have requested a resource currently owned by another process.

boundary conditions Values that separate two logical possibilities. These are important cases to check when testing a module.

boundary folding A variation on shift folding: in boundary folding, the digits of every other numeric section are reversed before the addition is performed.

branch In a tree, a link between a parent and its child node.

breadth-first traversal A visiting of all nodes in a graph; it proceeds from each node by first visiting all nodes adjacent to that node.

B-tree An efficient, flexible index structure that supports fast searches and is often used in database management systems.

bubble sort Rearranges elements of an array until they are in either ascending or descending order. Consecutive elements are compared to move (bubble) the elements to the top or bottom accordingly on each pass. *See also* **heap sort**, **insertion sort**, **merge sort**, **quick sort**, **radix sort**, **selection sort**, and **shell sort**.

bucket In bucket hashing, a contiguous region of storage locations.

bucket hashing Method of handling collisions whereby the hashing function sends the key to a bucket of locations rather than a single location. The key is then placed by performing a sequential search within the bucket.

child node A node that descends from another node in a tree.

children Nodes pointed to by a node in a tree.

circular linked list A linked list whose last node points to the first or head node in the list.

class A description of the attributes and behavior of a set of computational objects.

class template A special kind of class definition that allows clients to specify the component types of objects of that class.

client A computational object that receives a service from another computational object.

clustering Occurs when a hashing function is biased toward the placement of keys in a given region of the storage space.

collision Condition in which more than one key hashes to the same position with a given hashing function.

concordance A listing of the unique words and their frequencies in a text file.

context-free grammar A grammar that describes phrases in a language and uses recursion.

CRC modeling A type of analysis and design technique that makes use of classes, responsibilities, and collaborators.

cubic algorithm A polynomial algorithm in which the highest nonzero term is n^3.

deadlock An infinite wait state in which two processes each own system resources the other needs and will not release until they have obtained the remaining resources they need. Also referred to as fatal embrace.

density The number of storage locations used divided by the total number of storage locations available.

density-dependent search technique A search technique whose efficiency is determined solely by the density of the data.

depth-first traversal A visiting of all nodes in a graph, proceeding from each node by probing as deeply as possible along one path leading from that node.

dereference The operation by which a program uses a pointer to access the contents of dynamic memory. *See also* **dynamic memory** and **pointer variable**.

dereference operator The operator *, which is used as a pointer to an object.

derived class A class that inherits attributes and behavior from other classes. *See also* **inheritance**.

design phase The second phase of the software system life cycle. In this phase, a relatively detailed design plan is created from the formal specifications of the system produced in the analysis phase.

digit/character extraction In creating a hashing function, the process of removing from a key those digits of characters that may bias the results of the function.

digraph A graph having some edges that point in only one direction.

diminishing increment sort A sort in which the number of segments in any one pass decreases with each successive pass. *See also* **shell sort**.

directional graph *See* **digraph**.

divide-and-conquer algorithms A class of algorithms that solves problems by repeatedly dividing them into simpler problems. *See also* **recursion**.

division-remainder technique A hashing technique that ensures that the result will be a valid output. It uses the modulus operation to scale the value into the proper range.

dominant term The highest power of n in a polynomial. For large n, the behavior of the entire polynomial will approach the behavior of a polynomial that contains only that term.

doubly linked list A linked list in which each node has two pointers instead of one. One of these points to the previous node in the list and the other points to the next node in the list.

dynamic memory Memory allocated under program control from the heap and accessed by means of pointers. *See also* **heap** and **pointer variable**.

dynamic structure A data structure that may expand or contract during execution of a program. *See also* **dynamic memory**.

edge A direct connection between two nodes in a graph.

empty link A special value, usually 0, that indicates the absence of a pointer.

encapsulation The process of hiding implementation details of a data structure.

equivalence classes A partitioning of all the logical possibilities that can be checked when testing a module. All test cases within a single equivalence class are identical from the standpoint of the logic of the module.

expert system A program able to reason as an expert in a limited domain.

exponential algorithm An algorithm whose efficiency is dominated by a term of the form k^n.

external pointers A special pointer that locates the beginning of a linked structure.

fatal embrace *See* **deadlock**.

FIFO *See* **queue**.

first-in/first-out (FIFO) *See* **queue**.

folding A method of hashing in cases where the key is not an integer value. The nonnumeric characters are removed and the remaining digits are combined to produce an integer value.

free store *See* **heap**.

front pointer The pointer to the front of a queue.

garbage collector A software component that automates the recycling of dynamic storage.

generalized nested loops Loops whose nesting depth is determined at run time using recursive logic.

general list A collection of data items that are related by their relative position in the collection.

general tree A set of nodes that is either empty or has a designated node (called the root) from which descend zero or more subtrees.

generic abstract data type An abstract data type whose component types are specified as parameters. For example, a generic stack ADT could be used to create stacks of integers as well as stacks of characters.

grammar A set of rules for specifying well-formed sentences in a language.

graph A set of data elements called nodes and the paths between them called edges.

has-a relation The property of one class having an object of another class as a data member. *See also* **is-a relation**.

hashing A density-dependent search technique whereby the key for a given data item is transformed using a function to produce the address where that item is stored in memory.

head pointer A pointer to the first item in a list.

heap (1) An area of computer memory where storage for dynamic data is available. (2) A binary tree with the heap property.

heap property A binary tree has the heap property when the data at any given node are greater or equal to the data in its left and right subtrees.

heap sort A sort in which the array is treated like an array implementation of a binary tree. The items are repeatedly manipulated to create a heap from which the root is removed and added to the sorted portion of the array. *See also* **bubble sort**, **insertion sort**, **merge sort**, **quick sort**, **radix sort**, **selection sort**, and **shell sort**.

heap underflow An error that arises when no more dynamic storage is available to allocate for a data object.

height balancing A technique for ensuring that an ordered binary tree remains as full as possible in form.

heuristics Rules of thumb that cut down on the number of possible choices to examine. They often lead to quick solutions but do not guarantee a solution the way an algorithm does.

hierarchy A relation between nodes whereby one is viewed as above or prior to another.

index *See* **array index**.

indexed sequential access method (ISAM) The most common method of indexed sequential search.

indexed sequential search Use of a partial index based on disk-dependent factors to find the proper portion of the disk for sequential searching for a key.

index sort Sorting an array by ordering the indices of the components rather than exchanging the components.

infix Algebraic notation in which the operator appears between the two operands to which it will be applied.

infix priority A function that ranks the algebraic operators in terms of their precedence.

information hiding The process of suppressing the implementation details of a function or data structure so as to simplify its use in programming.

inheritance The process by which a derived class can reuse attributes and behavior defined in a base class. *See also* **derived class**.

inorder predecessor The node preceding a given node in an inorder traversal.

inorder successor The node following a given node in an inorder traversal.

inorder threads Pointers to the inorder predecessor and successor of a node.

inorder traversal A binary tree traversal in which a node's left subtree is visited first, then that node is processed, and finally the node's right subtree is visited.

insertion rule For binary trees, a rule whereby a new item is placed in the left subtree of an item greater than it or in the right subtree of an item less than it.

insertion sort Sorts an array of elements that starts with an empty array and inserts elements one at a time in their proper order. *See also* **bubble sort**, **heap sort**, **merge sort**, **quick sort**, **radix sort**, **selection sort**, and **shell sort**.

instance A computational object bearing the attributes and behavior specified by a class.

is-a relation The property of one class being a derived class of another class. *See also* **derived class** and **has-a relation**.

iterative prototyping A style of programming that starts with a simplified version of a complete system and fills it in gradually as it is tested.

key A field in a data structure that is used to access an element in that structure.

key-to-address transformation A transformation in which the key of a data item maps to the address at which the data are stored.

last-in/first-out (LIFO) *See* **stack**.

Leaf node In a tree, a node that has no children.

level All nodes in a tree with a path of the same length from the root node.

lexical analysis The task of recognizing valid words or tokens in an input stream of characters.

LIFO *See* **stack**.

linear algorithm A polynomial algorithm in which the highest nonzero term is n.

linear collision processing Method of handling a collision in which the storage space is searched sequentially from the location of the collision for an available location where the new key can be placed.

linear implementation (of binary tree) An implementation of a binary tree in an array. For a given node stored at index position K, that node's left child is at position $2K$, and the right child is at position $2K + 1$.

linear ordering Any ordering of data in which there is an identifiable first element, second element, and so forth.

linear search *See* **sequential search**.

linked collision processing Method of handling a collision in which the second key is stored in a linked list located in an overflow area.

linked implementation An implementation of a binary tree in which pointer fields are used to reference the right and left child of a node in the tree (as opposed to the linear representation of a binary tree).

linked list A list of data items where each item is linked to the next one by means of a pointer.

LISP (LISt Processor) A highly-recursive computer programming language used heavily in artificial intelligence (AI).

list traversal The process of sequentially visiting each node in a list.

logarithmic algorithm An algorithm whose efficiency is dominated by a term of the form $\log_i n$.

logically sorted Data have been logically sorted when pointers to the data have been sorted, even though the data itself have not been touched. Hence,

items that the sort places consecutively need not be physically adjacent.

logical order An ordering of data items according to some defined criterion such as alphabetic, increasing numeric, and so forth. That logical order of the data may or may not be the physical order of the data as stored in the computer.

logical size The number of data items actually available in a data structure at a given time. *See also* **physical size**.

logical structure The ordering of data in a structure that is independent of their ordering in memory.

logic error An error that does not appear until run time, in which the program does not produce the expected results.

$\log_2 n$ search algorithm A search algorithm whose efficiency is dominated by a term of the form $\log_2 n$.

maintenance phase The fifth phase of the software system life cycle. In this phase, changes must be made in the original program either to fix errors discovered by the users of the program or to meet new user needs.

mapping function A function that transforms row-column array coordinates to the linear address of that array entry.

members Functions and data within a class.

memory leakage A condition that occurs when the programmer does not return unused dynamic storage to the heap.

merge The process of combining lists. Typically refers to files or arrays.

merge sort Sort in which the array is repeatedly split in half and then these pieces are merged together. *See also* **bubble sort**, **heap sort**, **insertion sort**, **quick sort**, **radix sort**, **selection sort**, and **shell sort**.

message In object-oriented programming, a signal to perform an operation on an object.

message-passing In object-oriented programming, one object's telling another object to perform an operation that is part of its encapsulation.

multilinked list A linked list in which each node has two or more link fields.

natural language A language by which humans normally communicate (such as English), as opposed to a formal programming language (such as Pascal).

network A graph in which the edges have weight values associated with them.

node One data item in a linked list.

nonterminals Terms in a grammar that name phrases or rules.

object-oriented programming A programming paradigm in which a data object is viewed as the owner of operations, as opposed to procedural programming in which an operation is passed data objects as actual parameters. Object-oriented programming emphasizes the ADT approach and allows the users of an ADT to extend the operations of an ADT library in a convenient and efficient fashion.

one-key table A set of values each of which is accessed by specifying a unique key value, where the key values are ordered.

ordered collection A data structure that supports indexing for retrieval or change of data items, the detection of the logical size of the structure, and addition or removal of data items from the logical end of the structure.

ordering A means of arranging the elements in a list.

ordering property In a binary tree, the data in each node of the tree are greater than or equal to all of the data in that node's left subtree and less than or equal to all of the data in its right subtree.

order of magnitude Power of ten. Two numbers have the same order of magnitude if their representations in scientific notation have identical exponents to designate the power of ten.

overflow area In arithmetic operations, a value may be too large for the computer's memory location. A meaningless value may be assigned or an error message may result. *See also* **underflow**.

pages Chunks of code that are swapped in and out of memory during the execution of a program.

paging algorithm The method used to swap chunks of code in and out of memory during the execution of a program.

parent tree In a tree, the node that is pointing to its children.

parser A program that checks the syntax of an expression and represents that expression in a unique form.

parser generator A program that can take the input grammar for a language and produce the parser for that language.

parse tree Tree representation of the syntactic structure of a source program produced by a compiler. Also referred to as abstract syntax tree.

parsing The procedure of checking the syntax of an expression and representing it in one unique form.

partition In quick sort, the process of moving the pivot to the location where it belongs in the sorted array and arranging the remaining data items to the left of the pivot if they are less than or equal to the pivot and to the right if they are greater than the pivot.

path A sequence of edges that connect two nodes in a graph or network.

permutation An ordered arrangement of the first n positive integers in which each integer appears exactly once.

physical size The number of memory units available for storing data items in a data structure. *See also* **logical size**.

pivot Item used to direct the partitioning in quick sort.

pointer A memory location containing the location of another data item.

pointer sort A sort in which pointers to the data are manipulated rather than the data itself.

pointer to function A mechanism whereby a function can be passed as a parameter to another function.

pointer variable Frequently designated as `ptr`, a pointer variable is a variable that contains the address of a memory location. *See also* **address** and **dynamic memory**.

polymorphism The property of one operator symbol or function identifier having many meanings.

polynomial algorithm An algorithm whose efficiency can be expressed in terms of a polynomial.

popping Removing an item from a stack.

postcondition An assertion written after a segment of code.

postfix Unambiguous algebraic notation in which the arithmetic operator appears after the two operands upon which it is to be applied.

postorder traversal A binary tree traversal in which at any node, that node's left subtree is visited first, then that node's right subtree is visited, and finally that node is processed.

precondition An assertion written before a particular statement.

prefix Unambiguous algebraic notation in which the arithmetic operator appears before the two operands upon which it is to be applied.

preorder traversal A binary tree traversal in which at any node, that node is first processed, then that node's left subtree is visited, and finally that node's right subtree is visited.

primary key The first key used to locate a value in a table.

prime hash area In linked collision processing, the main storage area in which keys are placed if no collision occurs.

priority queue A queue in which the entries on the queue are ranked into groups according to priority. Such a queue requires a rear pointer for each different possible priority value.

private member A data member or member function that is accessible only within the scope of a class declaration.

productions Rules in a grammar.

profile an algorithm A means of empirically measuring the execution of an algorithm by inserting counters to keep track of the number of times certain instructions are executed during a run of the program.

program walk-through The process of carefully following, using pencil and paper, steps the computer uses to solve the problem given in a program. Also referred to as a trace diagram.

proportional Term applied to two algebraic functions whose quotient is a constant.

protected member A data member or member function that is accessible only within the scope of a class declaration or within the class declaration of a derived class.

public member A data member or member function that is accessible to any program component that uses the class.

pushing Inserting an item into a stack.

quadratic algorithm A polynomial algorithm in which the highest nonzero term is n^2.

quadratic collision processing Method of handling a collision in which the storage space is searched in the k^2 place, for successive integer values of k starting at the location of the collision, until an available spot is found.

queue A dynamic data structure where elements are entered at one end and removed from the other end. Referred to as a FIFO (first-in/first-out) structure.

quick sort A relatively fast sorting technique that uses recursion. *See also* **bubble sort**, **heap sort**, **insertion sort**, **merge sort**, **radix sort**, **selection sort**, and **shell sort**.

radix sort Sorts integer data by repeatedly placing the items into bins and then collecting the bins, starting with the least significant digit for the first pass and finishing with the most significant digit. Also referred to as bin sort. *See also* **bubble sort**, **heap sort**, **insertion sort**, **merge sort**, **quick sort**, **selection sort**, and **shell sort**.

RAM Random access memory, the primary storage area of a computer.

random access data structure Ability to access any elements in a list without first accessing all preceding elements.

randomized storage A name given to list access via a hashing function.

random number generator A function that returns a real number between 0 and 1 each time it is called. The numbers it returns are statistically random in that after repeated calls to the function, the sequence of numbers returned is evenly distributed over the interval yet each one is completely unpredictable.

ready queue In an operating system, the queue of processes with cleared access to all the resources the processes require to run.

rear pointer The pointer to the rear of a queue.

receiver object A computational object to which a request is sent for a service.

recursion The process of a subprogram calling itself. A clearly defined stopping state must exist. Any recursive subprogram can be rewritten using iteration.

recursive calls The process of a function calling itself.

recursive descent parsing A method of parsing that employs recursive functions.

recursive step A step in the recursive process that solves a similar problem of smaller size and eventually leads to a termination of the process.

recursive subprogram *See* **recursion**.

recursive termination condition The condition that causes a recursive function to return without further recursive calls.

rehashing Method of handling a collision in which a sequence of new hashing functions is applied to the key that caused the collision until an available location for that key is found.

rehashing collision processing Resolving a collision by invoking a sequence of hashing functions on a key.

relatively prime Two numbers are relatively prime if and only if their only common factor is 1.

relative ordering Ordering imposed on the entries in a list by their relative positions in that list.

root node The first or top node in a tree.

row-major order A means of traversing a two-dimensional array whereby all of the data in one row are accessed before the data in the next row.

run-time stack An area of memory that is reserved for activation records. *See also* **activation record**.

run-time trace diagram A diagram that depicts the calls of a function.

search algorithms Methods that are used to locate a given item in a data structure.

secondary key The second key that is used to locate a value in a two-key table.

sector A particular portion of a magnetic disk used at the machine language level in addressing information stored on the disk.

seed A global number used as the basis for generating random numbers in random number generating function.

selection sort A sorting algorithm that sorts the components of an array in either ascending or descending order. This process puts the smallest or largest element in the top position and repeats the process on the remaining array components. *See also*

bubble sort, heap sort, insertion sort, merge sort, quick sort, radix sort, and **shell sort**.

semaphore In an operating system, special flags that regulate the addition and removal of processes to and from the blocked and ready queues.

sender A computational object that requests a service from another computational object.

sequential access data structure Requirement that elements of a list must be accessed according to the list's ordering so that before a particular element can be accessed, all preceding elements must be accessed first.

sequential search The process of searching a list by examining the first component and then examining successive components in the order in which they occur. Also referred to as linear search.

sequential traversal The process of visiting items in a structure in positional order.

server A computational object that provides a service to another computational object.

shaker sort A variation on the bubble sort in which each pass through the data positions the (current) largest element in the (current) last array index *and* the (current) smallest element in the (current) first array index.

shell sort Sort that works by dividing the array into smaller, noncontiguous segments. These segments are separately sorted using the insertion sort algorithm. The number of these segments is repeatedly reduced on each successive pass until the entire array has been sorted. *See also* **bubble sort, heap sort, insertion sort, merge sort, quick sort, radix sort**, and **selection sort**.

shift folding A variation on folding in which each numeric part of the key is treated as a separate number, and these numbers are added to form an integer value. *See also* **boundary folding**.

siblings The child nodes of a given node.

simulation A computer model of a real-life situation.

simulation of system stack Technique used to eliminate recursion by making a program explicitly perform the duties of the system stack.

software engineering The process of developing and maintaining large software systems.

software reuse The process of building and maintaining software systems out of existing software components.

software system life cycle The process of development, maintenance, and demise of a software system. Phases include analysis, design, coding, testing/verification, maintenance, and obsolescence.

sorted collection A derived class of ordered collection, in which the data items are maintained in ascending or descending order. *See also* **ordered collection**.

sparse table A table in which a high percentage of data storage locations will be of one uniform value.

stack A dynamic data structure where access can be made from only one end. Referred to as a LIFO (last-in/first-out) structure.

stack frame *See* **activation record**.

stack priority Function to hierarchically rank algebraic operators in order of precedence.

start symbol A unique non terminal symbol that names the top-level rule in a grammar.

state space The space of all possible states that can be generated in the solution to a given problem.

stopping state The well-defined termination of a recursive process.

subtree A subset of a tree that is itself a tree.

symbol table A list of identifiers maintained by a compiler as it parses a source program.

synonyms Two keys that hash to the same position and therefore cause a collision.

systems analyst The person responsible for analyzing the needs of the users and then formally specifying the system and its requirements to meet those needs.

system testing Exercising the interfaces between modules instead of the logic of a particular module.

tail recursive The property that a recursive algorithm has of performing no work after each recursive step. *See also* **recursion**.

terminals Symbols in a grammar that appear in sentences in its language.

ternary tree A tree in which each node has three links to children.

test cases Collection of sets of test data that will exercise all the logical possibilities the module will encounter. Each test case has a corresponding expected result called the test oracle.

testing phase The fourth phase of the software system life cycle. In this phase, the program code is thoroughly tested in an effort to discover errors both in the design of the program and in the code itself.

test oracle The expected result for a particular test case when a module is being tested.

thread A pointer contained in a tree node that leads to the predecessor or successor of the node relative to a specified traversal.

threaded tree A tree in which threading is used.

threading A technique of avoiding recursion in tree traversal algorithms whereby the pointers unused in tree formation are turned into pointers to the inorder predecessor and inorder successor of that node.

time/space trade-off The maxim that an attempt to make a program more efficient in terms of time will come only as a result of a corresponding decrease in efficiency in terms of space, and vice versa.

token A language symbol comprised of one or more characters in an incoming stream of characters. The basic unit in lexical analysis.

trace diagram *See* **program walk-through**.

track A particular portion of a magnetic disk used at the machine language level in addressing information stored on the disk.

tree *See* **general tree**.

tree of recursive calls *See* **run-time trace diagram**.

tree traversal A means of processing every node in the tree.

trial-and-error backtracking Recursion in which more recursive calls may be made after the first return operation occurs.

trie index A type of indexing used when the keys are variable-length character strings. Although taken from the word *retrieve*, trie is pronounced "try."

two-dimensional array An array in which each element is accessed by a reference to a pair of indices.

two-key table A set of values each of which is accessed by two keys, where the set of primary keys is ordered and the set of secondary keys for each primary key is also ordered.

two-way merge The process of merging two sorted lists.

underflow If a value is too small to be represented by a computer, the value is automatically replaced by zero. *See also* **overflow**.

user requirements specification The part of the software engineering process in which the analyst describes what the system will do.

vertex A data object (or node) in a graph.

virtual memory The use of disk space to represent primary memory.

volatile list A list that undergoes frequent insertions and deletions.

weight The numeric value associated with an edge in a network.

white box testing The method of testing a module in which the tester is aware of the method of implementation and internal logic of that module. *See also* **black box testing**.

worst case The arrangement of data items prior to the beginning of the sort procedure which causes that procedure to take the longest amount of time for that particular set of items. *See also* **best case**.

INDEX

memory leakage, linked list, 207

merge sort algorithm. *See also* sort algorithm
    analysis, 491-493
    in general, 488-491

Microsoft, registration system, 480

"The military impact of information technology" (Johnson), 144

Milwaukee Journal, 480

modifiers, classes, 18

Murray, Janet, 436

The Mythical Man-Month (Brooks), 131, 137

N

"*N* choose *K*" computation, 335-337

Nance, Douglas W., 1

Naps, Thomas L., 411, 435

nested loop. *See also* recursion
    in bubble sort, 26
    efficiency and, 35
    in general, 339

network. *See also* graph
    implementation, 435-437
    use and abuse, 436

network ADT, 434-435

network algorithm. *See also* algorithm
    finding shortest paths, 442-446

Neumann, Peter G., 143

"No Silver Bullet" (Brooks), 131

node
    adding to binary search tree, 404-405
    child node, 375
    edge and, 430
    graph and, 430
    linked list, 178
    vertex and, 430

NP-complete problems, 441

Numerical Recipes (Press/Flannery/Teukolsky/Vetterling), 507

O

one-key table, 102
    binary search tree
        adding nodes, 404-405
        in general, 402-404

one-key table abstract data type. *See also* abstract data type; two-key table abstract data type
    C++ interface, 104-108
    formally specifying operations, 102-103
    in general, 101-102
    implementation, 108-112
        by hashing, 526
        comparing, 120-121
        using to implement two-key table, 118-120
    implementation with linked list
        in general, 211-212
        redefining one-key table class, 212-213
        reimplementing one-key table class, 213-215
    key, 101
    using to implement two-key table, 118-120

Operating System Concepts (Silberschatz/Galvin), 270

operations
    classes, 13
    formally specifying, 88-89, 97-98
    overloading, 18

operators. *See also* arrow operator
    assignment, 18-19
    deference, 19, 158
    expressions and assignment, 4-6
    polymorphic, 18

order of magnitude
    considerations, 36

ordered collection abstract data type. *See also* abstract data type
    declaring ordered collection class, 90-91
    defining, 85-88
    evaluating implementation, 93-94
        ADT implementation rule, 93
        ADT use rule, 93
    formally specifying operations, 88-89
    in general, 84-85
    implementing operations
        adding and removing elements, 92-93
        copy constructor, 91-92
        default constructor, 91
        indexing ordered collections, 92
        length operation, 92
    information hiding, 93-94
    interface, 90

output, interactive, 7

overflow area, 517

P

pages, virtual memory, 51

paging algorithm, 51

parameter, value and reference, 8

parameter object, 17

parameter passing modes, 8

parent node. *See also* node
    tree structure, 375

parse tree, 355

parsing. *See also* recursive descent parsing
    recursive descent parsing, 307
    stacks, 242-243

parsing expressions, discussed, 358-363

permutations problem
    discussed, 340-349
        binding time problem, 340

pivot, 475

pointer
    in binary search algorithm, 59-60
    with bubble sort, 48-51
    defined, 48
        to node, 192

breadth-first, 433
> graph algorithm, 440-442
depth-first, 433
> graph algorithm, 437,
>   438-440
general tree via binary tree,
>   425-428
sequential traversal of linked
>   list, 189

tree, defined, 377

tree structure, 375. *See also* data
> structure
ancestor, 375
child node, 375
leaf node, 375
parent node, 375
root, 375
siblings, 375
subtree, 375

trial-and-error methodology, 307.
> *See also* recursion
in general, 339

Trie indexing. *See also* indexed
> sequential search
efficiency considerations, 541
in general, 539-541

two-key table abstract data type.
> *See also* abstract data type;
> one-key table abstract data type
class template, 115
defined, 114
in general, 113-115
implementation, by hashing,
>   526-527
two-dimensional vector imple-
>   mentation, 116-118

type conversion, 6

typedef, 10

U

unordered search, one-key
> table, 112

update
concurrent, 531-533
record lock facility, 531-532

V

value, 108

value and reference parameters, 8

variables, 4
pointer, addresses and values,
>   200-202
simple, addresses and values,
>   198-199
vector, addresses and values,
>   199-200

vector
base type, 11
implementation of queue,
>   260-264
implementation of stack,
>   236-238
physical vs. logical size, 84-85

vector implementation, two-key
> table, 116-118

vertex, node and, 430

Vetterling, William T., 507

virtual memory
pages, 51
relation to performance, 51

W

watch, 66

Weiss, Stephen F., 405